OXFORD MONOGRAPHS ON CRIMINAL LAW AND JUSTICE

General Editors:
Jeremy Horder LLD, FBA, Professor of Criminal Law, London School of Economics
Michelle Madden Dempsey, Professor of Law, Villanova Law School

This series aims to cover all aspects of criminal law and procedure including criminal evidence. The scope of this series is wide, encompassing both practical and theoretical works.

OTHER TITLES IN THIS SERIES

The Insanity Defence
International and Comparative Perspectives
Ronnie Mackay, Warren Brookbanks

Justice In-Between
A Study of Intermediate Criminal Verdicts
Federico Picinali

Criminal Fraud and Election Disinformation
Law and Politics
Jeremy Horder

Policing the Borders Within
Ana Aliverti

Criminalizing Sex
A Unified Liberal Theory
Stuart P. Green

Reasons to Doubt
Wrongful Convictions and the Criminal Cases Review Commission
Carolyn Hoyle and Mai Sato

Fitness to Plead
International and Comparative Perspectives
Ronnie Mackay and Warren Brookbanks

Criminal Misconducts in Office
Law and Politics
Jeremy Horder

The Preventive Turn in Criminal Law
Henrique Carvalho

Criminal Justice and Taxation
Peter Alldridge

In Search of Criminal Responsibility
Ideas, Interests, and Institutions
Nicola Lacey

Preventive Justice
Andrew Ashworth and Lucia Zedner

Character in the Criminal Trial
Mike Redmayne

Homicide and the Politics of Law Reform
Jeremy Horder

The Insecurity State
Vulnerable Autonomy and the Right to Security in the Criminal Law
Peter Ramsay

Manifest Madness
Mental Incapacity in the Criminal Law
Arlie Loughnan

The Ethics of Plea Bargaining
Richard L. Lippke

Prosecuting Domestic Violence
A Philosophical Analysis
Michelle Madden Dempsey

Abuse of Process and Judicial Stays of Criminal Proceedings
Second Edition
Andrew L.-T. Choo

A Philosophy of Evidence Law
Justice in the Search of Truth
H. L. Ho

The Insanity Defence

The Insanity Defence

International and Comparative Perspectives

Edited by

RONNIE MACKAY AND WARREN BROOKBANKS

OXFORD
UNIVERSITY PRESS

OXFORD
UNIVERSITY PRESS

Great Clarendon Street, Oxford, OX2 6DP,
United Kingdom

Oxford University Press is a department of the University of Oxford.
It furthers the University's objective of excellence in research, scholarship,
and education by publishing worldwide. Oxford is a registered trade mark of
Oxford University Press in the UK and in certain other countries

First Edition published in 2022

Impression: 1

Published in the United States of America by Oxford University Press
198 Madison Avenue, New York, NY 10016, United States of America

British Library Cataloguing in Publication Data

Data available

Library of Congress Cataloging in Publication Data

Data available

ISBN 978–0–19–885494–4

DOI: 10.1093/oso/9780198854944.001.0001

Printed and bound by
CPI Group (UK) Ltd, Croydon, CR0 4YY

For Sally (M) and Glenys (B), for everything—just unending thanks!

Preface

The insanity defence has long been a topic of great controversy and debate which has amassed a considerable body of case law, legislation, and academic literature. However, this body of work is so disparate that there was in our view a need to bring together a range of different international perspectives on the insanity defence. That, in essence, is our justification for adding yet more literature to the corpus of work already devoted to the defence of insanity. In addition, this volume derives from the current international confusion and concern which surrounds the challenging issue of the relationship between mental impairment and crime.

This book seemed to us to be a natural sequel to our earlier collaboration in *Fitness to Plead: International and Comparative Perspectives* (Oxford University Press 2018). Of course, insanity and fitness to plead represent twin pillars of forensic psychiatric practice and together engage ethical, legal, and clinical matters of the greatest importance in securing the fair trial rights of offenders with mental disabilities. Mindful of the vast array of differing international approaches to exculpatory insanity we set about the task of identifying and approaching leading legal scholars in a range of jurisdictions who might wish to participate in a new comparative volume in this critical but fascinating domain. We were fortunate as a number of our contributors who had earlier contributed to *Fitness to Plead*, notably David Ormerod, Gerry Maher, Gerry Ferguson, Ian Freckelton, Stephen Morse, and Magda Karagiannakis, agreed to contribute chapters. We are deeply indebted to them, together with our new contributors—Mark Dsouza, Paul McCutcheon, Audrey Guinchard, Regina Rauxloh, Gerben Meynen, Linda Gröning, and Lilou Jiang—for their outstanding contributions to this volume. It is our sincere hope that the insights offered in these chapters will help to inform debate about the insanity defence and related mental state defences, especially in light of the host of new and emerging psychological, legal, and social challenges. The insanity defence is contentious and continues to attract publicity, much of it restrictive and negative. That is evident from the chapters in this book. Take, for example, the creation in Canada of the category of a 'high-risk accused' (Chapter 6), the new insanity verdict in New Zealand (Chapter 7), the United States Supreme Court decisions upholding restricting the scope of the insanity defence (Chapter 9), and the impact of the *Halimi* and *Breivik* cases in France (Chapter 10) and Norway (Chapter 13) respectively. All these initiatives stem from concerns about the defence of insanity which are driven by public safety and policy concerns but rarely are they informed by empirical research either before or after change takes place.

We believe that being well informed in relation to the many issues insanity gives rise to is essential to assist in the development of policy, and ultimately reform. Our sincere hope is that this book will contribute to that process, for until the current law in many jurisdictions is updated and modernized, numerous mentally abnormal defendants who should otherwise be exculpated will be convicted and those few who are found legally insane will continue to be the subject of stigma, fear, and suspicion.

RDM
WJB
April 2022

Contents

Table of Cases

UNITED KINGDOM JURISDICTIONS

England & Wales

Northern Ireland

Scotland

INTERNATIONAL COURTS AND TRIBUNALS

European Commission of Human Rights

European Court of Human Rights

International Criminal Court (ICC)

International Criminal Tribunal for Former Yugoslavia (ICTY)

International Military Tribunal (Nuremberg)

NATIONAL JURISDICTIONS

Australia

Canada

China

East Timor

France

Germany

Guernsey

Ireland

Jersey

Netherlands

New Zealand

Norway

Sierra Leone

United States

Table of Legislation

UNITED KINGDOM STATUTES

UNITED KINGDOM STATUTORY INSTRUMENTS

INTERNATIONAL INSTRUMENTS

INTERNATIONAL COURTS AND TRIBUNALS

International Criminal Court (ICC)

NATIONAL JURISDICTIONS

Australia

France

Germany

Ireland

Switzerland

United States

List of Abbreviations

AEDPA	Antiterrorism and Effective Death Penalty Act 1996
ALI	American Law Institute
CPMIP Act	Criminal Procedure (Mentally Impaired Persons) Act 2003
CRPD	Convention on the Rights of Persons with Disabilities
DP	Discussion Paper
DR	diminished responsibility
DSM	Diagnostic and Statistical Manual
ECHR	European Convention on Human Rights
ECtHR	European Court of Human Rights
GBMI	guilty but mentally ill
HRA	high-risk accused
ICC	International Criminal Court
ICD	International Classification of Diseases
ICTR	International Criminal Tribunal for Rwanda
ICTY	International Criminal Tribunal for the Former Yugoslavia
LC	Law Commission for England and Wales
LRA	Lord's Resistance Army
MPC	Model Penal Code
NCR	not criminally responsible
NCRMD	not criminally responsible due to mental disorder
NGRI	not guilty by reason of insanity
NIFP	Netherlands Institute for Forensic Psychiatry and Psychology
NRGD	Netherlands Register of Court Experts
PFC	prefrontal cortex
PTSD	post-traumatic stress disorder
QRMC	qualifying recognised medical condition
RPE	[ICTY] Rules of Procedure and Evidence
SCSL	Special Court for Sierra Leone
SIFER	Norwegian Board of Forensic Medicine and the National Network for Forensic Psychiatry
SPC	Supreme People's Court [of China]
UN	United Nations

List of Contributors

Warren Brookbanks, Professor of Criminal Law and Justice Studies, Director of the Centre for Non-Adversarial Justice at Auckland University of Technology, Auckland, New Zealand.

Mark Dsouza, Associate Professor, Faculty of Laws, University College London, UK.

Gerry Ferguson, University of Victoria Distinguished Professor, Faculty of Law, University of Victoria, Victoria, British Columbia, Canada.

Ian Freckelton, AO QC, Professor of Law and Professorial Fellow in Psychiatry, University of Melbourne, Australia; Judge, Supreme Court of Nauru.

Linda Gröning, Professor at the Faculty of Law, University of Bergen. Senior Researcher Regional Centre for Research and Education in Forensic Psychiatry and Psychology, Haukeland University Hospital of Bergen, Bergen, Norway.

Audrey Guinchard, Senior Lecturer in Law, University of Essex, UK.

Lilou Jiang, Intellectual Property Examiner of Canadian Intellectual Property Office, Canada.

Magda Karagiannakis, Barrister, Melbourne; Senior Lecturer, La Trobe University, Melbourne, Australia.

Ronnie Mackay, Professor of Criminal Policy and Mental Health, Leicester De Montfort Law School, De Montfort University, Leicester, UK.

Paul McCutcheon, Professor of Law, University of Limerick, Republic of Ireland.

Gerry Maher, Professor of Criminal Law, School of Law, Edinburgh University, Law Commissioner at the Scottish Law Commission from 2000 to 2008, Edinburgh, UK.

Gerben Meynen, Professor of Forensic Psychiatry, Utrecht University, and Professor of Ethics, in particular bioethics, Vrije University Amsterdam, The Netherlands.

Stephen J Morse, Ferdinand Wakeman Hubbell Professor of Law; Professor of Psychology and Law in Psychiatry, University of Pennsylvania, USA.

David Ormerod, QC, Professor of Criminal Law, Faculty of Laws, University College London, Law Commissioner for England and Wales from 2010 to 2019, UK.

Regina E Rauxloh, Former Associate Professor in International Crime Law and Contract Law, Southampton Law School, University of Southampton, UK.

1
Introduction

Ronnie Mackay and Warren Brookbanks

The insanity defence is an enigma. More than any other defence in the criminal law it has been and continues to be, the subject of heated debate. A debate that far outstrips its practical significance, as the defence is rarely encountered in practice and is even more rarely successful. On the one hand, the insanity defence represents a fundamental tenet of criminal responsibility which is designed to shield those who qualify within its criteria from a criminal conviction. On the other hand, however, the defence is not only deeply stigmatic in its nomenclature, but also presents real problems relating to disposal of the acquittee. These problems concern how to protect the public while giving recognition to the rights of the victim or to his or her family, and yet to be fair to a defendant who has been excused from all criminal responsibility.

In this book, we wish to confront the fact that too little is known about how the insanity defence operates in different jurisdictions, including in the United Kingdom and Ireland. Every law student is taught about the famous M'Naghten Rules, but few know how they operate in practice, and the same may be true for most criminal law practitioners. When it comes to how the insanity defence is applied in other countries, we are probably even more ignorant. The M'Naghten Rules are, of course, the common law test for the insanity defence in England and Wales and although they have influenced many other jurisdictions this influence has gradually been eroded, with many common law countries replacing the Rules with other statutory tests. Indeed, in Great Britain, England and Wales is now the only jurisdiction which continues to adhere to the Rules, with Scotland, Northern Ireland, and the Channel Island of Jersey all having adopted different insanity defences. As for other common law countries, with the exception of some states in the United States, many have altered or updated the Rules. By way of contrast, civil law jurisdictions have never adopted the M'Naghten Rules but instead have a range of, sometimes radically different, approaches to the insanity defence. This is also true of a country like China. In short, in this book, we are firmly of the view that by bringing together a range of domestic and international experts from a wide selection of jurisdictions, including the international criminal law arena which is becoming increasingly important, we will be able to inform readers of the multifaceted way in which the insanity defence operates. By doing so we believe that this publication has the potential to significantly influence debate around the insanity

Ronnie Mackay and Warren Brookbanks, *Introduction* In: *The Insanity Defence*. Edited by: Ronnie Mackay and Warren Brookbanks, Oxford University Press.
DOI: 10.1093/oso/9780198854944.003.0001

defence and to assist in the development of policy and legislation in a critical and evolving area of the law. We hope in turn to be able to reinvigorate the debate about the defence by discussing, within the book's framework, the theoretical basis for the defence, how different jurisdictions approach the insanity plea, not only in relation to an appropriate test and how it operates, but also from the perspective of disposal and how those who use the insanity defence successfully are dealt with. Accordingly, each chapter will address common issues surrounding the insanity defence, including normative, practical, and procedural issues as well as relevant empirical studies on the workings of the defence. This will also include disposal issues. In doing so we will ensure that the respective chapters give readers a unique and distinctively comparative insight into how the defence operates in those different jurisdictions.

The Theoretical Basis of the Insanity Defence

Theories concerning the origins, purpose, and outcomes of the insanity defence are legion. Such theories may be informed by history, politics, social science, and professional judgement but are seldom exhaustive or complete. The immediate problem is the sheer breadth and diversity of the aberrant mental states that constitute the 'stuff' of the insanity defence. To formulate a theory which adequately encompasses the legal elements of mental disturbance or aberration sufficient to confer immunity for otherwise criminal behaviour seems like an impossible task. And so it has proven to be. There is currently no universally agreed formula as to what constitutes legal insanity or how it should be expressed in legal language. Recent jurisprudence of the United States Supreme Court has identified four 'strains' of insanity defences '"yield[ing] a diversity of American standards" for when to absolve mentally ill defendants of criminal culpability'.[1] These are broadly identified as (1) the cognitive capacity test, (2) the moral capacity test, (3) the volitional incapacity test, and (4) the 'product- of-mental-illness' test. As the Court in *Clark* observed, even that taxonomy fails to capture the field's complexity.[2]

Whether a working test for insanity should capture either knowledge of *moral* wrong or knowledge of *legal* wrong, or both, has been an ongoing challenge since the M'Naghten Rules first provided that a relevant 'defect of reason' must be proved, amongst other things, to have caused the defendant not to know his act was 'wrong'. However, more problematic has been the interpretation of the M'Naghten Rules as providing an exclusively cognitive test for determining insanity. A consequence of the narrowness of this approach is that a person judged to be truly 'mad', in light of the application of clinical diagnostic criteria, may still be regarded

[1] *Kahler v Kansas*, 589 US 1 (2020) 1 and see *Clark v Arizona*, 548 US 735, 749 (2006).
[2] Cited in *Kahler v Kansas*, 589 US 1, 2 (2020).

as legally sane because they know the nature and quality of their act and that it is contrary to law. The harsh nature of this prescriptively narrow rule is powerfully demonstrated in the 1955 trial, conviction, and eventual hanging of Ruth Ellis on the charge of murdering David Blakely. Despite evidence of the physical violence and abuse experienced by Ellis at Blakely's hand, the true extent of her mental distress was never disclosed at the trial, and while juries had shown some willingness to bend the M'Naghten Rules to avoid the death penalty 'it was not wide enough, even under its most liberal interpretation, to encompass Ruth'.[3]

More recently it has become clear in English law that the narrow interpretation of the two limbs of the M'Naghten Rules is a major reason why the insanity defence is not used more often in that jurisdiction. Although the Criminal Procedure (Insanity and Unfitness to Plead) Act 1991 did introduce a wide range of disposal options for cases other than murder, there has not been a significant increase in successful insanity pleas.[4] Similarly, for example in New Zealand, where a modified version of the M'Naghten Rules has been in existence since 1893, the New Zealand Law Commission estimated in 2010 that the insanity defence was run between 30 and 40 times each year, and was successful about ten times.[5]

Future theoretical challenges to the insanity defence are likely to come from the movement towards abolition, discussed below, and as a result of fresh insights from neuroscience. This domain, in particular, has attempted to expose the inadequacy of existing statutory and case law definitions of insanity, which are increasingly criticized as 'obsolete, rudimentary and inconsistent with state-of-the-art science', although it is conceded that reform poses significant practical and conceptual difficulties.[6] To date, however, abolitionists have failed in their efforts to invalidate the insanity defence in most jurisdictions, although powerful criticisms of the utility of the defence still remain.

The debate surrounding the insanity defence is fraught with controversy. However, one matter that seems uncontroversial is that serious mental illness which leads to offending can, in some circumstances, interfere with a person's normal mental functioning to such a degree that he or she should be treated differently by the criminal law. This view, that the mentally ill offender should sometimes be treated differently by the criminal justice process, has led scholars to support a variety of different theories about the fundamental nature of criminal responsibility and the insanity defence. In this section, we will discuss these differing, but

[3] T Grant, *Court Number One: The Old Bailey Trials That Defined Modern Britain* (John Murray 2019) 222–23.

[4] See RD Mackay and G Kearns, 'More Fact(s) about the Insanity Defence' [1999] Crim LR 714; R Mackay, 'Ten More Years of the Insanity Defence' [2012] Crim LR 946–54. See Chapter 2.

[5] Law Commission, 'Mental Impairment Decision-making and Insanity Defence' (2010) para 6.1. See Chapter 7.

[6] S Moratti and D Patterson, 'Introduction' in S Moratti and D Patterson (eds), *Legal Insanity and the Brain* (Hart Publishing 2019) 3.

sometimes interrelated, approaches and how they have influenced the debate surrounding mental illness and criminal responsibility.

Lack of Rationality

The notion of lack of rationality, or 'irrationality', is central to many of the discussions surrounding the exculpatory nature of the insanity defence. Both Michael Moore and Stephen Morse have long advocated this approach. In *Law and Psychiatry—Rethinking the Relationship*[7] Moore states that the central question in assessing the insanity defence is for the jury to consider whether the accused's mental illness was severe enough for them to conclude that he was 'so irrational as to be nonresponsible'.[8] In a similar vein, Morse has consistently advocated that 'The moral basis for the insanity defense is that in some cases mental disorder affects the defendant's capacity to act rationally or to control his behavior.'[9] This incapacity in turn explains why it is fundamentally wrong to punish those who are legally insane. As Morse and Bonnie have put it the 'defense of legal insanity applies this fundamental principle by excusing those mentally disordered offenders whose disorder deprived them of rational understanding of their conduct at the time of the crime'.[10] While few, if any, would deny that punishing the legally insane is wrong, the idea of resting the excusatory basis of an insanity defence on the principle of 'irrationality' is one which deserves careful scrutiny.

If incapacity to act rationally is the basis of the insanity defence, then it may be useful to contrast this with the idea of capacity for 'rational' conduct, which Fingarette and Hasse consider has 'a far deeper and more global significance, than such traditional concepts as "intent", "knowledge", "deliberation", and "voluntariness" '.[11] Accordingly, it is 'rationality' which governs these traditional concepts in the sense that they only remain significant if the person in question is rational. While 'rationality', therefore, can be regarded as underpinning normal mental functioning, in the sense of being able to exercise reason and judgement, by way of contrast, 'irrationality' can be equated with inability to exercise normal powers of reason and judgement. This may be conveniently described as 'an aberration of normal mental functioning'. When interfered with to the extent that reason and judgement are lacking, it is then, if mental illness was present and operating at the

[7] M Moore, *Law and Psychiatry—Rethinking the Relationship* (Cambridge University Press 1984).

[8] ibid 245.

[9] SJ Morse 'Mental Disorder and Criminal Justice' in E Luna (ed), *Reforming Criminal Justice: A Report of the Academy for Justice Bridging the Gap between Scholarship and Reform* (Academy for Justice 2018) 290.

[10] SJ Morse and RJ Bonnie, 'Abolition of the Insanity Defense Violates Due Process' (2013) 4(1) J Am Acad Psychiatry Law 488, 489.

[11] H Fingarette and AF Hasse, *Mental Disabilities and Criminal Responsibility* (University of California Press 1979) 218.

relevant time, that an enquiry should consider whether this individual may have been acting 'irrationally'.

From a practical point of view, this approach to understanding the basis of the insanity defence seems to make a lot of sense. Certainly, the type of cognitively based insanity defence exemplified in the M'Naghten Rules seems to chime with this approach, in that the empirical studies of the operation of the Rules in England and Wales paint a consistent picture of cases where the accused were, to put it colloquially, 'crazy' or 'out of their minds' at the time of the commission of the alleged offences.[12] While such cases may be suitable candidates for an insanity defence based on 'irrationality', this does not detract from the criticisms that the notion of 'irrationality' is itself too vague and imprecise to rely upon; and further, that if its use is limited to a M'Naghten-based insanity defence then it will not assist in seeking a useful theoretical basis for a wider defence which can accommodate volitional impairment or a character or status-based approach. Each of these arguments merits consideration.

Is 'rationality' too vague?

The insanity defence is essentially a legal issue which also has moral aspects. As such, there is no consensus as to what form it should take with different jurisdictions, some of which are discussed in this book, opting for a variety of approaches. With this in mind, it follows that the notion of 'rationality' itself will vary according to the way in which the insanity defence in question is drafted. As Morse has emphasized 'rationality is the defining criterion of legal (and moral) responsibility, but it is not self-defining. It is a normative concept that can take on various meanings . . . '.[13] In the context of the insanity defence, there is no reason why one view of rationality should fit all defence models. In that sense, its imprecision is a strength as it is 'a continuum concept and individuals differ widely in their ability to get the facts straight, to understand the rules, and to reason'.[14] However, at the same time, this means that as a defining concept, 'rationality' will have a fundamental and multiform role to play as it applies to all insanity defences. But can it carry the freight or is this asking too much of it?

As mentioned above, insanity defences based on the M'Naghten Rules do not present a problem in this connection, as a test which is cognitively based seems to fit comfortably within the concept of 'rationality'. This is because those offenders who, as a result of mental illness, are proved not to know what they were doing or that it was wrong, are clear candidates for a finding of 'irrationality'. Although such a lack of cognitive ability sits squarely with a finding of irrationality, other forms

[12] See RD Mackay, BJ Mitchell, and Leonie Howe, 'Yet More Facts about the Insanity Defence' [2006] Crim LR 399, 411.

[13] SJ Morse, 'Rationality and Responsibility' (2000) 74 South Calif Law Rev 251, 254.

[14] ibid 255.

of insanity defence may present more of a problem. For example, what of those defences which have a volitional limb? Can it be said that those whose offending is the result of an impulse control disorder can be said to have acted 'irrationally'? Clearly, such defendants know what they are doing and that it is wrong. Is this awareness always indicative of rational behaviour or can it also, in some cases, qualify as 'irrational'? Importantly, if the idea of 'rationality' is a defining concept, then it must be applicable in such cases. Here it is of note that in his analysis Morse includes 'incapacity to control behaviour'. In doing so he argues 'that disorders of desire should excuse only in those cases in which the desire is so strong and overwhelming that the agent at least temporarily loses the capacity to be guided by reason ... intense desires ... only furnish an excuse if they produce irrationality'.[15] Of course, there is an empirical issue here as to whether desires to do something can become so extreme that the subject's ability to reason is itself so uncontrolled that his action can be adjudged 'irrational'. However, while there is understandable scepticism as to whether volitional impairment should qualify for an insanity defence, this is because it is difficult to distinguish between a desire which *cannot* be resisted as opposed to one which the subject chose not to resist.[16] At the same time, this does not mean that uncontrollable desires do not exist and if they do then many would argue that they may be a suitable candidate for an insanity defence. In that case, an approach which advocates that 'irrationality' is the root concept of all insanity defences, including those which accommodate volitional impairment, may go some way to answering the sceptics, as it will restrict the scope of any such impairment control defence to those which are so severe that the agent's actions are viewed as 'irrational'.[17]

A good example of how this might operate is to be found in the work of the Law Commission for England and Wales in its Discussion Paper on Insanity and Automatism. The Commission concludes 'that in some cases it is possible for a medical condition to deprive a person of the power to control his or her actions, and that it is right in principle for the law to allow a defence in such cases'.[18] Thus, the Commission provisionally recommends that a new defence of 'not criminally responsible by reason of a recognised medical condition' should be available where 'the defendant wholly lacked the capacity ... to control his or her physical acts in relation to the relevant conduct or circumstances'.[19] Although the Commission

[15] ibid 257 and 258.

[16] See SJ Morse, 'Culpability and Control' (1994) 142 U Pa L Rev 1587.

[17] See SJ Morse, 'Against Control Tests for Criminal Responsibility' in PH Robinson, S Garvey, and K Kessler Ferzan (eds), *Criminal Conversations* (Oxford University Press 2011) chapter 21.

[18] Law Commission, 'Insanity and Automatism—A Discussion Paper' (2013) para 4.53. The Commission is at pains to avoid using the term 'volition' by taking 'the practical view that whether a person is able to will not to do something is not the focus; rather, it is whether it is possible for him or her to make a choice': para 4.35. However, while this may indeed be a 'practical' way forward it is difficult to deny that the making of a choice is in turn not motivated by a desire to make that choice. In short, this approach does little to alleviate the problems surrounding volition and impulse control.

[19] ibid para 4.160.

questions whether the capacity to act rationally 'applies to all instances of loss of self-control',[20] this criticism rather misses the point, as it is only those cases of loss of self-control that do reach the level of 'irrationality' which will qualify for an insanity defence. In that respect, the Commission's requirement of a total or complete lack of capacity is likely to achieve that level and in doing so will restrict the availability of the defence to those cases of volitional impairment where the accused's total lack of capacity equates with 'irrationality'.

Having discussed the place of 'irrationality' in the defence of insanity it is now time to consider two alternatives, namely the character and status based approaches.

Character theory

The role of 'irrationality' and with it, the capacity for rational choice, have been questioned, with some seeking to replace this approach by advocating instead, that the insanity defence should concern itself with an enquiry into the agent's character. This approach, in focusing on a person's settled dispositions and character traits, claims that such traits and dispositions are 'severed by insanity, not because it alters the capacities of the insane person, but because it involves disordered thought and behaviour which is not patterned by the structure of thought (both in terms of reason and emotion) by which we normally communicate and interpret each other's actions'.[21] In short, an accused ought not to be held responsible if his actions are manifestly out of character, or as Tadros puts it, 'the claim that the defendant makes is "although I did it, I wasn't really myself"'.[22] If adopted, this approach would have the merit of extending the narrow cognitively based insanity defence exemplified in the M'Naghten Rules to allow consideration of whether 'the mental disorder was such that the belief formed was radically disconnected from the background beliefs of the defendant'.[23] This then enables the enquiry to probe the accused's 'attitudes, concerns and values'. However, it brings with it some serious criticism.

The focus on character and traits requires an investigation 'of the accused's general mindset over a long period of time prior to the alleged disorder which affected him or her at the time of the crime'. This, in turn, would require evidence that the accused's actions were so 'radically disconnected'[24] from his ordinary beliefs and desires that he ought not to be adjudged criminally responsible. It is not only the scope and reliability of such evidence which is open to question but also the premise that one's character is a sound yardstick for assessing criminal

[20] ibid para 4.48.

[21] N Lacey, *State Punishment* (Routledge 1988) 74; N Lacey, *In Search of Criminal Responsibility: Ideas, Interests, and Institutions* (Oxford University Press 2016) 33–42.

[22] V Tadros, 'The Characters of Excuse' (2001) 21 OJLS 495.

[23] V Tadros, *Criminal Responsibility* (Oxford University Press 2005) 339.

[24] ibid.

responsibility. Character flaws are commonplace but do not of themselves give rise to the type of disconnection which, as is suggested above, is the benchmark of an insanity defence. So at what stage would a disconnection become 'radical' enough to qualify for an insanity plea? How would this be measured? For this reason alone it does seem unlikely that a character-based approach is a practical way forward. As a result, it has been remarked that 'in light of the incoherence of theories more centrally based on character traits-choice remains the crucial issue, but considerations of character sometimes intrude, assisting the effort to punish only the morally blameworthy'.[25]

So it now seems appropriate to discuss the 'choice' model of excuse together with the important argument that insanity should be classed as a form of status exemption.

Choice, causation, and status exemption

The idea of free choice, which focuses on a person's ability to make rational choices, is often regarded as fundamental to notions of criminal responsibility. However, the 'choice' theory is wholly dependent on the actor's choices being free, unlike the 'character' theory, which 'can happily admit that responsible choices are caused by character, and that character, in turn, is caused by factors, not themselves chosen by the actor'.[26] Accordingly, provided we do not choose our characters then individuals can be held responsible for their acts which are 'in character', even in the face of determinism. It follows that for the 'choice' theorist determinism poses a problem, as it claims that choice and causation are incompatible. For a hard determinist like Robert Sapolsky this means that we must face the fact that we are not responsible for anything and that 'free choice' is an illusion. It follows, in his view, that the criminal justice system should be abolished and with it criminal responsibility and punishment. As a result, there would be no need for an insanity defence (or any other defence). In discussing this issue and the importance of the role of the prefrontal cortex (PFC) in cognition, emotional regulation, control of impulsive behaviour, and moral reasoning, Sapolsky concludes that 'Whereas ... a neurobiological framework may indeed eliminate blame, it does not eliminate the need for forceful intervention in the face of violence or antisocial behaviour. To understand is not to forgive or to do nothing; whereas you do not ponder whether to forgive a car that, because of problems with its brakes, has injured someone, you nevertheless protect society from it.'[27] In response to the accusation that it is 'dehumanizing

[25] AE Lelling, 'A Psychological Critique of Character-based Theories of Criminal Excuse' (1998) 49 Syracuse Law Rev 35, 97.

[26] M Moore, 'Choice, Character and Excuse' (1990) 7(2) Soc Philos Policy 50.

[27] RM Sapolsky, 'The Frontal Cortex and the Criminal Justice System' (2004) 359 Phil Trans R Soc Lond B 1787–96, 1794.

to medicalize people into being broken cars',[28] he states this approach 'can still be vastly more humane than moralizing them into being sinners'.[29]

The fundamental problem, of course, is whether claims of a neuroscientist like Sapolsky's are correct. There has certainly been a great deal of debate recently on the role of neuroscience and how it might help in our understanding of criminal responsibility.[30] However, the argument that free will does not exist goes much further, as it would eradicate the whole criminal justice process. In this connection, the neuroscientist has much to prove and in response, Morse has consistently argued that we are very far from reaching that level of proof.[31] So the criminal lawyer must continue to grapple with the complex issues surrounding criminal responsibility. A related point of interest here is that the reference to equating 'damaged humans as broken machines'[32] chimes with the notion that insanity is not an excuse but is a 'status' which exempts the actor from punishment. It follows, therefore, that much like 'infancy', in such cases the whole prosecution process and the criminal jurisdiction of the court become inappropriate to deal with these classes of defendants. Moore puts it this way, 'My own long-held view is that craziness is like infancy and non-personhood generally, in that it is truly a status excuse. The seriously crazy, like animals, stones, corpses, infants, and so on generally lack the attributes making them moral agents; as such, they are not blameable in general, without regard to there being some connection between their craziness and their wrongful and criminal acts.'[33] The problem here, of course, is that, unlike all the categories mentioned, the 'crazy' can be held criminally responsible for their acts unless they are 'seriously' crazy, in which case, presumably, their 'status' alters. And therein lies a serious practical problem for those who advocate the status excuse approach. For how, it may be asked, is it to be established that the accused's craziness was so serious that he should be accorded exemption status? Unlike 'infancy', where the child's age can be established with certainty, this does not apply to 'mental illness ... as psychiatrists often disagree over matters of diagnosis'.[34] And what is to happen where there is disagreement? Would further evidence be required as to the accused's state of mind at the time of the alleged offence? Once again it seems that rationality is the key here as Moore states: 'Although we may colloquially attribute particular actions to their insanity, we do not mean that they are to be excused because of some supposed causal relation. We mean that they cannot fairly be blamed

[28] Or more broadly 'broken machines'. See RM Sapolsky, *Behave: The Biology of Humans at Our Best and Worst* (Penguin Press 2017) 612.

[29] RM Sapolsky, 'The Frontal Cortex and the Criminal Justice System' (2004) 359 Phil Trans R Soc Lond B 1787, 1794

[30] See eg S Moratti and D Patterson (eds), *Legal Insanity and the Brain* (Hart Publishing 2016).

[31] SJ Morse, 'Legal Insanity in the Age of Neuroscience' in S Moratti and D Patterson (eds), *Legal Insanity and the Brain* (Hart Publishing 2016) chapter 9.

[32] RM Sapolsky, *Behave: The Biology of Humans at Our Best and Worst* (Penguin Press 2017) 612.

[33] M Moore, *Mechanical Choices: The Responsibility of the Human Machine* (Oxford University Press 2020) 189.

[34] RD Mackay, *Mental Condition Defences and the Criminal Law* (Clarendon 1995) 82.

because *in general* they lack our rational capacities.'[35] So infants and the seriously crazy are, because of their status, both 'generally' presumed to be incapable of rational thought and as a result, there is no need to prove any causal connection since 'It is not because their mental disease causes the insane to commit crimes that we excuse them ... Rather, ... we excuse because the actors lack the status of moral agents.'[36]

Certainly, the avoidance of the notion that there is any need for a causal connection between the accused's mental illness and the alleged offence is important. For example, no one suggests that being under a certain age, in English law under ten, causes the child to commit the alleged offence. So in much the same way for the status theorist 'the very status of being crazy precludes responsibility'.[37] And the same is true for those that support the 'irrationality' theory in that 'Causation is not the issue, nonculpable lack of rationality and compulsion is'.[38] This is not to say that a causal connection is not central to most, if not all, insanity defences built on the M'Naghten Rules. We will return to this matter shortly but before doing so a few more remarks will be made about the problems of drawing an analogy between children and the insanity defence as types of status exemptions. Gideon Yaffe has questioned the nature of the status of children in this connection. In his view, this is not based on the psychological aspects of developmental immaturity but rather on the basis of the status of citizenship which he describes as 'a necessary condition for holding someone to the standards of culpability applied in cases of unmitigated criminal responsibility. We have constructed our laws in such a way as to disable kids from full participation in the roles central to citizenship, and thereby imposed on them a disability analogous to that suffered by the mentally disabled, who are incapable of full participation in the roles central to personhood.'[39] Although Yaffe's thesis concerns all children rather than only those who are under the age of criminal responsibility, it is of note that he draws an analogy with the mentally disabled. However, it is also important to note that he states 'those, I contend, who are diminished in this status, the status of citizenship, are also diminished in criminal culpability. The more diminished their status as citizens, the more diminished their culpability. If they are not citizens at all, they have a citizen-based status excuse from criminal responsibility.'[40] Again, it is only those who are under the age of criminal responsibility who qualify for an excuse rather than merely reduced culpability. In much the same way only the insanity defence qualifies for an excuse

[35] M Moore, 'Causation and the Excuses' (1985) 73(4) California Law Review 1091, 1137 (emphasis in original).
[36] ibid 1137.
[37] ibid 1139.
[38] SJ Morse, 'Excusing the Crazy' (1980) South Calif Law Rev—The Insanity Defense Reconsidered 777, 789.
[39] G Yaffe, *The Age of Culpability: Children and the Nature of Criminal Responsibility* (Oxford University Press 2018) 15.
[40] ibid.

while in other cases the defendant's mental illness may result in reduced culpability as in the diminished responsibility plea, which in English law reduces murder to manslaughter.[41] But is this where the analogy ends or can it also be contended that the type of craziness which results in an insanity defence supports the type of citizen-based status excuse suggested by Yaffe? His main contention in support of this approach revolves around the fact that kids are disenfranchised, which means they are disabled 'from full participation in the roles central to citizenship, and thereby [have] imposed on them a disability analogous to that suffered by the mentally disabled, who are incapable of full participation in the roles central to personhood'.[42] While it is the case that most 'mentally disabled' persons do have the right to vote, the mental illnesses from which they suffer often mean they lack the capacity to engage fully in everyday roles. In particular, in the context of the criminal process, if adjudged unfit to plead, the defendant will be found to have lacked the ability to effectively engage in the criminal trial process,[43] while based on a status account of the insanity defence, the accused will similarly be regarded as not being an appropriate person to face a criminal prosecution. This then is another, more radical, basis for a status excuse formulated around the notion of citizenship. But in order to be regarded as a status exemption, the accused's craziness would have to be regarded as imposing upon him a disability which deprives him of citizenship, when clearly this is not the case, as the temporary nature of the mental condition which deprives the accused of capacity at the time of the offence[44] means that any status, whether of lack of citizenship or irrationality, is just that—temporary. It follows that citizenship and rationality will be recovered once the accused's mental state improves, which makes it very different from the nature of age which is certain and absolute insofar as it fixes an age for criminal responsibility, which will, of course, vary according to each jurisdiction. This, in turn, means that the age in question is not just a legal matter but is also a political judgement. This again makes it very different from the insanity defence, so different that it does seem difficult to support the status theory and we now return to the issue of the causal link in the insanity defence.

As mentioned above, the causal connection is central to most, if not all, insanity defences built on the M'Naghten Rules. As such the Rules require 'a defect of reason *from* disease of the mind'. What is important here is not to confuse the need for a connection between the disease of the mind and the knowledge requirements about the act or its wrongfulness as opposed to the insanity or craziness causing

[41] See Homicide Act 1957, s 2.

[42] G Yaffe, *The Age of Culpability: Children and the Nature of Criminal Responsibility* (Oxford University Press 2018) 15.

[43] See R Mackay and W Brookbanks, *Fitness to Plead—International and Comparative Perspectives* (Oxford University Press 2018).

[44] We are making a distinction here between the mental illness itself which will, like age, have a degree of permanence, and the 'craziness' which the illness gives rise to at the time of the offence which will be temporary.

the criminal behaviour. The latter is simply not relevant as 'all behaviour is caused. If causation were an excuse, no one would ever be held responsible for any behaviour, criminal or not ... '.[45] However, proof of the causal requirement contained in the M'Naghten Rules is not without its problems, especially for psychiatrists, and it led the Butler Report to propose a revised special verdict which would be returned in any case where it could be shown that, at the time of the commission of the alleged offence, the accused was suffering from severe mental illness or severe subnormality. According to the Butler Report, 'Such a person is exempted from responsibility on account of his disordered mental state notwithstanding technical proof of *mens rea*.'[46] While this seems closer to the notion of a status excuse, it was also made clear in the Butler Report that this revised special verdict would also be available to those who lacked mens rea because of mental disorder, thus retaining the need for a causal link.[47]

Neither proposal was implemented and one of the reasons for this is likely to have been the radical nature of the first limb, which in essence would have turned over part of the test of criminal responsibility to psychiatrists. In addition, the Law Commission, in its reconsideration of the Butler Report's first limb, stated:

> Some people take the view that it would be wrong in principle that a person should escape conviction if, although severely mentally ill, has committed a rational crime which was uninfluenced by his illness and for which he ought to be liable to be punished. They believe that the prosecution should be allowed to persuade the jury (if it can) that the offence was not attributable to the disorder. We agree.[48]

It seems likely, therefore, that this type of approach focusing on severe mental phenomena as being themselves sufficient to excuse has been regarded, in England at least,[49] as too extreme, as it tells us little about the fundamental nature of the insanity defence which, in many jurisdictions, continues to be embedded in notions of rationality.

[45] SJ Morse, 'Excusing the Crazy' (1980) South Calif Law Rev—The Insanity Defense Reconsidered 777, 789.

[46] Butler Report of the Committee on Mentally Abnormal Offenders, Cmnd6244 (HMSO 1975) para 18.17, emphasis in original.

[47] ibid para 18.20.

[48] The Law Commission, 'A Criminal Code for England and Wales' Vol 2 (Law Com No 177) (1989) para 11.16.

[49] The Law Commission in its more recent work on the insanity defence clearly thought as much stating; 'We conclude that there should be no passport to exemption. In other words, no category of people who are as a matter of law always exempt from prosecution on the grounds of their condition, and that the defence should be framed with reference to some kind of link between the accused's condition and the resultant lack of capacity.' See Law Commission, 'Insanity and Automatism—A Discussion Paper' 219, para A102.

Is the Insanity Defence Worth Keeping?

Until recently in most common law jurisdictions, with the exception of the United States, there has been no call for ridding the law of some form of an insanity defence.[50] Thus, the Law Commission's Discussion Paper in its chapter entitled 'Should there be an Insanity Defence at all?' concluded, 'The abolition of a special defence for the mentally disordered would result in conviction of people who could not, due to their mental disorder, have avoided committing the crime, and in our view that result is not just.'[51]

It is important to understand that the 'abolition' debate in the United States[52] has revolved around ridding the law of any separate insanity defence and only permitting evidence of mental disorder to be admissible to show a lack of mens rea or actus reus. As such, there has been no recent suggestion that there should be a 'total' abolition of the defence thus not allowing any evidence of mental disorder to be admitted even to negative mens rea. In the United States, all such attempts at 'total' abolition were, with good reason, ruled to be unconstitutional.[53] Rather it is the former which has assumed importance with four American states having adopted this position.[54] In *Kahler v Kansas*,[55] the US Supreme Court was asked to consider whether the law in Kansas which states that a defendant may raise mental illness to show that he 'lacked the culpable mental state required as an element of the offense charged',[56] infringed due process as not including a wrongness/moral-incapacity test. In following its earlier decision in *Clark v Arizona*,[57] which had confirmed that no single version of the insanity defence has become so ingrained in American law as to rank as 'fundamental', the majority of the court ruled that as the insanity defence is a project for state governance, not constitutional law, Kansas was not required to adopt an insanity test that turns on a defendant's ability to recognize that his crime was morally wrong. In a powerful dissent, Justice Breyer was of the clear view that 'Kansas' abolition of the second part of the M'Naghten test requires conviction of a broad swath of defendants who are obviously insane and would be adjudged not guilty under any traditional form of the defence. 'This result offends deeply entrenched and widely recognized moral principles underpinning our criminal laws.'[58] While a detailed discussion of both the *Kahler* and *Clark* decisions is contained in Chapter 9 it is worth noting that the confirmation of the mens

[50] See generally N Morris, *Madness and the Criminal Law* (University of Chicago Press 1982) chapter 2. See also N Morris, R Bonnie, and JJ Finer, 'Should the Insanity Defense be Abolished—An Introduction to the Debate' (1985–1987) 1(2) JL & Health 113.

[51] See Law Commission, 'Insanity and Automatism—A Discussion Paper' para 2.33.

[52] See Chapter 9.

[53] See J Robitcher and A K Haynes, 'In Defence of the Insanity Defence' (1982) 31 Emory LJ 9, 51.

[54] They are Idaho, Kansas, Montana, and Utah.

[55] 589 US (2020) 1.

[56] Kan Stat Ann §21-5209.

[57] 548 US (2006) 735.

[58] 589 US (2020) 21.

rea approach in *Kahler* has been the subject of trenchant academic criticism, much of which has centred on the need for a wrongness limb as, without it, 'in virtually all cases, even severe mental disorder does not prevent defendants from forming the mental state required by the charged offense',[59] with the result that most mentally ill offenders will be convicted. In addition, the decision in *Kahler* now means that there is nothing to prevent US state legislators from adopting this mens rea approach. And they only have to look at the many reasons given in the next section as to why this might be justified.

However, a separate and important strand to the 'abolition' debate relates to the United Nations (UN) in its Guidelines on Article 14 of the Convention on the Rights of Persons with Disabilities (CRPD) (also discussed below and in Chapter 16) which states in paragraph 16 'The Committee has established that declarations of unfitness to stand trial or non-responsibility in criminal justice systems and the detention of persons based on those declarations is contrary to article 14 of the Convention since it deprives the person of his or her right to due process and safeguards that are applicable to every defendant.' In effect, this means that the insanity defence should be abolished as it is contrary to Article 14.[60] An important aspect of this debate has been the 'integrationist' approach advocated by Christopher Slobogin who also argues 'that the insanity defense should be abolished and that people with mental disorder should have a complete defensive claim only when they lack mens rea or act for reasons that sound in justification or duress'.[61] Although this approach has been the subject of much critical debate,[62] one of its strengths is that as mental disorder would no longer be a requirement for any such complete defensive claim, all such claims would be compliant with Article 14.[63] This is undoubtedly an important issue which will need careful scrutiny by

[59] SJ Morse and RJ Bonnie, 'Don't Abolish the Insanity Defense' The Hill, 18 May 2020, https://thehill.com/opinion/judiciary/497726-dont-abolish-the-insanity-defense.

[60] Article 14 states:

1. States Parties shall ensure that persons with disabilities, on an equal basis with others:
   a) Enjoy the right to liberty and security of person;
   b) Are not deprived of their liberty unlawfully or arbitrarily, and that any deprivation of liberty is in conformity with the law, and that the existence of a disability shall in no case justify a deprivation of liberty.
2. States Parties shall ensure that if persons with disabilities are deprived of their liberty through any process, they are, on an equal basis with others, entitled to guarantees in accordance with international human rights law and shall be treated in compliance with the objectives and principles of the present Convention, including by provision of reasonable accommodation.

[61] C Slobogin, 'An End to Insanity: Recasting the Role of Mental Disability in Criminal Cases' (2000) 86 Virginial Law Rev 1199, 1246.

[62] See C Slobogin, 'A Defense of the Integrationist Test as a Replacement for the Special Defense of Insanity' (2009) 42 Tex Tech Law Rev 523.

[63] See C Slobogin, 'Eliminating Mental Disability as a Legal Criterion in Deprivation of Liberty Cases: The Impact of the Convention on the Rights of Persons with Disabilities on the Insanity Defense, Civil Commitment, and Competency Law' (2016) 40 Law & Psychol Rev 297.

the signatories to the CRPD. However, at its root is the worry that the integrationist approach fails to cater fully for those mentally disordered offenders who ought properly to be excused through the mechanism of an insanity defence and as such could be viewed as 'unduly harsh'[64] and potentially 'unjust'.[65]

The Problematical Nature of the Insanity Defence

The insanity defence is an enduring challenge for legislators, legal professionals, psychiatrists, and the public alike. Few criminal law concepts have generated more controversy, confusion, and hostility than the defence of insanity. Some of the reasons for this continuing hostility are explored in this book. Yet as an established doctrine of the criminal law its primary rationale is deceptively simple. Often referred to in American writings as the doctrine of mental nonresponsibility, and in Canada as the defence of 'not criminally responsible on account of mental disorder', insanity is concerned with an offender's mental state at the time of an alleged offence, as a basis for determining whether a person should be held criminally responsible for that offending. However, the apparent simplicity of this rationale is belied by the numerous conceptual, policy, and popular challenges that have accompanied the development of the defence. These are both adventitious as, for example, where the rapid growth of neuroscience exposes the narrowness of legal conceptions of mental state defences, or by design when lawmakers struggle to craft a workable statutory defence. In addition, the potential for confusion with other statutory threshold tests for mental capacity, including mental disorder, intellectual disability, mental impairment, and unfitness to stand trial, is a serious issue. Although insanity is conceptually distinct from trial competence, or unfitness to be tried, the two are regularly confused, despite playing quite different roles in the trial process.[66] Unfitness to stand trial is principally a procedural issue and is unrelated to the substantive law questions raised by legal insanity. Unfitness to stand trial is covered in an earlier book in this series and is not discussed in this volume.[67]

Insanity has been described as a 'protean defence, operating at several levels and in different ways'.[68] However, in real terms, it plays a minor role in the

[64] C Slobogin, 'An End to Insanity: Recasting the Role of Mental Disability in Criminal Cases' (2000) 86 Virginial Law Rev 1199, 1246.

[65] See Paul Litton's criticism Against Integrationism in PH Robinson, S Garvey, and K Kessler Ferzan (eds), *Criminal Law Conversations* (Oxford University Press 2011) 487. Chapter 22 contains both a defence and further criticism of the 'integration theory'.

[66] See further Chapter 15.

[67] See R Mackay and W Brookbanks (eds), *Fitness to Plead: International and Comparative Perspectives* (Oxford University Press 2018).

[68] PA Fairall, 'The Exculpatory Force of Delusions—A Note on the Insanity Defence' (1994) 6 Bond LR 57.

administration of justice.[69] Commentators have observed that the public at large, legal professionals, and legislators have dramatically and grossly overestimated the frequency and success rate of the insanity plea, abetted by media depictions and distortions in portraying mentally ill persons charged with crimes.[70] In the United States, and in many other jurisdictions, the determination of unfitness to stand trial affects a far larger number of criminal defendants than the insanity defence. It is estimated that insanity is pleaded in less than 1% of cases and is successful in about 26% of those cases.[71]

However, this well-attested fact has had little impact on the popular practice of the scapegoating of the insanity defence as the supposed source of a host of social ills. This prejudice may operate at several different levels. At a popular level, there may be a fear that certain predatory offenders, usually sexual offenders, will be acquitted on account of insanity and released prematurely back into the community. On this view, the defence is being misused and is a threat to public safety.[72] At yet another level, prejudice against the defence may be evident in the formulation of official policy which aims to amend the formulation of the special verdict, ostensibly to better designate the level of risk presented by insanity acquittees or enhance the rights of victims.[73] Finally, prejudice against the defence can be discerned in international conventions, in particular the CRPD, which advocates the complete abolition of the defence in states' jurisdictions on account of its alleged violation of the prohibition of deprivation of liberty on the grounds of disability.[74] Abolition is the ultimate call that can be made against a legal doctrine with as many perceived shortcomings as insanity. Violation of Convention rights is a serious charge that cannot be ignored. Yet the danger of such a radical solution is the risk of creating a new set of problems for putative insanity pleaders that would arise directly from the defence's demise. These, it has been suggested, could include violation of the rights to the highest attainable standard of health, access to justice, the right to liberty, and the right to life.[75] As a result, it has been strongly argued that there is a

[69] E Tanay, 'In Defence of the Insanity Defence' in SJ Hucker, CD Webster, and MH Ben-Aron (eds), *Mental Disorder and Criminal Responsibility*, (Butterworths 1981) 134.

[70] See ML Perlin, 'The Insanity Defense: Nine Myths That Will Not Go Away' in MD White (ed), *The Insanity Defense: Multidisciplinary Views on its History, Trends and Controversies* (Praeger 2017) 5.

[71] ibid 11.

[72] See eg EM Maeder, S Yamamoto, and KL Fenwick, 'Educating Canadian Jurors about the Not Criminally Responsible on Account of Mental Disorder Defence' (2015) 47(3) Can J Behav Sci 226–35; EM Maeder, S Yamamoto, and L Zannella, 'Putting Negative Attitudes on the Agenda? Not Criminally Responsible Reform Act Publicity and Juror Decision-Making' (2016) 49 Int J Law Psychiatry 154, 155.

[73] See eg the Not Criminally Responsible Reform Act (Bill C-54) passed by the Parliament of Canada on 11 July 2014 discussed in chapter 6 and Rights for Victims of Insane Offender Act 2021 discussed in chapter 7.

[74] See C Slobogin, 'Eliminating Mental Disability as a Legal Criterion in Deprivation of Liberty Cases: The Impact of the Convention on the Rights of Persons with Disabilities on the Insanity Defense, Civil Commitment and Competency Law' (2015) 40 Int J Law Psychiatry 36–42; L Malatesti, M Jurjako, and G Meynen, 'The Insanity Defence Without Mental Illness? Some Considerations' (2020) 71 Int J Law Psychiatry 1–7.

[75] MC Freeman and others, 'Reversing Hard Won Victories in the Name of Human Rights: A Critique of the General Comment on Article 12 of the UN Convention on the Rights of Persons with

need for urgent reconsideration of the General Comment on Article 12, with the full participation of practitioners and a wide range of user and family groups.[76]

Although calls for abolition are not new, and in some instances have resulted in legislative intervention to repeal existing insanity laws,[77] by and large the law has been remarkably ambivalent towards mental disorders generally and the defence of insanity especially. However, claims of societal ambivalence towards the insanity defence probably understate the degree of antipathy towards the doctrine. On one view society is fixated on the insanity defence as 'a symbol of all that is wrong with the criminal justice system and as a source of social and political anger'.[78] Arguably, the narrow range of disposal options available in many western jurisdictions for persons acquitted on account of insanity is a further expression of this particular cultural mentality. Often enough, however, anger towards the defence reflects not so much on the defence itself but the person who is claiming it. The defence is demonized because the accused is perceived as a 'bad' person. In this regard, Perlin's insights into the power of the 'vividness heuristic' are telling. He cautions that this cognitive simplifying device teaches us that 'when decisionmakers are in the thrall of a highly salient event, that event will so dominate their thinking that they will make aggregate decisions that are overdependent on the particular event and that overestimate the representativeness of that event within some larger array of events'. Perlin further states that 'one single vivid, memorable case overwhelms mountains of abstract, colorless data upon which rational choices should be made'.[79]

In addition to the popular prejudice that has afflicted the legitimacy of the insanity defence, a host of collateral conceptual challenges have bedevilled its ongoing development and application. These include agreeing a base threshold for determining criminal responsibility, determining the kinds of mental conditions sufficient to trigger the defence, distinguishing between relevant internal and external causal factors, the scope and legitimacy of irresistible impulse, and defining the parameters of knowledge of wrong. These and many other conceptual issues have sometimes led to difficult legal and moral distinctions having to be made, often challenging judges, jurors, and legal and medical professionals alike. A contemporary example is the notion of drug-induced psychosis and its place, if any,

Disabilities' (2015) 2(9) The Lancet Psychiatry 844–50; Editorial, 'Psychiatry Unlocked' (2017) 4 The Lancet Psychiatry 261.

[76] See ML Perlin, 'God Said to Abraham/Kill Me a Son: Why the Insanity Defense and the Incompetency Status Are Compatible with and Required by the Convention on the Rights of Persons with Disabilities and Basic Principles of Therapeutic Jurisprudence' (2017) 54(2) Am Crim Law Rev 477.

[77] In the United States the states of Idaho, Kansa, Montana, and Utah have abolished the insanity defence: see Chapter 9.

[78] ML Perlin, 'The Insanity Defense: Nine Myths That Will Not Go Away' in MD White (ed), *The Insanity Defense: Multidisciplinary Views on its History, Trends and Controversies* (Praeger 2017) 3.

[79] ibid 4.

within the insanity rules. In this and other domains in which exculpatory insanity is sought to be advanced, the accurate identification of offenders as either sane or insane is invariably dependent on the evidence of medical professionals, typically psychiatrists but increasingly neuropsychologists, whose professional insights will often be determinative of certain facts in issue. Yet there are no bright lines for determining when or whether a mental impairment constitutes a state of insanity sufficient to amount to an excuse for crime. Medical testimony is extremely variable, with highly qualified medical professionals often disagreeing on diagnoses in assessments of mental capacity, the more so when the instructing party is also a party to the proceedings in which testimony is given. Such disagreement amongst medical professionals may be misinterpreted by laypeople as indicating that insanity has no consistent foundation in medical science, reinforcing popular prejudice against the defence.

In this book, these and many other difficult questions raised by the insanity defence are explored in detail. While the focus of the book is primarily legal, comparative and interdisciplinary insights will also be discussed as a wide range of jurisdictions and different sociolegal perspectives are examined.

Organization of the Book

What follows is a brief outline of each chapter contained in this edited collection.

In Chapter 2, 'The Insanity Defence in English Law', Professor Ronnie Mackay traces the development of the M'Naghten Rules through the case and statute law and evaluates how the insanity defence, including that of automatism, operates in practice.

Chapter 3, 'Reforming the Insanity Defence in England and Wales' is authored by Professor David Ormerod, QC, formerly Law Commissioner for England and Wales and Dr Mark Dsouza. It discusses how with an increasingly enlightened attitude to mental health issues in the criminal justice system, there is an opportunity for law reform to create an insanity defence which deals fairly and equitably with mentally disordered offenders.

Chapter 4, 'The Mental Disorder Defence in Scots Law' is authored by Professor Gerry Maher formerly the Scottish Law Commissioner who led the law reform project dealing with reform of the insanity defence in Scots law. The chapter contains a detailed discussion of the history of the reform process in Scotland together with a full account of the Commission's law reform proposals duly implemented by statute.

In Chapter 5, 'The Insanity Defence in Irish Law', Professor Paul McCutcheon shows how the insanity defence in Ireland has altered from one based on the M'Naghten Rules to a statutory defence which codifies the judicial development of the plea.

In Chapter 6, 'The Mental Disorder Defence: Canadian Law and Practice', Professor Gerry Ferguson examines the defence of mental disorder in Canada. Significant legislative changes were made in 1992 to the procedures, evidence, and disposition options for the insanity defence. Many of these legislative changes contain significant improvements in the application of the mental disorder defence.

Professor Warren Brookbanks, in Chapter 7, 'The Insanity Defence: Conflict and Reform in New Zealand', discusses the development of the defence of insanity and how over the last 15 years, the insanity defence has been the subject of close attention, and criticism, in New Zealand.

In Chapter 8, 'The Insanity Defence under Australian Law', Professor Ian Freckelton reviews the extensive and distinctive jurisprudence that has evolved in Australia in relation to the defence of insanity/mental impairment by reference to High Court and Court of Appeal decisions. The chapter analyses the procedures for raising and establishing the defence, as well as the criteria for findings of not guilty by reason of insanity at common law and then the later, subtly different formulations for findings of not guilty by reason of mental impairment under the statutes of Australia's states and territories.

Chapter 9, 'Before and After Hinckley: Legal Insanity in the United States', is written by Professor Stephen J Morse. In the wake of the successful insanity defence raised by John Hinckley, Jr for the attempted assassination of President Reagan and others in 1981, there was intense criticism of the defence of legal insanity and a wave of legislative reform. This chapter considers the primary changes that followed the verdict and developments in the law of the defence since then, including abolition of the defence in four states.

Chapters 10–13 are devoted to the insanity defence in four civil law jurisdictions.

In Chapter 10, 'The Insanity Defence in French Law: Are Prisons the "New Asylums"?', Dr Audrey Guinchard traces how French criminal law has long recognized that a person lacking capacity due to lack of control or a mental disorder should not be held criminally liable. It did so through a single cause of non-liability, a structure that has not changed, even with the 1992 reform of the Criminal Code.

Chapter 11, 'Insanity in German Criminal Law', is authored by Dr Regina E Rauxloh and traces the development of the defence of insanity in German law where culpability is presumed for perpetrators from the age of 14 but can be excluded where, at the time of the commission of the offence, the offender is 'incapable of appreciating the unlawfulness of their actions or of acting in accordance with any such appreciation due to a pathological mental disorder, a profound consciousness disorder, debility or any other serious mental abnormality'.

In Chapter 12, 'Legal Insanity in the Netherlands: Regulations and Reflections', Professor Gerben Meynen discusses the insanity defence in the Dutch criminal justice system, which is markedly different from common law jurisdictions as it has no legal criterion specifying the conditions under which the presence of a mental illness supports an insanity plea. In addition, Dutch law has three levels of criminal responsibility namely: responsibility, diminished responsibility, and (complete) insanity.

Chapter 13, 'Criminal Insanity in Norwegian Law', by Professor Linda Gröning reviews the Norwegian rules and systems for criminal insanity. Focus is given to the unique medical model used in Norway; its content, historical/legal cultural background and justifications, and critique and proposals for change.

In Chapter 14, entitled 'The Insanity Defence in China', Dr Lilou Jiang critically examines the insanity defence regime in China and addresses the historical treatment of mental illness in Chinese society generally and in the criminal law in particular.

Chapter 15, 'The Insanity Defence under International Criminal Law', written by Professor Ian Freckelton and Magda Karagiannakis traces the history of the insanity defence from the Nuremberg trials. Insanity was the subject of extensive discussion in the lead-up to the Rome Conference which established the International Criminal Court.

The final Chapter 16, 'Conclusion', written by Professor Ronnie Mackay and Professor Warren Brookbanks offers a synthesis of the law around the insanity defence drawn from the different jurisdictions surveyed in the book. It seeks to identify common themes and to suggest areas where there is a clear consensus on the need for reform. It is hoped that the book will serve as a benchmark for the theory and practice relating to the defence of insanity and provide an opportunity for useful reflection and debate on the future direction of this unique defence.

2
The Insanity Defence in English Law

Ronnie Mackay

Introduction

The insanity defence in English law is based upon the famous M'Naghten Rules which have remained unchanged since 1843.[1] This is despite constant criticism and several official attempts at reform.[2] This chapter will trace the development of the Rules through the case and statute law in order to evaluate how the insanity defence, including that of automatism, is perceived to operate. The chapter will also contain an analysis of the author's empirical studies into the defence, together with a discussion of how the law in the channel island of Jersey came to reject the M'Naghten Rules in favour of a new test which incorporates volitional impairment.

It will be argued that although the M'Naghten Rules are in need of urgent statutory reform,[3] if, as seems likely, this is not forthcoming then the appellate courts, if given the opportunity, should develop the law by adopting an expansionary approach to the Rules in much the same way as has occurred in some other common law jurisdictions.

The Historical Development of the Insanity Defence

For present purposes, there are two historical landmarks which merit discussion given their impact and influence on the defence of insanity. The first was the trial and acquittal on the grounds of insanity of James Hadfield,[4] which resulted in the enactment of the Criminal Lunatics Act of 1800. This statute had a profound influence on the treatment of Hadfield and all those who were subsequently so acquitted, leading as it did to automatic detention for an indefinite period of time.[5] Indeed, Hadfield was held at Bethlem hospital for a period of 41 years until his

[1] (1843) 10 Cl & F 200, 210; [1843–60] All ER Rep 229.
[2] Referred to later in the concluding section of this chapter.
[3] See Chapter 3.
[4] (1800) 27 How St Tr 765.
[5] Although the 1800 Act was effectively replaced by the Criminal Procedure (Insanity) Act 1964, it was not until the enactment of the Criminal Procedure (Insanity and Unfitness to Plead) Act 1991 that such automatic detention was no longer mandatory (except where the charge was murder).

Ronnie Mackay, *The Insanity Defence in English Law* In: *The Insanity Defence*. Edited by: Ronnie Mackay and Warren Brookbanks, Oxford University Press. © Ronnie Mackay 2022. DOI: 10.1093/oso/9780198854944.003.0002

death from tuberculosis in 1841, only two years before the most significant historical landmark in the development of the insanity defence, namely the trial of Daniel M'Naghten and its aftermath.

Much has been written about M'Naghten's case.[6] The accused, who is said to have suffered from delusions of persecution, mistakenly assassinated the Private Secretary to the Prime Minister, Sir Robert Peel, in the belief that he was attacking the latter. It is well-known that the public outcry following M'Naghten's special acquittal on the grounds of insanity resulted in the formulation of the Rules which are named after him. What is perhaps less well-known is that historical research into the case and its aftermath strongly suggests that M'Naghten was not mentally ill and that his special acquittal was used to discredit him and to serve as an example to others as well as to incapacitate him:[7] a result which was successfully achieved, as M'Naghten died in Broadmoor from tuberculosis some 22 years later.

The importance of M'Naghten's case lies in the repercussions which followed from his acquittal on the ground of insanity. This resulted in debate in the House of Lords[8] which in turn led to the resolution that the opinion of all the judges should be sought as to the law governing such cases. Accordingly, on 19 June 1843, a number of questions were put to the judges, the answers to which have become known as the M'Naghten Rules.

Before turning to the Rules themselves, a point which is worthy of note is that until recently there was a lack of clarity as to which and how many of the judges had actually been signatories to the Rules. Thus, in an earlier discussion of the insanity defence I had concluded 'It has been generally assumed that all 15 judges were involved. However, the House of Lords' record speaks only of 11. Apart from Tindal LCJ, who delivered the collective ruling and Maule J who dissented, we cannot now be sure who the others were.'[9] From this, I surmised that all 15 of the judges had been actual signatories to the Rules. However, I was mistaken as my further research into the Parliamentary Archives at the House of Lords[10] revealed at the end of the actual manuscript containing the majority answers were 12 signatures, including that of Lord Tindal CJ.[11] This means that, with the addition of Maule J who dissented, we have a total of 13 judges who appear on the actual record. The two missing judges, namely, Lords Denman and Abinger, did not sign and we do not know why this is so. As a result, we can now only be sure that 12 judges approved

[6] See N Walker, *Crime and Insanity in England, Vol. I The Historical Perspective* (Edinburgh University Press 1968) chapter 5; D West and A Walk (eds), *Daniel McNaughton: His Trial and Aftermath* (Gaskell Books 1977).

[7] R Moran, *Knowing Right from Wrong: The Insanity Defence of Daniel M'Naghten* (Free Press 1981).

[8] See House of Lords Debates Hansard Vol 67, 6 March, cc 288–90 and 13 March, cc 714–44.

[9] RD Mackay, *Mental Condition Defences in the Criminal Law* (Clarendon Press 1995) 96, n 120.

[10] I wish to record my sincere thanks to Parliamentary Archives for all their help. They can be found at: https://archives.parliament.uk/

[11] For discussion and detail of the actual signatures see R Mackay, 'The M'Naghten Rules—A Brief Historical Note' [2019] Crim LR 966, 968.

the Rules. Of course, the Rules have been followed without question since 1843. However, the precise way they came about remains anomalous. So this added lack of certainty about the signatures might in some small way call into question their continued legal status as well as supporting the need to develop the Rules.[12] Let us now turn to the Rules themselves.

The M'Naghten Rules in Operation

The essentials of the rules are as follows:

> [T]he jurors ought to be told in all cases that every man is to be presumed to be sane, and to possess a sufficient degree of reason to be responsible for his crimes, until the contrary be proved to their satisfaction; and that to establish a defence on the ground of insanity, it must be clearly proved that, at the time of the committing of the act, the party accused was labouring under such a defect of reason, from disease of the mind, as not to know the nature and quality of the act he was doing; or, if he did know it, that he did not know he was doing what was wrong.
>
> If a person ... labours under [a] partial delusion only, and is not in other respects insane, we think he must be considered in the same situation as to responsibility as if the facts with respect to which the delusion exists were real.[13]

Although the Rules as quoted above have three limbs, only the 'nature and quality' and 'wrongness' limbs are of real importance; as the 'partial delusion' limb seems never to have achieved the same degree of authority, perhaps because it seems to add little of substance to the other limbs. Despite this, and the constant criticism to which they have been subject, the Rules have remained unaltered as the basic common law test for criminal responsibility in English law. The criticism in question has taken a variety of forms, the basis of which is that the Rules are (i) too narrow and so if interpreted strictly have the potential to exclude most mentally abnormal offenders and (ii) do not accord with current medical thinking, as they are based on antiquated and outmoded concepts.[14]

What now follows is an analysis of the case law which has interpreted the Rules, together with a discussion of automatism and finally a summary of my empirical research into how the insanity defence operates in practice. At the outset, it should be emphasized that the two 'knowledge' requirements contained in the Rules have

[12] This point is discussed below in the concluding section.

[13] (1843) 10 Cl & F 200, 210; [1843–60] All ER Rep 229, 233.

[14] See also Law Commission, 'Criminal Liability: Insanity and Automatism, A Scoping Paper' (2012) Part 2.

been interpreted by the courts as establishing a narrow cognitive test for both the 'nature and quality' and 'wrongness' limbs.

The 'Nature and Quality' Limb

This phrase has been interpreted in a restrictive sense so that no distinction has been drawn between 'nature' and 'quality'. Rather, the phrase refers only to the physical character of the act and not to its moral or legal quality.[15] In *R v Sullivan*[16] the phrase was updated by Lord Diplock when he remarked that 'it might be more clearly expressed as "He did not know what he was doing"'.[17] An obvious example is where the accused's acts were unconscious and involuntary and so were performed while the accused was in a state of automatism. In such cases, the crucial question tends to be whether the automatism is the result of a 'disease of the mind', in which case it will be classified as being of the insane variety. Cases of this type fall within the first limb of the Rules as they are obvious examples of where the accused (D) does not know what he was doing and so lacked any knowledge of the 'act' in question which gave rise to the offence. In short, the automatism strand of the insanity defence does not present any difficulty insofar as its place in the 'nature and quality' limb is concerned.

But what of cases where D's condition falls short of automatism but results in a lack of mens rea? This issue goes to the heart of a vital distinction between the two limbs of the M'Naghten Rules, for while it is clear that the 'wrongness' limb does not engage mens rea questions this is not true of the 'nature and quality' limb which does seem to have such relevance. If this is so then should not unawareness of the act lead to a simple acquittal irrespective of whether that lack of mens rea was the result of a 'disease of the mind'? The answer is not straightforward but depends not only on whether D was suffering from a 'disease of the mind' but also whether D's condition gave rise to a 'defect of reason'. In *Clarke*[18] it was held that a 'defect of reason' requires more than mere confusion or absentmindedness. Thus, where

[15] See *R v Codere* (1916) 12 Cr App Rep 21. AP Simester and others, *Simester and Sullivan's Criminal Law: Theory and Doctrine* (7th edn, Hart Publishing 2019) 772 suggest that in *Loake v CPS* [2018] QB 988, para 56, a wider approach may have been taken in a harassment case where the Divisional Court, in confirming that the insanity defence was available in respect of strict liability offences, stated that 'If a person suffering from severe dementia, such that they cannot recall events beyond a few minutes, repeatedly telephoned or texted the same individual, on each occasion believing they are doing so for the first time, they would not know the nature of their act: they would not know of the sustained nature of the texts or calls.' If this does indicate a wider approach then it is to be welcomed. However, this seems unlikely given the Court's concluding remark at para 63, 'We do not anticipate that someone who has engaged in such conduct will readily be able to show that throughout that period they did not know the nature and quality of their act, or that throughout that time they did not know what they were doing was wrong, in the necessary sense'.

[16] [1984] AC 156; [1983] 2 All ER 673.

[17] [1984] AC 156, 173.

[18] [1972] 1 All ER 219.

a mildly depressed accused was prosecuted for shoplifting, the Court of Appeal ruled that, even if the depression might qualify as a 'disease of the mind', the trial judge should not have left insanity to the jury. This makes it clear that something more fundamental is needed to satisfy the 'defect of reason' requirement. It is also noteworthy that the Rules require proof that the 'party accused was labouring under *such* a defect of reason, from disease of the mind' (emphasis added), which highlights the fact that for a disease of the mind to be able to ground an insanity plea it must have caused a distortion in D's reasoning powers of a particular kind or character in the sense of being severe enough to produce unawareness of the act. In short, this type of distortion alone will qualify as a 'defect of reason' under the M'Naghten Rules[19] which is why only very few Ds will fall within the nature and quality limb.[20]

The Wrongness Limb

This limb of the Rules has also been interpreted very narrowly by the English courts. So in *R v Windle*[21] the meaning of the word 'wrong' was restricted to legal wrong alone. Although in principle this meant that a defendant who was deluded into believing that his act was in compliance with the law might be found to be legally insane even if he knew that what he was doing was morally wrong this avenue of excuse is no longer possible as a result of the Court of Appeal's decision in *R v Keal*[22] referred to below.

The wrongness limb differs from its nature and quality counterpart as it does not go to an essential ingredient of the offence. This was confirmed in *Loake v CPS*[23] where the court stated that 'the principle underpinning the second limb of the M'Naghten Rules ... is a fundamental one' the rationale of which is 'when a person ought to be liable for criminal punishment'.[24] However, this did not prevent the court from confirming that '"he did not know it was wrong" means legally wrong, and not morally wrong'.[25] In doing so the court also approved *R v Johnson*,[26] where

[19] In H Fingarette, *The Meaning of Criminal Insanity* (University of California Press 1972), the author, in emphasizing the essential and distinctive nature of 'defect of reason', opines at 178: 'I believe that what the judges had in mind by "defect of reason" was what we also have in mind when we speak, in the context of insanity, of "losing one's reason," of being irrational, or reason being dethroned. They appreciated, as we all do in practice, that lack of capacity for rationality impairs responsibility.'

[20] For detailed discussion see R Mackay, '"Nature", "Quality" and Mens Rea—Some Observations on "Defect of Reason" and the First Limb of the M'Naghten Rules' [2020] Crim LR 588.

[21] [1952] 2 QB 826. For recent criticism of this decision see J Manwaring, 'Windle Revisited' [2018] Crim LR 987.

[22] [2022] EWCA Crim 341

[23] [2018] QB 998.

[24] ibid para 49.

[25] ibid para 23.

[26] [2007] EWCA 1978.

the Court of Appeal, in giving passing recognition to the fact that in practice strict adherence to this approach seems to have been ignored by psychiatrists and perhaps the courts themselves,[27] concluded that there was 'room for reconsideration of the rules and, in particular, rules which have their genesis in the early years of the 19th century. But it does not seem to us that that debate is a debate which can properly take place before us at this level in this case.'[28] This was confirmed by the Court of Appeal in *R v Keal*[29] where Lord Burnett CJ stated, 'An individual case does not provide an apt vehicle for the reconsideration of the "wrongdoing" elements of the M'Naghten rules'. [30] In dismissing the appeal his Lordship ruled:

> In order to establish the defence of insanity within the M'Naghten Rules on the ground of not knowing the act was 'wrong', the defendant must establish both that (a) he did not know that his act was unlawful (i.e. contrary to law) and (b) he did not know that his act was 'morally' wrong (also expressed as wrong 'by the standards of ordinary people'). In our judgment, 'wrong' means both against the law and wrong by the standards of ordinary reasonable people. [31]

What this means is that the interpretation of the wrongness limb in *Windle* and *Johnson* is now even stricter as 'in the reverse, and likely rare, case, where the defendant did not know what he was doing was "contrary to law", but did know it was "morally wrong", the defence is not available'. [32] Lord Burnett's justification for this approach is based on the fact that 'The focus in *Windle* (and *Johnson*) on "wrong" meaning "contrary to law" flowed from the nature of each case. On the facts of both, each defendant knew what he was doing was "contrary to law", but there was evidence that he did not consider that the act was "morally wrong".'[33] The result is that any knowledge of wrong, whether legal or moral, will ensure that D is outside the M'Naghten Rules.

So we must await either an appeal to go before the Supreme Court[34] or for statutory reform, while in the meantime many mentally abnormal offenders remain

[27] ibid para 23 where Latham LJ states 'The fact, however, remains that, although that has been the basis upon which the textbooks have set out the rule and its proper meaning, there is some evidence which is contained in material in articles, in particular, by Professor Mackay, for example, "Yet more facts about the Insanity Defence" [1999] Crim LR 714, that courts may have on occasions been prepared to approach the issue on a more relaxed basis. Nonetheless, in our view, the strict position at the moment remains as stated in Windle . . . '.

[28] ibid para 24.

[29] [2022] EWCA Crim 341.

[30] ibid para 50.

[31] ibid para 41.

[32] ibid para 42.

[33] ibid.

[34] But in *Keal* [2022] EWCA Crim 341, para 51 Lord Burnett CJ makes it clear that the judicial avenue is inappropriate stating, 'In our judgment significant changes to an aspect of our criminal law that has remained undisturbed for so long, laden with policy choices as they would be, are more properly for Parliament'.

excluded from the insanity plea[35] by virtue of the fact that it is not unusual for mentally ill Ds to be so deluded that they believe that their criminal act is morally right which, as emphasized above, will not fall within the 'wrongness' limb.

'Disease of the Mind' and Automatism

This phrase within the M'Naghten Rules has resulted in more debate and litigation than any other aspect of the Rules. In essence, the scope of 'disease of the mind' has influenced the parameters of the insanity defence as well as those of the closely related defence of automatism. This, in turn, has resulted in two conflicting principles which are difficult to reconcile. The first is the need to protect the public from certain types of mentally abnormal offenders, while at the same time recognizing that if such a person is found legally 'insane' then he is not criminally responsible and so cannot be punished, hence the special verdict of 'not guilty by reason of insanity'. The second—leading to the development of the automatism defence—is the need to control the scope of 'disease of the mind' so that certain types of conditions can be excluded where it would be 'an affront to common sense'[36] to declare such a person 'insane'.

As long ago as the decision in *Kemp*[37] it was clear that an expansionary interpretation of 'disease of the mind' was the accepted judicial approach. In that case, where D suffered from arteriosclerosis (a hardening of the arteries), Devlin J confirmed that such a condition could fall within 'disease of the mind' saying, 'In my judgement the condition of the brain is irrelevant and is so the question of whether the condition of the mind is curable, incurable, transitory or permanent'.[38] Two House of Lords decisions both dealing with epilepsy endorsed this approach. First in *Bratty v AG for N. Ireland*[39] Lord Denning famously opined 'It seems to me that any mental disorder which has manifested itself in violence and is prone to recur is a disease of the mind'.[40] Secondly, in *Sullivan*[41] Lord Diplock remarked:

> The nomenclature adopted by the medical profession may change from time to time … but the meaning of the expression 'disease of the mind', as a cause of a 'defect of reason' remains unchanged for the purposes of the application of the M'Naghten Rules. I agree with what was said by Devlin J. in *Kemp* that 'mind' in the M'Naghten Rules is used in the ordinary sense of mental faculties of reason,

[35] For further discussion see RD Mackay, 'Righting the Wrong?—Some Observations on the Second Limb of the M'Naghten Rules' [2009] Crim LR 80.

[36] See *R v Quick* [1973] QB 910, 918.

[37] [1957] QB 399.

[38] ibid 407.

[39] [1963] AC 386.

[40] ibid 412.

[41] [1984] AC 156; [1983] 2 All ER 673.

> memory and understanding. If the effect of a disease is to impair these faculties so severely as to have either of the consequences referred to in the latter part of the rules, it matters not whether the aetiology is organic, as in epilepsy, or functional, or whether the impairment itself is permanent or is transient and intermittent, provided that it subsisted at the time of the commission of the act.[42]

In rejecting the views of two psychiatrists that epilepsy was not a mental illness and should not be classified as a 'disease of the mind', Lord Diplock justified this approach in the following manner:

> The purpose of the legislation relating to the defence of insanity ... has been to protect society against the recurrence of dangerous conduct. The duration of a temporary suspension of the mental faculties of reason, memory and understanding ... cannot on any rational ground be relevant to the application by the courts of the M'Naghten Rules.[43]

Left like this, 'disease of the mind' would encompass almost every aberration of normal mental functioning irrespective of its cause. It was this concern which led to the development of the automatism defence, which Lord Diplock made clear should be available 'in cases where temporary impairment ... results from some external physical factor such as a blow on the head causing concussion or the administration of an anaesthetic for therapeutic purposes'.[44]

This itself has been deeply problematical as it has given rise to a sane/insane automatism dichotomy based on a distinction between internal and external factors.

Internal v external

Automatism was defined in *Bratty v AG for N Ireland* as 'connoting the state of a person who, though capable of action, is not conscious of what he is doing ... It means unconscious involuntary action, and it is a defence because the mind does not go with what is being done.'[45] This rather simplistic definition was somewhat clarified in *Coley and others v R*[46] which called for a consideration of the 'interplay between the law relating to voluntary intoxication and the law relating to insanity or (non-insane) automatism'.[47] In the course of his judgment, Hughes LJ emphasized that for an action to qualify as automatism, although this does not mean that D must be '*un*conscious, in the sense of comatose',[48] it does require 'movements

42 [1984] AC 156, 172.
43 ibid.
44 ibid.
45 [1963] AC 386, 401.
46 [2013] EWCA Crim 223.
47 ibid para 1.
48 ibid para 23.

or actions of the defendant at the material time that were wholly involuntary'.[49] In reaching this conclusion Hughes LJ cited the decision in *A-G's Reference (no 2 of 1992)*[50] and preferred the expression 'complete destruction of voluntary control'. Although this narrow approach to what constitutes automatism has been the subject of much criticism, it must now be regarded as the prevailing judicial approach. In addition, the Law Commission recently remarked, 'Our view is that, although the case law is not entirely consistent in requiring a total loss of control, the overwhelming weight of the recent authority supports the stricter view'.[51] The problem with this approach is that, as I have said before, it would seem to restrict the defence to 'spasms, convulsions and reflex acts'.[52] Thus, it will continue to cater for forms of epileptic automatism but is likely to exclude most forms of outwardly purposeful behaviour where D argues that his condition deprived him of 'effective control of the act'. In short, a state of reduced, partial, or altered consciousness will, in principle, no longer suffice. While this approach will in itself reduce the scope of the automatism defence, so also does what Hughes LJ referred to as 'the distinction drawn in *Quick*[53] between cases where external factors induce a condition of the mind and internal factors which can properly be described as a disease',[54] a distinction which his Lordship remarked 'can give rise to apparently strange results at the margin'.[55] No results are stranger than in relation to diabetes, where the Court of Appeal in *R v Quick*[56] recognized that a legal device was needed to prevent the 'affront to common sense' of 'a diabetic being sent to a [mental] hospital when in most cases the disordered mental condition can be rectified by pushing a lump of sugar or a teaspoonful of glucose into the patient's mouth'.[57] In that case, in order to prevent the accused's condition of hypoglycaemia from being classified as a 'disease of the mind', Lawton LJ ruled that the automatism 'was not caused by the diabetes but by the use of insulin … Such malfunctioning as there was, was caused by an external factor and not by a bodily disorder in the nature of a disease.'[58] In this way, the accused's automatism was able to be classified as sane rather than insane. But by relying on the need for any such malfunctioning of the mind of transitory effect to be attributable to 'the application to the body of some external factor', the court was conceding that if no such external factor is present then a condition, such as diabetes, will still qualify as a 'disease of the mind' irrespective of the

[49] ibid para 22.
[50] [1994] QB 91.
[51] Law Commission, 'Insanity and automatism: Supplementary Material to the Scoping Paper' (2012) para 2.64.
[52] RD Mackay, *Mental Condition Defences in the Criminal Law* (Clarendon Press 1995) 63.
[53] [1973] QB 910.
[54] [2013] EWCA Crim 223, para 22.
[55] ibid.
[56] [1973] 3 All ER 347.
[57] ibid 352.
[58] ibid 359.

'affront to common sense' argument. Such was the case in *R v Hennessy*,[59] where a diabetic's hyperglycaemic episode was ruled to fall within insane automatism as it was 'caused by an inherent defect'[60] and was, therefore, a 'disease of the mind'. Although this legally created distinction is manifestly unsatisfactory, in *Coley* the Court of Appeal had no choice but to conclude that '*Hennessy* approved and applied *Quick*, which represents the law binding on us'.[61] It would seem, therefore, that the only way forward is either for the Supreme Court to be asked to reconsider the status of the 'external factor' doctrine or for there to be wholesale statutory reform of both automatism and insanity. With regard to the latter, which is fully discussed in Chapter 3, it is this very distinction between 'internal' and 'external' factors which influenced the Law Commission provisionally to recommend a new 'not criminally responsible' defence based on a 'recognised medical condition'[62] which would not only encompass *Quick* but also most other cases of sane automatism having regard to the fact that such an approach would eradicate the 'internal/ external' dichotomy.[63] While such an approach may seem understandable, its consequences are far-reaching, as to deny an unqualified acquittal to those who at present plead sane automatism successfully is a major shift in respect of defence parameters. Instead, such cases would qualify for a new special verdict and be subject to such control and disposal as considered judicially appropriate.

In the light of this concern, together with the fact that comprehensive reform within this area seems unlikely, a better approach would be for the Supreme Court to be given the opportunity to re-evaluate the relationship between insanity and automatism.

The Canadian approach

In this respect, a comparison with the approach taken in Canada[64] seems instructive. Before considering this issue, it should be pointed out that the legal position in relation to self-induced intoxication has been altered by the Supreme Court of Canada. In two important decisions, the Court ruled that the statutory provision introduced by the Canadian Parliament, which precluded the defence of intoxication in respect of general intent offences of violence where the intoxication was self-induced,[65] is unconstitutional as it infringes the Canadian Charter of Rights. Thus in *R v Brown*[66] *and in R v Sullivan and Chan*[67] the defendants attacked

[59] [1989] 2 All ER 9.
[60] ibid 14.
[61] [2013] EWCA Crim 223, para 20.
[62] Law Commission, 'Criminal Liability: Insanity and Automatism—A Discussion Paper' chapter 3.
[63] ibid chapter 5.
[64] See also Chapter 6.
[65] Section 33.1 of the Criminal Code of Canada provided that a person is guilty of a violent offence even if they were so intoxicated that they did not know what they were doing, so long as that intoxication was self-induced.
[66] 2022 SCC 18
[67] 2022 SCC 19 .

thei victims, each claiming that at the time they were in a state of automatism. The accused's appeals against their convictions were allowed. In Brown's case the accused had consumed alcohol and magic mushrooms which gave rise to a state of automatism which resulted in his acquittal being restored. In the case of *Chan*, a new trial was ordered, as the trial judge had been wrong to refuse to allow D's defence, based on a state of extreme intoxication resulting from his consumption of 'magic mushrooms', to be considered by the jury. In *Brown*'s case, his state of extreme intoxication, arising from his consumption of alcohol and 'magic mushroms', was accepted as giving rise to an automatism defence and his convictions were set aside. Such an approach is in marked contrast to that in *Coley* where it is clear that self-induced intoxication cannot give rise to an automatism defence even though it is due to an 'external factor'. The reason is one of policy and based on the notion of fault, which is discussed in the following section. In the course of his decision in *Brown*, Kasirer J , citing the decision of the Supreme Court of Canada in *R v Stone*,[68] confirmed that automatism in the law of Canada is defined as 'a state of impaired consciousness, rather than unconsciousness, in which an individual, though capable of action, has no voluntary control over that action',[69] which again is markedly different from the definition adopted in *Coley*. In *Stone*,[70] a case dealing with psychological blow automatism, Bastarache J agreed with the court's earlier decision in *Parks*, a sleepwalking case, where La Forest J concluded that what he termed the 'internal cause' theory 'is really meant to be used only as an analytical tool, and not as an all-encompassing methodology'.[71] This, in turn, led Bastarache J to adopt 'a more holistic approach'[72] where it would be appropriate 'to refer to the internal cause factor and the continuing danger factor, rather than the internal cause theory and the continuing danger theory',[73] thus permitting a trial judge to 'find one, the other or both of these approaches of assistance'.[74] Further, in cases where 'the internal cause theory is not helpful because it is impossible to classify the alleged automatism as internal or external, and the continuing danger factor is inconclusive because there is no continuing danger of violence ... a more holistic approach to disease of the mind must also permit trial judges to consider other policy concerns which underlie this inquiry'.[75] In Bastarache J's view, policy concerns were not only relevant to distinguishing between sane and insane automatism but also to determining an appropriate legal burden of proof in all such cases. Concerning the latter, he concluded that 'because automatism is easily feigned and all knowledge of its occurrence rests with the accused, putting a legal burden on the accused

[68] [1999] 2 SCR 290, para 156; 173 DLR (4th) 66.
[69] 2022 SCC 18 at para 2 , para 2.
[70] [1999] 2 SCR 290.
[71] (1992) 95 DLR (4th) 27 (SCC), 48.
[72] [1999] 2 SCR 290, para 150.
[73] ibid para 154.
[74] ibid.
[75] ibid para 156.

to prove involuntariness on a balance of probabilities is necessary to further the objective behind the presumption of voluntariness. In contrast, saddling the Crown with the legal burden of proving voluntariness beyond a reasonable doubt actually defeats the purpose of the presumption of voluntariness.'[76] In reaching this conclusion Bastarache J made it clear that this legal burden on the defence applies to both sane and insane automatism.

Again this is different from the approach taken in English law, where the burden of proof remains on the prosecution in cases of sane automatism but rests on the defence in all cases of insanity, including those of insane automatism.[77] What difference this makes is open to question. On the one hand, it might be argued that it is unfair and contrary to principle to require the defence to prove that the act was both conscious and voluntary. On the other hand, it makes the law simpler to have the same burden of proof in all automatism cases.[78] Whether this change has had a significant effect on the success of sane automatism cases in Canada is difficult to assess as there are no official statistics kept. However, the number of reported cases suggests that placing the legal burden on the defence has not acted as a disincentive to pleading automatism.[79]

A good example of how the 'holistic' approach may lead to different results from those achieved by the application of the 'external factor' doctrine in England is in respect of epilepsy. In English law, as mentioned above, epileptic automatism was confirmed in *Sullivan* as being of the insane type. However, in *R v Bohak*[80] the accused, in answer to a charge of assault, claimed that at the time he had suffered an epileptic seizure. There was strong evidence to support this so the judge, Giesbrecht PJ, had no difficulty in deciding that the evidential burden had been satisfied. More difficult was how this form of automatism should be classified, sane or insane. To answer this question the judge relied on the holistic approach endorsed in *Stone*. In doing so he concluded that the internal cause theory which had resulted in epilepsy being categorized as a disease of the mind needed to be reconsidered as it was of limited value in the present case because both internal and external factors were operating.

He then proceeded to consider the continuing danger factor in the context of the two issues of particular relevance identified in *Stone*, namely 'the psychiatric history of the accused and the likelihood that the trigger that caused the automatistic

76 ibid para 180.

77 See *Bratty v AG for N Ireland* [1963] AC 386.

78 Interestingly, the Law Commission seeks to achieve this by provisionally proposing that the burden of proof should be the same for both the new defence of 'not criminally responsible by reason of recognised medical condition' and automatism. See 'Criminal Liability: Insanity and Automatism—A Discussion Paper' paras 10.26 and 10.27. However, unlike the position in Canada, the prosecution would bear the burden of proof.

79 It is also interesting to note that the evidential burden in automatism cases is low in Canada, see *R v Fontaine* [2004] 1 SCR 702. This means that many such cases will reach the consideration of the fact finder.

80 [2005] WWR 339.

episode will recur'.[81] In doing so he found that the accused, although diagnosed with epilepsy in 1977, had no psychiatric history. In addition, he found that although certain triggers such as lack of rest, lack of proper food, excitement, and the possibility that the accused had not taken his medication might recur, a consideration of such triggers was not very helpful in this case as epilepsy was far removed from Stone's condition of psychological blow automatism and the triggers which had been considered important in that case. As a result, he concluded that the continuing danger factor did not lead to any obvious result in the present case. This meant that it became necessary to consider other policy factors and in doing so he gave the following reasons for clearly distinguishing between epilepsy-related and psychological blow automatism which can be summarized as follows:

1) an epileptic seizure is not easily feigned;
2) epileptic automatism would not strain the credibility of the criminal justice system in the way psychological blow automatism would;
3) there was little support for the floodgates argument with epileptic automatisms; and
4) there were compelling public policy reasons for not labelling people with epilepsy mentally disordered or insane.[82]

In conclusion, the judge, being satisfied on the balance of probabilities that at the time of the alleged assault the accused was in a state of epileptic automatism, returned a verdict of simple acquittal.

Before leaving this case another interesting comment was made by the judge relating to burden of proof which was as follows:

> In view of the natural skepticism that courts have stated time and again in dealing with claims of automatism, it is perhaps not surprising that conditions were classified as a disease of the mind in order to ensure that the legal burden remained with the accused. All of this should change, however, in view of the fact that the legal burden in the case of mental disorder automatism and sane automatism is now the same. The legal burden in each case is on the accused to prove the defence on a balance of probabilities.[83]

Thus the change in the burden of proof, rather than acting against the accused's interests, might actually be in his favour. It certainly seems to have been one of the many factors which led the court to conclude that Bohak's epileptic automatism

[81] ibid para 101.
[82] ibid paras 111–18.
[83] ibid para 95.

should be classified as sane rather than insane.[84] It is also a salutary reminder that this more nuanced approach adopted in Canada is foreclosed in English law by the inflexibility of the 'external factor' doctrine. Further, English law has an additional complication in respect of sane automatism which is the 'fault factor' discussed in the next section.

The doctrine of 'fault' in automatism

The decision in *Quick* referred to above was the first to recognize that a legal device in the form of the 'external factor' doctrine was required to save an otherwise mentally normal diabetic from the special verdict and (then) mandatory hospitalization. However, in the course of his judgment Lawton LJ opined, 'Such malfunctioning, unlike that caused by a defect of reason from disease of the mind, will not always relieve an accused from criminal responsibility. A self-induced incapacity will not excuse (see *R. v. Lipman* [1970] 1 QB 152) nor will one which could have been reasonably foreseen as a result of either doing, or omitting to do something, as, for example, taking alcohol against medical advice after using certain prescribed drugs, or failing to have regular meals whilst taking insulin.'[85] The decision in *Lipman* concerns self-induced intoxication and it is clear that even if D's intoxicated condition gives rise to automatism, no defence is available to any basic intent offence.[86] However, the introduction of a similar 'fault' notion beyond voluntary intoxication is problematic both in relation to its operation and its scope. Following *Quick* two appellate decisions cast doubt upon using the analogy of voluntary intoxication in other cases of 'self-induced' incapacity. Thus in *Bailey*[87] and *Hardie*,[88] it was ruled that although the intoxicating effects of the consumption of alcohol and recreational drugs may be common knowledge, the same was not true for other cases of self-induced incapacity, whether it be the failure to take food after an insulin injection as in *Bailey* or taking too much Valium for sedative purposes as in *Hardie*. Rather, such Ds should not be convicted merely for consuming the drug in question but only if the consumption was proved to be 'reckless'. Although this restricts the scope of the 'fault' doctrine created in *Quick* it brings with it considerable problems concerning its application in terms of the precise scope of the recklessness required.[89]

[84] An approach followed in *R v Taylor* 2008 CanLII 10052 (ON SC) where, in answer to a charge of causing death by dangerous driving, D's epileptic automatism was classed as non-insane. Belobaba J stated at para 23, 'In my view, it is beyond dispute today that an epileptic seizure cannot be characterized as a disease of the mind. If automatism is available as a defence in the case of an epileptic seizure, then it should properly be described as non-mental disorder automatism.' See also *R v Bueckert* [2008] 5 WWR 724, para 56.

[85] [1973] 3 All ER 347, 356.

[86] See *DPP v Majewski* [1977] AC 443.

[87] [1983] 1 WLR 760; [1983] 2 All ER 503.

[88] [1985] 1 WLR 64; 1984] 3 All ER 848.

[89] For discussion see RD Mackay, *Mental Condition Defence in the Criminal Law* (Clarendon 1995) 169–71.

Extending the 'fault' doctrine

A decision of the Court of Appeal has extended the rule relating to self-induced intoxication and at the same time an earlier appellate decision has raised the possibility of introducing the notion of 'fault' into the defence of insanity. In *Taj*[90] it was ruled that the rule in *Majewski*[91] was not limited to cases where D was actually suffering from the immediate effects of voluntary intoxication at the time of the offence. In the case of *Taj* D's paranoia was held to be 'attributable' to intoxication even though he had not consumed alcohol or drugs for some time prior to the offence. Sir Brian Leveson P, giving the judgment of the court, stated:

> *DPP v. Majewski* focused on crime committed while specifically under the influence of drugs or alcohol. Having said that, however, it is difficult to see why the language (and the policy identified) is not equally apposite to the immediate and proximate consequences of such misuse. That is not to say that long standing mental illness which might at some stage have been triggered by misuse of drugs or alcohol would be covered. The point is that a defendant who is suffering the immediate effects of alcohol or drugs in the system is, in truth, not in a different position to a defendant who has triggered or precipitated an immediate psychotic illness as a consequence of proximate ingestion of or drugs in the system whether or not they remain present at the time of the offence.[92]
>
> … we have no doubt that, had the House in *Majewski* been presented with the same medical evidence and facts as in the present case, the House would have had no difficulty in applying the general common law principle with equal force to this case and holding that Taj had no defence because his state of mind had been brought about by his earlier voluntary intoxication. We see that as an application of *Majewski*, rather than an extension of that decision or, at the highest, a most incremental extension.[93]

While it is open to question whether this is merely an 'incremental extension' of the rule in *Majewski*, what is clear is that the decision in *Taj* is based on 'fault'. In addition, there is a further concern about the relationship between mental illness and the impact of abusing alcohol and drugs. In particular, in *R v Harris*[94] Hughes LJ opined:

> We agree that there is scope for the argument that an illness caused by his own fault ought as a matter of policy to be treated in the same way as is drunkenness at

[90] [2018] EWCA Crim 1743. For a critique of the decision see JJ Child, S Crombag, and GR Sullivan, 'Defending the Delusional, the Irrational and the Dangerous' [2020] Crim LR 306.

[91] [1977] AC 443.

[92] [2018] EWCA Crim 1743, para 56.

[93] ibid para 57.

[94] [2013] EWCA Crim 223.

> the time of the offence. This would, however, represent a significant extension of *DPP v Majewski* [1977] AC 443 and of the similar principle expounded in Quick which likewise concerned a case where what was asserted was an acute condition (there of automatism) induced arguably by the defendant's fault. A great many mental illnesses have their roots in culpable past misconduct of the sufferer: those attributable to many years of past drug abuse or alcohol abuse are perhaps the most obvious ... Whether the Majewski approach ought to be extended to such cases may be a topic which might be addressed in the forthcoming work of the Law Commission on loss of capacity and it should, no doubt, be the subject of proper public debate. But in the present state of the law, Majewski applies to offences committed by persons who are then voluntarily intoxicated but not to those who are suffering mental illness.[95]

Although in this case and in *Taj* insanity was held not to have been proved, the raising by the judiciary of extending 'fault' in the manner suggested, namely to remove the defence of insanity, is of considerable importance as it seems to have influenced the Law Commission in its Discussion Paper on Insanity and Automatism. At the law stands at present the 'fault' factor has no role to play in respect of the insanity defence. As long ago as 1920 the House of Lords in *DPP v Beard* stated that 'the law takes no notice of the cause of insanity'.[96] Of course, this gives rise to the inconsistency between cases like *Quick* and *Hennessy* where 'fault' applies in the former but not the latter and yet both Ds suffer from diabetes with the only distinction based on the 'external factor' of an insulin injection in the case of *Quick*. The Commission, in pointing out the absurdity of this distinction, was driven to remark:

> We have considered above the position of the individual who suffers from a recognised medical condition and who has, by his culpable conduct in not taking prescribed or authorised medicines at the appropriate time and/or in the appropriate dose, rendered him or herself completely lacking in a relevant capacity. Under the present law such a person would be treated as insane and liable to a not guilty by reason of insanity verdict. This seems to be out of step with the outcome in other cases in which the defendant has been at fault in bringing about his loss of capacity (whether he or she suffered from a medical condition or not).[97]

As a result, the Commission concluded that the newly proposed 'defence of recognised medical condition should not be available to any person who has culpably caused his complete loss of a relevant capacity, regardless of whether this is

[95] ibid para 25.
[96] [1920] AC 479, 500.
[97] 'Criminal Liability: Insanity and Automatism—A Discussion Paper' 6.75.

by ingesting a substance or failing to ingest a substance'.[98] While the Commission's quest for consistency is understandable, this provisional proposal sits uncomfortably where the medical condition is a serious mental illness.[99] Although the Commission concedes that 'for some people, the medical condition itself can lead to taking too much medication, or to the failure to take prescribed medication or to take it correctly'[100] the problem remains that distinguishing such cases from those who are at 'fault' is no easy matter. Accordingly, removing any new recognized medical condition defence from some defendants who are mentally ill, based on culpability in relation to his or her medication regimen, seems unduly harsh. Surely such individuals need help and support rather than a criminal conviction and penal sanction.

A better way to approach this complex issue could be to rid the law of the 'fault' doctrine, with the possible exception of the rule in *Majewski* relating to self-induced intoxication which it may be necessary to retain for policy reasons. This would permit all such cases, including those of sane automatism resulting from a 'recognised medical condition', to be subject to the disposal regime rather than conviction and punishment. It would also have the merit of simplifying the law. The argument against this is that it is inappropriate to excuse those who are clearly at 'fault' in ignoring the need to take prescribed medication. However, if such a D would otherwise qualify as a candidate for the recognized medical condition defence then he or she clearly lacks all responsibility for the offence in question. Better then to recognize this and to help him or her overcome the problems that led to the medication issues. In this connection, the Commission in its work on 'Unfitness to Plead'[101] has recommended a strengthening of supervision orders by extending the maximum period for such an order to three years[102] together with an optional review function where the court considers it appropriate[103] and finally, the introduction of a procedure for those that fail to comply with such an order which in turn may lead to a custodial sentence.[104] In other respects the disposal regime would remain essentially the same (presumably also for the new recognized medical condition defence), allowing for a hospital order where in-patient treatment is required and an absolute discharge where no formal treatment or supervision is needed.[105] By tightening up supervision orders in this way if, for example,

[98] ibid 6.77.

[99] See RD Mackay, Mental Condition Defence in the Criminal Law (Clarendon 1995) 178.

[100] See 'Criminal Liability: Insanity and Automatism—A Discussion Paper' 6.80.

[101] Law Commission No 364 (2016).

[102] ibid para 6.100. See M Bevan and D Ormerod, 'Reforming the Law of Unfitness to Plead in England and Wales—A Recent History' in R Mackay and W Brookbanks (eds), *Fitness to Plead—International And Comparative Perspectives* (Oxford University Press 2018) chapter 2.

[103] Law Commission No 364 (2016) para 6.75.

[104] ibid para 6.97.

[105] See R Mackay, 'The Development of Unfitness to Plead in English Law' in R Mackay and W Brookbanks (eds), *Fitness to Plead—International and Comparative Perspectives* (Oxford University Press 2018) 26–28.

a sane automaton (such as the accused in *Quick* who was found to be at 'fault' in not following his required diet and failing to adhere to his insulin regime or taking too much insulin), would be found 'not criminally responsible' and could be given a newly crafted supervision order to help him overcome his problems. If, subsequently, he failed to comply with the order conditions and kept flouting his medical regime, as a last resort he could be given a custodial sentence. But what is crucial here is that he would be convicted for his failure to comply with the supervision order conditions rather than having to base any conviction on his prior 'fault', a principle which would no longer trouble the law. In short, although it may seem attractive to extend the idea of 'fault' to the defence of insanity, it is submitted that the stance taken by English law of refusing to do so is correct and that the Law Commission's approach to reform would be better informed if the same were true for their provisionally proposed recognized medical condition defence.[106]

The operation of the insanity defence

The numbers

I have conducted several empirical studies of the M'Naghten Rules and they show a fairly consistent picture. At the outset, it should be emphasized that these studies relate to successful defences of insanity. So far as is known there is no empirical study which has examined unsuccessful insanity defences. However, it seems likely that cases of unsuccessful defences are rare since, as most successful insanity defences are uncontested, it also seems to follow that failed cases will be even rarer.

My first empirical study examined all verdicts of 'not guilty by reason of insanity' (NGRI) during the years 1975–88.[107] This study, conducted before the introduction of disposal flexibility, showed that during this 14-year period there were only 63 successful defences of insanity, an annual average of 4.5 and a maximum of six in any single year. The next two empirical studies examined all verdicts of NGRI during the first five years (1992–96)[108] and second five years (1997–2001)[109] of the new regime under the Criminal Procedure (Insanity and Unfitness to Plead) Act 1991,[110] which introduced flexibility of disposal. During the first five-year study the total number of findings of 'not guilty by reason of insanity' was 44 (average 8.8, maximum of 13 in any single year) compared to 72 (average 14.4, maximum of 17 in any single year) in the 1997–2001 study. This was followed by a final empirical

[106] For detailed discussion see R Mackay and D Hughes, 'Insanity and Blaming the Mentally Ill—a Critique of the Prior Fault Principle in the Law Commission's Discussion Paper' [2021] Crim LR 16.

[107] See RD Mackay, 'Fact and Fiction about the Insanity Defence' [1990] Crim LR 247. The three-year period 1989–91 is referred to in RD Mackay and G Kearns, 'More Fact(s) about the Insanity Defence' [1999] Crim LR 714.

[108] See RD Mackay and G Kearns, 'More Fact(s) about the Insanity Defence' [1999] Crim LR 714, 716 n 99.

[109] See RD Mackay, BJ Mitchell, and L Howe, 'Yet More Facts about the Insanity Defence' [2006] Crim LR 399.

[110] Now amended by the Domestic Violence, Crime and Victims Act 2004.

study for the Law Commission as part of its work on insanity and automatism[111] examining findings of NGRI during the ten-year period, 2002–11. The total of NGRI verdicts during this period was 223, giving an annual average of 22.3 (maximum of 34 in any single year). This means the annual average number of NGRI verdicts reached over 20 for the first time, with (also for the first time) a maximum of over 30 in any single year. Although it seems likely that the introduction of flexibility of disposal has impacted by increasing the successful use of the defence, it must be emphasized that, as the Law Commission remarked, the number of such verdicts remains 'surprisingly low'.[112] More importantly, it does seem as if the increase in the number of NGRI findings has levelled out. My ongoing research reveals totals of 30 and 26 such verdicts in 2017 and 2018 respectively. In short, it now seems likely that a plateau has been reached and that any future increase in numbers, if any, will be modest.

Offences and disposals

The main offence leading to an NGRI verdict has remained fairly consistent. Although there is a wide range of offences, non-fatal offences are most prevalent, particularly grievous bodily harm and attempted murder. Interestingly, murder charges remain minimal. The reason for this is unclear. In my first empirical study murder accounted for almost one-third of charges[113] while in my most recent study this had fallen to 1.8% (n = 4).[114] An obvious answer would be that diminished responsibility is being used in cases which might otherwise qualify for an insanity defence. However, my research into the diminished responsibility plea 'suggests that the insanity defence is considered in a relatively small proportion of cases'.[115]

With regard to the disposal of those found NGRI, it is important to realize that not all those subject to the special verdict are hospitalized and, of those, only around 59% are subject to a restriction order. Rather, the research shows that the majority (51.2%) are subject to community disposals, both supervision orders (36.8%) and absolute discharges (13.5%).[116] This is an important finding as it clearly indicates that the judiciary is taking full advantage of the flexibility of disposal introduced by the Criminal Procedure (Insanity and Unfitness to Plead) Act 1991.

111 RD Mackay, 'The Insanity Defence—Data on Verdicts of Not Guilty by Reason of Insanity from 2002 to 2011' Appendix E of Insanity and Automatism, Supplementary Material to the Scoping Paper, 18 July 2012. Summarized in RD Mackay, 'Ten more Years of the Insanity Defence' [2012] Crim LR 946.

112 Law Commission, 'Insanity and Automatism: A Scoping Paper' (2012) para 1.48.

113 RD Mackay, 'Fact and Fiction about the Insanity Defence' [1990] Crim LR 247, 248.

114 See RD Mackay, 'Ten More Years of the Insanity Defence' [2012] Crim LR 946,946 949.

115 See R Mackay and B Mitchell, 'The New Diminished Responsibility Plea in Operation: Some Initial Findings' [2017] Crim LR 18, 34. In no cases was use made of the Criminal Procedure (Insanity) Act 1964, s 6 which permits the prosecution to answer an insanity defence with diminished responsibility.

116 See RD Mackay, 'Ten More Years of the Insanity Defence' [2012] Crim LR 953–54. There were two guardianship orders given. This form of disposal for both insanity and unfitness to plead was abolished by the Domestic Violence, Crime and Victims Act 2004.

The role of psychiatric reports

My first three empirical studies included access to relevant psychiatric reports. These studies reveal that the diagnosis most likely to qualify as a 'disease of the mind' within the M'Naghten Rules is schizophrenia, which consistently accounted for around 50% of all such cases. There were also a number of insane automatism cases resulting mainly from epilepsy.[117]

An additional point of interest confirmed in these studies is that both courts and psychiatrists seem to continue to interpret the M'Naghten Rules, not in a narrow legalistic way, but instead apply the Rules more widely. The central question addressed by psychiatrists was not, in the majority of cases, essentially psychiatric. Rather, it was often a question of whether, if a delusion had in fact been reality, would the defendant's actions have been legally and/or morally justified? In short, as Latham LJ commented in *R v Johnson*, 'there is some evidence which is contained in material in articles[118] ... that courts may have on occasions been prepared to approach the issue on a more relaxed basis'. This 'more relaxed basis' seems to show that when applying the wrongness limb of the Rules, psychiatrists often focus on moral wrongness and that, in consequence, the strict position in *Windle* may not be adhered to in some cases.

The Channel Island of Jersey

The island of Jersey, as a self-governing entity, is not part of the United Kingdom. Its status is that of a British Crown Dependency. Although it has its own laws and customs many of which are influenced by English law, Jersey has not accepted the M'Naghten Rules. What follows is a brief discussion of the novel insanity defence adopted in Jersey.

In *A-G v Prior*[119] the defence raised the question as to whether, at the time of the alleged offence, the accused who had a long history of mental illness, was legally insane. This, in turn, resulted in a preliminary hearing to determine this question as the law on Jersey was unclear on the matter. In his judgment, the Bailiff, Sir Philip Bailhache, ruled that the M'Naghten Rules, any reference to which could not be found in the records of the Court, do not form part of the law of Jersey. He further opined that adopting the M'Naghten Rules would conflict with such evidence as there is as to the meaning of insanity in Jersey law in that the Rules do not admit of a volitional test.[120] Accordingly, the Bailiff ruled as follows:

[117] See RD Mackay and M Reuber, 'Epilepsy and the Defence of Insanity' [2007] Crim LR 782.

[118] [2007] EWCA Crim 1978, para 23, referring to RD Mackay and G Kearns, 'More Fact(s) about the Insanity Defence' [1999] Crim LR 714.

[119] 2001 JLR 146.

[120] ibid 158–59.

> I should therefore adopt a definition of 'insanity' which is consistent with the evidence given to the Royal Commissioners in 1846, compliant with Convention rights under the Human Rights (Jersey) Law 2000, and appropriate to the state of medical knowledge in the 21st century. Counsel for the defence laid out a number of options for me in the course of her submissions. I prefer, and I respectfully adopt, a definition suggested by Professor R. D. Mackay. I therefore hold that a person is insane within the meaning of Article 2 of the Criminal Justice (Insane Persons)(Jersey) Law 1964 if, *at the time of the commission of the offence, his unsoundness of mind affected his criminal behaviour to such a substantial degree that the jury consider that he ought not to be found criminally responsible.*[121]

In addition, in refusing to accept the M'Naghten Rules, the Jersey court introduced a new test which, in the Bailiff's opinion, 'will permit objective medical evidence of a defendant's unsoundness of mind to be given in the sense required by Convention jurisprudence while retaining a clear causal link between the offence and the mental disorder. It will also cater for defects of volition.'[122]

Interestingly although this is the first court in Great Britain to reject the M'Naghten Rules, the neighbouring channel island of Guernsey, in the case of *Derek Lee Harvey*,[123] refused to go down that route and instead confirmed that the Rules continue to form part of Guernsey law. While this demonstrates the fact that the two islands in question jealously guard the independence of their own legal regimes, it does not detract from the importance of the decision in *Prior*, which poses a fundamental question about the M'Naghten Rules as an appropriate test for legal insanity in the 21st century.

Conclusion

The M'Naghten Rules continue as the test for the defence of insanity in England and Wales. However, their influence, although profound and long-standing, is beginning to diminish. For example, in Great Britain, it is not just the island of Jersey which has refused to adopt the Rules. Both Scotland and Northern Ireland have also followed suit by enacting statutory provisions which introduce more liberal insanity defences. The former is discussed in Chapter 4[124] while the latter provides in section 1 of the Criminal Justice Act (Northern Ireland) 1966:

[121] ibid, emphasis added. Now enacted in the Mental Health (Jersey) Law 2016, s 72(2).

[122] ibid 159.

[123] Guernsey Unreported Judgements: 3 August 2001, available at Guernsey Legal Resources, see https://www.guernseylegalresources.gg/CHttpHandler.ashx?documentid=63368

[124] The new test in Scotland contained in the Criminal Justice and Licensing (Scotland) Act 2010, s 168(1) uses the word 'appreciate'. The Scottish Law Commission Report on Insanity and Diminished Responsibility, July 2004, SE/2004/92 states at para 2.47: 'In our view the particular value of the concept of appreciation is that it connotes something wider than simple knowledge and includes a level of

> 'insane person' means a person who suffers from mental abnormality which prevents him—
> (a) from appreciating what he is doing; or
> (b) from appreciating that what he is doing is either wrong or contrary to law; or
> (c) from controlling his own conduct; and
> 'insanity' shall be construed accordingly.[125]

Similarly, in many other common law jurisdictions such as Canada, New Zealand, and Australia, discussed in Chapters 6, 7, and 8 respectively, the M'Naghten rules have been augmented with a wider test.[126]

Few would argue against such an approach in England and Wales, and this is a view strongly supported by the Law Commission. But the history surrounding the proposed abrogation of the Rules is far from encouraging.

To date, five separate official reports from English law reform bodies have recommended changing the M'Naghten Rules, the most recent of which is contained in the Law Commission's Discussion Paper on Insanity and Automatism (discussed in Chapter 3). But none of these reform initiatives has been successful. Why is this? The repeated criticisms of the M'Naghten Rules are well made. But it seems this is not enough. A possible answer might revolve around the infrequency of use of the insanity defence, so that it is rarely encountered in practice. My empirical research reveals that there are only around 30 findings of 'not guilty by reason of insanity' annually. This may mean that for policymakers and legislators it is low priority and simply not worth the parliamentary time needed to take any reform proposals forward. However, if this is true then it is regrettable. The explanation for the small number of special verdicts each year is to be found in the narrowness of the M'Naghten Rules themselves together with the pejorative label of 'insanity' contained in the verdict. Accordingly, it is something of a self-defeating prophecy to use the paucity of cases as a reason to do nothing, since until the Rules are reformed, this minimal number of insanity findings will remain unaltered.

(rational) understanding. It therefore avoids the narrowness of the M'Naghten Rules, as they have been traditionally interpreted.'

125 This largely follows that recommended by Lord MacDermott in his Holdsworth Lecture entitled 'Murder in 1963'. It received Royal Assent on 7 July 1966 and came into force a month later on 7 August 1966. Interestingly, Lord MacDermott originally used the word 'knowing' which has been replaced with 'appreciating'. See *R v Mawhinney* [2008] NICC 44 where D was found NGRI for wounding with intent under this provision with one of the psychiatrists testifying that D 'was suffering from paranoid schizophrenia and would not have appreciated that what he had done was *morally* or legally wrong' (emphasis added).

126 Chapter 5 deals with Irish law where, although the M'Naghten rules are retained, there is an additional limb which provides for volitional impairment.

Although root and branch statutory reform is to be preferred, the chances of this seem slim as the Law Commission's recent work, which dates back to 2013, seems to have stalled.[127] This would leave as the only other realistic alternative an appellate decision of the Supreme Court.[128] Of course, this would mean getting an appeal case before the court which also seems unlikely. But in that unlikely event, there is surely a strong argument that the court should be willing to reinterpret the M'Naghten Rules with a view to updating them. This would not necessarily require a rewording of the Rules. However, there is another argument to be made that this ought to be considered, namely that given the legal uniqueness of the Rules, which are neither statutory nor the result of case law, there is nothing in principle to prevent the Supreme Court from adopting such an approach.

Concerning the former, a reinterpretation of the Rules could be achieved if the Supreme Court chose to overrule *Codere*,[129] *Windle*,[130] *Johnson*,[131] and *Keal*.[132] These decisions, as discussed above, perpetuate a narrow interpretation of the M'Naghten Rules which could be swept away by first drawing a distinction between the words 'nature' and 'quality' in limb one. While knowledge of the 'nature' of the act is limited to its physical ingredients, knowing its 'quality' should require a broader rational understanding of an act's circumstances and consequences. Secondly, in limb two, the meaning of 'wrong', which in *Windle* had been limited to knowledge of 'legal' wrongfulness but, since *Keal*,[133] now includes knowledge of 'moral' wrongfulness, could be changed to ensure that unawareness of either 'legal' or 'moral' wrongfulness is within the M'Naghten rules in much the same way as has been achieved in many other jurisdictions.[134] Both of these important changes could be achieved without in any way altering the wording of the M'Naghten Rules. However, if a rewording of the Rules was also held to be permissible then replacing the single word 'know' with that of 'appreciate' would go a long way to improving their meaning.[135] The first or both of these initiatives, if adopted by the Supreme Court, would do a great deal to give English law an insanity defence which is more appropriate for the 21st century.

127 See Chapter 3.

128 In *Johnson* [2007] EWCA 1978 [24] Latham LJ remarked, 'There is room for reconsideration of rules and, in particular, rules which have their genesis in the early years of the 19th century. But it does not seem to us that that debate is a debate which can properly take place before us at this level in this case.' Thus he made it clear that this is now a task for the Supreme Court.

129 (1916) 12 Cr App Rep 21.

130 [1952] 2 QB 826.

131 [2007] EWCA 1978.

132 [2022] EWCA Crim 341.

133 ibid.

134 See RD Mackay, 'Righting the Wrong—Some Observations on the Second Limb of the M'Naghten Rules' [2009] Crim LR 80, 87–89. For discussion of the importance of having a clear legal definition of 'wrongfulness' see K Bloch and J Goul, 'Legal Indeterminacy in Insanity Cases: Clarifying Wrongfulness and Applying a Triadic Approach to Forensic Evaluations' (2016) 67 Hastings LJ 913.

135 See n 124.

Failing that or any statutory reform, English law is likely to have to continue with the present-day M'Naghten Rules for many more years to come, ensuring that a small but important section of mentally ill offenders will continue to be denied a defence and so are inappropriately convicted rather than excused.

3

Reforming the Insanity Defence in England and Wales

David Ormerod and Mark Dsouza

Introduction

The numerous failings of the present law are examined in the preceding chapter.[1] The M'Naghten Rules[2] provide a 'defence' that is of unusual status,[3] lacking in sound psychiatric foundation,[4] ambiguous in its terms,[5] uncertain in its scope,[6] illogical in its outcomes,[7] stigmatizing in its labelling, potentially in conflict with European Convention rights,[8] and of no value to any but a tiny fraction of the (too many) people with mental health issues who become caught up in the criminal justice system.

Such a catalogue of failings might be thought to present an overwhelming case for reform.[9] That is not, however, a universally held view. For some, any changes made to this very specific plea in the substantive criminal law will lack practical

[1] See more generally A Loughnan, *Manifest Madness: Mental Incapacity in Criminal Law* (Oxford University Press 2012); RD Mackay, *Mental Condition Defences in Criminal Law* (Oxford University Press 1995) chapter 2. For a detailed discussion of the defence in application see D Ormerod and K Laird, *Smith, Hogan and Ormerod's Criminal Law* (16th edn, Oxford University Press 2021) chapter 9; and for a purely practical discussion see D Ormerod and D Perry (eds), *Blackstone's Criminal Practice* (Oxford University Press 2022) A4.

[2] (1843) 4 St Tr NS 847.

[3] As an opinion of the judges sought by the legislative committee of the legislative chamber of the House of Lords. See generally A Loughnan, 'M'Naghten's Case' in P Handler, H Mares, and I Williams (eds), *Landmark Cases in Criminal Law* (Hart Publishing 2017); R Moran, *Knowing Right From Wrong: The Insanity Defence of Daniel McNaughtan* (Free Press 1981).

[4] F McAuley, *Insanity, Psychiatry and Criminal Responsibility* (Round Hall Ltd 1993); A Loughnan and T Ward, 'Emergent Authority and Expert Knowledge: Psychiatry and Criminal Responsibility in the UK' (2014) 37 Int J Law Psychiatry 25.

[5] For a helpful guide to terminology see the Glossary in the Law Commission, 'Insanity and Automatism, A Scoping Paper' (2012), https://s3-eu-west-2.amazonaws.com/lawcom-prod-storage-11jsxou24uy7q/uploads/2015/06/insanity_scoping_supplementary.pdf

[6] eg in its relationship with other pleas. See *R v Oye* [2013] EWCA Crim 1725.

[7] See classically the dichotomy between the hypoglycaemic and hyperglycaemic attacks: *R v Bailey* [1983] 1 WLR 760 (sane-automatism); *R v Hennessy* [1989] 1 WLR 287 (insanity). See Law Commission, 'Criminal Liability: Insanity and Automatism, A Discussion Paper' (23 July 2013) para 1.42.

[8] The concern is longstanding: P Sutherland and C Gearty, 'Insanity and the European Court of Human Rights' [1992] Crim LR 418.

[9] See also Law Commission, 'Criminal Liability: Insanity and Automatism, A Discussion Paper' (23 July 2013) 6–17.

David Ormerod and Mark Dsouza, *Reforming the Insanity Defence in England and Wales* In: *The Insanity Defence*.
Edited by: Ronnie Mackay and Warren Brookbanks, Oxford University Press. © David Ormerod and Mark Dsouza 2022.
DOI: 10.1093/oso/9780198854944.003.0003

significance; it is reform for those who aspire to a theoretically purer criminal code but in terms of the everyday operation of the criminal justice system the reform is desirable rather than necessary. Of greater priority, perhaps, is reform to provide more effective criminal justice responses to mental health more generally and particularly in ensuring better assessment and treatment.[10] It is true that the number of cases in which insanity is pleaded or even contemplated as a plea each year is tiny. There are around 30 successful pleas in the 25,000 or so Crown Court trials conducted per annum.[11] Considering the prison population specifically, of almost 90,000 people imprisoned it is reported that '26% of women and 16% of men said they had received treatment for a mental health problem in the year before custody. 25% of women and 15% of men in prison reported symptoms indicative of psychosis. The rate among the general public is about 4%.'[12] On a pragmatic view then, reform of the technicalities of the insanity defence is only of real importance if it results in changes that would provide more appropriate processes and outcomes for these tens of thousands of individuals.[13] The Law Commission explicitly recognized this line of argument, being itself

> convinced, on the basis of [its] research to date, the vast wealth of academic literature and the reform proposals made by others, that there are significant problems with the law when examined from a theoretical perspective. There is, however, less evidence that the defences cause significant difficulties in practice and a dearth of published research into the operation of the defences.[14]

Against this pragmatism, several arguments can be marshalled to suggest that any reform of the insanity defence is of substantial value in and of itself. A civilized society should strive to define its criminal laws so that they are based on sound principles and policies that respect basic human rights and dignity. That should be true in the scope of their application, the processes adopted in their operation throughout the criminal justice system, and in the labels that are applied to such laws and those they affect. The illogical outcomes perpetuated by the

[10] See Lord Bradley's report, *Review of People With Mental Health Problems or Learning Disabilities in the Criminal Justice System* (2009), DoH.

[11] Taking figures from 2019 (the last pre-pandemic figures), the Crown Court disposed of 102,485 cases with 24,000 trials, https://data.justice.gov.uk/courts. R Mackay, 'Ten More Years of the Insanity Defence' [2012] Crim LR 946, notes the gradual increase in the number of special verdicts returned, plateauing at around 30; A Ashworth and L Zedner, *Preventive Justice* (Oxford University Press 2014) 209–14. See also Law Commission, 'Insanity and Automarism—A Scoping Paper' (2012).

[12] Prison Reform Trust, http://www.prisonreformtrust.org.uk/WhatWeDo/Projectsresearch/Menta lhealth

[13] The pathways through the criminal justice system for the mentally ill are considered in Law Commission Report No 364, *Unfitness to Plead* (2016) chapter 2 and Appendix A of supplementary material to Law Commission, 'Insanity and Automatism, A Scoping Paper' 18 July 2011.

[14] Law Commission, 'Criminal Liability: Insanity and Automatism, A Discussion Paper' (2013) paras 1.8 and 1.81, hereafter LCDP.

arcane definitions and processes of this archaic law, and the stigmatizing labelling of someone as 'insane' ought themselves to be sufficient in prompting reform.

Historical Reform Proposals

Despite profound deficiencies in the insanity defence having been recognized for a century, no one could describe the process of reform as having displayed any urgency. Attempts to reform the law date back to at least 1923. Lord Atkin's report of that year recommended that the M'Naghten Rules should be retained but recommended a defence where the accused acted under an irresistible impulse arising from mental disease.[15] That was rejected. A greater impact followed the 1953 recommendations of the Royal Commission on Capital Punishment[16] which led to the introduction of a partial defence of diminished responsibility—albeit available only to those accused of murder.[17] The Criminal Law Revision Committee in its Third Report, *Criminal Procedure (Insanity)*, in 1963[18] focused largely on the procedures for those who were unfit, but, echoing the Atkin Committee and the Royal Commission, concluded that the verdict should be an acquittal in the form 'not guilty by reason of insanity'.[19] It was successful in achieving that reform at least. A more comprehensive review of mental responsibility defences in criminal law was undertaken in 1975: *Report of the Committee on Mentally Abnormal Offenders*.[20]The 'Butler Committee' review based its proposals for a new form of insanity defence firmly on the basis of serious mental illnesses.[21] It proposed a new verdict of 'not guilty on evidence of mental disorder' and recommended that the defence be available even without a causal link being established between the illness and the wrongdoing. That approach was endorsed in the Law Commission's Draft Criminal Code in 1985 and 1989 (clauses 34 and 35) subject to a new rebuttable presumption that the commission of the offence was attributable to the defendant's disorder.[22]

[15] *Report of the Committee as to the Existing Law, Practice and Procedure relating to Criminal Trials in which the Plea of Insanity as a Defence is Raised* (1923) Cmnd 2005, or 'the Atkin report'. The Committee was established in response to a reprieve issued by the Home Secretary following *R v True* (1922) 16 Cr App R 164, on the grounds of the accused's mental condition even though his plea of insanity had not succeeded.

[16] *Report of the Royal Commission on Capital Punishment* (1953) Cmnd 8932.

[17] That defence was replaced by reforms in the Coroners and Justice Act 2009, substituting a new s 2 into the Homicide Act 1957 from October 2010.

[18] Cmnd 2149.

[19] ibid para 5.

[20] 1975, Cmnd 6244.

[21] See E Griew, 'Let's Implement Butler on Mental Disorder and Crime!' (1984) CLP 47.

[22] *Codification of the Criminal Law—A Report to the Law Commission* (1985) HC 270 Law Com No 143; *Criminal Law: A Criminal Code for England and Wales* (1989) Law Com No 177. For criticism, see J Horder, *Ashworth's Principles of Criminal Law* (9th edn, Oxford University Press 2019) 164.

After a century of eminent committees' comprehensive reviews and recommendations for fundamental changes to the M'Naghten Rules, the only reforms achieved were procedural and dealt primarily with verdicts and disposals.[23]

The Law Commission Insanity Project

The Law Commission for England and Wales (hereafter LC) undertook as part of its *Tenth Programme of Reform*[24] to reform insanity, specifying that 'the core of the project would be to identify better and more up to date legal tests and rules for determining fitness to plead and legal insanity'.[25]

The work commenced in 2009 with parallel streams tackling reform of the unfitness to plead procedure for those whose mental conditions affect their ability to participate effectively at trial, and the reform of the defence of insanity which focuses on the mental condition of the defendant at the time of the offence. The LC made more immediate progress on unfitness to plead with a Consultation Paper in 2010.[26] The further prioritization of that work over insanity reform was supported by consultees' responses to a Scoping Paper[27] on the relative merits of each stream of reform. In short, consultees supported prioritizing reform of unfitness to plead—that was likely to have a more positive impact on more individuals in the criminal justice system than reform of insanity.[28]

The LC insanity work was also initially more faltering because it was realized that the scope of that project would have to be wider than the original terms of reference if it was to have any practical significance. As is obvious from the discussion in Chapter 2, and the case law,[29] effective reform of insanity requires consideration of the closely related defence of sane-automatism and the plea of intoxication along with theoretical questions about the doctrine of prior fault underpinning them. All three pleas are concerned with an individual's denial that he was a responsible actor at the time of the commission of the offence.[30] By 2012, Commissioners accepted

[23] See RD Mackay, *Mental Condition Defences in Criminal Law* (Oxford University Press 1995) chapter 2.

[24] *Tenth Programme of Law Reform* (2008) Law Com No 311.

[25] *Tenth Programme*, para 2.46.

[26] *Unfitness to Plead* (2010), Law Commission Consultation Paper No 197.

[27] The LC sought evidence of problems in practice. See J Peay, 'Insanity and Automatism: Questions from and About the Law Commission's Scoping Paper' [2012] Crim LR 927. The supplementary materials to the Scoping Paper, chapters 2–4 set out the present law and problems in considerable detail.

[28] See Appendix B to the LCDP. The unfitness to plead work generated a Consultation Paper in 2014 and finally a report including a 70-clause draft Bill: Report No 364 *Unfitness to Plead* (2016). For further details see M Bevan and D Ormerod, 'Reforming the Law of Unfitness to Plead in England and Wales: A Recent History' in R Mackay and W Brookbanks (eds), *Fitness to Plead: International and Comparative Perspectives* (Oxford University Press 2018) 55. Note the government's current reform agenda to tackle mental health issues in the criminal justice system: see D Ormerod, 'Mental Health and Criminal Justice' [2021] Crim LR 247.

[29] Illustrated perfectly by the trilogy of cases: *R v Coley, McGhee and Harris* [2013] EWCA Crim 223.

[30] LCDP, chapter 6 analyses the relationship between insanity, automatism, and intoxication.

that the terms of reference should be read widely to allow for that scope of reform. The inanity reform then commenced in earnest.

As with the 20th-century reviews, the LC's focus was on practical reform. The aim was to understand the problems and their impact, and to provide solutions. The comprehensive nature of the LC's Scoping and Discussion Papers, and its extensive citation of academic legal, psychiatric, and philosophical literature, confirm that the reform process was also a rigorous one.

In 2013 the LC produced a 'Discussion Paper'[31] (DP) on Insanity. This was a bitter-sweet moment for those urging reform. From a positive perspective these were carefully considered, detailed, and far-reaching reforms. On the more negative side, it was clear that the Discussion Paper represented the conclusion of the LC's work for the foreseeable future. Typically, the LC would produce a Consultation Paper for each project followed by a formal Report to the Lord Chancellor, with recommendations and a draft Bill, which is laid before Parliament.[32] That was not possible for insanity reform because of the other demands on the LC's diminishing resources. Moreover, indications from the Ministry of Justice, even at that relatively early stage of the work, were that even if a report were produced, there was little prospect of that being taken forward in legislation.[33] The Commission nevertheless chose to publish as a DP the valuable work already completed to facilitate and influence public debate. In style and format, the Paper appears identical to a Consultation Paper. The difference is simply that the DP includes no request for responses to the questions posed—to have done so may have engendered false expectations that a Report would be produced. Despite the unusual labelling, there is no question that the DP contains developed albeit provisional proposals of the LC.[34]

The Proposed New Defence

Outline

The principal proposal is that the common law insanity defence should be abolished and replaced with a new statutory defence whereby a defendant would be 'not criminally responsible by reason of a qualifying recognized medical condition'.[35]

[31] Available from https://s3-eu-west-2.amazonaws.com/lawcom-prod-storage-11jsxou24uy7q/uploads/2015/06/insanity_discussion.pdf

[32] See more generally on the workings of the Commission: the Law Commissions Act 1965 and M Dyson, J Lee, and S Wilson Stark (eds), *Fifty Years of the Law Commissions: The Dynamics of Law Reform* (Hart Publishing 2016).

[33] LCDP, para 1.15.

[34] These were not just the published workings of the Criminal Team. The insanity DP was approved by the Commissioners.

[35] LCDP, para 4.159.

The party seeking to raise the defence would have to adduce expert evidence that at the time of the offence the defendant wholly lacked one of the following capacities in relation to the conduct they have been charged with having performed: (a) rationally to form a judgement; (b) to understand that they are doing something wrong; or (c) to control their actions. Any such lack of capacity would have to be due to a 'qualifying recognised medical condition'. Not all recognized medical conditions would qualify for the defence and it would be a matter of law, not medicine, whether the condition did qualify.[36]

Identifying a Rationale

As noted, the LC cannot be accused of superficiality in its approach, indeed the first substantive chapter of the DP poses such fundamental questions as whether any insanity defence (and indeed an automatism defence) is even needed in the criminal law. That chapter, (Chapter 2) considers wide ranging arguments, and is accompanied by a more detailed analysis of the theoretical aspects of the debate in an Appendix.[37] This analysis led the LC to conclude that a defence providing for a special verdict is necessary both 'where the case is not proved against the accused because of his or her mental disorder as well as where it is proved because of the mental disorder'.[38]

Its conclusion, founded on the moral argument 'that the foundation of criminal responsibility is the person's capacity not to do the act which would amount to an offence' is, it is submitted, a strong one. In the particular context of insanity, this translates to the need for the law to provide a defence for a person who lacks capacities for rational, practical reasoning and/or the ability to control physical actions.[39] The LC dismisses arguments: for abolition without replacement of a defence of insanity; for use of civil commitment powers instead of criminal proceedings; and claims that it is illogical to provide defences for a lack of capacity arising from medical conditions, but not other circumstances lying equally beyond a person's control. An insanity defence is necessary to reflect the lack of moral culpability from the lack of capacity and, relatedly but separately,[40] to provide the courts with control and disposal powers over the individuals concerned.

36 LCDP, para 4.161.

37 Appendix A addressing in particular arguments from some US academics including C Slobogin, author of, inter alia, 'An End to Insanity: Recasting the Role of Mental Illness in Criminal Cases' (2000) 86 Va Law Rev 1199.

38 LCDP, para 2.34.

39 LCDP, para 2.9. Appendix A and para 4.6. These are wider than the narrow focus of M'Naghten on cognitive capacity. See generally, R Schopp, *Automatism, Insanity and the Psychology of Criminal Responsibility* (Cambridge University Press 1991).

40 LCDP, para 2.14.

That discussion leads the Commission to several important conclusions about the scope of its proposed defence. These include that the defence should not be restricted to cases of serious 'mental' illness (even assuming that could be defined with precision); there can be as much a lack of capacity as a result of a physical condition. The resulting broader reach of the defence also allows for greater coherence with sane automatism. In addition, the Commission recognizes that its rationale for a new defence renders it irrelevant whether the offence against which it is pleaded depends on proof of mens rea or not:[41] the new defence should be available in relation to *any* kind of offence. Similarly, given its rationale, the new defence should not depend on the seriousness of the offence charged, and hence the defence and special verdict would be available in the magistrates' courts as well as in the Crown Court.

Qualifying Recognised Medical Condition

Central to the proposed new defence is the requirement to prove that the accused had a 'qualifying recognised medical condition' (QRMC).[42] While obviously founded on the concept of a 'recognised medical condition' at the heart of the diminished responsibility plea in murder[43] it has been refined in a number of ways.

The QRMC must be one that is *recognized* by professionals in the relevant field. This limitation would avoid idiosyncratic notions of what constitutes a medical condition. It would also help to deter spurious defences, and would define an issue on which expert evidence could be admitted in terms which the courts and medical experts can apply. Evidence that a condition is accepted by the relevant profession could arise from its listing in an accepted classificatory system, but that fact alone will not mean that it automatically constitutes a 'qualifying recognised medical condition' for the purposes of the new defence. Equally, in some very rare cases, a condition which is not listed might be accepted by the courts as a QRMC if there is adequate evidence of its general acceptance by professionals.[44]

A medical condition must not only be recognized by the medical profession, but must 'qualify' as a matter of *legal* policy before the defence applies. The DP makes this requirement explicit when it had been found by the courts to be implicit in the diminished responsibility defence to murder.[45] Medical conditions are defined and diagnosed primarily for medical purposes and it does not always

[41] LCDP, para 3.7.

[42] That concept is introduced in Chapter 3 and fully explained in Chapter 4 of the DP.

[43] On the operation of that partial defence see D Ormerod and K Laird, *Smith, Hogan and Ormerod's Criminal Law* (16th edn, Oxford University Press 2021) Chapter 13; D Ormerod and D Perry, *Blackstone's Criminal Practice* (Oxford University Press 2022) B1.

[44] LCDP, paras 4.67–8.

[45] *R v Dowds* [2012] 1 WLR 2576.

follow that a medical condition should form the basis for a defence in criminal law. As Lord Justice Hughes stated in interpreting the diminished responsibility defence, 'there will inevitably be considerations of legal policy which are irrelevant to the business of medical description, classification, and statistical analysis'.[46] An obvious example is acute intoxication, which appears as a condition in standard reference manuals. It would be odd, and contrary to well-established principles in the common law, to allow the state of being voluntarily heavily intoxicated to act as a non-responsibility defence. Acute intoxication, therefore, would not be a QRMC. Similarly, the LC concludes it would be wrong for the new defence to be based on a condition consisting of a personality disorder characterized solely or principally by abnormally aggressive or seriously irresponsible behaviour; in other words, where the evidence for the condition is simply evidence of what might broadly be called criminal behaviour.[47]

The significance of the QRMC is the impact it has on the accused's relevant capacities: it must have given rise to the total lack of a relevant capacity. The capacities that must be proved to have been negated, as discussed in Chapter 4 of the DP, are very similar to those in the diminished responsibility (DR) defence.[48] There are three significant differences worth noting. First, whereas the DR defence requires proof of the accused's capacities being 'substantially impaired'[49] the Not Criminally Responsible (NCR) defence will require a 'total' lack of control.[50] This aspect of the LC proposal has excited academic interest and is examined below. Secondly, the burden of proof is more sophisticated, with an elevated evidential burden on the accused and the legal burden on the prosecution (unlike DR where the burden is exclusively on the accused). Thirdly, the question of whether the condition is one that is a qualifying recognized one is explicitly acknowledged to be a question of law for the court to determine.[51] The judge will rule whether there is evidence from which a jury could conclude that the condition caused the accused's lack of capacity as alleged. Unless this initial threshold is met, then there will be no legal basis on which the defence could proceed.

[46] *R v Dowds* [2012] 1 WLR 2576, para 30.

[47] LCDP, para 4.107.

[48] Homicide Act 1957, s 2, as substituted by Coroners and Justice Act 2009, s 52.

[49] The Supreme Court has interpreted that expression in *Golds* [2016] UKSC 67 to mean something weighty as opposed to more than *de minimis*. For criticism and suggestion that the decision is flawed and not faithful to its own premise see D Ormerod and K Laird, *Smith, Hogan and Ormerod's Criminal Law* (16th edn, Oxford University Press 2021) chapter 13.

[50] LCDP, para 3.2.

[51] Thereby avoiding the ambiguity in diminished responsibility resolved in *R v Dowds* [2012] 1 WLR 2576.

A Relevant Capacity

Alongside the QRMC, the central element of the proposed defence is the requirement for a total loss of one or more relevant capacities. In its discussion of which capacities, when negated, should be relevant the LC is clearly influenced by the failings of *M'Naghten*, by the lessons learned from its reform work on diminished responsibility, and by the need for practical solutions. The LC concludes that the relevant capacities should be (i) the capacity for practical reasoning—expressed as the capacity rationally to form a judgement about the relevant conduct or circumstances and (ii) the capacity to understand the wrongfulness of the act or omission, and that wrongfulness should not be limited to illegality;[52] as well as (iii) the capacity to control bodily actions.[53] These address the major failings of the M'Naghten Rules since the focus is not limited to cognitive abilities nor awareness of legal wrongdoing.[54]

As a welcome additional proposal the LC calls for further consideration of the merits of a freestanding developmental immaturity defence. Although related to the 'recognised medical condition' defence because both depend on lack of the same specified capacities, a developmental immaturity defence is clearly a distinct concept and is not examined further here.[55] The courts have already acknowledged concerns regarding developmental immaturity in procedural terms[56] and in sentencing.[57]

Denying the Defence for 'Prior Fault'

One potentially controversial aspect of the DP proposals is that the NCR defence is subject to the principle of prior fault which exists in the current law in relation to intoxication and automatism.[58] (Where a defendant has voluntarily become intoxicated, his or her subsequent lack of fault at the time of the offence is no excuse where the voluntary intoxication involved an appreciation of the risk of

[52] The defence should be available to a defendant lacking capacity to appreciate the moral wrongfulness even if he was aware of the illegality.

[53] This involves the LC in a detailed discussion of whether 'irresistible impulse' should feature in the proposed defence. That knotty question has proved fatal to earlier reform proposals—see eg the 'Atkin' reforms above, n 15.

[54] Discussed in Chapter 2.

[55] On the significance of child development see eg S-J Blakemore and S Choudhury, 'Development of the Adolescent Brain: Implications for Executive Function and Social Cognition' (2006) 47 J Child Psychol Psychiatry 296–312.

[56] See Criminal Procedure Rules and Practice Directions 2020 (published at http://www.legislation.gov.uk) 3F.12; *R v Rashid* [2017] EWCA Crim 2.

[57] See eg *R v Clarke* [2018] EWCA Crim 185 and D Emmanuel and others, 'The Sentencing of Young Adults: A Distinct Group Requiring a Distinct Approach' [2021] Crim LR 203.

[58] See LCDP, paras 6.3ff.

unpredictable or aggressive behaviour).[59] Adopting this approach will promote coherence. It will mean that the NCR defence will *not* be available to any person who has culpably caused his or her total loss of capacity.[60] That coherence comes at a cost—the scheme becomes necessarily more complex as it adopts the common law distinction between specific and basic intent offences. The result is that where an individual is charged with a specific intent offence, to be consistent with the rules on intoxication, he or she ought to be acquitted but where, in those circumstances, he or she is charged with a basic intent offence a conviction should follow.[61]

Redefining the Boundary with Automatism

Since the proposed NCR defence is based on a total lack of capacity arising from *any* medical condition affecting the identified capacities, it would conflict with the common law sane-automatism defence[62] in a case where the condition giving rise to the defendant's lack of capacity potentially triggered both defences.

The LC's proposed solution is for the wider reaching NCR defence to be complemented by a new statutory automatism defence, as discussed in Chapter 5 of the DP. The new automatism defence would lead to an acquittal if the defendant may have suffered a total loss of control of his or her actions at the time of the alleged offence, other than as a result of a QRMC or prior fault. The NCR defence and the automatism defence would be mutually exclusive. Automatism would be a much narrower defence than under the present law, reflecting the fact that so many cases currently treated as automatism would be swept into the NCR defence. The reformed defence of automatism would, for example, apply where D's conduct that would otherwise be criminal was no more than a reflex action. If the loss of capacity was due to a QRMC, however, automatism would not apply and NCR would be the only plea.[63]

In combination, the NCR and reformed automatism defence would bring numerous advantages. First, the scheme would rid the law of the illogical and arbitrary distinctions based on internal or external causes that has done so much to bring the law into disrepute. The incoherent results will therefore disappear. The diabetic who, without fault, lapses into a coma and in that state commits the conduct element of an offence will be able to rely on the NCR defence in exactly the

[59] *Quick* [1973] QB 910. See A Loughnan and N Wake, 'Of Blurred Boundaries and Prior Fault: Insanity, Automatism and Intoxication' in A Reed and M Bohlander (with N Wake and E Smith) (eds), *General Defences in Criminal Law—Domestic and Comparative Perspectives* (Ashgate 2014) 118–19 and 124.

[60] LCPD, para 6.75.

[61] LCDP, para 4.124.

[62] On which see LCDP, para 5.65 et seq. The LC provides an extremely comprehensive analysis of the scope and application of automatism.

[63] LCDP, para 4.59.

same way whether the coma is a result of the diabetes or the insulin (in other words, whether it is hyperglycaemic or hypoglycaemic). Secondly, all cases in which the loss of control is caused by a QRMC will be treated alike, whether they are mental or physical conditions. Thirdly, the proposal will be better aligned with medical understanding. Fourthly, the proposals allow far greater public protection than the current law. Under the current law, a person who is acquitted on the grounds of automatism may have caused harm in circumstances which one might anticipate would readily recur. The court has no powers to take steps for the protection of the public if such a person is acquitted,[64] but under the NCR defence a person suffering from, say, a sleep disorder would receive the new special verdict triggering disposal powers for the court to reduce the likelihood of recurrence.

Relationship to Intoxication

Echoing the approach of the Butler Report, the DP[65] rightly recognizes the need for insanity reform to consider the interrelationship between mental condition defences: insanity, automatism, and intoxication cannot be seen in isolation. The new NCR and automatism defences are drafted to ensure coherence with the (heavily policy laden) common law rules on voluntary intoxication and prior fault.

In relation to voluntary intoxication, the LC recommends no change to the law, but proposes one change to involuntary intoxication. The NCR defence (rather than a complete acquittal) should apply where an accused who suffers from a QRMC has a total lack of capacity, having taken properly authorized medication for that condition in accordance with the prescription (or in circumstances where it was otherwise reasonable to do so), and the accused had no reason to believe that he or she would have an adverse reaction to that medication which would cause him or her to act in that way. This again promotes coherence[66] and public safety: an individual in those circumstances would be subject to a non stigmatizing NCR verdict, which is a 'more appropriate verdict than an absolute acquittal since it accurately reflects the true underlying cause of the defendant's conduct, namely the medical condition, and because it allows the court to address the risk of harm if he lost capacity again'.[67]

64 Subject to a restraining order under the Protection from Harassment Act 1997, s 5A.

65 LCDP, Chapter 6.

66 Albeit contradicting the earlier LC recommendations on intoxication—but those were rejected outright by the government in any event—*Intoxication and Criminal Liability* (2009) Law Com No 314, para 3.135.

67 LCDP, para 6.49.

Verdicts and Disposals

The proposed defence would lead to a new special verdict—'not criminally responsible by reason of a recognised medical condition'. Although cumbersome, it provides a more accurate and less stigmatizing label.[68] The defence would be further destigmatized because it would apply to all QRMCs not only serious *mental* conditions.

Following this NCR verdict, both the Crown Court and the magistrates' courts would have a range of available disposals: to make a hospital order, a supervision order, or an absolute discharge, and the Crown Court would be able to make a restriction order. As regards children and young people, the LC proposes that the courts should also have the option of making a non-penal Youth Supervision Order. A court could attach non-punitive requirements, such as a mental health treatment requirement, or a medical requirement, where such requirements would be beneficial. Since the defence would apply to physical as well as mental conditions, this broad range of supervisory disposals seems entirely appropriate.

Procedural Aspects

A longstanding controversy in the current law is that the legal burden is on the accused to prove the defence of insanity.[69] Despite recent explicit endorsement of the common law approach by the Court of Appeal[70] the LC takes the view that this is both wrong in principle and unnecessary.[71] Its more sophisticated proposal is that in the NCR defence the accused should have an 'elevated evidential burden' to be satisfied by calling evidence from two experts. If the accused satisfies that burden, the prosecution must satisfy the tribunal of fact, to the criminal standard of proof, that the accused did not suffer a complete loss of capacity by reason of a QRMC.

In a further demonstration of the desire to ensure that the defence is not only sound in principle, but of practical value, the LC proposes that a jury verdict can be dispensed with if: the accused is legally represented; no jury could reasonably reach any other verdict; and the judge records the reasons for the verdict.[72] This conclusion is based on the empirical research revealing that in some cases, the

[68] LCDP, para 3.26.

[69] T Jones, 'Insanity, Automatism and the Burden of Proof on the Accused' (1995) 111 LQR 475; A Loughnan, 'Manifest Madness' (2007) 70 MLR 379, 398. It is surprising that there has not been a direct challenge to the European Court of Human Rights (ECtHR) on this basis other than in 1990 in *H v UK* (App no 15023/89) in which the Commission dismissed the application.

[70] See eg *R v Foye* [2013] EWCA Crim 475 in which Lord Hughes stated at para 35: 'In the case of both insanity and diminished responsibility, the issue depends on the inner workings of the defendant's mind at the time of the offence. It would be a practical impossibility in many cases for the Crown to disprove (beyond reasonable doubt) an assertion that he was insane or suffering from diminished responsibility.'

[71] Discussed issue in detail in Chapter 8 of the LCDP.

[72] Discussed in Chapter 7 of the LCDP.

need for the jury to return a verdict of 'not guilty by reason of insanity' is a waste of court time and resources, when all parties are agreed on the outcome and the verdict is a formality.[73]

The Role of the Expert

Under the current law, to support a defence of insanity, evidence is required from two medical practitioners, one of whom must be a psychiatrist. That latter requirement would not be appropriate for the NCR defence which extends beyond mental health conditions to any QRMC. The kind of expert evidence which will best inform the court will depend on the kind of QRMC which is in issue, so the relevant expert might be a psychiatrist, a medical practitioner, a psychologist, or a person with another expertise. The LC therefore proposes retaining the requirement for two experts, but proposes that only one of them need be a medical practitioner.[74]

Expert evidence would be critical to the defence, being relevant to: (a) whether the condition is a medical condition recognized by the relevant profession; (b) whether the condition could cause a lack of capacity as is claimed in the particular case; (c) whether the accused did in fact have that condition at the time of the alleged offence; and (d) whether the accused did in fact lack the relevant capacity in relation to what he or she is alleged to have done.

Expert evidence will be necessary, though not determinative as to whether the defence is made out. The test for the defence is whether someone is 'criminally responsible'. Such a verdict contains a judgement which is not a physical fact about a person: 'Discovering and identifying a state of responsibility is not like discovering and identifying a brain tumour. Rather, it is a moral judgment about a person's motives and behaviour.'[75] The question whether a person is criminally responsible is a moral one rather than a scientific one, because it is about the relationship of the individual to the state, about public condemnation, and the attribution of blame. The ultimate question—whether a person is not responsible due to his or her lack of capacity—is not a matter of expert opinion; it is a judgement by the jury or magistrates, informed by expert opinion. That view taken by the LC aligns with the view

[73] The results from empirical studies suggested that, during the period studied, in over half of cases in which the insanity defence succeeded, the jury were directed by the judge to give a verdict of not guilty by reason of insanity. See RD Mackay, BJ Mitchell, and L Howe, 'Yet More Facts about the Insanity Defence' [2006] Crim LR 399.

[74] If a psychiatrist is the relevant expert, then he or she would still be subject to the requirement of Mental Health Act 1983, s 12.

[75] See EP Trager, 'The Insanity Defence Revisited' (1998) 4(1) MLJI 15, 18. See also the Bonnie's assertion that 'at bottom, the debate about the insanity defense and the idea of criminal responsibility raises fundamentally moral questions, not scientific ones': in R Bonnie, 'The Moral Basis of the Insanity Defense' (1983) 69(2) ABA Journal 194, 195 and that of Williams who writes: '[R]esponsibility (in the absence of further definition) is not a scientific or objective fact': G Williams, *Textbook of Criminal Law* (2nd edn, Stevens 1983) 640.

in the appellate courts in *Golds*,[76] *Brennan*,[77] *and Blackman*[78] in cases on similar issues for diminished responsibility decided since the Law Commission Discussion Paper (LCDP).

Developments Since the LCDP

Academic Challenges

The Commission's DP succeeded in drawing published discussion from eminent scholars in the field. In this section we offer a detailed analysis of their criticisms and comments on the DP proposals.

Antony Duff

Commenting on the LC's proposal, Antony Duff argues that persons who totally lacked the capacity to conform to the relevant law (by, for instance, lacking the capacities identified by the LC in its test for the NCR defence), ought always to have a defence, even without showing that the incapacity resulted from a QRMC. This 'rational incapacity' defence should, according to him, result in an unqualified 'not guilty' verdict.[79] This is because, for Duff, the only substantive role of the QRMC in the LC's proposal is to allow the court, if necessary, to order the accused's detention in a psychiatric institution for his or her own protection, and for the protection of the public. But, Duff says, the criminal court has no business making such an order—while the criminal court is equipped to address the issue of the accused's 'condition and capacities at the time of and in relation to the alleged crime', it is for a civil court, through the process of civil detention, to decide whether the accused's condition at the time of trial is such that he or she is likely to harm herself or others if freed. The criminal court should acquit persons determined to have lacked the capacity to conform to the law, but be empowered nevertheless to order their temporary detention pending a civil order.[80]

But consider the upshot of Duff's proposal. It will, of course, require the deployment of considerable additional resources (the time, effort, and cost of making a civil court acquainted with facts and evidence already examined at length by another court). But much more importantly, deploying these resources would not improve things for deserving defendants. Duff's proposal would mean that

[76] [2016] UKSC 61.
[77] [2014] EWCA Crim 2387.
[78] [2017] EWCA Crim 190.
[79] RA Duff, 'Incapacity and Insanity: Do We Need the Insanity Defence?' in B Livings, A Reed, and N Wake (eds), *Mental Condition Defences and the Criminal Justice System* (Cambridge Scholars Publishing 2015) 159, 167–73.
[80] ibid 168.

a criminal court concluding that a person lacked the capacity to conform to law would have to acquit them, but despite that acquittal, under the powers that Duff suggests, decide whether to release the person, or order that they be temporarily detained until a civil court can consider their case. On what basis would it make this decision? Presumably, based on an assessment of whether the individual posed a risk to themself and to others. But that is exactly the same basis on which it would make disposal orders under the proposed NCR defence. Recall also, that even under the LC's proposal, the court will have the discretion either to release the accused, or to direct his or her detention. The only difference is, under the LC's proposal, the discretion to direct detention applies to the narrow set of cases in which he or she lacked the capacity to conform to the law *and* this resulted from a QRMC. Many of the defendants, in cases in which their incapacity did not result from a QRMC, would be entitled to an unqualified acquittal and release on the basis that they acted involuntarily, or lacked the mens rea for their offences. Under Duff's proposal, every defendant who lacked the capacity to conform to the law, including those who would otherwise be entitled to an unqualified acquittal and release, would be liable to be detained pending a civil court's consideration of their case.

Finally, consider defendants who voluntarily choose to perform the actus reus of an offence because they lack the capacity to conform to the law owing to something that does not qualify, under the LC's proposals, as a QRMC—say, acute voluntary intoxication. Under existing law, no defence is available to such defendants. Duff's proposal would grant a complete defence to such defendants as well. But it is difficult to countenance such a significant change to the law in the absence of any positive argument for it.

Michael Moore

Michael Moore's work was cited extensively by the Commission in the DP, in particular, the LC noted his arguments to the effect that the insanity defence ought to take the form of a blanket exemption from criminal liability for people diagnosed with certain serious mental illnesses.[81] It rejected this proposal for various reasons, chief amongst which was that many people who ought to receive the defence are not 'globally incompetent' in the manner necessary for a blanket exemption, especially since the impact of a mental illness varies from person to person, from time to time, and from situation to situation, with people moving in and out of a category of mental illness. 'Insanity' as a status gives it permanency—it treats the group of legally insane persons as fixed. This does not reflect the realities of mental illness.

Recently, Moore has reiterated his argument for a status-based defence of insanity by sharpening his criticism of the general structure of existing tests for insanity.[82] Moore refers to tests for insanity with the following structure: insanity = mental

[81] LCDP, A.93–A.100.

[82] MS Moore, 'The Quest for a Responsible Responsibility Test: Norwegian Insanity Law After Breivik' (2015) 9 Crim Law Philos 645.

disease + some other 'Factor X' that is caused or accompanied by the mental illness, where Factor X is an exculpating condition that operates independently 'of any exculpation done by the mental disease itself'.[83] Amongst the conditions that Moore identifies as having played the role of Factor X, is the existence of ignorance or mistake of either fact or law, and the lack of a voluntary act.[84] Since the LC's proposed NCR defence also has this sort of structure, and it refers to 'Factor X' conditions that Moore addresses, his arguments are also directed at the LC's proposals. It is therefore worthwhile considering Moore's argument in further detail.

Moore notes that these 'Factor X' conditions eliminate or diminish responsibility independently of the mental illness. If a person acts involuntarily, he or she is not responsible for their conduct on that basis alone; if a person is ignorant of, or mistaken about, some key fact or rule, then he or she is excused on that basis alone. This, he says, sets up a dilemma.[85]

> The first horn of the dilemma is this: why is mental disease an element of any of these tests? If Factor X is already a responsibility eliminating or diminishing factor, independently of any exculpatory work done by mental disease itself, why does it matter how Factor X came to exist in a particular case?[86]

Moore suggests that this pushes us to limit the defence to cases in which Factor X is not itself excusing. But in respect of those cases, we are faced with the second horn of the dilemma, which is that

> if these variations of Factor X are not themselves excusing, then mental illness itself (i.e., without Factor X) must be relevant to responsibility. Take the mistake/ignorance of law prong of [the] M'Naghten [test] ... typically under Anglo-American law ignorance/mistake of law does not excuse. Yet the M'Naghten [test] broadly give[s] such an excuse to the mentally ill. Why do the mentally ill get excused when the non-mentally ill do not? Mental illness must itself do some excusing work, transforming generally non-excusing conditions into excusing ones ...
>
> Indeed ... isn't mental disorder doing all of the moral work in insanity cases?[87]

How so? Moore explains that even when all potential Factor X conditions are absent, we have strong intuitions that the insanity defence should apply. He cites

[83] ibid 658.

[84] ibid.

[85] ibid 661.

[86] ibid. See also RA Duff, 'Incapacity and Insanity: Do We Need the Insanity Defence?' in B Livings, A Reed, and N Wake (eds), *Mental Condition Defences and the Criminal Justice System* (Cambridge Scholars Publishing 2015) 159, 167.

[87] MS Moore, 'The Quest for a Responsible Responsibility Test: Norwegian Insanity Law After Breivik' (2015) 9 Crim Law Philos 645, 662.

the facts of the landmark *M'Naghten* case as an example. The defendant exhibited classic symptoms of paranoid schizophrenia when he fatally shot Edward Drummond, private secretary to the Prime Minister. Moore notes that M'Naghten had the intent required for murder in England (he intended to kill a human being); he knew the 'nature and quality of his act' (his shooting was calculated to kill); he knew of its wrongfulness (being aware of the legal and moral prohibitions against killing); and there was no evidence that he was compelled to do as he did. So, none of the potential Factor X conditions that might, in combination with a mental illness, have exculpated M'Naghten, existed. Yet we intuitively agree with his acquittal on murder charges. That intuition, Moore says, can only be traced to M'Naghten's mental illness.[88]

On this basis, Moore argues that we are drawn inexorably to the conclusion that all of the exculpatory work in the insanity defence is done by the mental disorder, and that therefore 'Factor X' is (or ought to be) superfluous.

But look again. As regards the first horn of the dilemma he sets up, Moore is too quick to conclude that the mental illness is essentially inert, since Factor X does all the exculpatory work. In fact, the mental illness may be doing plenty of other things:[89] it may provide evidence in support of the defendant's claim that Factor X existed (as, on some views of the intoxication defence, intoxication does in respect of a claim that D lacks the mens rea for an offence).[90] Additionally (and substantively), it gives the court powers to make directions in respect of the defendant despite him or her not being criminally liable. This mirrors how the voluntariness in voluntary intoxication, and the self-induced nature of self-induced automatism, vests the criminal court with powers over a defendant who would otherwise be acquitted. The difference is that in English law, insanity results in the special verdict of not guilty by reason of insanity (or under the LC's recommendations, the special verdict of 'not criminally responsible by reason of recognised medical condition') whereas the voluntariness of intoxication and the self-induced nature of automatism result in criminal liability.[91] But the point stands—the requirement for a mental disorder (or, in the context of the LC's recommendations, a QRMC) is not inert, even where Factor X can independently eliminate responsibility.

Now consider cases in which Factor X conditions cannot independently eliminate responsibility. As Moore notes, whereas ignorance of, or mistakes about, the law do not ordinarily exculpate, they do so when that ignorance or mistake was

[88] ibid 662.

[89] See also LCDP paras 2.1–2.34; RA Duff, 'Incapacity and Insanity: Do We Need the Insanity Defence?' in B Livings, A Reed, and N Wake (eds), *Mental Condition Defences and the Criminal Justice System* (Cambridge Scholars Publishing 2015) 159, 167.

[90] D Ormerod and K Laird, *Smith, Hogan and Ormerod's Criminal Law* (16th edn, Oxford University Press 2021) 334; *Simester and Sullivan's Criminal Law* (7th edn, Hart Publishing 2019) 742.

[91] AP Simester, 'Intoxication is Never a Defence' [2009] Crim LR 3, 6; D Ormerod and K Laird, *Smith, Hogan and Ormerod's Criminal Law* (16th edn, Oxford University Press 2021) 327–30; *R v Bailey* [1983] 1 WLR 760; *R v Coley, McGhee and Harris* [2013] EWCA Crim 223.

caused by mental illness. In these cases, Moore accepts that 'mental illness itself must be doing some excusing work'. But in fact, Moore argues by reference to the facts of *M'Naghten*, it is 'doing all of the moral work'. This is the second horn of his dilemma, and Moore says, it suggests that insanity is really a status defence, based purely on having a mental illness.

Again though, this is too quick. First, some might simply not share the strong intuition that M'Naghten ought to have been acquitted. And secondly, even if they did, as Moore himself notes:

> [U]nder the facts as [M'Naghten] believed them to be, he had a hard choice to make. He believed that he was being persecuted by [the Prime Minister, whom he mistook Drummond to be] and others and that if he did not strike first, he himself would be hurt or worse.[92]

If M'Naghten believed that he was defending himself against an unlawful threat, then arguably, he did not realize the wrongfulness of shooting at the person he believed to be the threatener.

Moore anticipates this objection, and responds that, 'for a sane person such beliefs [ie that one was being persecuted by the person one believes is the Prime Minister], even if true, would not give rise to any valid duress defense (there being no threats of immediate harm), nor can such pre-emptive strikes against non-imminent harm be justified as self-defense'.[93] But the fact that the objective absence of an immediate threat would render M'Naghten's beliefs incapable of grounding a valid defence of duress or self-defence, is beside the point. M'Naghten might, because of his paranoid schizophrenia, have believed the threat to be immediate. If so, his mental illness would have prevented him from realizing the legal and moral wrongfulness of his actions after all.

In sum, Moore's arguments against the standard formulations of the insanity defence (and indeed against the proposed NCR defence) do not stand up to scrutiny. The first horn of the dilemma he tries to set up disappears once we recognize the various roles that the mental illness may be playing in tests with the structure of the proposed NCR defence, even in cases in which a Factor X condition is independently capable of eliminating responsibility. The second horn of his dilemma dissolves once we realize that his strongest example of a case in which we might want the defence to apply despite Factor X being inert, is not in fact a case in which Factor X is inert.

[92] MS Moore, 'The Quest for a Responsible Responsibility Test: Norwegian Insanity Law After Breivik' (2015) 9 Crim Law Philos 645, 662.

[93] ibid.

John Stanton-Ife

Perhaps the most forceful criticism of the LC's proposals comes from Stanton-Ife. He has argued strongly against the LC's insistence on a *total* lack of capacity for the NCR defence on grounds that it is absurdly stringent. He suggests that an alternative explicitly rejected by the LC—that of effective incapacity—is clearly preferable.[94]

Stanton-Ife illustrates the supposed stringency of the proposed NCR defence by reference to an example taken from the DP:

> D lives in a flat. He has a history of sleepwalking. One night, he gets up, puts toast under the grill, turns the grill on and returns to bed. The kitchen catches light and the fire spreads to neighbouring flats. D is woken by the sirens of the fire engines. No one is hurt but several flats are badly damaged. He is charged with arson. His defence is that he was asleep throughout, including when he turned the grill on.
>
> In this case, the prosecution would have to prove that D damaged the flats, without lawful excuse, and intending to damage them or being reckless as to whether they would be damaged. D will be 'reckless' in this context where he was aware of a risk that the flats would be damaged by his actions and it was, in the circumstances known to him, unreasonable to take that risk.[95]

Stanton-Ife identifies the relevant question for the applicability of the NCR defence in this case as whether D was '"wholly incapable at the time of thinking rationally" or totally incapable of rationally forming a judgment at the time'.[96] He notes that as per the LC's preferred exegesis,[97] D is capable of rationally forming a judgement if he has the ability to form accurate beliefs, the ability to draw on existing wants and beliefs, and an accurate reasoning process that allows him to draw warranted conclusions about the probable relationships among various wants, acts, and consequences. Combining these, he argues that '[a]ny accurate belief, any drawing on an existing want or belief and so on provided it relates, albeit in the right way, to the incapacity to perform the physical actions and form the fault elements of a specific offence, will be enough to put the [NCR] defence out of reach on the basis of rational incapacity'.[98]

Stanton-Ife then points out that D clearly has some above-zero capacity on these criteria. D has the perfectly accurate belief that putting bread under a grill that has been switched on is a way of making toast. Furthermore, he seems to be able to

[94] J Stanton-Ife, 'Total Incapacity' in B Livings and others (eds), *Mental Condition Defences and the Criminal Justice System* (Cambridge Scholars Publishing 2015) 130, 141.

[95] ibid 149; LCDP, paras 1.97–98.

[96] J Stanton-Ife, 'Total Incapacity' in B Livings and others (eds), *Mental Condition Defences and the Criminal Justice System* (Cambridge Scholars Publishing 2015) 130, 150.

[97] LCDP, para 4.11.

[98] J Stanton-Ife, 'Total Incapacity' in B Livings and others (eds), *Mental Condition Defences and the Criminal Justice System* (Cambridge Scholars Publishing 2015) 130, 154.

draw on his beliefs together with existing wants, since (according to Stranton-Ife) D presumably makes the toast because he wants to eat, and he almost certainly chose to toast his bread because of some desire or belief he had—perhaps a preference for the taste of toast over bread, or a belief the bread was getting stale so toast was better than nothing. This too would be perfectly rational. Although Stanton-Ife admits that these capacities are being directed towards minor matters, they are significant, because (he says) all that appears necessary to exclude the proposed NCR defence is an above-zero capacity to form accurate beliefs and to draw on beliefs and desires. Moreover, it is not clear to Stanton-Ife that D totally lacks an accurate reasoning process that allows him to draw warranted conclusions about the probable relationships among various wants, acts, and consequences either, because sleepwalking often appears purposive.[99] So despite the fact that D ought to have a defence, Stanton-Ife argues that the NCR defence would be unavailable to him because of 'the bare existence of [this or these] above-zero pocket or pockets of capacity, irrespective of whether it avails or they avail [D] in any way or whether or not it is or they are trivial'.[100]

This analysis is, we suggest, flawed. First, there are no facts in the LC's example to suggest that D formed the belief that putting bread under a grill that had been switched on was a way to make toast *while he was sleepwalking*, or that D's sleepwalking actions were motivated by an actual desire to eat, and in particular, to eat toast, or that D had some desire or belief-based reasons to prefer toast to bread. And while D may *appear to* act purposively while sleepwalking, that does not suggest that D *actually* acts purposively—D is, after all, sleepwalking.

Even if we granted Stanton-Ife all of these dubious assumptions, the relevant part of the test for the proposed NCR defence does not refer to whether D was 'wholly incapable at the time of thinking rationally or totally incapable of rationally forming a judgment at the time'. It refers instead to whether D wholly lacked the capacity rationally to form a judgement *about the relevant conduct or circumstances of the offence*. Beliefs and desires about eating toast, and a reasoning process that is able to connect these to acts and consequences, are irrelevant to offences not constituted by eating toast. Undoubtedly, an awake person who actually committed a similar offence might have, inter alia, invoked the beliefs and reasoning processes that Stanton-Ife describes, in the course of committing the offence, but that is beside the point.

The NCR defence is designed to apply to people who are 'incapable of complying with the relevant law',[101] and so the key question in relation to an offence of criminal damage (including arson) is whether D was totally incapable of rationally forming a judgement about whether he was doing something in circumstances in

[99] ibid, 150.
[100] ibid, 154.
[101] LCDP, paras 3.3, 1.20.

which someone else's property might be damaged or destroyed. All that is needed for D to be wholly incapable of complying with this law, is for him to be wholly incapable of (a) forming accurate beliefs as to these matters, or (b) drawing on existing wants and beliefs in relation to them, or (c) drawing warranted conclusions about the probable relationships among the various relevant wants, acts, and consequences.[102] Even on the most generous reading of Stanton-Ife's analysis, D appears to wholly lack the ability to form beliefs and conclusions relevant to both, whether he might start a fire, and whether it might spread to other flats. Therefore, on a less uncharitable reading of the NCR defence, it would be available to D, and Stanton-Ife's main criticism of the proposed test dissolves.

As to his support for a test of effective incapacity, the foregoing analysis will have indicated that the distance between the Stanton-Ife's and the LC's positions is smaller than Stanton-Ife thinks it is. True, the LC expressly rejects an effective incapacity standard,[103] but it appears to mean something different by that standard than what Stanton-Ife means by it.

The only relatively sustained discussion of effective incapacity in the DP comes when the LC explains its departure from a previous recommendation in favour of using a loss of effective control standard for the automatism defence.[104] In that context, the LC notes that the loss of effective control standard 'would be a more flexible standard [than the total loss of control standard] for the courts to define'; and expresses concern that 'the courts [may not] interpret the notion of loss of effective control as amounting to something close to total loss of control in every case'.[105] In other words, the LC does not think that someone who could, with difficulty, control their conduct, ought to get the automatism defence, and it was concerned that an 'effective control' test might conduce to that outcome. In the absence of contrary indications, we may take it that the LC was using 'effective incapacity' in the same sense when discussing the NCR defence too. The concern in this context is the same: that someone who could, with difficulty, form a rational judgement about what they were charged with having done, or understand its wrongfulness, or control their relevant physical acts, might be found to have been 'effectively incapable' of exercising these capacities, and therefore qualify for the defence. Since the proposed NCR defence is meant to be a defence of no responsibility, and not one of reduced responsibility,[106] this is considered to be an inappropriate outcome.

Now consider how Stanton-Ife uses the term 'effective incapacity'. While arguing that an 'effective incapacity' standard would not unduly widen the defence,

[102] See also RA Duff, 'Incapacity and Insanity: Do We Need the Insanity Defence?' in B Livings, A Reed, and N Wake (eds), *Mental Condition Defences and the Criminal Justice System* (Cambridge Scholars Publishing 2015) 159, 160–67, who makes many of the same points.

[103] LCDP, para 3.3.

[104] 1989 Draft Criminal Code, cl 33(1)(a).

[105] LCDP, para 5.116.

[106] LCDP, para 3.3.

he explains that 'those who are able to control themselves, albeit with difficulty, are *not clearly "effectively" incapacitated*, even if they may possibly be "substantially" or "partially" incapacitated'.[107] On his view therefore, these people would, quite appropriately, not qualify for the NCR defence, even if the defence used what Stanton-Ife understands as an effective incapacity standard. But this is not how the LC fears the term 'effective incapacity' will be used—in fact, the LC wants to exclude this same set of people from the NCR defence by avoiding the language of 'effective incapacity'. While such people have less capacity than others whose capacity was 'merely' substantially impaired (either in the sense in which this term was used when the DP was published,[108] or in its current sense[109]) or partially impaired,[110] they still have some capacity and so should not qualify for the 'no responsibility' NCR defence.[111] Stanton-Ife agrees with the LC then, on how the NCR defence should operate—his criticism of the LC's proposed test seems to stem solely from the fact that he uses the term 'effective incapacity' in a sense different from that in which it is used in the DP.

Judicial Developments

Aside from the engagement from academics on the DP, the indications from case law and judicial comment are that, in the context of a new 'recognised medical condition' lack of capacity defence, the courts may well endorse the LC's approach.[112] There have also been some welcome judicial developments on the law relating to insanity generally. The Divisional Court has finally, correctly, accepted that insanity may be pleaded in respect of an offence irrespective of whether it is an offence of mens rea: *Loake v CPS*.[113] That does little to alleviate the practical problems inherent in the M'Naghten Rules and serves to illustrate that even appellate courts continue to struggle with the application of the Rules.

[107] J Stanton-Ife, 'Total Incapacity' in B Livings and others (eds), *Mental Condition Defences and the Criminal Justice System* (Cambridge Scholars Publishing 2015) 130, 144 (emphasis added).

[108] ie meaning 'more than minimal'. LCDP, para 4.81 read with 4.46 at fn 45 and *R v Brown* [2011] EWCA Crim 2796.

[109] ie the more demanding standard of significant or appreciable; not total, but something that is beyond merely more than trivial. *Golds* [2014] EWCA Crim 748, para 55.

[110] Again, the only other mentions of partial incapacity in the LCDP relate to the automatism defence, in which context, it is now settled law that nothing less than a total loss of voluntary control will trigger the defence. LCDP, paras 5.23, 5.32.

[111] Perhaps this supplies a normative case for a new defensive claim to sit between the 'no responsibility' NCR defence and the very limited diminished responsibility defence. But of course, making that case was not within the remit of the DP.

[112] See p 21 of the lecture given by Stanley Burnton LJ, 'Doctors, Patients and the Human Rights Act' (2011) 79 Med-Leg J 115–28 and the comments of Hughes LJ on the general approach of the English criminal law to voluntary drunkenness in *R v Dowds* [2012] 1 WLR 2576 and *R v Coley* [2013] EWCA Crim 223. Note also the approach of the Canadian Supreme Court in *Bouchard-Lebrun* [2011] SCC 58.

[113] [2017] EWHC 2855 (Admin).

A less welcome development has been the further tension created by recent decisions between the rules governing intoxication and insanity. The orthodox approach to these cases has been to maintain a strict distinction between (a) cases in which D is intoxicated at the time of the offence—if the intoxicant is in his body and continuing to affect capacity, intoxication rules apply; and (b) cases in which D was previously intoxicated and, although now sober, is affected by the after-effects (eg a paranoid or psychotic state)—the rules on insanity apply since this is a claim that the accused is affected by an internal malfunctioning. That orthodox position was reiterated as recently as 2013 in *Harris*, conjoined on appeal with *Coley*.[114] This orthodox position has been called into question by some broad *obiter dicta* in the recent case of *R v Taj*.[115] D was convicted of attempted murder having attacked V with a tyre lever on a street in London. It was not in dispute that D had the ability to form an intent at the time of the alleged offence. The cause of his belief was a drug induced/drug and alcohol induced paranoid state of mind. D sought to rely upon self-defence on the basis that the defence is available even if the defendant is mistaken as to the circumstances as he genuinely believed them to be, and that as there was no suggestion that he had alcohol or drugs present in his system at the time, he was not 'intoxicated' and should not be denied the defence. A five-member Court of Appeal dismissed his appeal. Read strictly, the *ratio* of the case is simply that on these facts D was not able to rely on the plea of self defence since his mistaken belief 'was attributable to intoxication' within the meaning of section 76(5) of the Criminal Justice and Immigration Act 2008. More controversial are the *obiter* comments of the court about the relationship between intoxication and insanity. The court suggested that D is also unable to rely on self defence where the mistaken state of mind is

> immediately and proximately consequent upon earlier drink or drug-taking, so that even though the person concerned is not drunk or intoxicated at the time, the short-term effects can be shown to have triggered subsequent episodes of *e.g.* paranoia. This is consistent with common law principles. We repeat that this conclusion does not extend to long term mental illness precipitated (perhaps over a considerable period) by alcohol or drug misuse. In the circumstances, we agree with Judge Dodgson, that the phrase 'attributable to intoxication' *is not confined to cases in which alcohol or drugs are still present in a defendant's system. It is unnecessary for us to consider whether this analysis affects the decision in Harris:* it is sufficient to underline that the potential significance of voluntary intoxication in the two cases differs' "[116]

[114] [2013] EWCA Crim 223.
[115] [2018] EWCA Crim 1743.
[116] ibid at para 60.

If the principles governing intoxication are applicable in such cases, that would generate confusion and further incoherence with the rules on insanity. Cases such as this demonstrate the desirability of a statutory scheme that deals in a coherent way with intoxication, insanity, and automatism—as in the DP—with consistent application of prior fault approaches.[117] The Law Commission has proposed a workable scheme to that effect. It is doubtful, in any event, whether in *Taj* the psychosis caused a total loss of one of the relevant capacities to trigger the NCR defence.

Future Reform Prospects

There is no doubt that the pressure for reform remains substantial, with campaign groups continuing to produce compelling evidence of unfairness and incoherence in the law.[118] That said, there is, as noted, a risk that the pressure for reform of the substantive law on insanity is overwhelmed by the calls for more wide-reaching reforms capable of greater impact across the sector. There are positive signs of agencies adopting policies that demonstrate more enlightened approaches to mental health issues,[119] and this is echoed as a clear commitment in many initiatives across the criminal justice system, as for example by the roll-out of liaison and diversion;[120] and the Sentencing Council guidelines on mental health.[121]

There is a generally positive move to address the needs of those with neurodiverse conditions in the criminal justice system. Against that, the prospects of imminent reform of the insanity defence look bleak. The LC has shown no signs of recommencing work on the next phase of the project. That would, presumably, involve producing a Consultation Paper and then finally a Report, which would commit the Commission to at least a further two years' work on the project. Its resources have been cut by over 50% in recent years and the pressure to deal with new

[117] It has been argued that the courts should reject *Taj* and interpret the insanity defence more permissively, taking account of circumstances and results when assessing the accused's understanding of his conduct, and taking account of belief in a defence when assessing his or her knowledge of wrongfulness and when applying the delusional limb of the M'Naghten Rules. See JJ Child, HS Crombag, and GR Sullivan, 'Defending the Delusional, the Irrational, and the Dangerous' [2020] Crim LR 306; M Dsouza, 'Intoxication, Psychoses, and Self-defence: Evaluating Taj' (2018) 9 Arch Rev 6

[118] See eg the Justice Report, https://justice.org.uk/wp-content/uploads/2017/11/JUSTICE-Mental-Health-and-Fair-Trial-Report-2.pdf

[119] eg CPS, https://www.cps.gov.uk/legal-guidance/mental-health-suspects-and-defendants-mental-health-conditions-or-disorders

[120] There were 56,000 cases in the Crown Court. See also the HL Select on the Constitution Report: *Covid 19 and the Courts* (2021), HL 257, https://publications.parliament.uk/pa/ld5801/ldselect/ldconst/257/257.pdf

[121] https://www.sentencingcouncil.org.uk/news/item/sentencing-offenders-with-mental-health-conditions-or-disorders-consultation-launched-on-providing-additional-information-in-sentencing-guidelines/

projects, recently referred to it, which reflect priorities of the current government is obvious.

It should also be noted in this context that the DP is almost ten years old. The Commission has had changes of Chairman and Commissioners and therefore it is distinctly likely that the Commission would wish to reopen the policy contained in the LCDP. That would also provide the opportunity for the proposals to take account of emerging developments which may be highly relevant in the way the law deals with mental illness and criminal law in the future.[122] In particular there are interesting neurolaw[123] developments to consider, and the potential impact of genomics in predicting likelihoods of certain conditions and behavioural patterns that might manifest themselves in criminal conduct.[124] It is not unlikely that the Commission will wish to explore those initiatives if its opportunity to address the insanity defence is going to 'future proof' the law rather than merely correct existing problems.

Even assuming that the Commission produced a report based on the DP proposal the prospects of any imminent enactment look slender. In a post-pandemic criminal justice system currently facing a backlog of almost half a million cases,[125] where resources are strained to breaking point, it is going to be a challenge to persuade a minister that a government Bill and precious parliamentary time should be devoted to reform of insanity. It is much more likely that the government will continue to prioritize its wider-ranging cross-departmental initiatives dealing with mental health and the criminal justice system.

Conclusion

The Commission's work has been well received. Academic comment was constructive and focused on refining the detail. The proposals would eradicate many of the illogicalities that bedevil the present law. The reforms would place the law on a more solid psychiatric foundation allowing for more accurate expert opinion to be advanced more confidently. Despite all of this, for reasons beyond the Law Commission's control, it seems unlikely that the proposals in the DP will form the basis of any imminent statutory reform.

[122] One of the Commission's present focuses is on emerging law and development.

[123] See eg the Kalisher lecture (2019) by Cheema-Grubb J, https://www.judiciary.uk/wp-content/uploads/2019/12/NEUROSCIENCE-MIND-READING-AND-THE-CRIMINAL-LAW-BCG-1.pdf

[124] See eg J Wertz and others, 'Genetics and Crime: Integrating New Genomic Discoveries Into Psychological Research About Antisocial Behavior' (2018) 29(5) Psychol Sci 791, https://journals.sagepub.com/doi/10.1177/0956797617744542

[125] See 'Justice undermined by lack of progress on backlog' Law Society Press Release 30 September 2021, https://www.lawsociety.org.uk/contact-or-visit-us/press-office/press-releases/justice-undermined-by-lack-of-progress-on-backlog

7. Postscript

Shortly after we finalized our draft of this chapter, the Court of Appeal had occasion to consider aspects of the insanity defence once again in *R v Keal*.[126] The defendant was convicted of three counts of attempted murder after attacking his father, mother, and grandmother with an array of weapons. He had a history of mental health problems, ADHD and drug addiction. In the weeks leading up to the attack, he had been behaving bizarrely, and on the day before the attack, he'd attempted suicide. During the unprovoked attack, he was apologetic, saying things like, 'I know I'm sorry I don't want to, I'm sorry I'm sorry dad',[127] and 'I'm sorry this isn't me it's the devil'.[128] After the attacks, he was found by the police on a country road dressed only in his underpants, and due to his condition, he underwent enforced Electroconvulsive Therapy. The defendant's mental health made it impossible for him to be present for large parts of his trial. Even so, the jury rejected the defendant's plea of insanity. The defence appealed, arguing that the trial judge misdirected the jury on the test of insanity. It argued that on a proper reading of the M'Naghten Rules, 'the defence of insanity is available to a psychotic defendant who is aware that his act is "wrong" (within the meaning of the M'Naghten Rules) but whose delusion is such that he is compelled to perform it or powerless to prevent it.'[129] The Court of Appeal rightly rejected this argument—as a matter of doctrinal law, nothing in the M'Naghten Rules supports it. But as a normative matter, the defendant's argument is compelling. If the defendant lacked control of his actions, then his knowledge that they were wrong is beside the point, since he could not have done anything with that knowledge. This was the Law Commission's position too—its Not Criminally Responsible defence would apply to someone who wholly lacked the capacity to control his or her physical acts in relation to the relevant conduct or circumstances as a result of a qualifying recognized medical condition.

The Court of Appeal went further and pronounced that under the M'Naghten Rules, to show that he did not know that his act was 'wrong', the defendant would have had to establish both (a) that he did not know that his act was unlawful (ie contrary to law) and (b) that he did not know that his act was 'morally' wrong (by reference to the standards of ordinary people). Strictly, this ruling is obiter dicta. Nothing in the appellant's arguments required it to be made. The court relied, on this point, upon observations made in a previous Court of Appeal ruling in *R v Johnson*,[130] which in turn relied on observations made in Archbold, Blackstone's Criminal Practice, and Smith and Hogan on Criminal Law (11th Ed, 2005). The

[126] [2022] EWCA Crim 341.
[127] ibid para 3.
[128] ibid para 4.
[129] ibid para 19.
[130] [2007] EWCA Crim 1978.

observation made in Johnson was itself obiter dicta; in fact, there is no reported case in which the court has had to adjudicate on whether the defendant must prove that he or she did not know that his or her actions were both legally and morally wrong. The observation in Smith and Hogan relates to whether it would be appropriate to extend the defence of insanity also to defendants' whose disease of mind gave rise to a defect of reason that manifested in their unawareness of the moral wrongness of their actions; as such, it is not directly on the point. The observations in Archbold and Blackstone's Criminal Practice are not backed by further authority, and are not in line with the Law Commission's understanding, based on a detailed survey of the authorities, of the M'Naghten test. That said, the Law Commission did indicate that it would like the law to develop in this way.

4

The Mental Disorder Defence in Scots law

Gerry Maher

The Current State of the Defence and Disposals

The Definition of the Defence

The common law defence of insanity was abolished in June 2012, and replaced by a new defence in the following terms:[1]

> (1) A person is not criminally responsible for conduct constituting an offence, and is to be acquitted of the offence, if the person was at the time of the conduct unable by reason of mental disorder to appreciate the nature or wrongfulness of the conduct.
> (2) But a person does not lack criminal responsibility for such conduct if the mental disorder in question consists only of a personality disorder which is characterised solely or principally by abnormally aggressive or seriously irresponsible conduct.
> ...
> (5) In this section, 'conduct' includes acts and omissions.

The expression mental disorder is defined as any (a) mental illness; (b) personality disorder; or (c) learning disability, however caused or manifested.[2]

This change to the test for the defence followed on from recommendations made by the Scottish Law Commission.[3]

Name of the defence

The Scottish Law Commission rejected the idea that a defence such as the insanity defence should be abolished altogether, but recommended that it should be

[1] Criminal Procedure (Scotland) Act 1995, s 51A, introduced by the Criminal Justice and Licensing (Scotland) Act 2010, s 168. It was brought into force on 25 June 2012 (SSI 2012 No 160. The Criminal Justice and Licensing (Scotland) Act 2010 (Commencement No 10 and Saving Provisions) Order 2012).
[2] Mental Health (Care and Treatment) (Scotland) Act 2013, s 328(1).
[3] Discussed below (n 5).

Gerry Maher, *The Mental Disorder Defence in Scots law* In: *The Insanity Defence*. Edited by: Ronnie Mackay and Warren Brookbanks, Oxford University Press. © Gerry Maher 2022. DOI: 10.1093/oso/9780198854944.003.0004

replaced by a new defence set out in statute. At the same time the Commission argued that the term 'insanity' should no longer be used, as it was stigmatizing and no longer in medical usage. However, the new statutory defence has no name apart from that contained in the title of section 51A of the amended Criminal Procedure (Scotland) 1995 Act[4] which is 'criminal responsibility of persons with mental disorder'.

In its initial recommendations the Commission were minded to call the defence the mental disorder defence. However, it later abandoned this view on the basis that this name did not fully capture the full scope of the defence as mental disorder was one, but only one, constituent part of the defence.[5] Furthermore, other defences such as diminished responsibility and unfitness for trial also involve mental disorder. However, some commentators do refer to the defence as the mental disorder defence,[6] but the courts have tended to use a version of the statutory section title.

It is also worth noting an oddity here about the location of the defence. The Scottish Law Commission envisaged that the reforms it recommended for its project would be implemented in a separate, free-standing statute.[7] However the implementation of the Commission's recommendations was made as part of a more general statute, the Criminal Justice and Licensing (Scotland) Act 2010, which added various new sections to the Criminal Procedure (Scotland) Act 1995, namely section 51A (criminal responsibility of mentally disordered persons), section 51B (diminished responsibility), and section 53F (unfitness for trial).

This seems odd, for as both the long and short titles of the 1995 Act make clear, the scope of the Act is limited to criminal procedure. It could possibly be argued that unfitness for trial relates to procedural matters but defences such as those in section 51A and 51B are clearly part of substantive criminal law. It is, of course, the case that there are many provisions in the 1995 Act which deal with mental disorder but these relate to the procedural consequences of establishing this defence, and there is little, if anything, on the procedural consequences of a finding of diminished responsibility. A more natural home for these provisions would have been another statute of 1995, namely the Criminal Law (Consolidation) (Scotland) Act 1995.

[4] References in this chapter to 'the 1995 Act' are to the Criminal Procedure (Scotland) Act 1995, which is a consolidating statute dealing with a very wide range of provisions on criminal procedure in Scotland.

[5] Scottish Law Commission, *Report on Insanity and Diminished Responsibility* (Report No 195, 2004), ('SLC Report'), paras 2.19–2.24.

[6] See eg E Shaw, 'Automatism and Mental Disorder in Scots Criminal Law' (2015) 19(2) Edin L R 210 and SD Barnes, 'Re-evaluating the Exclusion of Psychopathy from the Mental Disorder Defence in Scots Law' 2018 Jur Rev 1.

[7] The SLC Report contained a draft bill with the title Criminal Responsibility and Unfitness for Trial (Scotland) Bill.

The Disposal Consequences of the Defence

Where the defence in section 51A has been established by the accused or has been accepted by the Crown, the accused is acquitted of the offence he was charged with. However, this is not a simple acquittal as the verdict specifies that the accused is acquitted by reason of the defence set out in section 51A.[8] A verdict in this form gives rise to various consequences in terms of further disposal of the case.

A similar approach was taken in relation to the common law defence of insanity, where the acquittal was stated to be on the ground of insanity. But for a long time in Scots law the consequences of a verdict in this form were drastic, as the court had to order the detention of the accused in a state hospital without limitation of time.[9]

Concern was raised that this type of disposal was challengeable under the European Convention on Human Rights (ECHR). Article 5(1) of the Convention states that no one 'shall be deprived of his liberty save in the following cases and in accordance with a procedure prescribed by law'. One of the specified cases is in paragraph (e) of that article which provides for 'the lawful detention of persons for the prevention of the spreading of infectious diseases, of persons of unsound mind, alcoholics or drug addicts or vagrants'. The leading decision of the European Court of Human Rights (ECtHR) on this provision is *Winterwerp v The Netherlands*,[10] where the Court, in discussing the expression 'person of unsound mind', said:[11]

> This term is not one that can be given a definitive interpretation: as was pointed out by the Commission, the Government and the applicant, it is a term whose meaning is continually evolving as research in psychiatry progresses, an increasing flexibility in treatment is developing and society's attitudes to mental illness change, in particular so that a greater understanding of the problems of mental patients is becoming more widespread.

The Court also noted that the 'lawful detention' of such persons required that 'no one may be confined as "a person of unsound mind" in the absence of medical evidence establishing that his mental state is such as to justify his compulsory hospitalisation'.[12]

Accordingly, to be ECHR compliant in a disposal of a case where someone has been acquitted on the basis of the mental disorder defence, three pre-conditions must be satisfied: (i) there must be a mental condition at the time of making the disposal; (ii) the mental condition must be established by medical evidence; and

[8] 1995 Act, s 53E.
[9] As eg under the Criminal Procedure (Scotland) Act 1975, s 174(3), (4).
[10] (1979) 2 EHRR 387.
[11] ibid para 37.
[12] ibid para 39.

(iii) the mental condition requires compulsory detention, including detention in a hospital.

To make Scots law compatible with the Convention requirements, changes were introduced to the rules on disposal of cases involving the insanity defence,[13] and these now apply to the new statutory defence. Under section 57 of the 1995 Act, where a person has been acquitted on the ground of the section 51A defence, the court has the power to make the following orders:[14]

(a) a compulsion order which may (but not must) authorize the detention of the person in a hospital;
(b) a compulsion hospital order coupled with a restriction order;
(c) an interim compulsion order;
(d) a guardianship order;
(e) a supervision and treatment order; and
(f) a discharge with no further order made.

Use of mental disorder defence

There are no available data on the number of cases where the mental disorder defence under section 51A of the 1995 Act has been raised. However, the scale of the use of the defence can be surmised from the data on the disposals ordered by a court where the defence has been successfully established.

The tables below show the use of these various orders over the period 2010–19. However, these figures are combined totals for persons acquitted by reason of the mental disorder defence as well as those found unfit for trial and not acquitted after an examination of facts.

Note that these data do not include any cases where the court has made no mental health disposal order.

To put the data on disposal orders into context, the following table shows the figures for the number of persons against whom criminal proceedings were taken.

There are also figures available for interim compulsion orders, but these deal with orders applying not only to persons unfit for trial or acquitted on the non-responsibility ground but also to anyone convicted of an offence where no issue of unfitness or mental disorder arose at the trial.

[13] Criminal Justice (Scotland) Act 1995, s 50. These provisions were consolidated into the Criminal Procedure (Scotland) Act 1995, s 57. These changes came into effect in April 1996.

[14] For a detailed discussion of these provisions, see G Maher, 'Unfitness for Trial in Scots Law' in R Mackay and W Brookbanks (eds), *Fitness to Plead: International and Comparative Perspectives* (Oxford University Press 2018) 81, 98–102. It should be noted that the disposal must be based on a medical assessment of the acquitted person at the time of making the order.

Table 4.1 Persons proceeded against in Scottish Criminal Courts[a]

2010/11	2011/12	2012/13	2013/2014	2014/15	2015/16	2016/17	2017/18	2018/19	2019/20
130,268	124,736	116,678	121,753	123,369	116,678	107,362	95,557	89,725	85,726

[a]Source: Criminal Proceedings in Scotland 2010–11 to 2019–20.

Table 4.2 Disposals where a person has been acquitted by reason of mental disorder and unfitness for trial[a]

Order type	2010/11	2011/12	2012/13	2013/14	2014/15	2015/16	2016/17	2017/18	2018/19
Compulsion Order	8	8	11	15	21	24	28	50	33
Compulsion Order—Community	1	0	0	1	0	0	0	0	0
Compulsion Order with Restriction Order	0	4	4	8	7	3	5	4	6
Guardianship	0	1	0	0	0	1	0	0	0
Supervision and Treatment Order	0	0	0	0	1	0	3	1	1

[a]Source: Mental Welfare Commission for Scotland, *Mental Health Act Monitoring Report 2018-19. Annual Statistical Monitoring* (2019) 46, Table 6.2.2.

Table 4.3 Interim compulsion orders[a]

Order type	2010/11	2011/12	2012/13	2013/14	2014/15	2015/16	2016/17	2017/18	2018/19
Interim Compulsion Order	17	18	26	31	21	24	26	23	15

[a] Source: Mental Welfare Commission for Scotland, *Mental Health Act Monitoring Report 2018–19. Annual Statistical Monitoring* (2019) 47, Table 6.3.1.

History of the Insanity Defence in Scots Law

There are several general points to note about the more relatively modern history of the defence of insanity, in its development during the 19th and 20th centuries. The first is that, not surprisingly in a small jurisdiction, in terms of overall numbers there were relatively few cases where the defence was considered.[15] Furthermore, most cases of mental disorder involved insanity as a plea in bar of trial (in modern parlance unfitness for trial), rather than as a substantive defence. Although at times judges treated these instances of insanity as involving the same test or definition, most attention was given to evolving the definition of the plea in bar. Another important factor was that there was no court of appeal in the Scottish criminal justice system until 1926, and as a consequence, the mechanism for developing the law on the defence of insanity was to be found in the directions which trial judges gave to juries in cases where the defence was in issue, a factor which continued even after the establishment of the criminal appeal court. A related issue was a tendency for Scots criminal law to avoid detailed definitions of many of its key doctrines and concepts.

Hume on Absolute Alienation of Reason

As with many issues in Scots criminal law, the starting point in considering the historical development of insanity as a defence is the discussion in Hume's Commentaries.[16] Hume begins his exposition by referring to the 'miserable defence of idiocy or insanity'. He emphasizes that not every type of mental disorder will allow for the defence; it does not apply to 'mere weakness of intellect, or a strange and moody humour, or a crazy and capricious or irritable temper', as these conditions are consistent with the accused having a competent understanding of the true circumstances of the facts of the crime or of a criminal purpose. He continues:

> To serve the purpose of a defence in law, the disorder must therefore amount to an absolute alienation of reason, '*ut continua mentis alienatione, omni intellectu careat*'—such a disease as deprives the patient of the knowledge of the true aspect and position of things about him—hinders him from distinguishing friend from foe—and gives him up to the impulse of his own distempered fancy.

[15] See further text at Tables 4.1–4.3 above.

[16] D Hume, *Commentaries on the Law of Scotland Respecting Crimes* (4th edn, Bell & Bradfute 1844) I, 37.

This notion of absolute alienation of reason has survived into more modern authorities. In *HM Advocate v Kidd*,[17] the trial judge directed a jury on the definition of insanity on similar lines:

> [I]n order to excuse a person from responsibility for his acts on the ground of insanity, there must have been an alienation of the reason in relation to the act committed. There must have been some mental defect, to use a broad neutral word, a mental defect, by which his reason was overpowered, and he was thereby rendered incapable of exerting his reason to control his conduct and reactions. If his reason was alienated in relation to the act committed, he was not responsible for that act, even although otherwise he may have been apparently quite rational. What is required is some alienation of the reason in relation to the act committed.

In contrast to Hume, the test in *Kidd* refers to alienation without its being absolute in nature. In *Brennan v HM Advocate*,[18] a question for the court of appeal was whether the defence of insanity could be based on an extreme malfunctioning of the mind brought about by self-induced intoxication. The court rejected this argument and stated: 'insanity in our law requires proof of total alienation of reason in relation to the act charged as the result of mental illness, mental disease or defect or unsoundness of mind'.

The M'Naghten Rules and the Scots Law of Insanity

Another strand in the development of the defence of insanity is the extent to which the M'Naghten Rules were part of Scots law. Certainly during a period from 1844 onwards a test very like the Rules became dominant in judicial pronouncements on the defence.[19] The leading case was *HM Advocate v Jas Gibson*,[20] where the jury was instructed that the test of insanity required that the accused had believed that the particular act with which he was charged was not 'a crime against the law'. Gordon notes that the *Gibson* case expressly rejects a defence based on irresistible impulse.[21]

The use of a test akin to the M'Naghten Rules, based solely on cognitive factors, continued to feature as part of Scots law well into the 20th century, but in some cases judges would interpret the test more widely by adding a further element,

[17] 1960 JC 61, 70–71.

[18] 1977 JC 38, 45.

[19] GH Gordon, *The Criminal Law of Scotland* (1st edn, W Green & Son 1967) 319–21 argues that most of the early cases which advanced the use of the Rules were inspired by Lord Justice Clerk Hope. Gordon argues that Lord Hope's use of the Rules were inspired more by a religious principle of absolute free will than any medical or legal basis.

[20] (1844) 2 Broun 138.

[21] Gordon, *The Criminal Law of Scotland* (n 19) 320.

usually in terms of a volitional component involving loss of control of conduct. As Gordon notes, by the earlier part of the 20th century, the 'Rules were the law, though in some cases they were not the whole law'.[22] However, in the second part of the 20th century a view became established that the Rules were not part of the Scots law of insanity.[23]

Other Approaches to Insanity at Common Law

A quite different approach was to downplay the need to provide a legal definition of insanity but to concentrate on medical tests for insanity, an approach formulated by Lord Moncreiff in a series of decisions in the 1870s.[24] For example, in *HM Adv v Archibald Miller*,[25] he directed the jury that:

> it is not a question of knowledge but of soundness of mind. If the man have not a sane mind to apply his knowledge, the mere intellectual apprehension of an injunction or prohibition may stimulate his unsound mind to do an act simply because it is forbidden.... If a man has a sane apprehension of right and wrong, he is certainly responsible; but he may form and understand the idea of right and wrong and yet be hopelessly insane. You may discard these attempts at definition altogether. They only mislead.

On this approach the key issue was whether the conduct of the accused was a result of a mental disorder, and the existence of a mental disorder would be established by medical science.[26]

A version of this approach is hinted at by some of the evidence given to the Royal Commission on Capital Punishment[27] on the definition of insanity in Scots law. Some of the judges who gave evidence mentioned the M'Naghten Rules but emphasized that the Rules were not applied as strictly as they were in English law. Lord Cooper further noted that:[28]

22 ibid 329.

23 See *HM Advocate v Kidd* 1960 JC 61, 71:

> At one time, following English law, it was held in Scotland that if an accused did not know the nature and quality of the act committed, or if he did know it but did not know he was doing wrong, it was held that he was insane. That was the test, but that test has not been followed in Scotland in the most recent cases.

24 Lord Moncreiff was Lord Justice Clerk from 1869–88.

25 (1874) 3 Couper 16, 18.

26 Gordon, *The Criminal Law of Scotland* (n 19) 322 states that this view was broadly similar to the product test used in New Hampshire (the Durham test).

27 *Minutes of Evidence Taken Before the Royal Commission on Capital Punishment* (1950).

28 ibid para 5479. Note the reference to 'any other test'.

> However much you charge a jury as to the M'Naghten Rules or any other test, the question they would put to themselves when they retired is—'Is the man mad or is he not?'

The Insanity Defence in the Later 20th Century

It is not easy to be precise as to the definition of the defence of insanity in the later part of the 20th century. In the first edition of his book in 1967 Gordon suggested that Scots law was broadly similar to the definition in the American Law Institute's Model Penal Code 'in requiring the absence of a proper "appreciation" of the situation, and of the ability to control one's action in the light of such an appreciation'.[29] However, this statement reads more like a recommendation than a description of existing Scottish sources.

In the light of subsequent authorities, especially the *Brennan* decision, the situation can be summarized as follows. There was no hard-and-fast definition of the defence, and judges would adopt a flexible approach when charging juries on the matter. The M'Naghten Rules as such were not part of the Scots law of insanity and the dominant approach was a version of Hume's definition which used at its core the concept of an (absolute) alienation of reason which had the consequence that a person did not properly understand his situation and possibly also could not control his conduct.

The Reference to the Scottish Law Commission

The last but crucial stage in the development of the defence was the project conducted by the Scottish Law Commission, which is an official body whose task is to consider topics of Scots law which are thought to be outdated or undeveloped and to make recommendations as to reform the law.

Given the uncertainty about the definition of the insanity defence and the use of terminology and concepts derived from the 18th century, it might have been supposed that this area of law would have been identified by the Commission or by legal commentators as one suitable for consideration for reform. However, the initiative for the reform of the law came from a quite different source. In the late 1990s a comprehensive review was made of mental health law in Scotland by a committee chaired by the Rt Hon Bruce Millan.[30] In the course of preparing its Report, the committee had received representations that the tests used for insanity as a defence

[29] Gordon, *The Criminal Law of Scotland* (n 19) 329, referring to American Law Institute, Model Penal Code—Proposed Official Draft (1962) section 4.01(1).

[30] *New Directions: Report on the Review of the Mental Health (Scotland) Act 1984* (SE/2001/56).

and as a plea in bar of trial were causing problems for mental health practitioners when giving expert evidence.[31] The Committee concluded:[32]

> We were satisfied that the criticisms of the definition of insanity, both in relation to the special defence, and as a plea in bar of trial, carried considerable weight. It seems to us wrong that such an important issue as determining the responsibility of an individual for a serious criminal charge should depend on terms and definitions which are largely meaningless to those with the responsibility of giving expert evidence to the court.

The Millan Committee accepted that changes to the law of insanity in the criminal law would involve consideration of issues of theoretical and practical complexity and recommended that the Scottish Law Commission should examine this area of the law. This recommendation was taken forward by the Scottish Ministers,[33] who referred the issue to the Commission. The terms of reference for the project asked the Commission:[34]

> (1) To consider—
>   (a) The tests to establish insanity (either as a defence or as a plea in bar of trial) and the plea of diminished responsibility; and (b) issues of the law of evidence and procedure involved in raising and establishing insanity and diminished responsibility; and
> (2) To make recommendations for reform, if so advised.

The project started in October 2001. A Discussion Paper, containing a set of detailed proposals for reform, was published for consultation in January 2003.[35] However the Commission had been engaged in consultation prior to this wider public consultation. The Commission took the view that successful reform of the Scots law of insanity would require consideration not only of the law in other jurisdictions but also of law reform projects elsewhere. Towards the start of the project a seminar involving academic lawyers and legal and medical practitioners was held to discuss these issues.[36]

[31] ibid ch 29.
[32] ibid para 43.
[33] Later known as the Scottish Government.
[34] SLC Report, para 1.1.
[35] Scottish Law Commission, *Discussion Paper on Insanity and Diminished Responsibility* (Discussion Paper No 122, 2003).
[36] The seminar was held in April 2002. The speakers were Professor RA McCall Smith, University of Edinburgh; Professor RD Mackay, De Montfort University; Professor Richard J Bonnie, School of Law and Director, Institute of Law Psychiatry and Public Policy at the University of Virginia; Professor

To ensure that the Commission's recommendations for reform of the law cohered with medical practice and understanding, meetings with mental health experts were held throughout the project.[37] The Commission's final recommendations for reform were set out in its final Report, which was published in July 2004.[38]

As referred to above, the Commission's final recommendations were fully implemented by statute.[39] However, the statute in question dealt with a very wide range of issues and only brief consideration was given during the Parliamentary process to the provisions on mental disorder defences. Furthermore, since the new law came into force there have been, to date, few court decisions on it. Accordingly the Scottish Law Commission Report is still a good basis for a full description and interpretation of the current law.

Constituent Elements of the Defence

The definition of the defence in section 51A (1) contains four connected elements: (i) the presence of a mental disorder, (ii) which results in or links to (iii) an inability to appreciate (iv) certain aspects of conduct.

The Presence of Mental Disorder

Virtually all versions of the insanity defence include the requirement that at the time of the offence the accused suffered from a mental disorder. In Scots common law the disorder has been described in a variety of ways such as a disorder or disease (Hume); mental defect (*HM Adv v Kidd*); mental illness, mental disease or defect, or unsoundness of mind (*Brennan v HM Adv*). The M'Naghten Rules uses the expression a disease of the mind.

For purposes of the 1995 Act, including that relating to the defence, the definition of 'mental disorder' incorporates the definition from the Mental Health (Care and Treatment) (Scotland) Act 2003,[40] which is the main statute dealing with civil law aspects of mental health. Section 328(1) of the 2003 Act defines mental disorder as any (a) mental illness; (b) personality disorder; or (c) learning disability.[41]

Warren Brookbanks, University of Auckland; and Professor Finbarr McAuley, University College Dublin and Commissioner, Law Reform Commission of Ireland.

[37] A list of the mental health experts who assisted with the project is set out in Appendix C of the SLC Report.

[38] Scottish Law Commission, *Report on Insanity and Diminished Responsibility* (Report No 195, 2004).

[39] Criminal Justice and Licensing (Scotland) Act 2010 which added a new section, s 51A, to the 1995 Act to implement the recommendations relating to the new defence.

[40] 1995 Act, s 307 (as added by 2003 Act, s 331(1) and Sch 4, para 8(16)).

[41] 2003 Act, s 328(1). Note the definition of mental disorder for purposes of the 1995 Act does not include the provisions of s 328(2) of the 2003 Act. Section 328(2) states that 'a person is not mentally

The Scottish Law Commission had considered whether the defence used in the criminal law should use the same concept of mental disorder as that in the civil law, or even whether the term mental disorder should be defined at all. The Commission was concerned that as mental disorder played a different role in civil law (identifying the persons who fell within the care and treatment provisions) from that in the criminal law (attribution of criminal responsibility), it might be confusing to use the same concept in both. The problem with this approach was that if the civil law definition of mental disorder was not to be used in the criminal law, then for purposes of the defence either a different definition was to be adopted or the concept was to be left undefined, and neither of these options seemed desirable.

Consultees pointed out that mental health practitioners were familiar with the civil law concept and would find it confusing to use the same term but with a different definition in the criminal law context. Moreover, if mental disorder was not defined for purposes of the defence, mental health practitioners would be likely to use the civil law concept in relation to the defence. If there were particular mental health conditions that were not appropriate for issues of criminal responsibility the better approach was to make explicit exclusions of those conditions in the definition of the defence.

Connecting Link

A second element of the defence deals with the link between the accused's mental disorder and his criminal conduct. One possible view is that the presence of a mental disorder of a person at the time of committing a criminal act would by itself be sufficient to remove criminal responsibility for that act. The difficulty with this approach is that it gives no explanatory power to the mental disorder as a basis or justification for a defence where there is no link between the mental disorder and criminal conduct. For example, the defence would apply to someone who suffers from bi-polar disorder and commits a theft where the disorder is totally unconnected to the conduct.

Another approach is to accept the need for a connection between the mental disorder and the criminal conduct but to presume that in almost all cases such a link exists. This was the position adopted by the Butler Committee who argued that:[42]

disordered by reason only of any the following factors: (a) sexual orientation; (b) sexual deviancy; (c) transsexualism; (d) transvestism; (e) dependence on, or use of, alcohol or drugs; (f) behaviour that causes, or is likely to cause, harassment, alarm or distress to any other person; (g) acting as no prudent person would act'.

[42] *Report of the Committee on Mentally Abnormal Offenders*, chaired by the Rt Hon Lord Butler (Cmnd 6244, 1975) para 18.29.

> It is true that it is theoretically possible for a person to be suffering from a severe mental disorder which has in a causal sense nothing to do with the act or omission for which he is being tried: but in practice it is very difficult to imagine a case in which one could be sure of the absence of any such connection.

However, this approach does not advance the argument to any great extent. In the first place, as mentioned above, it is not too difficult to imagine cases where a person has a mental disorder but commits a crime which is unrelated to the disorder, for example someone with an obsessive disorder who commits a by-chance theft. Also, it uses the language of causation between mental disorder and criminal conduct but, as will be explored in the next section, this presents a too mechanistic a view of how mental disorders operate in the context of human action. And finally, it fails to explain why the presence of mental disorder operates as a reason for exempting a person from responsibility for his conduct.

Specific Effect of Mental Disorder: Lack of Appreciation of Conduct

The common law insanity defence provided for a specific effect which a mental order gives rise to as an (absolute) alienation of reason. However, this concept was largely unexplained and the terminology of 'alienation' is not used in current medical science.[43]

The defence in section 51A of the 1995 Act sets out a different type of effect of a mental disorder, namely lack of appreciation of conduct. This idea was used in order to capture current psychiatric thinking about how mental disorders operate. Arguments presented to the Scottish Law Commission by mental health experts indicated that although some types of disorder could be the direct cause of criminal action (eg where the existence of a hypoglycaemic episode results in a person striking out and hitting someone else), this was not typical of how mental disorders affected action. It cited a passage from Finbarr McAuley's book:[44]

> But diseases do not always affect behaviour in this way. Much more frequently, they do so through the medium of psychological states, such as thoughts, beliefs and desires. For example, Huntington's chorea and Pick's disease—both forms of genetically transmitted arteriosclerosis—typically affect the cerebral blood supply in a way that may lead to mental confusion and, consequently, to grossly

[43] Furthermore, as the Scottish Law Commission pointed out (SLC Report, para 2.41), the phrase is ambiguous. It could refer to (a) a total lack of the power of reasoning or (b) a form of reasoning which exists but is totally lacking in meaning

[44] F McAuley, *Insanity, Psychiatry and Criminal Responsibility* (Round Hall Press 1993) 12–13.

anti-social behaviour on the part of those suffering from them. Similarly, victims of a functional disorder like paranoia sometimes have extremely violent reactions as a direct result of their condition.

But notice that a completely different type of causation is at work in these examples. Here the disease causes the defendant to *do* something by influencing the content and direction of his thoughts and feelings (paranoia) or by generally interfering with his thought processes (Huntington's chorea or Pick's disease). Thus what follows are actions, not mere movements of the defendant's body such as might occur in the course of an epileptic seizure or during an attack of St Vitus' dance. In the result, the question of the defendant's responsibility for what happened arises in such cases in a way that it does not arise in cases where the effects of the disease are not mediated by psychological states.

Mental disorder in this context does not deprive a person of their powers of reasoning. Rather such a person has reasons for their actions but because of the mental disorder the reasons are distorted, they do not make sense. What is lacking is a proper understanding of their own conduct. The Scottish Law Commission gave the example of a woman who kills her children by smothering them with a pillow. She does this to drive out demons from their souls. In this example the woman in one sense 'knows' what she is doing in that she understands her own physical acts and their consequences but she lacks a full or rational understanding of her conduct. This situation is not fully captured by saying that there is a defect in her knowledge. Furthermore, the Commission wanted to avoid using the term 'knowledge' in case doing so would attract the narrow interpretation of that term as used in the M'Naghten Rules. Instead it preferred the use of the idea of appreciation as bringing with it a much wider meaning and application. The Commission further noted that the concept of appreciation was used in the definitions of the insanity defence in Australia,[45] the US Model Penal Code,[46] and the Criminal Code of Canada.[47]

The importance of using the idea of lack of appreciation of conduct at the core of the new defence is that it indicates the ways in which a mental disorder has distorted the accused's reasoning at the time of the relevant conduct and as such it provides a good reason for removing the accused's criminal responsibility for that conduct.

[45] *R v Porter* (1936) 55 CLR 182.

[46] The American Law Institute, Model Penal Code, Official Draft (1985), s 4.01(1).

[47] RS 1985 c. C-46, s 16(1).

Nature or Wrongfulness of Conduct

The final aspect of the definition of the defence relates to the aspects of a person's conduct which someone with a mental disorder fails to appreciate. These are specified as the nature or the wrongfulness of the conduct. These are similar to the criteria in the M'Naghten Rules which refer to the lack of knowledge of the nature and quality of a person's acts and to doing what was wrong. This similarity presents the danger that the new mental disorder defence in Scots law is simply repeating or incorporating the M'Naghten Rules, which would be ironic given the efforts of the Scottish courts in the later part of the 20th century to make clear that the Rules were not (or no longer) part of the insanity defence. The statutory-based defence could merely have referred to lack of an appreciation by an accused of the conduct involved in the criminal charge against him. However, this does not bring out the aspects of conduct which are relevant and appropriate to issues of criminal responsibility, which the nature and wrongfulness of the action do identify. The possibility of these elements being interpreted as they are under the M'Naghten Rules is lessened by the concept of appreciation which is at the core of the new defence. A person may 'know' in a narrow sense the physical attributes of what they are doing or that what they are doing breaches legal or moral norms but their mental disorder provides them with reasons for continuing with their actions or overriding such norms.[48]

In *Mackay v HM Advocate*,[49] the High Court of Justiciary, sitting as a court of appeal, gave some guidance on the proper interpretation of section 51A of the 1995 Act and in particular on the meaning of the key concept of appreciation. The accused had been charged with threatening behaviour by calling the police saying that he was armed with a machete and was going to kill Muslims. He said that he was going to approach a nearby Asian takeaway shop, and he was going to behead the shop workers. A police car had immediately responded to this call and the accused was arrested.

At his trial the accused advanced the new statutory defence. Psychiatric evidence was led by both the Crown and the defence. All the psychiatrists agreed that the accused suffered from a mental disorder and also that he had appreciated the nature of his conduct, but there was disagreement on whether he had appreciated its wrongfulness. The jury concluded that the defence had not been established and found the accused guilty. An appeal was made on the basis that the trial judge had misdirected the jury on a number of aspects of the defence.

[48] This was recognized in the common law insanity defence. In *HM Advocate v Kidd* 1960 JC 61, 71, Lord Strachan stated: 'A man may know very well what he is doing, and may know that it is wrong, and he may none the less be insane. It may be that some lunatics do an act just because they know it is wrong.'
[49] 2017 JC 311.

Part of the trial judge's direction was that in considering whether the accused had appreciated his conduct the jury should consider his 'awareness' of his actions and his ability to recognize the wrongfulness of his actions. The appeal court held that, while the charge to the jury contained some possibly inaccurate phrases, taken as a whole it did reflect the statutory language and would not mislead the jury, and the appeal was dismissed.

In its judgment the appeal court traced the background to the new defence in the recommendations of the Scottish Law Commission and comments during the Parliamentary proceedings on the implementing Bill. This no doubt reflected the fact that the submissions made during the appeal had referred to these sources. However, the court held that the defence was new law and something quite different from the common law defence of insanity. It followed that the common law concept of 'total alienation of reason' had no role in understanding the statutory-based defence. Furthermore, key terms such as 'appreciate' and 'wrongfulness' were words in common usage and did not pose any difficulty in interpretation. As the provisions on the defence had no ambiguity there was no need to consider external aids in interpreting the statute. Terms such as appreciate and wrongfulness were words of ordinary English and, the court added,[50] 'It is important, therefore, for the court not to put a spin or gloss on such words by using different words to explain, and thus to distort, their plain meaning.'

This is a somewhat surprisingly narrow approach to interpreting the new defence in section 51A of the 1995 Act. An important element to the context of the Scottish Law Commission's recommendation to adopt the term appreciation was that that concept was much wider than the idea of knowledge, at least as it is used in the M'Naghten Rules. Indeed in *Mackay* the appeal court accepted that in appropriate cases a jury should be directed that appreciation involved a level of 'rational understanding'. And the court provided a further gloss on the meaning of appreciation as part of the new test. Part of the model jury direction which the court recommended was that 'the phrase "appreciate the nature or wrongfulness of his conduct" is not limited to a lack of knowledge of these matters. It can also cover an inability to conduct oneself in accordance with a rational and normal understanding of them.'[51]

There are also certain issues which are not expressly mentioned in the definition of the defence or are excluded from the scope of the defence.

[50] ibid para 26.
[51] ibid para 30.

The Definition of the Mental Disorder Defence: A Volitional Element?

The definition of the new mental disorder defence in the 1995 Act makes no direct mention of a volitional element as part of the defence. This omission is no oversight and follows a recommendation of the Scottish Law Commission that the definition should not contain any reference to the volitional incapacities or disabilities of the accused.[52] This is perhaps surprising, as many legal systems incorporate a volitional element into the definition of the insanity defence, often as a supplement to the M'Naghten Rules which focus solely on a narrow conception of cognitive failings.[53] Indeed the Scots law on insanity defence seemed to use a volitional element. In his discussion of absolute alienation of reason Hume states that one effect on the accused is that it 'gives him up to the impulse of his own distempered fancy'.[54] In *HM Advocate v Kidd*, the trial judge stated that:[55]

> in order to excuse a person from responsibility for his acts on the grounds of insanity, there must have been an alienation of the reason in relation to the act committed. There must have been some mental defect, to use a broad neutral word, a mental defect, by which his reason was overpowered, *and he was thereby rendered incapable of exerting his reason to control his conduct and reactions.*

However, there is a need to be clear about what the Scottish Law Commission recommended on this issue. It did not suggest that volitional matters were irrelevant to questions of criminal responsibility based on mental disorder. Rather, it argued that a definition of the defence which used the key concept of lack of appreciation of conduct had no need to specify volitional failings by an accused as this idea was captured by the concept of appreciation. The Commission argued that an appreciation test would cover all cases where a person should not be found criminally responsible. It gave the example of a woman suffering from depression who feels she is 'driven' to killing her children to save them from her own bad parenting. This case involves a mixture of a cognitive failing (based on the depression which gives rise to her perception of inadequacy as a parent) and volitional effect, rather than a purely volitional one.

The Commission posed the question whether there could be a case where a person who committed criminal conduct would be found criminally responsible on the appreciation test but would or should be treated as lacking criminal responsibility in respect of a separate volitional incapacity. The Commission noted that

[52] SLC Report, para 2.56.

[53] This point is explored by McAuley, *Insanity, Psychiatry and Criminal Responsibility* (n 44) 52–61.

[54] Hume, *Commentaries on the Law of Scotland Respecting Crimes* (n 16) I, 37.

[55] 1960 JC 61, 70 (emphasis added).

during the consultation process consultees could not provide any example where a person might fail the test for the defence on the appreciation criterion but satisfy it purely on a volitional one. It also reported that the mental health experts who were advising the Commission tended to reject a category of mental disorder which was purely volitional in nature and which had no impact on cognitive functions.

Furthermore, if the defence specifically mentioned a separate element of volitional failings, that might lead to the concept of appreciation being given a narrow interpretation.

It is also worth noting that the omission from the statutory definition of a specific volitional element was one of the few aspects of the implementing Bill which attracted discussion during the Parliamentary process. In the Justice Committee which scrutinized the Bill, an amendment was proposed to the effect that the defence would be available where a person had appreciated the nature and wrongfulness of the act, but had nevertheless been unable to control his or her actions because of the mental disorder.[56] However, the amendment was withdrawn after the Minister who sponsored the Bill assured the Committee that the idea of appreciation of the nature or wrongfulness of conduct would encompass volitional failings.

The Psychopathy Exclusion

Section 51A(2) of the 1995 Act states that:

> a person does not lack criminal responsibility for ... conduct [constituting an offence] if the mental disorder in question consists only of a personality disorder which is characterised solely or principally by abnormally aggressive or seriously irresponsible conduct.

Although this provision does not explicitly use the term psychopathy, it is clear that it is that condition which is covered by this exclusion from the scope of the mental disorder defence.[57] The exclusion of psychopathy from the insanity defence is to be found in many legal systems. For example, the American Law Institute Model Penal Code contains a provision that the 'terms "mental disease or mental defect" do not include an abnormality of mind manifested only by repeated criminal or

[56] Scottish Parliament Official Report. Justice Committee (4 May 2010) Session 3, cols 3102–04.

[57] In *R v Secretary of State for Scotland* 1999 SC (HL) 17 Lord Hutton (at 44) stated: 'While I recognise that there is a medical debate as to the appropriateness of the term "psychopath" in modern times, it is convenient for the purpose of considering the construction of secs 17 and 64 [of the Mental Health (Scotland) Act 1984] to use that term in relation to a person whose mental disorder is "a persistent one manifested only by abnormally aggressive or seriously irresponsible conduct".'

otherwise antisocial conduct'.[58] The Law Commission for England and Wales recommended a similar exclusion in respect of a reformed definition of the insanity defence in English law.[59]

The Scottish Law Commission took the view that the condition of psychopathy would not meet the 'appreciation' part of the test for the new defence. It characterized the condition as 'associated with forms of anti-social (including criminal) behaviour by a person who cannot apply or is indifferent about applying normal moral standards and feelings to his actions'.[60] A person with this condition may have difficulties in complying with the requirements of the law. But such difficulties do not make the person's reasons for acting abnormal or disordered. He still has a rational understanding of his conduct and as such appreciates what he is doing. Furthermore, someone with a psychopathic disorder is not completely lacking in his ability to control his behaviour, even if he has difficulties in doing so. As the Commission expressed the point, the condition of psychopathy might be an extenuating circumstance but not an excusing one.[61]

Finally, it should be noted that the exclusion only refers to psychopathy as the sole or principal condition of an accused person and the defence would be available where someone with a psychopathic personality also suffered from a different mental disorder which did impact on their ability to appreciate their conduct.

During its consultation process there was considerable support for the Scottish Law Commission's recommendation that psychopathy should be excluded from the scope of the new defence.

However, there has been subsequent criticism of this provision.[62] Simon Barnes has argued that the Scottish Law Commission's approach to psychopathy is an oversimplification of what, from a scientific point of view, is a complex and multi-dimensional set of personality disorders. He examines these disorders from a range of scientific classification systems and from research on empirical moral psychology. His general conclusion is that some members of the group of psychopaths excluded from the defence lack capacity for criminal responsibility in a general sense. However, in relation to the section 51A defence, Barnes's views are stated more tentatively. He talks about the 'possibility' that 'some' psychopaths (as that term is used by the Commission) have an 'impaired' ability to appreciate the nature or wrongfulness of their action;[63] that 'some' psychopaths 'may' have

[58] Section 4.01(2). In Australia the exclusion is recognized at common law: *Willgoss v The Queen* (1960) 105 CLR 295 (High Court of Australia).

[59] Law Commission, *Criminal Liability; Insanity and Automatism* (Discussion Paper (2013)) para 4.93.

[60] SLC Report, para 2.57.

[61] For this reason the Commission recommended that the condition of psychopathic personality disorder should come within the scope of the plea of diminished responsibility (SLC Report, para 3.34).

[62] SD Barnes, 'Re-evaluating the Exclusion of Psychopathy from the Mental Disorder Defence in Scots Law' 2018 Jur Rev 1.

[63] ibid 13.

responsibility-relevant 'impairments';[64] and that it is 'possible' that at least 'some' psychopaths 'may' have severe impairments in this regard.[65]

But Barnes also offers a more general perspective that is worth noting. He argues that questions of the capacity of various types of psychopaths for criminal responsibility extend beyond the type of defence as set out in section 51A and the traditional insanity defence. He mentions two other issues which are a more apt focus for dealing with persons with a psychopathic personality disorder. One is fitness for trial.[66] The other is diminished responsibility, and Barnes's point here is that this doctrine should not be restricted to murder and should not be seen solely as a question of mitigation of sentencing in other types of case. These are interesting perspectives on how the criminal justice system should deal with psychopaths but they are consistent with the approach taken by the Scottish Law Commission in its law reform project.[67]

Scope of the Law Reform Project: The Absence of Automatism

The project by the Scottish Law Commission focused on three topics: insanity as a defence, insanity as a plea in bar of trial (unfitness to plead or unfitness for trial), and diminished responsibility. These were the three areas of the interaction between the criminal law and mental disorder which the Millan Committee had identified as causing problems for mental health practitioners and which should therefore be examined by the Scottish Law Commission.

One issue which the Commission did not consider as part of this project was the defence of automatism. This omission has been the subject of severe criticism.

The Law Commission for England and Wales included a project on unfitness to plead and the insanity defence as part of its 10th Programme of Law Reform (2008). The Commission had concluded that the project should include the automatism defence, and in 2012 published a Scoping Paper on automatism and insanity. In this paper, the Commission stated that 'One of the most problematic aspects of the law is the overlap between the law of insanity and automatism'. It further argued that its project required that both defences should be considered in tandem: 'The defence of automatism is so closely related to that of insanity that it would make no sense to attempt to reform one without the other.'[68]

[64] ibid 18.

[65] ibid. See also at 20 where he writes that 'the Commission's own analysis may apply to a subset of psychopathic persons'.

[66] The definition of fitness for trial is set out in s 53F of the 1995 Act. There is nothing in the test for that defence which would exclude psychopathy.

[67] As noted above (n 61), in its Report the Commission recommended that the condition of psychopathy should be a basis for diminished responsibility.

[68] *Insanity and Automatism—A Scoping Paper*, Law Commission for England and Wales (2012) paras 1.3 and 1.20 respectively. In its later Discussion Paper (Law Commission, *Criminal Liability: Insanity and Automatism* (Discussion Paper (2013)), the Commission stated (at para 1.29): 'The defence of

This is a striking claim as it suggests that a law reform project which focused on insanity but not also automatism (or vice versa) is misconceived. Reform proposals, such as the Scottish Law Commission's, which were restricted to law of insanity could be at best incomplete or provisional only.

Furthermore, the perspectives of the Law Commission for England and Wales on the scope of reform cannot be dismissed as reflecting the particular content of the defences of insanity and automatism in English law, for a similar point has been made about Scots law. Professor James Chalmers has written that in 'Scots law, therefore, the two common law defences are not simply closely related but two sides of the same coin'.[69]

A similar argument has been made by Elizabeth Shaw who, in discussing the Scottish Law Commission Report and the subsequent legislative changes based on it, noted: 'However, that report ignored automatism. This omission is unfortunate, since automatism and the mental disorder defence are very closely related. By looking at the mental disorder defence in isolation, the Commission missed an opportunity to make sure that the criminal law takes a philosophically coherent and practically workable approach to people with mental abnormalities.'[70]

So did the Scottish Law Commission's project on the defence of insanity, which did not examine automatism, make no sense? The Report of the Millan Committee, which was the immediate spur to the Commission's project, had not reported any problems encountered by mental health practitioners with the defence of automatism. The Scottish Law Commission itself had not identified automatism as a topic which should be included in its terms of reference, and during the consultation processes no contributor had pointed out that this topic was a useful or desirable, far less a necessary, component of reform.[71]

However, even if the Scottish Law Commission had been alerted to the issue of automatism, it is unlikely that it would have widened this particular project to include it along with the insanity defence. One reason reflects a pragmatic consideration in the process of law reform.[72] One aim of a project by a body dedicated

automatism is evidently so closely related to that of insanity that reform of one entails reform of the other.'

[69] J Chalmers, 'Insanity and Automatism: Notes from over the Border and across the Boundary' (2014) 65(2) NILQ 205, 207. He added: 'Both are based on a total alienation of reason, and are distinguished by reference to the cause of that alienation, with the further caveat that the automatism defence is unavailable where the alienation has been caused by the prior fault of the accused.'

[70] E Shaw, 'Automatism and Mental Disorder in Scots Criminal Law' (2015) 19(2) Edin L R 210, 211. However, Shaw does note that the 'close connections between automatism and insanity were not fully appreciated in the Scottish academic literature at the time and the SLC did not recognise the need to broaden the project'.

[71] Some of the participants at the seminar at the early stage of the project (see n 36 above) were familiar with reform of the insanity defence in other jurisdictions but did not make the point that these reforms were either successful or had failed because reform of the automatism defence had been included or ignored. However, this may reflect the lack of any conceptual overlap between insanity and automatism in the legal systems in question.

[72] For discussion of the range of factors involved in the strategy of law reform see G Maher, 'Principles and Politics in Law Reform: Sexual Offences in Scots Law' 2013 Jur Rev 563.

to law reform like a law commission is to convince the government to take the project's proposals forward to Parliament with a view to legislative implementation. Irrespective of the merits of proposals, one important factor is the scale and scope of the project in question. This particular project examined the substantive law and procedural and evidential aspects of the three topics, insanity as a defence, insanity as a plea in bar of trial, and diminished responsibility. Increasing the scope of the project to include automatism, and as a consequence the time needed to complete it, might have proved unattractive to a government in finding legislative opportunities for implementation.

In addition, there would have been more principled reasons for the Scottish Law Commission to keep to its original terms of reference and not to include automatism. As it currently exists in Scots law, automatism presents some major issues which have no direct equivalent in the insanity defence.[73] The automatism defence has a connection with the general principle of voluntary action yet it has also been described as operating by negating mens rea. Furthermore, a state of automatism cannot be raised as a defence if an accused was in prior fault in getting into that state, a feature absent from the common law insanity defence. Also automatism requires 'total alienation of reason'. This condition was also a requirement of the common law insanity defence but it is no longer used in the new statutory defence. But it is not clear whether total alienation of reason is the same concept in both the automatism and insanity defences and in this context there is virtually no discussion of the point noted by the Scottish Law Commission that alienation of reason has different meanings, which might apply differently in the two defences. In addition, many of the issues concerning automatism also apply to the defence of intoxication,[74] a topic which has received virtually no law reform consideration in Scotland.

This is not to say that the defence of automatism in Scots law is beyond criticism nor that it is not in need of reform. The point is rather that this topic should be a law reform project in its own right.[75]

[73] For a detailed account of automatism in Scots law, see J Chalmers and F Leverick, *Criminal Defences and Pleas in Bar of Trial* (W Green & Son Ltd 2006) chapter 7.

[74] In its Scoping Paper the Law Commission for England and Wales noted in discussing self-induced automatism (n 68, para 3.25): 'The law in this area is complex. It rests on a series of common law principles involving the law governing insanity, automatism, and intoxication.'

[75] More recently the Scottish Law Commission has raised the issue whether the law on automatism gives rise to any problems which should be considered for reform (Scottish Law Commission, *Discussion Paper on the Mental Element in Homicide* (SLC DP No 172 (2021) para 11.46). But it is doubtful whether the law of homicide is the correct context for considering reform of automatism.

Burden of Proof

Section 51A(4) of the 1995 Act states that the new statutory defence of not being criminally responsible by reason of mental disorder 'may be stated only by the person charged with the offence and it is for that person to establish it on the balance of probabilities'.[76]

This provision gives rise to two issues, first the nature of the burden of proof placed on an accused; and second whether the defence can be raised and proved by the Crown.

Burden of Proof on the Accused

To a large extent the statutory provision follows the rules on the burden and standard of proof which applied to the common law defence of insanity.[77] However, in its consultative Discussion Paper the Scottish Law Commission suggested that a different approach should be taken in respect of the new statutory defence. It identified two reasons for a change to the question of burden of proof.

The first was that it could identify no clear rationale for conferring a burden of proof on the accused for the insanity defence. The reason often advanced was that there is a presumption of sanity and therefore anyone asserting that someone was not sane bore the burden of proving so.[78] But this argument is both question-begging and circular. A presumption is a way of allocating a burden of proof. By itself a presumption of sanity can provide no independent basis for a burden of proof. Furthermore, much of the discussion on this issue takes little or no account of the key distinction between legal and evidential burdens of proof. A presumption of sanity could easily cohere with imposing on an accused person an evidential rather than a legal burden of proof, and this is the position with other common law defences.[79]

A second reason for the Scottish Law Commission's provisional proposal to depart from the common law position on the burden of proof of the new mental disorder defence was its understanding of the requirements of the ECHR.[80] At the time when the Commission's Discussion Paper was published, the House of Lords had recently issued its opinions in *R v Lambert*.[81] What that decision seemed to

[76] Section 51A (3) states that the defence is a 'special defence'. In modern practice, the distinguishing feature of a special defence is that the accused must, prior to a trial, give written notice of his intention to rely on it. See further GH Gordon, 'The Burden of Proof on the Accused' 1968 SLT (News) 29, 29–30.

[77] *HM Advocate v Kidd* 1960 JC 61, 68–69.

[78] See eg *Lambie v HM Advocate* 1973 JC 53, 57.

[79] Including the defence of automatism: *Ross v HM Advocate* 1991 JC 210, 220–21.

[80] See especially, ECHR Art 6(2) which states: 'Everyone charged with a criminal offence shall be presumed innocent until proved guilty according to law.'

[81] [2002] 2 AC 545.

be laying down was a general rule that where a statutory provision imposed a reverse burden of proof of a defence, interpreting the statute as imposing a full legal burden on a defendant was a disproportionate way of achieving the statute's aims. Instead, the Convention required that the statute should be read down as placing only an evidential burden of proof on the accused.

The Scottish Law Commission regarded this decision as equally applicable to the new mental disorder defence which it was proposing and recommended that for the new statutory defence an accused person should bear an evidential burden of proof, but if the accused satisfied that burden the Crown would have a legal burden of showing that the defence did not apply.

However, in the light of responses to its Discussion Paper the Commission had a change of mind on this issue, and its final recommendation, which was implemented in the statutory provisions on the new defence, was that the accused should bear the burden of establishing the defence on the balance of probabilities.[82] The Commission was persuaded by the arguments of consultees that there were good reasons why a defence like the insanity defence or its new statutory equivalent should place a legal burden of proof on the accused. What is at issue with a defence of this sort is the mental state of the accused at the time of the conduct in question. But the question arises how the Crown can obtain evidence which can show (beyond reasonable doubt) that the accused's then mental state was 'normal' or not disordered in terms of the definition of the defence. Under the existing law an accused could not be compelled to provide medical evidence of his mental state at the time nor could he be compelled to attend for medical examination for this purpose. The Commission were not attracted to changing the law on these issues.

A further factor concerns the requirements of the ECHR. By the time the Scottish Law Commission was preparing its final report, it had become clear that *R v Lambert*[83] could not be read as widely as the Commission had supposed. Subsequent case law had indicated that not every legal burden being placed on an accused was disproportionate or incompatible with Article 6(2) of the Convention.[84] All depended on the aims of the statute which contained the reverse burden and whether reading the provision as imposing a legal burden, rather than an evidential burden, on the accused was a proportionate way of achieving those aims. The Scottish Law Commission accepted that the practical difficulties facing the Crown in obtaining evidence for disproving the accused's mental disorder beyond reasonable doubt provided good reasons for imposing the full burden of proof on the accused.[85]

[82] It is generally accepted that the standard of proof of balance of probabilities is the appropriate one where there is a reverse burden on the accused.

[83] [2002] 2 AC 545.

[84] See especially *Sheldrake v DPP; Attorney General's Reference (No 4 of 2002)* [2005] 1 AC 264.

[85] In arriving at this conclusion the Scottish Law Commission gave detailed consideration to the decision of the Supreme Court of Canada in *R v Chaulk* [1990] 3 SCR 1303, where the Supreme Court had held that placing a legal burden of proving an insanity defence on the accused did not infringe the

Insanity Raised by the Prosecution

It was not entirely clear whether the common law defence of insanity could be raised and proved by the Crown. There is one case, *HM Advocate v Harrison*,[86] which suggests that this was possible where the accused had raised a plea of diminished responsibility to a charge of murder, but there was no authority on whether the Crown could raise the issue of the accused's insanity in other circumstances.

An important factor here is that the focus of attention is on the mental state of the accused at the time of the criminal conduct, and not at the time of the trial.[87] The Scottish Law Commission recommended that the proposed new statutory defence based on mental disorder could be raised only by the accused, and this recommendation was implemented in what became section 51A(4) of the 1995 Act. The Commission took the view that it was wrong in principle for the Crown to prove a 'defence' which had not been raised by the accused himself where the accused was mentally fit for trial. The Crown could lead evidence of the accused's mental state at the time of the conduct where that was relevant either in proving guilt or disproving a defence which the accused had raised (such as diminished responsibility). But the Crown could not go further and use such evidence to prove the mental disorder defence. Furthermore, the Crown would retain its power (and duty) to bring to the attention of the court any issues concerning the accused's mental health at the time of the proceedings. This could be done either in terms of a possible issue of fitness for trial or where matters of public safety might be involved, but evidence on these issues would have no relevance to proving the substantive defence.[88]

Interestingly the Crown Office[89] itself did not dissent from this proposal and agreed that it would not be in the public interest for the Crown to pursue a defence of mental disorder where the issue was not raised by the accused.

However, this provision has attracted very strong criticism. Professor Chalmers has described it as a dangerous loophole, as undesirable and unjustified, and as possibly giving rise to potential danger.[90] He notes that a defence such as insanity

provisions of the Canadian Charter of Rights and Freedoms. These provisions are broadly similar to those of the ECHR.

[86] High Court of Justiciary, Dundee October 1967, unreported but see (1968) 32 J Crim L 119.

[87] It may be noted that under s 52(1) of the 1995 Act, where it appears to the Crown in any proceedings that the accused may be suffering from a mental disorder, the Crown is under a duty to bring before the court any evidence as may be available as to the mental condition of the accused. However this provision focuses on the accused's mental condition at the time of the proceedings. As such it has implications for mental disorder as a plea in bar but not for the special defence.

[88] The amended 1995 Act also simplified the procedure in solemn proceedings to allow the Crown to accept the mental disorder defence raised by the accused without the need for a jury verdict (1995 Act, s 53E(1)).

[89] The 'Crown Office' is the generally-used short name of the Crown Office and Procurators Fiscal Service, which is the prosecuting authority in criminal proceedings in Scotland.

[90] J Chalmers, 'Section 117 of the Criminal Justice and Licensing (Scotland) Bill: A Dangerous Loophole?' Sc Crim L (November 2009) 1240.

can in many situations involve a denial of mens rea, and provides the following scenario:[91]

> Suppose that A kills B under the insane delusion that B is an animal. A person who believes they are killing an animal does not have the *mens rea* of murder. Is it therefore open to the accused in such a case simply to deny murder—on the basis of a lack of *mens rea*—without pleading insanity? Logically, unless some hitherto unknown rule of evidence which bars an accused from leading evidence of mental disorder without formally pleading insanity is discovered, the answer is yes. If so, s 51A(4) would debar the jury from considering insanity and they would be obliged to acquit *simpliciter*.

But it is far from clear what mischief this situation gives rise to. If there are concerns that the mental state of the now-acquitted accused raises issues of public safety, use can be made of the procedures under section 60C of the 1995 Act. This provision applies where an accused has been acquitted of a charge (but not where the acquittal was based on the s 51A defence of mental disorder). The court has power to make an order for the removal of the acquitted person to a place of safety to allow for a medical examination where it is not practicable to have that person immediately examined by a medical practitioner provided that there is written or oral evidence of two medical practitioners that:

(a) the person has a mental disorder;
(b) medical treatment is available which would be likely to (i) prevent the mental disorder worsening; or (ii) alleviate any of the symptoms, or effects, of the disorder, and
(c) if the person were not provided with such medical treatment there would be a significant risk (i) to the health, safety or welfare of the person; or (ii) to the safety of any other person.[92]

Conclusion

The criminal law of Scotland has for a long time recognized a defence based on a defect or abnormality in the mental state of an accused person at the time of committing a crime. The common law version of this defence, the insanity defence, was replaced in 2012 by a statutory-based defence which focuses on an accused's mental disorder and its effects on the accused's understanding of their conduct.

[91] ibid 1242 (footnotes in original omitted).
[92] Criminal Procedure (Scotland) Act 1995, s 54(2).

The definition and scope of the common law defence had started to settle by the late 18th century. The jurist, Hume, writing in 1797, noted a key characteristic of the defence as 'an absolute alienation of reason' on the part of the accused but further refinement and development of the defence during the 19th century was marked by a lack of uniformity in the approach of judges on this issue. For a brief period it seemed that the Scots law of insanity was based solely on the M'Naghten Rules borrowed from English law. However, the narrow approach to the Rules which developed in English law was rejected by the Scottish courts, and the defence was usually seen as using a wider test which incorporated both cognitive and volitional elements. During the 20th century it became clear that the M'Naghten Rules were not part of the Scots law on insanity. The courts accepted that insanity was based on the accused's alienation of reason (usually understood as being total or absolute in nature) but other elements of the defence were left largely undefined.

The uncertainty about the exact definition of the insanity defence did cause problems in giving the defence its application in practice. These problems were particularly acute for medical practitioners who were called upon to present expert evidence in criminal trials. Not only were elements of the defence unclear, the language in which it was expressed continued to use terms and ideas which were no longer part of medical science, as with the central notion of absolute alienation of reason. As a consequence of these problems, the Scottish Law Commission was asked to conduct a law reform project on the insanity defence. The Commission's recommendations were implemented by statute, which abolished the common law defence of insanity and replaced it with a defence which the statute refers to as 'criminal responsibility of persons with mental disorder'.

The term 'insanity' is no longer used in Scots law. It is not now an accepted concept within medical science and has stigmatic overtones. Instead of the now outdated concept of alienation of reason, the core principle of the new defence is that an accused is entitled to be acquitted of an offence where, at the time of the conduct in question, they had a mental disorder which resulted in their failing to appreciate the nature and wrongfulness of their conduct. Mental disorder is given a wide meaning in this context and corresponds to the definition of that concept in other parts of mental health law. The new defence, however, expressly excludes psychopathy from its scope, not on the basis that psychopathy is not a type of mental disorder but because although that condition may diminish a person's responsibility for their conduct, it does not remove that responsibility.

The idea of lack of appreciation of conduct is much wider in scope than the concept of knowledge which is found in insanity defences such as the M'Naghten Rules. The Scottish Law Commission argued that appreciation of conduct was to be understood as involving rational understanding of the whole circumstances of a person's conduct. Furthermore, the defence would apply not only to cognitive failings but also to any volitional defects which resulted in such a lack of understanding. The Commission expressly based its recommendation for Scots law to adopt this wider sense of appreciation on its use in the insanity defence in jurisdictions such the United States, Canada, and Australia. Although the appeal court in Scotland has suggested that appreciation should be understood in its ordinary meaning, it is to be hoped that in future cases the courts will be willing to consider the case law from those other legal systems in the development of the concept in Scots law.

One way in which the new defence mirrors the common law is that the legal burden of pleading and proving the defence rests with the accused. However, the new law makes clear that only the accused, and not the prosecution, can raise the defence.

5

The Insanity Defence in Irish Law

Paul McCutcheon

Overview

The defence of insanity in Irish law[1] was originally based on the M'Naghten Rules. However, since the absorption of the Rules into Irish law, the defence has undergone considerable development. This occurred in two stages: the theoretical acceptance of the plea of irresistible impulse in the 1930s and the recognition of a defence of volitional insanity by the Supreme Court in 1974. Both stages were made possible by the fact that, for many years, Irish judges were unwilling to accept the view that the insanity defence is confined to the limited category of insane delusions covered by the traditional interpretation of the M'Naghten Rules.

While the courts engineered a broadening of the defence, legislative intervention was slow in coming. Reform was recommended by an Interdepartmental Committee in 1978 but was not implemented at the time. Thus, the old version of the verdict—'guilty but insane'—was retained and indefinite detention was the outcome. By the early 1970s the courts adopted a practice of ordering the detention of persons found insane 'until further order of the court', but this was declared invalid in 1991: the release of a detainee was an executive function, not a judicial one. Later cases established basic procedural requirements governing the release of detainees.

The law was eventually overhauled by the Criminal Law (Insanity) Act 2006. The Act codified the judicial development of the plea and confirmed its extension beyond the M'Naghten Rules. However, the Oireachtas (the National Parliament) did not take the opportunity to flesh out the details of the defence and a number of matters await resolution. On the other hand, the 2006 Act significantly overhauled other aspects of the law: the form of verdict was altered to 'not guilty by reason of insanity' (NGRI); dispositional arrangements were liberalized; appeals are allowed against NGRI verdicts; independent and regular review of those detained in consequence of an insanity verdict is required, and the Mental Health (Criminal Law)

[1] See generally P Charleton, PA McDermott, C Herlihy, and S Byrne, *Charleton and McDermott's Criminal Law and Evidence* (2nd edn, Bloomsbury 2020) (hereafter, Charleton and McDermott) chapter 24; L Campbell and others, *Criminal Law in Ireland: Cases and Commentary* (2nd edn, Clarus Press 2020) (hereafter, Campbell and others) chapter 26; F McAuley and P McCutcheon, *Criminal Liability* (Round Hall Sweet & Maxwell 2000) chapter 14; F McAuley, *Insanity, Psychiatry and Criminal Responsibility* (Round Hall 1993).

Paul McCutcheon, *The Insanity Defence in Irish Law* In: *The Insanity Defence.* Edited by: Ronnie Mackay and Warren Brookbanks, Oxford University Press. © Paul McCutcheon 2022. DOI: 10.1093/oso/9780198854944.003.0005

Review Board was established. The Act also introduced the partial defence of diminished responsibility and reformed the law on unfitness to plead, replacing the latter with the concept of unfitness to stand trial.

Moving beyond the M'Naghten Rules

In the 1930s the Court of Criminal Appeal indicated a willingness to expand the defence beyond the cognitive impairments comprehended by the M'Naghten Rules, that is, inability to know the nature and quality of the act done or that the act was wrong. In *Attorney General v O'Brien*[2] it was contended that the jury ought to have been directed on the question of 'irresistible impulse', which, it was argued, would afford a good defence. The Court upheld the conviction, concluding that there was no evidence of irresistible impulse and that the points raised on appeal were inconsistent with the case made at trial. However, the Court suggested that Irish law might accommodate a broader conception of insanity than that encapsulated by the M'Naghten Rules, which only concerned defendants suffering from 'insane delusions'. The Court observed that the 'whole field of insanity . . . comprises a more extensive and varied range of cases of mental disease'[3] than insane delusions. The Court also noted that many legal and medical professionals were dissatisfied with the traditional stance that confined the defence to a narrow reading of the M'Naghten Rules. The Court cited Stephen's formulation of the defence, which included a mental disease that prevented the defendant 'from controlling his own conduct, unless that absence of the power of control has been produced by his own default'.[4] The Court observed that English authorities were divided on the question whether 'irresistible impulse' fell within the defence, but given that the issue did not arise on the facts of the instant case its resolution would await a suitable case.[5] While the plea of irresistible impulse ultimately failed in *O'Brien* it is significant that the Court of Criminal Appeal did not rule out its possible success where it is supported by appropriate evidence. Moreover, it recognized that the M'Naghten Rules were overtaken by developments in clinical understanding of mental illness, thus paving the way for a better alignment of the medical and legal conceptions of insanity.

The potential to recast the defence of insanity was realized in a series of rulings in the 1960s and 1970s where trial judges directed juries in terms that went beyond the M'Naghten Rules. In *People (Attorney General) v Hayes*[6] Henchy J directed the

[2] [1936] IR 263.

[3] ibid 269.

[4] Stephen, *Digest of Criminal Law* (Macmillan 1883) Art 28.

[5] See also *Attorney General v Boylan* [1937] IR 449; *People (DPP) v McGrath* (1960) 1 Frewen 192.

[6] Unreported, Central Criminal Court, 30 November 1967; this and other cases are documented in R O'Hanlon, 'Not Guilty Because of Insanity' (1968) 3 Ir Jur (n.s.) 61.

jury that if they were satisfied that at the time of the attack 'the accused man's mind was so affected by illness that he was unable to restrain himself, a verdict of guilty but insane should be returned'. In *People (Attorney General) v Coughlan*[7] Kenny J adopted Stephen's formula, ruling that the defence would lie if the defendant 'was prevented by defective mental power or disease affecting the mind from controlling his conduct unless the absence of control was produced by his own default'. In *People (Attorney General) v McDonagh*[8] Gannon J directed the jury that the defence would apply in the case of a defendant who 'was unable to control his actions and such defect was due to mental illness'. A clear trend is discernible in the foregoing rulings, namely that the defence in Irish law is broader than that envisaged by the M'Naghten Rules and extends to what would become known as 'volitional insanity'. Nevertheless, Kennedy CJ's observation 30 years earlier in *Attorney General v O'Brien* to the effect that 'directions in summing up to juries … do not settle the law'[9] remained apposite. However, the Supreme Court would soon confirm that those rulings represented Irish law on insanity.

Doyle v Wicklow County Council[10] involved a claim for compensation for criminal injuries. A 17-year-old youth had deliberately burned down the applicant's abattoir. There was psychiatric evidence that the youth was medically insane, in the sense that he was suffering from a mental disorder—unidentified in the law report—that caused him to believe that his love of animals entitled him to burn down the abattoir and that he would not be liable to criminal punishment for doing so. And there was uncontested evidence that he was so determined to carry out his plan that had police officers been present he would have waited until there was no one around to fulfil his mission.[11] The question of law turned on the criminal law's understanding of insanity. If the youth was insane no crime was committed and thus there would be no entitlement to compensation under the criminal injuries code.[12] In answering the questions posed on a case stated, the Supreme Court confirmed that the M'Naghten Rules did not represent the full extent of the defence of insanity in Irish law. Taking its cue from *Attorney General v O'Brien*, the Supreme Court concluded that the Rules were to be read in the light of the questions posed to the judges, namely as being concerned with 'insane delusions'. On the broader issue, the Court held that the defence would apply to a defendant who by reason of mental illness is unable to refrain from acting. Writing for the Court, Griffin J quoted Henchy J's ruling in *People (Attorney General) v Hayes* with approval:[13]

[7] Unreported, Central Criminal Court, 27 November 1968.
[8] (1973) 107 ILTR 169.
[9] [1939] IR 263, 271.
[10] [1974] IR 55.
[11] ibid 57.
[12] Grand Jury (Ireland) Act 1836, s 135; Local Government (Ireland) Act 1898, s 5.
[13] [1974] IR 55, 71.

> In the normal case, tried in accordance with the M'Naghten Rules, the test is solely one of knowledge: did [the defendant] know the nature and quality of his act or did he know that the act was wrong? The rules do not take into account the capacity of a man on the basis of his knowledge to act or to refrain from acting, and I believe it to be correct psychiatric science to accept that certain serious mental diseases, such as paranoia or schizophrenia, in certain cases enable a man to understand the morality or immorality of his act or the legality or illegality of it, or the nature and quality of it, but nevertheless prevent him from exercising a free volition as to whether he should or should not do that act. In the present case the medical witnesses are unanimous in saying that the accused man was, in medical terms, insane at the time of the act. However, legal insanity does not necessarily coincide with ... medical ... insanity, but if it is open to the jury to say, as say they must, on the evidence, that this man understood the nature and quality of his act, and understood its wrongfulness, morally and legally, but that nevertheless he was debarred from refraining from assaulting his wife fatally because of a defect of reason, due to his mental illness, it seems to me that it would be unjust, in the circumstances of this case not to allow the jury to consider the case on these grounds.

The decision in *Doyle* was reinforced by the Supreme Court in *People (DPP) v O'Mahony*[14] and its effect is that Irish law recognizes the form of insanity that is now referred to as 'volitional insanity'. While the courts have reiterated the familiar refrain that 'legal insanity does not necessarily coincide with ... medical ... insanity' it is clear that the judges thought it desirable to ensure a broad, if not complete, alignment between medical and legal conceptions of insanity. While this is to be welcomed, it not obvious that *Doyle* satisfactorily resolved the problems posed by a restrictive interpretation of the M'Naghten Rules. The judgment in *Doyle* begs the question of how a jury should determine the question of control and this may be interpreted either strictly or liberally.

The Slow March towards Reform

Doyle v Wicklow County Council brought some clarity to the defence of insanity, in particular by confirming the correctness of the approach adopted by trial judges from the 1960s onwards. However, other aspects of the law remained unchanged. In line with the Trial of Lunatics Act 1883, defendants who successfully raised the defence were subject to mandatory detention in the Central Mental Hospital[15]

[14] [1985] IR 517.

[15] The Central Mental Hospital (CMH), established by the Central Criminal Lunatic Asylum (Ireland) Act 1845, opened in 1850 in Dundrum, Co Dublin, 13 years before Broadmoor Hospital in England. Given its Victorian origins the CMH is considered no longer fit for purpose and it is to move

'until the government's pleasure be known'; moreover, no provision was made for independent review of such detention. In 1978 the Interdepartmental Committee on Mentally Ill and Maladjusted Persons (the Henchy Committee) recommended in its Third Interim Report,[16] inter alia, the abolition of mandatory detention and the establishment of a review body that would annually review all cases of detention that resulted from an insanity verdict. Part of the review body's function would be to ensure that detainees who were no longer a danger to themselves or others would be promptly released so that they would not be subjected to a regime of punishment.[17] In this regard, the Henchy Committee anticipated the decision in *Winterwerp v Netherlands*[18] and the Committee's recommendations would have met many of the concerns identified by the European Court of Human Rights (ECtHR) in that case. As matters transpired three decades would elapse before legislation was enacted. In the meantime, a number of cases came before the courts, which reinforced the need for legislative action.[19]

The catalyst for reform was a series of cases that questioned the exercise of the power to release a detainee who had been found legally insane. The practice of ordering the detention of such persons 'until further order of *the court*' was developed in *State (0) v O'Brien*,[20] apparently on the assumption that the decision as to how long a person should be detained was a matter for the courts. This practice, which enabled detainees to apply to the court of trial for release on the grounds that they no longer posed a danger to themselves or others, was declared invalid by the Supreme Court in *Application of Gallagher*.[21] The Court held that since the special verdict is an acquittal, trial courts ceased to have any role and the question of release was an executive matter. The Court observed that there was nothing constitutionally improper with this arrangement although, in considering whether to release a detainee, the government must adopt fair procedures. This state of affairs prompted concerns about the absence of a formal review process and dark hints that broader political considerations might play a part in the decision whether or not to release an individual.[22] Some of these concerns were allayed in *Application of Gallagher (No 2)*[23] which established basic procedural

to a new facility in Dublin; Central Mental Hospital (Relocation) Act 2020. At the time of writing that move has been delayed due to the Covid-19 pandemic.

[16] Interdepartmental Committee on Mentally Ill and Maladjusted Persons, *Treatment and Care of Persons Suffering from Mental Disorder who Appear before the Courts on Criminal Charges: Third Interim Report* (Prl. 8275 Dublin, Stationery Office) (hereafter Henchy Committee Report).

[17] ibid 39–43; see F McAuley, *Insanity, Psychiatry and Criminal Responsibility* (Round Hall 1993) 188–90.

[18] [1979] 2 EHRR 387.

[19] See *People (DPP) v Neilan* [1991] IRLM 185, 208 *per* Keane J: '[O]ur law in this entire area is archaic and in urgent need of statutory reform.'

[20] [1973] IR 50.

[21] [1991] 1 IR 31.

[22] Indeed, Gallagher's efforts to secure release had attracted considerable media attention, not always of a wholesome nature.

[23] [1996] 3 IR 10.

requirements[24] and anticipated that a detainee's status would be subject to periodic review. Moreover, in *Gallagher (No 2)* it was accepted that, in an appropriate case, a court could order the release of a detainee. However, as things stood there still was no statutory obligation to carry out a review in cases where a detainee has not sought one. The *Gallagher* litigation was a timely reminder of the need for reform and ultimately prompted the enactment of the Criminal Law (Insanity) Act 2006.

The Criminal Law (Insanity) Act 2006

Section 5(1) of the 2006 Act codified the common law defence as it had developed in Ireland, by providing:

> Where an accused person is tried for an offence and, in the case of the District Court or Special Criminal Court, the court or, in any other case, the jury finds that the accused person committed the act alleged against him or her and, having heard evidence relating to the mental condition of the accused given by a consultant psychiatrist, finds that—
> (*a*) the accused person was suffering at the time from a mental disorder, and
> (*b*) the mental disorder was such that the accused person ought not to be held responsible for the act alleged by reason of the fact that he or she—
> (i) did not know the nature and quality of the act, or
> (ii) did not know that what he or she was doing was wrong, or
> (iii) was unable to refrain from committing the act,
> the court or the jury, as the case may be, shall return a special verdict to the effect that the accused person is not guilty by reason of insanity.

Section 5(1)(b) specifies the effects the mental disorder must have in order that the defendant be relieved of liability: that provision essentially incorporates the M'Naghten Rules in subparagraphs (i) and (ii), while subparagraph (iii) reflects the extension of the defence to embrace volitional insanity, brought about as a result of *Doyle v Wicklow County Council*. Thus, the pre-Act law with its uncertainties and unresolved issues remains relevant.

A number of elements of the defence await clarification. The first is the interpretation of 'mental disorder'. Second, the extent to which the defendant's knowledge must be impaired under the M'Naghten Rules is uncertain with different

[24] In particular, the Court held that the executive was bound to act in a quasi-judicial manner and to observe the requirements of fair procedures.

approaches being taken in various jurisdictions. Third, the concept of volitional insanity that was recognized in *Doyle v Wicklow County Council* is open to either a broad or narrow interpretation. Thus, while the 2006 Act is generally to be welcomed for the reform it has bought about, it is unfortunate that the Oireachtas did not take the opportunity to clarify details of the defence.

'Mental Disorder'

'Mental disorder' is defined in section 1 of the Act as including 'mental illness, mental disability, dementia or any disease of the mind but does not include intoxication'. Clinicians will be familiar with the first three elements of that definition, but the expression 'disease of the mind' derives from the M'Naghten Rules. The inclusion of the latter concept invites the conclusion that the Oireachtas intended to preserve the received understanding of 'disease of the mind' albeit that Irish jurisprudence on that question is scarce. Case law in other jurisdictions has identified different tests to determine what constitutes a 'disease of the mind': whether the defendant's condition was produced by an internal or external factor; whether that condition is one that is liable to recur; and the 'holistic' test that was adopted by the Supreme Court of Canada. Irish courts have not determined which, if any, of those tests represents Irish law. Likewise, the courts have not been called on to determine whether conditions that psychiatrists do not consider to be mental disorders, such as arteriosclerosis[25] and epilepsy,[26] fall within the scope of the Irish defence. The test of what constitutes a 'mental disorder' remains a matter of speculation, but some observations are offered.

First, it seems clear that in reworking the defence of insanity the courts were concerned to ensure a better alignment between the legal and medical conceptions of insanity. This is evident in the remarks of Kennedy CJ in *Attorney General v O'Brien* and Henchy J in *People (Attorney General) v Hayes*, quoted above, which were cited with approval in *Doyle*. Given these views it would seem incongruous that conditions that clinicians unambiguously exclude from the category of 'mental disorders' could result in the special verdict. Second, the requirement in section 5(1) that the jury hears evidence of the defendant's mental condition from a 'consultant psychiatrist' is designed to ensure that a verdict of insanity is based on appropriate clinical opinion. Given the foregoing considerations, it is submitted that Irish law should reject a test that classifies non-pathological conditions as 'mental disorders'. This would seem to rule out both the internal/external factor or likelihood of recurrence tests as the *exclusive* determinant of what constitutes a 'mental disorder'. It is further submitted that there is considerable merit to the 'holistic' test

[25] *R v Kemp* [1957] 1 QB 399.
[26] *R v Sullivan* [1984] AC 156.

that was adopted by the Supreme Court of Canada in *R v Stone*.[27] That test incorporates a range of considerations: whether the defendant's condition was internally or externally generated; the likelihood of recurrence of the condition; and policy factors, including the need for public protection and whether the defendant should be subjected to the special regime associated with the insanity defence.[28]

The question of psychopathy requires consideration. In this context, the term 'psychopathy' is used as a layperson's synonym for a range of personality disorders variously described by clinicians as 'anti-social personality disorder' or 'dissocial personality disorder'. Psychopathy may be a personality disorder, but the predominant psychiatric view is that a personality disorder is not a mental disorder. However, there is a body of clinical opinion that recognizes psychopathy as a distinct syndrome and that 'psychopathy' is properly reserved for individuals who meet certain diagnostic criteria. Criminal lawyers cannot resolve the clinical debate, but the question is whether any of the conditions that might loosely be described as 'psychopathy' qualify as 'mental disorders' for the purposes of the defence of insanity. In *People (DPP) v O'Mahony*[29] the Supreme Court was invited to recognize a common law defence of diminished responsibility where the appellant was described as having a psychopathic personality. The Court expressed the view that a psychopath who found it impossible or difficult to control his violent desires would be entitled to the defence of insanity in Irish law. The Court also suggested that the appellant in *R v Byrne*[30] would, if tried in Ireland, have been found insane. This reflects a view that the defence of insanity, at least since *Doyle v Wicklow County Council*, is sufficiently wide to embrace what in English law was covered by a combination of the M'Naghten Rules and the statutory plea of diminished responsibility. If this is correct, it follows that the enactment of the partial defence of diminished responsibility in section 6 of the 2006 Act was unnecessary. However, *O'Mahony* is authority for a more limited proposition, namely that a common law doctrine of diminished responsibility was not recognized in Ireland. In cases where there is clear psychiatric evidence that a defendant's violent impulses interfered with his capacity for self-control, it is submitted that this should be done by means of the statutory plea of diminished responsibility.[31] The concept of diminished responsibility acknowledges that there are factors which clinicians accept interfere with self-control but do not negate it completely.[32]

[27] [1999] 2 SCR 290.
[28] Discussed further in Chapter 6.
[29] [1985] IR 517.
[30] [1960] 2 QB 396.
[31] Criminal Law (Insanity) Act 2006, s 6.
[32] Recent cases suggest that Irish courts subscribe to this view: *McD v Governor of X Prison* [2018] IEHC 668; *People (DPP) v Judge* [2018] IECA 242.

Knowledge Component

There are two limbs to the cognitive component of the defence. The question is whether mental disorder prevented the defendant from knowing the 'nature and quality' of his act (s 5(1)(b)(i)) or that it was 'wrong' (s 5(1)(b)(ii)). The terse language of that provision gives little indication of how the knowledge component should be interpreted and we are thrown back to the pre-Act law and jurisprudence of other common law jurisdictions for guidance.

What it means not to 'know the nature and quality' of an act is usually explained[33] by the hypotheticals provided by Stephen[34] and Kenny:[35] the defendant who kills 'under the delusion that he is breaking a jar' and 'the madman who cut a woman's throat under the idea that he was cutting a loaf of bread', respectively. These examples suggest that the defendant must be ignorant of the physical nature of what he is doing and this interpretation was confirmed in *R v Codere*[36] where it was decided that 'nature and quality' denote the 'physical character' of an action as distinct from its moral aspects.

However, the concept of 'physical character' itself is ambiguous. It could refer to the behaviour described by the act, namely the bodily movements involved in stabbing, shooting, poisoning, choking, and the like. In the alternative, the notion of 'physical character' might refer to the conduct as a whole, including relevant circumstances and consequences. The distinction is important: on the first interpretation, a defendant who knows he is engaging in the physical act of cutting the victim's throat would be denied the defence even if due to mental disorder he could not appreciate that death was a probable consequence of that act.

The alternative interpretation allows for consideration of more than the defendant's understanding of the 'physical character' of the act. Such an approach is consistent with basic principles of criminal liability. The actus reus of some offences includes a consequence of the defendant's conduct while that of other offences requires the existence of a particular circumstance. In general, mens rea on the part of the defendant is required as to the circumstances and consequences. It can hardly be right that a mentally disordered defendant is treated more harshly than a sane defendant and this suggests that knowledge of the nature and quality of the act points to a more meaningful understanding. There is support in Canadian law for this approach. In *R v O*,[37] there was evidence that the defendant had admitted to a neighbour that she had killed her children. Nevertheless, the jury was

[33] See eg D Ormerod and K Laird, *Smith, Hogan and Ormerod's Criminal Law* (16th edn, Oxford University Press 2021) 314 (hereafter, Smith, Hogan and Ormerod).

[34] *History of the Criminal Law of England* (Macmillan 1883) Vol II, 166. Stephen also gives the example of someone who cuts off a sleeper's head because 'it would be great fun looking for it when he woke up'.

[35] JWC Turner (ed), *Outlines of Criminal Law* (19th edn, Cambridge University Press 1966) 76.

[36] (1916) 12 Cr App R 21.

[37] (1959) 3 CLQ 151.

asked to consider whether her subsequent statement that she wanted to return to look after them showed that she did not 'appreciate the nature and quality' of her actions. Similarly, in *R v Adamcik*,[38] the jury was permitted to consider whether a defendant who attempted to rob a bank in order to obtain money to buy a crucifix which he believed was blasphemously displayed in a shop window was 'capable of appreciating the nature and quality of his actions'. Both defendants were acquitted notwithstanding that they knew what they were doing in the *R v Codere* sense and had not claimed that they did not know that their actions were contrary to law.

It is submitted that the knowledge component is better interpreted as going to the defendant's inability to evaluate his actions, including his reasons for committing them and the consequences normally associated with them, in the way that a sane person can. A defendant who cannot do this might know what he is doing in a literal sense, but he does not know why he is doing it and cannot assess its true effects. He may be quite clear about the 'physical character' of his actions, but he does not know what he is doing in an epistemologically significant sense. And, as the Canadian authorities demonstrate, it seems wrong to suppose that the insanity defence is tied to a conception of knowledge that cannot be defended on epistemological grounds.

The second limb of the knowledge component, namely knowledge that the act was wrong, is also open to different interpretations. In *R v Windle*[39] the English Court of Criminal Appeal stated that the word 'wrong', as used in the M'Naghten Rules, meant contrary to law and it follows that a delusional belief that the conduct was morally justified would not excuse the defendant. The proposition in *Windle* was taken to state the law in England,[40] and recent English decisions have confirmed this view.[41] If this statement represents the law in Ireland, and there is no reported decision on the point, it would introduce an unnecessary distinction into the law. Its effect would be to close off the possibility of expanding the interpretation of the word 'wrong' along the lines suggested by the trial judge in *M'Naghten*, namely, to include situations where the defendant's mental disorder prevented him from realizing that his actions could not be rationally justified.[42] If mental disorder prevents a defendant from knowing that something is wrong in this sense, it is arguable that he was not 'conscious that the act was one that he ought not to do', an option that is excluded if all that is required is awareness that the act contravenes a particular legal rule. This point has been accepted by Australian courts. In *R v Porter*, Dixon J observed that a defendant who 'could not reason about the matter

[38] (1977) 33 CCC (2d) 11.

[39] [1952] 2 QB 826.

[40] Smith, Hogan and Ormerod (n 33) 315–17; but RD Mackay, *Mental Condition Defences in the Criminal Law* (Oxford University Press 1995) 104–05 suggests that in practice the defendant's appreciation of wrongness is treated in a 'liberal fashion', ie one that is not confined to questioning his knowledge of the legal character of the act.

[41] *R v Johnson* [2007] EWCA 1978; *Loake v DPP* [2017] EWHC 2855 (Admin), [2018] QB 998.

[42] (1843) 4 St Tr (n.s.) 847, 931.

with a moderate degree of sense and composure ... could not know that what he was doing was wrong'.[43] In *Stapleton v The Queen*[44] the High Court of Australia affirmed that the word 'wrong' meant 'wrong having regard to the everyday standards of reasonable people' and that the crucial question was whether the defendant could 'think rationally' about the reasons that made his act 'right' or 'wrong' by those standards.

Canadian law has adopted the same approach. In *R v Chaulk*[45] the Supreme Court of Canada held that the concept of 'wrong' went beyond an appreciation of the legal quality of the act. The majority reasoned that individuals are held criminally responsible because of their ability to distinguish between right and wrong. Where insanity is raised as a defence, the issue is whether the defendant was rendered incapable by mental disorder of knowing that the act was one he ought not to have done. It was accepted by the majority that a person might know that the act is prohibited by the law but due to mental disorder be unable to appreciate that it is wrong according to the moral standards of society. The majority emphasized that the concept of wrongness is understood according to societal standards, 'not by the personal standards of the offender',[46] a qualification designed to exclude the psychopath whose acts are prompted by an individualized (im)moral code. In *R v Oommen*,[47] the same Court held that the trial judge erred when he rejected the defence of insanity on foot of psychiatric testimony that the defendant enjoyed a general capacity to distinguish right from wrong: the appropriate question was whether the defendant had the ability to apply that knowledge to the act in question.[48]

The approach adopted in Australia and Canada opens the insanity defence to the type of defendant excluded by the traditional interpretation based on *Windle*.[49] Paranoid schizophrenics and psychotics, who cannot claim any justification for their actions would seem to be covered by it, as would the depressive who kills his children in order to end their earthly plight, since in these cases the defendant's insane motives override his awareness of the legal and moral considerations governing his actions.[50]

43 (1933) 55 CLR 182, 189.

44 (1952) 86 CLR 358. See Chapter 8.

45 (1991) 2 CR (4th) 1. See Chapter 6.

46 (1991) 2 CR (4th) 1, para 111.

47 [2004] 2 SCR 507.

48 There is American authority to the same effect: *People v Serravo* (1992) 823 P 2d 128; *State v Wilson* (1997) 700 A 2d 633.

49 [1952] 2 QB 826.

50 Note *People (DPP) v Morley*, *Irish Times* 21 May 2021: clinical evidence was that the defendant, who was found NGRI, believed that her acts were morally right; but the defendant also admitted to clinicians that 'at some level' she knew the killings were wrong and that if she survived, she would spend her life in prison.

Inability to Refrain from Acting

The defence is also available where the defendant's mental disorder resulted in his being 'unable to refrain from committing the act' (s 5(1)(b)(iii)): this provision captures the concept of volitional insanity that was recognized in *Doyle v Wicklow County Council*. As we have seen this extends the plea to defendants who do not fall within traditional reading of the M'Naghten Rules. The defence is available if it is shown that the defendant was 'unable to refrain' from acting even though he understood the nature and quality of the act and that it was wrong. It can be accepted that a defendant who cannot exercise control due to mental illness does not deserve to be punished but the question remains: how should a jury determine the question of control?

The formula adopted by the Supreme Court is that the defendant must be 'debarred from refraining', but the Court did not elaborate. As it happens, a *Doyle*-type defendant might not satisfy this threshold given the facts outlined in the case stated and the psychiatric evidence that was adduced. Griffin J expressed doubts that it had been established that the youth was insane but, appropriately, he did not comment further as the case was to return to the Circuit Court for final resolution.[51] His misgivings reflect the fact that the claim that the youth was unable to control his behaviour did not sit easily with the evidence that he was determined to burn down the abattoir as a protest against the killing of animals and did burn it down for that reason; and that he would have waited until later to incinerate the building had police officers been present.[52]

Case law on the question of control is scarce. The matter was considered in *People (DPP) v Courtney*,[53] an unreported decision where the Court of Criminal Appeal approved the following direction on irresistible impulse:[54]

> There is a limited form of insanity recognised by our law, commonly called irresistible impulse. That means in this case an irresistible impulse caused by a defect of reason due to mental illness. Merely because an impulse is not in fact resisted does not mean that it is an irresistible impulse. If so, no one could ever be convicted of a crime—they would only have to say, I found the impulse irresistible. It must be an irresistible impulse, not an unresisted impulse, to constitute this form of insanity. Diminished self-control or weakened resistance to impulse is not necessarily the same as irresistible impulse. Diminished self-control makes the resistance to an impulse more difficult but does not necessarily make it irresistible.

[51] [1974] IR 55, 71. The law report notes the subsequent history of the case. The Circuit Court awarded the applicant compensation on the basis that the act was criminal but, on appeal, the High Court concluded on foot of 'evidence adduced at that appeal' that the youth was insane: [1974] IR 55, 74.

[52] ibid 56–57.

[53] Unreported, Court of Criminal Appeal, 21 July 1994.

[54] ibid 48.

That direction suggests a narrow interpretation of *Doyle v Wicklow County Council* and it is cited in Irish criminal law texts as establishing the relevant standard.[55] The distinction between an irresistible impulse and one that is not resisted is important, but it cannot be said that the *Courtney* ruling is definitive. Beyond approving the trial judge's direction, the Court of Criminal Appeal did not analyse the issue in any depth. In any event, given that the evidence of insanity was underwhelming, to say the least, it is arguable that the question of insanity should not have been put to the jury. The clinical evidence was that the appellant suffered from post-traumatic stress disorder (PTSD), arising from military service in Lebanon some years previously, to the point that his self-control was diminished but not lost; there was no evidence that he suffered from a pathological condition. However, the prosecution had agreed to allow the issue of insanity go to the jury and in the light of that stance the Court declined to comment on whether the issue 'by definition should have been left to the jury'.[56] It is submitted that had the reverse happened, namely had the trial judge *refused* to put the issue to the jury and that refusal been upheld on appeal, the decision would carry greater weight.

Despite the *Courtney* direction, there are hints of a more liberal approach to the question of impulse control being adopted in practice. This may be seen in the *Gallagher* litigation, mentioned above, where the applicant sought release from detention. The applicant was found insane on a charge of murdering his ex-girlfriend and her mother. Within 18 months of the trial, he sought release from detention on the basis that he no longer suffered from a 'disease of the mind' and, he contended, there was no legal justification for his continued detention. Clinical evidence supported the claim that he did not now suffer from a mental disorder and the opinion was expressed that he had probably never suffered from such a condition.[57] The *Gallagher* decisions did not deal with the appropriate test for irresistible impulse but the point being made here is that it may be inferred that a liberal approach is adopted, at least in some cases, at trial level. Moreover, the fact that the issue was put to the jury in *Courtney*, where the clinical evidence went no further than suggesting that the appellant had diminished self-control might also be taken as evidence of a liberal approach being taken in practice.

Raising and Proving Insanity

Section 5(4) of the 2006 Act specifies that, on a *trial for murder* where a defence of either insanity or diminished responsibility is raised, the prosecution may adduce evidence 'tending to prove the alternative contention'. This provision aside, the Act

[55] Charleton and McDermott (n 1) 1146; Campbell et al (n 1) 1009–10.
[56] Unreported, Court of Criminal Appeal, 21 July 1994, 50.
[57] *Application of Gallagher (No 2)* [1996] 3 IR 10, 17.

is silent on whether and in what circumstances the prosecution may raise the issue of insanity and, again, the pre-Act common law is relevant.

The opinion expressed by Lord Denning in *Bratty v Attorney-General for Northern Ireland* to the effect that if the issue of insanity arises on the evidence it is the duty of the trial judge to instruct the jury accordingly, irrespective of the views of the prosecution or the defence,[58] was reinforced by Kenny J in *People (Attorney General) v Messitt*.[59] However, in *People (DPP) v Redmond*[60] the Supreme Court, by a 4:1 majority, held that a trial judge may not reject a plea of guilty on grounds that he thought the defendant might be insane. In that case the defendant chose to plead guilty so that he would receive a determinate sentence of imprisonment, rather than the indefinite detention that the law at the time mandated for those found insane. The majority took the view that a defendant is entitled to manage his defence as he thinks appropriate and that, in the absence of exceptional circumstances such as duress, a trial judge may not query the motives for pleading guilty. The view was also expressed that the trial judge had a slender basis for his suspicion that the defendant was insane; different considerations might arise where a verdict of insanity 'seemed certain'.[61] *Redmond* concerned the role of the trial judge at the sentencing stage rather than during a contested trial. It does not necessarily follow that the prosecution or trial judge is precluded from raising the issue of insanity during the course of a trial. In this regard, the observations of Kearns J are relevant:[62]

> Common also to the submissions was an acceptance by all parties that an issue as to insanity, while normally raised as a matter of defence, may also be raised by the prosecution in an appropriate case.... It was further accepted however that the issue of possible insanity might be raised by a trial judge at any time during a trial.

The foregoing remarks reinforce the view that the decision in *Redmond* is confined to the role of the trial judge at sentencing and that it does not displace the observations in *Bratty* and *Messitt*. At the very least, the question whether the trial judge can intervene during the course of the trial remains open and its resolution will involve a balancing of a defendant's right to conduct his defence against the public interest in ensuring the fair administration of justice and the protection of the integrity of the judicial system. Moreover, it is submitted that considerations of public safety, namely ensuring the detention of dangerous individuals, should have little purchase. The primary function of the criminal process is to determine the responsibility of defendants: civil law, in the form of the Mental Health Act 2001, provides mechanisms to ensure public protection.

[58] [1963] AC 386, 411.
[59] [1972] IR 204, 213.
[60] [2006] IESC 25, [2006] 3 IR 188.
[61] ibid para 56.
[62] ibid para 91.

Section 5 of the 2006 Act is silent on the allocation of the burden of proof. This contrasts with the allocation of the burden of establishing diminished responsibility to the defendant.[63] Nevertheless, judicial practice in Ireland always conformed to the M'Naghten Rules to the extent that the allocation of the burden of proof to the defendant is not in question. The Supreme Court has confirmed this to be the position in *People (DPP) v Heffernan*,[64] a case that involved the burden of proof for diminished responsibility. The Court's reasoning was based on the assumption that the defendant bears the burden of proving insanity and it considered that the allocation of different burdens in cases of diminished responsibility and insanity would prove unworkable. Where the prosecution contends that the defendant was insane it will bear the burden of establishing that proposition, based on the general principle that the party that contends must prove. This was confirmed by the Court of Appeal in *People (DPP) v Henry*,[65] where the defence and prosecution advanced the alternate pleas of diminished responsibility and insanity, respectively.

It had once been thought that the standard of proof borne by the defendant was higher than the civil standard, based on the judgment of Sullivan CJ in *People (Attorney General) v Fennell (No 1)*,[66] where he suggested that proof to the 'satisfaction of the jury' equated to proof 'beyond reasonable doubt'. Subsequent jurisprudence has confirmed that the burden borne by the defendant is no greater than establishing his insanity on the balance of probabilities. This proposition was central to *People (DPP) v Heffernan* where, in equating the burdens and standards of proof for insanity and diminished responsibility, it was concluded that the defendant bears the burden of establishing the latter on the balance of probabilities: it inevitably follows that the balance of probabilities standard also applies to the defence of insanity.[67] Moreover, where the prosecution advances a claim that the defendant was insane the better view is that the burden it bears is discharged by proof on the balance of probabilities.[68] Finally, the Supreme Court has recently held that, given the burden and standard of proof, a verdict of NGRI 'demonstrates innocence';[69] in contrast, a standard 'not guilty' verdict is a conclusion that there is reasonable doubt regarding the defendant's guilt.

The constitutionality of the reverse onus must be considered. The Supreme Court has held that the presumption of innocence is constitutionally protected but, in general, the courts have upheld provisions that allocate an evidential burden to the defendant.[70] On the other hand, a measure that imposes the legal burden on the

[63] Criminal Law (Insanity) Act 2006, s 6(2).
[64] [2017] IESC 5, [2017] 1 IR 82.
[65] [2015] IECA 219, [2015] 4 IR 217.
[66] [1940] IR 445.
[67] See *People (DPP) v Ramzan* [2016] IECA 158, para 31.
[68] See *People (DPP) v Henry* [2015] IECA 219, [2015] 4 IR 217, para 29.
[69] *People (DPP) v Ali Abdi* [2022] IESC 24, para 53.
[70] *O'Leary v Attorney General* [1995] 1 IR 254; see D McGrath and E Egan McGrath, *Evidence* (3rd edn, Round Hall Thomson Reuters 2020) 2-25–2-44.

defendant will pass constitutional muster if it is proportionate.[71] The reverse onus for insanity has not been expressly considered but observations in cases involving other reverse onuses rest on an assumption that the reverse onus in insanity is constitutional.[72] Such 'thinking out loud' does not establish a definite proposition of law but it indicates the current state of judicial opinion. In *People (DPP) v Heffernan*[73] the Supreme Court avoided considering the constitutionality of the reverse onus for diminished responsibility. The Court reasoned that the onus did not violate the presumption of innocence on the grounds that the prosecution bears the legal burden of proving the ingredients of the offence, that is, of proving the actus reus and the mens rea. It followed, in the Court's view, that no question of the constitutionality of the reverse onus arose. Nevertheless, dicta in the judgments indicate that, had the issue arisen, the Court would have ruled that the reverse onus is a permissible limitation of the defendant's rights. It may be inferred that the Court would take the same view of the reverse onus for insanity.

The question of insanity is ultimately for the trier of fact (the jury, or trial judge in a non-jury trial) to determine. Section 5 stipulates that the jury (or judge) hears evidence from a 'consultant psychiatrist' relating to the defendant's mental condition. In *People (DPP) v Ramzan*,[74] 'consultant psychiatrist' was held to mean 'any medical doctor specialising in psychiatry and holding a consultant post at a hospital or clinic'. The Court also held that evidence of other health professionals may be adduced in addition to that of consultant psychiatrists. In *People (DPP) v Ali Abdi*[75] the Court of Appeal emphasized the primacy of the jury's role, stating that 'it is essential that every such decision be taken by a properly informed jury in a public forum'. The Court also observed that expert testimony should not be 'expressed in a form which suggests that the expert is trying to subvert the role of the finder of fact'. However, a verdict that rejects unchallenged clinical opinion is liable to be overturned on appeal. This occurred in *People (DPP) v Alchimionek*[76] where the Court of Appeal overturned a conviction for manslaughter in the face of unanimous psychiatric opinion that the defendant was a paranoid schizophrenic who experienced paranoid delusions. The Court did not cite any authority, but its approach is consistent with that adopted in *R v Oye*.[77] *Alchimionek* was an exceptional case and the Court is generally reluctant to overturn a verdict on grounds that it was perverse. In *People (DPP) v Kenna*,[78] the Court refused to overturn a

[71] *McNally v Ireland* [2009] IEHC 573, [2011] 4 IR 431.

[72] See *People (DPP) v Smyth* [2010] IECCA 34, [2010] 3 IR 688, para 20.

[73] [2017] IESC 5, [2017] 1 IR 82.

[74] [2016] IECA 158.

[75] [2005] 1 ILRM 382, 393; a second appeal, on grounds of newly discovered facts (consisting of a revised medical opinion) was successful: [2019] IECA 38; on retrial, the defendant was found NGRI and the court issued a miscarriage of justice certificate: [2020] IEHC 434, upheld on appeal [2021] IECA 237 and [2022] IESC 24.

[76] [2019] IECA 49.

[77] [2013] EWCA Crim 1725, [2014] 1 WLR 3354.

[78] [2020] IECA 265.

conviction where the jury rejected a plea of insanity. Conflicting clinical evidence had been adduced, with one witness stating that the appellant met the criteria for the defence and the other expressing the opposite view. The Court held that it could not be concluded that the verdict was perverse simply because the jury preferred the evidence of one witness over the other: the instant case 'could scarcely be more different' to that in *Alchimionek*.

Verdict and Disposition

The Criminal Law (Insanity) Act 2006 changed the form of the special verdict and the disposition of defendants who are found insane. The form of the insanity verdict was alerted from 'guilty but insane' to 'not guilty by reason of insanity'. The Act replaced the regime of mandatory detention that operated previously and established a formal review mechanism where detention has been ordered (considered in the next section) and introduced a right of appeal where the defendant has been found to be insane.[79]

The disposition of defendants found insane is governed by section 5(2) and section 5(3). Those provisions prompt a number of observations. The first point is that mandatory detention has been replaced by a flexible regime. Detention is restricted to cases where the defendant is found to suffer from certain mental disorders and requires in-patient care or treatment in a designated centre.[80]

Second, a procedure for determining whether the defendant should be detained is established. The trial court may commit the defendant to a designated centre for 14 days (which may be extended if appropriate) to facilitate his examination by an 'approved medical officer'.[81] The latter is defined in section 1 as 'a consultant psychiatrist (within the meaning of the Mental Health Act 2001)',[82] a potentially more limited category than that of 'consultant psychiatrist', whose testimony is required to support a defence of insanity. The evidence of an 'approved medical officer' is required in cases concerning involuntary committal of defendants who are found insane.

When it comes to the decision whether to order detention the trial court is required to 'consider' any psychiatric reports provided by the medical personnel who examined the defendant and 'such other evidence as may be adduced'.[83] It is clear

[79] Criminal Law (Insanity) Act 2006, s 8.

[80] At present, the CMH is the only 'designated centre' but the Minster for Health may designate other centres for the reception, detention, and treatment of people committed under the Act: Criminal Law (Insanity) Act 2006, s 3.

[81] Criminal Law (Insanity) Act 2006, s 5(3)(a).

[82] Mental Health Act 2001, s 2 defines 'consultant psychiatrist' as 'a consultant psychiatrist who is employed by the Health Service Executive or by an approved centre or a person whose name is entered on the division of psychiatry or the division of child and adolescent psychiatry of the Register of Medical Specialists maintained by the Medical Council in Ireland'.

[83] Criminal Law (Insanity) Act 2006, s 5(2).

from the term 'consider' that the court is not bound by any recommendation in the report. Moreover, the court is not restricted to the report prepared by the 'approved medical officer'. What other evidence the court may consider is not specified but prudence would dictate that a court would only act on appropriate clinical evidence. Moreover, natural justice demands that a defendant should be permitted to challenge the psychiatric report and to adduce evidence in support of a case not to be detained.

Third, detention may only be ordered where the court is satisfied that the defendant suffers from a 'mental disorder' as contemplated by the Mental Health Act 2001, which governs the involuntary detention of mentally disordered persons in non-forensic contexts. 'Mental disorder' in the 2001 Act is defined as 'mental illness, severe dementia or significant intellectual disability'.[84] Involuntary detention under the 2001 Act is permitted where there is a serious likelihood that the patient will cause harm to himself or another or where his judgment is so impaired that not detaining him would lead to a serious deterioration in his condition and detaining him would be likely to lead to an improvement in his condition. 'Mental disorder' under the 2001 Act is narrower than the equivalent category in the Criminal Law (Insanity) Act 2006.[85] It follows that there will be defendants who are found NGRI but who are not liable to detention because they do not suffer from a 'mental disorder', as that concept is understood under the 2001 Act. This will assume practical relevance to the extent that non-pathological conditions that are held to be 'diseases of the mind' fall within the Irish defence: those conditions do not match the strictures of the 2001 Act.

Fourth, the restriction on the range of defendants who may be detained post-verdict represents an attempt to align the detention of criminally accused persons with involuntary detention in civil contexts. Thus, a defendant should be detained only where his condition is such that, criminal charges aside, he would be involuntarily detained under the 2001 Act. This is appropriate: given that the special verdict is an acquittal, the defendant ought to be treated on the same footing as any other citizen and should only lose his liberty under the same conditions.

Review of Detention

The 2006 Act introduced a formal review mechanism of the detention of defendants who are found insane. Section 11 established the Mental Health (Criminal Law) Review Board (the Board), which is independent in the exercise of its functions and is required to have regard to the welfare and safety of the detainee and to the public interest.[86] Section 12 invests the Board with broad powers to direct

[84] Mental Health Act 2001, s 3.

[85] See *People (DPP) v MB* [2016] IECA 311, para 51.

[86] Criminal Law (Insanity) Act 2006, s 11(2).

the attendance of a detainee at a hearing, to compel the attendance of witnesses, to order the production of documents and other things, and to give such other directions as it thinks 'reasonable and just.' Section 12(6) authorizes the Board to determine its procedures, which are to include provision for granting legal aid, for notifying relevant parties, providing copies of reports, admitting written statements in evidence, examination and cross-examination of witnesses, determining whether evidence should be given on oath or otherwise, and the making of a record of the proceedings.[87]

Section 13 of the 2006 Act governs the review of detention. That section states that the Board should review a patient's detention at intervals of not more than six months' duration. The clinical director of the designated centre in which the patient is held is required to comply with any request issued by the Board. If the clinical director forms the opinion that a patient is no longer in need of in-patient treatment, he is required to notify the Board of this.[88] The Board must then hold a hearing to determine whether in-patient treatment is still required and to order what it considers proper in relation to the patient: this could be for his continued detention, or his conditional or unconditional discharge.[89] A patient may apply to the Board for a review of his detention and the Board is required to conduct a hearing unless it is satisfied that a review is not necessary because of any previous review that has been undertaken. Again, the Board is required to determine whether there is a need for continued in-patient treatment and it must make such order it thinks proper in relation to the patient: continued detention, conditional or unconditional discharge.[90] The Board is also authorized to act on its own initiative to review a patient's detention.[91]

Decisions of the Board are amenable to judicial review and it is bound to act rationally, judicially, and in accordance with the principles of constitutional justice.[92] The stipulation in section 11(2) of the 2006 Act that the Board must 'have regard' to the welfare and safety of the patient and to the public interest has been said to be a 'guide' for the Board in reaching a decision.[93] It follows that, while the Board may be guided by considerations of the patient's welfare and public safety, a decision to continue his detention should be based on a determination that in-patient treatment 'is still required'[94] or that the patient 'is still in need of in-patient treatment.'[95]

[87] See *Procedures of Mental Health (Criminal Law) Review Board* (2020) https://www.mhclrb.ie/wp-content/uploads/2020/06/Procedures-MHRB.pdf (accessed 18 June 2022).
[88] Criminal Law (Insanity) Act 2006, s 13(5).
[89] Criminal Law (Insanity) Act 2006, s 13(6).
[90] Criminal Law (Insanity) Act 2006, s 13(8).
[91] Criminal Law (Insanity) Act 2006, s 13(9).
[92] *L v Kennedy* [2010] IEHC 195, [2011] 2 IR 124, para 76.
[93] ibid para 77; a different emphasis is evident in *JB v Mental Health (Criminal Law) Review Board* [2008] IEHC 303, [2011] 2 IR 15, para 47: '... the Board is enjoined to have regard to the welfare and safety of the applicant and to the public interest ...'.
[94] Criminal Law (Insanity) Act 2006, s 13(6).
[95] Criminal Law (Insanity) Act 2006, s 13(8).

In *L v Kennedy*,[96] clinical evidence was that the applicant no longer suffered from his original mental disorder and the medical consensus was that his continued in-patient treatment was no longer required. The applicant contended that, since his condition was in remission, there was no longer any legal justification for this continued detention. Indeed, had the applicant been tried at the date of the application hearing he would have been entitled to the special verdict but would have been immune from detention, given that he no longer suffered from a mental disorder in the narrower sense of the 2001 Act. In effect, the argument was that continued detention is lawful if and only if a patient continues to suffer from a relevant mental disorder. The High Court rejected that contention, concluding that '[i]t does not follow that because he no longer suffers from the mental disorder which justified his or her detention at the Central Mental Hospital in the first place that he must be discharged.'[97]

The foregoing remarks were shaped by the context of the case: an application for release from detention under Article 40.4.2° of the Constitution (the *habeas corpus* procedure) rather than judicial review proceedings challenging the decision of the Board. Moreover, continued detention of a patient who has overcome his mental disorder might be justifiable for a limited period to allow clinicians to confirm that he is in remission and determine whether any further treatment or care is required. But a broader proposition to the effect that a patient who has recovered is not entitled to be discharged is questionable given that the purpose of a review process is to consider the release of a patient where his circumstances warrant it. Inasmuch as the Court's observations suggest otherwise it is submitted that they do not represent the law.

Conditional Discharges

Section 13 allows the Board to order a patient's conditional discharge. However, the 2006 Act, as originally enacted, did not contain any provision to enforce conditions that might be imposed. In contrast, section 14, which authorizes temporary release, contained enforcement provisions from the outset. The absence of enforcement provisions has proved problematic. In *JB v Criminal Law (Mental Health) Review Board*[98] the applicant responded well to treatment and the medical personnel considered that he no longer required in-patient treatment. However, they were of the view that his release should be subject to conditions. The Board agreed that a conditional discharge was appropriate, but it was concerned about the lack of enforcement provisions in the 2006 Act: in its view, the lack of such

[96] [2010] IEHC 195, [2011] 2 IR 124.
[97] ibid para 76.
[98] [2008] IEHC 303, [2011] 2 IR 15.

provisions, in effect, made a conditional discharge unconditional and it was unwilling to order such a discharge. The High Court considered the Board's concerns about the lack of enforcement provisions to be 'legitimate'[99] and concluded that the refusal to order the applicant's discharge, where the other options were unsuitable, was reasonable and made 'within jurisdiction'.[100] A different approach was evident in *L v Kennedy*[101] where conditional release was also refused. The ultimate decision turned on the appropriateness of the remedy that was sought, but there are strong hints in the judgment of concerns with the process by which the Board operated: the High Court observed that it was not permissible for the Board to adopt a general policy of refusing to order conditional releases.[102] The proper course of action was for the Board to identify the appropriate conditions on which the applicant might be released and then to determine whether he was likely to abide by those conditions.

The Criminal Law (Insanity) Act 2010 filled the lacuna identified in the foregoing decisions. The 2010 Act inserted two new sections (13A and 13B) into the 2006 Act. Section 13A outlines the process for ordering a conditional discharge but stipulates that the Board may not order a conditional release until 'it is satisfied that such arrangements as appear necessary to the clinical director' to facilitate release are in place (s 13A(2)). Section 13B provides enforcement procedures in the case of a material breach of a conditional discharge.

The Supreme Court considered the respective roles of the Board and the clinical director in *MC v Clinical Director of the Central Mental Hospital*.[103] The Board proposed to vary the applicant's conditional release. The applicant's treating psychiatrist opposed the variation and the respondent explained that he was unable to make the arrangements in question. The Court observed that the clinical director exercises a statutory obligation at the direction of the Board:[104] the stipulation that 'the clinical director … shall make such arrangements' does not mean that the making of a condition is 'by arrangement' with the clinical director.[105] The Court concluded that the Board's directions to the clinical director have legal effect that compel him to take the steps mandated by it.[106] If there are differences of clinical opinion between the Board and the clinical director the 'ultimate power'[107] resides in the Board. The clinical director's role is 'managerial or administrative'[108] and he is not entitled to refuse to take measures to support a conditional discharge.

[99] ibid para 54.
[100] ibid paras 56, 58.
[101] [2010] IEHC 195, [2011] 2 IR 124.
[102] [2010] IEHC 195, [2011] 2 IR 124, para 65.
[103] [2020] IESC 28.
[104] ibid para 67.
[105] ibid para 89.
[106] ibid para 112.
[107] ibid para 101.
[108] ibid para 102.

Consequently, the Court concluded that the applicant established that the clinical director was in breach of his statutory duty. However, the Court accepted that the making of an arrangement might be 'impossible in a technical or practical sense'[109] and it did 'not discount the possibility that more complex circumstances might arise were there to be a genuine impossibility and more complex questions might then arise for consideration which did not need to be argued in this appeal'.[110] The Court did not elaborate but the lack of appropriate support facilities or clinical expertise are matters that might inhibit the making of arrangements to support a conditional release. In this respect, it seems that the clinical director may reach a conclusion in his managerial (as opposed to clinical) opinion that is not possible to facilitate the conditions proposed by the Board. That said, such an opinion should be supported by evidence rather than assertion: there is a fine line between an opinion that it is not possible to fulfil conditions proposed by the Board and one that seeks to nullify the Board's decision.

Concluding Remarks

The Criminal Law (Insanity) Act 2006 provided welcome, if belated, reform of the treatment of defendants who are found NGRI, with the abolition of mandatory indefinite detention and the implementation of a statutory review mechanism of those who are detained. As far as the substantive defence is concerned that Act represents a terse codification of the plea as developed by Irish courts. However, the opportunity to clarify further the elements of the defence was missed and Irish law awaits definitive resolution of the legal test of 'mental disorder', the nature of the knowledge component, and how broadly the notion of 'inability to refrain from acting' should be interpreted. While the decision in *Doyle v Wicklow County Council* represents an understandable desire to move from the restrictions associated with the traditional interpretation of the M'Naghten Rules, that objective might better have been achieved by a reworking of the knowledge component along the lines suggested above.

[109] ibid para 94.
[110] ibid para 95.

6

The Mental Disorder Defence

Canadian Law and Practice

Gerry Ferguson

Introduction

The mental disorder defence in Canada is a direct descendent of the common law insanity defence developed in England in the 18th and 19th centuries.[1] The common law on insanity as a defence ultimately crystallized in law based on the answers given by the judges to a set of questions addressed to them by the House of Lords in respect to the scope of the insanity defence. The judges' answers are referred to as the M'Naghten Rules.[2] From the beginning, the M'Naghten Rules evoked significant medical and legal criticism. However, the essence of the M'Naghten Rules have shown themselves, at least in Canada, to be more resilient and adaptable than most critics would have expected, and that continues to be so in Canada even after a significant reform to the treatment of mental disorder in criminal law in 1992.[3] Admittedly, as other chapters in this book demonstrate, many countries have abolished or have significantly altered the M'Naghten Rules, but several countries, including Canada, still follow a basic M'Naghten-style test for insanity.[4]

In this chapter, I intend to briefly review the survival of the M'Naghten test in Canada, in large part due to the Supreme Court's highly pragmatic and somewhat chameleon interpretation of it. I will also describe the difficult line between insane and non-insane automatism, some of the key rules of evidence and procedure which shape the defence's application, and the disposition options which flow from a successful verdict of not criminally responsible due to mental disorder

[1] See AM Platt and BL Diamond, 'The Origins and Development of the "Wild Beast" Concept of Mental Illness and its Relation to Theories of Criminal Responsibility' (1965) 1 J Hist Behav Sci 335; DN Robinson, *Wild Beasts and Idle Humours: The Insanity Defense from Antiquity to the Present* (Harvard University Press 1996).

[2] 10 Cl & F 200; 8 ER 718 (1843). See also Chapter 2 of this book for a more detailed account of the history of the insanity defence in England.

[3] An Act to amend the Criminal Code SC 1991 C43.

[4] G Ferguson, 'Insanity' in WC Chan, B Wright, and S Yeo (eds), *Codification, Macaulay and the Indian Penal Code* (Ashgate 2011) chapter 10.

Gerry Ferguson, *The Mental Disorder Defence* In: *The Insanity Defence*. Edited by: Ronnie Mackay and Warren Brookbanks, Oxford University Press. © Gerry Ferguson 2022. DOI: 10.1093/oso/9780198854944.003.0006

(NCRMD). Finally, I will examine what the available empirical studies in Canada tell us about the characteristics of those persons who have been found NCRMD.

Substantive Law in Respect to the Mental Disorder Defence

Origins of Canada's Insanity Defence

Canada had no legislative provision on the insanity defence until it enacted its own Criminal Code in 1892.[5] The Canadian Attorney General and his small drafting team expressly relied on the English Commissioners' 1880 Draft Criminal Code for England as the primary basis for the first Canadian Criminal Code.[6] The English Commissioners had been directed by their Attorney General to examine and amend as they deemed appropriate a draft Criminal Code Bill completed by James Fitzjames Stephen in 1878.[7] The English Commissioners' 1880 Criminal Code is their amended version of Stephen's 1878 Criminal Code Bill. In drafting Canada's Criminal Code, the Canadian drafters blindly followed the English Commissioners' Draft Code. In other words, they adopted the English Commissioners' provision on the insanity defence, without examining whether the Commissioners' changes to Stephens' draft Bill were in fact improvements and without looking at any other alternative suggestions for an insanity test.[8] Often the Commissioners' changes were not improvements, and arguably, that was the case with the insanity defence. The English Commissioners' insanity defence, and therefore, Canada's first codified insanity defence, are a direct replica of the M'Naghten Rules. Stephen's draft insanity defence was not.

Judicial Interpretation of the Canadian Insanity Defence

Canada's insanity test, as amended in 1992, currently states:

> 16(1) No person is criminally responsible for an act committed or an omission made while suffering from a mental disorder that rendered the person

[5] G Ferguson, 'From Jeremy Bentham to Anne McLellan: Lessons on Criminal Law Codification' in D Stuart (ed), *Towards a Clear and Just Criminal Law* (Carswell 1999) 192–218.

[6] The English Draft Criminal Code 1879 and the Report of the Royal Commission Appointed to Consider the Law Related to Indictable Offences (1879) and the Draft Code are reproduced in the British Parliamentary Papers, *Legal Administration: Criminal Law* (vol 6, Irish University Press 1971) 286.

[7] See House of Commons, Bill 178, 1878. See also JF Stephen, *A History of the Criminal Law of England* (vol 2, MacMillan & Co 1883) 167–80.

[8] G Parker, 'The Origins of the Canadian *Criminal Code*' in D Flaherty (ed), *Essays in the History of Canadian Law* (vol 1, Osgoode Society 1989) 249.

incapable of appreciating the nature and quality of the act or omission or knowing that it was wrong.

(2) Every person is presumed not to suffer from a mental disorder so as to be exempt from criminal responsibility by virtue of subsection (1), until the contrary is proven on the balance of probabilities.

(3) The burden of proof that an accused was suffering from a mental disorder so as to be exempt from criminal responsibility is on the party that raises the issue.

Canadian courts have focused primarily on the following eight issues in their interpretation of the insanity defence.

The meaning of 'disease of the mind'

The first requirement for the insanity defence is proof that the accused was suffering from 'a mental disorder' at the time of the criminal act. The M'Naghten Rules use the expression, 'a defect of reason, from his disease of the mind'. The English Commissioners in their 1879 Draft Code also used the words 'disease of the mind' in their insanity defence provision and therefore Canada followed suit in its 1892 Code. The words 'disease of the mind' continued to be used until 1992, when section 16 of the Criminal Code was amended by deleting the words 'disease of the mind' and substituting the words 'mental disorder'. But that deletion was nothing more than a 'sleight of hand'. Parliament resurrected 'disease of the mind' in the same amending statute by defining 'mental disorder' in section 2 of the Criminal Code as follows: 'mental disorder means a disease of the mind'. Hence, 'disease of the mind' is in fact, still part of the insanity defence in Canada.

The definition of 'disease of the mind' has always been left to the courts. At first, there was little controversy in Canadian courts over its meaning. However, by the 1950s, some debate and disagreement had arisen. In large part, this arose from some courts treating 'disease of the mind' as a medical, psychiatric expression. The courts were often faced with applying conflicting psychiatric expert testimony as to whether the accused's medical condition was a 'disease of the mind' according to *medical* standards. This resulted, for example, in 'psychopathy' being interpreted as a 'disease of the mind' in some cases, but not in others, depending on the psychiatric classification the expert psychiatric witnesses adhered to. This nonsense was finally ended in *R v Cooper*,[9] where the Supreme Court of Canada held that 'disease of the mind' has a legal meaning when used in section 16 of the Criminal Code, and therefore its meaning must be determined as a matter of law by judges, not as a question of scientific classification by the medical profession.[10] Since the 1980s, appeal courts, including the Supreme Court of Canada, have given a very wide

[9] (1980) 51 CCC (2d) 129 (SCC).

[10] ibid.

definition to the expression 'disease of the mind'. This is quite appropriate since determining whether the accused had a 'disease of the mind' is only a precondition to the real question: what effect did the disease or disorder have on the functioning of the accused's mind? The Supreme Court stated that 'disease of the mind' includes, 'any illness, disorder, or abnormal condition which impairs the human mind and its functioning'.[11] This broad definition now ensures that a wide range of mental impairments are not automatically excluded from consideration based on psychiatric labels. The Supreme Court's definition does, however, expressly exclude two forms of abnormal mental functioning based on policy grounds:

First, if the mental disorder is of a temporary nature as a result of voluntary intoxication, the accused must rely upon the rules that govern voluntary intoxication as a defence and is not permitted to rely on the insanity defence.

Second, if the accused's mental disorder arises from non-insane automatism (eg, by a physical blow to the head), the accused may rely on the defence of automatism, which results in an unqualified acquittal. However, if the mental impairment arises from insane automatism, only the insanity defence, not the more favourable automatism defence, is available. The difficult distinction between the legal categories of insanity and non-insane automatism will be canvassed later in this chapter.[12]

Incapable of knowing or appreciating versus not actually knowing or appreciating

There appears to be an anomaly in the language used to describe the defence of insanity compared to the defence of intoxication. The M'Naghten Rules refer specifically in both branches of the insanity test to an absence of *actual knowledge* (ie 'did not know'), rather than an *incapacity to know*.[13] The 1879 English Commissioners' Draft Code, and section 16 of the Canadian Criminal Code, use the expression, 'incapable of appreciating or knowing' rather than 'did not in fact appreciate or know'.[14] The expression 'incapable of appreciating' is a higher test than 'actually appreciating'. Obviously, if an accused is *not capable* of appreciating or knowing, then they did not actually appreciate or know. However, it is possible for an accused not to appreciate or know some fact even though they retain the *capacity* to appreciate or know it, had their mind been directed to it. Very little attention, until recently, has been drawn to this distinction in the insanity defence.

By contrast, the classic statement on the defence of intoxication by the House of Lords in *DPP v Beard*[15] in 1920 uses the words 'incapable of forming the specific

[11] ibid 144.

[12] See 'Sane and insane automatism'.

[13] According to the M'Naghten Rules, the defence of insanity applies where the accused is 'labouring under such a defect of reason from disease of the mind as not to know the nature and quality of the act he was doing, or if he did know it, that he did not know he was doing what was wrong'.

[14] Section 22 of the English Commissions Draft Code states in part, 'incapable of appreciating the nature and quality of the act or that the act was wrong'.

[15] [1920] AC 479 (PC).

intent' essential to constitute the crime. But in 1964, in *Broadhurst v the Queen*,[16] the Judicial Committee of the Privy Council criticized the use of 'incapacity' in the intoxication defence. Lord Devlin recognized that the proper test for intoxication as a defence was to inquire into the accused's 'actual intent' rather than the accused's 'incapacity to intend'.[17] This distinction was ignored in Canadian case law until the mid-1980s. However, it is now considered an error of law which may result in a new trial to instruct a jury on 'capacity' without making it clear that the ultimate issue is whether the accused 'actually had' the required intent for the offence.[18]

In regard to the defence of insanity, recent case law has adopted the exact opposite to what applies to the intoxication defence. To describe the insanity test as 'not appreciating' rather than 'incapable of appreciating' the nature and quality of the act is now considered a serious error.[19] However, reliance on 'incapacity' as the proper test leaves an anomalous gap in the insanity defence. Suppose A shoots and kills B at a time when A is suffering from a 'disease of the mind'. Under his paranoid delusion, A thinks that the person entering his house is a dangerous assailant coming to kill him. Instead, it turns out that B is his eldest son. A *did not appreciate* that his act was an unlawful attack on an innocent person. He thought it was a lawful act of self-defence. But despite his paranoia, he was *capable of appreciating* that fact and not shooting the person, if someone simply had told him it was his son, not an assailant. Since he was 'capable of appreciating the nature of his act' he does not, strictly speaking, qualify for the insanity defence. But, since he thought he was acting in self-defence, he does not have the mens rea for murder and therefore he is entitled to an acquittal on a charge of murder. Surely, Parliament would want A to be found NCRMD, not simply acquitted of murder in such circumstances. After all, his mistake of fact arose out of his paranoid delusion.

Are the words 'appreciate' and 'know' synonymous?

The M'Naghten Rules used the word 'know' for both branches of the insanity defence. Stephen, in his draft Bill, also used the word 'know' in both branches whereas the English Commissioners used the word 'appreciate' rather than 'know' for both branches. And just to make things interesting, the Canadian codifiers used the word 'appreciate' for the first branch, and 'know' for the second branch. Neither the English Commissioners nor the Canadian drafters made any mention of the fact that 'appreciate' was being used instead of 'know' or that they expressly chose 'appreciate' because they thought it had a broader meaning. To the contrary, the fact that the English Commissioners stated that their insanity provision 'expresses the

[16] [1964] AC 441 (PC 1963).

[17] G Ferguson, '*Mens Rea* Evaluated in Terms of Essential Elements of a Crime: Specific Intent, and Drunkenness' (1971) 4 Ottawa LR 356–88.

[18] *R v Daley* 2007 SCC 53, para 102.

[19] *R v McBride* (2018) 45 CR 7th 341 (Ont CA).

existing law' (ie the M'Naghten Rules) seems to suggest that the Commissioners did not think they were expanding the law by inserting 'appreciate' in place of 'know'.

However, in 1956, the Royal Commission on Insanity[20] concluded that the Canadian insanity test was not in need of expansion because the Canadian test was much wider than the M'Naghten test. The Canadian Commission stated that the word 'know' in the M'Naghten Rules restricted the insanity defence to a mere cognitive test, whereas the words 'incapable of appreciating' in the Canadian test went far beyond that. In 1980, the Supreme Court of Canada in the cases of *R v Cooper*[21] and *R v Barnier*[22] cited the Royal Commission's opinion on the wider meaning of 'appreciate'. In particular, the Supreme Court held that the words 'know' and 'appreciate' are not synonymous and that the word 'appreciate' was used by the drafters of the Code, 'to make it clear that cognition was not to be the sole criterion'.[23] The Court held that 'appreciate' involves an '[e]motional, as well as intellectual awareness of the significance of the conduct'.[24] The Court also added that the word appreciate 'imports an additional requirement to mere knowledge of the physical quality of the act. The requirement, unique to Canada, is that of perception, an ability to perceive the consequences, impact and results of a physical act.'[25]

However, in the subsequent cases of *R v Kjeldsen*[26] and *R v Abbey*,[27] in which the insanity defence was rejected on the facts of those cases, the Supreme Court of Canada effectively narrowed, if not completely eliminated, this 'unique' Canadian requirement. The Supreme Court applied a narrow cognitive test to the requirement that the accused 'appreciate' the nature and quality of his act. Thus, the Canadian test reverted back to a narrow M'Naghten cognitive test. The Court's judgment in *Kjeldsen* was no doubt driven by the different types of mental impairment in *Cooper* and *Barnier* versus the type of mental disorders in *Kjeldsen* and *Abbey*. *Cooper* and *Barnier* were cases involving accused persons with paranoid psychoses. On the other hand, *Kjeldsen* was a dangerous sexual psychopath, devoid of any emotional understanding of his conduct but not suffering from psychosis. In *Kjeldsen*, the Supreme Court held that 'appreciating' the nature of an act *only* requires 'knowing the nature of the act and its *physical* consequences'. The emotional component of appreciating an act was dispensed with. The fact that the accused had no emotional appreciation of the impact of his conduct was not a basis for finding the accused NCRMD.

[20] Report of the Royal Commission on the Law of Insanity as a Defence in Criminal Cases (Ottawa, Canada, 1956).
[21] (1980) 51 CCC (2d) 129 (SCC).
[22] (1980) 51 CCC (2d) 193 (SCC).
[23] (1980) 51 CCC (2d) 129 (SCC), 145.
[24] ibid.
[25] ibid 147.
[26] (1981) 24 CR (3d) 289 (SCC).
[27] (1982) 68 CCC (2d) 394 (SCC).

After *Kjeldsen*, courts of appeal partially revived the wider *Cooper* definition of appreciate. Those courts held that appreciate involves more than the barest cognitive awareness of the physical act and its physical consequences.[28] But in 1991, the Supreme Court again reasserted a bare minimum meaning for the word 'appreciates' in *R v Landry*.[29] The accused in *Landry* was a paranoid schizophrenic who believed that the person he shot was Satan and that he was on a Divine mission, whereby it became necessary to kill that person. The Court of Appeal held that under these circumstances, the accused was not capable of 'appreciating' the nature and quality of his act. But the Supreme Court reversed that finding and held that the accused did know he was shooting another person (albeit he thought that person was Satan] and knew the physical consequences of shooting a person could cause death. The Supreme Court held that knowledge of those facts was enough to find the accused 'appreciated' the nature and quality of his act. Wow, what a narrowing of the meaning of 'appreciate'! The Supreme Court did nonetheless find the accused NCRMD, but on the basis of the second branch of the test, that is, the accused was incapable of knowing that his act was wrong.

Knowing that the act was wrong

The second branch of the M'Naghten test, that is, 'the accused did not know he was doing what was wrong' left some uncertainty as to the intended meaning of the word 'wrong'. Did it mean wrong according to law, or wrong in the moral sense, that is, that it was an act he ought not do? In 1952, the English Court of Appeal in *R v Windle*[30] held that the word 'wrong' meant contrary to law, rather than morally wrong. That interpretation was confirmed by the English Court of Appeal in 2007 in *R v Johnson*.[31] On the other hand, the High Court of Australia in *Stapleton v The Queen*[32] expressly declined to follow *Windle*. The High Court held that an accused can rely on the insanity defence if he knew his act was contrary to law but believed his act was morally right according to the ordinary moral standards of reasonable persons. In Canada, the Supreme Court flip-flopped on the meaning of 'wrong'. In 1976, in *R v Schwartz*,[33] the Supreme Court followed *Windle* and held that wrong only meant legally wrong, not morally wrong. However, in 1990, in *R v Chaulk*,[34] the Supreme Court reversed *Schwartz*, and held that the insanity defence applies if the accused 'is incapable of understanding that the act is wrong according to the ordinary moral standards of reasonable members of society'.[35]

[28] See *R v Kirkby* (1985) 21 CCC (3d) 31 (ONCA); *R v Swain* (1986) 24 CCC (3d) 385 (ONCA); and *R v Charest* (1990) 57 CCC (3d) 312, 333–34 (QUECA).
[29] [1991] 1 SCR 99.
[30] [1952] 2 QB 826.
[31] [2007] EWCA Crim 1978.
[32] (1952) 86 CLR 358.
[33] (1976) 29 CCC (2d) 1 (SCC).
[34] (1990) 62 CCC (3d) 193 (SCC).
[35] ibid 232–33.

The combination of the narrow definition of 'appreciate' in the first branch of the insanity defence in *Landry*, and the broad definition of 'wrong' in the second branch in *Chaulk* has meant that the majority of successful insanity pleas are now decided under the second branch rather than the first branch as they once were. Thankfully, the second branch was given some real traction in 1990 by a majority of the Supreme Court in *Chaulk*,[36] and by a unanimous Supreme Court in 1994 in *R v Oommen*.[37] In *Oommen*, the accused suffered from psychosis with paranoid delusions. He believed that members of his Union wanted to 'destroy' him and that a Union member had been sent to kill him. The accused believed that he had to kill that person to prevent her from killing him. Expert evidence suggested that the accused had not lost the intellectual capacity to understand right from wrong, or that killing a person except in self-defence is wrong, but that the accused's delusions would affect his interpretation of events. In a unanimous Supreme Court decision, the accused's conviction was reversed and a new trial ordered. The Court held, 'the crux of the inquiry is whether the accused lacks the capacity to *rationally* [evaluate and] decide whether the act is right or wrong and hence to make a *rational* choice about whether to do it or not' (emphasis added).[38] The Court further added that the accused's 'delusion would have deprived the accused of the ability to know that his act was wrong; in his eyes it was right'.[39] And the Court also stated, '[W]e are not here concerned with the psychopath or person who follows a personal and deviant code of right and wrong ... s.16(1) of the *Criminal Code* embraces not only the intellectual ability to know right from wrong, but the capacity to apply that knowledge to the situation at hand'.[40] *Oommen* was liberally applied for the next 20 years,[41] but during the past five years or so, some cases have given *Oommen* a more restrictive application.[42]

Irresistible impulse

In Canada, the Supreme Court has clearly rejected the argument that irresistible impulse is part of the insanity defence, in cases such as *R v Borg*[43] and *R v Chartrand*,[44] notwithstanding that Stephen and Canada's Royal Commission on Insanity were of the view that the words 'incapable of appreciating the nature and quality of the act' were broad enough to include true cases of irresistible impulse. The M'Naghten Rules do not recognize any form of volitional incapacity arising

[36] ibid 1351–56.
[37] [1994] 2 SCR 507, 516–23.
[38] ibid.
[39] ibid.
[40] ibid.
[41] See eg *R v Szostack*, 2012 ONCA 503.
[42] See eg *R v Campione*, 2015 ONCA 67; *R v Dobson*, 2018 ONCA 589; *R v McBride*, 2018 ONCA 323; and *R v Baker*, 2010 SCC 9.
[43] [1969] SCR 551.
[44] [1977] 1 SCR 314.

from a 'disease of the mind' as a separate basis for insanity. Although Stephen argued that the insanity defence should include an irresistible impulse provision, the English Commissioners expressly excluded Stephen's recommendation in their Draft Code of 1879. Canada and New Zealand[45] followed the English Commissioners' provision and therefore did not include that component in the insanity provisions in their first Criminal Codes in 1892 and 1893 respectively.[46]

Absence of a volitional component is a fatal flaw

The Supreme Court has stated many times that there can be no criminal liability unless the accused's conduct was voluntary. Thus, a very strong claim can be made that the basic principles of criminal liability require the inclusion of a volitional limb in the insanity defence. Put simply, the criminal law and the imposition of criminal sanctions are based on the assumption that human beings are both rational and autonomous. The criminal law assumes that ordinary persons have the capacity to reason right from wrong and the capacity to choose right or wrong. These assumptions may be incorrect, or at least not in perfect accord with modern, social-scientific insights into human behaviour, but they are, and are likely to remain for a long time, the theoretical assumptions underlying our criminal law. It is these dual capacities—reason and choice—which give moral justification to imposing criminal responsibility and punishment on offenders. In other words, if a person can reason right from wrong and has the ability to choose between right or wrong, then if that person consciously chooses wrong, the attribution of responsibility and punishment is morally justified or deserved. To the extent that criminal law theory is based on a conception of human beings as rational and autonomous individuals, both attributes—reason and will—are relevant to imposing criminal responsibility on an individual. If there is no ability to reason, or no ability to choose, due to mental impairment, then conviction and punishment for conduct committed under such circumstances would be immoral. It is for this reason that a morally defensible insanity test must include some consideration of both cognitive and volitional impairment.

An influential formulation of the volitional limb of the insanity defence can be found in the 1962 US Model Penal Code provision on insanity (s 4.01(1)) where the drafters used the expression 'lacks substantial capacity ... to conform his conduct to the requirements of the law'.[47] Goldstein favourably comments on the inclusion of this volitional component in the insanity test, further noting that the word 'conform' is preferable to the word 'control' and that the proposal is a vast improvement over the misleading words 'irresistible impulse'.[48] In Australia,[49] most

[45] See Chapter 7.
[46] Ferguson (n 4) 251–53.
[47] Ferguson (n 4) 252. See Chapter 9.
[48] Ferguson (n 4) 91.
[49] See Chapter 8.

jurisdictions have adopted a volitional limb as part of their insanity test and have adopted the words 'capacity to control his or her actions' or 'unable to control his or her actions'.[50] The Australian expressions seem preferable to me.

Is a defence of diminished responsibility needed?

Because the test for proving insanity has traditionally been quite high in many jurisdictions, the insanity defence very often fails even in cases where the accused was seriously mentally disordered at the time of the offence. This reality has prompted a few jurisdictions to introduce a partial defence of diminished responsibility where mental disorder short of the legal definition of insanity can reduce murder (including a few jurisdictions where murder is still punishable by death) to manslaughter, with flexible sentencing options.[51] However, Canada is one of the countries that has not created a diminished responsibility defence at common law or statutorily.[52]

Sane and insane automatism

As already noted, it is a fundamental principle of criminal liability that no conduct can be criminal unless it has been done voluntarily, that is, through a willed physical act or omission. The word 'automatism' describes a condition in which the accused is still capable of performing some acts but does not have conscious control over what he or she is doing. This absence of conscious control renders the accused's conduct involuntary, and therefore not deserving of conviction and punishment.[53] Perhaps the biggest challenge for the insanity defence is making it clear which cases of automatism should be considered under the insanity defence (ie insane automatism) and which cases should be classified as non-insane automatism, whereby the result is an unqualified acquittal.

In Canada, the distinction between sane and insane automatism (now named mental disorder and non-mental disorder automatism) is governed by the 1999 Supreme Court decision in *R v Stone*,[54] in which the majority significantly restricted the scope of the defence of sane automatism. When there is some evidence that the accused's conduct was performed while the accused was totally or substantially unconscious, the cause of that unconsciousness must be determined:

[50] Ferguson (n 4) 253.

[51] See eg Scotland, Criminal Justice and Licensing (Scotland) Act 2010, s 168 (see Chapter 4); England, Homicide Act 1957, UK, c11 s 2, significantly revised in 2009, see RD Mackay, The Coroners and Justice Act 2009 (2) 'The New Diminished Responsibility Plea' [2010] Crim LR 290; Singapore, Penal Code, Singapore, s 300, exception 7 (1961); Queensland, Criminal Code, Queensland, s 304A (1961); New South Wales, Crimes Act, New South Wales, s 23A (1974) (see Chapter 8).

[52] In *R v Dobson*, 2018 ONCA 589, paras 34–38, the court held that it is only Parliament, and not the courts, that can create such a defence.

[53] See the previous section, 'Absence of a volitional component is a fatal flaw'.

[54] [1999] 2 SCR 290.

(i) if it was caused by voluntary intoxication by alcohol or drugs, the accused's only defence is intoxication;[55]
(ii) if it was caused by a 'disease of the mind,' the accused's only defence is insanity;[56] and
(iii) if it was caused by a factor other than voluntary intoxication or a 'disease of the mind' (e.g. a concussion caused by a blow to the head), then the accused can rely on (sane) automatism as a defence, and thereby obtain an unqualified acquittal.

In deciding whether the accused's substantially impaired consciousness was caused by a 'disease of the mind', the Supreme Court in *Stone* applied a 'holistic' test, composed of three distinct strands or theories: (1) the internal cause theory, (2) the continuing danger theory, and (3) the holistic approach. The holistic approach is informed by the internal cause and continuing danger theories, as well as policy concerns which include (a) fear of fabrication, (b) public disillusionment with an outright acquittal under automatism, and (c) public safety concerns based on the unqualified acquittal for automatism which does not provide for subsequent monitoring or treatment if required.

The Supreme Court held that it will only be in rare cases that automatism is not caused by a 'disease of the mind', and therefore trial judges should start from that position and decide if the evidence is strong enough to take the case out of the 'disease of the mind' category. The Supreme Court listed a number of factors (not intended to be a closed list) that should be considered in determining whether the alleged automatism was caused by 'a disease of the mind':[57]

- the severity of the stimulus that allegedly triggered automatism;
- corroborating evidence of the accused's behaviour by others;
- corroborating medical history of automatistic-like dissociative states;
- the presence or absence of a motive for the criminal offence; and
- the relationship between the alleged trigger of automatism and the victim of the automatistic violence.

While there is some judicial disagreement, the following conditions, which have resulted in claims of unconsciousness, have been treated as a 'disease of the mind' and therefore classified as insanity:[58]

[55] *R v Bouchard-Lebrun*, 2011 SCC 58.
[56] (1980) 51 CCC (2d) 129 (SCC).
[57] *Stone* [1999] 2 SCR 290, paras 189–91. In *Ghiorghita*, 2019 BCCA 59, the court clarified that no single factor is determinative and that a person could be found to be in a state of sane automatism even if the aforementioned factors are present (or vice versa). The presence or absence of the factors will simply make it more difficult to prove automatism.
[58] Ferguson (n 4) 246–47.

- epilepsy;
- cerebral arteriosclerosis;
- diabetic hypoglycaemic attacks;
- sleepwalking/somnambulism; and
- dissociative state caused by ordinary stresses and disappointments of life (eg loss of a job, breakup or rejection in a relationship with others, etc).

On the other hand, while there is some judicial disagreement, the following conditions which have resulted in claims of unconsciousness have been classified as sane automatism:[59]

- a concussion caused by a physical blow to the head;
- a psychological blow from an *extraordinary external event* which could cause an average, normal person to go into a dissociative state;
- sudden stroke;
- delirium from illness or infection;
- sleepwalking, if the risk of reoccurrence is low; and
- involuntary intoxication.

If a person is acting in a state of substantially altered consciousness (eg sleepwalking, concussion, or a severe dissociative state), that person will not normally know the nature and quality of his or her act, or that it is wrong. In such cases, it is the definition of 'disease of the mind' which will determine whether that form of automatism will be classified as insane or non-insane. In most jurisdictions, the distinction is based on pragmatic policy grounds, fair and appropriate labelling, and perhaps most dominantly, protection of the public from the predicted risk of future harm. Although there are concerns with labelling epileptic, diabetic, or sleepwalking accused persons as insane, the perceived concerns for public protection very often trump fair labelling concerns, and thus those conditions are frequently classified as insane automatism. The question becomes how should the law distinguish between sane and insane automatism? I have discussed three options elsewhere:[60]

1) treat all forms of automatism as insanity;
2) treat automatism as a special verdict (ie not criminally responsible due to automatism), followed by optional special disposition provisions when public safety is at stake; or
3) draft a code provision which specifically classifies the common forms of automatism as either non-insane automatism or insane automatism.

[59] ibid.
[60] ibid 244–47.

In my opinion, option one is not appropriate, primarily on the basis of unfair labelling concerns. Option two solves unfair labelling concerns and satisfies public safety concerns, but strangely, it has faced widespread opposition by many others.[61] Consequentially, option three, which currently exists in various forms in many countries, is likely to continue as the most popular choice.

Some Procedural and Evidentiary Issues

Burden and Quantum of Proof

The M'Naghten Rules state that 'every man is presumed to be sane … until the contrary be proved to their satisfaction'.[62] I consider this reverse onus and burden of proof a historic anomaly which should have been overruled years ago.[63] However, this evidentiary rule has been followed in Canada ever since M'Naghten. Section 16(2) of the current Criminal Code provides that an accused is presumed sane until the contrary is proven 'on the balance of probabilities'. This is a higher standard and quantum of proof than for most other defences. Most defences (eg mistake of fact, intoxication negating specific intent, self defence, etc) succeed unless the Crown can disprove the defence beyond a reasonable doubt, once there is *some* evidence that the defence may have existed. But in the case of insanity, the defence will not succeed unless it is proven on a balance of probabilities by the party that raises the defence that the defence existed. I have argued elsewhere that placing the burden of proof on a balance of probabilities is an unreasonable violation of principles of fundamental justice,[64] but that argument was rejected by all but one of the Supreme Court justices in *Chaulk*.[65] It is regrettable that the Supreme Court has not reconsidered that holding in *Chaulk* for the past 25 years.[66] Instead, the Supreme Court has in effect expanded the reverse onus in the insanity defence by applying it to two other defences that are somewhat akin to the insanity defence: non-insane automatism[67] and extreme intoxication akin to automatism.[68]

[61] ibid 245. I am not aware of any jurisdiction which currently uses option two. My proposal of option two was adopted in a government White Paper entitled 'Proposals to Amend the *Criminal Code* (General Principles) (June 1993)'. However, it was subsequently rejected by most groups including the Parliamentary Subcommittee, the Canadian Bar Association Criminal Code Taskforce, and the Canadian Association of Law Teachers Submission.

[62] Ibid. See (n 2).

[63] G Ferguson, 'The Insanity Defence in Canada, Malaysia, and Singapore: A Tale of Two Codes' (1990) 1 JMCL 20–25.

[64] ibid; and G Ferguson, 'A Critique of Proposals to Reform the Insanity Defence' (1989) 14 Queen's LJ 135, 147–49.

[65] (1990) 62 CCC (3d) 193 (SCC).

[66] eg Davies J in *R v Ejigu*, 2016 BCSC 1487, disagreed with *Chaulk* (1990) 62 CCC (3d) 193 (SCC) on the burden of proof issue, and had the trial judge not been bound by stare decisis to follow *Chaulk*, the judge would have reached a different conclusion by reading down s 16(2) and (3), see paras 436–38.

[67] *R v Stone*, 1999 CanLII 688 (SCC) reversing the holding in *R v Rabey*, 1980 CanLII 44 (SCC).

[68] *R v Daviault*, 1994 CanLII 61 (SCC).

Who Can Raise the Mental Disorder Defence?

It sounds strange to ask the above question—generally speaking, it is the accused who raises defences. Why would the prosecutor raise a defence? In the case of the insanity defence, for a very long time, the consequences of the NGRI verdict resulted in an automatic indeterminate order for confinement in an asylum (potentially for life) with virtually no legal oversight or appeal. That disposition was far more severe and, from the prosecutor's point of view, potentially provided more public protection than a conviction and sentence for the offence. Thus, the NGRI verdict was often favoured by prosecutors and often resisted by accused persons.

The Supreme Court addressed the appropriateness of this practice in 1991 in *R v Swain*.[69] The Court held that the common law rule, which allowed the Crown to raise evidence of insanity during the trial against the accused's wishes, was an unreasonable violation of principles of fundamental justice guaranteed in section 7 of the Charter. The majority took the view that the decision whether or not to raise the issue of insanity is part and parcel of an accused's right to control his or her own defence, which is a fundamental precept of our adversarial system and founded on respect for the autonomy and dignity of human beings. The majority replaced the common law rule with the following set of rules, including the possibility of a bifurcated trial process: (1) the insanity defence may be raised *during the trial* by the accused; or (2) *during the trial* by the prosecutor, but only if, in the trial judge's opinion, the accused has put his or her mental capacity for criminal intent in issue;[70] or (3) by either the accused or the Crown *after* the trier of fact has concluded that the accused was guilty of the offence, but before that verdict of guilty is formally entered by the trial judge (in which case, the so-called bifurcated trial is held to decide the insanity defence issue).[71] If there is some evidence of insanity, but the accused and prosecutor, for their own reasons, choose not to raise the defence, it is has not been conclusively settled whether the trial judge should raise it of their own accord.[72]

[69] *R v Swain* (1986) 24 CCC (3d) 385 (ONCA).

[70] In *R v Faire*, 2020 BCCA 110, the Court held that the trial judge wrongly concluded that the accused had put his mental capacity for criminal intent in issue, and therefore the trial judge had no authority at that point to allow the Crown to raise the NCRMD defence. See also other cases on the Crown's right to raise the insanity defence during trial: *R v Kindersley*, 2020 ONCJ 349 and *R v Brown*, 2006 BCSC 1581.

[71] For the unusual circumstance where a trial judge dismisses the jury before the NCRMD issue is heard, see *R v Watts*, 2020 ONSC 4671. Here, the court decided they could proceed hearing the NCRMD issue without a jury after the jury returned a verdict, even in the case that the jury had not been dismissed because of the potentially indefinite delays involved due to the COVID-19 pandemic. The trial judge found that this 'remedy' (being able to hear and adjudicate the NCRMD issue) was part of the inherent jurisdiction of the provincial superior court and accorded with the principles of fundamental justice: para 38.

[72] While the court in *R v Piette* [2005] BCJ No 2688 found that the court could not do so, and cited *R v Swain* (1986) 24 CCC (3d) 385 (ONCA) as the authority for this proposition, this conclusion was questioned in *R v Fluxgold*, 2009 ONCJ 201, where the court was ready to consider NCRMD on its own, until the Crown changed its mind and raised the issue. See to the same effect, *R v Harvey*, 2014 BCSC 1692.

NCRMD Accused in Canada

Canada lacks centralized and comprehensive data on persons found NCRMD, and on their subsequent dispositions and supervision under provincial Review Boards. This lack of national data extends to the number of cases in which NCRMD is pleaded and the number of times it succeeds. The shortfall in data has four significant impacts:

(1) it can lead to policy and legislative decisions that do not reflect empirical evidence on recidivism and risk;
(2) it can leave hidden the unwarranted discrepancies in the trends of decisions by courts and provincial Review Boards;
(3) it can obscure the true nature of the impact of the NCRMD verdict on mentally ill persons, causing misconceptions in the general public; and
(4) it can cloud the impact of dwindling mental health resources on mentally ill persons.[73]

Together, these shortcomings in data aid and abet legislative and policy decisions that are at odds with balancing the rights of the NCRMD person and public safety concerns, and that disregard the moral imperative of the NCRMD verdict. That imperative proclaims that such persons are not to be *punished* for their actions because they were not morally responsible for the offence due to their mental disorder.

Despite the lack of centralized data, some recent inquiries, particularly the National Trajectory Project, give some insight into people generally found NCRMD and their subsequent dispositions.[74]

The dominant number of NCRMD accused are male, and are an average of 37 years old.[75] Approximately 50% have a high school diploma, 75% were single at the time of the index offence, more than 33% lived alone, while less than 50% resided with a spouse, family, or friends, 66% were born in Canada, around 10% were homeless, and nearly 75% were receiving governmental income support.[76] Perhaps the most startling statistic was that only 2.9% of NCRMD accused were Aboriginal. Since Aboriginal people are overrepresented by a multiple of seven in the Canadian justice system, this low statistic suggests that this defence is being

[73] See AG Crocker and others, 'The National Trajectory Project of Individuals Found Not Criminally Responsible on Account of Mental Disorder in Canada. Part 2: The People Behind the Label' (2015) 60(3) Can J Psychiatry 106, 107.

[74] For an outline of the study, and its limitations, see AG Crocker, 'The National Trajectory Project on Individuals Found Not Criminally Responsible on Account of Mental Disorder' (2015) 60(3) Can J Psychiatry 96.

[75] Crocker (n 73) 108.

[76] ibid.

disproportionally underemployed for Aboriginal accused.[77] Troublingly, after Aboriginal persons are found NCRMD, they spend 'substantially more' time under Review Board control.[78]

Most NCRMD accused had a serious mental illness at the time of the index verdict, with the most common being a psychotic spectrum disorder.[79] Substance use disorders appeared in 33% of NCRMD accused, with 32.7% having a serious mental illness alongside a personality or substance use disorder.[80] Only around 10% had a personality disorder diagnosis at the time of verdict.[81] At the time of the offence, nearly 50% of cases mentioned delusions, almost 20% mentioned hallucinations, less than 10% mentioned suicidal or homicidal ideation and around 25% mentioned alcohol or drug abuse.[82] However, it is notable that there were significant differences between provinces on all of these statistics, except for substance use.[83] Additionally, 72% of NCRMD accused had at least one psychiatric hospitalization prior to the offence, with two being the median number of psychiatric hospitalizations prior to the offence.[84]

Despite public perception to the contrary, only 7% of index offences for NCRMD accused were homicides or attempted murder.[85] That said, 65% of cases involved offences against the person,[86] while only 17% were property offences.[87] Family members, parents in particular, are the most likely to be victims, with children being victims in less than 3% of cases.[88] Strangers are the most likely victims for sexual offences, whereas family members and partners or ex-partners are the most likely victims in homicides or attempted homicides.[89] Professionals (ie health care workers and police) are the second most likely victims in NCRMD offences.[90]

[77] The exact reason for this discrepancy is unknown. However, it is not unreasonable to suggest that this results from lack of adequate legal representation, reflecting the often low socioeconomic status of Aboriginal persons in Canada. It may also be due to implicit biases about Aboriginal persons and criminality. More data and inquiry in this respect are essential. ibid 114.

[78] J Latimer and A Lawrence, *Review Board Systems in Canada: An Overview of Results from the Mentally Disordered Accused Data Collection Study* (Department of Justice, Research and Statistics Division 2006) 39.

[79] Crocker (n 73) 108.

[80] ibid.

[81] ibid.

[82] ibid.

[83] ibid.

[84] ibid. Further details on the number of previous hospitalizations and psychiatric history can be found at ibid 108–09.

[85] ibid 114.

[86] It is not entirely clear what constitutes an 'offence against the person' in the National Trajectory study. More specifically, 2.3% of offences were sex offences, 26.5% were assaults, 1.8% were deprivation of freedom, and 27.4% were threats and/or other offences against a person: ibid 110.

[87] ibid 109. The relatively low number of property offences is somewhat surprising, considering that in 2013, Statistics Canada found that over half of all reported criminal offences were property crime violations: see A Thatcher, 'Property Crime' Royal Canadian Mounted Police Gazette 77(3) (2015) (<https://www.rcmp-grc.gc.ca/en/gazette/property-crime>).

[88] Crocker (n 73) 106.

[89] ibid.

[90] ibid.

Around 50% of NCRMD accused have a prior conviction or NCRMD verdict.[91] Perhaps surprisingly, only 8.2% had a previous NCRMD verdict.[92]

While the National Trajectory Project did provide statistics to generate a vision of the NCRMD accused, the project also emphasized the heterogeneity of those found NCRMD, and that this heterogeneity varied by province.[93] Quebec, which had the highest rates of NCRMD accused, also had the greatest degree of heterogeneity.[94] British Columbia had the highest rates of substance use disorders being concomitant with serious mental illness.[95] Such discrepancies suggest two key insights: the application of the NCRMD defence appears to vary by province, and *place and setting* may impact the number of persons who manifest symptoms of NCRMD.

Review Boards

In addition to the above data on NCRMD persons, it is also essential to scrutinize the treatment and supervision of persons found NCRMD.[96] The little data that exists raises some cause for concern. While the rates of recidivism after an NCRMD verdict are quite low, particularly for violent index offences,[97] 22% of NCRMD persons spend at least ten years in the Review Board system.[98] This may, but need not, suggest that NCRMD patients are being held in custody or under supervision longer than necessary. This further suggests that the factors being taken into consideration in order to continue supervision of an NCRMD accused under a Review Board are not driven by evidence, but by emotion and public perception. Indeed, causing an NCRMD person to be held under Review Board supervision for longer durations to complement the severity of an offence looks unnervingly like the application of punishment and therefore contrary to the moral basis for the NCRMD verdict.[99]

Data suggests that there is little consistency among Review Boards in the consideration of variables in making a disposition decision.[100] This lack of consistency

[91] ibid.
[92] ibid 112.
[93] ibid 114.
[94] ibid.
[95] ibid.
[96] The National Trajectory Project provides some data in AG Crocker and others, 'The National Trajectory Project of Individuals Found Not Criminally Responsible on Account of Mental Disorder in Canada. Part 3: Trajectories and Outcomes Through the Forensic System' (2015) 60(3) Can J Psychiatry 117.
[97] ibid 125.
[98] Latimer and Lawrence (n 78) 34.
[99] Crocker (n 96) 125.
[100] AG Crocker and others, 'Dynamic and Static Factors Associated with Discharge Dispositions: The National Trajectory Project of Individuals Found Not Criminally Responsible on Account of Mental Disorder (NCRMD) in Canada' 32 Behav Sci Law (2014) 577, 577–95.

undermines procedural justice and may result in unduly limiting the freedoms of NCRMD accused. In particular, the lack of consistency in using structured forensic risk assessments is a cause for concern. Where such risk assessments are used, conditional discharges are significantly more common than when they are not.[101] With Review Boards consistently being faced with more cases, remedying these procedural gaps is necessary to ensure the rights of NCRMD accused.

Dispositions

Once a verdict of NCRMD is pronounced by a judge or jury, then a disposition hearing will be held by the court or, if the court wishes, the case will be referred to the provincial Review Board for the purpose of making a disposition order. There are three dispositions available:[102]

a) absolute discharge;[103]
b) conditional discharge;[104] or
c) detained in custody in a hospital, subject to any appropriate conditions.

The choice of disposition must represent a balancing of the 'twin goals': the protection of the public and the protection of the rights of the accused and their fair and appropriate treatment.[105] This balancing is achieved when the disposition order meets the criteria set out in section 672.54. Prior to an amendment in 2014, section 672.54 stated that the primary concern was to find the 'least onerous and least restrictive' disposition considering the need to protect the public, the accused's mental condition, the reintegration of the accused into society, and other needs of the accused.[106] However, the 2014 amendments replaced the terminology 'least onerous and least restrictive' disposition with terminology that stated the primary requirement is to impose the disposition that is 'necessary and appropriate in the circumstances' and the amending provision added that the safety of the public was 'the paramount consideration' in determining NCRMD dispositions. It is hard to identify the exact impact of this change of emphasis on public safety (arguably at the expense of the NCRMD persons' rights): most cases continue

[101] ibid 588.

[102] Criminal Code, s 672.54.

[103] An absolute discharge shall be made where the NCRMD person 'is not a significant threat to the safety of the public'. Those who are absolutely discharged are no longer within the criminal justice system, nor are they subject to Review Board: *R v Conway*, 2010 SCC 22, para 92.

[104] Conditional dispositions include supervision, and often prescribe that an NCRMD accused must reside in a particular place, refrain from substance use and/or possessing weapons, follow a treatment plan, and check in with a professional, like a psychiatrist, on a schedule. The National Trajectory Project found that the imposition of conditions varied by province (n 96).

[105] *R v Conway*, 2010 SCC 22, para 88.

[106] Latimer and Lawrence (n 78) 2.

to follow the proposition that the 'least onerous and least restrictive' disposition must be found, citing *Winko* for this proposition.[107] Additionally, in *R v Winko*,[108] the Supreme Court of Canada stated that unless the accused presents a 'significant threat' to the safety of the public, a Review Board or the court must order an absolute discharge.[109] This assertion by the Supreme Court confirms that the disposition system following an NCRMD verdict is not intended to be punitive. Perhaps it is the strong assertions in *Winko* on the appropriate balance between an NCRMD person's rights and public safety that have somewhat insulated the rights of NCRMD persons against the 2014 changes that strive to encumber them.

If the accused is not given an absolute discharge, they remain under the supervision of the Review Board. Despite the fact that the NCRMD person is *not* guilty of the index offence, continued supervision has been held not to be contrary to the Charter of Rights and Freedoms, as long as the accused has access to the procedural safeguards provided by the NCRMD regime: that is, that the disposition presents the least restrictive and onerous conditions to achieve the objectives set out in section 672.54, and the accused's case is reviewed on a yearly basis.[110] To this end, the Supreme Court in *Winko* stated:

> [I]t has been determined that the NCR offender is not morally responsible for his or her criminal act. Punishment is morally inappropriate and ineffective in such a case because the NCR accused was incapable of making meaningful choice upon which the punishment model is premised. Because the NCR accused's liberty is not restricted for the purpose of punishment, there is no corresponding reason for finitude. The purposes of restriction on his liberty are to protect society and to allow the NCR accused to seek treatment. This requires a flexible approach that treats the length of the restriction as a function of these dual aims and renders a mechanistic comparison of the duration of confinement inappropriate.[111]

Perhaps it is notable that the actual practice of Review Board supervision arguably operates *contrary* to the principles mentioned above. One of the primary determinants in long-standing supervision under the Review Board is the violence of the index offence, despite evidence that most NCRMD persons who commit violent offences are unlikely to commit a similar offence. This suggests that the

[107] See eg *Guthrie v British Columbia (Adult Forensic Psychiatric Services)*, 2019 BCCA 430; *R v Jones*, 2019 ABCA 313 (CanLII); *Collins (Re)*, 2018 ONCA 563 (CanLII); and *R v WCR*, 2019 ABCA 170 (CanLII).

[108] [1999] 2 SCR 625 (SCC).

[109] ibid paras 46, 49, and 54.

[110] Criminal Code, s 672.81. How effective this procedural safeguard is, is debatable, considering that the National Trajectory Project found that most disposition hearings result in an affirmation and continuation of the previous disposition. See Crocker (n 96) 578, where the authors state: 'Disposition stability was the most common trajectory, meaning that a patient with a prior CD (conditional discharge) disposition was most likely to receive another CD disposition at the next hearing.'

[111] *Winko* [1999] 2 SCR 625 (SCC), para 93.

guiding principles for longstanding supervision may be unduly impacted by prevailing or biased attitudes about mentally ill individuals, violence, and capacity for future violent acts, and that these principles are unfairly impacting the rights of NCRMD accused.

High-Risk Accused

In 2014, the Harper government introduced the high-risk NCRMD accused designation as a facet of their 'tough on crime' political agenda.[112] Under section 672.64, a prosecutor can now apply to have this special disposition imposed on an NCRMD person pursuant to section 672.64(3) before an absolute discharge is ordered. The alleged purpose of this disposition is to 'ensure the protection of the public against NCR accused who are considered dangerous and present an unacceptable risk to society based on an assessment of current dangerousness'.[113] In *R c FJ*,[114] the Court stated the following:

> Section 672.64 of the *Criminal Code* sets up an exceptional regime, applicable to particularly dangerous offenders, compared to the usual rules provided for in the *Criminal Code* in matters of mental disorder. Essentially, the effect of this provision is twofold. First, it has the effect of limiting the range of decisions that can be rendered under section 672.54. High-risk accused conviction results in restricted hospital detention. Second, the provision has the effect of giving the courts a greater role than the role normally assigned to the Review Board. The high-risk offender declaration can only be issued and reviewed by a court of law.

An NCRMD accused may be designated as a 'high-risk accused' (HRA) if they are found NCRMD for a serious personal injury offence (defined in s 672.81(1.3)), were over 18 years old when the index offence occurred, and if '(a) the court is satisfied that there is a substantial likelihood that the accused will use violence that could endanger the life or safety of another person; or (b) the court is of the opinion that the acts that constitute the offence were of such a brutal nature as to indicate a risk of grave physical or psychological harm to another person'.[115] Thus, there are two routes for the HRA designation: the first branch of the test suggests a prospective requirement, while the second branch emphasizes the particular nature of the index offence.

[112] R Lacroix, R O'Shaughnessy, D McNeil, and R Binder, 'Controversies Concerning the Canadian Not Criminally Responsible Reform Act' (2017) 45(1) J Am Acad Psychiatry Law 44–51, 46.

[113] *R v Schoenborn*, 2017 BCSC 1556, para 26.

[114] 2017 QCCS 4267. Note: the original text is in French, and as such, the translation may vary.

[115] *R v Schoenborn*, 2017 BCSC 1556, para 22; Criminal Code, s 672.64(1).

To make an HRA determination, the court considers the nature and circumstances of the offence, patterns of repetitive behaviour, the accused's mental condition and course of treatment, and the opinion of experts.[116] The limited case law gives significant weight to repetitive behaviour, even if prior behaviour is not of the same severity as the present index offence.[117] Lack of insight into their mental illness or the seriousness of the index offence also appears to be given emphasis.[118] The HRA designation raises several questions: what is meant by the expressions 'substantial likelihood' of the use of violence, acts of a 'brutal' nature, and 'grave psychological harm'? The Court in *Schoenborn* considered these questions in some detail.[119] The Court in *Schoenborn* also held that the description of 'brutal' in the dangerous offender regime was fitting for the HRA regime.[120]

Being designated as an HRA removes some of the procedural safeguards in the NCRMD regime for non-HRA patients. HRA individuals are not eligible for conditional or absolute discharge, are automatically detained in a hospital setting, and are only guaranteed a Review Board hearing every 36 months.[121] In doing so, it significantly impacts the liberties of NCRMD persons without providing due justification. Dispositions and procedures already exist to balance the safety of the public with the rights of the accused. Beyond creating further stigma surrounding violent mentally ill offenders and pandering to public fear, there seems to be little virtue in this addition to Canadian criminal law. Thus far, the provision has been sparingly applied; however, there have been at least four designations.[122] While the cases on this subject are relatively few, a Charter challenge could render this disposition invalid, considering it does not seem to give due weight to the rights of the NCRMD person while overemphasizing predictions of future violent behaviour.[123]

[116] Criminal Code, s 672.64(2).

[117] *R v Schoenborn*, 2017 BCSC 1556, para 115.

[118] See *R c Gaudette*, 2020 QCCS 3649; and *R v Grant*, 2018 ONSC 3581.

[119] *R v Schoenborn*, 2017 BCSC 1556, paras 48 and 86.

[120] ibid para 90. For a discussion of 'brutal' in the dangerous offender regime, see *R v Campbell*, [2004] OJ No 2151 (SC), 56.

[121] Pursuant to s 672.81(1), further reviews must generally occur every 12 months as long as the disposition remains in force; however, the Review Board may extend the time for holding a review hearing in respect of a HRA to a maximum of 36 months if the accused is represented by counsel and both the accused and the Attorney General consent to the extension, or if the Review Board is satisfied on the basis of any relevant information that the accused's condition is not likely to improve and that detention remains necessary for the period of the extension: s 672.81(1.31) and (1.32). The latter extension may be appealed to the Court of Appeal: s 672.81(1.5).

[122] *R v Gaudette*, 2020 QCCS 3649; *R v Grant*, 2018 ONSC 3581; *R c SF* [2016] QCCS 4803; and *R v Raymond* [2020] NBQB 251.

[123] Allan Schoenborn challenged the constitutionality of the HRA regime under ss 7 and 11(h) of the Charter. However, the Court was not convinced that the accused presented a substantial likelihood of causing harm to another person and was spared from addressing the constitutional question: *R v Schoenborn*, 2017 BCSC 1556, para 6.

Conclusion

The mental disorder defence in Canada remains a M'Naghten-style two-branch cognitive test. Canadian courts have shown their ability over the years to interpret each element of the two-branch cognitive test both broadly and narrowly. At the moment, the judicial interpretation is on the narrow side. Even if the broadest interpretation is given to section 16, the defence is still seriously flawed. The defence does not include the absence of volition due to mental disorder as a ground for establishing the defence; it fails to distinguish adequately between sane and insane automatism; it violates the presumption of innocence by requiring the defence to be proven on a balance of probabilities; and it fails to recognize serious mental impairments that fall just short of the high requirements for the defence. Further, the scheme of dispositions and ongoing supervision of NCRMD accused by Review Boards are unduly driven by public perception, fear, and misconceptions about recidivism and potential danger to the public. The current mental disorder defence in Canada is well beyond its 'best before' date. It is high time to throw it out and start anew, including consideration of the collection of current data on the operation of the mental disorder defence in Canada.[124]

[124] The author would like to thank Rachael Carlson for her excellent research and writing assistance.

7
The Insanity Defence
Conflict and Reform in New Zealand

Warren Brookbanks

Introduction

Relative to its existence at common law, New Zealand's experience of legal insanity is brief. The defence was first enacted in section 23 of the Criminal Code Act 1893 and was substantially based on section 22 of the Draft Code of the Criminal Code Bill Commission. As late as 1981 it was the accepted view that the current section 23 substantially preserved the common law as laid down in *M'Naghten's Case*[1] and reaffirmed in *R v Brooks*.[2] While insanity is generally regarded as a 'ground of defence, the proof of which lies upon the accused',[3] it has more recently been observed that 'it is not a defence in the sense that it is some sort of legal construct that permits the guilty to go free. Rather, it is a recognition by the law that a person may, because of mental illness, be so disordered in their thinking that at the time they act, they lack the capacity to be held responsible for the crime they commit. As the law has developed, that is not a low threshold to meet.'[4] For this, and other reasons, insanity is seldom pleaded in New Zealand, despite popular perceptions that the defence is overused and allows many dangerous offenders to wander at large in the community.

The presumption of sanity, although deeply embedded in many jurisdictions, is not without controversy. But it will not be considered further in this chapter. However, the fact that the insanity defence is still, in most common law jurisdictions, exclusively a test of cognitive ability is a matter of some concern. Writing nearly 50 years ago Sir Francis Adams commented that the fact that the M'Naghten Rules still rest on a requirement of knowledge 'without reference to defects of will or disorder of the *emotions*'[5] rendered insanity a 'highly controversial topic'.[6] It remains so today, for reasons that will be discussed below.

[1] (1843) 4 St Rt (NS) 847, 10 Cl & F 200. See RA Caldwell, *Garrow and Caldwell's Criminal Law in New Zealand* (Butterworths 1981) 44.
[2] [1945] NZLR 584, 596, *per* Myers CJ.
[3] ibid.
[4] *R v Chand* [2012] NZHC 2745, para 19 (*per* Winkelmann J).
[5] *FB Adams Criminal Law and Practice in New Zealand* (2nd edn, Sweet & Maxwell 1971) para 413 (emphasis added).
[6] ibid.

Warren Brookbanks, *The Insanity Defence* In: *The Insanity Defence*. Edited by: Ronnie Mackay and Warren Brookbanks, Oxford University Press. © Warren Brookbanks 2022. DOI: 10.1093/oso/9780198854944.003.0007

In a commentary on the substance of section 22 of the Draft Code, the Criminal Code Bill Commissioners noted that 'obscurity' hangs over the subject of insanity which could not be dispelled 'until our existing ignorance as to the nature of the will and the mind, the nature of the organs by which they operate, the manner and degree in which those operations are interfered with by disease, and the nature of the diseases which interfere with them, are greatly diminished'.[7] While acknowledging that framing the definition had caused the Commissioners 'much labour and anxiety'[8] the final result was 'as satisfactory as the nature of the subject admits of'.[9] This somewhat bleak assessment essentially encapsulates the present state of the law in this area, some 140 years later. Little has changed in the formulation of the insanity test, despite the significant advancements in scientific knowledge generally, and neuropsychology in particular, which have given greater insights into the workings of the human mind.

Regrettably, the only major review of the insanity provisions in New Zealand's Crimes Act 1961, undertaken by the New Zealand Law Commission in 2010, did not result in any significant reform recommendations other than a proposal for a new tribunal to take over ministerial responsibility for mental health and intellectual disability decision-making. Thirteen years on no action has yet been taken to establish an independent tribunal. As regards the insanity defence, in the Commission's view the defence was, broadly speaking, 'workable' so that in spite of its flaws, it should not be changed.[10]

The insanity defence in New Zealand has not been the subject of significant debate for most of its duration. Its relative lack of use, and an unwillingness to examine other models with a view to reform, has meant that judicial commentary has focused on the elements of the statutory defence within a narrow cognitive incapacity framework. While the defence has, for the most part, served the interests of New Zealand society tolerably well, new challenges presented by neurodisability and the gross abuse of methamphetamine in New Zealand raise serious questions concerning the future fitness for purpose of the defence.

The issue of automatism and its relationship to insanity, although the subject of intense scrutiny in other jurisdictions, is not discussed in this chapter.

The chapter proceeds as follows. I begin with a discussion of the legislative changes to the defence over its 127-year history. The next section examines the debate concerning knowledge versus lack of capacity in the application of the defence, as reflected in recent case law. The chapter considers current attempts to alter the insanity verdict to one of 'proven but insane', a move effectively countermanded by the unexpected intervention of New Zealand's Chief Justice. A brief discussion

[7] Criminal Code Bill Commission: Report (London, 1879) 17.

[8] ibid.

[9] ibid.

[10] See Law Commission, *Mental Impairment Decision-making and the Insanity Defence*—Report 120 (Law Commission 2010) paras 6.05 and 6.11.

of the Law Commission Report of 2010 precedes an exploration of issues around the growing problem of methamphetamine abuse and its relationship to legal insanity. The penultimate section briefly examines dispositional issues before offering some concluding comments on the implications for the insanity defence of the Convention on the Rights of Persons with Disabilities (CRPD).

Legislative Changes

A statutory insanity defence has now existed in New Zealand for 127 years without substantial modification. The current provision in section 23 of the Crimes Act 1961[11] states:

Section 23:

(1) Everyone shall be presumed sane at the time of doing or omitting any act until the contrary is proved.
(2) No person shall be convicted of an offence by reason of an act done or omitted by him when labouring under natural imbecility or disease of the mind to such an extent as to render him incapable-
  (a) of understanding the nature and quality of the act or omission; or
  (b) of knowing that the act or omission was morally wrong, having regard to the commonly accepted standards of right and wrong.
(3) Insanity before or after the time when he or she did or omitted the act, and insane delusions, though only partial, may be evidence that the offender was, at the time when he or she did or omitted the act, in such a condition of mind as to render him or her irresponsible for the act or omission.
(4) The fact that by virtue of this section any person has not been or is not liable to be convicted of an offence shall not affect the question whether any other person who is alleged to be party to that offence is guilty of that offence.

The section is substantially the same as its predecessor sections, namely, section 23 of the Criminal Code Act 1893 and section 43 of the Crimes Act 1908. The principal substantive provision is subsection (2) which contains the essence of the M'Naghten Rules. Subsection (3), which provides for insanity occurring before or after the alleged offence, together with insane delusions, has not been the subject of detailed judicial consideration in New Zealand. However, the effect of the

[11] The section defines the only mental state defence under current New Zealand law. New Zealand has never enacted a defence of diminished responsibility and has never pursued the possibility of having a volitional arm within the insanity defence structure.

provision is that insane delusions, whatever their character, may be evidence that the offender lacked mental responsibility for the act or omission. The issue was briefly considered in *R v Green*,[12] where the New Zealand Court of Appeal doubted whether delusions as to factual matters which, if true, would make the act morally justifiable could be sufficient to show that a person was incapable of knowing that an act or omission was morally wrong.

There are two distinct differences between the current version of the insanity defence and its predecessors. First, in subsection (2)(a) the word 'and', which appeared in the predecessor sections, is substituted with the word 'or'. This was done to reflect the interpretation of the Court of Appeal in *Murdoch v British Israel World Federation (New Zealand) and Another*[13] which aimed to bring the New Zealand provision into conformity with *M'Naghten's Case*. In particular, it meant that the subsection allowed for two lines of defence, requiring separate consideration, once it was established to the court's satisfaction, that the accused was 'labouring under natural imbecility or disease of the mind'. Most insanity defence acquittals in New Zealand are based on proof of lack of knowledge of *moral wrong* and seldom on the basis of incapacity to understand the 'nature and quality of the act or omission'.[14] However, it has been suggested that if a defendant was unaware of the nature and quality of his or her act 'for some other cause', this would mean he would be entitled to a simple acquittal on the basis of lack of mens rea.[15] In such circumstances the onus would remain on the Crown, only shifting to the defendant once he has offered evidence of 'a defect of reason from disease of the mind'.[16] Absent reference to 'defect of reason from disease of the mind', the same principle would, presumably, apply in New Zealand, although this question does not appear to have been tested by New Zealand courts.

The second major statutory change to the insanity test was the addition in the 1961 Act of the word 'morally' before 'wrong' in section 23(2)(b). This amendment has had a controversial history, although there is now a well-settled understanding that the test is a subjective, not an objective one. The test is 'moral wrongfulness in the eyes of the accused himself, regardless of the "commonly accepted standards"'.[17] Although FB Adams soundly criticized this articulation of the test as being

[12] [1993] 2 NZLR 513, 525, (1993) 9 CRNZ 523 (CA) 525, 535–36.

[13] [1942] NZLR 600, [1943] GLR 390.

[14] See, however, *R v Rawson* [2019] NZHC 1381, where a psychiatric expert had testified that the defendant considered he had been ordered by God to assault his father and stepmother, a direction he was unable to resist. The Court held that the schizophrenic psychosis from which the defendant suffered meant that he was 'incapable of knowing the *quality of the acts* constituting the offences at the time the offences were committed.... he did not apprehend that they were voluntary acts for which he was responsible' (para 40, *per* Toogood J). Emphasis added.

[15] See Smith, Hogan, and Ormerod's, *Criminal Law* (16th edn, Butterworths 2021) 315. But see R Mackay, '"Nature", "Quality" and Mens Rea—Some Observations on "Defect of Reason" and the First Limb of the M'Naghten Rules' [2012] Crim LR 585.

[16] Smith, Hogan, and Ormerod, above, 314.

[17] FB Adams, *Criminal Law and Practice in New Zealand* (2nd edn, Sweet & Maxwell 1971) para 418.

'directly contrary to the words of the Act',[18] it has, nevertheless, endured as the prevailing interpretation of section 23(2)(b). The rationale for the rejection of what was apparently an objective standard was the view that to maintain an objective test would have effectively disenfranchised a 'large and substantial class of persons clinically demonstrable as persons of unsound mind'.[19] While this undoubtedly remains the case, in reality the number of offenders successfully pleading insanity in New Zealand has always been small, relative to the total number of offenders prosecuted. There is no evidence whatsoever that the liberal approach to the test adopted in *McMillan* has led to an opening of the floodgates of successful insanity defences.

Insanity by Agreement

A legislative change which, in all probability, has had an impact on the numbers of successful insanity pleas in New Zealand, is not substantive but procedural. The Criminal Procedure (Mentally Impaired Persons) Act (CPMIP Act) 2003 introduced a new procedure allowing for a verdict of 'not guilty on account of his or her insanity' without the matter proceeding to trial. The new procedure, defined in section 20 of the Act of 2003, is designed to allow for a verdict of not guilty by reason of insanity (NGRI) to be recorded where there is no dispute as to the defendant's mental health status, in particular, where the defendant having indicated an intention to raise the defence of insanity, the prosecution agrees that the only reasonable verdict is not guilty on account of insanity.[20] The matter then goes to the judge who must be satisfied, on the basis of expert evidence, that the defendant was insane in terms of section 23 of the Crimes Act 1961 at the time the offence was committed.[21]

The principal benefits of this new model are twofold. First, it eliminates the need for lengthy jury trials, with the risk of re-traumatizing witnesses, by allowing an insanity verdict to be recorded pre-trial and without the need for a judge or jury to determine the factual questions concerning the defendant's insanity. Secondly, the new procedure reduces the likelihood of juries entering perverse verdicts of guilty against defendants who are manifestly legally insane, but where the emotional impact of the alleged offence generates significant popular prejudice against the defendant.[22] In practice, most New Zealand cases where insanity is raised as a defence are now resolved using the section 20 procedure. Insanity is now seldom litigated in a defended criminal trial.

[18] ibid.

[19] *R v McMillan* [1966] NZLR 616, 620.

[20] CPMIP Act 2003, s 20(2)(a) and (b).

[21] CPMIP Act Act) 2003, s 20(2)(c).

[22] A Simester and W Brookbanks, *Principles of Criminal Law* (5th edn, Thomson Reuters 2019) 472.

During the period 2010–19, there was a total of 677 charges where the person was found 'not guilty by reason of insanity' based on their mental state at the time of the offence.[23] Over this period an average of 3.9% of charges was for homicide and related offences, while the highest percentage of charges involved acts intended to cause injury (32.3%) and property damage and environmental pollution (14%). These figures tend to dispel any perceptions either that the insanity defence is overused in New Zealand or that it is limited to murder cases.

Incapacity Versus Lack of Knowledge

One interpretative issue which has engaged New Zealand courts in recent years concerns the nature and the level of incapacity required to establish relevant knowledge under the second limb of the insanity defence in section 23 of the Crimes Act 1961.

In *R v McMillan*[24] the New Zealand Court of Appeal held that section 23(2)(b) was intended to be a restatement of the law of insanity as first expounded in *M'Naghten's Case*,[25] in particular, the part of the Rules which states:

> to establish a defence on the ground of insanity, it must be clearly proved that, at the time of committing the act, the party accused was labouring under such a defect of reason, from disease of the mind, ... *that he did not know he was doing what was wrong.*[26]

It was observed that when section 43(2) of the Crimes Act 1908, the predecessor to section 23(2), was enacted, the italicized words from the M'Naghten Rules had been changed in the section to 'such an extent as to render such person *incapable ... of knowing* that such act or omission was wrong'. The Court concluded, nevertheless, that it did not think that any difference in meaning was intended by using the word 'incapable' in section 43 of the 1908 Act, or that the use of the word was intended to alter in any way the test proposed in the M'Naghten Rules.

Turner J concluded:

> If it can be shown that the accused, by reason of disease of the mind, did not know that his act or omission was wrong, then he will be excused on the ground of insanity; ...[27]

[23] Ministry of Justice Data Sheets, Table 4: Number and percentage of charges where people were found not guilty by reason of insanity by offence type, 2010–19.

[24] [1966] NZLR 616.

[25] (1843) 8 ER 718.

[26] ibid 722. Italics supplied in the judgment in *R v McMillan*. This material is under Crown copyright.

[27] [1966] NZLR 622. This material is under Crown copyright.

The decision in *McMillan* was considered at some length in *R v Dixon*[28] which affirmed that *McMillan* represents the law in New Zealand. The Court of Appeal in *Dixon* said:

> What it makes clear is that the question under subs (2)(b) is simply:
>
> Did the accused, because of the disease of his mind, not know that what he was doing was morally wrong? The focus is on the accused's state of mind and whether he appreciated that what he was doing was wrong.[29]

This question was an issue in *Dixon*, where the appellant had appealed against his conviction for murder on the ground, inter alia, that the trial judge had misdirected the jury in her treatment of the second limb of the insanity defence in section 23(2)(b). The judge had directed that this limb of the defence could be established only if the jury was satisfied that the state of the appellant's brain was such that he was totally incapable of understanding what was right and what was wrong.[30] The Court of Appeal rejected this approach and warned that what is to be avoided in such an inquiry is any suggestion that the task of the jurors is to perform a neurological or psychiatric assessment of the accused's brain or its workings, with a view to establishing its capacity.[31]

The Court of Appeal also held that since the trial judge in *Dixon* had applied a literal reading of the section, she had been led into error, since the Court of Appeal's interpretation of section 23(2)(b) in *MacMillan* was not the literal interpretation.

> [I]t is an interpretation based on historical context, and in particular on an understanding of *M'Naghten's Case* and decisions based on it.[32]

Furthermore, the Court of Appeal found that the trial judge may have been misled when she modelled part of her summing up on a dictum from the Court of Appeal in *R v Lipsey- McCarthy*,[33] where the Court had said that: 'Incapability is an absolute, not a relative concept.'[34]

Although the Court of Appeal has reiterated that the test for insanity in New Zealand is based on a subjective test of knowledge of moral wrong and is not dependent on a literal interpretation of the section, New Zealand judges continue to apply the test as though *incapability* were the standard. The risk, therefore, arises that without a proper direction from the court, defendants pleading insanity may

[28] [2008] 2 NZLR 617.
[29] ibid para 29. This material is under Crown copyright.
[30] *R v Dixon* [2008] 2 NZLR 617, para 31.
[31] ibid para 32.
[32] ibid para 34. This material is under Crown copyright.
[33] Court of Appeal CA 237/04, 28 October 2004.
[34] *R v Lipsey-McCarthy* [2004] NZCA 364 (28 October 2004).

be required to prove a degree of incapability that is not warranted by the subjective knowledge test. In other words, it will be more onerous for a defendant to prove that he or she was *totally incapable* of understanding that his or her act was morally wrong than in simply proving, on the balance of probabilities, that she *did not know* the relevant fact. This distinction proved to be decisive in the appeal in *Dixon*, the Court of Appeal finding that the summing up was not correct in its treatment of the second limb of the insanity defence.[35]

More recently several High Court decisions have further exemplified the tension. The defendant in *R v Yad-Elohim*[36] was convicted of murder after violently assaulting an elderly defenceless victim. The key issue at trial had been whether he was legally insane at the time of the assault. Two psychiatric experts called by the Crown and the defence agreed that the defendant was psychotic, was suffering from a disease of the mind at the time of the assault and that he continued to display active psychotic symptoms after arrest and subsequently. Although in agreement that the defendant's schizophrenia was a continuing condition, the experts failed to agree on whether it had rendered the defendant *incapable* of understanding the nature and morality of his actions.[37] The Court found, nevertheless, that the jury's verdict of guilty of murder meant it must have concluded that, by reason of his illness, the defendant was 'not *rendered incapable*' of understanding the nature and quality of his actions or of knowing that his actions were morally wrong, having regard to the commonly accepted standards of right and wrong.[38]

Two points may be made. First, in using the expression 'not rendered incapable', in the jury's eyes this may have been taken to imply, wrongly, that the state of the defendant's brain was not such that he was totally incapable of understanding what was right and what was wrong contrary to established authority.[39] Secondly, in reciting the literal words of the statute without any qualification the judge was in error since, as noted above, the correct interpretation is not the literal interpretation but one based on historical context and an understanding of *M'Naghten's Case*,[40] in particular subjective knowledge of moral wrong.

The same error was repeated in *R v Brackenridge*,[41] where the High Court distinguished between drug-induced schizophrenia and an exclusively drug-induced state of mind, suggesting that the latter, which was indistinguishable from intoxication,

[35] *R v Dixon* [2008] NZLR 617, 625.
[36] [2018] NZHC 2494.
[37] ibid para 6.
[38] ibid para 7.
[39] See *R v Dixon* [2008] 2 NZLR 617, para 31.
[40] ibid para 34.
[41] [2019] NZHC 1004.

may only render the offender 'unable', rather than the 'qualifying incapable'.[42] Similarly, in *R v Rawson*,[43] in a hearing conducted under s 20 of the CPMIP Act, in finding the defendant to be insane within the meaning of s23 of the Crimes Act 1961, the Judge was satisfied that the schizophrenic process from which the defendant was suffering meant that he was '*incapable* of knowing the quality of the acts constituting the offences at the time the offences were committed'.[44]

In light of the analysis in *Dixon*, it is clear that the 'qualifying incapable' referred to in *Brackenridge* is not a qualification at all. The question is simply 'Did the accused, because of his disease of the mind, not know that what he was doing was morally wrong?'.[45] If he or she did not know the relevant facts, then the question of whether he was *incapable* of knowing adds nothing to the inquiry.

Rights for Victims of Insane Offenders Act 2021

Public concerns around the insanity defence typically include that the test for insanity is outdated and inconsistent with advances in psychiatry, that psychiatrists are unaccountable for release decisions in respect of dangerous patients, and that the insanity verdict should be replaced by a verdict of 'proven but insane'. Such arguments are often supported by claims of dramatic increases in insanity acquittals even though in New Zealand the numbers of offenders acquitted on account of insanity in any one year are extremely low.[46]

In April 2019 a Private Members' Bill was pulled from the ballot which aimed to ensure that victims of legally insane offenders would be treated the same as other victims of crime.[47] The Bill purported to formalize a requirement for the court to make a ruling that the defendant caused the act or omission forming the basis of the offence, despite the traditional verdict of not guilty on account of insanity and despite the offender's lack of criminal responsibility. Such a determination would need to be recorded on the official record.

[42] ibid para 10.
[43] [2019] NZHC. 1381
[44] Ibid, [40].This material is under Crown copyright.
[45] *R v Dixon* [2008] 2 NZLR 617, para 29.
[46] eg see Sensible Sentencing Trust, 'Mental Health Review' (Undated). 'There was a 300% increase in "not guilty by reason of insanity" verdicts between 2000 and 2010, rising from 4 to 13.' https://sst.org.nz/our-aims/mental-health-review/

The official statistics reveal that for the year 2009–10 the number of people found not guilty by reason of insanity was 12 and that this number rose to 42 in 2020–21. See Ministry of Justice, Research and Data.

https://www.justice.govt.nz/justice-sector-policy/research-data/justice-statistics/data-tables/

[47] See Rights for Victims of Insane Offenders Bill—Member's Bill 129–1. Explanatory Note. The Bill received the Royal Assent on 13 December 2021. The Rights for Victims of Insane Offenders Act 2021, came into force on 13 December 2022.

The proposed amendment to the CPMIP Act 2003 was driven by the view that victims of an offender found not guilty by reason of insanity do not have the same rights as victims of an offender found guilty.[48] It is said that the description of 'not guilty' can leave victims feeling that the court has found no crime has occurred even where the act or omission constituting the offence has been proved on the facts. The rationale for the newly enacted legislation, which renames the verdict of 'not guilty on account of insanity' to 'the acts or omissions are proven but the defendant is not criminally responsible on account of insanity', is that by changing the formal finding of the court, victims are provided with an acknowledgement that the person has been proven to have acted 'grievously', 'even if they lacked the intent to be guilty of the action'.[49] This is a surprising concession, given that in other trial contexts a finding that the accused 'lacked ... intent' would necessarily result in a not guilty verdict, with no obligation to advise the jury of the meaning of the verdict. In supporting this Members' Bill the National Opposition reasoned that victims 'should be at the heart of our justice system', noting that the Bill would also ensure certain victims of legally insane offenders would be notified of any unescorted leaves of absence, or unescorted overnight leaves of absence, from a secure health care facility into the community.[50] Other more detailed provisions would have given victims the right to make submissions on the proposed leave of absence of special patients, and clarifying any ongoing risk concerns the victim may have. The Bill would also have given victims the right to make a submission to the Mental Health Review Tribunal on the patient's special conditions.

The Bill went through its second reading and was reported back to Parliament on 16 April 2021 with the recommendation that it be passed with amendments. It had the unanimous support of the Select Committee and was due to be passed into law on 30 June 2021. However, before the Bill could be enacted there was an unexpected intervention by New Zealand's Chief Justice, Dame Helen Winkelmann, resulting in the Bill being returned to the Justice Committee to consider the Chief Justice's concerns raised in a letter to the Attorney General on 24 May 2021, in which Dame Helen argued strongly for the existing law. Her Honour re-affirmed the 'well-established position' of insanity at common law, namely, that defendants who were legally insane at the time of the alleged offending could not be guilty of the crime they were charged with because the necessary mental element was missing. On this view mens rea is said to be lacking either because defendants are incapable of forming the necessary intent or because the intent formed was an insane one. Her Honour's comments should not, however, be taken to exclude the other possibility, namely, that not all insane offenders lack mens rea but may be exculpated because they do not appreciate the moral wrongness of their acts.

48 Explanatory Note.

49 ibid.

50 See Law and Order Discussion Document 'Have your say', November 2019.

Her Honour nevertheless reiterated that such defendants are not guilty since the charge against them has not been proven because the 'mental element' has not been proven. As a matter of principle, it was inaccurate to use the term 'proven' against an insane defendant.[51]

Her Honour also made the important point that the proposed verdict of 'proven but insane' failed to accommodate the possibility that the defendant had a good defence to the charge even if they committed the relevant act but may have done so, for example, in self-defence.[52] This raises the additional question that if the proposed law change requires, in effect, a declaration that the offender committed a criminal act while lacking criminal responsibility, will this analysis also apply to other defence circumstances, including automatism, compulsion, mistake, and accident? These questions are not addressed in the Bill proposals.

On 19 November 2021 the Bill was reported back from the Justice Committee for a second time with a unanimous recommendation that it be passed.[53] After having considered the Chief Justice's concerns the Committee has recommended replacing the proposed verdict of 'proven but insane' with a new finding of 'act proven but not criminally responsible on account of insanity'.[54] In the Committee's view this would clarify that the charge itself has not been proven while acknowledging that the defendant has engaged in the conduct which is the subject of the charge. The new verdict also avoids the implication that the mental element of the charge has been proven.[55]

Law Commission Report

In December 2010 the New Zealand Law Commission released its Report, *Mental Impairment Decision-making and the Insanity Defence*.[56] The Commission had been requested by the New Zealand government to review the defence of insanity, considering in particular whether the defence was appropriate in its nature and scope, whether or not it should be abolished, the way the defence should be put to and considered by the court, and issues relating to the burden and standard of proof.

[51] 'Government puts brakes on insanity bill after Chief Justice intervenes' *New Zealand Herald*, 30 June 2021.

[52] ibid.

[53] Rights for Victims of Offenders Bill, as reported from the Justice Committee, *Commentary*, 1. https://www.parliament.nz/resource/en-NZ/SCR_117875/07c3b437c20de2394565226680df0650c44a7d70

[54] ibid 2.

[55] ibid 3.

[56] *Mental Impairment Decision-making and the Insanity Defence*, New Zealand Law Commission, December 2010, Wellington, New Zealand, Report 120.

In examining issues around the insanity defence the Commission commented on the mixed purpose of the defence, namely to protect defendants by shielding them from a criminal conviction, and protecting the community by ensuring that a defendant who would otherwise be entitled to an acquittal could be detained. The Commission noted the limitations of both rationales, especially that the availability of public protection in any given case could well depend on choices made by the defence as to whether insanity is explicitly relied upon as a defence or put in issue.[57] The Commission also noted the archaic and inappropriate terminology (eg 'natural imbecility') and the gulf existing between language and case law on the one hand and psychiatric concepts and practices on the other. It also highlighted the anomalous results produced in some cases, in particular, the classification of hyperglycaemia as a disease of the mind, and hypoglycaemia as not.

Yet despite these acknowledged limitations, the Law Commission did not think that other options, including abolition, revising the language of qualifying mental conditions, or revising the cognitive impairment part of the defence were worthwhile options. It concluded that 'broadly speaking, the defence is workable, in spite of its flaws'.[58] Although the Commission recognized that the problems with the insanity defence were not insignificant, it did not recommend its reform. It did, however, recommend that the model of ministerial decision-making which accompanied a special verdict of not guilty by reason of insanity, where an offender was made a 'special patient' should be replaced with a new Special Patient's Review Tribunal which would take over the ministerial functions. However, despite the government's agreeing in 2012 that this recommendation had merit, it has not yet been the subject of law reform. But regardless of this lack of official action in implementing the recommendation, other waves are shaking the foundations and structure of the insanity defence in New Zealand, in particular, the tsunami of lives being destroyed by methamphetamine abuse.[59]

Methamphetamine and Disease of the Mind

The insanity defence is infrequently used in New Zealand, although there is some evidence of a slight increase in its use in recent years.[60] Over the same period, there was a significant increase in the number of convictions for methamphetamine

[57] ibid 2.4.

[58] ibid 7.

[59] See I Freckelton, 'Methamphetamine Induced Psychosis and Mental Impairment: A Challenge from New Zealand' (2019) 27(2) J Law Med 284–93; M Black, 'Getting the Measure of Meth: Just How Bad a Problem Has New Zealand Got?" (2015) 26(2) Matters of Substance 6–13; C Wilkins and others, 'Determinants of High Availability of Methamphetamine, Cannabis and Ecstasy in New Zealand: Are Drug Dealers Promoting Methamphetamine rather than Cannabis?' (2018) Drug Alcohol Rev 37.

[60] See n 46.

offences in New Zealand from 1,230 in 2011–12 to 2,392 in 2020–21.[61] Whether there is a connection between the increase in insanity acquittals and the rise in methamphetamine offences is unclear. However, it seems likely that the increase in insanity acquittals is at least partly attributable to the increase in methamphetamine use simply on the basis of the increasing number of cases coming before New Zealand courts where insanity is pleaded in the context of methamphetamine use.

The difficulty for courts in applying traditional insanity jurisprudence to the challenge of methamphetamine is that the types of psychoses which traditionally undergirded a claim that the offender was suffering from a 'disease of the mind' were the product of organic, endogenous, or environmental distress, and when the most relevant abused substance was alcohol.[62] But for the most part such mental diseases were not the result of the consumption of illicit substances, whether or not they were treatable conditions. Their characterization as 'internal' causes is now well established. However, where psychoses arise from substance abuse, as in the case of methamphetamine, the situation has become much more complex. In fact, most countries are currently experiencing greatly increased rates of illicit drug-induced psychosis, especially methamphetamine-related.[63] Yet applying traditional jurisprudential models, such drug use constitutes an 'external' factor which would normally negate the availability of the insanity defence, being an artefact of intoxication. The rationale has the appearance of simplicity. If a defendant chooses to take a drug that produces psychosis, the cause is considered to be voluntary psychosis. Because the cause did not originate within the person, and being voluntarily consumed is something over which they, at least in theory, have some control, the altered mental state can have no exculpatory effect.

However, because of the psychological complexities which typically accompany the abuse of methamphetamine, the distinction between internal and external causes of altered mental states may be of little utility in assessing culpability in offenders whose criminal offending was associated with methamphetamine use. Identifying a primary cause when both drug use and psychosis are present is extremely challenging for expert witnesses, especially given that in this highly conflicted domain, real-world clinical complexities often do not align well with legal definitions.[64] Recent case law in both Australia and New Zealand now differentiates

[61] See Ministry of Justice, Research and Data, https://www.justice.govt.nz/justice-sector-policy/research-data/justice-statistics/data-tables. See also Justice Statistics data tables Notes and trends for 2020/2021 at 5 https://www.justice.govt.nz/assets/Documents/Publications/Justice-Statistics-data-tables-notes-and-trends-jun21-v1.0.pdf

See also 'Methamphetamine in New Zealand: A Snapshot of Recent Trends' March 2021, Parliamentary Service https://www.parliament.nz/media/7832/methamphetamine_in_new-zealand_-a_snapshot_of_recent_trends.pdf

[62] G Mellsop and others, 'Drug Driven Psychoses and Legal Responsibility or Insanity in Six Western Pacific Nations' (2016) 47 Int J Law Psychiatry 68, 72.

[63] ibid.

[64] See K Thom, M Finlayson, and B McKenna, 'Insanity, Methamphetamine and Psychiatric Expertise in New Zealand Courtrooms' (2011) JLM 749, 756 and see Mellsop and others (n 62) 70.

between patients experiencing drug-induced psychosis, which may be characterized as an exclusively drug-induced state of mind and indistinguishable from intoxication,[65] and those with an authentic mental illness either derivative of or closely associated with methamphetamine use. Whether such a distinction is ethical, on the basis that both categories may produce significant psychological distress, is a live question. However, for the purposes of the current discussion, public policy at the present time seems to be firmly set against privileging criminal behaviour resulting from voluntarily consumed drugs, other than where consumption of drugs has produced an authentic schizophrenic process that is the equivalent to a disease of the mind and that is distinguishable from a drug-induced state of mind.[66]

An Emerging Jurisprudence of Methamphetamine

Since 2004 there has been a tranche of New Zealand cases where methamphetamine use has been associated with dangerous criminal behaviour, commonly involving either the death or serious injury of the victim or victims of the offending, where issues of mental health status have arisen. Issues of concern as regards the relevance of the insanity defence in such cases relate to the characterization of the meth-induced state of mind (ie whether it is properly characterized as a mental disease) and its impact on the offender's cognitive capacity. As these cases demonstrate, this analysis is complex and highly fact-specific.

R v Lipsey-McCarthy[67] was an appeal against conviction for a vicious assault on a 72-year-old woman in a public street, resulting in serious injury to the victim. Shortly after the initial assault the accused had assaulted two young girls, stealing the mobile phone of one, leading to a robbery charge. On conviction, the accused was sentenced to three years' imprisonment. The principal issue at trial was whether the appellant was insane in terms of section 23 of the Crimes Act 1961. She had started experimenting with methamphetamine ('P') about two weeks before the events in question and was smoking P heavily in the three days leading up to the incidents. She had ingested a large quantity of P on the day of the assault, leading to a psychotic state involving delusions and paranoia. She had not experienced similar psychosis prior to bingeing on P. Her diagnosis at the time was one of methamphetamine-induced psychotic disorder with delusions. At trial, it was accepted that the defendant had pre-existing, albeit mild symptoms of illness, which were substantially exacerbated by the consumption of amphetamines

[65] See *R v Brackenridge* [2019] NZHC 1004, para 10.

[66] See *Fang v The Queen* (2018) 274 A Crim R 323. '[A] drug induced psychosis (unaccompanied by a separate psychiatric illness) does not constitute a disease of the mind as understood in the common law' (at para 76).

[67] [2004] NZCA 364.

which, according to one forensic expert, had led to a schizophrenia-type disorder to which she was predisposed. The Court acknowledged that 'difficulties of evaluation of mental disorder, in terms of disease of the mind, arise where a mental state may be attributable both to an inherent psychiatric condition and external causes such as the influence of drugs'.[68] The Court emphasized that to come within the terms of section 23 the mental state must be such as to 'render a person incapable of understanding the nature and quality of the conduct or of knowing that it was morally wrong'.[69] The Court observed that the psychiatric evidence provided a rational basis to conclude if the appellant did not know her conduct was morally wrong, then her disability was attributable to an underlying psychiatric condition which could be characterized as a disease of the mind, rather than the transient effects on the appellant's mental processes of the methamphetamine she had consumed.[70] The appeal, however, was dismissed because the Court of Appeal was not satisfied that the trial judge's direction on insanity was in any way flawed. There was also evidence, apparently accepted by the jury, that the appellant knew that her behaviour was wrong, despite forensic evidence that her consumption of methamphetamine had triggered schizophrenia, to which she was predisposed. On this basis, insanity was excluded.

However, as noted above a matter that arose in the appeal decision, that was critical to the outcome in the appeal in *R v Dixon*[71] was the Court of Appeal's observation in discussing the 'incapable of understanding test' in section 23(2) that 'incapability is an absolute, not a relative concept'.[72]

R v Dixon[73] was a notorious case where the defendant had gone on a violent rampage, in which he murdered one person, very nearly killed two others, and committed numerous other offences while continuing to consume methamphetamine. Insanity was rejected at the trial, although at sentencing it was conceded that the accused's consumption of considerable amounts of methamphetamine in the months prior to the offending might have had the effect of exacerbating a disordered mental state short of insanity, namely personality disorder and may have fuelled grandiose ideas. But the court did not accept that it had resulted in reduced responsibility. The court found the accused understood well what he was doing and intended the outcome. However, the appeal was allowed on the basis of the trial judge's misdirection in relation to the second limb of the insanity defence and ordered a new trial. At the retrial, at which the accused was also found guilty on the eight charges he faced, a written jury direction stated that 'temporary mental

[68] *R v Lipsey-McCarthy* [2004] NZCA 364, para 16.
[69] ibid.
[70] ibid para 17.
[71] [2007] 2 NZLR 617.
[72] *R v Lipsey -McCarthy* [2004] NZCA 364, para 20.
[73] [2007] 2 NZLR 617.

disorder caused by some factor external to the accused such as the taking of drugs' does not amount to a disease of the mind.[74]

Literalism vs Intent

The successful appeal against conviction and sentence in *Dixon* had turned on the applicability of an incapability standard.[75] The Court of Appeal observed, in rejecting a literal approach to the interpretation of section 23(2), that the courts 'never support literalism at the expense of purpose and intent'.[76] This dictum may have an important bearing on the interpretation of New Zealand's insanity offence where, as has already been demonstrated, courts continue to apply a literalist approach to section 23. The non-literalist approach allows judges some flexibility to interpret existing statutory criteria in ways which might give better expression to legislative intention, that is, to protect the public and the interests of mentally impaired defendants, while also supporting the principle that the law is always speaking.[77] On this basis, common law defences, like insanity, that might have been recognized at an earlier period, should not be regarded as frozen in time[78] and ought to be open to judicial interpretation which reflects contemporary values and social aspirations. Furthermore, this principle suggests that a particular defence may be developed in a way that has regard to what has happened in other common law jurisdictions. It has been noted, for example, that most current insanity laws were drafted when the most relevant abused substance was alcohol. Today, however, the universal experience of a much-increased rate of illicit *drug*-induced psychoses, especially related to methamphetamine,[79] might suggest a need for further legislative intervention. The aim would be to accommodate the complex reality of the relationship between the consumption of illicit substances and the development of psychoses that may be brief or ongoing.[80] It has been contended that 'changes in drug usage, in psychiatric knowledge and quite possibly evolving social values requires countries to reconsider how they wish their courts and justice systems to interpret or deal with those who offend while suffering from conditions aetiologically related to and sustained by, voluntary, use of psychoactive substances'.[81] This observation suggests a changing conceptualization of the drugs/insanity debate, that may be moving it from a morality to a public health discourse. What this looks like as regards the structure of a modified defence remains to be seen.

74 *R v Dixon* HC, Auckland, CRI 2003-092-026923, 21 June 2008.
75 See discussion in the earlier section, at page 146 et seq.
76 *R v Dixon* [2007] 2 NZLR 617, para 28.
77 *R v Hutchinson* [2004] NZAR 303, para 44 CA.
78 See *R v Hutchinson* [2004] NZAR 303 (CA).
79 Mellsop and others (n 62).
80 ibid.
81 ibid.

Nevertheless, it is clear that the current insanity formulation fails to adequately account for offenders who may have committed extremely grave crimes, yet whose mental condition, as a result of, or concurrent with illicit substance consumption, has rendered their rational capacity highly questionable. At present, rejection by the courts of insanity may not be inconsistent with a high degree of rational impairment, provided the evidence shows a measure of knowledge of the conduct undertaken and/or knowledge of 'moral wrong'.

The problem is well illustrated in *R v Yad-Elohim*.[82] The accused had been charged with the murder of an elderly victim following a brutal and sustained assault. The victim happened to be in the wrong place at the wrong time when the defendant came to his apartment pursuing a drug debt in relation to another person. It was accepted that the appellant suffered from a severe mental disorder, namely chronic schizophrenia, possibly exacerbated by his consumption of methamphetamine sometime earlier. Forensic evidence given at trial confirmed the appellant's diagnosis of paranoid schizophrenia and meth dependence; and that during treatment his psychotic symptoms persisted in a way that was consistent with chronic schizophrenia, rather than drug-induced psychosis. The defence and Crown experts at trial agreed that he was psychotic and suffering from a disease of the mind at the time of the attack and that he continued to display active psychotic symptoms after arrest and subsequently. It was also agreed his schizophrenia was a continuing condition. However, the experts failed to agree on whether the disease had rendered him 'incapable of understanding the nature and morality of [his] actions'.[83] He was found guilty of murder by the jury which 'must have concluded that you were not, by reason of your illness, rendered *incapable of understanding the* nature and quality of your actions or of knowing that your actions were morally wrong, having regard to the commonly accepted standards of right and wrong'.[84]

A contrasting outcome is the case of *R v Rawson*,[85] where the appellant was found NGRI following assaults on his father and stepmother that resulted in charges of attempted murder and assault with a weapon. In this case, all three forensic experts *agreed* that the defendant was probably insane at the time of the offending, providing the basis for Crown and defence concurrence that not guilty by reason of insanity was the only reasonable verdict, and thus triggering the procedure under section 20 of the CPMIP Act 2003. It was agreed that he experienced

[82] [2018] NZHC 2494.

[83] ibid para 6.

[84] ibid para 7 (emphasis added). An interesting comparison can be drawn with the US case of Eddie Ray Routh, a Marine Corps veteran charged with the shooting murder of celebrated war hero, Chris Kyle. Although Routh suffered from schizophrenia and PTSD arising from his tours of duty in Iraq and Haiti and suffered bouts of psychosis and paranoid delusions in the period prior to the event, the evidence was insufficient to persuade the jury of his insanity. It is noted that the public nature of the trial, together with Kyle's war hero reputation 'aroused intense public disapproval towards Ruth'. See L Kachulis, 'Insane in the Mens Rea: Why Insanity Defence Reform is Long Overdue' [2017] 26(3) Review of Law and Social Justice 245, 256.

[85] [2019] NZHC 1381.

florid psychotic symptoms, including delusions of grandeur and religiosity, that could have impacted on his actions at the time of the offending.

In finding that the defendant was insane in terms of section 23 of the Crimes Act 1961, Toogood J found that while the defendant may have appreciated that what he was doing was assaulting both his father and stepmother, the schizophrenic psychosis from which he suffered meant he was 'incapable of knowing the quality of the acts constituting the offences at the time the offences were committed. That is, he did not apprehend that they were voluntary acts for which he was responsible.'[86] In this case, the literal incapability test was applied to the defendant's advantage, as suggesting a degree of global rational impairment, in contrast to *Yad-Elohim*, whose incapability was insufficiently advanced to excuse his criminal behaviour.

Two further cases demonstrate how schizophrenia, co-occurring with methamphetamine abuse can be differentiated for the purposes of discerning legal insanity.

In *Tarapata v R*[87] the accused had been convicted on two counts of murder. He had attacked two men with a knife without warning, at their workplace, and killed them. It was agreed he was psychotic at the time of the murders but there was considerable disagreement as to the *cause* of the psychosis and its consequences. The defence argued he suffered from schizophrenia, while the prosecution said the cause was methamphetamine. At trial, he was unable to discharge the burden of proof on the balance of probabilities and was convicted of murder.

Two defence experts at trial had testified that the appellant suffered from schizophrenia, which amounted to a disease of the mind. However, a Crown expert argued that he suffered from a drug-induced psychosis rather than a disease of the mind and that he knew his actions were morally wrong. Here the critical questions were the timing, frequency, and quantity of the appellant's methamphetamine use. Evidence was led by the defence that the appellant had discontinued use of meth two to three months prior to the homicides, while the prosecution case was that he had been using methamphetamine right up until the killings.

However, on appeal the Court of Appeal accepted as cogent and reliable the evidence of a very senior forensic psychiatrist who said:

> I would not consider methamphetamine-induced psychotic disorder to be a better explanation of his condition at this time, even though it is apparent that his psychotic disorder emerged during a time period when he was abusing methamphetamine, and it is known that methamphetamine can induce a clinical syndrome indistinguishable from schizophrenia. The persistence of psychotic symptoms over this extended time period without methamphetamine and in the context of high dose antipsychotic treatment renders schizophrenia the more clinically appropriate diagnosis at this time.[88]

[86] ibid para 40.
[87] [2016] NZCA 500.
[88] [2016] NZCA 500, at [25]. This material is under Crown copyright.

In this case, because defence counsel had made an error in handling the evidence of drug use in fact and propensity evidence, the court found there had been a miscarriage of justice and ordered a retrial. At the retrial, it was agreed that T suffered from a disease of the mind, namely schizophrenia, and the jury's verdict of not guilty by reason of insanity necessarily meant that the defence had satisfied the jury it was more likely than not that T did not know his acts were morally wrong.[89] At the disposition hearing, in which the accused was made a special patient pursuant to section 24(2)(a) of the CPMIP Act, the court acknowledged that the victims had died from a 'frenzied attack driven by delusional paranoia' and that as a person suffering from treatment-resistant paranoia, the accused posed a continued risk of serious harm to the public.[90]

The second, more recent, case concerned a trial ruling given in the course of a murder trial where the judge ruled that drug-induced schizophrenia is a disease of the mind.

In *R v Brackenridge*[91] the accused had been charged with the murder of his mother. He was found guilty at trial and sentenced to life imprisonment with a minimum term of ten years' imprisonment.

However, during the trial, the Court was required to rule on whether methamphetamine-induced psychosis was a disease of the mind. In finding that it was the Court said this:

> Schizophrenia facilitates a state of mind that may affect an offender to the extent s/he is incapable of the requisite knowledge or understanding. That schizophrenia may be drug-induced is immaterial because the operative state of mind is schizophrenic, however induced. That is quite distinct from an exclusively drug-induced state of mind, which seems indistinguishable from intoxication (which may not provide excuse or justification). Such only may render the offender 'unable', rather than the qualifying 'incapable'.[92]

In light of the earlier comments arising from the *Dixon* case, clearly the qualifying 'incapable' is no longer a qualification at all. The Court's distinction between being 'unable' and being 'incapable' actually is irrelevant in this context. Either way, the question is simply 'Did the accused, because of his disease of the mind, *not know* that what he was doing was morally wrong?'[93] If he didn't actually know the relevant facts, the question of whether he was *(in)capable* of knowing is otiose.

However, this decision does provide some useful clarification on the issue of drug-induced schizophrenia. It represents the clearest statement that wherever

[89] *R v Tarapata* [2018] NZHC 85, para 3.
[90] ibid para 17.
[91] [2019] NZHC 1004. This material is under Crown copyright.
[92] *R v Brackenridge* [2019] NZHC, para 10.
[93] See *R v Dixon* [2008] 2 NZLR 617, para 29, emphasis added.

schizophrenia is caused by the consumption of drugs (of whatever kind), it is necessarily a disease of the mind, whether or not the condition proceeds to full-blown insanity. The distinction is between a condition clinically recognized as bearing the indicators of schizophrenia as opposed to a lesser mental state that is merely 'drug-induced' or a 'self-induced state caused by alcohol or drugs',[94] a form of intoxication.

Analysis

This is clearly a very vexed area of law and practice. Bright lines of distinction are absent. Many questions arise: Is 'disease of the mind' an appropriate descriptor for an acknowledged mental impairment that is closely tied to methamphetamine consumption? Is the focus of the test in section 23 on knowledge of moral wrong appropriate, or even meaningful, in this context? Should the impact of paranoia be assessed independently of the insanity model?

Contemplating these matters leads to another line of thinking. Cases like *Tarapata*, *Brackenridge*, *Dixon*, and *Yad-Elohim* clearly stretch the utility and applicability of the traditional insanity model. In each case, the defendants were profoundly paranoid and delusional yet in three of the four cases, they failed to meet the narrow insanity formulation. But who is to say that they did, or did not, understand that their conduct was 'morally wrong', given the impact of their profound paranoia and the cascading effects of minds in total disarray? These are metaphysical questions that few are competent to answer. It is little wonder forensic professionals may, and often do, disagree as to whether the accused knew their actions were morally wrong.

Disposition Issues

The disposal of insanity cases in New Zealand is governed by the CPMIP Act 2003. The Act is a statutory code the purpose of which was to provide courts with appropriate options for the detention, assessment, and care of defendants and offenders with an intellectual disability.[95] However, the options for disposal are limited. A court may either order an offender acquitted on account of insanity to be detained as a 'special patient', where there are public safety concerns[96] or, if detention as a special patient is deemed not necessary, that they be treated as a committed 'patient' under the Mental Health (Compulsory Assessment & Treatment)

[94] See *Cooper v R* [1980] 1 SCR 1149, 1159, cited in *Brackenridge v R* [2019] NZHC 1004, para 7.
[95] CPMIP Act 2003, s 3(a).
[96] See CPMIP Act 2003, s 24(2)(a).

Act 1992.[97] There is parallel provision for offenders acquitted on account of insanity on the basis of 'natural imbecility'[98] to be detained either as 'special care recipients',[99] where there are public safety concerns, or as 'care recipients' pursuant to the Intellectual Disability (Compulsory Care and Rehabilitation) Act 2003.[100] Offenders who are made special patients, where such an order is 'necessary in the interests of the public',[101] are subject to indeterminate detention until such time as clinicians or the Mental Health Review Tribunal certify that the defendant's continued detention is no longer necessary to safeguard the defendants own interests or the safety of the public and the Minister of Health directs a change of status to 'patient' or 'care recipient', or directs the person's discharge.[102]

Immediate Release

Orders that the offender be immediately released,[103] as an alternative to detention as a special patient or special care recipient, or committal under the Mental Health (Compulsory Assessment & Treatment) Act 1992, are rare and likely to be made only where there is a very low risk of the behaviour being repeated and therapeutic detention is no longer appropriate. Although courts tend to be resistant to making orders for immediate release, in situations where the defendant has experienced serious cognitive decline with the unlikelihood of improvement, such an order may be warranted.[104] However, even where the offender has developed severe dementia, such that the offender would never recover capacity to undergo a trial, it has been held not to justify an order for immediate release, when balanced against the seriousness of the harm caused, and the views of victims.[105]

New Zealand judges have been critical of the shortcomings of the statutory regime which does not permit the court to impose any form of supervisory oversight following an immediate release order.[106] However, in *R v Kalolo*[107] Lang J suggested that this deficiency might be resolved by the addition of the words 'upon such conditions as the Court may deem fit' at the end of the relevant provision.[108] To date this suggestion has not been acted upon by the legislature and uncertainty remains around the appropriate circumstances for the use of the immediate release order.

97 CPMIP Act 2003, s 25(1)(a).
98 See Crimes Act 1961, s 23(2).
99 CPMIP Act 2003, s 24(2)(b).
100 CPMIP Act 2003, s 25(1)(b).
101 CPMIP Act 2003.
102 CPMIP Act 2003, s 33(3).
103 CPMIP Act 2003, s 25(1)(d).
104 See eg *R v I* [2017] NZHC 1021.
105 *R v Mulholland* [2015] NZHC 881.
106 *R v I* [2017] NZHC 1021.
107 [2017] NZHC 518.
108 See CPMIP Act 2003, s 25(1)(d).

In other respects, the experience of clinicians suggests that while many would regard the present disposal options as adequate, the bigger concern is the real-world availability of appropriately supported places. In New Zealand, community mental health services are more reluctant to tolerate violence, meaning that places in supported housing may not be offered to mentally impaired offenders, or in some cases, even agree to follow them up. Similarly, supported placements in secure care for intellectually disabled offenders are often scarce, making the provision of appropriate care a challenging exercise.

A Balancing Exercise

New Zealand judges have observed that the decision whether to make a special patient or special care recipient order often involves a difficult balancing exercise. In *H v The Queen*[109] the Court of Appeal said:

> In determining whether to make either a special care or a care order, the court is undertaking a balancing exercise which involves the need to protect the public from persons who may reoffend while subject to an incapacity (on the one hand) and the desirability of rehabilitating the defendant (on the other). The court must consider relevant aspects of public interest, the purposes for which the disposition is being made, and the consequences (both to the public and the defendant) of making either a special care or a care order.

The necessary balancing reflects the fact that the 'special' designation serves as a flag concerning the patient's potential dangerousness, as revealed in their forensic history, and implies that the patient is brought under the control and care of specialist forensic services. More careful scrutiny of leave arrangements is also a feature of special status,[110] and discharge from compulsory treatment can only be determined by the non-clinical authorization of the Minister of Health.[111]

Implications of the CRPD

However, more recent commentary questions the appropriateness of this model of supervision and, in particular, its compliance with the terms of the Convention on the Rights of Persons with Disabilities (CRPD). It has been noted that special patients do not need to be 'mentally disordered' in order to be subject to detention

[109] CA 841/2012 [2013] NZCA 628.
[110] See Mental Health (Compulsory Assessment & Treatment) Act 1992, s 50.
[111] CPMIP Act 2003, s 33(3).

and compulsory treatment and are not entitled to release if they are not or are no longer mentally disordered. Rather, as noted above, New Zealand legislation authorized post-insanity acquittal committal where an insanity acquittee has been judged to be dangerous, whether or not the person suffers from a contemporaneous mental disorder and with no requirement that a court make such a finding.[112] It is argued that the indefinite detention of such persons, simply because they pose a danger to the community, amounts to arbitrary preventive detention and violates their civil and human rights.[113]

There are two elements to this argument. First, detention as a 'special patient' found not guilty by reason of insanity does not include a requirement that the defendant be presently mentally disordered. Of greater significance, however, is the fact that such persons are not entitled to release, whether or not they are mentally disordered. Discharge from compulsory treatment, or simply from detention if no longer mentally disordered, can only occur if the Minister of Health decides that the person may be discharged or their status downgraded to that of a civilly committed patient under the Mental Health (Compulsory Assessment) Treatment) Act 1992.[114] This discretion delegated to a senior politician has been criticized as involving a 'perceived lack of independence, and risk of political decision-making'.[115] The recommendation of the Law Commission to make the process more transparent by removing Ministers from the process and the creation of a Special Patients' Review Tribunal to take over the ministerial functions,[116] has yet to be acted upon.

The second, and perhaps more pressing point, is that it is said that the insanity disposal regime under current New Zealand law breaches the requirements of the CRPD in a number of important respects. Arguably some reformulation of the defence might achieve greater compliance with CRPD values to better reflect modern human rights law. However, the CRPD Committee's aspirations are significantly more radical. Article 12 section 2 of the CRPD says: 'State Parties shall recognise that persons with disabilities enjoy legal capacity on an equal basis with others in all aspects of life.' On the basis it is claimed that any use of compulsory admission in mental health care directly violates basic principles of human rights, the Committee on the Rights of Persons with Disabilities has asserted that substituted decision-making, compulsory treatment, involuntary admissions, and diversion from criminal system processes on the grounds of mental disability, should be abolished.[117] This would necessarily include the insanity defence.

[112] C Leonetti, 'The Arbitrary Detention of Insanity Acquittees in New Zealand' [2020] NZ Law Rev 493.

[113] ibid.

[114] See CPMIP Act 2003, s 33(3).

[115] New Zealand Law Commission, Report 120: *Mental Impairment Decision-Making and the Insanity Defence* (Wellington, December 2010) 9, cited in Leonetti (n 112) 10.

[116] Report 120, 9.

[117] Editorial, 'Psychiatry Unlocked' (2017) 4 Lancet Psychiatry 261.

However, a recent decision of the New Zealand Court of Appeal makes it clear that under New Zealand law, international instruments, including the CRPD, do not prevail over primary legislation.[118] It was held that the CRPD does not override New Zealand legislation and that where a New Zealand statute clearly provides for a particular outcome, that outcome is lawful, even if it is not consistent with the CRPD.[119] More particularly, in *M(CA677/2017) v AG* it was held that it is not the role of New Zealand courts to make findings about whether New Zealand legislation is consistent with international instruments such as the CRPD.

> If the legislation that governs a particular issue is clear then it is neither necessary nor appropriate for this Court to go on to make findings about the consistency of that legislation with the CRPD.[120]

A further difficulty with the potential impact of the CRPD in this area of the law has been expressed by a group of mental health professionals concerned with the broad scope of the Article 12 provision. It has been suggested that instead of enhancing human rights, other fundamental rights like the enjoyment of the highest attainable health standards, access to justice, right to liberty, and even the right to life could be violated in the event that the processes identified were to be abolished.[121] The authors suggest that a consensus, or near-consensus 'would be needed to replace existing mental health laws with new laws consistent with all the CRPD principles, and compatible with the other rights, including to the highest attainable standards of health of people with severe mental disorders who might at times have impaired decision-making capacity'.[122] They suggest there is an urgent need for advocacy and action by clinicians, practitioners, and professional organization and service user groups to ensure that the implementation of the CRPD 'generates laws and practices that ... safeguard the rights of persons with mental disabilities'.[123] This is an issue of critical concern since the unchallenged interpretation of the CRPD offered in the General Comment by the Committee on the Rights of Persons with Disabilities would radically impact both the interpretation and, indeed, the very existence of an exculpatory insanity defence which, in many jurisdictions, still prevails as hornbook law.

[118] *M (CA677/2017) v Attorney- General* [2020] NZCA 311, para 35.
[119] ibid.
[120] ibid para 36.
[121] MC Freeman and others, 'Reversing Hard Won Victories in the Name of Human Rights: A Critique of the General Comment on Article 12 of the UN. Convention on the Rights of Persons with Disabilities' (2015) 2 Lancet Psychiatry 844–50.
[122] ibid 849.
[123] ibid.

Conclusion

The insanity defence in New Zealand, despite its longevity, has an unsettled history. Broadly modelled on the M'Naghten Rules, the New Zealand defence has largely adopted prevailing English common law jurisprudence on insanity, including the troublesome distinction between 'internal' and 'external' causes and the elusive concept of 'disease of the mind'. However, distinctively New Zealand jurisdictional questions have centred around the degree and nature of incapacity sufficient to trigger the defence and the meaning and scope of knowledge of *moral* wrong in the second limb of the defence. These issues have generated lively judicial debate but may be regarded as a mere sideshow compared to the challenging issues now confronting the defence in New Zealand and further afield.

An especially pressing concern is the ability of the defence to respond to the clinical and legal demands presented by the upsurge in illicit drug use, in particular methamphetamine, and its ability to redefine the parameters of exculpatory insanity. It is clear from the burgeoning case law in this area in several jurisdictions discussed in this volume that judges and clinicians are troubled by the binary sane/insane which, when aligned with the requirement to distinguish drug-induced psychosis from an authentic schizophrenia-type process, may demand more than competent professionals are reasonably able to deliver. In this regard, we may well ask whether the current statutory defence of insanity is fit for purpose as the chosen means of assessing criminal culpability in such cases.

Finally, while the insanity defence has a well-established history in all common law jurisdictions, including New Zealand, its future, at least in its current form, is by no means secure. In addition to the growing calls for the defence to better accommodate the demands of both volitional and affective disorders, the charge that it is inconsistent with international human rights norms, in particular the CRPD, and should be abolished, is especially troubling. Clearly, the halcyon days when an 'insanity' trial was clustered around the conflicting evidence of two or more forensic psychiatric professionals as an effective 'trial of the experts', are largely in the past, at least in New Zealand. Increasingly, with the 'insanity by agreement' procedure defined in section 20 of the CPMIPAct 2003 changing how the issue of exculpatory insanity is determined, there is less occasion for highly publicized and stigmatizing hearings. While populist concerns are periodically expressed concerning the perceived overuse of the defence, sometimes accompanied by calls for the defence's abolition, these lack the urgency and insistence of the promptings of the Committee on the CRPD. For New Zealand and other comparable jurisdictions, reimagining substantive criminal law without an insanity defence, will be a major practical and conceptual challenge. At the time of writing, no steps have yet been taken by New Zealand authorities seriously to address this issue. While reforms consequent upon a major review of the provision of mental health services in New Zealand are now well underway,[124] evaluation of the insanity defence is not a part of this review. Any further evaluation of the usefulness and legitimacy of the defence will need to be the subject of a separate review process which is not, however, likely in the foreseeable future.

[124] Recommendations for major reform of New Zealand's mental health services were made in the 2018 report *He Ara Oranga—Report of the Government Inquiry into Mental Health and Addiction* (Ministry of Health, Wellington, 2018). In addition to making far-reaching recommendations for the reform of mental health and addiction services, the Report recommended the repeal of the Mental Health (Compulsory Assessment & Treatment) Act 1992 and its replacement with a statute that better reflected a human rights approach and aligned with modern mental health and wellbeing models, see Chapter 11.

8

The Insanity Defence under Australian Law

Ian Freckelton

Introduction

The core of Australian law in relation to the insanity defence, now known in most jurisdictions as the mental impairment defence, remains based upon the English *M'Naghten* formulation from 1843.[1] However, its legislative formulations, along with what occurs by way of disposition for those found not guilty by reason of their mental condition, are remarkably diverse throughout Australia. In addition, key aspects of the defence are the subject of ongoing controversy amongst scholars, practitioners, and law reform bodies. In the courts, practical and conceptual difficulties continue to be encountered as thinking evolves about conditions which have the potential to erode criminal responsibility.

The general power of the Crown over 'lunaticks' and 'ideots' was transported to Australia, along with the convicts, from England in 1788. As Shea noted in 1999, 'When Governor Phillip landed at Port Jackson in 1788 he had with him a commission from King George III containing all the powers necessary for him to establish the colony. Amongst these powers were those relating to "lunaticks" and "ideots", (the mentally ill and the mentally retarded). Inter alia, the Governor was entrusted with "the care and commitment of the custody of .... 'Ideots' and 'lunaticks' and their estates"'.[2] The modern era of 'mental impairment' legislation dates back to 1995 when the Community Development Committee of the Victorian Parliament[3] recommended thoroughgoing legislative reforms to the pre-existing system under

[1] See A Loughnan, *Manifest Madness: Mental Incapacity in Criminal Law* (Oxford University Press 2012); S Yannoulidis, *Mental State Defences in Criminal Law* (Taylor & Francis 2016).

[2] P Shea, *Defining Madness* (Hawkins Press 1999) 22.

[3] Community Development Committee, Victorian Parliament, *Review of Legislation under which Persons Are Detained at the Governor's Pleasure* (Victorian Government Printer 1995). See too Victorian Law Reform Commission, *Mental Malfunction and Criminal Responsibility*, Report No 34 (Victorian Government Printer 1990); Inter-Departmental Committee of Western Australia, *The Treatment of Mentally Disordered Offenders* (1989) which recommended: '(1) An order as to the defendant's disposition should be made by the trial court; and (2) That order would not be mandatory but discretionary; and (3) In exercising that discretion, the court should have power to make (i) an order for the safe custody of the defendant in some institution or place appropriate to the circumstances of the case. Where the person is mentally ill that would ordinarily be an approved psychiatric hospital with a secure ward. In the case of an intellectually handicapped person that place might be a hospital or other institution, including a prison. (ii) an order releasing the defendant by way of conditional discharge into an appropriate after cate program.'

Ian Freckelton, *The Insanity Defence under Australian Law* In: *The Insanity Defence*. Edited by: Ronnie Mackay and Warren Brookbanks, Oxford University Press. © Ian Freckelton 2022. DOI: 10.1093/oso/9780198854944.003.0008

which persons found not guilty by reason of insanity or unfit to plead[4] were detained indefinitely, at the Governor's pleasure,[5] often for longer than if they had been found guilty.[6] The outcome of the legislative reforms for Victoria, and progressively throughout Australian jurisdictions (save in Western Australia), was a reformulation of terminology and a recalibration of the outcomes for persons found not guilty by reason of their mental illness or other conditions, as well as a reworking of the processes for their being reintegrated under supervision into the community.

A further generation of reforms commenced in 2013 when the Sentencing Council of South Australia and the New South Wales Law Reform Commission made recommendations about changes to the law relating to the defence of what in South Australia was 'unsoundness of mind' and in New South Wales had become known as 'mental impairment'.[7] The following year, 17 years after the legislation which followed the recommendations of the Community Development Committee of the Victorian Parliament, the Victorian Law Reform Commission reviewed the mental impairment regime in that state and made further recommendations for its improvement and modernization.[8]

This chapter identifies the multifarious variations in Australia's law on the insanity defence from state to state, for reasons of brevity omitting reference to the law in the Australian Capital Territory[9] and the Northern Territory,[10] and reviews the controversies that have been particularly prominent in judicial, law reform, and scholarly debates.

[4] See I Freckelton, 'Fitness to Stand Trial under Australian Law' in R Mackay and W Brookbanks (eds), *Fitness to Plead: International and Comparative Perspectives* (Oxford University Press 2018) 153.

[5] Crimes Act 1958 (Vic), ss 393, 420.

[6] See S Delaney, 'Controlling the Governor's Pleasure—Some Gain, Some Pain' (1998) 72(1) LIJ 46; J Lightfoot, 'Striking the Balance—Abolition of the Governor's Pleasure System' (2009) 5(2) Psychiatr Psychol Law 265; C Porter, 'At the Governor's Pleasure' (1994) 26 Aust J Forensic Sci 25. See too the criticisms made by Wickham J in *Wilsmore v Court* [1983] WAR 190, 201; Law Reform Commission of Tasmania, *Insanity, Intoxication and Automatism* (TLRC 61, 1988); I Campbell, 'Dangerousness and Detention: An Agenda for Reform of the Insanity Defence' (1988) 18 Univ WAL Rev 175; J Cockram, 'Justice or Differential Treatment? Sentencing of Offenders with Intellectual Disability' (2005) 30 J Intellect Dev Disabil 3.

[7] New South Wales Law Reform Commission, *People with Cognitive and Mental Health Impairments in the Criminal Justice System: Criminal Responsibility and Consequences* (NSWLRC 2013). https://www.lawreform.justice.nsw.gov.au/Documents/Publications/Reports/Report-138.pdf; Law Reform Commission of Victoria, Mental Malfunction and Criminal Responsibility (VLRC 34, 1990) paras 76–93.

[8] Victorian Law Reform Commission, *Review of the Crimes (Mental Impairment and Unfitness to Be Tried) Act 1997* (VLRC 2014), https://www.lawreform.vic.gov.au/wp-content/uploads/2021/07/Review_of_the_Crimes_Mental_Impairment_and_Unfitness_to_be_Tried_Act_0.pdf

[9] *Criminal Code 2002* (ACT), s 28(1); *R v Steurer* (2009) 3 ACTLR 272, para 49; *R v Aranyi* 278 FLR 409 *per* Nield AJ; *R v Smith* 269 FLR 233 *per* Refshauge J in *R v Aleer* [2016] ACTSC 75, and *R v Barker* [2014] ACTSC 374; *R v Cross* [2017] ACTSC 91.

[10] Criminal Code Act 1983 (NT), Sch 1, cl 43C(1).

Diverse State Statutory Formulations

Criteria for the acquittal of persons by reason of mental impairment bear significant features in common in the nine criminal jurisdictions of Australia—at Commonwealth level, the six states and the two territories. However, they also employ different terms and significantly varying definitions and attributes with the result that both the law and procedure are different from one part of Australia to another.

The Commonwealth

Under section 7.3(1) of the Commonwealth Criminal Code a person is 'not criminally responsible' for an offence if, at the time of carrying the conduct constituting the offence, the person was suffering from a 'mental impairment' that had the effect that:

(a) the person did not know the nature and quality of the conduct; or
(b) the person did not know that the conduct was wrong (that is, the person could not reason with a moderate degree of sense and composure about whether the conduct, as perceived by reasonable people, was wrong); or
(c) the person was unable to control the conduct.

Thus, the term 'mental impairment' is fundamental. It is defined to include 'senility, intellectual disability, mental illness, brain damage and severe personality disorder'.[11] The terminology has the potential to cause a number of challenges because each of the conditions exists on a spectrum, at the low end not necessarily being relevantly exculpating and at the high end potentially being wholly exculpating. In addition, the symptoms for certain of the conditions have the potential to vary according to both context and time. 'Mental illness' is stipulated to be a 'reference to an underlying pathological infirmity of the mind, whether of long or short duration and whether permanent or temporary, but does not include a condition that results from the reaction of a healthy mind to extraordinary external stimuli. However, such a condition may be evidence of a mental illness if it involves some abnormality and is prone to recur.'[12] 'Senility', which is not the same as dementia,[13] and is not a medical term, is not defined.

[11] Criminal Code, s 7.3(8).
[12] Criminal Code, s 7.3(8). See B McSherry, 'The Reformulated Defence of Insanity in the Australian Criminal Code Act 1995 (Cth)' (1997) 20(2) Int J Law Psychiatry 183.
[13] See A Barrell, 'What to Know about Senility and Dementia' (24 November 2020) Medical News Today, https://www.medicalnewstoday.com/articles/senile; A Leibing and L Cohen (eds), *Thinking about Dementia: Culture, Loss, and the Anthropology of Senility* (Rutgers University Press 2006).

New South Wales

In New South Wales, section 28 of the Mental Health and Cognitive Impairment Forensic Provisions Act 2020 (NSW) provides that a person is not criminally responsible for an offence if, at the time of carrying out the act constituting the offence, the person had a 'mental impairment' or a 'cognitive impairment', or both, that had the effect that the person:

(a) did not know the nature and quality of the act; or
(b) did not know that the act was wrong (that is, the person could not reason with a moderate degree of sense and composure about whether the act, as perceived by reasonable people, was wrong).[14]

A person is stated to have a 'mental health impairment' if:

(a) the person has a temporary or ongoing disturbance of thought, mood, volition, perception or memory, and
(b) the disturbance would be regarded as significant for clinical diagnostic purposes, and
(c) the disturbance impairs the emotional wellbeing, judgment or behaviour of the person.[15]

Notably there is no requirement for a particular degree of impairment and there are three domains in respect of which there can be impairment. A distinctive feature of the New South Wales legislation is that it is explicitly provided that a mental health impairment may arise from any of the following disorders but may also arise for other reasons:

(a) an anxiety disorder,
(b) an affective disorder, including clinical depression and bipolar disorder,
(c) a psychotic disorder,
(d) a substance induced mental disorder that is not temporary.[16]

The controversial aspect of this definition is the final component which recognizes that substance abuse may give rise to a mental disorder which is enduring and potentially such as to allow for exculpation of criminality. However, a person is stipulated not to have a mental health impairment if their impairment is caused solely by the temporary effect of ingesting a substance, or a substance use disorder.[17]

[14] For the prior law, see D Howard and B Westmore, *Crime and Mental Health Law in New South Wales: A Practical Guide for Lawyers and Health Care Professionals* (2nd edn, LexisNexis 2010).
[15] Mental Health and Cognitive Impairment Forensic Provisions Act 2020 (NSW), s 4(1).
[16] Mental Health and Cognitive Impairment Forensic Provisions Act 2020 (NSW), s 4(2).
[17] Mental Health and Cognitive Impairment Forensic Provisions Act 2020 (NSW), s 4(3).

A person is stated to have a 'cognitive impairment' if:

(a) the person has an ongoing impairment in adaptive functioning, and
(b) the person has an ongoing impairment in comprehension, reason, judgment, learning or memory, and
(c) the impairments result from damage to or dysfunction, developmental delay or deterioration of the person's brain or mind that may arise from a condition set out in subsection (2) or for other reasons.[18]

A cognitive impairment is prescribed to have the potential to arise from any of the following conditions but may also arise for other reasons:

(a) intellectual disability,
(b) borderline intellectual functioning,
(c) dementia,
(d) an acquired brain injury,
(e) drug or alcohol related brain damage, including foetal alcohol spectrum disorder,
(f) autism spectrum disorder.[19]

The reference to foetal alcohol spectrum disorder[20] is another distinctive and modern component of the New South Wales legislation that is yet to be emulated by other Australian jurisdictions. The reference to autism spectrum disorder is also innovative; high-functioning autism, also known as Asperger's disorder, has been held in a number of cases to have limited relevance to sentencing. It has the potential too to be such as to amount to a wholly exculpating condition.[21]

It is obligatory for a judge to explain to a jury if the question of whether the defendant has a mental health impairment or a cognitive impairment, or both, is raised:

(a) the findings which may be made on the trial,
(b) the legal and practical consequences of those findings,
(c) the composition of the [Mental Health Review] Tribunal and its relevant functions with respect to forensic patients,

[18] Mental Health and Cognitive Impairment Forensic Provisions Act 2020 (NSW), s 5(1).

[19] Mental Health and Cognitive Impairment Forensic Provisions Act 2020 (NSW), s 5(2).

[20] See I Freckelton, 'Sentencing Offenders with Foetal Alcohol Spectrum Disorder' (2016) 23(6) Psychiatr Psychol Law 815; I Freckelton, 'Assessment and Evaluation of Fetal Alcohol Spectrum Disorder (FASD) and its Potential Relevance for Sentencing: A Clarion Call from Western Australia' (2017) 24(4) Psychiatr Psychol Law 485.

[21] See I Freckelton, 'Expert Evidence about Autism Spectrum Disorder' in F Volkmar and others (eds), *Handbook of Autism and the Law* (Springer 2021) 36–69.

(d) without limiting paragraph (b), that a defendant who is found to have committed the act constituting the offence but not to be criminally responsible because of a mental health impairment or cognitive impairment, or both, may be ordered to be released by the Tribunal only if the Tribunal is satisfied, on the evidence available to it, that the safety of the defendant or any member of the public will not be seriously endangered by the defendant's release,

(e) that the jury should not be influenced by the consequences of a special verdict of act proven but not criminally responsible in deciding a verdict.[22]

A jury is obliged to return a special verdict of 'act proven but not criminally responsible' if it is satisfied that the defence of mental health impairment or cognitive impairment has been established.[23] A decision can be made without a jury—a court can enter a special verdict of act proven but not criminally responsible at any time in the proceedings (including before the jury is empanelled) if—

(a) the defendant and the prosecutor agree that the proposed evidence in the proceedings establishes a defence of mental health impairment or cognitive impairment, and

(b) the defendant is represented by an Australian legal practitioner, and

(c) the court, after considering that evidence, is satisfied that the defence is so established.[24]

Queensland

In Queensland, section 27 of the Criminal Code 1899 (Qld) provides that:

(1) A person is not criminally responsible for an act or omission if at the time of doing the act or making the omission the person is in such a state of mental disease[25] or natural mental infirmity as to deprive the person of capacity to understand what the person is doing, or of capacity to control the person's actions, or of capacity to know that the person ought not to do the act or make the omission.

(2) A person whose mind, at the time of the person's doing or omitting to do an act, is affected by delusions on some specific matter or matters, but who is not otherwise entitled to the benefit of subsection (1), is criminally responsible for the act or omission to the same extent as if the real state of things had been such as the person was induced by the delusions to believe to exist.

22 Mental Health and Cognitive Impairment Forensic Provisions Act 2020 (NSW), s 29.
23 Mental Health and Cognitive Impairment Forensic Provisions Act 2020 (NSW), s 30.
24 Mental Health and Cognitive Impairment Forensic Provisions Act 2020 (NSW), s 31.
25 By contrast with 'mental illness' which is defined by the Mental Health Act 2016 (Qld), s 10.

Every person is presumed to be of sound mind until the contrary is proved.[26] Notably, by contrast, for instance with the New South Wales provisions, the provision omits reference to the word 'wrong'.[27] The notion of 'unsound mind' does not include 'a state of mind resulting, to any extent, from intentional intoxication or stupefaction alone or in combination with some other agent at or about the time of the alleged offence'.[28] 'Stupefaction' is not defined and is not a medical term.

The Mental Health Court, which sits with a Supreme Court judge and two assisting psychiatrists,[29] determines whether a section 27 defence is made out[30] on a referral under section 109 of the Mental Health Act 2016 (Qld) with expert evidence playing a pivotal role in assisting the court.[31]

South Australia

In South Australia section 269C(1) of the Criminal Law Consolidation Act 1935 (SA) uses distinctive terminology—that of 'mental incompetence'. It provides that a person is 'mentally incompetent to commit an offence' if at the time of the conduct alleged to give rise to the offence, the person is suffering from a mental impairment in consequence of which the person:

(a) Does not know the nature and quality of the conduct; or
(b) Does not know that the conduct is wrong; that is, the person could not reason about whether the conduct, as perceived by reasonable people, is wrong; or
(c) Is *totally* unable to control the conduct. [Emphasis added]

The inability to exercise control is required to reach a very high bar—total inability.

There is no explicit reference to the person being able to reason with a 'moderate degree of sense and composure'. A 'mental impairment' is defined to include:

(a) A mental illness;
(b) An intellectual disability; and
(c) A disability or impairment of mind resulting from insanity.[32]

[26] Criminal Code 1899 (Qld), s 26.

[27] See CR Williams, 'Development and Change in Insanity and Related Defences' (2000) 24(3) Melb Univ Law Rev 711.

[28] Mental Health Act 2016 (Qld), s 109(2).

[29] See R Scott, 'The Function of the Assisting Psychiatrists in the Queensland Mental Health Court' (2009) 16(1) Psychiatr Psychol Law 7.

[30] See S Coghlan and S Harden, 'The Queensland Mental Health Court: A Unique Model' (2019) 16(4) BJ Psych Int 86.

[31] See R Scott, 'Expert Evidence in the Queensland Mental Health Court' (2009) 16 (Supp 1) Psychiatr Psychol Law S13.

[32] Criminal Law Consolidation Act 1935 (SA), s 269A.

A 'mental illness' is defined to mean 'a pathological infirmity of the mind (including one of short duration)', with a note stating that 'a condition that results from the reaction of a healthy mind to extraordinary stimuli is not a mental illness, although it may be evidence if it involves some abnormality and is prone to recur'.[33] Neither 'intellectual disability'[34] nor 'senility' are defined in the Criminal Law Consolidation Act.

When a mental incompetence defence is raised successfully, a person is found 'not guilty by reason of mental incompetence' and is subject to the 'special powers' of the court in respect of disposition.

Tasmania

In Tasmania a person is stated not to be 'criminally responsible' for an act done or an omission made:

> (a) when afflicted with mental disease to such an extent as to render him incapable of:
> (i) understanding the physical character of such act or omission; or
> (ii) knowing that such act or omission was one which he ought not to do or make; or
>
> (b) when such act or omission was done or made under an impulse which, by reason of mental disease, he was in substance deprived of any power to resist.[35]

Again, as in New South Wales, there is no reference to the accused knowing that their conduct was 'wrong'. It has been held that the term 'mental disease' is 'not necessarily synonymous' with the definition of 'mental illness' in Tasmania's mental health legislation.[36] However, the defence is still referred to as 'insanity'. The formulation of 'understanding the physical character of the act' reflects the language of the English Court of Appeal decision in 1913 of *R v Codere*.[37] It may be that the word 'understand' 'reflects the need for a deeper appreciation of the effect of the conduct upon other people, and may be an important discrepancy in relation to the scope and effect of the mental impairment on the accused's mental capacities'.[38]

The fact that at the time at which he or she is alleged to have done an act or made an omission a person was incapable of controlling their conduct generally,

[33] Criminal Law Consolidation Act 1935 (SA), s 269A.
[34] See though Child Sex Offenders Registration Act 2006 (SA), s 4; Disability Inclusion Act 2018 (SA).
[35] Criminal Code Act 1924 (Tas), Sch 1, cl 16(1).
[36] *R v Howe* [2004] TASSC 61, para 12; *Jeffrey v The Queen* [1982] Tas R 199.
[37] (1916) 12 Cr App R 21.
[38] Sentencing Advisory Council of South Australia, *A Discussion Paper Considering the Operation of Part 8A of the Criminal Law Consolidation Act 1935 (SA)* (2013) para 2.35.

is relevant to the question whether he or she did such an act or made such an omission under an impulse which by reason of mental disease he or she was in substance deprived of any power to resist.[39] The provision contrasts with that in section 269C(1) of the Criminal Law Consolidation Act 1935 (SA) which requires total inability to control conduct.

It is provided that a person whose mind at the time of doing an act or making an omission is affected by a delusion on some specific matter, but who is not otherwise exempted from criminal responsibility, is criminally responsible for the act or omission to the same extent as if the fact which he or she was induced by such delusion to believe to exist really existed.[40] For the purpose of the provision, the term 'mental disease' includes 'natural imbecility',[41] an anachronistic term that used to be employed as a synonym for mental retardation or intellectual disability.[42] If a person is exculpated on this basis a jury must find specially that it was on the ground that he or she was 'insane so as not to be responsible according to law'.[43]

Victoria

In Victoria, the relevant formulation exists under section 20 of the Crimes (Mental Impairment and Unfitness to be Tried) Act 1997 (Vic):

> (1) The defence of mental impairment is established for a person charged with an offence if, at the time of engaging in conduct constituting the offence, the person was suffering from a mental impairment that had the effect that—
> (a) he or she did not know the nature and quality of the conduct; or
> (b) he or she did not know that the conduct was wrong (that is, he or she could not reason with a moderate degree of sense and composure about whether the conduct, as perceived by reasonable people, was wrong).
>
> (2) If the defence of mental impairment is established, the person must be found not guilty because of mental impairment.

If the defence of mental impairment is raised by the prosecution or the defence, the party raising it bears the onus of rebutting the presumption that the accused was not suffering from a mental impairment.[44] Whether a person was suffering from a mental impairment is a question to be determined by a jury on the balance of probabilities, save that if the prosecution and defence agree that the evidence establishes the defence of mental impairment, the trial judge (alone) may hear the evidence

[39] Criminal Code Act 1924 (Tas), Sch 1, cl 16(2).
[40] Criminal Code Act 1924 (Tas), Sch 1, cl 16(3).
[41] Criminal Code Act 1924 (Tas), Sch 1, cl 16(4).
[42] See AM Clarke, 'The Study of Imbecile Behaviour' (1961) 3 Cerebral Palsy Bulletin 465.
[43] Criminal Code Act 1924 (Tas), Sch 1, cl 383(2).
[44] Crimes (Mental Impairment and Unfitness to be Tried) Act 1997 (Vic), s 21(3).

and make the decision as to whether the person is not guilty by reason of mental impairment.[45]

Western Australia

In Western Australia, section 27 of the Criminal Code (WA) employs the terminology of 'unsoundness of mind'. It provides that:

> A person is not criminally responsible for an act or omission on account of unsoundness of mind if at the time of doing the act or making the omission he is in such a state of mental impairment as to deprive him of capacity to understand what he is doing, or of capacity to control his actions, or of capacity to know that he ought not to do the act or make the omission.

This permits of a variety of conditions, including psychotic depression, to enable the defence.[46] Section 27 contains a similar provision in respect of delusions as exists in Tasmania. Section 1 of the Criminal Code defines 'mental impairment' as 'intellectual disability, mental illness, brain damage or senility' and 'mental illness' as 'an underlying pathological infirmity of mind, whether of short or long duration and whether permanent or temporary, but does not include a condition that results from the reaction of a healthy mind to extraordinary stimuli'.[47]

The component of section 27 relating to delusions has been controversial[48] although in 2007 the Western Australian Law Reform Commission rejected the argument it was redundant because most delusions will fall under the first limb of the insanity defence, concluding that:

> it is not in the public interest to allow a complete acquittal in circumstances where an accused has suffered such delusion as to be capable of killing another person. It is possible . . . that an accused's delusions spring from a mental disorder, but that the accused does not qualify for the first limb of the insanity defence because the disorder was not an 'underlying pathological infirmity of the mind' or did not completely deprive the accused of one of the named capacities.[49]

Earlier, in 1991 the Western Australian Law Reform Commission observed that: 'The second paragraph is likely to be difficult to apply because it involves an inquiry into the defendant's state of mind to determine whether the defendant

[45] Crimes (Mental Impairment and Unfitness to be Tried) Act 1997 (Vic), s 21(2), (4).

[46] See eg *State of Western Australia v Pearson* [2022] WASC 191.

[47] Law Reform Commission of Western Australia, *The Criminal Process and Persons Suffering from Mental Disorder* (WALRC 69, 1991), https://www.lrc.justice.wa.gov.au/_files/P69-R.pdf, para 2.16.

[48] See eg P Fairall, 'The Exculpatory Force of Delusions—A Note on the Insanity Defence' (1994) 6 Bond Law Rev 57.

[49] Western Australian Law Reform Commission, *The Law of Homicide* (WALRC 97, 2007), https://www.lrc.justice.wa.gov.au/_files//P97-ch05.pdf, 233.

believed, for example, that the defendant was threatened with "actual and unlawful violence". It noted too that acts committed during sleepwalking or as a result of conditions such as epilepsy, a cerebral tumour, or hyperglaecemia may all take place without a person's capacity to control their actions.[50]

Application of Mental Impairment Provisions by the Courts

The threshold statutory term 'disease of the mind' arising from the *M'Naghten* judgment has proved problematic in Australia. It has been accepted by the High Court as being synonymous with the term 'mental illness'[51] without the need to satisfy any specific diagnostic category. As Campbell put it, the disease of the mind requirement provides a means by which to distinguish exculpatory from non-exculpatory conditions.[52] Scholarly commentary has identified a number of strands in court decisions, which are not easily reconcilable. As long ago as 1993, McSherry maintained that three tests had emerged in the case law to determine whether an accused person suffers from a disease of the mind:

- 'The recurrence test', which focuses upon the likelihood the mental state's recurrence—where it is likely to recur it is likely to be a disease of the mind;
- The internal/external test, which provides that where a condition is internal or organic, as against external, it is likely to be a disease of the mind; and
- The 'sound/unsound mind test', which postulates a standard of mental strength below which a mind is 'infirm' or unsound.[53]

Each of these tests has deficiencies.

The most authoritative interpretation of the law on the issue is that of the High Court in *R v Falconer*[54] where Mason CJ, Brennan, and McHugh JJ approved the following passage in the Canadian decision of *Rabey v The Queen*:[55]

> In general, the distinction to be drawn is between a malfunctioning of the mind arising from some cause that is primarily internal to the accused, having its source in his psychological or emotional make-up, or in some organic pathology, as opposed to a malfunctioning of the mind which is the transient effect

[50] ibid 229.

[51] *R v Falconer* (1990) 171 CLR 30, 53, approving a passage from *R v Radford* (1985) 42 SASR 266, 274–75, where King CJ expressly accepted that the term 'disease of the mind' had the same meaning as 'mental illness'.

[52] IG Campbell, *Mental Disorder and Criminal Law in Australia* (Butterworths 1988) 128.

[53] B McSherry, 'Defining What is a "Disease of the Mind" The Untenability of Current Legal Interpretations' (1993) 1 *J Law Med* 76.

[54] (1990) 171 CLR 30, para 22.

[55] (1977) 79 DLR (3d) 414, 430.

> produced by some specific external factor such as, for example, concussion. Any malfunctioning of the mind, or mental disorder having its source primarily in some subjective condition or weakness internal to the accused (whether fully understood or not), may be a 'disease of the mind' if it prevents the accused from knowing what he is doing, but transient disturbances of consciousness due to certain specific external factors do not fall within the concept of disease of the mind.

Their Honours held that a temporary mental disorder must not be prone to recur if it is to avoid classification as a disease of the mind because a malfunction of the mind which is prone to recur reveals an underlying pathological infirmity.[56] This has meant that conditions such as self-induced intoxication (from alcohol or drugs) are excluded from the concept of 'disease of the mind'.[57] However, it is common for such scenarios to involve comorbidities—namely, an underlying (often schizophrenic) condition compounded or exacerbated by substance use.[58] Where a person suffers from a temporary disorder of the mind associated with the ingestion of intoxicating substances, the question asked in Australia tends to be whether the person suffered from a mental illness in the legal sense or whether the person was acting under an external stimulus such as drugs or alcohol but was otherwise of sound mind.[59]

However, whether conditions such as 'amphetamine-induced psychosis' should be permitted as a basis for the mental impairment defence has been controversial and, as yet, has not been finally resolved,[60] although in South Australia it has been accepted that there can be more than one cause of mental impairment.[61]

It is common for there to be an aggravation of psychotic symptomatology by substances such as Ice, GHB (and its variants) and cannabis.[62] It has been held that for the defence of mental impairment to be open, a psychiatric illness must be operative at the time of the act giving rise to the charge, even if there is a drug-induced psychosis.[63]

A personality disorder has been held not to constitute a 'disease of the mind'[64] and in 1991 the Law Reform Commission of Western Australia recommended no

[56] *R v Falconer* (1990) 171 CLR 30, para 24, applying *R v Radford* (1985) 42 SASR 266, 274–75.

[57] *R v Carter* [1959] VR 105, 110; *R v Meddings* [1966] VR 306; *R v Martin (No 1)* (2005) 159 A Crim R 314; [2005] VSC 518; *R v Sebalj* [2006] VSCA 106; *R v Konidaris* [2014] VSC 89; *R v Gibson* [2016] VSC 634.

[58] See A Carroll and others, 'Drug-Assisted Psychoses and Criminal Responsibility' (2008) 26 Behav Sci Law 633.

[59] *Fang v The Queen* [2018] NSWCCA 210, para 90.

[60] See eg A Carroll, B McSherry, and S Yannoulidis, 'Drug-associated Psychoses and Criminal Responsibility' (2008) 26(5) Behavioral Sciences and the Law 633; R Scott and W Kingswell, 'Amphetamines, Psychosis and the Insanity Defence: Disturbing Trends in Queensland' (2003) 23 Queensland Lawyer 151; S Yannoulidis, 'Drug Use and the Defence of Mental Impairment: Some Conceptual and Explanatory Issues' (2006) 182 Bond Law Rev 165.

[61] *Question of Law Reserved (No 1 of 2021)* [2021] SASCA 148.

[62] See eg *R v Hammond* [2020] VSC 515, para 28.

[63] See *R v Derbin* [2000] NSWCCA 361; *R v Ham* [2009] NSWSC 296; *R v Doolan* [2010] NSWSC 147.

[64] *R v Hodge* (1985) 19 A Crim R 129, 133.

change to the law in this respect, concluding: 'It is inconsistent with fundamental notions of criminal responsibility to excuse a person's acts or omissions arising from a personality disorder evidenced merely by a lack of self-control or indifference to standards of morality.'[65] However, the position on this issue is not wholly uniform. For instance in *McDermott v Director of Mental Health; Ex parte A-G (Qld)* the Queensland Court of Appeal held that it was not the law that a personality disorder could never constitute an 'abnormality of mind' for the purpose of the Queensland Criminal Code and that the determination is 'a question of fact, necessarily influenced by the question of degree, which the finder of fact is entitled to approach in a broad common sense way and not necessarily in accordance with medical evidence'.[66] This will not be the last word on the issue as more is learned about the physical attributes of the brains of persons with personality disorders.

The concept of what constitutes 'knowledge of wrongness' is difficult. Australia's major authority on the issue is that of *R v Porter*[67] where Dixon J stated that:

> We are not dealing with right or wrong in the abstract. The question is whether he was able to appreciate the wrongness of the particular act he was doing at the particular time ... If through the disordered condition of the mind he could not reason about the matter with a moderate degree of sense and composure it may be said that he could not know that what he was doing was wrong. What is meant by 'wrong'? What is meant by wrong is wrong having regard to the everyday standards of reasonable people. If you think that at the time when he administered the poison to the child he had such a mental disorder or disturbance or derangement that he was incapable of reasoning about the right or wrongness, according to ordinary standards, of the thing which he was doing, not that he reasoned wrongly, or that being a responsible person he had queer or unsound ideas, but that he was quite incapable of taking into account the considerations which go to make right or wrong, then you should find him not guilty upon the ground that he was insane at the time he committed the acts charged. In considering these matters from the point of view of fact you must be guided by his outward actions to a very large extent. The only other matter which can help you really is the medical opinion. I think the evidence may be described as his outward conduct and the medical opinion. It is upon this you must act. The medical opinion included explanations of the course of mental conditions in human beings generally.
>
> In conclusion I go back to what I consider the main question of the case and it is whether you are of the opinion that at the stage of administering the poison to

[65] Law Reform Commission of Western Australia, *The Criminal Process and Persons Suffering from Mental Disorder* (WALRC 69, 1991), https://www.lrc.justice.wa.gov.au/_files/P69-R.pdf, para 2.13; see too PA Fairall and PW Johnson, 'Antisocial Personality Disorder (APD) and the Insanity Defence' (1987) 11 Crim LJ 78.

[66] [2007] QCA 51, para 124 *per* Jerrard JA.

[67] (1933) 55 CLR 182, 190.

> the child the man whom you are trying had such a mental disorder or diseased intelligence at that moment that he was disabled from knowing that it was a wrong act to commit in the sense that ordinary reasonable men understand right and wrong and that he was disabled from considering with some degree of composure and reason what he was doing and its wrongness. If you answer that question in his favour you will find him not guilty on the ground of insanity at the time of the commission of the offence charged.

'The *Porter* gloss' was applied in *Sodeman v The King*[68] and *Stapleton v The Queen*[69] where the High Court referred to *Porter* and stated that 'given a disease disorder or defect of reason, then it is enough if it so governed the faculties at the time of the commission of the act that the accused was incapable of reasoning with some moderate degree of calmness as to the wrongness of the act or of comprehending the nature or emotion or significance of the act of killing'.[70] The '*Porter* gloss' was further considered in *Willgoss v The Queen*, an application for special leave to appeal to the High Court, where Dixon CJ and McTiernan, Fullagar, Menzies, and Windeyer JJ held: 'Such a direction well may be called for in cases where the acts which but for insanity would form the crime charged are committed in a state of frenzy, uncontrolled emotion or suspended reason, the product of mental disease or disorder'.[71] In Western Australia it has been held that a person is deprived of the capacity to know that they ought not to do a criminal act or make an omission 'if they have a complete incapacity of understand, appreciate or comprehend that the act ... is wrong according to ordinary standards (as distinct from unlawful)'.[72] In South Australia, it has been stated that 'the disease, disorder or disturbance must have been of such a character as to prevent a defendant from knowing what he or she was doing was wrong. One must draw attention to the defendant's understanding, and whether the defendant's functions of understanding are "thrown into derangement or disorder" by reason of the mental impairment'.[73] And in New Zealand, it has been observed that even amongstsane defendants it is unrealistic to expect rationality, sense, and composure in situations that are fraught and emotional.[74]

In *R v Martin (No 1)*[75] Bongiorno J held that the Crimes (Mental Impairment and Unfitness to be Tried) Act 1997 (Vic) had not, so far as the defence of mental impairment was concerned, altered the common law and that the term 'mental impairment' is synonymous with the term 'disease of the mind'. This led him to

68 *Sodeman v The King* (1936) 55 CLR 192, 215.
69 *Stapleton v The Queen* (1952) 86 CLR 358, 367.
70 See too *State of Western Australia v Davidson* [2022] WASC 70, para 44.
71 *Willgoss v The Queen* (1960) 105 CLR 295, 301.
72 *State of Western Australia v Taylor* [2021] WASC 34, para 31; *State of Western Australia v Davidson* [2022] WASC 70, para 45.
73 See eg *R v EY (No 2)* [2012] SASC 116, para 36.
74 See *R v Macmillan* [1966] NZLR 616.
75 (2005) 159 A Crim R 314; [2005] VSC 518, para 21; see too *DPP v Taleski* [2007] VSC 183.

conclude on the evidence before him that the condition of cannabis-induced psychosis was not a disease of the mind which would be such as to entitle the accused to an acquittal on the ground of mental impairment.

In the challenging decision of *R v Sebalj*,[76] Smith J reaffirmed that mental impairment means no more and no less than 'disease of the mind' as that concept was used in the common law M'Naghten defence of insanity. However, the complexity of the situation is illustrated by the facts of the case, in which Sebalj was charged with murder committed when he was in a psychotic state after extensive earlier use of heroin and amphetamines. The Supreme Court formed the view that Sebalj's condition was temporary and associated with the use of substances, or at least withdrawal from them, and so his condition was drug-induced and not a disease of the mind. However, after his plea but before he was sentenced, Sebalj had developed symptoms of schizophrenia. It has been argued that the distinction between methamphetamine-induced psychosis and schizophrenia is of little utility, given the parallels between the two,[77] especially in light of the prevalence of hallucinations and delusions in methamphetamine-induced psychoses.[78]

The term 'defect of reason' under *R v M'Naghten* was viewed in *R v Porter*[79] as involving the accused person's faculties being 'disordered' with there being 'some diminution or malfunction of the normal capacity for rational thought'.[80] This issue was reviewed by the Victorian Court of Appeal in *Kosian v The Queen*[81] which held that the Victorian formulation of the defence of mental impairment required 'an evaluation ... of how the [mental impairment] affected the offender's reasoning capacity, his understanding of what would be "wrong" and whether that understanding accorded with reasonable standards'. It confirmed the decision by the same court in *R v White*[82] that the test 'is not directed to moral or legal concepts ... but to the accused's awareness that reasonable people would disapprove as wrong the actions he is performing'. However, the Court of Appeal in *Kosian* emphasized that the comprehension of the accused as to whether his or her actions

76 [2003] VSC 181.

77 See eg TA Wearne and JL Cornish, 'A Comparison of Methamphetamine-Induced Psychosis and Schizophrenia: A Review of Positive, Negative and Cognitive Symptomatology' (2018) 9 Front Psychiatry 491. See also I Freckelton, 'Methamphetamine-induced Psychosis and Mental Impairment: A Challenge from New Zealand' (2019) 27(2) J Law Med 284, discussing *R v Brackenridge* [2019] NZHC 1004.

78 See H Gan and others, 'A Research of Methamphetamine Induced Psychosis in 1430 Individuals with Methamphetamine Induced Use Disorder: Clinical Features and Possible Risk Factors' (2018) 9 Front Psychiatry 551; H Zarrabi and others, 'Clinical Features, Course and Treatment of Methamphetamine-induced Psychosis in Psychiatric Inpatients' (2016) 16 BMC Psychiatry 44.

79 (1933) 55 CLR 182, 185.

80 See also Howard and Westmore (n 14); S Bronitt and B McSherry, *Principles of Criminal Law* (4th edn, Thomson Reuters 2017); S Yannoulidis, *Mental State Defences in Criminal Law* (Ashgate 2012); Loughnan (n 1); see too S Allnutt, A Samuels, and C O'Driscoll, 'The Insanity Defence: From Wild Beasts to M'Naghten' (2007) 15(40) Australasian Psychiatry 292.

81 [2013] VSCA 357, para 64.

82 (2003) 7 VR 422, 451.

were morally or legally wrong 'is not irrelevant to the evaluative task'.[83] This was in the context of expert evidence that the thinking capacity of the accused was impaired by his schizophrenic symptomatology which impacted upon his capacity to reason rationally. The outcome of this line of authority is that an impairment of the capacity for rationality may well result in a decision that the person suffered 'a disease of the mind'.

While mental health legislation defines 'mental illness' for the purpose of determining when coercive measures may be taken to mandate treatment of a person as a hospital inpatient or as an outpatient on a community treatment order, Australian criminal courts have tended to wrestle with the concept of mental illness at a more abstract level. For instance, for the purposes of the insanity/mental impairment defence, mental illness has been distinguished from 'mere excitability or a normal man, passion, even stupidity, obtuseness, lack of self control and impulsiveness'.[84]

While it is orthodox for accused persons seeking to plead insanity or mental impairment to adduce expert evidence from mental health professionals (usually from psychiatrists because of the need for a 'disease of the mind' to be established), on rare occasions the plea has been made out in the absence of expert evidence. For example, in *Lucas v The Queen*,[85] it was claimed on behalf of the accused that, first, due to an excessive consumption of methylated spirits he was in a state of delirium tremens at the time of the commission of the acts constituting the offences and, second, some statements attributed to him indicated a lack of comprehension of events that were taking place. No medical evidence was called as to the existence of any mental disease or disorder. The court held (at para 5) that:

> Whilst medical evidence may not always be indispensable to the establishment of a defence of insanity, its absence in this case meant, in our opinion, that the material before the jury was insufficient to found such a defence. Whilst the jury could have concluded that the applicant was at relevant times very intoxicated, there was, in our opinion, nothing on which it could have been concluded that any mental disease or disorder had supervened so that by reason of that disease or disorder he was unable to know what he was doing or to appreciate its quality. However, the trial judge left the defence of insanity to the jury. As we have said, the facts in the case were few and at the time of the summing up had been but recently evidenced and canvassed before the jury. In our opinion, the trial judge did not fail adequately in the circumstances of the case to place the defence before the jury and to instruct them in its legal elements. In so far as leave to appeal may be necessary, we would refuse it.

83 *Kosian v The Queen* [2013] VSCA 357, para 67.
84 *R v Porter* (1933) 55 CLR 182, 189, applied in *Falconer v The Queen* (1990) 171 CLR 30, 53.
85 (1970) 120 CLR 171.

The authorities on insanity/mental impairment prominently discuss the role of expert opinions, with many of the major authorities containing evaluation of conflicting expert evidence.

In *Taylor v The Queen*,[86] for example, Connor and Franki JJ held that a jury could not reject unanimous medical evidence where there was no other evidence casting doubt on it. Smithers J, in a separate judgment, held that the judicial direction might have induced an impression that the distinction it drew between evidence of fact and opinion meant that jurors could decide the question of insanity on facts other than the opinion stated by the expert witnesses, thus calling on the latter evidence only if they felt the need to be assisted by it in reaching their conclusions. Were they to have approached the case in that way, then the jury, his Honour held, would not have properly understood the evidentiary basis of the case for the accused where 'the only real evidentiary basis of that case was that constituted by the medical opinions considered as evidence of the critical facts'.

In *Taylor*, Smithers J observed that in a case where insanity was an issue it might well be, for practical purposes, that the only evidence on the critical facts bearing on the question of insanity was to be found in the opinion of the expert witnesses.[87] He observed:

> Where the fact in issue was the state and capacity of mind and the only evidence thereof is expert opinion, the jury should understand that where the competence and honesty of the expert are accepted his skill in the area should be respected and should only be rejected for good reason. But if the jury are under the impression that on the relevant issue they must look at the 'facts' given in evidence other than by the experts as the source or primary source of proof of insanity, and that they are not bound by the opinions and are free to make up their own mind contrary to those opinions, then it is hard to think that they would be performing their task according to law. And it appears to me that there was great danger that the impression of the jury would have been that referred to above. If so, that would explain the verdict which it is reasonable to think was quite unexpected.[88]

However, the orthodox position is that evaluating the differences between experts on the question of insanity is a question with which juries are well capable of dealing.[89] The fact that such evidence trespasses upon the 'ultimate issue rule', in principle a proscribed area of common law, has never inhibited its admissibility.[90]

[86] (1978) 22 ALR 599, 616–17.
[87] (1978) 22 ALR 599, 609–10.
[88] (1978) 22 ALR 599, 611.
[89] See eg *R v Gemmill* (2004) 8 VR 242; [2004] VSCA 72.
[90] See I Freckelton, *Expert Evidence: Law, Practice, Procedure and Advocacy* (6th edn, Thomson Reuters 2019).

Consequence of a Finding of Insanity/Mental Impairment/ Mental Incompetence/Unsoundness of Mind

The insanity law reform changes commencing in the 1990s resulted in the creation of 'special verdicts' (in some jurisdictions), the abolition of open-ended Governor's pleasure detention, and the creation of a procedure for the courts or, in the case of New South Wales and Queensland, the Mental Health Review Tribunal to reintegrate the offender into the community by a graduated process that reviewed the ongoing level of risk posed by the offender.

If an Australian court finds a person not guilty of a serious offence by reason of mental impairment it must determine whether to impose a custodial or non-custodial supervision order. Acquittal by reason of mental illness is contemplated by section 20BJ of the Commonwealth Crimes Act 1914 (Cth) where it is required that the court must order the person to be detained in safe custody in prison or in a hospital for a person specified in the order, for a period not exceeding the maximum period of imprisonment that could have been imposed if the person had been convicted of the person charged.

In New South Wales a court must refer the defendant to the Tribunal if a 'special verdict' of act proven but not criminally responsible is returned or entered and an order is not made for the unconditional release of the defendant.[91] Upon such a special verdict being delivered, the court can make a number of orders:

(a) an order that the defendant be remanded in custody until a further order is made under this section,
(b) an order that the defendant be detained in the place and manner that the court thinks fit until released by due process of law,
(c) an order for the unconditional or conditional release of the defendant from custody,
(d) other orders that the court thinks appropriate.[92]

Before making an order for the release of a defendant, a court may request a report from a forensic psychiatrist or other person of a class prescribed by the regulations, who is not currently involved in treating the defendant, as to the condition of the defendant and whether the release of the defendant is likely to seriously endanger the safety of the defendant or any member of the public.[93] A court must not make an order for the release of a defendant unless it is satisfied, on the balance of probabilities, that the safety of the defendant or any member of the public will not be seriously endangered by the defendant's release.[94]

[91] Mental Health and Cognitive Impairment Forensic Provisions Act 2020 (NSW), s 34.
[92] Mental Health and Cognitive Impairment Forensic Provisions Act 2020 (NSW), s 33(1).
[93] Mental Health and Cognitive Impairment Forensic Provisions Act 2020 (NSW), s 33(2).
[94] Mental Health and Cognitive Impairment Forensic Provisions Act 2020 (NSW), s 33(3).

Evaluation of such matters involves a balancing of competing considerations with the likelihood of the person being a danger to herself or himself or another person and the need to protect others needing to be balanced against the desire to ensure the liberty of the individual:

> The consequences for the individual who, it must be remembered, has been found not guilty of criminal activity by virtue of mental impairment, may be quite serious including ongoing detention or living under onerous supervision. The risk assessment must reflect both the likelihood of conduct of concern occurring and the magnitude of the harm that may result from any such conduct. The legislation calls for an assessment of the degree of likelihood of the occurrence of the risk along with the nature of the risk and its consequences. Some level of risk will, almost always, be present. The extent of the risk must be weighed in the balance in determining the nature of the supervision order to be imposed.[95]

If a person constitutes a significant risk of committing further offences or of absconding and thereby undermining the court's order for supervision if placed on a non-custodial supervision order, these will be powerful considerations, even if there is an absence of suitable custodial supervisory options.[96] However, the court is obliged to refer the defendant to the Mental Health Tribunal if a special verdict of act proven but not criminally responsible is made and an order is not made for the unconditional release of the defendant.[97] The person becomes a 'forensic patient'[98] and must be reviewed at intervals of six months.[99]

In Queensland, if the Mental Health Court decides a person was of unsound mind when an offence was committed, it will generally make a 'forensic order' and can make a 'non-revocation period' of not more than 10 years during which the Mental Health Tribunal cannot revoke the order.[100] While the Mental Health Court makes the initial disposition, the Mental Health Review Tribunal then reviews the person under the forensic order at least every six months.

Similarly in South Australia, if a court records a finding that the defendant was mentally incompetent to commit an offence, it is obliged to hear evidence and representations put to the court by the prosecution and the defence relevant to whether it should find the 'objective elements' of the offence are established.[101] By

[95] *R v KMD* [2015] NTSC 31, para 39 *per* Riley CJ.
[96] *The Queen v GC* [2021] NTSC 29, paras 28–35 *per* Grant CJ.
[97] Mental Health and Cognitive Impairment Forensic Provisions Act 2020 (NSW), s 34.
[98] Mental Health and Cognitive Impairment Forensic Provisions Act 2020 (NSW), s 72.
[99] Mental Health and Cognitive Impairment Forensic Provisions Act 2020 (NSW), s 78(d).
[100] Mental Health Act 2016 (Qld), s 137.
[101] Criminal Law Consolidation Act 1935 (SA), s 269F(B)(1).

2013 the existence of this option was identified by the Sentencing Advisory Council as having generated a 'significant increase in the number of defendants raising the defence of mental incompetence'.[102]

In Tasmania, as in Victoria, special hearings exist where an accused person is found unfit to stand trial[103] but not if a person is found not guilty by reason of insanity. Upon an insanity finding, a court is obliged to:

(a) make a restriction order; or
(b) release the defendant and make a supervision order; or
(c) make a treatment order; or
(d) …
(e) release the defendant on such conditions as the court considers appropriate; or
(f) release the defendant unconditionally.[104]

A restriction order is an order requiring a person to be admitted to and detained in a secure mental health unit until the order is discharged by the Supreme Court,[105] while a supervision order is an order releasing a person under the supervision of the Chief Forensic Psychiatrist, subject to such conditions as the court considers appropriate.[106] In making such decisions a court is obliged to have regard to:

(a) the nature of the defendant's mental impairment or other condition or disability; and
(b) whether the defendant is, or would if released be, likely to endanger another person or other persons generally; and
(c) whether there are adequate resources available for the treatment and support of the defendant in the community; and
(d) whether the defendant is likely to comply with the conditions of a supervision order; and
(e) other matters that the court thinks relevant.[107]

In Victoria, a special hearing, when a person has been found unfit to stand trial, is held to determine whether, on the evidence available, the accused:

[102] Sentencing Advisory Council of South Australia, *A Discussion Paper Considering the Operation of Part 8A of the Criminal Law Consolidation Act 1935 (SA)* (2013), para 3.41.
[103] Criminal Justice (Mental Impairment) Act 1999 (Tas), s 21. See *State of Tasmania v Bosworth* [2005] TASSC 29.
[104] See eg *H v DPP (No 2)* [2008] TASSC 10; *R v Howe* [2004] TASSC 61.
[105] Criminal Justice (Mental Impairment) Act 1999 (Tas), s 24.
[106] Criminal Justice (Mental Impairment) Act 1999 (Tas), s 29A.
[107] Criminal Justice (Mental Impairment) Act 1999 (Tas), s 35.

(a) is not guilty of the offence; or
(b) is not guilty of the offence because of mental impairment; or
(c) committed the offence charged or an offence available as an alternative.[108]

A special hearing has to be conducted as nearly as possible as if it were a criminal trial, with the accused being taken to have pleaded not guilty.[109] A judge is able to give a direction with the consent of the prosecution and the defence that expert witnesses give their evidence on the issue concurrently and consecutively, including before the prosecution has closed its case.[110] If a finding is made that the person committed the offence, it constitutes 'a qualified finding of guilt and does not constitute a basis in law for any conviction for the offence'. It constitutes a bar to further prosecution and is subject to appeal in the same manner as if the person had been convicted.[111]

If a judge in Victoria declares a person not guilty by reason of mental impairment they must declare them liable to custodial or non-custodial supervision or release them unconditionally, which is almost unknown. If they are found liable to supervision, they tend to be remanded in custody in an appropriate place (Victoria's forensic psychiatric hospital) or in a prison.[112] Persons can be subject to a prison detention order if no certificate of available services is issued by a designated mental health facility or if there is no practicable alternative to prison in the circumstances. This has the potential to occur if the offender is unpredictably dangerous and the circumstances are not such that the person can be detained at the mental health facility with safety for fellow detainees or staff[113] or if the view is formed that the person is not amenable to treatment—such as if they are a psychopath.[114]

Pending the making of a supervision order, the court can order the person to be examined by a medical practitioner or psychologist.[115] A supervision order after a finding of not guilty by reason of mental impairment is for an indefinite term[116] but a sentencing court must set a 'nominal term'[117] which prescribes the minimum time before a 'major review' of the order must occur.[118] Processes for review of supervision orders are prescribed, as well as for downgrading of such orders so that the person has the potential to transition from being 'custodial' to 'non-custodial'

[108] Crimes (Mental Impairment and Unfitness to be Tried) Act 1997 (Vic), s 17.
[109] Crimes (Mental Impairment and Unfitness to be Tried) Act 1997 (Vic), s 16.
[110] Under the Criminal Procedure Act 2009 (Vic), s 232A.
[111] Crimes (Mental Impairment and Unfitness to be Tried) Act 1997 (Vic), s 18.
[112] Crimes (Mental Impairment and Unfitness to be Tried) Act 1997 (Vic), s 19.
[113] See eg *Re AB* [2018] VSC 349.
[114] *In the matter of s35 Crimes (Mental Impairment and Unfitness to be Tried Act) 1997 In the matter of major review of: Derek Ernest Percy* [1998] VSC 90.
[115] Crimes (Mental Impairment and Unfitness to be Tried) Act 1997 (Vic), s 19(d).
[116] Crimes (Mental Impairment and Unfitness to be Tried) Act 1997 (Vic), s 27.
[117] Crimes (Mental Impairment and Unfitness to be Tried) Act 1997 (Vic), s 28. See too Criminal Code (NT), s 43ZC.
[118] Crimes (Mental Impairment and Unfitness to be Tried) Act 1997 (Vic), s 35.

by court order, the principal yardstick for which is whether the person or members of the public will be seriously endangered.

In South Australia alternatives to indeterminate detention came into force in March 1996 with the Criminal Law Consolidation (Mental Impairment) Amendment Act 1995 (SA). In determining the disposal of persons found not guilty by reason of mental incompetence, but made subject to supervision, section 269T(1) requires a court to have regard to:

- the nature of the defendant's mental impairment;
- whether the defendant is, or would if released, be likely to endanger another person, or other persons generally;
- whether there are adequate resources available for the treatment and support of the defendant in the community; and
- whether the defendant is likely to comply with the conditions of the licence; and other matters the court thinks relevant.

In the ACT, it is the Civil and Administrative Tribunal that reviews the supervision order.

In Western Australia, if a question arises under section 27 of the Criminal Code as to whether the accused was or was not criminally responsible for an act or omission on account of unsoundness of the mind, the trial judge must direct the jury that if it finds the accused not guilty by reason of the charge on account of unsoundness of mind and return a 'special verdict' to that effect.[119] In its review of the law of homicide,[120] the Western Australian Law Reform Commission reviewed the decision of *Walsh*[121] in which a combat veteran shot and killed his friend under the delusion he was in Korea defending himself against an enemy soldier. The accused expressly disclaimed reliance on the defence of insanity but claimed he suffered from post-traumatic stress disorder (PTSD) and was entitled to avail himself of the defence of self-defence. The Commission recommended that section 113 of the Criminal Procedure Act 2004 (WA) be amended to provide that if in a trial the question arises whether, under section 27 of the Criminal Code, 'the accused was not criminally responsible for an act or omission by reason of mental impairment or by the effect of delusions, the judge must direct the jury that if it finds the accused not guilty of the charge on this basis, it must return a special verdict of not guilty by reason of mental impairment'.[122]

When an accused person is acquitted by a superior court or on appeal of an offence on account of unsoundness of mind of a serious (Sch 1) offence, it must

[119] Criminal Procedure Act 2004 (WA), s 113(1).

[120] Western Australian Law Reform Commission, *The Law of Homicide* (WALRC 97, 2007), https://www.lrc.justice.wa.gov.au/_files//P97-ch05.pdf

[121] (1991) 60 A Crim R 419.

[122] Western Australian Law Reform Commission, *The Law of Homicide* (WALRC 97, 2007) 233.

make a 'custody order'.[123] A mentally impaired accused is detained in an authorized hospital, a declared place, a detention centre, or a prison, as determined by the Mentally Impaired Accused Review Board ('the Board') until released by an order of the Governor[124] who can release the person unconditionally or on conditions.[125] A mentally impaired accused can be detained in an authorized hospital only if the Board is satisfied:

(a) the accused has a mental illness requiring treatment; and
(b) that, because of the mental illness, there is—
  (i) a significant risk to the health or safety of the accused or to the safety of another person; or
  (ii) a significant risk of serious harm to the accused or to another person; and
(c) the accused does not have the capacity to consent to treatment; and
(d) the treatment can only be provided satisfactorily in an authorised hospital.[126]

Controversies

In the period subsequent to the progressive abolition of Governor's pleasure detention for persons found not guilty on the basis of insanity/mental impairment/unsoundness of mind/mental incapacity, there have been three major law reform reports. The first was a 2013 discussion paper by the Sentencing Advisory Council of South Australia.[127]

The second was the 2013 report of the New South Wales Law Reform Commission[128] which recommended the adoption of a definition of 'mental impairment' which included a volitional impairment—to incorporate mental health disorders (including independent substance-induced mental disorders); cognitive impairments (intellectual disability, borderline intellectual functioning, dementias, acquired brain injuries, drug- or alcohol-related brain damage, and autism spectrum disorders), but not personality disorders.[129]

[123] Criminal Law (Mentally Impaired Accused) Act 1996 (WA), s 21.
[124] Criminal Law (Mentally Impaired Accused) Act 1996 (WA), s 24.
[125] Criminal Law (Mentally Impaired Accused) Act 1996 (WA), s 35.
[126] Criminal Law (Mentally Impaired Accused) Act 1996 (WA), s 24.
[127] Sentencing Advisory Council of South Australia, *A Discussion Paper Considering the Operation of Part 8A of the Criminal Law Consolidation Act 1935 (SA)* (2013), https://www.agd.sa.gov.au/sites/default/files/discussion_paper_-_part_8a_criminal_law_consolidation_act.pdf?v=1491268750
[128] New South Wales Law Reform Commission, *People with Cognitive and Mental Health Impairments in the Criminal Justice System: Criminal Responsibility and Consequences* (NSWLRC Report No 138, 2013), https://www.lawreform.justice.nsw.gov.au/Documents/Publications/Reports/Report-138.pdf
[129] ibid 61–62.

The 2014 report of the Victorian Law Reform Commission into the 17 years of operation of the Crimes (Mental Impairment and Unfitness to be Tried) Act 1997 (Vic) was the third of the reports. A threshold issue identified by the Commission was whether 'mental impairment' should be given an explicit definition, rather than reliance being placed upon the common law test for insanity.[130] The Commission expressed concern that the *Falconer* test for the sound/unsound mind approach to what constitutes a 'disease of the mind' requires an unhealthy mind reacting to extraordinary stimuli, leaving it unclear whether conditions such as an intellectual disability of other cognitive impairment constitute a mental impairment.[131] The Commission concluded that the law was unclear about those conditions which constitute a 'disease of the mind' and expressed concern that this might be affecting the consistency of the application of the defence of mental impairment.[132] It advocated for a broad and inclusive definition which excluded self-induced conditions resulting from the temporary effects of ingesting substances so as to avoid widening of the definition of mental impairment in a way that would be inconsistent with its underlying policy. However, it recommended inclusion of self-induced independent conditions resulting from ingesting substances, instancing the *Sebalj* case as an example of a condition that should be included.[133] It noted that this was consistent with the recommendation of the New South Wales Law Reform Commission.

The Victorian Law Reform Commission identified that it is far more common for the defence of mental impairment to be established on the second limb of the M'Naghten test, this relating to the way in which a person processes knowledge about the nature and quality of their conduct in terms of whether it is wrong. The 2013 Sentencing Advisory Council in South Australia estimated that approximately 87% of findings of what is termed 'mental incompetence' are based on the second limb of the test.[134] While the Victorian Commission noted the recommendation of the New South Wales Law Reform Commission to include a volitional element, it did not endorse such a course. However, it did recommend clarification of the phrase 'to reason with a moderate degree of sense and composure about whether the conduct, as perceived by reasonable people, was wrong', replacing it with: 'that is, he or she did not have the capacity to think rationally about whether the conduct, as perceived by reasonable people, was wrong'.[135]

[130] The Victorian Law Reform Committee, in its Inquiry into Access to and Interaction with the Justice System by People with an Intellectual Disability and their Families and Carers (2013, at 243) recommended a definition to encompass 'mental illness, intellectual disability, acquired brain injuries and severe personality disorders'.

[131] Victorian Law Reform Commission, *Review of the Crimes (Mental Impairment and Unfitness to Be Tried) Act 1997* (VLRC, 2014) para 4.29.

[132] ibid para 4.62.

[133] ibid para 4.73.

[134] Sentencing Advisory Council of South Australia, *A Discussion Paper Considering the Operation of Part 8A of the Criminal Law Consolidation Act 1935 (SA)* (2013) 8.

[135] Victorian Law Reform Commission, Review of the Crimes (Mental Impairment and Unfitness to Be Tried) Act 1997 (VLRC, 2014) para 4.108.

The Victorian Law Reform Commission considered the advantages of a review model in relation to supervision orders, based on the role of the Queensland and New South Wales Mental Health Review Tribunals:

- Expertise could be better embedded in an alternative model. For example, judges and barristers would develop expertise practising in that field and independent psychiatrists could assist the court or tribunal.
- It would reduce the workload that is now being placed on the judiciary in the criminal jurisdiction, which can detract from their principal responsibility of conducting jury trials.
- It may be more appropriate for a separate tribunal to be involved in decisions under the processes for review, variation and revocation of supervision orders and extended leave rather than judges of a court where the original supervision order was made.[136]

However, it was not satisfied that there was sufficient support for a mental health court for Victoria to sustain a recommendation for a change from the judicial model of decision-making and concluded that 'the benefits of a judicial model of decision making currently outweigh the benefits of an alternative model'.[137] In this regard its approach was the same as that of the Western Australian Law Reform Commission which in 2007 expressed the 'tentative view ... that there is no reason to remove determination of the issue of insanity from the normal trial process'.[138]

The Victorian Commission recommended a higher level of supervision, recommending the abolition of nominal terms and their replacement with provisions that:

(a) a supervision order is for an indefinite term and that the matter is to be brought back to the court at the end of every five years for a 'progress review'
(b) the court must set a term of five years before the first progress review of a supervision order to run from the day the person was first made subject to the supervision order, and
(c) the court that made the supervision order must conduct the first progress review of the order before the end of the five-year term and thereafter at intervals not exceeding five years for the duration of the order.[139]

[136] ibid para 10.29.
[137] ibid para 10.31.
[138] Western Australian Law Reform Commission, *The Law of Homicide* (WALRC 97, 2007), https://www.lrc.justice.wa.gov.au/_files//P97-ch05.pdf, 235.
[139] Victorian Law Reform Commission, Review of the Crimes (Mental Impairment and Unfitness to Be Tried) Act 1997 (VLRC, 2014) para 10.160.

Many of the decisions in relation to major reviews, extended leave for patients subject to custodial supervision orders, change of custodial supervision orders to non-custodial supervision orders, and revocation of supervision orders are inaccessible by reason of non-publication orders. There has been some scholarly analysis of the jurisprudence, principally in Victoria.[140] The decisions about such matters have a discretionary character[141] and are focused upon assessment of risk of endangerment to the public and the person should the level of restrictions be eased. The Victorian Court of Appeal has observed: 'The function which the court is to perform is essentially an inquisitorial or administrative one in which it is not bound by defined rules or practices but may inform itself in any manner it thinks fit ... The court is required by the statute, amongst other things, to balance the competing interests of the detainee and the public and, in doing so, to assess risk factors which, in turn, depend upon value judgments in respect of which reasonable minds might differ.'[142]

As in most mental impairment cases, the offender has committed a serious crime of violence, decision-making about release from custody is strongly influenced by expert evidence from treating forensic psychiatrists and forensic psychologists and is conservative in terms of the prediction of risk. Decisions are usually heavily focused upon the extent to which the offender has complied with required pharmacotherapy but also takes into account the persistence of symptomatology which played a role in their committing the index offence, the person's level of insight about warning signs of relapse, the extent of any therapeutic rapport which they have formed with those who have provided them with treatment, their use of alcohol and drugs, and the stability of their personal circumstances. In Victoria, the Law Reform Commission recommended in 2014 a realignment of the criteria for decision-making to focus upon whether the person would pose an 'unacceptable risk of causing physical or psychological harm' if restrictions on their autonomy of decision-making, living situation, and obligations to co-operate with treatment were eased.[143]

In Western Australia, however, the system of Governor's pleasure detention remains,[144] with the role of the Mentally Impaired Accused Review Board being to assess the detainee's suitability for release every 12 months and to report to the

[140] See eg I Freckelton, 'Applications for Release by Australian in Victoria to be released Having Been Found Not Guilty of Offences of Violence by Reason of Mental Impairment' (2005) 28(4) Int J Law Psychiatry 375; I Freckelton, 'Involuntary Detention of Persons Found Not Guilty of Murder by Reason of Mental Impairment or Found Unfit to Stand Trial: A New Jurisprudence from Victoria' in I Freckelton and K Diesfeld (eds) *Involuntary Detention and Therapeutic Jurisprudence: International Perspectives on Civil Commitment* (Ashgate 2003) 383.

[141] See *NOM v DPP* [2012] VSCA 198.

[142] *RDM v DPP* [1999] VSCA 86, para 64; see too *NOM v DPP* [2012] VSCA 198, paras 47, 58.

[143] Victorian Law Reform Commission, Review of the Crimes (Mental Impairment and Unfitness to Be Tried) Act 1997 (VLRC, 2014) para 10.215.

[144] See I Freckelton, 'Indefinite Detention in Australia: The Ongoing Risk of Governor's Pleasure Detention' (2014) 21(4) Psychiatr Psychol Law 469; *Yates v The Queen* [2013] HCA 8.

Executive.[145] In its 1991 Report, the Western Australian Law Reform Commission argued that:

> The mandatory imposition of detention, whether in a hospital or in a prison, is unjustified because it is based on an assumption that a person who succeeds with a defence of insanity is dangerous and in need of restraint at the time of the trial, a prediction that is apparently based on the commission of the alleged offence. However, the person's mental condition may have improved between the time of the alleged offence and the time of the trial or the conduct may have arisen from a periodic disturbance such as epilepsy which can be treated with medication while the person leads a normal life in the community.[146]

It reiterated its view in its 2007 report on homicide, contending that 'a trial or appeal court should be given discretion to impose a range of dispositions following a finding of not guilty by reason of mental impairment for any offence'[147] and recommending a supervised release order for mentally impaired release regime with a limiting term similar to that in Victoria.[148]

Conclusions

Australia's statutory law relating to determination of a person's guilt on the basis of their mental state is an incoherent patchwork of inconsistent provisions. The variation in legislative regimes even extends to its terminology—insanity (Queensland, South Australia, Tasmania), mental impairment (Commonwealth, Victoria, ACT, Northern Territory), mental health impairment (New South Wales, South Australia), mental incompetence (South Australia), and unsoundness of mind (Queensland, Western Australia). In some jurisdictions anachronistic references exist to phenomena such as 'natural imbecility' (Tasmania). Unclear terms such as 'senility' (Commonwealth, South Australia), 'borderline intellectual functioning' (New South Wales), and 'disability of mind' (South Australia) confuse the position. In most jurisdictions (South Australia, Victoria, Tasmania, Western Australia, and the Northern Territory) decision-making about disposition of persons found not guilty by reason of their mental condition is by the sentencing court but in Queensland and New South Wales it is by a Mental Health Review Tribunal

[145] Criminal Law (Mentally Impaired Accused) Act 1996 (WA), s 33(2)(d).

[146] Law Reform Commission of Western Australia, *The Criminal Process and Persons Suffering from Mental Disorder* (WALRC 69, 1991), https://www.lrc.justice.wa.gov.au/_files/P69-R.pdf, para 2.40. See too DK Malcolm, 'Western Australia and the High Court Centenary: A Reason to Celebrate?' (29 November 2003) Constitutional Centre of Western Australia: https://www.supremecourt.wa.gov.au/_files/HighCrt-Cent2003.pdf

[147] Western Australian Law Reform Commission, *The Law of Homicide* (WALRC 97, 2007), https://www.lrc.justice.wa.gov.au/_files//P97-ch05.pdf, 242.

[148] ibid 246.

and in the ACT by the Civil and Administrative Tribunal. In Western Australia the Governor's pleasure system lingers anachronistically, with involvement from the Mentally Impaired Accused Review Board.

In some jurisdictions mental impairment or its equivalent is defined, including by reference to specific mental health conditions (see eg New South Wales, the Commonwealth of Australia). Under Commonwealth legislation this includes 'severe personality disorder' and 'mental illness' which is defined by reference to the quaint descriptor, 'pathological infirmity of the mind', a term that is also employed in Western Australia. In Queensland there is a cognate term—'natural mental infirmity'. In New South Wales 'mental health impairment' is stated to include a 'substance induced mental disorder that is not temporary' whereas in most jurisdictions this conundrum is not explicitly addressed. In New South Wales too 'foetal alcohol spectrum disorder' and 'autism spectrum disorder' are brought explicitly under the mental impairment umbrella, but not in any other jurisdiction, leaving uncertainty about their status as potential aetiologies for mental impairment. In Queensland, Tasmania, and Western Australia there is specific reference to the effect of delusions.

At Commonwealth level, and in Tasmania and Western Australia, a volitional component is retained for the defence but in South Australia the inability to control the conduct must be 'total'. There are diverse formulations of the second M'Naghten limb, with some jurisdictions referring to knowledge of wrongfulness, and others using alternative formulations with uncertainty about the extent such formulations are endeavouring to deal with the same issue. In some jurisdictions a special verdict of not guilty or not criminally responsible but act proven is provided for (see eg New South Wales) but in most jurisdictions such an option does not exist.

Diverse formulations and procedures exist for decision-making about gradual reintegration into the community of those found not guilty by reason of their mental state. This can assume an extra level of complexity when it comes time for a detainee to be moved from one jurisdiction to another to facilitate their mental health and psycho-social rehabilitation.

However, the essence of the law throughout Australia is derived from the M'Naghten rules, although some variation occurs in relation to both drug-induced mental health impairments and personality disorders, as well as the need for the accused to be able to understand that what he or she did was 'wrong' in order to avail himself or herself of the defence. Challenges, including issues arising as a result of human rights, autism spectrum disorders, and substance use-generated brain injuries[149] remain for determining the extent to which conditions such as

[149] See P Gooding and others, 'Unfitness to Stand Trial and the Indefinite Detention of Persons with Cognitive Disabilities in Australia: Human Rights Challenges and Proposals for Change' (2017) 40 Melb Univ Law Rev 817.

foetal alcohol spectrum is incorporated within the conditions that have the potential to exculpate from criminal responsibility.

Predicting the likely evolution in the complex tapestry of insanity law in its diverse incarnations in Australia is far from straightforward. There are few clear signposts for future law reform. The Queensland experiment of a specialist Mental Health Court appears unlikely to be emulated elsewhere but it may well be that there will be extension of the mental health conditions that qualify for the defence, and the emergence of some level of consensus. In addition, it may be that there will be a convergence in the availability of a finding of act proven but not guilty on the basis of mental impairment. Such a finding has many benefits in terms of clarity. In addition, it is probable that there will be uniform abolition and streamlining of the role of the executive in decision-making about progressive release of persons found not guilty on the basis of the risk that they pose to the community becoming acceptable. However, it is likely that the responsibility for such sensitive decision-making will continue to be split amongst jurisdictions that favour courts and those that prefer administrative tribunals, a question for some jurisdictions being whether the responsibility for such a high stakes predictive issue ought to remain that of judges while for others it will be preferred that the decision-making be undertaken by a specialist multi-disciplinary panel.

9

Before and After Hinckley

Legal Insanity in the United States

Stephen J Morse

Introduction

This chapter first considers the scope of the affirmative defence of legal insanity in the United States before John Hinckley was acquitted by reason of insanity in 1982 for attempting to assassinate President Reagan and others and the immediate aftermath of that acquittal. Since the middle of the 20th century, the tale is one of the rise and fall of the American Law Institute's Model Penal Code test for legal insanity.[1] The chapter then turns to the constitutional decisions of the United States Supreme Court concerning the status of legal insanity. Finally, it addresses the substantive and procedural changes that have occurred in the insanity defence since the wave of legal changes following the *Hinckley* decision.

Before and in the Wake of Hinckley

The affirmative defence of legal insanity has always been controversial, but every state had some form of the defence until the time of Hinckley. In the early part of the 20th century, a few states tried to abolish the defence legislatively,[2] but all such attempts were rejected by the states' appellate courts. After *M'Naghten*,[3] virtually all US jurisdictions adopted some form of the English cognitive test, although starting with the *Parsons*[4] case in Alabama, a minority of jurisdictions also adopted a control[5] test in addition to the M'Naghten standard. There were, of course,

[1] The American Law Institute is a private, non-profit organization of lawyers, judges, law professors, and others dedicated to reform of various areas of the law.

[2] See *State v Lange*, 123 So 639, 641–42 (La 1929) (finding a violation of the state due process clause); *Sinclair v State*, 132 So 581, 584–87 (Miss 1931) (finding a violation of the federal due process, equal protection, and cruel and unusual punishment clauses); *State v Strasburg*, 110 P 1020, 1023–24 (Wash 1910) (finding a violation of the state due process clause).

[3] *Cl & Fin* [1843] 8 Eng Rep 718.

[4] *Parsons v State*, 81 Ala 577 (1887).

[5] These tests are sometimes referred to as 'irresistible impulse' or 'volitional' tests, but both alternatives sow confusion for various reasons. 'Control' is a preferable generic term that I shall use throughout this chapter.

Stephen J Morse, *Before and After Hinckley* In: *The Insanity Defence*. Edited by: Ronnie Mackay and Warren Brookbanks, Oxford University Press. © Stephen J Morse 2022. DOI: 10.1093/oso/9780198854944.003.0009

criticisms of *M'Naghten*. It was allegedly too inflexible because its test is expressed in all-or-none terms, is too unscientific, and it unduly limited the scope of expert testimony. In practice, however, most of these alleged flaws were unproblematic. Experts were not cabined, and there is no evidence that the test was applied narrowly as a result of its narrow language. It was, of course, open to the criticism that an independent control test was necessary. Nonetheless, M'Naghten remained the dominant test until the second half of the 20th century. Jurisdictions were given great freedom to allocate the burden of persuasion at any level, including requiring the defendant to prove legal insanity beyond a reasonable doubt,[6] thus increasing the risk of wrongful conviction. Jurisdictions were permitted to place the persuasion burden on the prosecution beyond a reasonable doubt once the defendant met the production burden, and most did so.

In 1952, the American Law Institute (ALI) began work in earnest on the Model Penal Code (MPC), an attempt to bring order, rigour, and precision to the common law of crimes. After the publication of numerous preliminary drafts, a final official draft was published in 1962. Its insanity defence provision is as follows:

> Section 4.01. Mental Disease or Defect Excluding Responsibility.
>
> (1) A person is not responsible for criminal conduct if at the time of such conduct as a result of mental disease or defect he lacks substantial capacity either to appreciate the criminality [wrongfulness] of his conduct or to conform his conduct to the requirements of law.
> (2) As used in this Article, the terms 'mental disease or defect' do not include an abnormality manifested only by repeated criminal or otherwise anti-social conduct.[7]

The drafters had consulted with mental health professionals and believed the new test was an improvement on both M'Naghten and control tests. It notably included a control prong. It required only lack of substantial capacity, not lack of all capacity to appreciate or to conform. Further, its cognitive prong gave lawmakers the choice between appreciation, not knowledge, of criminality (legal appreciation) or of wrongfulness (moral appreciation), and did not focus on 'knowledge' narrowly conceived. State lawmakers and judges were convinced. After publication of the MPC test, every state that seriously considered insanity defence reform legislatively or judicially adopted the MPC test. There was no uniform federal insanity test extant at the time, but before *Hinckley*, all federal circuits but one had judicially

[6] *Leland v Oregon*, 343 US 790 (1952); re-aff'd, *Rivera v Delaware*, 429 US 877 (1976).

[7] American Law Institute, *Model Penal Code & Commentaries* §4.01 (American Law Institute 1962, 1985).

adopted the MPC test. At the time of *Hinckley*, the MPC test was probably the majority rule.

In March 1982, John W Hinckley, the 25-year-old son of a prosperous Colorado family, attempted to assassinate President Reagan and others in the District of Columbia. He was charged with attempted murder under both federal and local District law.[8] As is often the case, the prosecutions were consolidated in the federal district court. At the time, the MPC test was the applicable federal rule in the District of Columbia and the prosecution bore the burden of persuasion beyond a reasonable doubt once the production burden had been met. Both sides were represented by excellent attorneys and experts. There was not profound disagreement among the experts about the facts, including those pertaining to Hinckley's mental state. The crucial question was whether those facts amounted to delusional beliefs or evidence of a disturbed but non-delusional agent. I did not attend the trial, but I did read the complete transcript. In my experience, it is rare for the evidence to be in such exquisite equipoise. The prosecution's weighty burden of persuasion made it almost inevitable that a proper jury would acquit Hinckley by reason of insanity and in June 1982, they did so.

The verdict caused a public uproar. President Reagan was popular and the insanity defence was not. Many thought that the control prong of the MPC test was the culprit, but there is no convincing evidence for this allegation. There were the usual complaints that this was another example of the 'circus atmosphere' of duelling experts that insanity cases too often produced. And so on. The result was a wave of legislative reform at the federal and state levels, much of it aimed at narrowing and even abolishing the defence.

The Justice Department and the Attorney General were both initially in favour of abolishing the insanity defence in federal criminal trials, but were ultimately convinced that this change was too extreme.[9] In the event, Congress passed the Insanity Defense Reform Act in 1984, which for the first time established a uniform federal rule. The legislation adopted a M'Naghten variant that used 'appreciation' of the nature and quality of one's acts or wrongfulness, that contained no control test, that required the necessary mental disorder component to be 'severe', and that placed the burden of persuasion on the defendant by clear and convincing evidence.[10] Many states followed suit, typically abolishing a control test, narrowing the cognitive substantive test, and allocating the burden or persuasion to the defendant by either a preponderance of the evidence or the more onerous clear

[8] Under the dual sovereignty doctrine, the US Constitution permits successive prosecution in federal and local courts for the same criminal acts without violating the double jeopardy clause. *Bartkus v Illinois*, 359 US 121 (1959), re-affirm'd, *Gamble v United States*, 139 S Ct 1960 (2019).

[9] I testified twice on behalf of the American Psychological Association concerning what the federal insanity rule ought to be. I know from staffers and some member of the House that abolition was considered too extreme by members of both parties in both the legislative and executive branches of government.

[10] 18 USC § 17 (1984).

and convincing standard.[11] Five states abolished the affirmative defence of legal insanity. Four of the state supreme courts upheld the legislation against constitutional attack, but one held the reform unconstitutional.[12]

The triumphal march of the MPC test had come to an end. The *Hinckley* verdict had done its work. In the ensuing decades, there were no major changes to the law of legal insanity nationwide, although criticism of a narrow cognitive test persisted. Cases like those of Andrea Yates,[13] who had drowned her five children in a bathtub in response to the delusion that she needed to do so to save them from Satan, increased calls to once again adopt a control test. Such claims made little headway. Most important, a question the Supreme Court had never answered remained open: whether the Constitution required some form of the affirmative defence of legal insanity. Three Supreme Court cases addressed the issue, to which we will now turn.

The Deconstitutionalization of the Affirmative Defence of Legal Insanity

The United States Supreme Court is admirably reluctant to interfere with substantive criminal law. The definition of crimes and defences is largely left to the states and Congress in deference to our federal system of government. The standard trope is that the individual jurisdictions are 'laboratories' to test the validity of the will of the people expressed through legislative enactments, and the Supreme Court should not interfere except in extreme cases. Thus, any petitioner making a substantive due process claim that some state statute is unconstitutional faces a difficult task to show that the remedy is implicit in ordered liberty or that the law 'offends some principle of justice so rooted in the traditions and conscience of our people as to be ranked as fundamental'.[14] The historical record is a crucial part of this analysis. A frequently quoted opinion expressing the Court's deference to the states in substantive criminal law is from Justice Marshall's plurality opinion in *Powell v Texas*,[15] in which the Court was asked to constitutionalize an affirmative

[11] There has been one good study in a sample of states of the naturalistic experiment that reforms and abolition produced that found that narrowing the substantive defence made little difference in outcomes but allocating the burden of persuasion to the defendant produced fewer acquittals. HJ Steadman and others, *Before and After Hinckley: Evaluating the Insanity Defense Reform* (The Guilford Press 1993).

[12] *State v Searcy*, 118 Idaho 632, 798 P 2d 914 (1990); *State v Bethel*, 66 P 3d 840 (Kansas 2003); *State v Korell*, 690 P 2d 992 (Montana 1984); *State v Herrera*, 895 P 2d 359 (Ut 1995). *Finger v State*, 27 P 3d 66 (Nevada 2001) ruled that abolition violated the due process clauses of the US and Nevada Constitutions.

[13] See DW Denno, 'Who is Andrea Yates? A Short Story About Insanity' (2003) 10 Duke J Gend Law Policy 1.

[14] *Leland v Oregon*, 343 US 790, 798 (1952).

[15] *Powell v Texas*, 392 US 514 (1968).

defence for behaviour associated with an addiction which was allegedly a compulsion symptomatic of the disease.

> We cannot cast aside the centuries-long evolution of the collection of interlocking and overlapping concepts which the common law has utilized to assess the moral accountability of an individual for his antisocial deeds. The doctrines of *actus reus*, *mens rea*, insanity, mistake, justification, and duress have historically provided the tools for a constantly shifting adjustment of the tension between the evolving aims of the criminal law and changing religious, moral, philosophical, and medical views of the nature of man. *This process of adjustment has always been thought to be the province of the States.*[16]

The Court thus refused to adopt such a one-size-fits-all constitutional defence as not fruitful and as something that should be left to the province of the states.

An unusual exception to the Court's deference was *Robinson v California*.[17] Walter Lawrence Robinson was a needle-injecting drug addict who was convicted under a California statute that made it a crime to 'be addicted to the use of narcotics' and he was sentenced to 90 days in jail. The only evidence that he was an addict was needle marks. Robinson appealed to the Supreme Court on the ground that punishing him for being an addict was a violation of the 8th and 14th Amendments' prohibition of cruel and unusual punishment. There were many different opinions written in the case, but a majority agreed that punishing for addiction was unconstitutional. (As a sad footnote, Robinson died of an overdose before the case was decided.)

It is difficult to determine precisely what reasoning was the foundation for the Court's constitutional conclusion, but for our purposes three stand out: it is unconstitutional to punish for status alone or because addiction is a disease or because addiction is 'involuntary'. Herbert Fingarette and Anne Fingarette Hasse demonstrated conclusively decades ago that the disease rationale collapses into either the status rationale or the involuntariness rationale (1979), so let us examine what implications follow from each of these two. The status rationale is far more modest and simply builds on the foundational criminal law requirement that criminal liability generally requires action (or an intentional omission in appropriate cases). Robinson was not charged with possession or use, but simply with the status of being an addict. In dissent, Justice White pointed out that if it was unfair to punish an addict for his status, why would it not be equally unfair to punish him for the actions that are signs of that status. It is a clever question, but it ignores the view of addiction as a chronic and relapsing disorder. On this view, one can be an addict even if one is not using at the moment so there is no action. Again, the status argument is

16 ibid 536–37 (emphasis added).

17 370 US 660 (1962).

modest because it betokens no genuine widening of non-responsibility conditions. Indeed, it is a narrowing holding because the older common law permitted punishment for prohibited statuses.

The 'involuntariness' claim more extensively suggests that punishing people for abnormal conditions and their associated behaviours that they are helpless to prevent is also unconstitutional. Adopting the involuntariness position would be an invitation to undermine the choice model of addiction in light of some powerfully supported arguments that use by addicts is indeed a choice. More important, if the Court adopted an 'involuntariness' defence, it could not be limited to addiction-related behaviour.

Those who wanted to test the meaning of *Robinson* did not have long to wait because *Powell v Texas* settled the issue just six years later. Leroy Powell was a chronic alcoholic who spent all his money on wine and who had been frequently arrested and convicted for public drunkenness. We have already seen that the Court rejected constitutionalizing a control test in *Powell*, but the *Powell* plurality made clear that *Robinson* should *not* be read extensively as based on an involuntariness rationale. Instead, it was simply based on the rationale that the Constitution does not permit punishment for status alone.[18] Culpable action was required before the state could justifiably blame and punish. There have been attempts since then to claim that Justice White's confusing concurrence,[19] which envisioned some circumstances in which a constitutional excuse might be required, should be read as the holding of *Powell*.[20] These attempts have been fruitless to date, but claims based on accumulating scientific knowledge might motivate further such attempts. In short, as of 1968, there was no definitive statement from the High Court about the constitutionality of some form of the insanity defence.

That status quo did not change in 2006 when the Court decided *Clark v Arizona*.[21] In the early morning of 21 June 2000, Eric Clark, a 17-year-old resident of Flagstaff, Arizona, was riding around in his pickup truck blaring loud music. Responding to complaints about the noise, Officer Jeffrey Moritz, who was in uniform, turned on the emergency lights and siren of his marked patrol car and pulled Clark over. Moritz left the patrol car and told Clark to remain where he was. Less than a minute later, Clark shot and killed Moritz. Clark was charged with intentionally killing a police officer knowing that the officer was acting in the line of duty.[22]

Clark did not contest the shooting and death. But he did claim he was suffering from paranoid schizophrenia at the time of the crime. He claimed both that his

[18] *Powell v Texas*, 392 US 514, 532 (1968).

[19] ibid 548.

[20] *Manning v Caldwell*, 930 F 3d 264 (4th Cir 2019). The case ultimately settled, however, so there was no definitive opinion on the issue.

[21] 548 US 735 (2006).

[22] All statements of the facts are taken from the Supreme Court opinion.

mental disorder negated the required mens rea for the crime charged (because he lacked the intent to kill a person and the knowledge that the victim was a police officer) and that in any event his mental disorder rendered him legally insane.

There was substantial evidence to suggest that Clark knew Moritz was a police officer and that he had planned just such a shooting, including Clark's statements to classmates a few weeks earlier that he wanted to shoot police officers. He had arguably even lured Officer Moritz to the scene by driving his truck with its radio blaring in a residential area. On the other hand, Clark presented testimony from family, classmates, and school officials about his bizarre behaviour during the preceding year, including rigging his bedroom with fishing line, beads, and chimes to warn him of intruders, and keeping a bird in his car to warn him of airborne poison. These actions were plausibly a result of his paranoid delusions. Indeed, lay and expert testimony reported that Clark thought Flagstaff was populated with 'aliens', including some that were impersonating police officers, that the aliens were trying to kill him, and that only bullets could stop the aliens. The defence expert also testified that Clark had turned the radio up to drown out auditory hallucinations.

The operative Arizona legal insanity test under which Clark was tried was limited to the cognitive right/wrong test: once the burden of production was met, the defendant had the burden of proving by clear and convincing evidence that 'at the time of the commission of the criminal act [he] was afflicted with a mental disease or defect of such severity that [he] did not know the criminal act was wrong'.[23]

Clark argued that the full M'Naghten rule was the minimum test necessary to satisfy due process and that Arizona's truncated test was therefore unconstitutional. Writing for the five-Justice majority, Justice Souter rejected this claim, concluding that the full M'Naghten Rule is not a fundamental principle of justice subsumed by the due process clause.[24]

The Court correctly noted that the history of legal insanity defences in this country demonstrates that there is substantial diversity of language and interpretation within the broad cognitive and control categories. As Justice Souter pointed out, insanity definitions vary widely across the United States, and four states had abolished the defence entirely. The Court also observed that the test for legal insanity is not a test for mental disorder. The tests for insanity and disorder have been devised for different purposes—assessing criminal responsibility and justifying mental health treatment—and there is controversy about both. This is inevitable because the test for legal insanity is a matter of policy. The Court concluded that because there is so much variation, 'no particular formulation has evolved into a baseline for due process, and ... the insanity rule, like the conceptualization of criminal offenses, is substantially open to state choice'.[25]

[23] Arizona Revised Statutes Annotated Sec 13–502(A) (West 2001).

[24] *Clark v Arizona*, 548 US 735 (2006). Chief Justice Roberts and Justices Scalia, Thomas, and Alito joined Justice Souter's majority opinion. Justice Breyer concurred in the majority's analysis.

[25] ibid 752.

Although reasonable people might believe that Arizona's truncated insanity test is not optimally just, the Court's holding on this issue—that due process does not require 'any single canonical formulation of legal insanity'[26]—seems plainly right. But in the course of reaching this rather unremarkable conclusion, the Court may have confounded the two M'Naghten prongs.

In its original characterization of the disjunctive M'Naghten Rule, as well as in its categorization of types of insanity rules, it referred to knowledge of the nature and quality of one's act as a question of 'cognitive capacity' and knowledge of right and wrong as a question of 'moral capacity'.[27] But, in fact, both are cognitive questions, and indeed that is why both are usually alternative prongs of cognitive tests such as M'Naghten. They differ only in the object of the knowledge required. Moreover, mental disorder seldom disables a person's moral compass. The person may be making a 'moral mistake' because his or her perceptions and beliefs are distorted by disorder, but the moral sense generally remains intact. Andrea Yates might genuinely have thought her behaviour was morally justified, but her moral capacity was hardly disabled. Indeed, one could view her act as an indication that her moral sense was perfectly intact, albeit driven by a delusional belief.

The Court also consistently referred to control tests as 'volitional' and characterized them as asking 'whether a person was so lacking in volition due to a mental defect or illness that he could not have controlled his actions'.[28] It is common to refer to control tests as volitional but this is a confused locution that should be abandoned. Whether Clark thought he was killing an alien to save himself or thought he was killing an officer because he was angry at the police, his volition or will perfectly and competently executed the intention he formed. Yates too perfectly executed her intention to kill, motivated by her desire to save the children from Satan's eternal torments. Both may have experienced grave difficulty conforming to the law because they suffered profound delusions about the nature of the world, but in neither case was a defect of the will the source of the problem.

The Court also decided that the narrow Arizona legal insanity rule was constitutionally acceptable because evidence of so-called cognitive incapacity—lack of knowledge of what one was doing—is relevant to the right/wrong test and has the same significance for both. The Court recognized that one might show lack of moral knowledge without showing lack of factual knowledge about what one was doing, but it correctly observed that lack of the latter was almost always sufficient to show lack of moral knowledge.[29] After all, if the agent does not know what he

[26] ibid 753.

[27] ibid 747, 753–54.

[28] ibid 749.

[29] Contrary to the Court's assertion, it is quite possible that a defendant might not know what he or she was doing but would know that it was wrong. eg suppose a defendant violently attacked a person with the belief that the person was a dog. See J Livermore and PE Meehl, 'The Virtues of M'Naghten' (1967) 51 Minn L Rev 769, 809. In such a case, the defendant would not know what he or she was doing, but would know that cruelty to animals was a moral and legal wrong. It is not clear from *Clark*'s reasoning if a rule like Arizona's that produced such an outcome would be constitutional because the Court

is doing, he cannot know that it is right or wrong. Indeed, the Court interpreted Arizona's legislative narrowing of the rule as a 'streamlining'[30] change rather than a genuinely substantive alteration. Even under the narrow rule, then, all evidence of lack of factual knowledge would apparently be relevant and admissible, as it was at trial.

Before we leave *Clark*, we should take note of the case's other important holding: a state was free to exclude all expert evidence of mental disorder to negate mens rea, as Arizona did. A state had to allow introduction of observational evidence of mental disorder, whether from lay people or experts on the mens rea issue, but expert evidence about mental disorder generally and the defendant's capacities could constitutionally be excluded. The Court noted that Arizona was free to 'channel'[31] all such expert evidence into the issue of legal insanity. In its discussion of the mens rea issue, the Court sometimes confused that issue with legal insanity. It is true that the same evidence may often support claims that mens rea is negated and that the defendant is legally insane, but they are nonetheless legally distinct doctrines with equally distinct consequences. Mens rea negation is a denial of the prima facie case that can lead to outright acquittal; legal insanity is an affirmative defence that leads to a form of involuntary civil commitment to a forensic facility. I raise this mens rea issue because the same confusion about the relation between mens rea and legal insanity bedevilled both the ancient authorities and the Supreme Court majority effectively upholding the complete abolition of the defence of legal insanity in *Kahler v Kansas*,[32] which will be discussed below.

Whether a jurisdiction could constitutionally both abolish the insanity defence and exclude expert testimony on mens rea was unclear because Arizona did have an insanity defence, even if it was the narrowest in the nation. Thus, the effect of mental disorder on culpability assessment was not completely forbidden. In holding that Arizona's very narrow legal insanity formulation was constitutional, the Court took no position on whether a jurisdiction had to have some form of an affirmative defence. The case did not present that question. But *Delling v Idaho* did.

In late March and early April 2007, John Joseph Delling planned and committed the intentional homicide of two people he believed were stealing his 'aura' and 'powers'. He further believed that he needed to kill the victims to prevent the victims from harming him. There was uniform agreement that Delling was psychotic and delusional. He was charged with first degree murder. Idaho was one of the first states to abolish the insanity defence in the wake of *Hinckley*. State law did permit the defendant to introduce evidence of mental disorder to negate mens rea,

did not envisage this possibility. There is a serious question about whether such a rule would permit unjust blame and punishment. Nevertheless, although such cases are a theoretical possibility, they will be so rare that the Court's analysis is reasonable. See *Clark v Arizona*, 548 US 735, 753–55 and n 24.

30 *Clark v Arizona*, 548 US 735, 755 and n 24.

31 *Clark v Arizona*, 548 US 735, 770–71.

32 140 S Ct 1021 (2020).

the so-called mens rea alternative to the insanity defence. In this case, however, there was no doubt that rather than negating the mens rea of intent, Delling's severe mental disorder gave him reason to form it. After all, his delusional beliefs led him to kill the victims on purpose to save his own life. In the event, Delling pleaded guilty to second degree murder, but the trial judge who accepted taking the plea and imposed sentence noted the following:

> I don't believe that the defendant has the ability to appreciate the wrongfulness of his conduct or to conform his conduct to the requirements of the law. I do not believe it existed at the time he committed the offenses. I do think that he was in such a severe grip of his delusions that he would not have conformed his conduct to the law, and I do think the crimes do arise directly from his illness.[33]

In other words, although Delling formed the mens rea and was fully guilty under Idaho law, in the judge's opinion, Delling was legally insane. The facts were perfect to test whether Idaho's abolition of legal insanity and adoption of only the mens rea alternative were unconstitutional. Delling appealed on that ground and asked the Supreme Court to grant *certiorari* (discretionary review).

In the United States Supreme Court, it takes the vote of only four of the nine justices for the Court to grant review. The Court declined to hear the case, 6:3.[34] Although written dissents to denials of *certiorari* are relatively infrequent, Justice Breyer filed one that was joined by Justices Ginsburg and Sotomayor.[35] In his argument that review should have been granted, Justice Breyer noted the long, virtually uniform acceptance of an affirmative defence of legal insanity and the criticisms that the mens rea alternative was not adequate because it would convict defendants who would otherwise be found insane and because mental disorder seldom negates mens rea. The constitutional status of the insanity defence remained an open question.

On the evening of 28 November 2009, James Kraig Kahler entered the home of his former grandmother-in-law and shot and killed his former wife, his two daughters, and the wife's grandmother. Kahler was charged with capital murder. Prior to the killings, the Kahlers had seemed to be a 'perfect' family, but infidelity and other factors caused the marriage to disintegrate and end in divorce. Kahler had been leading an exemplary personal life as a family man and a professional life as an engineer and city manager. As his personal life deteriorated, so did Kahler. He had been fired from his job and was living at his family's Kansas farm. On the

[33] Brief for Respondent in the Supreme Court of Idaho, *Idaho v John Joseph Delling*. Nos 36920 and 36921 (2010) 3–4.

[34] Full disclosure: Professor Richard J Bonnie of the University of Virginia and I wrote an amicus brief urging the Court to grant review on behalf of a large number of criminal and mental health law professors. Such 'friend of the court' briefs are meant to advise the Court's decision-making.

[35] *Delling v Idaho*, 133 S Ct 504 (2012).

evening of the homicides, Kahler was angry at his ex-wife. His son was staying with him and they were having a good time. Kahler called his ex-wife and asked if he could extend the son's stay for a day. She refused, and while Kahler was doing an errand, she came by Kahler's residence and took the son away with her. Kahler then obtained the weapon, went to the homicide scene, and shot his victims.

Like Idaho, Kansas had abolished the affirmative defence of legal insanity and adopted the mens rea rule. Like Delling, there was little doubt that Kahler planned the homicides and formed the intent to kill. Unlike Delling, however, for whom the evidence of gross loss of contact with reality was overwhelming, Kahler was not obviously crazy. Nevertheless, he had been examined by a psychiatrist who concluded that Kahler suffered from a number of mental disorders, including a major mental disorder, severe depression. As a result, the expert opined, Kahler's perception and judgement were so distorted that he may have become dissociated from reality at the time of the crime. The expert also testified that Kahler could not refrain from his conduct. Severe depression can have psychotic features, but distorted perceptions and judgement do not necessarily rise to that level. Moreover, in contrast, Delling's motivating reason for forming the intent to kill—the need to save his own life—might have been a justification if true, whereas Kahler's actions were arguably an anger-driven reaction that had no justification whatsoever. Nevertheless, if Kansas did have an insanity defence, Kahler's expert testimony would have been sufficient to raise a jury issue and to warrant an instruction.

Because an insanity defence was not available and Kahler's conduct met the criteria for capital murder, his conviction for the most serious crime in the criminal law was improperly a foregone conclusion. He had no realistic prospect of exculpation. Kahler was convicted of capital murder and appealed on the ground that the Kansas law abolishing the insanity defence was unconstitutional. The Supreme Court agreed to hear the case.[36] Justice Kagan wrote the majority opinion upholding the Kansas law 6:3, with Justice Breyer once again in dissent, joined by Justices Ginsburg and Sotomayor.

Recall that the Court has repeatedly held that history is a prime guide to the analysis of whether a rule 'offends some principle of justice so rooted in the traditions and conscience of our people as to be ranked as fundamental'. As a result, a large part of both opinions was devoted to consideration of the earlier cases and authoritative commentaries concerning the relation of mental disorder to culpability. Unsurprisingly each claimed the history supported their own opinion. I claim that analysis of the history is clouded by the authorities' loose language that often left unclear whether the mens rea required by the prima facie case or

[36] Full disclosure: Professor Bonnie and I again co-authored an amicus brief on behalf of 290 criminal and mental health law professors, arguing that the Kansas law was unconstitutional. Amicus briefs arguing against the law were also submitted by the American Bar Association and a group of philosophers.

the affirmative defence of legal insanity was being referred to. The clear distinction between the two in legal writing did not emerge until recently, however, and even the Supreme Court conflates the two as it did in *Clark* and would do in *Kahler*. The more important observation about the history, however, is that everyone concedes that some form of an insanity defence has existed in English law since the 1300s and everywhere in American law since the founding until *Hinckley*. Even as of the year of the opinion, 2020, only four states have effectively abolished the defence. It is hard to imagine that anyone could characterize the ubiquity of legal insanity as anything other than a fundamental principle of justice rooted in our history and tradition. But the majority did just that, in part because a number of unclear historical sources were read as if they reasonably led to the contrary result.

The majority's traditional legal analysis began with the correct observation noted in *Clark* that there is much variation in the tests various jurisdictions use for legal insanity and no formulation is or ever has been 'canonical'. As a result, the petitioner had a heavy burden to convince the Court that at a minimum, the Constitution compels adoption of some form of the moral capacity prong of M'Naghten (the knowing right from wrong prong). Although the dissent conceded that no particular test was required, the majority seems on firm ground when it claimed that the dissent's analysis in fact accepted the moral incapacity test as a minimum requirement.[37]

This was probably a strategic error on the dissent's part, but it is not clear that it would have made a difference because the majority claimed that Kansas' mens rea rule in fact adopted the 'cognitive' prong of M'Naghten (nature and quality of the act).[38] The dissent argument about abolition is thus eviscerated because Kansas allegedly had *not* abolished the insanity defence and the Court did not need to address whether outright abolition was constitutional. That question was left open.[39]

The Court further argued that Kansas had decided that moral culpability was captured by the 'nature and quality' prong indirectly expressed through the mens rea rule. Consequently, Kansas' scheme was not untethered from judgements about moral culpability.[40] The Court noted that the Kansas moral judgement rule might differ from the dissent's or from many of the justices and other jurisdictions, but Kansas was constitutionally entitled to make that judgement without judicial interference. Further, the majority asserted that the dissent was wrong to claim that jurisdictions retain leeway concerning the content of the standard because they are free to go beyond the minimum moral capacity standard. But again, why should that be the canonical minimum? Jurisdictional freedom is indeed abridged. If the defendant lacked moral capacity, that does not eliminate culpability in Kansas, it

37 *Kahler v Kansas*, 140 S Ct 1021, 1031 n 5.

38 ibid 1026. The majority claimed without support that everyone agreed to this, but as we shall see, this is an unjustified claim.

39 ibid 1031 n 6.

40 ibid 1031 n 7.

simply diminishes it, the majority argued. Such considerations can be addressed at sentencing, which is clearly permitted in the Kansas scheme. Indeed, if the reason for moral incapacity, such as major mental disorder, requires diversion to inpatient psychiatric care, Kansas also directly permits this outcome.

The majority's reasoning is attractive on its face, but it is massively flawed. The Kansas rule is not the equivalent of the cognitive prong of M'Naghten because it is much narrower depending on how the 'nature and quality' of one's actions is interpreted. A defendant may know what he or she is doing in a narrow sense. Consider Andrea Yates again. She knew the victims were her children and that she was causing their biological death by drowning them. Please recall that she delusionally believed that she was saving them from eternal torment by Satan in hell. That was her material motivation for her action. She clearly formed the mens rea for premeditated, intentional homicide, but did she know what she was doing in any sensible sense? Defendants virtually never mistake their victim for a lemon or a dog, the silly examples used by the MPC and the *Kahler* dissent respectively. Few if any insanity claimants are acquitted by the factual cognitive prong. To the extent that any insanity rule is meant to express a moral judgement, the cognitive prong fails to do so. If the 'nature and quality' is interpreted more broadly, as I just suggested, then the cognitive prong does become a genuine moral standard, but note that Ms Yates would have been convicted under the Kansas mens rea rule because, unlike the 'nature and quality' standard, the Kansas mens rea alternative does not permit a broad interpretation. Mens rea is defined narrowly. The defendant did or did not form it, and in almost all cases, even the most abnormal defendants will form it, as the dissent clearly recognized and powerfully argued. No jurisdiction has ever adopted solely the cognitive prong as its insanity rule because essentially no one would ever be acquitted under this standard. Kansas has effectively abolished the insanity defence despite the majority's slippery claim to the contrary.

The ability of the judge to consider moral incapacity at sentencing and to commit the convicted felon to psychiatric care do not cure the central moral defect of the Kansas scheme. Conviction of a defendant who is morally innocent is legally and morally objectionable. A just criminal law would not permit this. The acquitted defendant is not stigmatized and blamed as a criminal, and the conditions of confinement should be required to be less onerous than prison. But Kansas judges are not required to take mental abnormality into account at sentencing or to order psychiatric care. Doing so is entirely discretionary, even in cases that seem to demand such actions.

For good measure, Kansas advanced the claim that the insanity defence is too hard and confusing for adequate jury assessment, but if the Court is correct that the mens rea rule is really a form of insanity defence, then mens rea evaluation faces the same difficulties. In addition to this logical flaw, the empirics of Kansas' claim were refuted by both the dissent and by the law professors' amicus brief. Of course it is difficult to reconstruct past mental states, but the insanity defence is adjudicated in 46 states and the federal jurisdiction without undue difficulty. Even the four abolitionist states permit such reconstruction for purposes of sentencing. And there is no evidence whatsoever that it is more difficult to assess past mental disorder than past mens rea. In my experience as a practicing forensic psychologist, I would claim the opposite is true. The gross mental abnormality typically needed for a successful insanity claim is easier to evaluate than mens rea because it is so gross and obvious in most cases.

The majority opinion concluded by noting that psychiatry is an inexact science and thus courts should be reluctant to intrude in the fraught relation between mental disorder and criminal culpability.

> Defining the precise relationship between criminal culpability and mental illness involves examining the workings of the brain, the purposes of the criminal law, the ideas of free will and responsibility. It is a project demanding hard choices among values, in a context replete with uncertainty, even at a single moment in time. And it is a project, if any is, that should be open to revision over time, as new medical knowledge emerges and as legal and moral norms evolve. Which is all to say that it is a project for state governance, not constitutional law.[41]

The Court is correct that the content of the test is a project for state governance, but wrong to imply that a state can constitutionally do without at least some affirmative defence of legal insanity. Moreover, at present, the working of the brain need not be examined to understand the behaviour of defendants and to decide how the law should respond to particular behaviours, such as gross loss of contact with reality. Even if we could 'read' the content of mental states from knowing the subject's brain states, which is entirely a fantasy, it would not entail how the law should respond because behaviour, not the brain, is crucial to responsibility assessment. Finally, the metaphysical concept of free will is not a criterion in criminal law nor even foundational for it.[42]

In conclusion, it is now constitutional to effectively abolish the insanity defence. No state has done so, however, since the original four states did so decades ago.[43] One hopes that no further jurisdictions will follow these examples.

[41] ibid 1037.

[42] SJ Morse, 'The Non-Problem of Free Will in Forensic Psychiatry and Psychology' (2007) 25 Behav Sci Law 203.

[43] Some believe that Alaska did so in 2018 because it adopted the mens rea alternative. Alaska Statutes §12.47.020. At the same time, however, it also adopted an affirmative defence of legal insanity. Alaska Statutes §12.47.010.

Substantive Law and Procedure Since Hinckley

This section of the chapter first considers the substantive law of legal insanity since *Hinckley*. As we shall see there have been few changes since the changes immediately post-*Hinckley*. Then it turns to the procedures associated with legal insanity.

Substance

There have been few substantive changes since the general tightening of the tests in the wake of *Hinckley*. Some variant of M'Naghten is by far the dominant rule. There continue to be skirmishes over its interpretation, especially about whether 'wrong' means legal or moral wrong. The states are split on this issue and some have given no definitive answer. The four abolitionist states have continued to reject the affirmative defence. A minority of states continue to include a control test. The unique New Hampshire doctrine simply acquits a defendant if he was 'insane' at the time of the crime.[44]

In the federal courts, most cases are on habeas corpus appeal from state convictions for very serious crimes, such as capital murder and murder. Most of the claims are for some variant of ineffective assistance of counsel or other non-substantive failures. Such claimants face a legal challenge because Congress enacted the Antiterrorism and Effective Death Penalty Act of 1996 (AEDPA) in 1996,[45] which applies to all federal petitions for habeas corpus filed on or after its effective date. Title I of AEDPA substantially changed the way federal courts handle habeas corpus actions. A state prisoner may not obtain relief with respect to any claim that was adjudicated on the merits in state court proceedings unless the adjudication of the claim:

(1) resulted in a decision that was contrary to, or involved an unreasonable application of, clearly established Federal law, as determined by the Supreme Court of the United States; or
(2) resulted in a decision that was based on an unreasonable determination of the facts in light of the evidence presented in the State court proceeding.[46]

[44] New Hampshire Statutes SA §628.2. This test relies on common law precedents dating from the late 19th century to determine if a defendant was insane. For example, if a defendant committed an act that would be criminal if he were sane, but the act was the product of mental disease, the defendant should be found insane. *State v Pike*, 49 NH 399, 402 (1869). The federal court in *Durham* that adopted the much-discussed but later rejected 'product' test, thought it was adopting New Hampshire's rule, but in fact there were differences. J Reid, 'Understanding the New Hampshire Doctrine of Legal Insanity' (1960) 69 Yale LJ 367.

[45] Pub L 104–32, 110 Stat 1217.

[46] 28 USC § 2254(d), as amended by AEDPA. A decision on the merits means a substantive and not procedural claim. AEDPA was not a response to *Hinckley*, to be sure. It was an attempt to make habeas corpus appeals more efficient. Nonetheless, since it was passed, it has had a large impact on appeals of convictions in insanity defence cases and related issues.

This provision makes it difficult to prevail, especially under subsection (2), and few claimants do so.

The state cases are similar to those in the federal courts. The dominant M'Naghten test has a surfeit of common law history, even in those jurisdictions that abandoned it in favour of the MPC rule in the middle of the 20th century. Thus, there are few surprises concerning the interpretation of the content of the test. Most involve questions regarding sufficiency of the evidence, ineffective assistance of counsel and like claims. In short, there has been little substantive activity since the post-*Hinckley* legislative changes.

Every now and then, an unusual case comes along, but it is not representative of any trend. For example, in the wake of *Hinckley*, the State of California jettisoned the MPC test for legal insanity and opted for a traditional M'Naghten Rule with the amendment that the two prongs were now conjunctive, separated by 'and', rather than traditionally disjunctive, separated by 'or'. In other words, a defendant could be found legally insane only if the defendant both did not know the nature and quality of the act *and* did not know it was wrong. In *People v Skinner*, the defendant challenged the constitutionality of the California legislation.[47] A number of the Court's assumptions are noteworthy. Although conceding that the United States Supreme Court had never ruled that a state must adopt some insanity defence, the Court inferred from Supreme Court jurisprudence that it was probably required. Also, the California history of the insanity defence was complicated, but the traditional California M'Naghten Rule before the MPC test was adopted was disjunctive, as was traditional everywhere. Finally, the conjunctive California test was massively narrow, indeed so narrow that few could succeed because few defendants would not know the nature and quality of their acts narrowly conceived. With these assumptions, the Court further assumed that the conjunctive test might be unconstitutional. To save its constitutionality, interpretation of the legislation was therefore required, and the Court opined the legislature must have made a simple drafting error, mistakenly using 'and' instead of 'or'. Consequently, the Court ruled the test must be interpreted to be disjunctive and found it constitutional. Now the California Supreme Court's creativity is often remarked upon, but this is a remarkable example. Such cases are rare, however.

Starting in the state of Michigan in the middle 1970s, between 15 and 20 states have adopted the 'Guilty But Mentally Ill Verdict' (GBMI) in addition to existing rules of legal insanity. It is an alternative, not a replacement. Although the first adoptions antedate *Hinckley*, the majority of jurisdictions adopting GBMI have done so since *Hinckley* and it is now a substantial minority rule.

A GBMI verdict does not indicate reduced culpability, it does not require lesser punishment, and it does not provide for hospitalization and treatment that would

[47] *People v Skinner*, 704 P 2d 752 (1985).

not otherwise be available to the convict. Essentially, the finder of fact is being asked to make a diagnosis in addition to a guilt determination. It is not different from 'guilty but herpes'. In short, GBMI is a fraudulent verdict because it does not address any issue relevant to just criminal blame and punishment and it has the potential to deflect juries from proper insanity acquittals because they do not understand the insanity defence or fear that it will cause the release of a dangerous offender.[48] When GBMI is available, jurors may falsely believe that they are 'taking account' of the defendant's impairment and thus may improperly return the GBMI verdict when an acquittal of insanity was appropriate. Paradoxically, defendants who raise the verdict may receive even harsher sentences, so there is evidence that its use is declining.[49]

Procedure

The standard rule in the United States is that an insanity defence cannot be imposed on a competent, unwilling defendant,[50] and, of course, all defendants must be competent to plead. Defendants who are incompetent to plead or to stand trial may not do so.[51] This is as it should be because the decision may be momentous for the defendant's future. As we shall see when discussing post-insanity acquittal procedures below, in many jurisdictions, a successful insanity defence may result in incarceration in a secure forensic facility for longer than the prison term for the crime charged. In other jurisdictions, the defendant may be committed to a secure forensic facility that is little different from a prison for as long as the prison term permitted. Release in both cases depends largely on the discretion of the facility's professional staff because judges are inclined to trust their judgement about whether release is safe. A competent defendant might well want to forego a potential insanity defence and should be permitted to do so.

Although in general the 'playing field' in criminal prosecutions is not 'level' between the prosecution and the defence, it would be unfair to the prosecution to permit the defendant to raise an insanity defence only at trial and to prevent the prosecution from appointing its own expert to evaluate a defendant who will raise the insanity defence. As a result, defendants are required to give advance notice to the prosecution that an insanity defence will be raised and to make the defendant

48 Steadman and others (n 11)102–20 (describing the verdict as a compromise).

49 ibid.

50 eg *US v Marble*, 940 F 2d 1543 (DC Cir 1991) (basing the decision on the Insanity Defense Reform Act). The Court did note that if the defendant gave no clear indication about this issue, the Court might give an instruction on the insanity defence sua sponte, but I assume such cases would be rare. Most competent defendants can express a simple choice.

51 See eg *Godinez v Moran*, 509 US 389 (1993) (defendant must be competent to plead guilty and to waive the right to counsel); *Drope v Missouri*, 420 US 162 (1975) (defendant must be competent to stand trial).

available for evaluation by a prosecution expert.[52] Failure to do so will prevent the defendant from raising the insanity defence.[53] An issue rarely raised is what the remedy should be if the defendant refuses to cooperate with the prosecution's expert. There are so few cases that it is difficult to state a general rule, but the dominant view seems to be similar to the consequence of not giving advance notice: the defence is barred. Another approach, for example, is to permit raising the defence, but using only lay evidence, which all defendants are entitled to do if they wish. Such cases are very rare. Most defendants cooperate.

Experts are usually indispensable to help prepare the case and testify for defendants who wish to raise an insanity defence. Without such an expert, the playing field is exceedingly unlevel. Very many criminal defendants in the United States are indigent and cannot afford to retain an expert. Moreover, the budgets of public defenders are rarely sufficient to afford adequate expert assistance. Consequently, many jurisdictions provided indigent defendants with an expert, but the Supreme Court had never ruled that this was a necessity, unlike the provision of an attorney in serious cases. A few years after Hinckley, in *Ake v Oklahoma*,[54] the Supreme Court held that such assistance was constitutionally required in insanity and death penalty cases. In *Ake v Oklahoma*,[55] the Supreme Court finally recognized the unfairness of not providing the defendant with a mental health expert. It noted that fundamental fairness entitles indigent defendants to an adequate opportunity to present their claims.[56] The Court further held that a mental health expert is necessary when the defendant needs expert assistance at capital sentencing hearings to rebut expert predictions of dangerousness.[57] As the Court held:

> [T]he State must, at a minimum, assure the defendant access to a competent psychiatrist who will conduct an appropriate examination and assist in evaluation, preparation, and presentation of the defense. This is not to say, of course, that the indigent defendant has a constitutional right to choose a psychiatrist of his personal liking or to receive funds to hire his own. Our concern is that the indigent defendant have access to a competent psychiatrist for the purpose we have discussed, and as in the case of the provision of counsel we leave to the States the decision on how to implement this right.[58]

The decision is correct, but it left open important questions.

[52] eg Federal Rules of Criminal Procedure §12.2 (US Government Printing Office).
[53] ibid.
[54] 470 US 68 (1985). In practice, the decision has been extended to obtain also in mens rea cases.
[55] *Ake v Oklahoma*, 470 US 68 (1985).
[56] ibid 77.
[57] ibid 83–84.
[58] ibid 83.

The problem is how the right has been implemented in many jurisdictions. *Ake* has not been interpreted to guarantee the defendant a mental health professional that the defence chooses.[59] If a defendant has resources, he can 'shop around' to try to obtain a mental health professional who will support his claims, but indigent defendants do not have that ability.[60] If the professional consulted will not render a favourable opinion, the defendant's mental health-based argument will almost certainly fail. In some jurisdictions with a sizeable number of forensic professionals, some experts may have a reputation for being favourable to the defence and the problem may be somewhat alleviated. There is no guarantee, however, that even a favourably inclined forensic professional will reach the expected conclusion, and the possibility of using a predisposed expert may not arise in jurisdictions with fewer forensic specialists. What is worse, in some jurisdictions an indigent defendant may be assigned a mental health professional who is an employee of the state and the prosecution may immediately have access to the report.[61] A state employee inevitably has a conflict of interest. The indigent defendant should be entitled to an independent professional, as some jurisdictions, including a majority of the federal circuits, hold.[62] Of course, an indigent defendant should not be entitled to shop around indefinitely for a genuine defence expert, but in my opinion at least a second opinion should be required, given what is at stake.

The Supreme Court had a perfect opportunity to clarify the issue, but avoided doing so in *McWilliams v Dunn*.[63] *McWilliams* held that the defence had not received the minimum assistance necessary under any interpretation of *Ake* because it had not had sufficient access to an available expert. Consequently, the Court overturned his conviction and noted that they had no need to decide the broader question of whether *Ake* required an expert who is not only independent of the prosecution, but also who would be part of the defence team. The Court should have ruled that the defendant is entitled to a genuinely independent evaluator, but that does not go far enough. The expert should not be an employee of the state. Further, the independent expert's report should not be disclosed to the prosecution unless the defendant decides to go forward with a mental health-based argument. An independent expert's report should be confidential work product unless the claim is raised. The fruits of an evaluation of a potential claim should not be of benefit to the prosecution.

Virtually all jurisdictions permit experts on both sides to offer an opinion about the ultimate legal issue—whether the defendant is legally sane or insane—but the federal jurisdiction is a notable exception. The expert cannot give an ultimate

[59] eg *United States v Osoba*, 213 F 3d 913 (6th Cir 2000).

[60] *Ake v Oklahoma*, 470 US 68, 83 (1985).

[61] *Granviel v Texas*, 495 US 963, 963–64 (1990) (Marshall J, dissenting from denial of *certiorari*).

[62] J Parry, *Criminal Mental Health and Disability Law, Evidence and Testimony* (American Bar Association 2009) 131–32.

[63] 137 S Ct 1790 (2017).

legal opinion in federal legal insanity cases.[64] This innovation was adopted by the Insanity Defense Reform Act in the wake of *Hinckley*. The thinking behind it is that the ultimate legal issue is just that, a legal issue to be decided by the trier of fact, and therefore beyond the expertise of mental health experts. When experts give such opinions, jurors may be misled into thinking that the issue is medical or psychological. Here is an example. After the *Hinckley* verdict, some jurors stated that if the experts couldn't agree on his legal sanity, how could the jurors.[65] I am a long-time proponent of this limitation on expert testimony, but proponents have had little success.

The traditional rule after the case is tried is that legal insanity is a jury question and the jury is free to credit or disregard any expert of lay testimony. As a result, jury verdicts are seldom overturned even if the defence experts are unanimous that the defendant was legally insane and the prosecution uses only lay testimony and cross-examination of the defence experts to defeat the insanity plea. In egregious cases, the trial judge or an appellate tribunal may decide that the verdict is so inconsistent with the weight of the evidence that the jury verdict will be overturned. Such cases are rare, however.

An interesting, oft-raised issue is whether the trial judge should instruct the jury concerning the consequences of finding the defendant legally insane, namely, some form of involuntary commitment to a secure forensic mental health facility, including indefinite confinement in some jurisdictions. In *Shannon v United States*,[66] the Court held that federal trial courts need not instruct the jury about commitment unless the prosecution affirmatively misleads the jury about the consequences. Justice Thomas' majority opinion focused primarily on the traditional assumption that juries should decide whether the defendant is culpable and should not be concerned with the consequences of their verdict.[67] Although this assumption may make sense for the vast majority of cases in which the defendant will be imprisoned or freed depending on the verdict—a fact jurors know—the insanity defence is the only form of exculpation that does not result in the defendant being immediately freed. I recognize that jurors may not fully understand what sentence will follow a conviction, but the insanity defence is *sui generis* because the acquitted defendant is not freed. It would be understandable if a juror voted to convict a legally insane defendant because the juror feared that a disordered and dangerous person might be freed. Similarly, jurors may be far more inclined to reach the just result if they learn that the insanity acquittee will be preventively detained by post-acquittal commitment, which will be discussed presently. Thus, I conclude that the

64 Federal Rules of Evidence, § 704(b) (The National Court Rules Committee).

65 '"Verdict was unjust": 2 jurors' *Chicago Tribune* (Chicago, 23 June 2014) A1.

66 512 US 573 (1994). This was not a constitutional decision. It was issued under the Supreme Court's supervisory authority over the procedures used in federal cases.

67 ibid 579–80, 586–887. In fact, Justice Thomas' entire majority opinion relies on the validity of this assumption.

defendant should be entitled to a 'consequences' instruction upon request. I would not make it mandatory because, as Justice Thomas recognized, there may be situations when the defendant would think it is not in his interest to have the jury learn of the consequences.

In all jurisdictions, a defendant acquitted by reason of insanity may be automatically civilly committed, either for an evaluation that will be followed by formal civil commitment, or by formal commitment itself without a prior evaluation.[68] Although not punishment for crime—the defendant has been acquitted after all—these civil commitments have been justified because the defendant is allegedly still dangerous and not responsible for the condition. The terms of such possible commitments vary across jurisdictions, but in some jurisdictions the term may be indefinite with periodic review. In *Jones v United States*,[69] the Supreme Court upheld both an automatic commitment for evaluation and the potentially indefinite commitment of a defendant acquitted by reason of insanity for shoplifting a leather jacket. The Court argued that, based on an insanity acquittal, it is rational to presume that the subject was still mentally disordered and dangerous.[70] The Court was unwilling to equate 'dangerousness' with violence. It claimed that the legislative purpose to confine was the same for violent and nonviolent offences and that the former often led to the latter.[71] Moreover, for this type of commitment, the Court was willing to accept a lesser burden of persuasion than the constitutionally-imposed standard civil commitment standard of clear and convincing evidence.[72] Post-insanity commitments are different, the Court claimed, because the defendant himself raised the issue of mental disorder, and so the risk of error is decreased.[73]

Finally, the Court approved potentially indefinite confinement on the ground that such confinement did bear a rational relation to the purpose of the commitment, which is to confine dangerous, non-responsible agents. The defendant was acquitted so the length of the confinement need not be limited by the deserved punishment. The subject is properly confined as long the defendant remains disordered *and* dangerous and need not be released until either condition is no longer met. This might happen at any time, or never.[74] In *Foucha v Louisiana*,[75] the Court affirmed that a post-insanity commitment must end if the subject is no longer mentally ill, even if he is still dangerous.[76]

[68] See Parry (n 62) 168–70.

[69] 463 US 354 (1983).

[70] ibid 365.

[71] ibid 365 n 14.

[72] ibid 367–68; see also *Addington v Texas*, 441 US 418, 431–33 (1979) (holding that traditional civil commitment required a finding by clear and convincing evidence, a standard between a preponderance and beyond a reasonable doubt).

[73] *Jones v United States*, 463 US 354, 367 (1983).

[74] ibid 368–69.

[75] 504 US 71 (1992).

[76] ibid 81. Justice O'Connor partially concurred. She noted that an insanity acquittee had been found to have committed the prima facie case beyond a reasonable doubt. She then wrote cryptically, as follows:

I think that the Court was correct to decouple the potential length of the civil commitment from the sentence for the crime charged. The defendant has been acquitted and the usual justifications for a sentence length do not apply. Roughly, the legislature sets sentences that are proportionate to culpability and that reflect an ordinary, rational offender's dangerousness. The insanity acquittee is neither culpable nor dangerous in the ordinary manner, however. If the basis for the commitment is non-responsible dangerousness, the commitment can justifiably continue until these conditions are no longer met. Although this is true as a theoretical matter, it seems useless to have lengthy commitments for nonviolent offenders. They do not present much danger and the risk that they will be erroneously held longer than necessary is substantial. I would have limited terms of confinement for nonviolent acquittees. These could be longer than ordinary involuntary civil commitment terms because the acquittee was prima facie guilty of a criminal offence, which is seldom the case in involuntary civil commitment and never required.[77] Nonetheless, the terms of post-insanity commitment for nonviolent offenders should be short. Even for those acquitted for crimes of violence, if the subject has a clean disciplinary record in the hospital for a substantial period of time, he should be released at the end of the period or the state can seek ordinary involuntary civil commitment. Another possibility is conditional or probationary release.[78] If the

> It might therefore be permissible for Louisiana to confine an insanity acquittee who has regained sanity [sic] if, unlike the situation in this case, the nature and duration of detention were tailored to reflect pressing public safety concerns related to the acquittee's continuing dangerousness ... [A]cquittees could not be confined as mental patients absent some medical justification for doing so; in such a case the necessary connection between the nature and purposes of confinement would be absent.

ibid 87–88 (O'Connor J, concurring). Justice O'Connor also noted that the seriousness of the crime should also affect whether the state's interest in continued confinement would be strong enough. See ibid 88.

If the subject is no longer mentally disordered and therefore no longer non-responsible, it is hard to imagine what possible 'medical justification' there could be for continuing civil commitment to protect the public. It is not clear from the O'Connor concurrence if she would require some finding of mental abnormality, as did the statute upheld in *Kansas v Hendricks*, to make the commitment analogous to traditional civil commitment. 521 US 346, 355 (1997). If not, however, then five justices of the Supreme Court, the four *Foucha* dissenters and Justice O'Connor, would have been willing to countenance pure preventive detention, at least of a person who had committed a crime without being responsible and who continued to be dangerous.

For an attempt to apply Justice O'Connor's suggestion, see *State v Randall*, 532 N W 2d 94, 109 (Wisconsin 1995) (permitting continued confinement if there were a medical justification and the subject was still dangerous, but limiting the term to the maximum sentence for the crime charged). Needless to say, I believe that this practice is simply criminal punishment by other means. The 'medical justification' criterion is a transparent and fraudulent attempt to bring this type of commitment within the disease justification for preemptive confinement. The limitation on the term of the commitment to the maximum term for the crime charged is simply a salve to the legislative conscience and a signal that the continued commitment is punitive.

[77] See Parry (n 62) 476–77 (discussing the criteria for commitments for dangerousness, which do not include a finding of prima facie guilt for a criminal offence or the equivalent thereof). In my experience, seriously violent conduct is virtually always processed through the criminal justice system. Moreover, traditional civil commitment requires only the lower, clear and convincing burden of persuasion. *Addington v Texas*, 441 US 418, 431–33 (1979).

[78] See California Penal Code § 1026.2(e)–(f) (West 2010).

acquittee has an unproblematic probationary period in the community, the commitment should end.

The Court in *Jones* never noted that the mental disorder and dangerousness had to be linked to ensure that the subject was not responsible for his dangerousness.[79] After all, non-responsibility for the legally relevant behaviour, in this case dangerousness, is necessary to justify involuntary commitment. It is possible for a person to be independently crazy and bad, with no link between them suggesting that the defendant's dangerousness is irrational. For example, a defendant may be wildly jealous because he delusionally believes that his partner has been unfaithful and might have some form of mitigation if he attacked the partner, but there will be no excuse if he robs a bank.[80] There probably will be such a link in most cases of insanity acquittal, but it cannot be taken for granted empirically.

More important, there is reason to doubt the Court's presumption of continuing mental disorder and dangerousness. By definition, the defendant must have been sufficiently rational to be competent to stand trial. If that state of rational capacity continues, then it is not clear that he continues to be mentally ill for the purpose of involuntary commitment. Moreover, to the extent that the mental disorder played a causal role in the practical reasoning that accompanied the offence, it is perfectly possible that the defendant is no longer dangerous either. This will be especially possible if the prosecution bears the burden of persuasion on legal insanity and the defendant only needs to cast a reasonable doubt about his sanity. Even if the defendant bears the burden of persuasion, as is commonly the case at present, the considerations just adduced apply.

My suggestion, therefore, is that all post-acquittal commitments should be for evaluation only and should not be for full commitment. There is little need to deprive the defendant of more liberty to protect the public. Preventive commitment should occur only if the evaluation indicates that the criteria for commitment are met at present. The evaluations need not last more than a few weeks. That is more than sufficient for the state's mental health professionals to reach a conclusion. I once again think that a subject facing potentially indefinite commitment and those facing substantial limited terms should be entitled to the services of an independent mental health professional to help defend against the commitment. Without such help, they have essentially no chance if the state's professional recommends commitment. These forms of commitment are more onerous than ordinary involuntary commitment and fairness requires that insanity acquittees should

[79] *Jones v United States*, 463 US 354, 363–65 (1983) (discussing the need for a showing of both mental disorder and dangerousness to justify these commitments and apparently assuming that the fact of an insanity acquittal supplies a link between the two criteria, but not explicitly requiring the causal link at the time of commitment).

[80] I recognize that a narrow interpretation of the standards for legal insanity would not excuse the person because he would neither be justified nor excused if the facts were as he believed them to be. On a broader reading, however, the defendant is not a rational agent and might have a plausible claim for legal insanity.

have a chance to avoid long-term incarceration in secure forensic facilities. For the same reason, the state should have to prove the commitment criteria by the higher, clear and convincing standard that *Addington* imposed for ordinary involuntary commitment to avoid imposing too much risk of error on the individual.[81]

Conclusion

Since the wave of changes to insanity tests and procedure in the wake of *Hinckley* there has been little substantive change in the test for legal insanity. Only the procedural change of shifting the burden of persuasion to the defendant seems to have been outcome determinative. In contrast, there have been considerable further procedural changes. The Supreme Court unjustifiably held that jurisdictions were constitutionally permitted to effectively abolish the insanity defence, but few have done so. The insanity defence continues to work reasonably well despite its critics.

[81] *Addington v Texas*, 441 US 418, 425–33 (1979).

10

The Insanity Defence in French Law

Are Prisons the 'New Asylums'?

Audrey Guinchard

Introduction

In 2006, 35% to 42% of inmates in French prisons were *de facie* extremely or seriously mentally ill,[1] supporting an earlier conclusion that the prisons have become the 'new asylums'.[2] Ten years later, the Human Rights Watch report on French prisons confirmed 'a double punishment', as more mentally ill offenders are sentenced to prison, for longer and with inadequate care.[3] Covid seems to have made the situation more visible.[4] The problem is, of course, multi-faceted, but one identified factor is the over-criminalization of offenders suffering from a disorder under Article 122-1 of the Criminal Code (CP), which defines the French 'insanity'[5] defence.[6] Yet, when the defence was recodified in 1992, the Article was presented

[1] Haute Autorité de Santé, *Audition publique. Expertise psychiatrique pénale. Rapport de la commission d'audition*, 2007) 18–20 (hereafter HAS, *Rapport*); J-P Michel, *Rapport n° 216 sur la proposition de loi relative à l'atténuation de responsabilité pénale applicable aux personnes atteintes d'un trouble mental ayant altéré leur discernement au moment des faits*, 2011, 15–16 (hereafter, Michel, *Rapport* n° 216). This chapter concentrates on mainland France and leaves aside its overseas regions and territories which still suffer from the traumatic effects of slavery and colonisation. eg A Charles-Nicolas, 'Folie et psychiatrie dans la Martinique d'antan. Des questions pour le temps présent' (2015) 173 Ann Méd Psychol 313; N Guerda and A Wheatley, 'Historical and Socio-political Perspectives on Mental Health in the Caribbean Region' (2013) 47 Interamerican Journal of Psychology 167.

[2] JL Senon, 'Soins ambulatoires sous contrainte: une mise en place indispensable pour préserver une psychiatrie publique moderne' (2005) 81 Inf Psychiatr 627.

[3] Human Rights Watch, *Double Punishment. Inadequate Conditions for Prisoners with Psychosocial Disabilities in France*, 2016 <https://www.hrw.org/report/2016/04/05/double-punishment/inadequate-conditions-prisoners-psychosocial-disabilities> accessed 5 April 2021; A Garib and others, 'General Medical Care in French Psychiatric Units for Inmates: A National Survey' (2018) 45(2) Encéphale 139.

[4] T Fovet and P Thomas, 'Troubles psychiatriques à l'entrée de prison: un enjeu de santé publique' *The Conversation* (4 March 2021) <https://theconversation.com/troubles-psychiatriques-a-lentree-en-prison-un-enjeu-de-sante-publique-153600> accessed 5 April 2021; T Fovet and others, 'Mental Health Care in French Correctional Facilities during the Covid-19 Pandemic' (2020) 46(3S) Encéphale S60.

[5] Hereafter, I will not use the terms insane or insanity as the French law defence is broader than its English and other common law counterparts. It encompasses insanity, automatism, intoxication, and diminished responsibility. Loss of control (provocation), abolished in 1992, was outside the scope of the French defence for mental disorder, an excuse leading to the mitigation of sentences.

[6] Inspection générale des services judiciaires and Inspection générale des affaires sociales, *L'organisation des soins aux détenus. Rapport d'évaluation* (2001) 85 <https://igas.gouv.fr> accessed 5 April 2021; HAS, *Rapport* (n 1); Gilbert Barbier and others, *Sénat. Rapport n° 434 d'information par le groupe de travail sur la prise en charge des personnes atteintes de troubles mentaux ayant commis des*

Audrey Guinchard, *The Insanity Defence in French Law* In: *The Insanity Defence.* Edited by: Ronnie Mackay and Warren Brookbanks, Oxford University Press. © Audrey Guinchard 2022. DOI: 10.1093/oso/9780198854944.003.0010

as just 'officialis[ing] for the most part a daily judicial practice which considered mental disorders as a mitigating cause of liability.'[7] Has the defence then failed to safeguard offenders suffering from a 'psychological or neuropsychological disorder'?

Using a historical perspective, as well as contemporary medico-legal writings, this chapter will demonstrate that the re-codification of the defence in Article 122-1 CP has exposed and accentuated perennial fault lines in French criminal law's articulation of the defence. Determining the boundaries between responsibility, irresponsibility and attenuated responsibility has never been as straightforward, as often claimed. The fraught and tense debates surrounding the case of Halimi, which the Cour de cassation, the French Supreme Court, decided in April 2021, confirm the need for clarification and reform. This evolution of the French law defence in turn sheds light on English criminal law's own approach to the insanity defence and its satellites: automatism, diminished responsibility and intoxication.

Legal scholars in France fear that the principle of irresponsibility under Article 122-1 al.1 CP is being eroded or abandoned in favour of an attenuated responsibility increasingly used to sentence more severely mentally ill than non-mentally ill offenders, because of their perceived dangerousness.[8] Yet, over the last 20–30 years, the literature outside the pure legal field[9] has depicted a more nuanced picture of how the defence has been structured and used over time. Historical and sociological studies have demonstrated how the work of the alienists, that is, the 19th-century psychiatrists, who could also be experts to the courts, led the courts and legal scholars to accept that mentally ill offenders could be liable under the 1810 Criminal Code applicable until 1992.[10] Studies also contextualized the defence by

infractions, 2010, 28–30 (hereafter, Sénat, *Rapport* n° 434); C Lafaye, C Lancelevée, and C Protais, *L'irresponsabilité pénale au prisme des représentations sociales de la folie et de la responsabilité des personnes souffrant de troubles men-taux. [Rapport de recherche] Mission de recherche Droit et Justice*, 2016, chapter 1 <https://halshs.archives-ouvertes.fr/halshs-01480984> accessed 5 April 2021 (hereafter, Lafaye, *Rapport*).

[7] Sénat, séance 9 May 1989, JO 10 May 1989 n° 18 S.(C.R.) p555.

[8] L Leturmy, 'La pénalisation des personnes atteintes de troubles mentaux' AJ Pénal 2018, 491; D Salas, 'La responsabilisation des fous criminels à l'ère néolibérale' (2012) 88 L'information psychiatrique 423; C Lazergues, 'Le choix de la fuite en avant au nom de la dangerosité: les lois 1, 2, 3, 4, 5, etc. sur la prévention et la répression de la récidive' RSC 2012, 274; P-J Delage, 'La dangerosité comme éclipse de l'imputabilité et de la dignité' RSC 2007, 797; J Danet and C Saas, 'Le fou et sa 'dangerosité', un risque spécifique pour la justice pénale' RSC 2007, 779; E Bonis, *Répertoire de droit pénal et de procédure pénale*. V° Troubles psychiques—Malades mentaux (Dalloz 2018) (hereafter, Bonis, *Répertoire*).

[9] For structural reasons, French legal scholarship tends to be narrow in its outlook to other disciplines, see J Bell, *French Legal Cultures* (Butterworths 2001) 46–48 (hereafter, Bell, *French Legal Cultures*).

[10] Notably, L Guignard, 'Le corps criminel au XIXe siècle: du trouble des facultés de l'âme à la dégénérescence' (2012) 118 Cahiers d'histoire. Revue d'histoire critique 61 (hereafter, Guignard, 'Corps criminel'); L Guignard, 'Les lectures de l'intériorité devant la justice pénale au XIXe siècle' (2008) 141 Romantisme 23; M Renneville, 'Les deux figures de la déraison criminelle' AJ Pénal 2004, 309; M Renneville, 'Psychiatrie et prison: une histoire parallèle' (2004) 162 Ann Méd Psychol 653; Y Hémery, 'Irresponsabilité pénale, évolutions du concept' (2009) 85 Inf Psychiatr 727 (hereafter Hémery, 'Irresponsabilité'); D Bouley and others, 'Les fondements historiques de la responsabilité pénale' (2002) 160 Ann Méd Psychol 396.

looking at the period before 1810, that is, during the French Revolution (1789–99), and earlier during the Ancien Regime (1600–1789).[11] Moreover, medical experts and regulators have reflected on the modern challenges faced by psychiatry both generally, in light of the penal laws' obsession with dangerousness, and specifically, in relation to Article 122-1 CP.[12] They notably pointed out how the legal concepts have never been easy to grasp from a medical perspective.[13]

Legal scholars do not completely ignore these works.[14] They do not, however, articulate well how the scope of the defence and its outcome continue to be shaped by the two interrelated matters the other disciplines have highlighted: first, the challenges the criminal law has faced over time when confronted with medical knowledge on mental disorders; and secondly, the technical and conceptual choices made, and not made, to determine who should or should not be answerable to society.

This chapter aims to fill this gap by showing that the 1992 codification exposed perennial fault lines in the structure of the defence, as the *Halimi* case illustrates. The chapter will start by briefly outlining the defence, its criminal justice context, and the *Halimi* case; it will then retrace the evolution of the defence to uncover these fault lines for each of the defence's defining features: the definition of the disorder to trigger the defence; the understanding of the impact the disorder should have for the defence to be accepted; and the modulation of the outcome of the defence in light of prior fault. The final section will bring together the various findings, with a brief comparison with English law, to show how this renewed perspective on the defence could allow for outlining pathways to improvement.

[11] C Mangin-Lazarus, 'L'affaire Firmin (1794–1799) et l'absence de législation sur le crime en « démence » pendant la Révolution française' (2012) 46 Hist Sci Méd 145; L Guignard, 'La genèse de l'article 64 du code pénal' (2016) Criminocorpus <https://journals.openedition.org/criminocorpus/3215?lang=it> accessed 5 April 2021 (hereafter, Guignard, 'Génèse'); C Peny, 'Le droit et les institutions de l'insanité d'esprit en France sous l'Ancien Régime' (2008) 2 Biomedical Law & Ethics 249 (hereafter, Peny, 'Le droit'); M Caire, 'Psychiatrie et ordre public, de l'Ancien Régime à la Restauration. L'exemple parisien' (2014) 172 Ann Méd Psychol 41.

[12] M Bénézech, 'La législation actuelle face à l'évaluation des comportements criminels violents: l'urgence d'une réforme' (2018) 176 Ann Méd Psychol 404; M Bénézech, 'Dangerosité psychiatrique et responsabilité pénale atténuée: à propos de la condamnation à la réclusion à perpétuité d'un schizophrène auteur d'un homicide sexuel sadique' (2020) 178 Ann Méd Psychol, revue psychiatrique 949; J-P Bouchard, 'Irresponsabilité et responsabilité pénales: faut-il réformer l'article 122-1 du Code pénal français?' (2018) 176 Ann Méd Psychol 421 (hereafter, Bouchard, 'Irresponsabilité'); D Zagury, 'Vers une clinique de l'abolition du discernement' (2006) 164 Ann Méd Psychol 847 (hereafter, Zagury, 'Clinique'); D Zagury and J-P Bouchard, 'Le psychiatre expert judiciaire et les auteurs d'homicides' (2020) 178 Ann Méd Psychol 938 (hereafter, Zagury and Bouchard, 'Le psychiatre expert'); Senon (n 2).

[13] Bouchard, 'Irresponsabilité' (n 12); Sénat, *Rapport* n° 434 (n 6) 28–30.

[14] Leturmy (n 8); Bonis, *Répertoire* (n 8).

The Defence in Context: Its Structure, the Criminal Justice System, and the Halimi Case

The defence is a long-standing feature of French criminal law.[15] Inherited from Roman law and consolidated by case law (without the doctrine of precedent), it was never stated in any written text of the Ancien Regime (1600–1789), although it was generally accepted that 'the mad (*fous*) d[id] not sin neither before God, nor before men'.[16] The Revolution (1789–99) brought sweeping legal reforms, with notably a Bill of Rights, still in force today, a new judiciary, one Criminal Code (1791) and two Criminal Procedure Codes (1791, 1795).[17] The context in which the defence operated had thus been transformed, acquiring many of its modern features. Paradoxically, the defence remained 'an implicit [principle] that d[id] not require further precision'.[18] As Bexon, former President of the Paris Assises Court, put it in 1799, the rules were 'so present in the heart of the French citizens that it was not needed to write them down'.[19]

This absence of a legal framework led to occasional challenges; yet, the defence gained statutory footing only in 1810, when a new Criminal Code was enacted.[20] In line with French legal style, Article 64 CP was laconic: 'There is neither *crime* nor *délit* when the defendant was in a state of *démence* at the time of the act', leaving the courts to fill in the gaps and to slowly return to the practice of sentence individualization abolished by the Revolution. By 1885, the Supreme Court had accepted that madness could also be a mitigating circumstance at the sentencing stage.[21] The Ministry of Justice confirmed the practice in a 1905 Instruction.[22] Committal to a mental health institution was not systematic, and the 1838 statute confirmed it was outside the courts' jurisdiction.[23]

Replacing Article 64 CP in 1992,[24] Article 122-1 CP encapsulates the defence's two-tiered structure, while replacing the old-fashioned '*démence*' with the more modern and neutral expression of a psychological or neuropsychological disorder

[15] For a presentation of French criminal law history, see C Elliott, *French Criminal Law* (William Publishing 2001) chapter 1 (hereafter, Elliott, *French Criminal Law*).

[16] F Serpillon, *Code criminel, ou commentaire sur l'ordonnance de 1670, Tome 1* (les frères Perisse 1784) 398 (hereafter, Serpillon, *Code criminel*); D Jousse, *Nouveau commentaire sur l'ordonnance criminelle du mois d'août 1670*, t. 1 (Debure Père 1763) v fn (e) (hereafter, Jousse, *Nouveau commentaire*). All sources prior to 1930 have been accessed in their digital format at gallica.bnf.fr, the website of the Bibliothèque nationale de France (the French 'British Library').

[17] P Lascoumes, P Poncela, and P Lenoël, *Au nom de l'ordre: une histoire politique du code pénal* (Hachette 1989) Part 1–2; Bell, *French Legal Cultures* (n 9) 53–58.

[18] Guignard, 'Génèse' (n 11) para 4.

[19] S-J Bexon, *Parallèle du code pénal d'Angleterre avec les lois pénales françaises, et considérations sur les moyens de rendre celles-ci plus utiles* (Fauvelle et Sagnier 1799) 155.

[20] Guignard, 'Génèse' (n 11).

[21] Bull crim T90, n170, année 1885, 1887, 285.

[22] Guignard, 'Génèse' (n 11).

[23] Caire (n 11).

[24] The code came in force on 1 March 1994, M Delmas-Marty, 'Nouveau code pénal, avant-propos' RSC 1993, 433 (hereafter, Delmas-Marty, 'Nouveau code pénal').

('*trouble psychique ou neuropsychique*').[25] When the disorder 'abolished [the offender's] discernment or his ability to control his actions', he 'is not criminally liable' (Art 122-1 al.1 CP). When the disorder only 'altered his discernment or ability to exercise control', he 'remains criminally liable' (Art 122-1 al. 2 CP).

The criminal procedure code adds details as to who raises the defence, who decides on liability, and how the relevant authority should do so. For offences other than *crimes* (those liable to less than ten years' imprisonment), the prosecutor can close the case without taking further action (Art 40-1 al.3 CPP) if he or she concludes that Article 122-1 al.1 CP applies. This represents less than 2% of all decisions to close cases.[26] If in doubt, the prosecutor can transfer the case to a trial court. The *tribunal de police* (one professional judge) will have jurisdiction for the *contraventions* (misdemeanours with no imprisonment, maximum fine €1500), and *the tribunal correctionnel* (with three professional judges, but increasingly with one judge) for the *délits*, that is, offences liable to less than ten years' imprisonment, for example, theft, involuntary manslaughter, or sexual assault.

Until 2008, there were no special findings for irresponsibility (Art 122-1 al.1 CP) and no court could order committal to a hospital. Breaking with this long tradition, stemming from the 1789 Revolution, the 2008 reform introduced both the disposal order and the equivalent of the English law verdict of 'not guilty by reason of insanity' when the disorder completely abolished the defendant's capacities. Courts must now make a decision 'of criminal irresponsibility for reason of mental disorder' after having confirmed that the defendant committed the actus reus of the offence.[27] The statistics do not record these court decisions when the offence is not a *crime*.

[25] Professor J Spencer's 2005 translation, <https://www.legislationline.org/download/id/3316/file/France_Criminal%20Code%20updated%20on%2012-10-2005.pdf>; Professor Bell referred to a 'psychiatric or neuropsychiatric disorder', J Bell, 'Criminal Law' in J Bell, S Boyron, and S Whittaker (eds), *Principles of French Law* (Oxford University Press 2008) 226. Professor Spencer's version is more reflective of the neutrality the French Parliament intended to achieve (see Defining the Disorder: A Legal Definition Grounded in Medical Knowledge). All primary sources of French law are available in French at the official website of Legifrance.gouv.fr. My translation of the text is as follows:

> A person is not criminally liable who, when the act was committed, was suffering from a psychological or neuropsychological disorder which abolished his discernment or his ability to control his actions.

A person who, at the time he acted, was suffering from a psychological or neuropsychological disorder which reduced his discernment or impeded his ability to control his actions, remains punishable. However, the court shall take this circumstance into account when it decides the penalty and determines its regime. If the sentence is of imprisonment, it is reduced by one third or, in the case of a *crime* with an imprisonment penalty or life imprisonment penalty, the sentence is brought down to 30 years' imprisonment. In case of liability for a *delit*, the court can, however, decide not to reduce the sentence after having extensively stated its reasons. When, after medical advice, the court considers that the nature of the disorder justifies it, the chosen sentence may allow for the convicted person to undertake treatment adapted to his health status.

[26] Références statistiques Justice 2019, ch 7, 11 at <http://www.justice.gouv.fr/statistiques-10054/references-statistiques-justice-12837/>

[27] Criminal Procedure Code, Arts 706-119–706-140 following Loi n° 2008-174, 25 February 2008.

When the offence committed is a *crime* (a statutory minimum of ten years' imprisonment, eg for murder and rape), the prosecutor cannot close a case and has to transfer it to the investigatory judge (Art 79 CPP). The latter can make a discharge order on the grounds of Article 122-1 al.1 CP which, since 2008, has to be made after hearing the victims who are parties to the trial and the defendant's lawyers or the defendant himself or herself should he or she be fit to plead. Since 2008, the decision to discharge on the grounds of Article 122-1 al. 1 CP can be appealed before the investigatory court, then before the regional appeal court. A final appeal on the law can be presented to the Supreme Court. Conversely, the investigatory judge may decide to transfer the case to the trial court, the *Cour d'assises*. The latter, composed of three professional judges and seven jurors deciding together on liability,[28] has, since 2000, to answer a specific question on Article 122-1 CP. As for the other courts, the 2008 reform introduced the special verdict of non-guilty for reason of mental disorder and the power to commit to a mental health hospital. Only decisions of irresponsibility are recorded.

All the courts' first instance decisions can be automatically appealed to the regional appeal courts on law and facts, including those of the Assises Courts since 2000 (which includes acquittals since 2002). Appeals, on the law only, to the Supreme Court, are also automatic.

Whichever trial court is considered, when the disorder only 'altered [the defendant's] discernment or ability to exercise control' (Art 122-1 al. 2 CP), the court will declare the defendant liable, with no specific 'verdict'. No statistics record the proportion of these decisions. The courts have to take the disorder into account at the sentencing stage. The original text of Article 122-1 al.2 CP did not specify that courts should mitigate the sentence. The different actors of the criminal justice system noticed that the practice quickly evolved towards an aggravation of the sentences, to account for the perceived dangerousness of the mentally ill offenders.[29] The 2014 reform attempted to curb this unexpected development. Mitigation became an obligation for Assises Courts, yet, the *tribunaux correctionnels* can still refuse mitigation. The impact of the reform is unknown[30] but may prove ill-fated. The obligation to mitigate concerns less than 1% of the cases going to trial, since the *tribunaux correctionnels* decide 99.74% of the prosecuted cases.[31] More importantly, the reform stopped short of tackling the origin of the problem. The issue of mitigation arose because of the steady decrease in the use of Article 122-1 al.1

[28] The composition of the Court has profoundly changed since its creation in 1791, see Elliott, *French Criminal Law* (n 15) chapter 2.

[29] Sénat, *Rapport* n° 434 (n 6) 23–27; C Ménabé, 'L'irresponsabilité pénale pour cause de trouble mental' 2008 AJ Pénal 488.

[30] J-J Urvoas, Ministre de la Justice, *Rapport sur la mise en œuvre de la loi du 15 août 2014 relative à l'individualisation des peines et renforçant l'efficacité des sanctions pénales*, 2016 <http://www.justice.gouv.fr/publication/rap_loi_15082014.pdf> accessed 5 April 2021.

[31] Ministre de la Justice, *Les Chiffres-clés de la Justice 2019*, <http://www.justice.gouv.fr/art_pix/Chiffres%20Cles%202020.pdf> accessed 5 April 2021.

CP, a pattern identifiable by the statistics on discharge orders. Where they would have been declared irresponsible, offenders are now sent to trial and convicted. Socio-legal research demonstrated that this pattern predates the Article, going back to at least the 1950s, but has accelerated since 1992.[32] So the question is: 'how did we come to the idea that a criminal is mentally ill but responsible enough to go to prison?'[33]

The *Halimi* case has crystallized the tensions surrounding the determination of the boundary between irresponsibility and liability when a defendant is mentally ill. In April 2017 Kobili Traoré entered a friend's apartment; fearing for their lives, the friend and his family locked themselves in one bedroom. Traoré then chose to access their neighbour's apartment from the balcony. He killed Sarah Halimi by throwing her over the balcony, after having beaten her up, while shouting 'Allah Akbar', 'I killed a daemon'. Sarah was Jewish, Kobili Muslim.

The investigatory judge called for a first expert report. The expert concluded that a severe psychotic episode, which was not acute intoxication, existed at the time of the offence. Traoré completely lost control and discernment. The episode, however, did not originate in a disorder such as schizophrenia, but from the regular and excessive consumption of cannabis (up to 15 joints a day) over the previous 11 years.[34] Therefore, instead of recommending irresponsibility, the expert favoured liability under Article 122-1 al.2 CP.

The two additional groups of experts settled on the same medical diagnosis. However, they supported irresponsibility because the defendant had started to develop schizophrenia and was not aware of the dangers his cannabis consumption created to his mental health.[35]

The investigatory judge made a discharge order on the grounds of Article 122-1 al.1 CP. Benefiting from the 2008 reform, the victim's family appealed. For them, the prior fault of voluntarily consuming cannabis for 11 years barred the use of Article 122-1 al.1 CP; the Assises court should have heard the case, as the defendant's hate speech demonstrated enough consciousness to consider attenuated liability under Article 122-1 al.2 CP. The investigatory court rejected the appeal; as did the Paris Court of Appeal in 2019 and the Supreme Court on 14 April 2021 because Article 122-1 al.1 CP did not distinguish according to the origin of the disorder.[36] The case raises a variety of questions that feed into the wider debates surrounding the defence. Let us start with the first one: how to define the disorder that may trigger the defence.

[32] Lafaye, *Rapport* (n 6) chapter 1.

[33] M Renneville, *Crime et folie. Deux siècles d'enquêtes médicales et judiciaires* (Fayard 2003) 10.

[34] CA Paris, pôle 7, ch instr 6, 19 December 2019, n° 2019/05058 *Halimi*, Dalloz Actualité 3 February 2020, 11–13 <https://www.dalloz-actualite.fr/flash/affaire-sarah-halimi-declaration-d-irresponsabilite-penale-pour-cause-de-trouble-mental#.YGstSS1Q1TY> accessed 5 April 2021.

[35] ibid.

[36] Crim 14 April 2001 Arrêt no 404 (20-80.135) para 29, <https://www.courdecassation.fr/jurisprudence_2/chambre_criminelle_578/404_14_46872.html>

Defining the Disorder: A Legal Definition Grounded in Medical Knowledge

How the disorder has been understood has evolved over time. It first shed its religious roots to become a medical condition called 'disease of the brain'. This concept—developed before the 1789 Revolution—was integrated into the original understanding of '*démence*' in Article 64 of the 1810 CP, before disappearing a century later. By the time Article 122-1 CP replaced Article 64 CP, the disorder was already considered to be a 'psychological or neuropsychological disorder'.

From a Religious Concept to a 'Disease of the Brain': the Ancien Droit or Old Law (1600–1789)

By the mid-17th century, the mentally ill, those with learning disabilities, epileptics, and their families ceased to be considered to be punished by God.[37]Madness became a medical condition, with no possibility that the mentally ill should be liable for witchcraft,[38] a 'crime de lèse-majesté divine' as serious as the offences against the King's person.[39]

Jousse and Muyart de Vouglans, the two main judges and criminal law scholars of the 18th century, considered madness a 'disease of the brain', both citing Paolo Zacchias, the Pope's doctor[40] who identified madness as a medical condition.[41] The insane lacked 'will (*volonté*) and knowledge of the wrong committed', like 'a child who does not have yet the use of reason'.[42] Based on medical knowledge of the time, legal scholars distinguished three forms of madness: the furious ('*furieux*'), who are extravagant, violent, and cannot control their impulses; the idiot ('*dément*'), whose reason is weak, with physical signs of lack of reason, childish behaviours or those akin to an animal; and the melancholic, who present no symptom of

[37] Peny, 'Le droit' (n 11) 253.

[38] J-M Carbasse, *Histoire du droit pénal et de la justice criminelle* (Droit fondamental, Presses Universitaires de France 2000) 200–01 (hereafter, Carbasse, *Histoire*); A Soman, 'Les procès de sorcellerie au Parlement de Paris (1565–1640)' (1977) 32 Ann Hist Sci Soc 790; A Soman, 'The Parlement of Paris and the Great Witch Hunt (1565–1640)' (1978) 9 Sixt Century J 31.

[39] Peny, 'Le droit' (n 11) 253–55; A Soman, 'La décriminalisation de la sorcellerie en France' (1985) 4 Hist Écon Soc 179, 196–98. Thereafter, the target shifted to infanticide, A Soman, 'La justice criminelle vitrine de la Monarchie française' (1995) 153 BEC 291, 302–03.

[40] Hémery, 'Irresponsabilité' (n 10) 729; J Doyon, 'Les enjeux médico-judiciaires de la folie parricide au XVIIIe siècle' (2011) 15 Crime, Histoire & Sociétés 5, 15–17 (hereafter, Doyon, 'Les enjeux').

[41] P-F Muyart de Vouglans, *Institutes au droit criminel, ou principes généraux sur ces matières, suivant le droit civil, canonique, et la Jurisprudence du Royaume; avec un traité particulier des crimes* (Le Breton 1757) 76; Jousse, *Nouveau commentaire* (n 16).

[42] Jousse, *Nouveau commentaire* (n 16) xci, 440–41; D Jousse, *Traité de la justice criminelle de France, t. 2* (Debure Pere 1771) 619–24 (hereafter, Jousse, *Traité*). Similarly, P-F Muyart de Vouglans, *Les loix criminelles de France dans leur ordre naturel* (1780) 11 (hereafter, Muyart de Vouglans, *Les loix*); Serpillon, *Code criminel* (n 16) 439.

excessive agitations and often have suicidal tendencies.[43] Epilepsy was incorporated into madness.

Despite sleepwalkers being 'deprived of the use of reason', they were not considered to be suffering from madness.[44] They were nevertheless not liable unless there was proof of prior fault (liability but with mitigated sentence).[45] Madness also excluded intoxication, with Muyart de Vouglans recognizing non-liability for involuntary intoxication,[46] but not Jousse for whom intoxication, voluntary or not, was a crime.[47] Finally, madness was distinguished from '*l'amour violent*', literally violent love, which could only be a mitigating circumstance but not for rape or violent kidnapping (full liability).[48] Despite the use of the language of madness ('*une espèce de fureur*'), violent love could at best be a mitigating factor to the sentence.[49]

This conception persisted not only during the Revolution,[50] when psychiatry was still in its infancy[51] but also well into the 19th century.

The Persistence of the Biological Origin in the '*Démence*' of the 19th Century

Article 64 CP, enacted in 1810, did not define '*démence*', but the legal scholarship confirmed an understanding anchored in the Ancien Droit. They restricted *démence* to 'the diseases of the brain', epilepsy,[52] and 'idiocy'.[53] 'Intoxication ... did not have madness's essential character, the biological disorder of intellectual faculties'.[54]

[43] With references, Doyon, 'Les enjeux' (n 40) 21–22.

[44] Muyart de Vouglans, *Les loix* (n 42) 29; Jousse, *Traité* (n 42); Serpillon, *Code criminel* (n 16) 398.

[45] Jousse, *Traité* (n 42) 628–29; Muyart de Vouglans, *Les loix* (n 42) 29; Serpillon, *Code criminel* (n 16) 399; N Laurent-Bonne, 'Les origines de l'irresponsabilité du somnambule' RSC 2013, 547.

[46] Muyart de Vouglans, *Les loix* (n 42) 79.

[47] D Jousse, *Traité de la justice criminelle de France, t. 3* (Desure Pere 1771) 671.

[48] Jousse, *Traité* (n 42) 629; Muyart de Vouglans, *Les loix* (n 42) 14.

[49] Muyart de Vouglans, *Les loix* (n 42) 15.

[50] L-N Lemercier, *Opinion de Lemercier, député de la Charente-Inférieure, sur la résolution du 16 messidor an 5, relative aux accusés en démence: séance du 3 prairial, an 6* (De l'imprimerie nationale) <https://archive.org/details/opinion00unse_20> accessed 1 April 2021.

[51] J Garrabé, 'Nosography and Classification of Mental Diseases in the History of Psychiatry' (2019) 84 Évol Psychiatr e31 (hereafter, Garrabé, 'Nosography'); J-F Pelletier and L Davidson, 'À l'origine même de la psychiatrie comme nouvelle spécialité médicale: le partenariat Pinel-Pussin' (2015) 40 Santé mentale au Québec 19.

[52] Crim 8 brumaire an XIIII; Crim 17 January 1822, Edouard Dalloz, Charles (père et fils) Vergé and Gaston Griolet, *Les codes annotés. Code d'instruction criminelle annoté et expliqué d'après la jurisprudence et la doctrine* (Bureau de la jurisprudence générale 1898) under Art 339 CIC, para 176.

[53] A Chauveau and F Hélie, *Théorie du code pénal*, vol 1 (Société typographique belge 1837) 216 (the passages are repeated in the 1852, 1872, and 1887 versions) (hereafter, Chauveau and Hélie, *Théorie*); R Garraud, *Précis de droit criminel contenant l'explication élémentaire de la partie générale du code pénal, du code d'instruction criminelle, et des lois qui ont modifié ces deux codes* (11 edn, Sirey 1912) 217–18 (hereafter, Garraud, *Précis*).

[54] Chauveau and Hélie, *Théorie* (n 53) 216.

Intoxication and sleepwalking could exclude liability, but outside the scope of Article 64 CP, as before.[55]

In medical circles, the term *démence* had quickly acquired its specific meaning of 'dementia'. Lawyers nevertheless considered the term to be generic, to describe the situation of those deprived of reason (*de-mens*). *Démence* meant madness, mental alienation by reference to the alienists' new vocabulary.[56] It was a legal term informed by medical knowledge but not solely defined by it.

This definition of madness, with its mixture of medical knowledge and Ancien Droit, should be viewed in light of the contemporary medical context. The first generation of alienists tried to move away from the purely biological understanding of mental illness, with the concepts of mania (Pinel) and homicidal monomania (Esquirol) based on passions.[57] Lawyers baulked at the idea, afraid that every passion would become madness, that criminals would simulate madness and escape liability when they should be punished.[58]

When the next generation of alienists discredited monomania in the 1850s, tensions eased.[59] Judges were receptive to the alienists' conception of madness as a spectrum where responsibility would remain but would be attenuated by the disorder.[60] It helped that at the same time the alienists defended a biological vision of madness based on the ideas of degeneration (Morel, Lombroso, Ferri, Garoffallo).[61]

When exactly this biological origin of madness disappeared is difficult to pinpoint. In 1887, Hélie, by then Honorary President of the Cour de cassation, continued to define madness as disease of the brain,[62] but in 1872, Lallement already included under Article 64 CP sleepwalking and intoxication when the disorders abolished discernment.[63] In the 1905 *circulaire*, the Minister of Justice Chaumié

[55] ibid 213; Garraud, *Précis* (n 53) 218; J-L-E Ortolan, *Éléments de droit pénal: pénalité, juridictions, procédure: suivant la science rationale, la législation positive et la jurisprudence*, vol 1 (3rd edn, Librairie de Plon 1863) 138–39 (hereafter, Ortolan, *Éléments*).

[56] Chauveau and Hélie, *Théorie* (n 53) 205–07; Ortolan, *Éléments* (n 55) 128–29; Garraud, *Précis* (n 53) 216.

[57] Guignard, 'Corps criminel' (n 10).

[58] Chauveau and Hélie, *Théorie* (n 53) 210–11; Guignard, 'Corps criminel' (n 10); C Protais, 'Psychiatric Care or Social Defense?: The Origins of a Controversy over the Responsibility of the Mentally Ill in French Forensic Psychiatry' (2014) 37 Int J Law Psychiatry 17, 21–22 (hereafter, Protais, 'Psychiatric Care'); M Renneville, 'L'anthropologie du criminel en France' (1994) 27 Criminologie 185, 187 (hereafter, Renneville, 'L'anthropologie'); L Bogani, 'Le vol sous l'œil des médecins légistes. Étude du concept de kleptomanie au cours du XIXe siècle' (2016) Criminocorpus [En ligne] <https://journals.openedition.org/criminocorpus/3253> accessed 5 April 2021 (hereafter, Bogani, 'Le vol')

[59] Protais, 'Psychiatric Care' (n 58) 22.

[60] T Lepoutre and T Dening, '« De la non-existence de la monomanie », by Jean-Pierre Falret (1854)' (2012) 23 Hist Psychiatry 356; B Lévy, 'Entre tribunaux et asiles—des « aliénés persécuteurs » aux « revendicateur »' (2016) Criminocorpus [En ligne] <https://journals.openedition.org/criminocorpus/3266 accessed 5 April 2021; R Huertas and CM Winston, 'Madness and degeneration, I: From "Fallen Angel" to Mentally Ill' (1992) 3 Hist Psychiatry 391.

[61] Guignard, 'Corps criminel' (n 10) paras 16–20.

[62] Chauveau and Hélie, *Théorie* (n 53) 576.

[63] L Lallement, *De la condition des aliénés en droit romain et en droit français* (E. Aubert 1872) 234 (hereafter, Lallement, *De la condition*); contra, Garraud, *Précis* (n 53).

asked the psychiatric experts to search for 'physical, psychic or mental anomalies' as a basis for the judicial practice of mitigated sentences by reason of *démence*.[64] The law did not, however, completely switch to a deterministic vision of criminal liability where mental disorders would be based on inherited physical characteristics. It remained centred on the concepts of reason and free will.[65]

By mid-20th century, the '*démence*' of Article 64 CP had become a neutral term not defined by its biological origins. Post-1945, the case law on '*démence*' included the following disorders: amnesia,[66] epilepsy,[67] schizophrenia,[68] sleepwalking, and intoxication.[69] Legal scholarship ceased to make any reference to the brain. It would not be surprising if the experience of the Nazi Occupation, and its extermination programme of the mentally ill, especially if Jewish, finally led to the abandoning of any biological reference.[70] In that regard, the movement of *L'école de la défense sociale nouvelle*, launched in 1954 by the judge Marc Ancel, insisted on the need to shred any preconceived ideas on crime and defendants.[71] Viewed as obsolete, the term '*démence*' was abandoned in 1992.[72]

A More Modern and Neutral Terminology: The Current Article 122-1 CP

Article 122-1 CP refers to a 'psychological or neuro-psychological disorder'. Chosen for its neutrality, the expression encompasses any medical condition an expert would consider as affecting the defendant's intellectual and volitional capacities. There is no legal requirement for the disorder to be recognized in a particular medical classification, whether the World Health Organization (WHO) International Classification of Diseases (ICD) or its French equivalents.[73] The disorder is thus a legal concept.

This conception was tested in the *Halimi* case. In her non-binding *avis* to the Cour de cassation to reject the appeal, the *Avocate générale* explained that the notion of psychological or neuropsychological disorder should not be interpreted, as

64 Guignard, 'Corps criminel' (n 10) paras 19–20; Protais, 'Psychiatric Care' (n 58) 18.

65 Guignard, 'Corps criminel' (n 10) paras 15–20; J-L Halpérin, 'Ambivalences des doctrines pénales modernes' RSC 2010, 9.

66 CA Alger, 18 December 1948 D 1949, 382 note Vouin.

67 Crim 14 December 1982 Gaz Pal 1983 1. pan 178.

68 CA Paris 21 May 1996 Droit pénql 1996 comm 240 obs Véron; Crim 18 February 1998 Bull Crim n 66.

69 Y Mayaud, *Droit pénal général* (Presses universitaires de France 2004) 397–407.

70 Y Mouchenik and V Fau-Vincenti, 'The Fate of Jews Hospitalized in Mental Hospitals in France during World War II' (2020) 31 Hist Psychiatry 178; Freudian ideas may also have played a role in accepting that un/consciousness is not the biological functioning of the brain, Renneville, 'L'anthropologie' (n 58).

71 R Merle and A Vitu, *Traité de droit criminel*, vol 1 (7th edn, Cujas) 134–36.

72 Delmas-Marty, 'Nouveau code pénal' (n 24).

73 Garrabé, 'Nosography' (n 51) e41–43.

the victim's family argued, as 'restricted to a psychiatric pathology, [such as schizophrenia,] but should include any cause leading to the abolition of discernment'[74] such as the 'psychic reaction' to cannabis consumption. 'To conclude otherwise contradicts the letter and spirit of the text, its historical origins and its judicial application.'[75] The Cour de cassation confirmed this conception of the 'psychological and neuro-psychological disorder'.[76] The disorder is a legal concept, neither based on the biological roots of the mental illness, as it was until the early 20th century, nor dependent on a particular pathology, as the *Halimi* case illustrated. What matters is for the experts to attest to the disorder and its impact on the defendant's capacities. But how has French law attempted to define this impact?

Defining the Impact of the Disorder: Some Perennial Fault Lines

The impact of the disorder focuses on capacities of discernment and control, terms that have never been defined in depth. The debates have instead concentrated on how the disorder has affected these capacities: is there abolition or alteration of capacities? The question is closely tied to the defence's outcome: abolition justifies irresponsibility; alteration [justifies] attenuated responsibility. How to define abolition/alteration continues to raise a number of challenges.

The Continuous Focus on Capacities of Discernment and Control

For the first time in the history of the defence, Article 122-1 CP identified discernment and control as capacities the defence requires. In doing so, it recognized a long tradition going as far back as the Ancien Regime.[77] It also fits within the wider theory of criminal law underpinning the 1791 Criminal Code and integrated in the 1810 Criminal Code. Only an individual who can reason, control, and exercise moral autonomy can be criminally liable.

The terms of discernment and control have never been defined, even in Article 122-1 CP. The courts have remained silent, probably because of three combined factors: a legal tradition of laconic and formulistic drafting of judicial decisions;[78]

[74] Avis, Crim 14 April 2021 (n 36).

[75] ibid 24.

[76] Crim (n 36).

[77] See From a Religious Concept to a 'Disease of the Brain': the Ancien Droit or Old Law (1600–1789).

[78] Bell, *French Legal Cultures* (n 9) 96. The 2019 reform barely dented this style, See, in French, <https://www.courdecassation.fr/acces-rapide-judilibre/comprendre-une-decision-de-la-cour/le-nouveau-mode-de-redaction-des>

the absence of directions given to juries;[79] and the decision on the defence being a question of fact outside the control of the Supreme Court.

Neither 19th-century authors,[80] nor 20th/21st-century scholars,[81] are specific beyond generic references to free will, reason or discernment, control, and intellectual and cognitive faculties.[82] The absence of definitions and analysis does not preoccupy the legal scholarship, but for psychiatric experts, the notions are problematic. Medical practice does not aim to measure the capacity to discern.[83] Experts are even less at ease with the concept of 'control', which they hardly use.[84] Discernment and control are not medical concepts. The terms abolition and alteration add to these difficulties. The fault line appeared in the 19th century.

Emerging Fault Line in the 19th Century: Alteration, Abolition, or Causality?

In 1810, the impact of the disorder under Article 64 CP was understood as an all or nothing matter. Either the person lost capacity and was not liable; or he or she did not and was liable, with no mitigating circumstances.[85] Medical knowledge challenged the status quo in two ways.

The first generation of alienists, notably Esquirol, identified monomania, specifically 'homicidal monomania', as a delusion fixated on a unique 'object', an irresistible impulse to kill.[86] For them, a person should be legally irresponsible when the overpowering delusion they suffered from explained the criminal act, even if they otherwise appeared sane.[87] Madness did not have to lead to a complete and absolute loss of the defendant's capacities to discern and control.

The second challenge was brought about by the second generation of alienists, around the 1850s. They viewed madness as a spectrum. The 'half-mad', those defendants who were not severely affected by their mental illness, remained

[79] E Boitard and F Hélie, *Leçons de droit criminel, contenant l'explication complète des Codes pénal et d'instruction criminelle (11e éd., revue, complétée et mise en harmonie avec toutes les lois modificatives des deux codes)* (11 edn, A. Cotillon et Cte, Librairies du Conseil d'Etat 1876) 735.

[80] Chauveau and Hélie, *Théorie* (n 53); Garraud, *Précis* (n 53); Ortolan, *Éléments* (n 55); L Guignard, 'Michel Foucault et la pratique des discours de vérité: droit et psychiatrie au XIXe siècle' in D Boquet, B Dufal, and P Labey (eds), *Une histoire au présent: les historiens et Michel Foucault* (CNRS éditions 2013) 183, 190–91 (hereafter, Guignard, 'Foucault').

[81] Merle and Vitu (n 71); Mayaud (n 69); Bonis, *Répertoire* (n 8).

[82] Protais, 'Psychiatric Care' (n 58) 18.

[83] Sénat, *Rapport* n° 434 (n 6) 75.

[84] ibid.

[85] Chauveau and Hélie, *Théorie* (n 53) 214.

[86] Guignard, 'Corps criminel' (n 10).

[87] L Guignard, 'Crime et Psychiatrie. Antoine Léger, le lycanthrope: une étape dans la généalogie des perversions sexuelles (1824–1903)' (2017) 82 Évol Psychiatr 579, 584–85; Renneville, 'L'anthropologie' (n 58) 187; Guignard, 'Corps criminel' (n 10); D Bouley and others, 'Les fondements historiques de la responsabilité pénale' (2002) 160 Ann Méd Psychol 396, 402–03.

criminally liable and should benefit from mitigating circumstances at the sentencing stage.[88] It was a different perspective from that of Esquirol. How did the lawyers receive this medical knowledge?

The possibility for the disorder to justify attenuated responsibility, rather than irresponsibility, was well received, but needed a statutory basis. Bound by the principle of strict interpretation of the criminal law, the courts could not expand the scope of Article 64 CP to include attenuated liability. Its wording clearly indicated that the disorder excluded liability. With the 1832 statute giving judges the power to individualize the sentence between a minimum and maximum, courts acquired the legal authority to recognize the disorder at the sentencing stage. The Supreme Court recognized the practice in 1885,[89] and the Ministry of Justice in its 1905 Instruction. Both the case law and the Instruction had no binding legal authority, but the system remained until its codification in Article 122-1 CP. The 19th century thus saw a return to the Ancien Regime practice of sentence individualization to accommodate the alienists' ideas about madness.[90]

Legal scholarship was also receptive to the concept of attenuated responsibility for the 'half-mad'. In response, the theories of imputability (for irresponsibility) and culpability (for attenuated responsibility) were developed, the concepts still in use today.[91] Imputability is the capacity to be accountable because of 'the author's existing free will and lucid intelligence'.[92] It captures the 'requisite of rationality'[93] underlying Article 64 CP. Culpability affects the mens rea in different degrees. The criminal law integrated the medical understanding that madness was a spectrum.

One would therefore infer that the boundaries between irresponsibility and attenuated responsibility were settled along clear lines. Abolition of the defendant's capacities to discern and control led to irresponsibility. Attenuated liability meant that their capacities partially remained. As the 19th-century debates surrounding homicidal monomania illustrate, medical knowledge and legal scholarship however presented a far more complex picture, where abolition and irresponsibility did not solely equate to complete loss of capacity.

The second generation of alienists discredited monomania, preferring the expression of 'partial alienation', but they did not entirely discard the factual situation Esquirol attempted to describe and the legal outcome of irresponsibility if

[88] Guignard, 'Corps criminel' (n 10).

[89] See n 21 above.

[90] On the broader aspects of sentence individualization, Carbasse, *Histoire* (n 38) 408–12; Guignard, 'Corps criminel' (n 10); Guignard, 'Foucault' (n 80) 192–96.

[91] Merle and Vitu (n 71).

[92] Ortolan, *Éléments* (n 55) 98–130; Merle and Vitu (n 71) 773; Protais, 'Psychiatric Care' (n 58) 18.

[93] Citing Foucault, L Guignard, 'L'irresponsabilité pénale dans la première moitié du XIXe siècle, entre classicisme et défense sociale' (2005) Champ pénal/Penal field [En ligne], XXXIVe Congrès français de criminologie, Responsabilité/Irresponsabilité Pénale, para 10 <https://journals.openedition.org/champpenal/368> accessed 5 April 2021.

further conditions were met.[94] For them, irresponsibility should ensue when the delusion had a broader impact on the individual's capacities than the first alienists described. Upon scrutiny, the individual would not appear of sound mind: their mental illness would have affected more widely their capacities to discern and control, making them alien to their surroundings.

Initially rejecting monomania, by the late 1830s juries declared defendants irresponsible despite their mental illness not having completely abolished their capacities to discern and control.[95] However, for the same reasons they did not define discernment and control, the courts did not define abolition and alteration. Legal scholarship provided more details, but not necessarily more clarity.[96] Chauveau and Hélie stated that '*démence*, in the legal meaning of the word, is not a complete abolition of intelligence' as otherwise too few mentally ill defendants would benefit from the defence.[97] Citing medical knowledge on monomania and partial alienation, they recommended irresponsibility,[98] enjoining judges to 'examine the relationships between this idea [on which the *démence* rests] and the apparent causes of the offence'.[99] Similarly, Ortolan considered that when the defendant suffered from 'this dominant and exclusive idea that led to the crime itself, the person submitted to an irresistible passion or impulse'. Having lost his will, but not his reason, he was not liable.[100] The legal test is thus in terms of causality and the effects on the defendant's capacities. Garraud was more ambiguous, stating that *démence* justifies irresponsibility 'where there was a *sufficient alteration* of his mental faculties to *destroy* his culpability' (emphasis added).[101] Lallement did not take a position, citing three contradictory verdicts of Assises Courts.[102]

Probably the most enlightening summary of the legal scholarship is by legal scholar Acollas in 1887, two years after the Supreme Court's decision. For him, two conceptions of *démence* were competing. Some considered that when 'convinced that the agent was in one of these states at the time of the offence, the courts could base the acquittal on the *general cause of démence*'. Others defended a '*more restrictive and more subtle*' view, that the courts could acquit only when the agent 'did not possess, in fact, the *full exercise* of his will' (emphasis added).[103] 'Anyway, they [all] agree ... that the same causes [of *démence*] can lead, at least, to an attenuation of culpability.'[104]

[94] J-P Falret, *Des maladies mentales et des asiles d'aliénés: leçons cliniques et considérations générales* (Librairies de l'Académie de médecine 1864) 443–48.

[95] Guignard, 'Corps criminel' (n 10) para 14.

[96] E Acollas, *Les délits et les peines* (Libraire Ch. Delagrave 1887) 74–75; Chauveau and Hélie, *Théorie* (n 53) 528–31; Guignard, 'Foucault' (n 80) 192.

[97] Chauveau and Hélie, *Théorie* (n 53) 497–98.

[98] ibid 502.

[99] ibid 531.

[100] Ortolan, *Éléments* (n 55) 131.

[101] Garraud, *Précis* (n 53) 217.

[102] Lallement, *De la condition* (n 63) 240–41.

[103] Acollas (n 96) 75.

[104] ibid.

As Acollas pointed out, the difference in understanding the impact of madness on the defendant is subtle but, I argue, crucial when establishing the boundaries between no liability and attenuated liability. When the focus is on the illness being the dominant cause of the offence, as in the words of Ortolan, a decision to acquit can be taken even when the illness had not destroyed the defendant's faculties. With the second conception, establishing the causality between the disorder and the offence will not suffice: only when the illness destroyed the defendant's intelligence and will can liability be excluded.

By the time Article 64 CP was to be abolished in 1992, the Supreme Court referred to the disorder having *totally* abolished capacity or control.[105] The legal scholarship adopted similar wording,[106] although Decocq added that the disorder must 'be related to the offence', that is, must explain the offence.[107] When this shift happened is difficult to identify in the absence of studies having focused on the exact legal test used to define abolition and alteration. It also does not account for the profound changes in psychiatric practice and how this fed into the boundaries between abolition and alteration without the legal test changing!

Protais has demonstrated that the increased use of attenuated liability did not start with Article 122-1 CP. From the 1960s onwards, medical experts began to recommend attenuated responsibility for conditions that were predominantly viewed, until the 1950s, as obvious cases of abolition and irresponsibility. The shift was gradual: first, the behavioural problems, low and medium debility (1950s/1960s), then the 'borderline' or 'psychopathic personality with psychotic decompensation' (1970s); finally the decompensated psychoses which include dissociated states with hallucination and paranoia (1990s).[108] In other words, the legal test remained centred on abolition/alteration, but the medical use of the test changed so much that cases of irresponsibility shrank, while conversely cases of attenuated responsibility increased. Many reasons explain these changes, not the least viewing criminal liability as a form of treatment;[109] but medical experts do not work alone. Judges have to be receptive to their conclusions. The treatment of kleptomania in the 19th century illustrates the point. For most of the 19th century, judges rejected kleptomania as a mental disorder excluding liability. However, by the late 19th century, the courts accepted kleptomania could result in the acquittal of defendants from theft under Article 64 CP. Why? The defendants were often women among the middle classes, if not upper classes, educated, and who had the means to pay for the goods; thus they were seen as having no motives to steal. Greed explained

[105] Crim 14 December 1982 Gaz Pal 1983.

[106] Bonis, *Répertoire* (n 8) 117; A Decocq, *Droit pénal général* (Armand Colin 1971) 338–39; M Puech, *Droit pénal général* (Litec 1988) 398–400.

[107] Decocq, *Droit pénal* (n 106) 339.

[108] Protais, 'Psychiatric Care' (n 58) 22–23.

[109] ibid.

theft by the working class; mental disorder, and gender, excused the middle-class thieves![110]

Therefore, the boundaries between abolition and attenuation have fluctuated because of evolving medical knowledge and because social factors interplayed with the perception of who was 'mad' and who was not, or not mad enough to be irresponsible. This flexibility was in a way facilitated by the terms of Article 64 CP itself. The diagnosis of *démence* at the time of the offence established a factual presumption that the defendant would not be liable unless the expert demonstrated that the defendant's capacities were only altered.[111] With Article 122-1 CP, establishing a diagnosis is no longer sufficient. How the disorder affected the defendant at the time of the offence needs to be carefully articulated in light of Article 122-1 CP's express reference to abolition and alteration. This subtle change made the experts' task more demanding, leaving less space for imprecision in the medico-legal interpretation.[112] It is thus not surprising that the shift towards more recommendations for attenuation, which started in the 1950s, finally became visible under Article 122-1 CP. In turn, the previous difficulties in defining the impact of the disorder resurfaced: is the dichotomy abolition/alteration the correct legal test?

Renewed Questions under Article 122-1CP: Abolition/Alteration or Causality?

Following concerns that Article 122-1 al. 2 CP was overused, a parliamentary commission led in 2010 to an inquiry.[113] The resulting consensus was that experts generally agreed on a diagnosis on the disorder(s), but they tended to disagree on the medico-legal interpretation of that diagnosis because the concepts of abolition, alteration, discernment, and control remained outside the scope of a diagnosis.[114] The Commission asked whether a list of pathologies should be added to Article 122-1 al.1 CP, since some medical conditions, such as delusional psychoses, tend to fit within the concept of abolition/destruction of reason and will. This option was rejected on the basis that a list would further reduce the use of Article 122-1 al.1 CP. Indeed, other pathologies, especially those at the borderlines, are difficult

[110] Lallement, *De la condition* (n 63) 241; P O'Brien, 'The Kleptomania Diagnosis: Bourgeois Women and Theft in Late Nineteenth-Century France' (1983) 17 J Soc Hist 65, 67–68, 71–73; Bogani, 'Le vol' (n 58) para 32.

[111] In that sense, Zagury and Bouchard, 'Le psychiatre expert' (n 12) 944; C Protais, 'Le psychiatre et le juge' 2018 AJ Pénal 494.

[112] HAS, *Rapport* (n 1) 30; Lafaye, *Rapport* (n 6) 77; Zagury and Bouchard, 'Le psychiatre expert' (n 12).

[113] Sénat, *Rapport n° 434* (n 6).

[114] ibid; HAS, *Rapport* (n 1) 30–31; B Godechot, 'Psychiatrie et droit pénal: discernement ou contrôle des actes, un dilemme médico-légal? Analyse de la littérature professionnelle et de la position d'un échantillon d'experts psychiatres'. Thèse Médecine humaine et pathologie 2014 <https://dumas.ccsd.cnrs.fr/dumas-01082093> accessed 5 April 2021.

to interpret, in the sense of altering or abolishing capacities according to the facts of the case.[115]

The report also considered whether the distinction between abolition and diminution should be abandoned. Some experts consider that even the 'core' disorders associated with abolition, such as schizophrenia and paranoia, do not deprive a person of their cognitive and volitional capacities unless in a middle of a crisis.[116] As in the 19th century, questions endure as to whether a person can be irresponsible when appearing sane, except for the object of her delusion. The dichotomy abolition/alteration was ultimately retained on the basis that the vast majority of experts wished to keep it. They appreciated the opportunity to establish 'a direct and exclusive link between the disorder at the time of the offence and the offence committed'.[117]

Yet, establishing a link does not completely equate to establishing abolition, as the 2018 proposal by Dr Bouchard, medical expert since 1979, shows. For him, irresponsibility under Article 122-1 al.1 CP would be when the disorder was the 'exclusive cause of the facts for which s/he is guilty'. Article 122-1 al.2 CP should apply when the disorder is 'the non-exclusive cause'. He also recommended a reflection to form a 'consensus clinically and semantically on what the disorders are' and on the legal test, which could be taught to both medical experts, judges and lawyers.[118] His justification for the change rests on the absence of definitions of the key words (abolition, alteration, discernment, and will) and the fact that the legal concept of abolition does not match the clinician's reality: a person can be suffering from a mental disorder and still retain their reason and intention to commit crime,[119] an observation the alienists made long ago through the concepts of monomania and partial alienation.[120] Interestingly, his causality test recommendation echoes 19th-century legal scholar Ortolan's test of a 'dominant and exclusive' idea leading to the crime and Acollas' explanation of the debates before the courts.

There is certainly a difference between a test based on causality and one based on abolition/alteration. A disorder can be the dominant or exclusive cause of the offence, while not completely destroying the defendant's capacities. The test would bring within the orbit of 'abolition' a broader range of disorders than are likely to be currently dealt with under 'alteration'. In addition, it shifts the focus away from discernment and control towards understanding how the disorder is the dominant or exclusive explanation for the offence. Thus it brings the work of experts closer

[115] HAS, *Rapport* (n 1) 30; Lafaye, *Rapport* (n 6) 72–73.

[116] Lafaye, *Rapport* (n 6) 71–72.

[117] Sénat, *Rapport n° 434* (n 6) 76.

[118] Bouchard, 'Irresponsabilité' (n 12) 423; similarly, Zagury, 'Clinique' (n 12); Godechot, 'Psychiatrie' (n 114).

[119] Bouchard, 'Irresponsabilité' (n 12) 422; HAS, *Rapport* (n 1) 31; Zagury, 'Clinique' (n 12); M Bénézech, 'Folie où es-tu?: Libre dissertation critique sur la responsabilisation des psychotiques' (2010) 168(1) Ann Méd Psychol 48.

[120] Bénézech (n 119) 52.

to their actual expertise, that is, that of establishing a medical diagnosis at the time of the offence. Discernment, control, abolition, and alteration, could still be taken into account, but they would no longer be the focal point. It would also bring more transparency to the decisional process; it could even be used to explain a decision to the victim.

In the *Halimi* case, for example, the victim's family argued that the judges could not simultaneously recognize the antisemitic nature of the defendant's speech and conclude that his capacity to discern was abolished. Citing the experts' reports, the Court of Appeal and the Avocate Generale took care to explain that the contradiction was only apparent, that the antisemitic words were part of the delusion.[121] The Supreme Court reached the same conclusion.[122] Nevertheless, when the legal test focuses on the defendant's capacities, it can be difficult to convince the victim's family that the defendant, in using the victim's religion to fuel his delusion, has lost his reasoning faculties. Viewing the test in causal terms on the other hand helps to shift the focus slightly away from discernment and volition. It requires an understanding of how a delusion works and how the psychotic episode dominated the defendant despite his apparent ability to reason. The causality test does not, however, provide an answer to the thorny issue of prior fault, when, for example, the episode results from a voluntary consumption of cannabis.

The Outcome of the Defence: The Modulation of Prior Fault?

Once the disorder is identified and is considered to have affected the defendant's capacities, the decision can still be influenced by the defendant's prior fault, a controversial question even today.

The State of the Law until the Halimi Case

The question of prior fault is longstanding. The Ancien Droit considered that prior fault for madness and sleepwalking meant conviction, with a mitigated sentence. For intoxication, scholars disagreed as to whether it was full liability in any case or just for voluntary intoxication.[123] Little is known of the revolutionary period. One wide-ranging study of historical records of the juries between 1791 and 1801 however mentioned that madness was often pleaded as a mitigating circumstance for sentencing purposes, after a conviction. Why is not clear, but madness seemed to have been accepted along with voluntary intoxication, learning difficulties, and

[121] CA Paris Halimi (n 34) 23–24.
[122] Crim (n 36).
[123] See From a Religious Concept to a 'Disease of the Brain': the Ancien Droit or Old Law (1600–1789).

destitution,[124] confirming Ortolan's observations in 1863.[125] Therefore, it may well be that the jury did not want to exclude liability, because there was prior fault and/or an altered state of mind (as with intoxication). France may have continued the Ancien Regime practice, despite the revolutionaries' wide-ranging ban on individualization of sentences by judges.

Article 64 CP makes no mention of the question. At first, the Supreme Court seemed divided,[126] but over time it settled on the fact that voluntary intoxication, when it altered the defendant's capacities, cannot justify mitigating circumstances, whichever type of offence is considered (intentional or non-intentional).[127] The question of prior fault when there is complete loss of discernment or control does not seem to have been resolved, as the *Avocate Générale* demonstrated in her *avis* to the *Halimi* case.[128]

The 19th-century legal scholarship on prior fault focused on intoxication and sleepwalking rather than on *démence*/mental alienation. They all agreed intoxication cannot be an excuse in the situation dubbed in English 'Dutch courage' as the author premeditated his crime while drinking. They also all agreed that involuntary intoxication leading to complete loss of consciousness or control should exclude liability; if it only altered the defendant's capacities, mitigating circumstances should be recognized.[129]

For voluntary intoxication, the authors are divided. Ortolan rejected liability as long as the person completely lost his faculties, even if drunkenness is habitual and not an accident, because the person stopped being just intoxicated and entered a state of mental alienation; when the person has not lost capacity, then the judge could consider intoxication as a mitigating or aggravating circumstance.[130] Garraud differentiated according to the type of offence (intentional/non-intentional) if intoxication led to total incapacity. Voluntary intoxication without abolition of capacities may be considered at the sentencing stage. Nevertheless, if the 'habitual use of alcohol, opium, hashish, morphine' leads to a state of mental alienation recognized by medical experts, then the person is in a state of *démence* and is not liable.[131] Lallement has a similar outlook, noting

[124] R Allen, *Les tribunaux criminels sous la Révolution et l'Empire: 1792–1811* (Presses universitaires de Rennes 2005) chapters 2, 3.

[125] Ortolan, *Éléments* (n 55) 466–67.

[126] Against mitigating circumstances (voluntary intoxication): Crim 7 prairial an 9; Crim 15 thermidor an 12; for, when intoxication is not total, Crim 8 frimaire an 7; Crim 11 florial an 10, in J-B Sirey, L-M Devilleneuve, and A-A Carrette, *Recueil général des lois et des arrêts, avec notes et commentaires (1791–1830)* vol 1 (M. Pouleur 1843).

[127] Crim 1 June 1843 S 1843, 1, 844; Crim 3 December 1963 Bull Crim 343; Bouloc, *Droit pénal général* (25th edn, Dalloz 2017) para 464.

[128] *Avis*, Crim (n 36).

[129] Garraud, *Précis* (n 53) 226–27; Lallement, 'De la condition' (n 63) 242; Chauveau and Hélie, *Théorie* (n 53) 214–15; Ortolan, *Éléments* (n 55) 132–33.

[130] Ortolan, *Éléments* (n 55) 225.

[131] Garraud, *Précis* (n 53) 224, 226–27.

that for Esquirol 'intoxication is far less the cause than the first symptom of madness'.[132]

For Chauveau and Hélie, intoxication which altered the defendant's capacities justifies mitigating circumstances, whether it is habitual or accidental. When voluntary intoxication leads to complete loss of capacity, in theory, the offender should not be liable, but in practice, only involuntary intoxication may be admissible.[133]

Modern authors' developments testify of a persisting fault line. They observe that Parliament has criminalized certain behaviours when the defendant is voluntarily intoxicated (mostly driving). They acknowledge the scholarly controversy. Furthermore, observing that the question is one of fact, outside the control of the Supreme Court, they explain that the case law, pre- and post-1992, is unfavourable to recognizing voluntary intoxication as a mitigating factor at sentencing, let alone as a cause to exclude liability.[134] Professor Mayaud quotes a long extract of a *tribunal correctionnel*'s decision (so a trial court) to explain why voluntary intoxication cannot be accepted as part of the defence: '[W]hen the person knows well the intoxicating qualities of the multiple drinks he consumed, which is strongly indicative of his intention to gradually reach a state of no-return in the state of drunkenness and a degree of excitement particularly dangerous for a habitual drinker'.[135] This rationale was put to the test in the *Halimi* case.

The Halimi Case

Nobody disputed that the defendant voluntarily consumed cannabis for 11 years, up to 15 joints a day. One expert, and the victim's family, considered however that this consumption, because it was voluntary, meant that the defendant understood the risks associated with cannabis. The defendant was at fault in terms echoing the extract above. The Paris Court of Appeal reached a very different assessment. It repeated twice that the defendant did not know, when he was consuming cannabis, that its use could cause an acute psychotic disorder.[136] His three convictions for possessing cannabis did not demonstrate either that the defendant understood the dangers of using cannabis. The Paris Appeal Court, therefore, rejected prior fault; so did the Supreme Court: Article 122-1 al.1 CP does 'not distinguish according to the origin of the disorder which led to the abolition of [the defendant's] discernment'.[137] The *Avocate Générale* reached a similar conclusion,[138] suggesting that at

[132] Lallement, *De la condition* (n 63) 247.

[133] Chauveau and Hélie, *Théorie* (n 53) 213–16.

[134] Bouloc (n 127); Bonis, *Répertoire* (n 8) paras 71–72; V Tellier-Cayrol, 'La turpitude du fou' [2020] Recueil Dalloz 349.

[135] Mayaud (n 69) 402.

[136] CA Paris Halimi (n 66).

[137] Crim (n 36) para 29

[138] *Avis*, ibid 68–70.

best, the investigatory court could have considered a charge for involuntary manslaughter, since the consumption demonstrated indifference to its dangers.[139]

Prior fault thus raises issues of causality, showing the relevance of the debates about the legal test to define the impact of the disorder. It also illustrates that defining the disorder's impact is not just a legal choice but a political and social choice. Who does society wish to punish? Would prior fault for example apply if the defendant had refused treatment? It is a controversial question among psychiatrists.[140] In early 2020, three senators proposed an amendment to Article 122-1 CP which would criminalize any form of prior fault, the refusal of treatment included.[141] Yet refusal of treatment is often symptomatic of the disorder,[142] and raises the question as to the degree of autonomy our society wants to give to a patient in choosing his treatment. Kobili's excessive consumption of cannabis could be a sign that he was already so ill that he could not seek medical help and thus was not at fault. The question would certainly deserve a parliamentary debate, informed if possible by clinical experience and the patients' own views. The Loi n° 2022-52 of 24 January 2022, enacted in reaction to the Halimi case, missed an opportunity to clarify the issues. Adding two articles to Article 121-1 CP, it excludes the benefit of the defence, both for abolition and attenuation, where the defendant 'has voluntarily consumed psychoactive substances with the objective to commit the offence or similar, or to facilitate its commission'. The problem in *Halimi* is that Kobili did not consume cannabis in order to kill his neighbour or commit a similar offence. The reform has thus not provided a resolution to the situation which the *Halimi* case represents.

A Conclusion with a Comparative Law Outlook

This chapter has presented the evolution of the French law defence of mental disorder over four centuries. French law has always accepted that the defence could have two outcomes: if total lack of capacity, liability is excluded. If capacity is only altered, liability is attenuated; the disorder justifies conviction with the court applying mitigating circumstances. Even the Revolution, which banned individualization of sentencing by judges, seemed to have continued with the practice of a mitigated sentence via the concept of excuse. Contrary to the claim often made, it has always punished offenders suffering from a medical condition, as long as the conditions of the defence have been met.

139 ibid 75–77.
140 Lafaye, *Rapport* (n 6) 82.
141 J-L Masson, Ch Herzog, and Cl Kauffmann, Sénat, *Proposition de loi n. 252*, 16 January 2020.
142 Tellier-Cayrol, 'Turpitude' (n 134).

Over the centuries, the definition of the disorder has changed. Anchored in the Ancien Droit, the *démence* of Article 64 CP (1810 Criminal Code) was initially a disease of the brain, an expression not dissimilar to the 1843 'disease of the mind' in the M'Naghten Rules in English law. In their own ways and in their own time, both laws stopped being defined by biology and evolved to encompass different conditions that do not reside in the brain.[143]

By the first half of the 20th century, *démence* was understood generically, including intoxication and sleepwalking which before were recognized by, but outside, Article 64 CP. The 1992 codification solidified this understanding by using the neutral expression of 'psychological or neuro-psychological disorder'. English law however developed the separate defence of automatism, and thus the insanity defence never extended as far as the French defence. In that sense, the modern French expression of 'psychological or neuropsychological disorder' is closer to the 'recognised medical condition' of diminished responsibility[144] and the Law Commission's suggested concept of 'a medically recognised condition' in its proposals relating to insanity, automatism, and intoxication.[145] As the *Halimi* case illustrated, the French law concept is a legal concept, where the disorder does not have to be a specific pathology such as schizophrenia and can include a wider range of medical conditions.

Once identified, the disorder has to have an impact, which has always been defined in French law along the lines of abolition/alteration of capacities, both cognitive and volitional. There is no exclusion of control like in the English insanity defence, and thus no separation between insanity and automatism. With perhaps the exclusion of the revolutionary period, French law always had two outcomes: exclusion of liability based on abolition and attenuated responsibility based on alteration. By contrast, English law does not formally recognize attenuated responsibility, except indirectly with diminished responsibility which only applies to murder charges. The Law Commission's reform proposal continues that tradition. English law, though, does not ignore mitigating circumstances based on a mental disorder. The current sentencing guidelines indicate that 'when the offender appears to be mentally disordered, the court must obtain and consider a medical report'.[146] The ultimate outcome may therefore be similar in both countries.

The legal test to decide between irresponsibility and responsibility focuses in both laws on abolition—total incapacity—to justify excluding criminal liability, in contrast to the Dutch legal test for insanity, for example, which focuses on

[143] Kemp [1957] 1 QB 399, 407.

[144] Homicide Act 1957 cl 11, s 2.

[145] Law Commission, *Criminal Liability: Insanity and Automatism. A Discussion Paper* (2013).

[146] Paragraph 6, <https://www.sentencingcouncil.org.uk/overarching-guides/magistrates-court/item/sentencing-offenders-with-mental-disorders-developmental-disorders-or-neurological-impairments/>

causality.[147] Yet, following recurring difficulties for medical experts in interpreting the terms abolition/alteration and discernment/control, which remained undefined in French law, I suggest amending Article 122-1 CP to switch to a causality test. The test for Article 122-1 al.1 CP would become slightly wider, bringing within its orbit cases where defendants have not completely lost capacity but where the disorder, nevertheless, is the dominant or exclusive cause of the offence.

Articulating such a test would bring additional clarity with regard to prior fault as Parliament would have to decide whether a disorder, which is the dominant or exclusive cause of the offence, should be excluded if brought about by the defendant's prior fault.

The question of prior fault has always been controversial in French law. The 19th-century authors did not agree, and modern scholars remain divided as to the effect of voluntary consumption of alcohol or cannabis. English law has long refused to conclude that the regular consumption of alcohol constitutes prior fault when the defendant has developed a mental illness and a defence or partial defence applies.[148] French courts had no opportunity to answer this question until the *Halimi* case. The Supreme Court rejected prior fault: judges cannot distinguish where Parliament never intended to make such a distinction when it enacted Article 122-1 CP. If prior fault is to be recognized in French law, it would be through a Parliamentary reform, as partially undertaken by the Loi n° 2022-52 of 24 January 2022.

More generally, the *Halimi* case illustrated how the application of the defence cannot be dissociated from the fact that Article 122-1 CP and embodies a choice French society made based on how it sees its relationship with those who commit a crime while suffering from a medical condition affecting their capacities. Psychiatric experts have their own conceptions of liability and treatment, but their participation in criminal proceedings is in practice limited. For offences which attract less than ten years' imprisonment, which represent 99.74% of tried cases, the multiplication of summary proceedings akin to guilty pleas has led to defendants rarely, if ever, seeing an expert before entering a prison after conviction.[149] Article 122-1 CP has its defects, but perhaps it is a sign of a wider problem: what is the purpose of a criminal sanction when often those offenders suffering from a mental disorder are the most vulnerable? It is time for France to confront the startling question as to why its prisons can be seen as the new asylums. Article 122-1 CP is only part of the solution.

[147] J Keiler and D Roef (eds), *Comparative Concepts of Criminal Law* (3rd edn, Intersentia) 243. The Dutch Criminal Code is built on the 1810 French Criminal Code.

[148] Law Commission (n 145) para 4.87.

[149] Lafaye, *Rapport* (n 6) 210.

11
Insanity in German Criminal Law

Regina E Rauxloh[*]

Introduction

The Concept of Guilt

Strictly speaking, German criminal law does not recognize a defence of insanity. The English legal expression 'insanity' corresponds to the German legal term '*Unzurechnungsfähigkeit*' which literally means 'inability to be allocated blame' as well as '*Schuldunfähigkeit*' which can be translated as the 'incapacity of being guilty'. This terminology reflects the understanding that even though the elements of the crimes such as actus reus and mens rea are present, no guilt can be attached to the defendant. Thus, in German criminal law, the role of mental disorders is conceptually different from the Anglo-American understanding. They are not considered a criminal defence but rather exclude the criminal responsibility of the defendant. The reason for this lies in the different concept of the elements of crime in the understanding of German criminal justice. In Germany, a conviction for a criminal offence requires three factors:

1) the presence of the necessary subjective and objective elements of the offence (*Tatbestand*),
2) the illegality of the action, which is assumed unless there are special circumstances such as self-defence (*Rechtswidrigkeit*), and
3) the culpability (individual criminal responsibility) of the offender (*Schuld*).

A mental illness does not affect the illegality of the act and thus cannot be raised as a defence, but it might exclude the culpability of the defendant.[1] It is therefore necessary to understand the notion of culpability in German criminal law. The term

* I would like to express my deepest gratitude to Professor Dr Carsten Momsen (Freie Universität Berlin), who allowed me to work as a guest researcher at the Law School and without whose help this research would not have been possible during the travel restrictions in 2020 and 2021.

[1] In the remainder of this chapter the author will use the terms 'culpability' and 'criminal responsibility' synonymously.

Regina E Rauxloh, *Insanity in German Criminal Law* In: *The Insanity Defence.* Edited by: Ronnie Mackay and Warren Brookbanks, Oxford University Press. © Regina E Rauxloh 2022. DOI: 10.1093/oso/9780198854944.003.0011

Schuld can be translated as guilt, culpability, or criminal responsibility which is seen as the capacity to adjust will and action to the law.[2] Unlike illegality, which is concerned with the question of whether the legal system condemns the act, the question of guilt concerns the defendant and is based on the autonomy and personal responsibility of the individual, who can self-determine their actions and, due to their free will, decide between right and wrong.[3] This requires that at the time of the commission of the crime the defendant must have been aware that their actions were wrong and must have had the ability to control them. As early as 1952, the Grand Chamber of the Federal Court of Justice[4] declared that

> [p]unishment presupposes guilt. Guilt is reproachable. With the judgment of guilt, the perpetrator is accused of not behaving lawfully, that he has decided in favour of the wrong, although he could have behaved lawfully, could have decided in favour of the right. The deep reason for the reproach lies in the fact that a person has free, responsible, and moral self-determination and is therefore able to decide in favour of the right and against injustice, to organise his behaviour according to the requirements of the legal norms and to avoid what is legally forbidden, from the moment he has reached moral maturity and as long as the system for free moral self-determination is not temporarily paralyzed or permanently destroyed by the pathological processes mentioned in § [20[5]] STGB.... Anyone who knows that what he freely decides to do is wrong, is acting culpably if he so acts anyway.[6]

This notion of guilt is the foundation on which German criminal justice is built. The very first section of the German Criminal Code declares the maxim of *nulla poena sine culpa*: 'An act can only incur a penalty if criminal liability was established by law before the act was committed.'[7] Indeed, the culpability principle is elevated to constitutional status in Germany.[8] Though the Constitution does not explicitly mention the culpability principle, it has been declared to be not just part of the rule of law protected in Article 20 III[9] but moreover an aspect of the inviolable right to human dignity in Article 1 I.[10] The constitutional status of this principle is especially important, as Germany does not recognize Parliamentary

[2] H Fuchs and I Zerbes, *Strafrecht Allgemeiner Teil I—Grundlagen und Lehre von der Straftat* (10th edn, Verlag Österreich 2018) (hereafter, Fuchs and Zerbes, *Strafrecht Allgemeiner Teil*) 228.

[3] BVergE 123, 267, 413.

[4] *Bundesgerichtshof.*

[5] At the time of this decision, the relevant provision was s 51 StGB. Unless otherwise stated all sections referred to are those of the German Criminal Code.

[6] BGHSt 2, 194 (all translations by the author).

[7] Section 1 German Criminal Code.

[8] T Fischer, *Strafgesetzbuch mit Nebengesetzten* (66th edn, C.H. Beck Verlag 2019) (hereafter Fischer, *Strafgesetzbuch*) 93.

[9] Rechtsstaatsprinzip. BVerfGE 20, 323, 332.

[10] Menschenwürde. BVerfGE 57, 250. Article 1 I reads: 'Human dignity shall be inviolable. To respect and protect it shall be the duty of all state authority.'

sovereignty and the Constitution binds all organs of the state. Moreover, the culpability principle counts among those core constitutional principles which cannot be changed even through constitutional amendment.[11]

Lack of Criminal Responsibility Due to Mental Illness

The German Criminal Code is built on the assumption that every person over the age of 14 has the ability to recognize the unlawfulness of their actions and act according to this discernment.[12] Section 20, which concerns criminal culpability, is therefore formulated negatively, stating the exceptional circumstances under which the wrongfulness of an act cannot be attributed to the perpetrator.[13] Its formulation illustrates the underlying understanding of German criminal law that culpability is directly linked to a person's freedom of will and their capacity to control their behaviour. Section 20 reads:

> Whoever, at the time of the commission of the offence, is incapable of appreciating the unlawfulness of their actions or of acting in accordance with any such appreciation due to a pathological mental disorder, a profound disturbance of consciousness, mental deficiency or any other serious mental abnormality is deemed to act without guilt.[14]

The analysis of section 20 consists of two stages, the second of which includes two alternatives. The biological cause (stage 1), that is, a mental disorder under section 20, results in the psychological effect (stage 2), namely the defendant's inability to recognize the wrongness of their actions[15] or the inability to react accordingly.[16] For simplicity, this chapter follows the common terminology of biological and psychological levels but acknowledges that this terminology is not strictly speaking correct as there is some overlap between the two stages.[17] Further, the category of 'profound disturbance of consciousness' as well as 'serious mental abnormality' are detached from the understanding of a biological root.[18] Also, the Federal Court

[11] BVergE 123, 267, 413.

[12] Section 19 German Criminal Code.

[13] W Perron and B Weißer, '§ 20 StGB Schuldunfähigkeit wegen seelischer Störungen' in A Eser (ed), *Schönke/Schröder Strafgesetzbuch Kommentar* (30th edn, C.H. Beck Verlag 2019) (hereafter Perron and Weißer, *Schönke/Schröder Kommentar*) 375. Another example where culpability is excluded is where the offender lacks the awareness of acting unlawfully because of an unavoidable mistake of law (s 17).

[14] All translations of provisions of the German Criminal Code are from the Bundesamt für Justiz available at https://www.gesetze-im-internet.de/englisch_stgb/.

[15] *Einsichtsfähigkeit.*

[16] *Steuerungsfähigkeit.*

[17] Also, the fourth alternative includes non-biological roots.

[18] F Streng, '§20 StGB Schuldunfähigkeit wegen seelischer Störungen' in CH Beck (ed), *Münchener Kommentar zum StGB* (4th edn, C.H. Beck Verlag 2020) (hereafter Streng, *Münchener Kommentar*) para 13.

of Justice included early on in the list of biological causes, severe states of affect[19] and sexual aberrations,[20] which have no biological root cause. Moreover, in the field of psychiatry too, the diagnosis has moved away from etiological diagnosis of a disease towards a descriptive diagnosis of the psychological disorder, which can be observed in the increased use of the international Diagnostic and Statistical Manual (DSM) and the International Classification of Diseases (ICD-11).[21] Thus, the biological elements lose significance not only in the legal concept but also in the medical scientific understanding, while it is still a basis of distinction of section 20.

If the court finds that culpability is excluded under section 20, the defendant is deemed not criminally responsible for the offence in question and will be acquitted. The court might, however, order the defendant's placement in a psychiatric hospital (see below)[22] or in an addiction treatment facility.[23] Where the ability to recognize the wrong or the ability to act accordingly is not completely lost but only reduced, the offender is considered culpable and deserving of punishment. However, as the offender is only partially responsible the court might mitigate the sentence under section 21 (Diminished Responsibility).[24] Unlike the lack of culpability in section 20, section 21 gives the judge discretion, and the mitigating effect of section 21 must be weighed against any possible aggravating factors. In cases of diminished responsibility the sentence can be split, for example between a prison sentence and placement in a forensic psychiatric hospital.

It is difficult to evaluate what quantitative relevance sections 20 and 21 have in practice, as the official statistics only capture those cases in which the court found lack of or diminished culpability, but not those in which the court considered but then rejected it.[25] In 2017, out of 4.9 million cases dealt with by the prosecution, 10,812 (0.2%) were discontinued by the prosecution because the offender was considered lacking culpability under section 20.[26] In 2017, 813 (0.09%) of criminal trials ended with an acquittal of the defendant due to lack of culpability under section 20.[27] In the same year, in 16,753 (2.34%) cases the defendants were judged to have diminished responsibility under section 21.[28] There is considerable variation within the different crimes. In violent crimes, including sexual violence, the

[19] BGH NJW 1958, 266.
[20] BGH NJW 1960, 1393.
[21] ibid.
[22] Section 63 (Placement in Psychiatric Hospital).
[23] Section 64.
[24] Section 21 (Diminished Responsibility). If the offender's capacity to appreciate the unlawfulness of the act or to act in accordance with any such appreciation is substantially diminished at the time of the commission of the offence due to one of the reasons indicated in s 20, the penalty may be mitigated pursuant to s 49(1).
[25] Streng, *Münchener Kommentar* (n 18) para 8.
[26] G Wolf and W Schrag, '#Faktenfuchs: Schuldunfähig—wie oft kommt das vor und warum?' BR24 (21.08.2019) accessible at https://www.br.de/nachrichten/deutschland-welt/faktenfuchs-schuldunfaehig-wie-oft-kommt-das-vor-und-warum,RZn3N1e.
[27] ibid.
[28] ibid.

number of exculpations can be twice as high as nonviolent crimes against property such as theft or embezzlement.[29] In homicide, the number is as high as 19% and there is an increasing trend.[30] The number of homicide convictions in which the sentence is reduced because of diminished culpability is as high as 45%.[31] Unfortunately, the data does not record the underlying pathological disorder in cases in which the court found a lack of or limited culpability. In general, these numbers are very constant, but Streng points out that there are local differences, which he suspects are based on regional conventions, for example in different courts and prosecution offices the number of requested expert opinions differs considerably. This is a worrying trend as it could mean that in other regions mental disorders might more easily be overlooked.[32]

The second and third sections of this chapter will examine the two levels of the test in section 20. The main difficulties, both in practice and in theory, lie however in the question of voluntary causation of a pathological mental disorder in the form of voluntary intoxication, as a large number of crimes, especially violent crimes, are committed under the influence of drugs or alcohol or a combination of both. The difficult question of how to balance the principle of individual criminal responsibility with the voluntary act of disabling one's own faculties will be discussed in the fourth section. The following section will examine the situation of patients who are placed in forensic psychiatric hospitals, before the chapter is concluded in the final section.

Biological Cause

The first part of the two-level test in section 20 asks whether, at the time of the crime, the defendant had a mental disorder which meets the threshold of section 20. An example would be a psychosis caused by brain damage, alcohol-induced delirium, drug abuse, or mental illnesses such as schizophrenia, which leads to a loss of reality perception. Section 20 lists four psychological states which, if they cause the second level, that is, the psychological effect, can exclude culpability. These states are:

1) a pathological mental disorder;
2) a profound disturbance of consciousness;
3) a mental deficiency;
4) or any other serious mental abnormality.

29 Streng, *Münchener Kommentar* (n 18) para 8.
30 ibid para 9. This statistic is from 2017.
31 Fischer, *Strafgesetzbuch* (n 8) 152.
32 Streng, *Münchener Kommentar* (n 18) para 11.

While this list is exclusive, the chosen terminology is so wide that it includes nearly all mental conditions.[33]

Pathological Mental Disorder

The first listed psychological state is called pathological mental disorder, although this use of 'pathological' is slightly outdated. Following the current International Statistical Classification of Diseases and Related Health Problems (ICD-11) these cases are nowadays referred to as disturbances or disorders rather than illnesses.[34] This means in today's terminology there is no distinction between psychological disorders and pathological mental disorders. 'Mental' is referring here to all areas of the human psyche, both intellectual and emotional.[35]

The disorder has to be caused by an abnormality which is based on a biological cause. The biological causes are, however, not yet explained for all disorders[36] and the exact meaning of 'pathological' has not been clearly defined. Included are disorders which are hereditary as well as those which have developed later in life.[37] They do not have to be permanent as long as it has had an effect at the time of the crime.[38] Recognized causes include exogenous psychoses (based on brain damage or infection psychoses) such as dementia,[39] age-related degeneration[40] and loss of intelligence due to drug abuse or chronic alcoholism,[41] and endogenous psychoses, including disturbances for which the biological or genetic causation is assumed but not yet scientifically proven, such as schizophrenia[42] and manic-depressive illnesses,[43] and major depressive disorders.[44] Inebriety caused by alcohol, medication, or other drugs are included too, as the subsequent toxic impairment affects the cerebral functions.[45]

33 Perron and Weißer, *Schönke/Schröder Kommentar* (n 13) 376.
34 ibid.
35 ibid.
36 W Schild, '§ 20 StGB Schuldunfähigkeit wegen seelischer Störungen' in U Kindhäuser, U Neumann, and H-U Paeffgen (eds), *Strafgesetzbuch* (5th edn, C.H. Beck Verlag 2017) para 85 (hereafter, Schild, '§ 20 StGB').
37 K Kühl, § 20 StGB Schuldunfähigkeit wegen seelischer Störungen in K Kühl and K Lackner (eds), *StGB Strafgesetzbuch: Kommentar* (29th edn, C.H. Beck 2018) para 3.
38 Perron and Weißer, *Schönke/Schröder Kommentar* (n 13) 376.
39 BGH 5 StR 499/88.
40 BGH 4 StR 240/64.
41 BGH 5 StR 560/68.
42 BGH 2 StR 128/13.
43 BGH 2 StR 500/00.
44 BGH 5 StR 306/03.
45 BGHSt 43, 66, 69.

Profound Disturbance of Consciousness

The second listed group of profound disturbance of consciousness are impairments of the ability to realize and comprehend the intellectual and emotional experience. The most important examples are affects, such as states of high excitement, anger and hatred, panic, shock, and asthenic reactions.[46] Included are non-pathological psychological disturbances such as states of exhaustion or overtiredness, or extreme emotional states.[47] In practice, the most prevalent cause is alcohol, as very often under intoxication the ability to discern the wrong of the situation is unaffected but the inhibition threshold is lowered to such an extent that there is a lack of ability to act according to realization of the wrong. To exclude those disturbances of consciousness which fall within the spectrum of normal, such as usual states of exhaustion or fatigue, the term 'profound' limits the application to exceptional circumstances.[48] A disturbance can only be classified as 'profound' if its impact on the offender's ability to appreciate the unlawfulness of their actions or to act in accordance with any such appreciation is equivalent to a pathological psychological disturbance.[49] To establish the exact line between normal reactions and changes in consciousness on the one hand and profound disturbances of consciousness on the other is extremely difficult and there is no agreement on relevant criteria.[50] This evaluation can only be carried out by examining the actual effects of the impairment at the time of the crime and therefore overlaps with the second level of the test, as seen later in this chapter.

Mental Deficiency

Until 1 January 2021, the German title for this third category was '*Schwachsinn*', which means hereditary weakness of intelligence or reduction of the cognitive capabilities without verifiable cause.[51] As this antiquated term has nowadays rather derogatory connotations it has been replaced with 'mental retardation'.[52] Since any mental deficiency with a known physical cause, such as Down's Syndrome, belongs to the first group of pathological mental disorder, only learning difficulties without medical physical cause fall into this category.[53]

[46] Perron and Weißer, *Schönke/Schröder Kommentar* (n 13) 378.
[47] Streng, *Münchener Kommentar* (n 18) 36.
[48] Schild, '§ 20 StGB' (n 36) para 87.
[49] BGH NStZ 90, 231.
[50] Perron and Weißer, *Schönke/Schröder Kommentar* (n 13) 378.
[51] R Eschelbach, '§ 20 StGB Schuldunfähigkeit wegen seelischer Störungen' in B von Heintschel-Heinegg (ed), *Beckscher Online Kommentar StGB* (48th edn, C.H. Beck Verlag 2020) para 45 (hereafter, Eschelbach, '§ 20 StGB').
[52] BGBl. I S. 2600.
[53] G van Gemmeren, '§63 StGB Unterbringung in einem psychiatrischen Krankenhaus' in *Münchener Kommentar zum StGB* (4th edn, C.H. Beck Verlag 2020) (hereafter, van Gemmeren, 'Münchener Kommentar') para 22.

Included are only cases where the low intellectual capacities of the defendant have an impact on the offender, not only in their intellectual capacity but in their whole personality.[54] This means the offender must be profoundly disturbed in the entirety of their personality structure.[55] The mere reduction of mental abilities alone is therefore not sufficient and there has to be a direct link with the offender's culpability at the time of the offence.[56]

Other Serious Mental Abnormality

The open formulation of this last category includes all other abnormal psychological phenomena, which diverge from the average psychological state and are not caused by biological causes or malfunctions and therefore cannot be considered pathological disturbances. An example would be an endogenous psychosis, which is so grave that it has an impact on personal development in the same way as a psychosis in the narrow sense.[57] Other serious mental abnormalities are neurosis, personality disorders such as dissocial or borderline personality disorders.[58] For example, paedophilia could qualify as a serious mental abnormality within the meaning of section 20 in cases where the sexual urges have changed the personality of the offender to such an extent that they were not any longer able to muster the necessary self-restraint to suppress their urges.[59] It is debated is whether personality disorders such as sexual dependence, *paranoia querulans*, or gambling addiction should be included.[60]

The criteria 'other serious mental abnormality' was added to section 20 in 1969.[61] This reform was strongly contested during the legislative debate as it was feared that it would give courts too much discretion and open the floodgates to a wave of exculpations which would obliterate the general preventative efficiency of the criminal justice system.[62] This fear proved not to be justified, however, as the number of exculpations has not increased since the new provision came into force in 1975. Indeed, the number of exculpations has remained surprisingly constant throughout the years.[63]

[54] BGH NJW 67, 299.

[55] Eschelbach, '§ 20 StGB' (n 51) para 46.

[56] BGH 4Str 287/13; K Detter, 'Zum Strafzumessungsrecht' [2021] NStZ 22 (hereafter, Detter, 'Strafzumessungsrecht') 24.

[57] BGH NJW 1986, 2893.

[58] van Gemmeren, '*Münchener Kommentar*' (n 53) para 23.

[59] BGH 1 StR 395/17.

[60] Schild, '§ 20 StGB' (n 36) para 102.

[61] Zweites Gesetz zur Reform des Strafrechts 4 July 1969 (BGBl I S. 717) which came into force in 1975.

[62] Streng, *Münchener Kommentar* (n 18) para 7.

[63] ibid para 10.

Drunkenness as a Biological Cause

Drug and alcohol abuse are the most common causes of psychoses relevant for section 20.[64] The question whether intoxication qualifies as disturbance of consciousness or pathological mental disorder has been left open by the Federal Court of Justice, as the exact classification is irrelevant as long as it is a biological cause listed in section 20.[65] The difficult question for the court is whether the degree of intoxication at the time of the crime has crossed the threshold of section 20. This will depend on the perpetrator's physique as well as how much they are used to drinking.[66] Whilst the court needs to examine all the circumstances to evaluate the overall picture, some guidelines have been developed in case law over the years. As a rough guide, the courts assume lack of culpability under section 20 where at the time of the offence the defendant had a blood alcohol concentration of $3^{0}/_{00}$. In cases of blood alcohol concentration of $2^{0}/_{00}$, the courts assume diminished responsibility under section 21.[67] These numbers are higher for grave violent crimes and homicide because the courts assume that for such crimes a person has a higher inhibition threshold and thus a greater degree of intoxication is needed to overcome this high inhibition.[68] While there is ample case law establishing these points of reference for alcohol consumption, there is no equivalent scale available for other forms of intoxication. This is due simply to the fact that there is less scientific data available for the impact that different drugs in varying quantities have on the abilities of an individual.

A common difficulty in practice is how to determine the extent of the drunkenness and its link to the alleged lack of culpability. One problem lies in the exact determination of the blood alcohol concentration at the time of the offence. Where a blood test cannot be carried out the court will need to rely on witness statements, for example how much alcohol was consumed at what time and other factors such as whether the defendant had eaten.[69] The court is allowed to estimate the blood alcohol concentration and according to the principle *in dubio pro reo*, the court has to assume the highest possible alcohol consumption.[70] In each case however, the trial judge has to consider all circumstances. In one murder case, no blood test had been taken from the defendant, but at court the expert witness testified that considering how much the defendant had been drinking according to various eyewitnesses, his blood alcohol concentration must have been at least $4.5^{0}/_{00}$. Yet, the trial judge dismissed the eyewitness statements as implausible because the defendant acted in

[64] Streng, *Münchener Kommentar* (n 18) para 32.

[65] BGH NJW 1991, 852, 853.

[66] R Rengier, *Strafrecht Allgemeiner Teil* (11th edn, C.H. Beck Verlag 2019) (hereafter, Rengier, *Strafrecht Allgemeiner Teil*) 232.

[67] BGHSt 37, 231, 235.

[68] BGH 5 StR 260/87; BGH 5 StR 405/84; BGH 5 StR 266/68.

[69] Perron and Weißer, *Schönke/Schröder Kommentar* (n 13) 382.

[70] BGH NStZ-RR 2010, 257, 258; BGH NStZ 2020, 473 f.

a controlled manner over several hours during which he had held the victim captive before killing him. The judge therefore dismissed the claim of insanity.[71] The Federal Court of Justice upheld the decision and confirmed that the judge has to consider all circumstances rather than exclusively following the opinion of expert witnesses.

The prevalence of intoxication as biological cause in section 20 raises the difficult question of whether the defendant lacks criminal responsibility even if they caused the lack of culpability voluntarily. This question will be discussed in the section on 'Voluntary Intoxication'.

Psychological Effect

The second step of the analysis of section 20 requires the court to evaluate what impact the disorder had on the defendant's capability at the time of the offence. The disorder established in the first step must impair the psychological capabilities of the offender at the time of the crime in such a way that the offender was either unable to appreciate the wrongfulness of their actions or incapable of acting accordingly.[72] Only one of the alternatives needs to be fulfilled, but either way, the ability must be lacking completely.[73] This means the court has to establish the concrete impact of the biological cause in relation to the specific crime. The exact line of when the second level is met, that is, at what point the defendant is deemed not to be sufficiently able to either appreciate the wrongfulness or act accordingly, is incredibly difficult to establish. The court has to examine whether the defendant displayed characteristics and behaviour patterns which fall outside of what can be considered normal reasons for criminal behaviour.[74] For example, crimes against the person are regularly committed by offenders with strong affects, such as anger, without excluding criminal responsibility.

As the German criminal process is based on the inquisitorial model, the trial judge can call expert witnesses to enquire about the facts concerning the mental state of the defendant and what influence such illness normally has on the ability to appreciate the wrongfulness of an act or behave accordingly. Therefore, the court regularly bases evaluations on the testimony of expert witnesses, such as a psychiatrist or toxicologist (in case of intoxication). Nevertheless, as early as 1955 the Federal Court of Justice made it very clear that the evaluation of the psychological

[71] BGH 5 StR 260/87.

[72] W Pfister, 'Die Beurteilung der Schuldfähigkeit in der Rechtsprechung des Bundesgerichtshofs' [2020] NStZ-RR 233 (hereafter, Pfister, 'Beurteilung der Schuldfähigkeit') 234. Where the offender is completely unable to control their actions, there would be no actus reus and thus no criminal offence at all.

[73] BGH NStZ 2019, 78. Partial reduction cannot lead to a lack of culpability, although in cases of substantial impairment, the court might find diminished responsibility under s 21 and reduce the sentence.

[74] BGH NStZ 1997, 383, recently confirmed in 4 StR 566/18.

cause is a normative question and therefore for the judge to decide.[75] Since then, the Federal Court of Justice has repeatedly emphasized the importance of the trial judge reaching their own conclusion which might be based on, but can never be bound by, the assessment of the medical expert.[76]

Furthermore, the court frequently underlined that this legal question requires a substantiated and consistent explanation from the trial judge.[77] The judge must not only scrutinize the evaluation of the medical expert but in addition, explain the court's conclusions in a way that can be reviewed and verified by the appellate court.[78] For example, the trial court must explain in their reasoning the connection between the attested biological cause and the commission of the crime.[79] Even the first step evaluation, namely the establishment of a mental disorder, cannot be left completely to the medical experts, as the criteria for the biological case go beyond describing the psychological state of the offender and include normative elements, such as 'profound' and 'serious'.[80] Since the underlying biological cause does not have to be permanent but only be present during the time of the offence,[81] the severity of the first level can only be measured through the perspective of the second level, namely by evaluating the impact the deficiency had on the control capacity of the offender at the time of the crime. Thus, there is no clear delineation of descriptive diagnosis of causes and the normative effect. There is however consensus that both questions are, in the end, legal rather than medical questions which have to be decided by the judge and not the medical expert.[82]

The normative aspect is even more prevalent on the second level, that is, the psychological impact the biological cause has created with a view of the specific crime. This is especially important in cases of personality disorders, for which there is no uniform systematic classification and many of which describe normal psychological manifestations and impairments of feelings and behaviours. The personality disorder of the defendant established by the expert witness must be distinguished from characteristics and behavioural patterns, which still lie in the ordinary spectrum of human behaviours and might be the cause for criminal behaviour without excluding or even substantially diminishing the defendant's culpability.[83] The diagnosis of a common disorder such as a narcissistic personality disorder, for example, is not sufficient to determine lack of culpability at the time of the crime.[84]

[75] BGHSt 8, 113, 124.
[76] BGH 5StR 385/18.
[77] BGH NStZ-RR 2019, 334.
[78] Pfister, 'Beurteilung der Schuldfähigkeit' (n 72) 234.
[79] BGH 2StR1/03.
[80] Perron and Weißer, *Schönke/Schröder Kommentar* (n 13) 375.
[81] ibid.
[82] Pfister, 'Beurteilung der Schuldfähigkeit' (n 72) 234.
[83] BGHSt 42, 385, 388.
[84] BGH BeckRS 2003, 8164.

Voluntary Intoxication

One of the most important questions is the legal impact of a temporary mental disorder which has been induced by voluntary intoxication. As seen above, intoxication can cause a pathological mental disorder or a profound disturbance of consciousness. Since alcohol and many drugs have a direct impact on the prefrontal cortex, which is the part of the brain which controls willpower and inhibition, intoxication can reduce the ability to appreciate the wrongfulness of the act or may limit the offender's inhibition and their ability to act accordingly. It is therefore not surprising that a high number of crimes are committed under the influence of drugs or alcohol or a combination of both.

Section 323a: Intoxication

This inherent risk of intoxication is recognized in section 323a which deals with the case that the defendant has put themselves in a state of intoxication before committing a criminal offence:

> (1) Whoever puts themselves into a state of intoxication by consuming alcoholic drinks or other intoxicating substances incurs a penalty of imprisonment for a term not exceeding five years or a fine if they commit an unlawful act whilst in this state and cannot be punished on account thereof because they lacked criminal responsibility due to the intoxication or if this cannot be ruled out.[85]

This provision tries to uphold the foundational concept of *nulla poena sine culpa* while at the same time seeks to avoid exonerating the high numbers of offences which are committed under the influence of intoxication. Section 323a reflects the fact that it is well known that intoxication lowers the inhibition threshold and thereby increases the risk of criminal behaviour. It does not, however, punish the creation of this danger (ie act of self-intoxication)[86] unless this danger has been manifested in a crime.[87] The sentence is therefore dependent on the crime which has been committed during the intoxicated state, but what is punished is the act of intoxication, not the crime as such. Section 323a punishes the breach of the underlying duty not to disable one's own capability to appreciate wrong and act accordingly through self-intoxication, but not the offence itself which has been committed without culpability. For this reason, the sentence in Section 323a is

[85] Section 323a(1) StGB.
[86] H Salger and N Mutzbauer, 'Die actio libera in causa—eine rechtswidrige Rechtsfigur' [1993] NStZ, 561 (hereafter Salger and Mutzbauer, 'Die actio libera in causa'), 561.
[87] Detter, 'Strafzumessungsrecht' (n 60) 28.

limited to the penalty provided for the offence which was committed in a state of intoxication[88] but cannot exceed five years. Thus, the act of voluntary intoxication which leads to homicide is punishable but not to the same degree as a commission of homicide without lack of culpability.

This limited sentence is seen as unsatisfactory considering the consequences, especially in violent crimes. But the dissatisfaction with section 323a goes deeper than only the five years' maximum sentence. The criminal offence of 'intoxication' in section 323a only captures the creation of an abstract risk of being intoxicated, not the specific wrong that was realized through the commission of the later crime in the state of intoxication.[89] The underlying problem is the fact that the defendant is not punished for the crime they have committed but only for the act of voluntary self-exculpation. On the basis that section 323a does not offer a satisfactory solution for cases where the offender puts themselves in a state of intoxication and then commits violent crimes, case law and the literature have resorted to the legal construct of *actio libera in causa*, which will be discussed next.

Actio libera in causa

The core of the principle of *actio libera in causa* is that where a defendant in the state of insanity within the meaning of section 20 commits a crime, they cannot claim lack of culpability if they themselves voluntarily caused this state by self-intoxication.[90] Thus, culpability is not excluded in cases where the offender knows or could have known that they will commit the offence, for example where they know that they tend to engage in violent behaviour when drunk.[91] The act of self-intoxication is seen as the first link in the chain of causation of the later crime.[92] For years it has been debated whether resorting to the principle of *actio libera in causa* is permissible, as it in fact constitutes an exception to section 20 which would operate against the defendant. This principle could therefore violate both the legality principle (*nulla poene sine legem*) and the presumption of innocence (*in dubio pro reo*). This is especially true since section 323a which provides for direct regulation of self-induced intoxication, was added to the Criminal Code.[93] As the legislator explicitly limited the penalty to five years' imprisonment, there seems to be little

[88] Section 323a(2) StGB.

[89] G Freund, 'Vorbemerkung zu § 13' in CH Beck (ed), *Münchener Kommentar zum StGB* (4th edn, C.H. Beck Verlag 2020) para 274.

[90] Rengier, *Strafrecht Allgemeiner Teil* (n 66) 235. All cases so far are based on consumption of drugs or alcohol but in theory there is no reason why the *actio libera in causa* should not apply to other voluntary acts which cause the state of lack of culpability.

[91] Fuchs and Zerbes also list the example of omission where the level crossing attendant gets drunk so that he will later omit to lower the barriers when the train is coming, and someone gets killed. Fuchs and Zerbes, *Strafrecht Allgemeiner Teil* (n 2) 232.

[92] Salger and Mutzbauer, 'Die actio libera in causa' (n 86) 563.

[93] RGBl. I 995, 24.11.1933.

room to exclude section 20 and thereby allow for conviction and punishment of the committed offence itself. In addition, Article 103 II of the German Constitution forbids development of customary law in criminal law. In response to these criticisms the literature has developed a number of theories which try to justify the application of *actio libera in causa.* This chapter will only introduce the prevailing theory, namely the Elements of Crime Theory.[94] This theory includes the act of intoxication in the elements of crime, so that the act of becoming intoxicated is seen as part of the commission of the offence. It claims that the *actio libera in causa* has its foundation in existing legal criminal law concepts and is therefore reconcilable with written German criminal law.

Indirect perpetration and attempt

The first concept the Element of Crime Theory draws parallels with is the concept of indirect perpetration of crime.[95] In indirect perpetration, the principal perpetrator commits the crime through a person who is not themselves the perpetrator or accomplice. For example, the principal perpetrator directs a child under the age of criminal responsibility to carry out the criminal act. The Elements of Crime Theory argues that this concept can be applied to cases of *actio libera in causa* in the sense that the perpetrator uses their own person in an intoxicated state to carry out the crime while lacking culpability.[96]

This construction has caused a number of criticisms. First, section 25 I speaks of 'another' which would exclude the idea that a person can use themselves as an innocent agent.[97] Rengier on the other hand, argues that the Elements of Crime Theory does not apply section 25 I 2 directly but only uses the concept of indirect perpetration to demonstrate that the relevant elements of crime (here the act of self-intoxication) can be carried out temporally and locally removed from the actual crime.[98] Thus, intoxication can be compared to a perpetrator handing over control to an agent, because through the act of intoxication the sober self releases control to a less controllable self. Indeed, as early as 1892, the Supreme Court[99] saw in the act of self-intoxication the cause for the later crime.[100] In this case, a street cobbler working on the pavement was seriously injured by a horse-drawn dairy cart when the heavily drunk milkman lost control over his horse. The Court held that when the milkman became intoxicated, he knew that his horse was difficult to control, and that he would drive through a very busy part of the town and thereby

[94] *Tatbestandsmodell.*
[95] *Mittelbare Täterschaft*, s 25 I.
[96] Rengier, *Strafrecht Allgemeiner Teil* (n 66) 237.
[97] M Hettinger, 'Referat 11.3 actio libera in causa 11.3, Abschlußbericht der Kommission zur Reform des strafrechtlichen Sanktionensystems' (2000) Bonn: Internet-Publikation 185 (hereafter, Hettinger, 'Referat'), 187.
[98] Rengier, *Strafrecht Allgemeiner Teil* (n 66) 237.
[99] *Reichsgerichtshof.*
[100] RG22, 413 (415).

pose a danger to others. The Court compared getting drunk with this knowledge to handing over the reins of a wild horse to an unconscious third person. In both cases, the defendant would have deliberately caused the vehicle to be driven by a person who is lacking culpability and therefore would be criminally responsible for any foreseeable harm.[101]

The second legal basis for the *actio libera in causa*, according to the Elements of Crime Theory, is the law of attempt. The comparison with the law of attempt shows that culpability does not always have to be present throughout the offence. Where, for example, the offender launches a missile just before they lose culpability, they will still be found criminally responsible for the consequences.[102] It is therefore sufficient that the defendant was culpable during some part of the crime, and the crime begins with entering the phase of attempt. Where the defendant intentionally causes themselves to be in a state of intoxication (and thereby in a state of lack of culpability) and at this time intends to commit the later crime, they have already entered the phase of attempt.

One problem with this line of argument is that section 22 (Attempt) requires that the offender has taken 'direct and immediate step towards the realisation of the offence'. In cases of self-induced intoxication, on the other hand, there might be numerous stages between intoxication and beginning of the criminal act, for example the offender might still need to travel to the location of the victim. One has to remember however that the Elements of Crime Theory combines aspects of indirect perpetration and criminal attempt. As seen above, in cases of indirect commission, the criminal act begins before the criminal offence itself, namely in the act which causes the innocent agent to commit the crime. Where, for example, the perpetrator sends the innocent agent to serve poisoned food to the victim, the principal is guilty of homicide through indirect perpetration even if a number of steps are still needed before the result is caused. Thus, under the concept of *actio libera in causa*, the act of self-induced intoxication is not seen as the direct and immediate step towards the realization of the crime itself but rather towards handing control over to a person lacking criminal responsibility.

This means that the combination of principles found in the law of criminal attempt and in the direct perpetration can explain the *actio libera in causa* without having to take recourse to unwritten law or contradicting the explicit wording of the Criminal Code.

With regards to the required fault element, one needs to distinguish between intentional and negligent *actio libera in causa*. The intentional *actio libera in causa* means that the defendant caused their own lack of culpability intentionally and voluntarily with the knowledge or at least reckless disregard that they will commit a specific criminal offence.[103] The defendant does not need to have decided all the

[101] ibid (415, 416).
[102] Rengier, *Strafrecht Allgemeiner Teil* (n 66) 237.
[103] Salger and Mutzbauer, 'Die actio libera in causa' (n 86) 562.

details but they must have already decided on an 'adequately concrete offence'.[104] What is required, therefore, is a double intent including both the act of intoxication and the later offence, but conditional intent is sufficient.[105] It suffices that the defendant intended to carry out the crime and intentionally intoxicated themselves with the expectation to commit the crime in the intoxicated state.[106] In the case of negligent *actio libera in causa*, the requirement of negligence refers only to the later crime. It requires that the offender (either intentionally or negligently) self-intoxicates and negligently fails to consider or negligently disregards the risk that they would commit a criminal act in this state.[107] This concept is based on the idea that the perpetrator should only be punished based on *actio libera in causa*, if at the time of self-induced intoxication, they could have anticipated the later events.[108] This is limited to cases where the specific offence includes negligence. The Federal Court of Justice declared, however, that the construction of a negligent *actio libera in causa* is unnecessary. The relevant landmark decision concerned a fatal car accident and the conviction for negligent killing under section 222. The defendant had consumed high quantities of beer and spirits in the Netherlands, before driving in his car to the German-Dutch border which he passed at speeds exceeding 70kmh. There he veered off the road and collided with a car on the other side, hitting two border guards who died at the crash site. With regards to negligent killing, the Federal Court of Justice explained that it was not necessary to resort to *actio libera in causa* to attribute culpability to the defendant. The act of self-intoxication is part of the offender's negligent acts causing the later death of the victims and this act is carried out while still in a state of culpability. In the present case, the defendant had acted negligently because, at the time when he started drinking, he had not yet found accommodation for the night and therefore must have known that he would still need to drive on the same evening. Furthermore, he had veered off the road in at least two previous incidents of drink driving. Hence, the risk of an accident was clearly foreseeable at the time of the act of self-induced intoxication. Thus, the Court made clear that in negligent offences any act of the offender can form the actus reus, as long as it causes or at least partially causes the result. Consequently, the *actio libera in causa* is only needed for intentional crimes, not negligence offences.

Limits of actio libera in causa

Unfortunately, the suggested construction leads to significant limits of the application of the principle of *actio libera in causa*. Basing the *actio libera in causa* on the concept of indirect perpetration limits its application to result crimes because only

[104] BGH NJW 1977, 590.
[105] (Bedinger Vorsatz) Salger and Mutzbauer, 'Die actio libera in causa' (n 86) 562.
[106] BGH NstZ 2002, 28.
[107] Salger and Mutzbauer, 'Die actio libera in causa' (n 86) 562.
[108] Rengier, *Strafrecht Allgemeiner Teil* (n 66) 240.

if the core of the wrongdoing lies in the causation of the result, can the beginning of the causation, namely the self-intoxication, be part of the relevant criminal act.[109] Thus it is not applicable in conduct crimes, such as perjury,[110] endangering road traffic,[111] or driving under the influence of drink or drugs,[112] because the conduct (eg driving the car) only begins with the driving itself. Even when the offender sits in the car intending to drive and starts the engine, the act of driving has not yet started. In a landmark decision in 1997, the Federal Court of Justice explicitly declared that the self-intoxication cannot be seen as the beginning of the offence of driving under influence of drink or drugs.[113] The result is that, when basing the *actio libera in causa* on the Elements of Crime Theory, it is limited to result crimes and that self-induced intoxication still leads to exculpation in conduct crimes. The consequence, namely conviction in result crimes based on *actio libera in causa* but acquittal in conduct crimes under section 20, is highly unsatisfactory as there is no justification why voluntary self-induced intoxication should have such different legal consequences.[114] To some extent, this is mitigated by section 323a which prevents the defendant from walking away sentence free,[115] but the fundamental discrepancy remains. The huge gap in the *actio libera in causa*, namely that it can only be applied to result crimes, means that there is a great sentencing and labelling discrepancy between different offences which cannot be justified by the danger or harm caused. The only fully satisfactory solution to the question of voluntary intoxication is legislative reform and the literature has been advocating for decades to codify the *actio libera in causa* which would allow allocation of full criminal responsibility for the act carried out during the self-induced act of lack of culpability.[116] The present author agrees that the legislator should include an exception to section 20 which itself is an exception to the general assumption of capacity of guilt for adults. Examples for such codification can be found in other German-speaking jurisdictions. Article 19(4) Suisse Criminal Penal Code for consideration states:

> If it was possible for the person concerned to avoid his state of mental incapacity or diminished responsibility and had he done so to foresee the act that may be committed in that state, paragraphs 1–3 [which exclude culpability] do not apply.

Likewise, the former German Democratic Republic (GDR) excluded self-intoxication from the general culpability principle:

[109] Rengier, *Strafrecht Allgemeiner Teil* (n 66) 238.
[110] Section 154.
[111] Section 315c.
[112] Section 316.
[113] BGH NJW 1997, 138, 139.
[114] Salger and Mutzbauer, 'Die actio libera in causa' (n 86) 565.
[115] Rengier, *Strafrecht Allgemeiner Teil* (n 66) 239.
[116] Salger and Mutzbauer, 'Die actio libera in causa' (n 86) 565.

> Whoever culpably puts themselves in a state of intoxication which excludes their criminal responsibility and in this state commits a punishable offence will be punished according to the violated law.[117]

A reform of this area was considered in 1997 when the then conservative-liberal government coalition appointed the Commission for the Reform of Criminal Sentencing System which recommended including the *actio libera in causa* in section 20.[118] Amending section 20 would avoid the unsatisfactory situation that very often it is a question of luck whether it was possible to establish the blood alcohol concentration for the time of the crime.[119] More importantly, it would avoid the necessity to resort to the Elements of Crime Theory and would thereby close the huge sentence and labelling discrepancy between result and conduct crimes. Considering the practical relevance of intoxication in crimes, especially violent crimes, and the common consensus that the current regulation in section 323a is not sufficient, it is regrettable that the legislator has still not codified the *actio libera in causa*, even though it has been applied in courts since the 19th century.

Placement in a Forensic Psychiatric Hospital

After having considered the requirements for a finding of lack of culpability due to a mental disorder and the important exception for self-induced incapability, the second essential question is the legal consequences of such an acquittal. Germany is based on the so-called two-track system of imprisonment and placement in a forensic psychiatric hospital.[120] Under section 63, when a defendant is acquitted because of lack of culpability, the court can commit them to a forensic psychiatric hospital. Indeed, once an offender is acquitted due to lack of culpability, the likelihood that they will receive a committal order is very high. Of the 686 offenders acquitted under section 20 in 2014,[121] 583 (85%) were placed in a forensic psychiatric hospital.[122]

[117] Section 15(3) Criminal Penal Code of the GDR.

[118] Hettinger, 'Referat' (n 97).

[119] A Hennig, 'Referat 11.2 Vollrausch' in *Abschlußbericht der Kommission zur Reform des strafrechtlichen Sanktionensystems* (Internet-Publikation 2000) 181.

[120] Other measures of reform and prevention include placement in an addiction treatment facility, placement in preventive detention, supervision of conduct, disqualification from driving, and disqualification from exercising a profession (s 61). Comparing regular prison sentences with committal orders, research by Weithmann and others showed that between 1995 and 2009, out of 14,100,329 criminal court decisions, 170,182 (1.2%) cases ended in a prison sentence of two years and above. (Only prison sentences not exceeding two years can be suspended on probation (s 56II).) In comparison, in 12,019 (0.09%) cases the defendant received an order of forensic treatment. G Weithmann and others, Comparison of Offenders in Forensic-Psychiatric Treatment or Prison in Germany (2019) 66 Int J Law Psychiatry 101502, 3.

[121] This is the last available date.

[122] H Pollähne, '§ 63 StGB Unterbringung in einem psychiatrischen Krankenhaus' in U Kindhäuser, U Neumann, and H- Paeffgen (eds), *Strafgesetzbuch* (5th edn, C.H. Beck Verlag 2017) (hereafter, Pollähne, '§ 63 StGB') para 8.

Forensic psychiatric hospitals are separate institutions with between 250 and 380 beds which exclusively treat criminal offenders.[123] The annual cost of a forensic bed is around €100,000 per year, which is about double of the cost of a prison place.[124] Unlike inmates in ordinary prisons, a discharge from section 63 measure is always conditional, that is, the court suspends the remainder of the measure on probation.[125] After release, patients in forensic hospitals are automatically placed under the supervision of the court.[126] Moreover, a placement order in a psychiatric hospital lasts as long as necessary, which means it is indefinite and patients are potentially interned for life.[127] Indeed, about 10% of patients in a forensic psychiatric hospital are detained for their whole life.[128]

Most offences which resulted in a placement order are homicide and other violent crimes against the person (57% or 439 patients) and this number is growing. This is followed by arson (nearly 12% or 92 patients) and robbery (11.6% or 89 patients). Interestingly, sexual violence cases, which caused most concern about early release cases, are actually decreasing (10% or 74 patients).[129] There is not much empirical research in Germany about the demographic of patients in forensic hospitals but work in the 1980s found that most were unmarried, and many were born out of wedlock, raised in children's homes, had a high number of siblings, and nearly half (43%) had been at a school for special needs, 46.8% belonged to the working class, 20.8% were unemployed, and 14.3% were pensioners.[130]

Development

The two-track sentencing system of punishment through imprisonment on the one hand and rehabilitation in a forensic psychiatric hospital on the other goes back to the 19th century when the conventional aims of retribution and proportional punishment, which had informed the new Criminal Code in 1870, were challenged

[123] Sometimes forensic patients are treated in separate forensic departments within general psychiatric hospitals. RL Trestman, S Eucker, and R Müller-Isberner, 'The Treatment of Personality-Disordered Offenders in Germany' (2007) 35(2) J Am Acad Psychiatry Law 229–34. There also have been attempts to decentralize the system and integrate forensic patients with non-forensic patients. The so-called '63-patients' were perceived as strange and hostile both by staff and other patients.

[124] van Gemmeren, 'Münchener Kommentar' (n 53) para 7. There are however considerable differences in the costs between the different German states.

[125] Section 67d (II).

[126] Section 67d (III). It was only in 2019, that patients of forensic psychiatric hospitals would not automatically lose their right to vote regardless of their crime. Gesetz zur Änderung des Bundeswahlgesetzes und anderer Gesetze 18 June 2019 (BGBl. I S. 834 (No 23)) which came into force on 1 July 2019.

[127] J Kinzig, '§ 63 StGB Unterbringung in einem psychiatrischen Krankenhaus' in A Eser (ed), *Schönke/Schröder Strafgesetzbuch Kommentar* (30th edn, C.H. Beck Verlag 2019) (hereafter, Kinzig, '§ 63 StGB') para 34.

[128] van Gemmeren, 'Münchener Kommentar' (n 54) para 7.

[129] Pollähne, '§ 63 StGB' (n 122) para 7.

[130] ibid para 8.

by new movements supported by legal theorists such as Gustaf Radbruch and Franz von Liszt, who emphasized the need to focus on prevention and risk adequate measures. This debate was ended by the Law Against Dangerous Habitual Criminals and on Measures of Security and Reform of 24 November 1933, which added preventive detention to conventional prison sentences and thus created the current two-track system. With the Nazis coming to power the same year, the new law was soon blatantly abused to dispose of political opponents, and patients of forensic psychiatric hospitals were among the first to be transported to death camps.[131] Nonetheless, the law remained unchanged until the major criminal law reform in 1969 (which came into force in 1973).[132] Even after the end of the Second World War, medical internment acted as a prison substitute to lock patients away to protect the public rather than offering meaningful healing chances. At the end of the 1960s, the system of detention in forensic psychiatric hospitals had been widely described as a scandal as both judges' committal orders as well as length of the detention showed that the sole aim was public safety rather than healing or improvement of the individual.[133] Often patients were accommodated in vast dormitories with small cross-barred windows or foul-smelling solitary cells.[134] The 1969 criminal law reform maintained the two-track system but emphasized the aim of individual treatment above protection of the public and introduced additional legal requirements for a placement order.[135] Yet, since the 1990s Germany observed a trend towards punitive priorities and away from treatment (which means *de facto* a reversal of the hierarchy of the legislator) which led to an increase in placement orders which is still continuing today.[136]

While the general rules on sentencing and punishment are under federal legislation, each of the 16 German states has its own laws regarding patients' rights and treatment, as well as organization, supervision, and funding of psychiatric hospitals.[137] For this reason, receiving reliable and comparable statistics for the whole of Germany has proven to be difficult to such an extent that in 2014 the Federal Office of Statistics ceased collecting nationwide data on psychiatric hospitals.[138] Consequently, it is difficult to get precise numbers about the occupancy

[131] H Pollähne, '§ 61 StGB Übersicht' in U Kindhäuser, U Neumann, and H-U Paeffgen (eds), *Strafgesetzbuch* (5th edn, C.H. Beck Verlag 2017) (hereafter, Pollähne, '§ 61 StGB') para 2.

[132] Pollähne, '§ 63 StGB' (n 122) para 1.

[133] ibid para 10.

[134] ibid.

[135] ibid para 1.

[136] Pollähne, '§ 61 StGB' (n 131) para 30.

[137] R Edworthy, S Sampson, and B Völlm, 'Impatient Forensic-Psychiatric Care: Legal Frameworks and Service Provision in Three European Countries' (2016) 47 Int J Law Psychiatry 18, 20, 22.

[138] Rat für Sozial- und Wirtschaftsdaten (RatSWD) (Ed.) (2020): Weiterentwicklung der Kriminal- und Strafrechtspflegestatistik in Deutschland, RatSWD Output, No. 7 (6), Rat für Sozial- und Wirtschaftsdaten (RatSWD), Berlin, 38.

or the duration of detention in psychiatric hospitals, but it is possible to discern several trends. During the 1970s until the mid-1980s the number of occupancies of psychiatric hospitals nearly halved from 4,222 to 2,362. Since then, however, the numbers have grown continuously, in particular since the end of the 1990s, and reached a high in 2014 of 6,540 patients.[139] This growth is considerably higher than the increase of inmates in conventional prisons. Traub and others found that in the period between 1995 and 2009 there was a 50% increase of the total number of hospital orders, which is 4.3 times greater than the increase in the number of prison sentences over more than two years given in the same period.[140]

If one looks at the average number of annual orders, one can observe that in the time leading up to the 1969 criminal law reform annual orders decreased from 602 to 306. While until 1990, the numbers levelled out at around 430, there was a strong increase since then with the highest point being 948 hospital orders in 2010.[141] The numbers decreased again to some extent in 2014 to 770[142] but this downwards trend does not seem to be permanent. In 2016, in the former West Germany, there are more patients in forensic psychiatric hospitals (with a potentially indefinite detention) than prison inmates with a sentence of five years and above.[143] The latest figures available are for 2019, when orders went up again to 969.[144] This means that currently every year, nearly a thousand mentally ill individuals are placed indefinitely in a forensic institution against their will. The continuous increase in numbers of forensic patients, who are often interned for many years and can potentially be kept inside indefinitely, led Lewe to call forensic psychiatry 'the black hole in the psychiatry universe'.[145]

The practical situation in psychiatric hospitals improved only slowly after the 1969 criminal law reform. Fourteen years after the reform came into force, Leygraf still condemned the 'desolate, depressing and inadequate' conditions[146] and even in 2002 the same author described the psychiatric hospital system as a 'gigantic human seepage facility'.[147] Staffing levels at the notoriously overburdened psychiatric hospitals had temporarily improved but since then, austerity measures and privatization of institutions have meant that these improvements have often been

[139] Kinzig, '§ 63 StGB' (n 127) para 2. Of these, 6% were below the age of 25 and 8% are female.

[140] H-J Traub and others, 'Court Sentences to Forensic-Psychiatric Treatment and Imprisonment in Germany: Types of Crimes and Changes from 1995 to 2009' (2020) 71 Int J Law Psychiatry 71 (2020) 101577, (hereafter, Traub and others, 'Sentences') 6.

[141] Pollähne, '§ 63 StGB' (n 122) para 5.

[142] ibid.

[143] Rat für Sozial- und Wirtschaftsdaten (RatSWD) (Ed.) (2020): Weiterentwicklung der Kriminal- und Strafrechtspflegestatistik in Deutschland, RatSWD Output, No. 7 (6), Rat für Sozial- und Wirtschaftsdaten (RatSWD), Berlin, 37.

[144] Bunderamt für Statistik 2019, Fachserie 3, 338.

[145] U Lewe, 'Forensik—Das Schwarze Loch des Pychiatrieuniversums' 2016 (2) Sozialpsychiartrische Informationen 30 (hereafter, Lewe, 'Schwarze Loch'), 34.

[146] *Leygraf*, Psychisch kranke Straftäter. Epidemiologie und aktuelle Praxis des psychiatrischen Maßregelvollzugs, 1988, 183 cited by Pollähne, '§ 63 StGB' (n 122) para 11 n 54.

[147] ibid.

reversed.[148] Likewise, treatment is seen by many as insufficient. Although since the 1980s, treatment has been improved and new therapies such as group therapy for personality disorders, especially sexual offenders, have been established, the necessary specific individual therapies, especially needed for borderline patients, are still very rare.[149] Pollähne even speaks of 'therapeutic nihilism'.[150] Furthermore, there is rigorous use of medicinal treatment which is often exaggerated and misdiagnosed and frequently administered forcefully.[151] Indeed, research has shown that in cases of psychological disorders, improvement could be diagnosed in only 14.8% of cases. In 66.9%, no change in the condition could be found and in 18.3% the situation had even deteriorated.[152] While these numbers compare with therapeutic success rates in general psychiatric hospitals, the therapy success there is achieved on average in 25 days.[153] Even if one takes into account that on average a schizophrenic patient needs to be readmitted 14 times before they can lead a normal life, this would still mean a healing duration of about only one year. The average duration of detention in forensic hospitals on the other hand is 8.6 years.[154] An additional particular concern is that the average length differs considerably both between German regions and between different mental forensic hospitals.[155] For example, in 2001, the average detention length in forensic psychiatric hospitals was 2.2 years in Bremen but 9.8 years in Schleswig-Holstein[156] which is only 80 miles away. This huge variance cannot be explained by differences in individual patients.

Balancing Individual Freedom and Public Safety

For both the prognosis for arrangement and continuation of the placement in a forensic psychiatric hospital the judge needs to carefully balance the interests of the individual and the interest in public safety. Under section 63, a committal to a forensic psychiatric hospital is only permissible if

> the overall evaluation of the offender and of the offence reveals that, due to the offender's condition, he or she represents a danger to the general public on account of it being expected that he or she will in future commit serious unlawful acts which will result in the victims of the offence suffering or being exposed to

[148] Pollähne, '§ 63 StGB' (n 122) para 13.
[149] ibid para 11.
[150] ibid.
[151] ibid.
[152] ibid para 15.
[153] Lewe, 'Schwarze Loch' (n 145) 33.
[154] ibid.
[155] Pollähne, '§ 63 StGB' (n 122) para 6. The organization of forensic hospitals is under Länder jurisdiction.
[156] Lewe, 'Schwarze Loch' (n 145) 33.

the considerable danger of severe emotional trauma or physical injury or which will cause serious economic damage.[157]

If these requirements are fulfilled the placement order is compulsory, which means that in theory there is no judicial discretion,[158] but in practice the judge has of course huge leeway when evaluating the required elements, for example the risk of future crimes.[159] The legislator has repeatedly emphasized the need for proportionality between the protection of the public and the protection of the individual from unnecessary loss of freedom. Section 62, which had been included in the 1969 criminal law reform, explicitly orders that each decision has to be proportional[160] and the 2016 reform of section 63 included a more detailed test to establish for detention in a forensic psychiatric hospital. In practice, however, this evaluation is highly tipped in favour of detention. Pollähne speaks of 'structural inherent disproportionality'.[161]

One problem is that the two compared interests are of a very different nature. On the one hand there is the risk to public safety, presented by a potential victim of an unspecified crime. On the other hand, the internment or continuation of the placement poses real and already manifested harm to the actual victim of the prognosis. Intuitively one would suspect that the comparison between danger and actual harm would tip the balance against internment, but on the contrary, the 'danger of dangerousness'[162] of the offender is so difficult to prove or to disprove that in fact it opens the way for more placement orders. The problem is that one can only observe the negative wrongs, that is, where an offender is released and then commits a relevant crime but it is impossible to prove a positive wrong, that is, a patient who should have been released because they would not commit a crime.[163] A number of research projects have however shown that the risk of reoffending of forensic patients are overestimated.[164] Indeed, it is estimated that two thirds of forensic patients probably do not pose a danger to the public and could be released.[165]

This problem of potentially wrong diagnosis is amplified by the fact that the judicial prognosis is, in practice, often formalistic and lacking transparent reasoning. Judges regularly simply repeat the medical report which is based on clinical prognosis rather than explaining how the legal requirements of section 63

[157] The same is true for cases of diminished responsibility, where the sentence can be split between imprisonment and detention in a forensic psychiatric hospital.

[158] BGH NStZ 90, 123.

[159] Pollähne, '§ 63 StGB' (n 122) para 77.

[160] Section 62 (Principle of Proportionality). A measure of reform and prevention may not be ordered if it is disproportionate to the severity of the offence committed by or expected to be committed by the offender and to the degree of danger which the offender poses to society.

[161] Pollähne, '§ 63 StGB' (n 122) para 5.

[162] ibid para 49.

[163] Pollähne, '§ 61 StGB' (n 131) para 54.

[164] Lewe, 'Schwarze Loch' (n 145) 32.

[165] Pollähne, '§ 63 StGB' (n 122) para 13.

are fulfilled.[166] Frequently the judge simply states that the order is proportional without explaining how this conclusion was reached.[167] Section 67e requires annual reviews by the court but these too are often perfunctory, short, and without individual examination. Pollähne states that marathon reviews with individual hearings of no more than ten minutes are still widespread.[168] Because of this high reliance on expert reports, the treating staff in the forensic hospitals have *de facto* decision-making power.[169]At the same time, staff are understandably reluctant to take the responsibility for a release of a possibly dangerous patient.[170] This reluctance is extenuated for sexual offenders. Especially since the 1990s, when cases of sexual violence were increasingly covered in the media and politicized, the sacrifice of the individual in favour of public safety became acceptable. This power of public opinion is demonstrated by the fact that while general crime at this time saw an increase of 20% (including a 10% increase in violent crime) the number of sexual offences actually decreased by 13%.[171]

Case law of the higher courts demonstrates a worryingly high discontent with the decisions of the lower courts. In the five years 2010–14, the Federal Court of Justice overturned the placement order in 59 out of 88 cases (67%) and confirmed the trial court's rejection of an order (which had been appealed against by the prosecution) in another nine cases.[172] Likewise, the Constitutional Court has ordered the release of forensic patients wrongfully committed for decades and continuously demanded from courts a more careful test of proportionality. In a landmark decision in 1985, the Court declared that the principle of proportionality has constitutional status and covers both the arrangement and continuation of placement in a psychiatric hospital.[173] In this case, the offender had been diagnosed with a schizophrenic psychosis and subsequently found guilty with diminished responsibility for the theft of a fur coat. He was convicted and sentenced to nine months' imprisonment but based on his diagnosis and because of his numerous previous convictions, the court ordered placement in a psychiatric hospital, as it saw a risk that he might commit similar crimes in future. This decision was later confirmed by the Court of Appeal which stated that it could not be certain that he would not commit a criminal offence again. This view was based on the fact that he had proven to be a difficult patient who had escaped a few times from the forensic hospital, had refused medication, and had threatened other patients, even though none of this behaviour had any connection with the original offence or was linked to a possible

[166] ibid para 58.
[167] ibid para 74.
[168] ibid para 18.
[169] This also means that the patient is especially dependent on the staff who is treating him or her.
[170] Pollähne, '§ 63 StGB' (n 122) para 17.
[171] ibid para 51.
[172] H Pollähne, 'Maßregelvollzug (§ 63 StGB) im Reformstau: Forensische Psychiatrie—ein Behandlungsfall?' (2015) 27(1) Neue Kriminalpolitik 25 (hereafter, Pollähne, 'Reformstau'), 32.
[173] BVerfGE70, 297.

new serious crime. When the case finally reached the Constitutional Court, the applicant was released after having been detained in a forensic psychiatric hospital for 11.5 years. This lengthy detention was shocking not only because the prognosis was not linked to any indication to public danger but also because of the sheer disproportionality to the minor original offence and original sentence of nine months. Unfortunately, this extreme case is far from being an exception,[174] as the more recent *Mollath* case demonstrates. In 2006, Gustl Mollath was tried among others for offences against the person against his wife, but acquitted under section 20 due to mental illness. He was diagnosed with paranoid delusions which included a money laundering network involving his former wife and the bank she worked for. Being considered violent and dangerous for the general public, Mollath was committed to a forensic psychiatric hospital.[175] After a number of court proceedings, Mollath was eventually released in 2014. In the meantime, it turned out that rather than Mollath suffering from paranoid delusions, the accusations of money laundering had indeed been factually true.

The case of *Mollath*, together with the constant increase in placement orders, are perceived as one of the driving factors behind the so-called 'proportionality amendment' in 2016, which for the first time since the great reform in 1969, limited circumstances under which a person can be committed under section 63.[176] Whether this amendment will be able to reverse the trend towards more and longer placements in forensic psychiatric hospitals remains to be seen and is doubted by many academics.[177] It does not seem that the German Länder expect a trend reversal as the number of forensic beds keeps rising, in spite of the fact that both crime rates and prison population continue to decline in Germany.[178] North Rhine-Westphalia, for example, decided in 2015 (at the time when the 2016 amendment was passed by both houses of Parliament), to open five new forensic hospitals with 750 new beds, an increase of 31%.[179]

Conclusion

While the term *Schuld* is not defined anywhere in the Criminal Code, the analysis of when it is excluded under section 20 provides valuable insights into the German understanding of what it means to commit a crime. There is a clear moral overlap between culpability and causation. It cannot be right to condemn someone who

174 Pollähne, 'Reformstau' (n 172) 26.

175 J Hauer, 'Anmerkungen und Gedanken zum Fall Mollath—Verschwörung oder Gleichgültigkeit?' (2013) ZRP 209.

176 Kinzig, '§ 63 StGB' (n 127) para 2a.

177 van Gemmeren, 'Münchener Kommentar' (n 53) para 135.

178 Traub and others, 'Sentences' (n 150).

179 Lewe, 'Schwarze Loch' (n 145) 34.

did not have the capability to understand the unlawfulness of their actions or to act accordingly. At the same time, an acquittal does not seem to serve justice where this incapability has been caused by the defendant themselves. So far, this difficult relationship between causing harm and being responsible has not been satisfactorily resolved in German criminal law. Related to this are questions about the underlying beliefs on which the traditional culpability principle is based. The basic assumption rests on the conception of the person as a rational moral being who has the free will to decide between right and wrong. Adam, Schmidt, and Schumacher ask, however, to what extent this anthropology is realistic as the idea of free will has been debated for centuries.[180] Instead of rationally balancing the advantages and disadvantages of one's actions, human behaviour is influenced and maybe even controlled by any number of factors. These influences might be based not only on pathological brain factors but also personality traits which have developed during lifelong learning processes, often formed in very early childhood.[181] Consequently, even the defendants themselves are often not conscious of all contributing motives. How difficult it is to be aware of the various causes for decisions has been explained in detail by Daniel Kahneman.[182] With growing research both in psychology and neuroscience the culpability principle is likely to face increasing challenges which may shake the foundations of our current understanding of criminal justice.

This uneasy relationship between law and medicine is also reflected in the poor state of forensic psychiatry. The high proportion of section 20 defendants who are acquitted but committed to a forensic psychiatric hospital and the long duration of such internments, are a sign of an irrational fear of the twice stigmatized 'bad and mad' and a strong reluctance to reintegrate these defendants into society. The length of the average stay in forensic psychiatric hospitals compared to prison sentences for the same crime could even be seen as discrimination against those with mental disorders.[183] Statistically, there is no reason to fear forensic patients more than released prison inmates. Research has shown that the ratio between the risk of committing violent crimes between schizophrenic individuals and non-schizophrenic persons was only 1:2. This only slightly higher statistical risk does not justify such extreme different treatment.[184] Furthermore, when comparing re-offending of released forensic patients with ordinary prisoners, there is no statistical difference at all.[185] So far, neither jurisdiction of the Federal Court of Justice

[180] J Adam, 'Karsten Schmidt and Jörg Schumacher, Nulla poena sine culpa—Was besagt das verfassungsrechtliche Schuldprinzip?' (2017) NStZ 7, 8.

[181] ibid.

[182] D Kahneman, *Thinking, Fast and Slow* (Penguin 2012).

[183] N Konrad and B Völlm, 'Forensic Psychiatric Expert Witnessing within the Criminal Justice System in Germany' (2014) 37 Int J Law Psychiatry 149, 153.

[184] Lewe, 'Schwarze Loch' (n 145) 32.

[185] ibid.

nor the German Constitutional Court, nor legislative reforms have succeeded in establishing a proportionate balance between individual freedom and public safety in the prognosis for arrangement and continuation of the placement in forensic psychiatric hospitals. While it remains to be seen whether the latest law reform in 2016 will result in a trend reversal and a decrease in incarceration in forensic psychiatric hospitals, based on the developments presented in this chapter, this author at least remains sceptical.

12

Legal Insanity in the Netherlands

Regulations and Reflections

Gerben Meynen

Introduction

In this chapter, the characteristics of legal insanity (*ontoerekeningsvatbaarheid*) in the Dutch criminal justice system will be discussed.[1] Three main features can be identified. First, there is no legal criterion specifying the conditions under which the presence of a mental illness substantiates an insanity plea. This is different from other legal systems, where the criteria for insanity are usually specified—an example is the M'Naghten Rule in Anglo-American jurisdictions. The Netherlands has a so-called 'open norm'. A second feature is that, while many jurisdictions use the dichotomy 'sane' versus 'insane', in the Netherlands three grades of criminal responsibility are used: responsibility, diminished responsibility, and (complete) insanity. A third characteristic concerns the fact that forensic psychiatrists and psychologists must render an explicit opinion about the defendant's (degree of) criminal responsibility—notably, this is done in the absence of a legal criterion for insanity.

In many countries, legal insanity has led to intense debates, and the Netherlands is no exception.[2] In fact, the three features of the Dutch system continue to be a

[1] On matters discussed in this chapter, see also L Gröning and others, 'Constructing Criminal Insanity: The roles of Legislators, Judges and Experts in Norway, Sweden and the Netherlands' (2020) 11 New J Eur Crim Law 390 (hereafter Gröning and others, 'Constructing Criminal Insanity'); G Meynen, 'Legal Insanity and Neurolaw in the Netherlands: Developments and Debates' in S Moratti and D Patterson (eds), *Legal Insanity and the Brain: Science, Law and European Courts* (Hart Publishing 2016) (hereafter Meynen, 'Legal Insanity and Neurolaw in the Netherlands'; G Meynen, *Legal Insanity. Explorations in Psychiatry, Law, and Ethics* (Springer 2016) (hereafter Meynen, *Legal Insanity*); G Meynen, 'The Insanity Defense' in B Brożek, J Hage, and N Vincent (eds), *Law and Mind: A Survey of Law and the Cognitive Sciences* (Cambridge University Press 2021) 317–41.

Where I refer to actual legal cases (eg as illustration) in this chapter, my presentation and interpretation are based merely on information from generally accessible sources, and is nowhere meant as 'expert opinion'. I was not involved in the cases I mention. I am grateful to Johannes Bijlsma for his helpful suggestions for this chapter.

[2] See eg Mackay: 'Perhaps more than any other area of the criminal law, the insanity defence generates heated discussion and debate.' RD Mackay, *Mental Condition Defences in the Criminal Law* (Clarendon Press 1995) 73. And more recently, Slobogin wrote, 'The insanity defense is perhaps the most widely discussed doctrine in criminal law.' C Slobogin, 'Introduction to this Special Issue: The Characteristics of Insanity and the Insanity Evaluation Process' (2018) 36 Behav Sci Law 271. And see Adjorlolo and others: 'The insanity defense is among the most controversial legal constructs that has

Gerben Meynen, *Legal Insanity in the Netherlands* In: *The Insanity Defence*. Edited by: Ronnie Mackay and Warren Brookbanks, Oxford University Press. © Gerben Meynen 2022. DOI: 10.1093/oso/9780198854944.003.0012

topic of debate. In this chapter, I will not only discuss relevant regulations, practices, and some case law, but I will also consider practical problems of, and scholarly reflections on, insanity in the Netherlands.

The outline of the chapter is as follows. The next section provides some background and practical information about legal insanity in the Netherlands. This is followed by a section considering the 'open norm' for legal insanity used in the Netherlands. In this section, I will also discuss the fact that behavioural experts have to provide explicit advice regarding the level of the defendant's criminal responsibility (even though this is, in fact, a legal matter). In the next section, the three grades of criminal responsibility will be considered. The chapter then looks at the role neuroscience currently plays in answering the question of legal responsibility in the Netherlands. In the final section, some conclusions will be drawn.

Background and Practical Issues

In the Netherlands, a state with a moderately inquisitorial system, a defendant's sanity is presumed. Yet, according to Article 39 of the Dutch Criminal Code (CC), anyone who commits an offence for which he cannot be held responsible due to a mental disorder, is not punishable. The legal principle that underlies this regulation is 'no punishment without guilt'.[3] In case of doubt about a defendant's sanity, an insanity evaluation by one or more behavioural experts can be ordered by the prosecution or by the court. Only in a small minority of cases is the evaluation requested by the defendant and in this sense, legal insanity in the Netherlands is only rarely a 'defence'. This means that a so-called 'battle of the experts', sometimes associated with adversarial systems,[4] is less likely to occur in the Dutch courtrooms. The experts will advise the court, and ultimately the judge will decide about the defendant's legal responsibility. Usually, the expert's advice will be followed. In general, the matter of legal insanity will arise in more severe cases, which are decided by three judges. In the Netherlands, all judges are professional judges; there are no lay judges and no juries.

attracted the attention of scholars, practitioners and policy makers.' S Adjorlolo, HCO Chan, and M DeLisi, 'Mentally Disordered Offenders and the Law: Research Update on the Insanity Defense, 2004–2019' (2019) 67 Int J Law Psychiatry 101507 (abstract).

[3] On what follows, see also Meynen, 'Legal Insanity and Neurolaw in the Netherlands' (n 1), E Messina and others, 'Forensic Psychiatric Evaluations of Defendants: Italy and the Netherlands Compared' (2019) 66 Int J Law Psychiatry (hereafter Messina and others, 'Forensic Psychiatric Evaluations'); S Radovic, G Meynen, and T Bennet, 'Introducing a Standard of Legal Insanity: The Case of Sweden Compared to The Netherlands' (2015) 40 Int J Law Psychiatry 43 (hereafter, Radovic, Meynen, and Bennet, 'Introducing a Standard of Legal Insanity').

[4] RG Beran, 'The Role of the Expert Witness in the Adversarial Legal System' (2009) 17 J Law Med 133; AA Stone, 'The Ethical Boundaries of Forensic Psychiatry: A View from the Ivory Tower. Bull Am Acad Psychiatry Law 12:209–19, 1984' (2008) 36 J Am Acad Psychiatry Law 167.

Approximately five thousand insanity assessments are made by behavioural experts annually[5]—the Dutch population is 17 million. These evaluations can be performed by a psychologist, psychiatrist, or by both. So, in principle, the behavioural experts who work on a case have different backgrounds. Most evaluations are performed by psychologists.[6] Sometimes another type of expert is also involved, such as a neurologist or neuropsychologist, for example in cases where a neurodegenerative disease is suspected (see the section below on 'Neuroscience').[7] Usually, the Netherlands Institute for Forensic Psychiatry and Psychology (NIFP) acts as an intermediary between the prosecution or court requesting the evaluation on the one hand and the expert on the other. The NIFP also offers a training programme for court experts, consisting of a theoretical part (covering, eg, relevant legal issues and risk assessment) and a practical part, which involves writing at least five reports under supervision. In addition, the NIFP offers a course for supervisors. In 2010, the Netherlands Register of Court Experts (NRGD) was established.[8] This is a national register for experts for the court, with several subdivisions, including one for behavioural experts. In principle, behavioural experts who perform evaluations of defendants have to be registered, but exceptions are possible, for instance, because the expert's specific expertise is valuable in a particular case. If experts are not registered in the NRGD, they have to be appointed by a judge.

In a small minority of the cases—about two hundred annually—the evaluation of the defendant takes place at the Pieter Baan Centre, a specialized observation clinic in Almere, founded in 1949.[9] This clinic is well known in the Netherlands and many defendants in highly publicized criminal cases have been evaluated in this clinic. Defendants can be sent there for observation for several weeks, often about six weeks. Reasons for such an observation can be, for example, the severity of the crime the person is charged with or the fact that during ambulatory evaluation it was not possible to make a proper evaluation because the defendant did not sufficiently cooperate.[10] Since in the Netherlands the evaluation

[5] JF Ter Harmsel and others, 'Forensic Assessments from the Netherlands Institute of Forensic Psychiatry and Psychology in Retrospect; Applications of Genetics and Neuroscience, in 2000 and 2009' (2016) 58 Tijdschrift voor Psychiatrie 20 (hereafter Ter Harmsel and others, 'Forensic Assessments').

[6] Messina and others, 'Forensic Psychiatric Evaluations' (n 3).

[7] SN Schouws, C Jonker, and G Meynen, 'The Importance of Neuropsychological Assessment for Forensic Psychiatric Evaluations of Defendants' (2016) 58 Tijdschr Psychiatr 872 (hereafter Schouws, Jonker, and Meynen, 'The Importance of Neuropsychological Assessment').

[8] http://www.nrgd.nl. On its website, the NRGD writes: 'The Netherlands Register of Court Experts (NRGD) guarantees and promotes the consistent quality of the contribution made by court experts to the legal process.'

[9] At the time, its name was 'Psychiatrische observatiekliniek van het gevangeniswezen', later it was given the name of its founder and the psychiatrist responsible for the clinic during the first years, Professor Pieter Baan. See T Bolt, J Gijzeman, and J Vijselaar, *Ter observatie opgenomen. Pieter Baan Centrum 1949–2019* (Boom 2019). Until recently, the clinic was located in Utrecht.

[10] See also E Muller and M Kempes, 'Gender Differences in a Dutch Forensic Sample of Severe Violent Offenders' (2016) 15 Int J Forensic Ment Health 164. They write: 'Possible reasons for the court to order a clinical assessment of defendants include the severity of the crime, the severity of the assumed psychopathology, the maximum security level within the PBC, and potential societal disturbance or media attention associated with the defendant's case. As a result, the population of the PBC covers the

is usually ordered by the prosecution or the judge, the defendant may or may not be willing to cooperate—and the defendant cannot be forced to cooperate. At the Pieter Baan Centre, the defendant will not only have conversations with a psychiatrist and a psychologist, but he or she will also be observed by a multidisciplinary team during daily activities, such as cooking and sports. This can provide valuable information about the presence of psychopathological phenomena. Such observation may make it possible to establish a disorder even in uncooperative defendants.

The behavioural expert has to answer specific questions the standard format for which is as follows:

- If the defendant refuses to be examined, what is your opinion about this refusal?
- Is the examinee suffering from a mental disorder, intellectual disability, and/or psychogeriatric condition, and if so, how can this be described in diagnostic terms?
- What was the mental condition during the time of the alleged offence?
- Did the (possible) mental disorder, intellectual disability, and/or psychogeriatric condition influence the examinee's behavioural choices and actions at the time of the alleged offence?
- If this was the case, could you indicate (with a motivation):
  - How this happened
  - Whether this leads to the advice that the examinee's accountability was diminished or absent
  - If the advice considers the accountability to be diminished, specify this in behavioral terms.[11]

The behavioural expert will answer these questions in a report. In the standard case, a draft of the report will be sent to the NIFP, and it will provide feedback on the draft. However, the responsibility for the report lies with the behavioural expert. Also, during the evaluation and writing of the report, the expert may confer with the NIFP, for instance regarding legal matters. Usually, no testimony will be given in the courtroom, but experts may be asked to provide testimony, for instance, to clarify their conclusions.

more severe criminological and psychiatric cases, and cannot be seen as representative of the entire forensic population whose mental status is assessed.'

[11] CM van Esch, JW Hummelen, E Blaauw, *Het kritisch beoordelen van gedragskundige rapportages in strafzaken* (Uitgeverij Paris 2021), my translation. The formulation has recently been changed—as far as the disorder/illness is concerned—because the terminology of Art 39 of the Criminal Code was changed in 2020. See Gröning and others, 'Constructing Criminal Insanity' (n 1). There are more questions in this standard format concerning the risk of recidivism and possible risk-reducing interventions, but they have been omitted as they do not concern legal insanity.

The defendant's criminal responsibility is evaluated using three categories: criminally responsible; diminished responsibility; and not responsible (legally insane). If a person is legally insane, he or she cannot be punished, as Article 39 CC states that anyone who commits an offence for which he cannot be held responsible due to a mental disorder/condition is not punishable.[12] Even though punishment is not an option if the defendant is found insane, a 'measure' can still be ordered. In Dutch criminal law, a distinction is made between punishments and measures—the latter do not have the objective to punish (even though they may be perceived by the person as 'punishment').[13] Regarding mental illness, such a measure can be imposed because of safety concerns, based on risk assessment. Under Dutch law, a defendant who had a mental disorder at the time of the crime and constitutes a danger to society may be sentenced to *terbeschikkingstelling* (*tbs*, hospital order, Art 37a Dutch CC).[14] This is the most far-reaching measure that, in many cases, can, in principle, be extended indefinitely.[15] The court can only order tbs if two forensic experts—one of them being a psychiatrist—have been appointed to evaluate the defendant. The primary purpose of tbs is to protect society, but it is also aimed at rehabilitation (through treatment and other interventions). The tbs setting is different from a prison and can be considered a therapeutic environment with a high level of security.[16]

If the person's responsibility is diminished (which implies that a mental disorder was present at the time of the crime), the court may impose a combination of punishment (prison) and tbs. In those cases, prison time will be served first, and thereafter, the person will become a patient in tbs. In recent years, the prison time that has to be served before tbs has increased. Nowadays, prison sentences of up to 30 years are combined with tbs. An example is a case in which a defendant was convicted of the manslaughter of his partner, and raping and murdering his stepdaughter. He hid their bodies in the crawlspace. He was also charged with possession of child pornography. Regarding manslaughter, his responsibility was considered diminished, however, for the other charges he was considered fully

[12] See also T Kooijmans and G Meynen, 'Who Establishes the Presence of a Mental Disorder in Defendants? Medicolegal Considerations on a European Court of Human Rights Case' (2017) 8 Front Psychiatry 199 (hereafter, Kooijmans and Meynen, 'Who Establishes the Presence of a Mental Disorder in Defendants?') for this translation.

[13] T Kooijmans, *Op maat geregeld. Een onderzoek naar de grondslag en de normering van de strafrechtelijke maatregel* (Kluwer 2002).

[14] There are further requirements, in particular concerning the nature of the crime. On tbs, see also MV Smeekens and P Braun, 'Long-Term Forensic Psychiatric Care: The Dutch Perspective' in B Völlm and P Braun (eds), *Long-Term Forensic Psychiatric Care: Clinical, Ethical and Legal Challenges* (Springer 2019) 235–50.

[15] In some cases, tbs cannot be extended, this depends on the nature of the crime. Notably, in a substantial part of the cases, the court orders *conditional* tbs, without compulsory admittance to a tbs facility, but with certain conditions, eg the use of medication.

[16] See HJC Marle, 'The Dutch Entrustment Act (TBS): Its Principles and Innovations' (2002) 1 Int J Forensic Ment Health 83.

responsible. He was sentenced to 30 years' imprisonment plus tbs.[17] The court reasoned that this combination of prison and tbs provides maximum protection to society, even more than a life prison sentence, because, in the Netherlands, after 25 years of a life prison sentence, there will be an assessment to evaluate whether the person can start rehabilitation. The court argued that this person should be prevented from re-entering society without tbs treatment—as was advised by the behavioural experts. This decision by the court illustrates that if a defendant is charged with more than one crime, his or her criminal responsibility is evaluated for each charge independently. Legal insanity and diminished responsibility are always related to a specific charge or crime, they are not regarded as a general condition of the defendant.

Over the last decade, an increasing problem has been the decision by some defendants not to cooperate with the evaluation. It is generally supposed that this refusal is often because of fear of tbs. Apparently, defendants assume that if no disorder can be established by the psychiatrist and psychologist, the chances of tbs are decreased. As noted above, not cooperating with the evaluation can be a reason for observation in the Pieter Baan Centre. And even if a defendant does not cooperate, the behavioural expert may nevertheless be able to establish a mental disorder because of clinical observation in combination with additional information. If the psychiatrist and psychologist (after weeks of observation) are unable to establish a disorder, the judge may still find a mental disorder. In addition, the judge may rule that the defendant's criminal responsibility was reduced as a result of that disorder and sentence the defendant to tbs.[18] In my view, in principle, establishing the presence and influence of a mental disorder falls in the medical domain, while making a judgment about the defendant's sanity falls in the legal domain (see the next section). This entails a certain division of labour between psychiatrists—establishing the illness and its impact—and the judge—determining the defendant's legal sanity.[19] Nevertheless, in the Netherlands, psychiatrists are asked to give advice regarding insanity (see standard questions), while judges may establish the presence of a disorder without behavioural experts having determined the presence of a mental illness.

In the Netherlands, the legal threshold for insanity is not specified exactly. In the United States, we find specific thresholds for insanity such as by *preponderance of the evidence* or by *clear and convincing evidence*. In the Netherlands, however, insanity must be '*aannemelijk*', which can be translated as 'plausible'. Obviously, this

[17] Court of Appeal Arnhem-Leeuwarden, 13-11-2017. ECLI:NL:GHARL:2017:9826. For another example, see District Court Gelderland, 14-02-2018, ECLI:NL:RBGEL:2018:666.

[18] MH Nagtegaal and DL Janssen, 'Weigerende verdachten en afdoeningen door de rechter: welke beslissing is gebruikelijk?' (2018/40) Sancties (hereafter Nagtegaal and Janssen, 'Weigerende verdachten en afdoeningen door de rechter'). This practice has been criticized, see Kooijmans and Meynen, 'Who Establishes the Presence of a Mental Disorder in Defendants?' (n 12).

[19] See also Gröning and others, 'Constructing Criminal Insanity' (n 1).

threshold is lower than 'beyond a reasonable doubt'. Yet, it is not clear whether this term—'plausible'—would be more like a 'preponderance of the evidence' or rather 'clear and convincing' evidence.[20] Given the importance of the matter, it has been suggested that the meaning of this threshold should be clarified.[21]

Finally, it is noteworthy that the insanity evaluation takes place before the facts have been established. So, it may well be that the defendant denies the charges—and it may also be that the defendant is eventually acquitted. This means that the behavioural expert should never reason or conclude as if the defendant has already been found guilty. Rather, experts must use conditional formulations like 'if the charges are proven, the advice is to consider the defendant insane'. In addition, the psychiatric guidelines, as a matter of principle, explicitly advise the expert not to infer the existence of a mental disorder from the crime the defendant has been charged with.[22]

An Open Norm

The first feature of the Dutch insanity defence, which will be discussed in some more detail, is that there is no legal criterion specifying the conditions under which the presence of a mental illness supports an insanity plea.[23] According to Article 39 of the Dutch Criminal Code:

> A person who commits an offence for which he cannot be held responsible by reason of the mental disorder, psychogeriatric condition or intellectual disability is not criminally liable.[24]

This article, which provides the legal basis for the Dutch insanity defence, merely states that a person who, as a result of a mental illness, is not responsible, cannot be punished. But it does not spell out how a mental disorder can result in exculpation in the first place. This is different from other legal systems, where the criteria for insanity are usually specified. An example is the M'Naghten Rule in Anglo-American jurisdictions,[25] which determines that a mental disease can render a defendant insane if, as a result of that disorder, he did not know the nature, quality, or

[20] J Bijlsma and G Meynen, 'Wat is 'aannemelijk'? Over het belang van een helder sanctierechtelijk bewijscriterium' (2018) Nederlands Juristenblad 2514. This article is mainly concerned with sanctions.
[21] ibid.
[22] NVvP, *Richtlijn Psychiatrisch onderzoek en rapportage in strafzaken* (De Tijdstroom 2012) 43.
[23] Meynen, *Legal Insanity* (n 1); Radovic, Meynen, and Bennet, 'Introducing a Standard of Legal Insanity' (n 3); Meynen, 'Legal Insanity and Neurolaw in the Netherlands' (n 1).
[24] Netherlands, *The Dutch Penal Code. The American Series of Foreign Penal Codes* (FB Rothman & co 1997). With an adaptation because the terminology of mental illness in Art 39 CC was changed in 2020.
[25] Meynen, *Legal Insanity* (n 1).

wrongfulness of what he was doing.[26] An open criterion as used in the Netherlands is unusual and, at least in my view, problematic.

The reasons behind this open criterion can be traced back to the 19th century when debates about what would become the Dutch Criminal Code were still ongoing (the Dutch Criminal Code entered into force in 1886). At the time, the Minister of Justice, Modderman, argued for an 'open' formulation of the insanity criterion, as he felt that neither the psychiatrist nor the court should be restricted by a legal criterion. They should have all the leeway they needed to reach a conclusion about the defendant's sanity in an individual case.[27] Not everyone agreed with this line of reasoning, however. Modderman, in order to resolve the matter, proposed to define insanity in terms of not 'understanding the nature and criminality of the act' or lacking the ability to act in accordance with one's behavioural choice—a formulation quite similar to standards in many other legal systems.[28] Yet, this criterion turned out not to be acceptable. Ultimately, the open norm became the criterion for legal insanity in 1886 and, with minor modifications, it has remained until today—leaving the behavioural experts and eventually the judge ample room to decide on the defendant's sanity.

Whilst Article 39 CC provides an 'open' norm, it has been interpreted in specific ways. For instance, in an influential Dutch criminal law textbook, De Hullu argues that, regarding legal insanity, it is of the essence to determine a *causal* connection between the disorder and the crime.[29] However, such a causal connection between the disorder and the crime is not reflected in the M'Naghten Rule, which merely requires that the disorder resulted in a lack of knowledge regarding the nature, quality, or wrongfulness of the act (not in the act itself). Meanwhile, the causal connection mentioned by De Hullu may remind us of the *product test* in the United States which, soon after it was introduced, became unpopular.[30]

While De Hullu emphasizes a causal link as an element of the insanity criterion, Tak, another Dutch legal scholar, writes that 'in practice a person is not held responsible for his criminal conduct if at the time of such conduct, as a result of a mental disorder or disease, he lacks substantial capacity either to appreciate the wrongfulness of his conduct, or to bring his conduct into conformity with the

[26] M'Naghten Rule: 'At the time of committing the act, the party accused was labouring under such a defect of reason, from disease of the mind, as not to know the nature and quality of the act he was doing; or if he did know it, that he did not know what he was doing was wrong.' *M'Naghten's Case*, 10 Cl & Fin 200, 8 Eng Rep 718 (HL 1843).

[27] The material on the history of Art 39 is based on J Bijlsma, *Stoornis en strafuitsluiting. Op zoek naar een toetsingskader voor ontoerekenbaarheid* (Wolf Legal Publishers 2016) (hereafter Bijlsma, *Stoornis en strafuitsluiting*). See also Gröning and others, 'Constructing Criminal Insanity' (n 1).

[28] Bijlsma, *Stoornis en strafuitsluiting* (n 27) 38.

[29] J de Hullu, *Materieel strafrecht* (6th edn, Wolters Kluwer 2015).

[30] The interpretation in terms of 'causation' is more like the *Durham rule* or 'product test', according to which a defendant is 'not criminally responsible if his unlawful act was the product of mental disease or mental defect'. *Durham v United States*, 214 F 2d 862 (DC Cir, 1954). See on this matter also Meynen, *Legal Insanity* (n 1).

requirements of law'.[31] Tak's quote reflects the components of the Model Penal Code test, according to which 'a person is not responsible for criminal conduct if at the time of such conduct as a result of mental disease or defect he lacks substantial capacity either to appreciate the criminality (wrongfulness) of his conduct or to conform his conduct to the requirements of the law'.[32]

Not only scholars but also courts have interpreted the Dutch 'open norm' in dissimilar—and sometimes wrong or problematic—ways.[33] For instance, behavioural experts and courts occasionally refer to a lack of 'free will' as a criterion for legal insanity.[34] Let us consider in more detail a recent case in which the Court of Appeal of The Hague explicitly formulated a norm for legal insanity.[35] This case received a lot of media attention as the defendant stood trial for killing two victims: his own sister and the former Minister of Health in the Netherlands.

The court of first instance had considered the defendant legally insane, even though the behavioural experts—after observation in the Pieter Baan Centre—did not agree. Both experts, a psychologist and a psychiatrist, stated that the defendant suffered from schizophrenia and concluded that his criminal responsibility was *strongly diminished*.[36] This case shows that the judge has the freedom to disagree with the experts' advice regarding the defendant's legal insanity. The fundamental point is that it is up to the judge to decide about the exclusion of criminal liability, as this concerns a legal matter. Here, even though both experts advised that the defendant's responsibility was strongly diminished, the Court considered him completely insane. However, such a departure from the advice of experts from the Pieter Baan Centre is unusual.[37]

The ruling was appealed to the Court of Appeal in The Hague. In the absence of a standard for legal insanity and given the discussion about this defendant's sanity, the Court of Appeal formulated the following criterion:

> [I]t has to be plausible that the defendant's actions are *not (partly) prompted by realistic/real, non-pathological motives*. Only then, can impunity be the result.

[31] PJP Tak, *The Dutch Criminal Justice System* (Wolf Legal Publishers 2008) 74.

[32] The Model Penal Code test (American Law Institute) is used in a minority of the states; most US states have M'Naghten, CL Scott and PJ Resnick, 'Forensic Psychiatry' in SH Fatemi and PJ Clayton (eds), *The Medical Basis of Psychiatry* (Springer 2016) 799–808.

[33] Bijlsma, *Stoornis en strafuitsluiting* (n 27); SLTJ Ligthart, T Kooijmans, and G Meynen, 'Een juridisch criterium voor de ontoerekeningsvatbaarheid: een uitspraak van het gerechtshof Den Haag geanalyseerd' (2018) 1 Delikt en Delinkwent 101 (hereafter Ligthart, Kooijmans, and Meynen, 'Een juridisch criterium voor de ontoerekeningsvatbaarheid').

[34] District Court Overijssel, 07-06-2018, ECLI:NL:RBOVE:2018:1957; District Court Overijssel, 24-09-2018, ECLI:NL:RBOVE:2018:3477; District Court Rotterdam, 16-11-2017, ECLI:NL:RBROT:2017.

[35] What follows is mainly based on Ligthart, Kooijmans, and Meynen, 'Een juridisch criterium voor de ontoerekeningsvatbaarheid' (n 31). Reference to the Court of Appeal: Hof Den Haag 16 maart 2017, ECLI:NL:GHDHA:2017:684.

[36] District Court Rotterdam 13-04-2016, ECLI:NL:RBROT:2016:2699.

[37] Nagtegaal and Janssen, 'Weigerende verdachten en afdoeningen door de rechter: welke beslissing is gebruikelijk?' (n 18).

To form a judgment about whether the suspect can be punished it is important to consider:

1) whether the suspect at the time of the crime was suffering from a mental or developmental mental disorder;
2) if so, whether there is a *causal* connection between that mental or developmental mental disorder and the proven facts;
3) if so, whether the suspect has been able to understand the *unlawfulness* of his actions;
4) if so, whether the developmental or mental disorder at the time of the proven facts completely determined the defendant's actions, in the sense that the defendant was *unable or not sufficiently able to act in accordance* with his understanding of the unlawfulness of the facts.[38]

As this norm requires several criteria to be fulfilled, it can be considered very strict. First, there should be a *causal* relationship between the disorder and the crime. This is in line with the interpretation provided by De Hullu (see above). Furthermore, the defendant should not know the *unlawfulness* of the act, and if he knew it, he should not be sufficiently able to *act in accordance* with such knowledge. The latter part of these criteria (nos 3 and 4) reflects components of Tak's interpretation of the Dutch standard (resembling the Model Penal Code test, see earlier). Finally, *no non-pathological or realistic motives* should influence the defendant's actions in order to justify legal insanity.

As it appears, this insanity test, used by the Court of Appeal of The Hague, stacks one criterion (resembling the Model Penal Code test) on the other (resembling the Product test).[39] Moreover, the criterion adds to these combined standards that no non-pathological or realistic motives should have influenced the defendant's actions. This not only leads to an (extremely) strict criterion, but also appears to be in conflict with a court ruling in another case. In that case, a mother dropped her 19-month-old daughter from the fourth floor of a department store in the centre of Amsterdam.[40] A few moments later, the mother jumped. The child did not survive, but the mother did. The mother, the behavioural experts established, suffered from a delusion at the time of the crime. She believed that Satanists were on the verge of killing her and her daughter. The mother had contemplated what to do and she chose to take her daughter's life, so that her daughter would not be in pain.[41] The

[38] My translation (emphasis added). Translated from Court of Appeal: Hof Den Haag 16 March 2017, ECLI:NL:GHDHA:2017:684.

[39] Ligthart, Kooijmans, and Meynen, 'Een juridisch criterium voor de ontoerekeningsvatbaarheid' (n 33).

[40] ECLI:NL:RBAMS:2009:BH8888. As discussed by Ligthart, Kooijmans, and Meynen, 'Een juridisch criterium voor de ontoerekeningsvatbaarheid' (n 33).

[41] ECLI:NL:RBAMS:2009:BH8888 'zodat haar dochter geen pijn zou hebben'.

motive that one's daughter should not be in pain cannot plausibly be considered a pathological motive. It is perfectly normal for parents not to want their children to suffer. In other words, apparently, a non-pathological motive played a role in this case. This mother, meanwhile—in apparent contrast with the Court of Appeal's criterion—was considered completely insane.

As the above illustrates, the Dutch open insanity norm provides scope for different interpretations—and it has received criticism for that reason.[42] The problems of the open norm start with the legal expert. As is clear from the format of questions discussed in the previous section, the expert has to explicitly advise regarding the (level of the) defendant's criminal responsibility *in the absence* of a legal standard for insanity (such as M'Naghten). In practice, this means that the behavioural expert has to come up with some implicit or explicit criterion to support and explain his or her conclusion about the level of the defendant's criminal responsibility. Given the various views on, and profound and complicated debates about, legal insanity, illustrated in this volume, this is obviously a challenge as the behavioural expert is not a lawyer, while legal insanity and criminal responsibility are *legal* notions. Such concepts have no meaning or relevance outside of the realm of criminal law. In particular, they have no meaning in health care, either mental or physical. Because the behavioural expert is required to provide explicit advice regarding a defendant's sanity in the absence of a legal criterion, psychiatrists are asked to go beyond the boundaries of their medical expertise, and to enter the legal realm. In general, it is recognized as important—if not crucial—that experts in the courtroom remain within the limits of their own expertise.

Legal insanity is often considered an ultimate legal issue—an issue for the court and/or jury. From a US perspective, psychiatrist and ethicist Paul Appelbaum states within this context:

> Part of the problem here relates to the proclivity of forensic psychiatrists and other experts to offer 'ultimate issue' testimony—that is, to attempt to answer legal/moral questions like whether a defendant is criminally responsible, as opposed merely to presenting descriptive information about a defendant's mental state. With no special expertise in addressing legal or moral questions, psychiatrists who make such judgments are treading on morally perilous terrain. Indeed, I have long believed that psychiatrists should avoid ultimate issue testimony, focusing their attention on descriptions of mental and functional states that they are much better qualified to address.[43]

[42] Bijlsma, *Stoornis en strafuitsluiting* (n 25) and G Meynen and T Kooijmans, 'Een standaard voor ontoerekeningsvatbaarheid en de functionele diagnostiek' (2015) 5 Expertise en Recht.

[43] PS Appelbaum, 'Ethics and Forensic Psychiatry: Translating Principles into Practice' (2008) 36 J Am Acad Psychiatry Law 195 (hereafter, Appelbaum, 'Ethics and Forensic Psychiatry').

In my view, this is a clear argument for staying away from ultimate issues as a forensic psychiatrist.[44]

The absence of a norm does not only constitute a problem for the experts. If we move to the court, there is also a problem or challenge: judges have interpreted the legal norm, as was already mentioned, in dissimilar ways. Such disparity may well result in inequality before the law.[45] Needless to say, in principle, inequality of justice is undesirable, especially if the consequences are grave, as is the case, at least potentially, regarding legal insanity. Apart from the issue of inequality of justice, this open criterion in practice also creates a lack of transparency and unpredictability: it is unclear what framework the court will use when deciding about this important matter. This may only become clear in the psychiatrist's report or in the verdict.

Bijlsma (2016) and Meynen (2013) have put forward proposals for an insanity standard. Both proposals reflect control (volitional) and knowledge/appreciation components.[46] This is in line with the norm in many other jurisdictions. For instance, the Model Penal Code test (see above) incorporates these elements and another example is China's article 15 of the criminal law which provides:

> A mentally ill person who causes dangerous consequences at a time when he is *unable to recognize or unable to control* his own conduct is not to bear criminal responsibility after being established through accreditation of legal procedures.[47]

An issue of debate is whether the epistemic component—knowing that what one is doing is wrong—should be taken to refer to *legal* or *moral* understanding. The Court of Appeal in The Hague, in the case discussed earlier, formulated its criterion in terms of understanding the unlawfulness, which reflects the legal interpretation. Ligthart and others, however, argued that a moral understanding would be preferable, referring to the case about the mother who killed her own daughter.[48]

[44] See eg TMS Neal, 'Discerning Bias in Forensic Psychological Reports in Insanity Cases' (2018) 36 Behav Sci Law 325, 239: 'Many legal and behavioral science scholars argue that psychologists should not address the "ultimate legal issue" in writing forensic reports. That is, they argue that the categorical legal issue should not be addressed (e.g., whether or not the defendant was "sane" at the time of offense or whether s/he should be held criminally responsible).... Regardless of the opinion a particular examiner holds on the issue, the Federal Rules of Evidence (FRE 704b) prohibit experts from reporting an opinion on the ultimate legal issue in insanity evaluations in federal cases, and several states follow suit. Similarly, the American Bar Association's Criminal Justice Mental Health Standards (2016) recommend that mental health professionals should not be allowed to offer ultimate opinions in insanity cases.' (References omitted.)

[45] G Meynen, 'Een juridische standaard voor ontoerekeningsvatbaarheid?' (2013) 88 Nederlands Juristenblad 1384.

[46] See on both components also Meynen, *Legal Insanity* (n 1).

[47] See Chapter 14 (emphasis added).

[48] The legal interpretation has been advanced by Bijlsma, *Stoornis en strafuitsluiting* (n 27), while the moral interpretation has been suggested by Ligthart, Kooijmans, and Meynen, 'Een juridisch criterium voor de ontoerekeningsvatbaarheid' (n 33).

She may have known that it was unlawful to kill her own child, but still she may have felt that it was morally the right thing to do—as she apparently believed her daughter would otherwise suffer.

Clearly, there is a debate in the international literature and throughout this volume about how wrongfulness should be interpreted: either in the legal or in the moral sense.[49] Elsewhere, I have argued that legal wrongfulness may lead to insanity in cases where the defendant delusionally believed he was acting in *self-defence*.[50] People are allowed to defend themselves when attacked or threatened. So, if one delusionally believes that one is under attack, one may honestly feel that one has the legal right to defend oneself against the attacker. But there is also another category of delusion cases, that do not fall in the category of 'delusional self-defence'. Suppose that a mother delusionally believes that her newborn son will go to hell and suffer eternally unless she kills him today. She knows very well that killing is prohibited by the law and therefore she is fully aware that such an act is unlawful. Yet, morally the situation is different: she feels that, as a mother, her concern above all should be her son's eternal wellbeing. The fact that she may be punished in her earthly life for her act, as it is unlawful, seems a finite sacrifice for this mother to save her son from eternal damnation. Such a situation is different from the self-defence cases: there is no imminent attack the action aims to neutralize. Rather, in the second category of cases, some delusionally motivated duty may *dwarf* the duty to obey the law. The delusion the person suffers from may involve supernatural entities, such as demons and angels. Cases in which mothers, driven by a delusional motive, kill their own children, may be among the most tragic insanity cases. Due to their deluded ideas, they not only take another person's life, but they also rob themselves and their loved ones of a beloved and innocent child—and all of this believing that they are doing something that is morally good. In my view, such sad cases should, in principle, also be covered by the insanity criterion. The strict legal interpretation however, excludes these cases as long as the parent knows that her action is unlawful.[51]

[49] On the debate in the US context, see W Sinnott-Armstrong and K Levy, 'Insanity Defenses' in J Deigh and D Dolinko (eds), *The Oxford Handbook of Philosophy of Criminal Law* (Oxford University Press 2011) 299–334.

[50] See, on what follows, also G Meynen, 'The Relevance of Free Will, Rationality, and Aristotle for Legal Insanity' in AM Waltermann and others (eds), *Law, Science, and Rationality* (Eleven International Publishing 2020) 113–39; G Meynen, 'The Insanity Defense' in Hage and others (eds), *Law and Mind* (Cambridge University Press 2021) 317–41.

[51] See also Ligthart, Kooijmans, and Meynen, 'Een juridisch criterium voor de ontoerekeningsvatbaarheid' (n 33). And on this matter, see also Morse: 'To the extent that an outcome might turn on moral versus legal wrong, the former should be preferred because it is more action guiding and provides a better fit with the underlying rationale for the defence.' S Morse, 'Legal Insanity in the Age of Neuroscience' in S Moratti and D Patterson (eds), *Legal Insanity and the Brain: Science, Law and European Courts* (Hart Publishing 2016) chapter 9, 239–76, 257. Interestingly, Bijlsma recently published a Dutch paper that brings the legal and the moral interpretation, to some extent, together, in short, by broadening the scope of the legal interpretation. J Bijlsma, 'Wederrechtelijkheid of morele ongeoorloofdheid: welk inzicht moet de ontoerekenbare verdachte ontberen?' (2019/61) Delikt en Delinkwent.

Diminished Responsibility

A second characteristic of legal insanity in the Netherlands is that, while many jurisdictions use the dichotomy 'sane' versus 'insane', three categories of criminal responsibility are used: responsibility, diminished responsibility, and (complete) insanity. However, until September 2016, five grades of criminal responsibility were used, and they had been used for decades. These were: responsible, somewhat diminished responsibility; diminished responsibility; severely diminished responsibility; insanity. But in 2012, the Guidelines for Forensic Evaluations in Criminal Cases were published. Remarkably, these Guidelines recommended a *new* practice: no longer using five grades, but, instead, three grades of criminal responsibility. The reason provided for this—rather drastic—change of practice was that the five grades, particularly the three in the middle, were not supported by state-of-the-art medical science.[52] In fact, the Guidelines state that there is 'no evidence for any scale, neither for five, nor for three grades'.[53] The Guidelines advise, as much as possible, conducting an analysis of the defendant's mental functions.

In this context of grades of responsibility, Morse's comment may be of interest: 'Although an agent's degree of responsibility depends on facts about either the agent's rationality or the hard choices the agent faced, we only have the limited ability to make the fine-grained responsibility judgments that are possible in theory.'[54] In other words, even though theoretically five grades (or possibly more) could be justified, there are limits to the distinctions we—behavioural experts, judges, jury members—can make in the actual practice of evaluating a defendant.

Of note, the change concerned the psychiatric Guidelines, although most reports are made by psychologists, and they are not bound by psychiatric guidelines. After the reduction of grades of criminal responsibility, a period of intense debate followed about the number of grades—three or five? Professor emeritus Van Marle, involved in developing the Guidelines, wrote: 'Before and after [its] publication, there was a fierce debate between proponents and opponents of these Guidelines, which abandon the five grades of criminal responsibility. The debate is not over yet . . . '.[55]

Initially, the NIFP decided that experts could choose between the framework of either three or five grades when making their reports. In 2016, however, the NIFP adopted the three grades. Still, some experts prefer the five grades. A study

52 Meynen, 'Legal Insanity and Neurolaw in the Netherlands' (n 1).

53 NVvP, *Richtlijn Psychiatrisch onderzoek en rapportage in strafzaken*, 65 (author's own translation).

54 SJ Morse, 'Diminished Rationality, Diminished Responsibility' (2003) 1 Ohio State J Crim Law 289 (hereafter, Morse, 'Diminished Rationality, Diminished Responsibility').

55 HJ van Marle, 'Determining Freedom of Choice in Forensic Psychiatry Is of Great Importance to Psychiatry as a Whole' (2016) 58 Tijdschr Psychiatr 92. See also J Bijlsma and G Meynen, 'Heeft ons strafrecht de "verminderde" toerekeningsvatbaarheid wel nodig?' (2017) Nederlands Juristenblad 304 (hereafter, Bijlsma and Meynen, 'Heeft ons strafrecht de "verminderde" toerekeningsvatbaarheid wel nodig?').

performed at the time the five grades were in use showed that the vast majority of the defendants who were evaluated by behavioural experts were considered to fall into the category of diminished responsibility (either slightly diminished responsibility, diminished responsibility, or strongly diminished responsibility).[56] This group was followed by those defendants considered fully responsible (about 20%), and only a small percentage of the defendants who were evaluated were considered completely insane.

Interestingly, however, even though there was much debate about the grades, this question was not asked: Do we need these grades in the first place? From an international perspective, this would have been an obvious question, as many legal systems do not have degrees of responsibility, but a dichotomy: sane versus insane. In 2017, the question was addressed in a Dutch law journal under the title 'Do We Actually Need "Diminished" Responsibility in Our Criminal Law?'.[57] The first point in that article is that, formally, diminished responsibility is not relevant for the question *whether* a defendant can be punished. Article 39 makes clear that *only* complete insanity renders punishment impossible. So, regarding this crucial issue—exemption from punishment—it has no value. Still, in principle, it could be relevant when deciding about the (severity of the) sanction.[58] However, it is important to realize that the judge in the Netherlands has considerable leeway in determining the sentence. In addition, the judge does not have an obligation to justify the factors he or she takes into account—as either mitigating or aggravating circumstances—when determining the sentence. Such factors could, at least in principle, be a risk of recidivism or diminished responsibility. While diminished responsibility could lead to a lower sentence, other factors, such as the risk related to a particular mental illness, can be considered weightier, and lead to a more severe sentence. Of note, in the Netherlands, the judge does not have to punish in accordance with the level of responsibility. In sum, there is considerable freedom on the part of the judge, and the formal category of 'diminished' responsibility does not really add to the discretion the judge already has—at least in the Dutch context.

In the article, this situation was contrasted with the legal position in the United States, where Federal judges have to consider the United States Sentencing Guidelines.[59] These not only provide a certain 'bandwidth' for sentencing but also formulate criteria for *departing* from the bandwidth. In such a system, it is crucial

[56] DJ Vinkers and others, 'Pre-trial Psychiatric Evaluations and Ethnicity in the Netherlands' (2010) 33 Int J Law Psychiatry 192. Even though the study focused on ethnicity, the findings are also informative regarding the percentage of defendants falling into each of the three categories.

[57] Bijlsma and Meynen, 'Heeft ons strafrecht de "verminderde" toerekeningsvatbaarheid wel nodig?' (n 55). What follows is based in this article.

[58] See AWM Mooij, 'De toerekeningsvatbaarheid: hoe verder?' (2012) 42 Delikt en Delinkwent 36 (hereafter, Mooij, 'De toerekeningsvatbaarheid').

[59] Bijlsma and Meynen, 'Heeft ons strafrecht de "verminderde" toerekeningsvatbaarheid wel nodig?' (n 55).

to define certain factors that allow for departures from the bandwidth.[60] This is not the case in the Netherlands, however, where no minimum—only maximum—sentences have been formulated and the judge, as already described, has freedom regarding mitigating and aggravating circumstances. Notably, for no other ground for exemption from punishment, does the Dutch criminal law have such a formalized 'diminished' grade. In fact, as legal scholar De Hullu writes, legal insanity was originally meant to be a dichotomous matter: 'The dichotomy [sanity vs insanity] was explicitly intended' and he adds: 'and it seems to me inevitable regarding grounds that make punishment *impossible*'.[61] Finally, in the article, it was argued that 'diminished' responsibility is not a formal criterion for tbs (even though some may feel it is). For tbs, the presence of a disorder at the time of the crime is required, but it is not required that the disorder resulted in 'diminished' responsibility (or insanity). All in all, it was concluded that the formal category 'diminished responsibility' does not serve a clear purpose in Dutch criminal law.

Neuroscience

Neuroscience has been discussed regarding the insanity defence in at least two ways. First, there is an ongoing debate, partly philosophical in nature, about the implications of neuroscience for free will.[62] It has been argued that neuroscience (allegedly) shows that free will is an illusion.[63] Proponents of this idea may refer to the deterministic nature of brain processes as such and to specific experiments, such as the Libet experiment.[64]

Libet and his colleagues reported that about 300 milliseconds before subjects became aware of the urge or intention to act, characteristic brain activity could

[60] Interestingly, Stephen Morse has argued for introducing 'diminished responsibility' in the United States: 'This Commentary proposes that the criminal law should include a generic, doctrinal mitigating excuse of partial responsibility that would apply to all crimes, and that would be determined by the trier of fact. This partial excuse would apply in cases in which a defendant's behavior satisfied the elements of the crime charged, but the defendant's rationality was non-culpably compromised and thus the defendant was not fully responsible for the crime charged. Current Anglo-American criminal law contains no such generic partial excuse. Some doctrines, such as provocation/passion and extreme mental or emotional disturbance for which there is reasonable explanation or excuse, appear to operate in effect as partial excuses. They typically apply only in limited contexts, however, such as to reduce a homicide that would otherwise be murder to manslaughter.' Morse, 'Diminished Rationality, Diminished Responsibility' (n 54) 289.

[61] J De Hullu, *Materieel strafrecht. Over algemene leerstukken van strafrechtelijke aansprakelijkheid naar Nederlands recht* (Kluwer 2012) 336.

[62] See on this debate, eg A Bigenwald and V Chambon, 'Criminal Responsibility and Neuroscience: No Revolution Yet' (2019) 10 Front Psychology 1406 (hereafter, Bigenwald and Chambon, 'Criminal Responsibility and Neuroscience').

[63] See on this debate A Lavazza, 'Free Will and Neuroscience: From Explaining Freedom Away to New Ways of Operationalizing and Measuring It' (2016) 10 Front Hum Neurosci 262.

[64] B Libet and others, 'Time of Conscious Intention to Act in Relation to Onset of Cerebral Activity (Readiness-Potential). The Unconscious Initiation of a Freely Voluntary Act' (1983) 106 (Pt 3) Brain 623.

already be registered using an EEG—a signal called the 'readiness potential'. Libet concluded that the brain activity—rather than our conscious decision-making—is first. The experiment and the conclusions that can be drawn from the findings are still the topic of debate, also in the Netherlands.[65] And some hold that since neuroscience (allegedly) shows that free will is an illusion, nobody is criminally responsible, and psychiatric assessments of criminal responsibility are no longer meaningful (assessments of future dangerousness, meanwhile, may still be valuable). Some best-selling books on the brain contributed to this discussion, such as Dick Swaab's *We Are Our Brains* and Victor Lamme's *Free Will Does Not Exist*—both authors renowned neuroscientists.[66] Although these discussions may also have had an impact on some forensic psychiatrists,[67] the further theoretical debate will not be entered into here.[68]

I will instead focus on the second way in which neuroscience has been discussed regarding legal insanity: the extent to which it could be helpful in actual assessments of criminal responsibility or legal insanity. While in the free will debate neuroscience allegedly undermines the *rationale* for legal insanity assessments by denying moral and legal responsibility altogether, regarding the *actual* assessments, it could be supportive in the diagnostic process.

In the Netherlands, neuroscience is sometimes used in the behavioural evaluations of defendants.[69] In 2015, De Kogel and Westgeest published an article on the use of neuroscientific and behavioural genetic information in criminal cases in the Netherlands from 2000 to 2012.[70] They searched the Dutch online database from the judiciary, *rechtspraak.nl*. Neuroscience information had been used in 207 cases, while behavioural genetic information was mentioned in 14 cases, and in ten cases both types of information could be found. Interestingly, the authors also looked into the 'Judicial questions with respect to which neuroscientific or behavioural genetic information is introduced', such as intent (20 cases), premeditation (two cases), and competency to stand trial (four cases).[71] As it turned out, the legal question with respect to which neuroscience/genetic information was most often introduced, was criminal responsibility: 72 cases.

[65] V Lamme, *De vrije wil bestaat niet. Over wie er echt de baas is in het brein* (Bert Bakker 2010) (hereafter, Lamme, *De vrije wil bestaat niet*).

[66] DF Swaab, *Wij zijn ons brein. Van baarmoeder tot Alzheimer* (Atlas Contact 2010); Lamme, *De vrije wil bestaat niet* (n 65).

[67] Mooij, 'De toerekeningsvatbaarheid: hoe verder?' (n 58).

[68] See on this topic, eg Bigenwald and Chambon, 'Criminal Responsibility and Neuroscience' (n 62).

[69] See, on what follows in this section, also G Meynen, 'Neuroscience-based Psychiatric Assessments of Criminal Responsibility: Beyond Self-Report?' (2020) 29 Camb Q Healthc Ethics 446.

[70] CH de Kogel and EJ Westgeest, 'Neuroscientific and Behavioral Genetic Information in Criminal Cases in the Netherlands' (2015) 2 JLB 580 (hereafter, De Kogel and Westgeest, 'Neuroscientific and Behavioral Genetic Information'). Of note, not all criminal cases are in this online database.

[71] In the Netherlands, unlike in the United States, competency to stand trial is rarely an issue in criminal cases, see EM Gremmen, *De kwetsbare psychisch gestoorde verdachte in het strafproces. Regelgeving, praktijk en Europese standaarden (Thesis)* (Wolf Legal Publishers 2018).

De Kogel and Westgeest provide one of these cases as an example:

> An example is a case of a man who is accused of fornication with a neighbor-girl. The abuse took place four or five times when she was about nine years old. The defendant is examined by a neurologist who finds a beginning of fronto-subcortical dementia in relation to Parkinson's disease. The behavioural choices of the defendant at the time of the offense were according to the neurologist, undoubtedly affected by the organic brain dysfunction. He reports: Directly related to the front-subcortical dementia is, in addition to the characteristic cognitive impairments, impulsivity, which occurs particularly in complex situations in which the defendant lacks an overview. As a result, the defendant was unable to control his impulses. He acted reflexively without overseeing the consequences. The defendant lacks the capacity for self-reflection, which prevents him from relating his actions to an appropriate framework of norms and values. In addition he was as a result of his cognitive impairment not able to interrupt his behavior once started. The other behavioral expert, a psychologist reports that the dementia is in an early phase and that the behavior of the defendant shows not a general disinhibition yet. She reasons that there is a realistic risk of criminal recidivism. The court adopts the advice of the experts and considers the defendant of diminished accountability for the offense. The verdict is a 297 days prison sentence, of which 60 days conditional and with two years of probation and psychogeriatric treatment as a special condition.[72]

In this case, a neurologist evaluated the defendant. During an evaluation of a defendant, a psychiatrist may feel that a neurological evaluation is required in case a tumour, neurodegenerative disease, brain damage, or other neurological condition is suspected. Then, the psychiatrist may ask the prosecutor or the judge to appoint a neurologist. If that request is granted, the NIFP will approach a neurologist to perform the evaluation, which may well include neuroimaging and neuropsychological assessment.[73] The neurologist writes an independent report, but also consults with the other behavioural experts about the findings.

In 2016, Ter Harmsel and colleagues published a study on 'whether and how genetic and neuroscientific applications are being used in forensic psychiatric assessments'.[74] They did not examine court decisions as De Kogel and Westgeest did, but, instead, analysed 60 forensic psychiatric assessments; 30 from the Pieter Baan

[72] De Kogel and Westgeest, 'Neuroscientific and Behavioral Genetic Information' (n 66) 592–93. (Minor textual changes made by this author.)

[73] G Meynen, 'Antwoord aan Goethals (Antwoord op Reactie op 'Neurolaw: de relevantie voor de forensische psychiatrie' en 'Forensisch psychiaters en forensisch psychologen: mind the gap')' (2014) 56 Tijdschrift voor psychiatrie 842 and see Schouws, Jonker, and Meynen, 'The Importance of Neuropsychological Assessment' (n 7).

[74] Ter Harmsel and others, 'Forensic Assessments' (n 6).

Centre and 30 non-clinical evaluations. They observed that from 2000–09 '(behavioral) genetic, neurological and neuropsychological applications played only a modest role in forensic psychiatric assessment'. Even though the value of neuroscience for psychiatric evaluations of criminal responsibility is still under debate,[75] it is my impression that in the Netherlands attention regarding neuro(bio)logical factors in the assessment of defendants is growing. At present, at the Pieter Baan Centre, annually, in about 40 cases (20% of those evaluated at the Centre) brain scans, most of them MRI, are performed.[76]

In any case, it is crucial to keep in mind the current limitations of neuroscience for forensic psychiatric assessments.[77] At the same time, at least in my view, we should not overlook the value of neurological evaluations because in some cases for justice to be done a thorough neurological evaluation is required. Behavioural experts should be alert for signs and symptoms that are indicative of neurological illness and ensure defendants receive proper evaluation in cases where neurological assessment is warranted.

Concluding Remarks

An important characteristic of the Dutch insanity defence is that there is no legal criterion specifying the conditions under which the presence of a mental illness supports an insanity plea. The 'open' Dutch criterion has, so it appears, several disadvantages. First, it may lead to inequality of justice as different criteria may be—and have been—used in legal practice. Another disadvantage is that behavioural experts do not have a legal criterion which they can apply when performing their evaluation—consequently, they have to apply their own criterion, even though insanity is a legal matter and behavioural experts are not lawyers. Recently, suggestions for a legal standard have been formulated, containing control and epistemic components. However, there may be an advantage to the open criterion because

[75] Bigenwald and Chambon, 'Criminal Responsibility and Neuroscience' (n 62); G Meynen, 'Neuroscience-Based Psychiatric Assessments of Criminal Responsibility: Beyond Self-Report?' (2020) 29(3) Cambridge Quarterly of Healthcare Ethics 446–58.

[76]. G Meynen, *Neurorecht: hoop of hersenschim?* Nr. 97 Pompe Reeks (Boom juridisch 2020).

[77] At this point, it may be useful to refer to Appelbaum, who mentions 'the current tendency of some forensic experts grossly to overstate what contemporary neuroscience can tell us about the causal links between various aspects of brain function and crime, especially crimes of violence. Whether basing their contentions on genetics, anatomic imaging, functional MRI, positron emission tomography, or other techniques, these witnesses make leaps worthy of the late Evel Knievel from the test findings themselves to conclusions regarding a defendant's responsibility for criminal acts.' Appelbaum, 'Ethics and Forensic Psychiatry' (n 43) 197. And see also Stephen Morse, who states: 'At present, neuroscience has little to contribute to more just and accurate criminal law decision-making concerning policy, doctrine, and individual case adjudication.' SJ Morse, 'Neuroscience and Criminal Law: Perils and Promises' in L Alexander and KK Ferzan (eds), *The Palgrave Handbook of Applied Ethics and the Criminal Law* (Palgrave Macmillan 2019) 492.

it does, as intended by Minister Modderman in the 19th century, provide ample leeway for the experts and the court.

I noted above that psychiatrists are not only allowed but are explicitly asked to advise the court about a defendant's level of criminal responsibility. In many jurisdictions, legal insanity is considered an 'ultimate' legal issue, something experts should avoid. Appelbaum has provided a good reason for such restraint, as it is crucial for experts to limit themselves in their testimony to their own domain of expertise.

We also noticed that the courts may tread on—what at least appears to be—medical terrain, by finding a mental disorder in cases where experts cannot confirm the presence of a mental illness. To me, it is clear that when two (or more) experts disagree, the court should find its own answer, but, in my view, this should—at least in principle—be done within the boundaries of the psychiatric and psychological reports and testimonies. This will often mean that the court should choose one of the reports. Alternatively, the court may request an additional report or observation from the Pieter Baan Centre. Yet, in the Netherlands, we have now had several cases in which behavioural experts, after weeks of observation of an uncooperative defendant in the Pieter Baan Centre, have concluded that the presence of a mental disorder could not be confirmed, but where the court itself found the presence of a 'mental disorder' and considered the defendant's criminal responsibility to be diminished (and sentenced the defendant to tbs).

A second characteristic is that, while many jurisdictions use the dichotomy 'sane' versus 'insane', in the Netherlands three levels of criminal responsibility are used: responsibility, diminished responsibility, and (complete) insanity. Even though the dichotomy sane versus insane was, apparently, intended, the grades evolved in legal practice. Until 2016, no less than five grades were used, since then only three grades. A positive point about the grades is that the level of criminal responsibility may be tailored to the defendant in a particular case. In addition, it seems reasonable to hold that, in a way, responsibility is a matter of shades of grey rather than black and white. However, five levels may be a bit too much by overstretching the expert's ability to make clear distinctions regarding the level of responsibility. The Guidelines for psychiatric evaluations of defendants emphasizes the lack of medical evidence in this matter. It has also been argued that, while a category of diminished responsibility may definitely be useful in other legal systems, for the Dutch criminal law it is not clear why we should have such a formal category of 'diminished' responsibility in the first place. For instance, punishment is only excluded if the defendant is completely insane. Also, the Dutch legal system does not have any rule that states that the punishment or duration of the prison sentence should be proportionate to the level of responsibility. Depending on the crime, the judge still has the freedom to impose a long prison sentence even if a defendant's responsibility is considered to be diminished.

The role of neuroscience in the assessment of legal insanity appears to be growing in the Netherlands. A study by De Kogel and Westgeest found that *the* legal question with respect to which neuroscience data had been used in court cases concerned legal insanity. Nevertheless, in general, the role of neuroscience in psychiatric assessments is very limited.

In conclusion, legal insanity is a fascinating and complex element of criminal law where two disciplines meet: law and psychiatry. These disciplines have to collaborate for justice to be done—and legal systems have sought and found disparate solutions to the challenges this collaboration creates. In my view, it is important to emphasize that psychiatrists and psychologists establish mental illness and its impact (a medical and psychological matter), while judges and juries must determine the implications of these findings for the defendant's legal insanity (a legal matter). In any case, legal insanity is likely to continue to play an important role in Dutch legal practice, as well as in scholarly debates.

13
Criminal Insanity in Norwegian Law

Linda Gröning

Introduction

The current criminal insanity rules in Norway came into force on 1 October 2020. These rules were the result of the law reform process that was initiated in the aftermath of the case concerning Anders Behring Breivik, who killed 77 people in Oslo and at Utøya on 22 July 2011.[1] The case highlighted the fact that the Norwegian regulation of criminal insanity reflected a specific 'medical model'.[2] This regulation equated insanity with being 'psychotic' at the time of the act and provided for experts to have a significant role in insanity cases. However, the Norwegian insanity rule has now been changed as a result of law reform post-22 July.[3] The contested criterion 'psychotic' has now been removed and replaced with criteria that provide for greater judicial discretion, and the role of the experts has been delimited.[4]

This chapter will discuss the current Norwegian rules concerning criminal incapacity and insanity as defined in section 20 of the Penal Code,[5] considered from both historical and comparative perspectives. Norwegian law, in addition to infancy, distinguishes between mental disorder, impairments of consciousness, and intellectual disability as different kinds of conditions that may entail *criminal incapacity*.[6] The Norwegian translation of criminal *insanity*—'*galskap*'—is primarily associated with mental disorder. This is different from how criminal insanity is conceptualized in many of the other countries included in this book, where 'insanity' may refer also to conditions of intellectual disability and consciousness

[1] The final judgment of Anders Behring Breivik in the 22 July case: TOSLO-2011-188627-24- RG-2012-1153, available in English at <https://lovdata.no/info/information_in_English> accessed 12 June 2020 (hereafter, 'the *Breivik* case').

[2] See, inter alia, S Wessely, 'Anders Breivik, the Public, and Psychiatry' (2012) 379 Lancet 1563–64, P Wittig, 'Anders Breivik: Evil, Insane or Just Criminal?'(2013) Kyushu University LRB 1–9 Online edition ISSN: 2186-6791, L Bortolotti, M Broome, and M Mameli, 'Delusions and Responsibility for Action: Insights from the Breivik Case' (2014) 7 Neuroethics 377–82, C Jacobsen and D Maier-Katkin, 'Breivik's Sanity: Terrorism, Mass Murder, and the Insanity Defense' (2015) 37 Hum Rights Q 137–52.

[3] For a discussion about the legal reform, and its background, see L Gröning, 'Has Norway Abandoned Its Medical Model? Thoughts about the Criminal Insanity Reform Post 22 July' [2021] Crim LR 191–202.

[4] See below in section on 'The Current Regulation of Criminal Incapacity'.

[5] The Norwegian Penal Code (LOV-2005-05-20-28). Available in English at <https://lovdata.no/dokument/LTI/lov/2019-06-21-48> accessed 12 June 2020 (hereafter, the Norwegian Penal code).

[6] See below in 'The Basic Criteria of Included Conditions'.

Linda Gröning, *Criminal Insanity in Norwegian Law* In: *The Insanity Defence.* Edited by: Ronnie Mackay and Warren Brookbanks, Oxford University Press. © Linda Gröning 2022. DOI: 10.1093/oso/9780198854944.003.0013

impairments. In order to provide a proper basis for a comparative discussion, this chapter will include a broader explanation of mental disorder, intellectual disability, and consciousness impairments as different grounds for criminal incapacity in Norwegian law.[7] By drawing on a broader perspective, the discussion will also highlight inconsistencies within the Norwegian law.

The chapter is structured as follows. First, in the following section, an overview of the central approaches and systems in Norwegian insanity law will be provided. The next section will explain the development of the current rules, including the 2020 reform. With this background, the current rules in section 20 of the Penal Code will be presented and discussed in the following section. The final section provides a concluding reflection.

Central Legal Approaches and Systems

In Norwegian law, criminal capacity at the time of the offence is a basic condition for criminal responsibility. What criminal capacity entails is, however, not legally defined and is also considered a difficult matter. Instead, criminal *incapacity* is defined in section 20 of the Penal Code[8] to include conditions amounting to a 'severely deviant state of mind' (cf serious mental disorder), 'severely impaired consciousness', and 'severe mental disability'.[9] When the defendant is considered to lack criminal capacity due to such a condition (that is not a result of self-induced intoxication or incapacity[10]), he or she is fully absolved from criminal responsibility. Unlike some other countries, Norway does not have rules about diminished responsibility.[11]

Criminal insanity/incapacity in Norway is considered an *excuse* in the doctrinal structure of the criminal law. Norwegian law is, in this regard, founded on the *principle of fault* that states that 'only those who could or should have acted differently should be blamed and held criminally responsible'. Conditions that entail criminal incapacity are those where it seems unfair to blame a defendant who has committed an unlawful act—because he or she could not be expected to act differently.

[7] Criminal incapacity due to infancy will not be included in the discussion. See further L Gröning, J Jacobsen, and E Husabø, *Frihet, forbrytelse og straff: En systematisk fremstilling av norsk strafferett* (2nd edn, Fagbokforlaget 2019)492–93 (hereafter Gröning and others, *Frihet, forbrytelse og straff*).

[8] The Norwegian Penal Code (LOV-2005-05-20-28) (n 5).

[9] See below in 'Overview of the Content of Section 20 of the Penal Code'.

[10] The rules about intoxication and incapacity are provided by the Penal Code, s 20 fourth paragraph, see below in 'Overview of the Content of Section 20 of the Penal Code'. These rules are not discussed further in this chapter. For a discussion, see L Gröning and I Myklebust, 'Intoxication and Self-induced Criminal Incapacity in Norwegian Law' (2018) BJCLCJ 68–69 <https://boap.uib.no/index.php/BJCLCJ/article/view/1554> accessed 20 October 2020.

[11] That the defendant suffered from a mental disorder at the time of the act can, however, be a mitigating circumstance in sentencing, cf the Penal Code, s 78(d), and a reason for setting the penalty below the minimum penalty for the relevant crime, cf the Penal Code, s 80(f).

This link to the fault principle is clearly reflected in the Norwegian term for criminal capacity '*skyldevne*', which literally means 'ability to guilt'. Norwegian criminal law emphasizes the fault principle as a basis for the concept of criminal (in)capacity, which has historical connections to German law.[12] In contrast to Germany and most other countries, however, the Norwegian rules concerning criminal incapacity do not imply any assessment in court of how the defendant's condition influenced the commission of the crime. This is a core characteristic of the medical model tradition in Norway that will be further elaborated on below.

The construction of criminal incapacity as an excuse is procedurally different from the insanity *defence* construction in Anglo-American law. In Norway, it is in this context the prosecution, and not the defendant, that bears the burden of proof, and the object of proof is whether the defendant was criminally *capable* at the time of the offence.[13] After considering all available evidence, the court must then determine the issue. The standard of proof is not fully clear from the legal sources,[14] but many argue that it is slightly lower than the general criminal standard requiring that the accused shall be given the benefit of any reasonable doubt.[15] The implications of the experts' diagnostic insecurity, that is, what evidential impact it has when the expert expresses doubt about the defendant's diagnosis, has in this context been debated but not yet fully clarified.[16]

Moreover, forensic experts in Norway can only be appointed by the courts, and not by the parties.[17] Typically, two independent experts are appointed. The minimum requirement for appointment as a psychiatric expert is that the expert is a qualified physician or psychologist and has general authorization.[18] Moreover, at least one of the experts must have approved specialization in a field that is relevant for the forensic examination at issue. If two or more experts are appointed, one of them must also work at least 50% of their time in a clinic or be a specialist in a public forensic unit in a field relevant for the examination.[19] The experts are

[12] See further J Jacobsen, 'Fiksjon uten moral eller konstruksjon uten verdi? Om det ideologiske grunnlaget for straffansvar for juridiske personer' (2009) TFS 52–55. <https://www.idunn.no/tidsskrift_for_strafferett/2009/01/fiksjon_utan_moral_eller_konstruksjon_utan_verdi> accessed 20 October 2020.

[13] The prosecution has, according to the Norwegian Criminal Procedure Act, ss 55 and 226, a duty to be objective. See further Gert Kjelby, *Påtalerett* (1st edn, Cappelen damm 2017) 241–57.

[14] For a review of the discussion in English, see the *Breivik* case (n 1).

[15] See S Asbjørn, *Uskyldspresumsjonen: 'In dubio pro reo'* (Fagbokforlaget 2003) 407 and A Løvlie, *Rettslige faktabegreper* (Gyldendal 2014) 359.

[16] The assessment in the 22 July case (n 1), cf 47–50, was subject to such a debate, and many have expressed the view that the court did in fact apply a lower standard of proof than that required.

[17] Note that also the parties may engage forensic experts, but without a court appointment these have the role of ordinary witnesses. Cf. the Criminal Procedure Act (LOV-1981-05-22-25) section 149, available at <lovdata.no> accessed 20 June 2022.

[18] See the Health Personnel Act (LOV-1999-05-07-34), s 48.

[19] A scientific position may also fulfil this requirement of a clinical position. See regulation about forensic examinations and experts (FOR-2020-09-30-1921), <https://lovdata.no/dokument/LTI/forskrift/2020-09-30-1921> accessed 17 June 2021. This regulation was enacted after the law reform in 2020 and subjects the experts to stricter requirements concerning their qualifications and the content of their report than before. See also below in 'The Role of the Experts'.

expected to follow a two-stage course that is arranged by the Norwegian Board of Forensic Medicine and the National Network for Forensic Psychiatry (SIFER).[20] In recent years, the first stage of this course has had a general focus on forensic medicine, while the second stage has concerned forensic psychiatry in criminal proceedings. The latter has involved learning about the rules about criminal capacity and compulsory care and especially about related clinical evaluations. The course has been provided annually as three-day modules, and each stage has had a total duration of six days. Because of the law reform, and the changed role of the experts, the content of the second stage has now been altered.[21]

The experts deliver their evaluation as a written report, usually 30–40 pages long. To secure a certain quality and a uniform forensic practice, the Norwegian Board of Forensic Medicine controls all evaluations. In 2019, there were 547 psychiatric evaluations, in 2020, there were 652, and in 2021, there were 657 psychiatric evaluations.[22] Only a minority of these result in acquittals by reason of insanity. As in many other countries, Norway does not record complete official statistics about insanity cases tried in courts. My investigations indicate, however, that there are annually fewer than 250 insanity cases that are tried in court, and that most of these result in a conviction.[23] In 2020, there were 50 defendants who were found insane and were sentenced to compulsory psychiatric care and compulsory care (see below about these reactions).[24] In addition, a few defendants are acquitted by reason of insanity without being subjected to any criminal reaction. Anecdotally the number of insanity verdicts seems to have increased since Norway established in 2016 a new type of time-limited compulsory care, provided by section 62 second paragraph of the Penal Code. We also seem to witness a new increase after the insanity law reform in 2020, where the threshold for time-unlimited compulsory care were lowered.[25] By comparison, England has around 30 successful insanity cases per annum, ie, by estimate half as many as Norway, despite a population ten times larger.[26] From a Nordic perspective, however, Norway has a high threshold for insanity.[27] As in many countries, most insanity cases are concluded at first instance,

[20] See The Official Norwegian Report 'NOU 2014:10 Skyldevne, sakkyndighet og samfunnsvern', 219–220 (Ministry of Justice and Public Security, 2020) (hereafter, NOU 2014:10).

[21] See further below in 'The Role of the Experts'.

[22] See the annual reports from the Norwegian Board of Forensic Medicine for further statistics, available at <https://www.sivilrett.no/arsmeldinger.339263.no.html> accessed 12 June 2020.

[23] Many of these cases are available in the database 'lovdata', see <https://lovdata.no/> accessed 2 November 2020.

[24] Of these 50 defendants, 44 were sentenced to compulsory psychiatric care according to section 62 of the Penal Code, and 6 were sentenced to compulsory care for intellectually disabled offenders according to section 63 of the Penal Code. See public criminal statistics at Statistics Norway, available at <www.ssb.no> accessed 20 June 2022.

[25] See below in 'The Breivik Case and the 2020 Legal Reform'.

[26] R Mackay, 'Ten More Years of the Insanity Defence' [2013] Crim LR 946, 948.

[27] See for a comparison of the Nordic countries in NOU 2014:10 66–84 (n 20).

that is, in the district courts. There is, in this regard, a significant variation in the number of cases between different regions in Norway.[28]

According to sections 62 and 63 of the Penal Code, the court may decide to commit a defendant who is acquitted by reason of criminal incapacity, to compulsory psychiatric care and compulsory care for mentally disabled offenders.[29] There are two forms of these reactions. The first is limited to a maximum of three years and can be used for offenders who have 'repeatedly committed offences that are harmful to society or particularly bothersome'. This form of compulsory psychiatric care and compulsory care was established in 2016 and seems, as mentioned above, to have led to an increase in the number of insanity verdicts.[30] The other form is time-unlimited and requires serious criminality and a risk of re-offending.[31]

Compulsory psychiatric care is administered in general psychiatric hospitals under the Mental Health Act.[32] There are no separate forensic hospitals for offenders who are sentenced to compulsory care.[33] Compulsory care for mentally disabled offenders is carried out in special units, but still within the general hospital structure. At the present time, Norway does not have any specific units for compulsory psychiatric care and compulsory care for young offenders, and in the period 2010–2020 only two defendants under the age of 18 have been sentenced to these reactions.[34] In October 2020, an initiative was undertaken to establish such a Unit.[35] It is likely that this will come into existence in the relatively near future. It remains to be seen whether this will also affect the number of insanity cases.

[28] For discussion of this variation, see Ø Holst, 'Samfunnsvernets begrensninger. En kritisk analyse av lovverket for gjennomføring av dom på tvungent psykisk helsevern' [2020] 23–26 (Doctoral thesis, Universitetet i Bergen).

[29] Compulsory psychiatric care is regulated in the Penal Code as a 'criminal sanction that is formally not amounting to a penalty', cf the Penal Code (n 5), ss 29 and 30.

[30] Legislative decision no 46 (2015–16) regarding amendments in the Penal Code.

[31] See further Gröning and others, *Frihet, forbrytelse og straff* (n 7) 658–61.

[32] The Mental Health Care Act (LOV-1999-07-02-62). Available in English at <https://app.uio.no/ub/ujur/oversatte-lover/data/lov-19990702-062-eng.pdf> accessed 30 September 2020.

[33] The Mental Health Act contains, in chapter 5, rules for the treatment of insane offenders. The prosecution authority has a control function. See Ø Holst, 'Court-Ordered Compulsory Care and the Prosecutor's Control Function' (2019) 7(1) BJCLCJ 136–47 <https://boap.uib.no/index.php/BJCLCJ/article/view/2884> accessed 20 October 2020.

[34] The numbers are provided by the Norwegian Civil Affairs Authority, <https://www.sivilrett.no/index.php?cat=305212> accessed 19 October 2020.

[35] This initiative was taken by Helse Vest, the regional health authority in western Norway. See protocol from the board meeting, Helse Bergen Helseforetak, sak 75/20 A, available at <https://helse-bergen.no/om-oss/styret-i-helse-bergen#styredokument-til-styremote-1-oktober-2020> accessed 14 October 2020.

Background and Development

The Medical Model Tradition in Norway

It is difficult to understand the current rules without first considering the specific 'medical model' tradition in Norway. The essence of the medical model is that *insanity is identified exclusively with a medical or biological condition*, such as some kind of mental disorder, intellectual disability, or consciousness impairment.[36] Whether the condition affected the defendant's commission of the crime is not relevant. It is, however, a common misunderstanding that a psychiatric diagnosis, such as schizophrenia, is sufficient. Under the Norwegian medical model criminal incapacity and insanity essentially requires a certain *seriousness and character* of the defendant's mental condition. As an *ideal type regulation model*, the medical model does not require the condition criterion to be specified in 'medical' terms. As we shall see, the early operationalization of the medical model used ordinary language to define the relevant conditions and the new rule reflects an 'ordinary language approach'. To a certain extent, the development of the Norwegian regulation about criminal incapacity also reflects this tension between the medical and legal approaches.

The Norwegian medical model has, however, above all been associated with the previous insanity rule in section 20 of the Penal Code that turned on the medical concept of psychosis. Until 1 October 2020, this rule defined insanity as a matter of being 'psychotic' at the time of the offence. The criterion 'psychotic' was introduced into Norwegian criminal law by an amendment in 1997 of section 44 in the former 1902 Penal Code. The amendment came into force in 2002.[37] The criterion 'psychotic' referred to the medical concept of psychosis, but also stipulated a specific legal threshold for insanity. More precisely, the threshold was that the perpetrator's ability to make a realistic assessment of his or her relationship to the surrounding world was 'significantly impaired'.[38] Commonly, this meant that it was not sufficient that the defendant suffered from a psychotic disorder, but the psychotic condition had to be discernible at the time of the offence through obvious symptoms.[39] Although Norway's requirement that being (actively) psychotic has been *sufficient*

[36] See further L Gröning, UK Haukvik, and KH Melle, 'Criminal Insanity, Psychosis and Impaired Reality Testing in Norwegian Law' [2019] BJCLCJ 27–59. L Gröning and others, 'Remodelling Criminal Insanity: Exploring Philosophical, Legal, and Medical Premises of the Medical Model Used in Norwegian Law' (2022) 81 Int J Law and Psychiatry 101766. <https://boap.uib.no/index.php/BJCLCJ/article/view/2879> accessed 20 October 2020 (hereafter, Gröning and others, 'Criminal Insanity, Psychosis and Impaired Reality Testing in Norwegian Law').

[37] For this amendment see the preparatory work regarding the Penal Code 'Ot. Prp. no. 87 (1993–1994)' (hereafter, Ot Prp no 87).

[38] Ot Prp no 87 (n 37) 22, Official Norwegian rapport 'NOU 1990:5', 38 (Ministry of Justice and Police 1990) NOU 2014:10 (n 20) 49.

[39] See further Gröning and others, *Frihet, forbrytelse og straff* (n 7) 495–96 and Gröning and others, 'Criminal Insanity, Psychosis and Impaired Reality Testing in Norwegian law' (n 36) 27–59.

for insanity is distinct from other jurisdictions, it is not unique for Norway to associate insanity mainly with psychosis. In fact, psychosis is commonly associated with the notion of insanity in western jurisdictions.[40] An interesting comparative research task would be to assess whether countries with mixed-model approaches, in the end associate insanity with mental disorder exclusively, in the same way as Norway.[41]

The medical model, as an ideal type regulation model, has existed for much longer than the criterion psychotic. By 1842 the Criminal Code was to a certain extent built upon a medical model, and it was fully established in 1929 when the 1902 Penal Code was revised.[42] At that time, Norwegian law did not have separate rules for incapacity due to mental disorder and intellectual disability, but regulated these in a common rule, while incapacity due to consciousness impairments was regulated separately. Thus, the structure of the rules more closely resembled current Anglo-American law.

More specifically, in the 1902 Penal Code the relevant legal criterion for criminal insanity was initially '*sinnssyk*', which translated precisely means 'insane'. At the core of the criterion were those who would have been understood today as being psychotic. But the criterion also included intellectual disability of a high degree and serious levels of autism spectrum disorders. This criterion was removed in the 1997 amendment and split into two new criteria, namely, 'psychotic' and 'intellectually disabled to high degree'.[43] The removal of the term 'insane' was to a significant extent based on a desire to move away from unmodern and potentially stigmatising labels, while the new criteria were considered to reflect adequate medical terminology.[44] The criterion about consciousness disturbances remained unchanged. The 1997 version of the criminal incapacity rules was retained without change in the 2005 Penal Code, until the *Breivik* case triggered legal reform.[45] On 1 October 2020, new rules came into force. These rules remove the criterion 'psychotic', and replace it with the 'ordinary language' criterion 'severely deviant state of mind', change the content of the criterion about intellectual disability and provide a new 'two-step structure' for assessing criminal incapacity.[46] As we shall see, however, the new rules also fit within the Norwegian medical model tradition.

Why then a medical model? The establishment of the medical model in Norway was largely justified by arguments about *legal certainty* and an adequate functional

[40] See M Moore, 'The Quest for a Responsible Responsibility Test: Norwegian Insanity Law After Breivik' (2015) 9 Crim Law Philos 645–93 <https://doi.org/10.1007/s11572-014-9305-6>accessed 20 October 2020 (hereafter, Moore, 'The Quest for a Responsible Responsibility Test').

[41] See ibid for a challenging perspective.

[42] For an explanation of the historical development of the medical model, see SA Skålevåg, *Utilregnelighet: En historie om rett og medisin* (Pax forlag 2016) (hereafter, Skålevåg, *Utilregnelighet*).

[43] These were before the 2020 law reform specified in s 20 first paragraph letters b and c.

[44] See further L Gröning, 'Utilregnelighetsreglenes moderne historie' in *Rett i vest—Festskrift til 50-årsjubileet for jurist-utdanningen ved Universitetet i Bergen* (Fagbokforlaget 2019) 317.

[45] See further below in 'The Breivik Case and the 2020 Legal Reform'.

[46] See further below in 'The Current Regulation of Criminal Incapacity'.

division between the legislature and the courts.[47] The preparatory work stated that questions regarding exemption from punishment should depend as little as possible on the judges' own discretion. Therefore, conditions of criminal insanity must be described in terminology which are recognized in psychiatric science.[48] In Norwegian criminal law, this focus on legal certainty and the role of the legislator is generally strong.[49]

Furthermore, the Norwegian medical model is tied to *general justifications for punishment*. More specifically, the justifications for identifying criminal insanity (only) with certain serious disorders have been tied to both retributive and preventive aims of punishment. The principle of fault, that is, that only those who could and should have acted differently can be blamed and punished, has here been a central part of the justification for psychosis as a proxy for insanity.[50] In addition, the justification of the medical model has been related to arguments of crime prevention, that is, that there is no benefit in holding accountable those who are in a severely confused and abnormal state of mind.[51]

Most importantly, the establishment of the medical model must be understood in the light of the *development of psychiatry* in Norway, and its influence on the legal understanding of insanity. The establishment and early development of the medical model in Norway were accompanied by scientific optimism and a belief that insanity could be identified by psychiatry, through scientific methods.[52] To a certain extent, criminal insanity in Norway has solidified through the interplay between judges and experts. The influence of psychiatry in law has been particularly clear since the 1997 amendment and the establishment of the criterion 'psychotic'. This amendment provided a certain 'medicalization' of the insanity problem. During this period the experts have also had a significant role in the determination of insanity cases. According to established practice, the experts have first provided a clinical evaluation of the defendant, including establishing a diagnosis based on the criteria listed in the International Statistical of Diseases and Related Health Problems (ICD-10) manual.[53] Under mandates from the courts, the experts have also evaluated whether the defendant was insane according to the criteria of

[47] On this matter for a comparative perspective, see L Gröning and others, 'Constructing Criminal Insanity: The Roles of Legislators, Judges and Experts in Norway, Sweden and the Netherlands' (2020) 11(3) New J Eur Crim Law 390–410. <https://doi.org/10.1177%2F2032284420950485> accessed 20 October 2020.

[48] See Ot Prp no 87 (n 37) 28. See also NOU 2014:10 (n 20) 91 with further references.

[49] See Gröning and others, *Frihet, Forbrytelse og Straff* (n 7) 63–65.

[50] See NOU 2014:10 (n 20) 111. See further Gröning and others, *Frihet, Forbrytelse og Straff* (n 7) 485–86.

[51] NOU 2014:10 (n 20) 85–86. See also L Gröning and GF Rieber Mohn, 'NOU 2014:10—Proposal for New Rules Regarding Criminal Insanity and Related Issues, Norway post-22 July' (2015) 113 BJCLCJ 109 <https://doi.org/10.15845/bjclcj.v3i1.830> accessed 20 October 2020.

[52] See Skålevåg, *Utilregnelighet* (n 42) 128–29.

[53] This practice involved a distinct recommendation that every person observed should be diagnosed according to the criteria in ICD-10. See the Norwegian Board of Forensic Medicine, Newsletter no 10 (2004). Available at <http://www.sivilrett.no/nyhetsbrev.339568.no.html> accessed 1 October 2020.

the Penal Code, which thus required them to interpret the *legal* meaning of these criteria.[54]

Although judges always have the final say regarding whether a defendant is insane, practice concerning the criterion 'psychotic' shows that judges have relied, to a significant extent, on the experts. In many insanity cases regarding the criterion 'psychotic', the legal verdicts have been justified through clinical and diagnostic evaluations.[55] To a certain extent, insanity has been associated with diagnostic categories. Paranoid schizophrenia has in recent years been the most frequent diagnosis where experts have concluded that the defendant was psychotic and insane.[56]

Despite this 'medicalization' of the insanity problem, the medical model was not subject to much attention, or criticism, until the criminal case of the terrorist attack which happened on 22 July 2011. This case triggered a wide-ranging debate about the Norwegian insanity rules and the criterion 'psychotic'. Eventually, as we shall see, this led to a new emphasis on criminal insanity as a *legal*—and not a medical—problem.

The Breivik Case and the 2020 Legal Reform

Was Breivik driven by ideology or insanity? Was his ability to plan reconcilable with insanity? In the *Breivik* case, two pairs of experts concluded differently about his condition. The first pair of experts that the court appointed evaluated him as psychotic and insane. While there was public pressure to hold him criminally responsible, the court decided to appoint another pair of experts who evaluated him as non-psychotic.[57] The experts' disagreement here reflected the lack of a clear and unified medical understanding of what is required for a psychotic state.[58] Breivik himself wanted to be considered sane.

After reviewing the statements of the experts, along with other medical evidence, the court finally concluded that Breivik was not psychotic, and was therefore

[54] The courts have in previous years used a standard mandate, composed in collaboration between the Prosecutor General, the Court Administration, and the Norwegian Board of Forensic Medicine. For the content of this mandate see the Norwegian Board of Forensic Medicine, Newsletter no 22 (2016), available at <http://www.sivilrett.no/nyhetsbrev.339568.no.html> accessed 12 June 2020.

[55] See further Gröning and others, 'Criminal Insanity, Psychosis and Impaired Reality Testing in Norwegian Law' (n 36) 27–59.

[56] See the annual reports from the Norwegian Board of Forensic Medicine at <https://sivilrett.no/arsmeldinger.339263.no.html> accessed 12 June 2020.

[57] For a discussion of this case, see also I Melle, 'The Breivik Case and What Psychiatrists Can Learn from It' (2013) World Psychiatry 16–21 <DOI: 10.1002/wps.20002> accessed 20 October 2020.

[58] See further Gröning and others, 'Criminal Insanity, Psychosis and Impaired Reality Testing in Norwegian Law' (n 36) 27–59. For a study of how the experts have reported psychosis symptoms, see also PJ Løvgren and others, 'Assessing Psychotic Symptoms in Forensic Evaluations of Criminal Responsibility—A Pilot Study Using the Positive and Negative Syndrome Scale' (2020) 31 J Forens Psychiatry Psychol <https://doi.org/10.1080/14789949.2020.1771402> accessed 20 October 2020.

responsible for his acts. The court reached this conclusion mainly by showing that he did not suffer from a psychotic disorder as defined in ICD-10, rather than clarifying the *legal* threshold for insanity. The judgment was also criticized for being based on incorrect statements that Breivik's ability to plan was hard to reconcile with schizophrenia.[59]

As such, the *Breivik* case revealed to the public how psychiatry influences insanity judgments and triggered a wide-ranging discussion about the adequacy of equating insanity with being 'psychotic'. It was also questioned whether the criterion 'psychotic' provided the experts with too much power in the determination of a defendant's criminal (in)sanity. At the same time, psychiatrists claimed that the lawyers did not have a sufficient understanding of the medical concept of psychosis, and how it has evolved over recent decades.

With the *Breivik* case as a backdrop, the government appointed, by Royal Decree of 25 January 2013, a law commission to investigate the need for change. The commission was asked to review the rules in section 20 of the Penal Code with special emphasis on the psychosis criterion, whilst also addressing the criteria regarding consciousness impairments and mental disability if deemed appropriate. In this context, the commission was also asked to perform a comprehensive assessment of the role of forensic experts.[60]

The commission presented its recommendation on 28 October 2014 in the report NOU 2014:10: *Skyldevne, sakkyndighet og samfunnsvern*.[61] The commission emphasized that the 22 July case ought not to have a decisive effect on the formulation of rules which will usually be applied in much less serious cases. After having considered both aspects of principle and practice, the commission finally proposed only minor changes to the insanity rule. Contrary to the political expectations, the commission proposed to preserve the medical model and the criterion 'psychotic', but with a specification that a certain seriousness of the psychotic condition is required.[62] According to the commission, a pronounced state of psychosis has a significant and confusing effect on the mind.[63] Thus, it is suited to distinguishing

[59] See A Dahl, 'Erklæringer og dom i 22. juli-saken—Hva kan vi lære?' (2013) Tidsskrift for Den norske legeforening 1289–90. <https://tidsskriftet.no/2013/06/kommentarartikkel/erklaeringer-og-dom-i-22-juli-saken-hva-kan-vi-laere> accessed 20 October 2020.

[60] The commission's mandate also involved issues regarding intoxication and criminal incapacity and regarding the rules for compulsory psychiatric care and compulsory care for mentally disabled defendants. For a fuller explanation of the law commission, its mandate, and report, see L Gröning and GF Rieber-Mohn, 'Proposal for New Rules Regarding Criminal Insanity and Related Issues, Norway post-22 July' (2015) BJCLCJ 109–31. <https://boap.uib.no/index.php/BJCLCJ/article/view/830> accessed 20 October 2020. The author of this chapter was a member of this committee.

[61] Excerpts of the report are available in English at <https://www.regjeringen.no/en/dokumenter/nou-2014-10/id2008986/> accessed 12 June 2020.

[62] It should be noted that the author of this chapter criticized the criterion 'psychotic' in an article attached to the report and presented contra-arguments to the decision to keep it, see L Gröning, 'Tilregnelighet og utilregnelighet: Begreper og regler' (2015) attachment to NOU 2014:10 (n 20) <http://bora.uib.no/bitstream/handle/1956/20886/Tilregnelighet+og+utilregnelighet,+Groning,2015.pdf?sequence=4> accessed 20 October 2020.

[63] See NOU 2014:10 (n 20) 110–12, 138–40.

those mentally disordered offenders who should be held accountable, from those who should not. The commission also recalled the tradition of the strong emphasis on legal certainty in Norwegian criminal law, and the view that it is the legislator—and not the judge—who should define the threshold for insanity.

In the commission's view, it would be too narrow to strictly limit insanity to offenders who satisfy the legal definition of psychosis. To avoid unfair convictions, the commission proposed to include conditions that are *equally as serious* as a psychotic condition, measured in relation to disordered thinking, reduced functioning, or distorted reality understanding.[64] The commission proposed no changes in the criteria concerning intellectual disability and consciousness impairments.

Closer to the political expectations than the proposed insanity rule, the commission proposed to change the role of the experts. To reduce their possible influence on insanity judgements, the commission proposed that the experts should limit their participation to their field of expertise. The experts should not conclude on the ultimate issue of whether the law's requirements for insanity are fulfilled.[65]

The commission's proposals were subjected to a broad official hearing by the Norwegian Ministry of Justice and Public Security, where many supported the suggested amendments.[66] However, the proposal to preserve the criterion 'psychotic' was not well received by the government. While the Ministry agreed with the law commission on the role for the experts, it proposed another insanity rule.

The Ministry published its Bill in June 2017.[67] In contrast to the law commission, the Ministry proposed to remove the psychosis criterion, and replace it with the criterion 'serious mental illness'. Contrary to the situation in 1997, the Ministry's Bill expressed the view that the medical terminology 'psychotic' was now inappropriate in an insanity rule and may stigmatize people with psychotic illnesses.[68] This view was also expressed in public hearing of NOU 2014:10 by mental health user organizations and must be taken seriously.[69]

Furthermore, the Ministry proposed an entirely new rule for regulating criminal incapacity and insanity, requiring that the defendant was 'unaccountable due to' his or her condition. The intention here was to provide much room for judicial discretion, and so allow the courts, in the last instance the Supreme Court, to

[64] These conditions have, to a certain extent, been included in the criterion 'psychotic' in previous forensic practice. See NOU 2014:10 (n 20) 123–31, 138–40.

[65] See NOU 2014:10 (n 20) 216–18.

[66] The responses are available at <https://www.regjeringen.no/no/dokumenter/Horing--Tilregnelighetsutvalgets-utredning-NOU-2014-10-Skyldevne-sakkyndighet-og-samfunnsvern/id2341869/> accessed 12 June 2020.

[67] For a commentary on this proposal, see L Gröning, 'Hvordan skal vi avgjøre om alvorlig sinnslidelse innebærer utilregenlighet? Refleksjoner om lovforslaget i Prop. 153 L' (2016–17) BJCLCJ 77–85 <https://doi.org/10.15845/bjclcj.v5i1.1384> accessed 20 October 2020

[68] See Prop 154 L (2016–2017) 66 (hereafter Prop 154 L).

[69] See for an elaboration of this argument, L Gröning, 'Er de norske utilregnelighetsreglene i strid med rettsfølelsen?' in *Rettsfølelsen i strafferettssystemet—perspektiver fra teori og praksis* (Gyldendal Juridisk 2016) 147–65.

define the threshold for insanity. The Ministry described this as a 'new direction for the evaluation of accountability' that can better target those who should reasonably be understood as insane.[70] As such, the Ministry's proposal broke with the long tradition of emphasizing legal certainty and the role of the legislator in Norwegian criminal law.

Mainly for this reason, the Ministry's Bill was widely criticized. It was argued that the lack of statutory certainty and the large room for judicial discretion would result in unequal treatment. It was also questioned why the Ministry had chosen to propose an entirely different rule than the law commission, without subjecting it to a broad public hearing. The majority of the Justice Committee in the Parliament shared these critical views and recommended that the proposal be sent back to the Ministry for further consideration.[71] The minority, which recommended that the Ministry's proposal be enacted, consisted, however, of representatives from the political parties in the government. These parties have the majority in the Parliament. Therefore, the voting in the Parliament was in favour of the proposal, with 52 votes for and 46 against, and it was enacted.[72] In the final version of the rule, the Parliament changed the criterion 'serious mental disorder' to the even more elusive 'severely deviant state of mind', but with no substantive difference intended.[73] Seen in an historical light, however, it is interesting that we are now witnessing a return to ordinary language in Norwegian insanity regulation. The new rule came into force on 1 October 2020.[74]

The Current Regulation of Criminal Incapacity

Overview of the Content of Section 20 of the Penal Code

The current regulation of criminal incapacity is provided by section 20 of the Penal Code that has the following wording:[75]

> A person who at the time of committing the act is under 15 years old, is not criminally liable.

[70] Prop 154 L (n 68) 12–14.

[71] Preparatory work from the Standing Committee on Justice regarding amendments in The Penal Code and Act of Criminal Proceedings 'Innst. 296 L (2018–2019)' 3–4, 8–9 (hereafter, Innst 296 L).

[72] Legislative decision no 60 (2018–19) regarding amendments in the Penal Code and Act of Criminal Proceedings concerning criminal capacity, social protection, and expertise.

[73] This change was made because the criterion 'serious mental disorder', which is also used in mental health legislation, has a meaning other than that intended for the criminal insanity rule. Innst 296 L (n 71) 10, cf Prop 154 L (n 68) 229.

[74] Amendments to the Act of The Penal Code and the Act of Criminal Proceedings (LOV-2019-06-21-48), s 20. Available at <https://lovdata.no/dokument/LTI/lov/2019-06-21-48> accessed 19 October 2020.

[75] The Norwegian Penal Code, official English translation (n 5).

> The same applies to a person who at the time of the act is unaccountable due to a
> a) severely deviant state of mind,
> b) severely impaired consciousness or
> c) severe mental disability
>
> When assessing unaccountability pursuant to the second paragraph, emphasis shall be given to the degree of failure in the person's perception of reality and functional capacity.
>
> A person who is temporally unaccountable as a result of self-induced intoxication, shall not be exempt from punishment, unless special reasons so indicate. A person who has a permanent condition as mentioned in the second paragraph a and who deliberately induces a state of unaccountability, is liable to punishment if special reasons so indicate.

Section 20 of the Penal Code is thus structured into four paragraphs. The first paragraph is the minimum age of criminal capacity, which is 15 years. The second and third paragraphs concern criminal incapacity for defendants over this age, which is the focus for this chapter. The determination of criminal incapacity here requires a *two-step evaluation*.

First, it must be considered whether the defendant's condition fulfils one or more of the criteria specified in the first and second paragraph letters a to c. To note is here that letter c in the original Norwegian version of the Penal Code, the wording is 'high degree of intellectual disability' [høygradig psykisk utviklingshemming], which will be used in the following.

Second, it must be evaluated whether the defendant was 'unaccountable due to' his or her condition. In the third paragraph of the rule, it is prescribed that the emphasis in this evaluation shall be given to the 'degree of failure of the person's perception of reality and functional capacity'. It should be noted here that the Norwegian rule still equates incapacity exclusively with a (sufficiently serious) medical condition. Whether the defendant's condition has affected his or her commission of the crime should not be relevant in the insanity assessment.[76] The required evaluation of the defendant's failure in reality perception and functional capacity thus concerns the seriousness of the disorder, but not how it influenced the specific crime. Finally, the fourth paragraph provides rules for self-induced intoxication and incapacity.

[76] Prop 154 L (n 68) 13.

The Basic Criteria of Included Conditions

Letters a to c in the second paragraph of section 20 provide the so-called 'basic criteria' for criminal incapacity. These criteria are exhaustive and alternative so that the defendant, at the time of the act, must be in a condition that is included in at least one of them to be considered criminally incapable. However, the criteria, as discussed below, may include different kinds of medical conditions and their demarcation is also open to judicial discretion.

The criterion in letter a, 'severely deviant state of mind', primarily targets mental disorder conditions and has replaced the previous criterion 'psychotic'. Psychotic conditions are, however, still at the core of this criterion, which in this regard also should be understood in accordance with previous practice.[77] A diagnosis of a specific psychotic disorder is thus not sufficient, but the psychotic condition must be discernible at the time of the offence through obvious symptoms. In addition, the category includes other disorders *equally serious as being psychotic*, measured in relation to how it affects the functional capacity and perception of reality of the defendant.[78] In the Ministry's Bill, severe autism disorders and dementia are mentioned as possible candidates.[79]

Generally, a 'severely deviant state of mind' can be the result of many different psychiatric and somatic disorders, such as brain tumours or infectious diseases, and what caused the condition is irrelevant. The focus on failures in functional capacity and reality perception also allows for a 'severely deviant state of mind' to be the result not only of one but of several co-existing disorders or dysfunctions. A practical example here concerns young offenders over 15 years who are borderline psychotic and/or mentally disabled (but not sufficiently disabled to qualify for letter c).[80] Since 2017, there have been several cases where young defendants have 'fallen between all stools' and have been considered accountable because they did not qualify for any of the categorical criteria.[81] In this regard, the new rules may result in acquittals in such cases, which in any event will be a significant improvement.

At the same time, it is emphasized in the preparatory work that certain conditions, particularly personality disorders (cf psychopathy), are excluded.[82] The Ministry explained in its Bill that: 'A considerable number of inmates in Norwegian

[77] Innst 296 L (n 71) 10, Prop 154 L (n 68) 229.

[78] Prop 154 L (n 68) 76, 229.

[79] Prop 154 L (n 68) 76, cf NOU 2014:10 (n 20) 112–14.

[80] See also Circular from The Director of Public Prosecutions (no 2) (2020) 5–6.

[81] Of significance are cases where children under the age of 18, and with severe mental dysfunctions, have been sentenced to time-unlimited preventive detention. See the Norwegian Supreme Court (HR-2017-290-A) and (HR-2019-00832-A). For a critical discussion, see L Grøning and HS Sætre, 'Criminal Justice and Detention' (2019) Children's Rights in Norway: An Implementation Paradox? 167–201 <https://doi.org/10.18261/9788215031415-2019-06> accessed 21 October 2020.

[82] Prop 154 L 8 (n 68) 13, 67, 76, cf Innst 296 L (n 71) 13–14.

prisons have different kinds of personality disorders, for instance of dissocial or paranoid type', and that as a rule defendants with these kinds of disorders should not be included.[83] This justification is difficult to accept from a principled point of view and also seems to be inconsistent with the emphasis that the reason for a 'severely deviant state of mind' is irrelevant as long as the defendant's failures are severe enough. Here, Norwegian law rather reflects a traditional folk-psychological view based on the distinction between 'madness' and 'evilness' that in my view should be reconsidered in light of current knowledge about severe personality disorders.[84]

The criterion in letter b has not been subject to any change through the law reform.[85] 'Severely impaired consciousness' still includes both so-called 'absolute unconsciousness' (coma) and 'relative' unconsciousness, where the latter is of most practical relevance for the demarcation of the category. In previous practice, relative unconsciousness has been explained as conditions where 'the connection to one's normal self is broken' and that sensory impressions are not 'registered, processed and stored in the memory'.[86] Such conditions may occur, for instance, due to epilepsy, head injuries, and sleepwalking—disregarding, in contrast to English law, whether the cause was 'internal' or 'external'.[87] Notable, however, is the fact that 'absolute unconsciousness' in most cases implies that the defendant did in fact not commit any criminal *act* at all, and it can be argued that this systematically should be dealt with under the actus reus requirement and not as a part of an excuse. Norway, however, compared to Anglo-American law, has a theoretical tradition with a limited focus and elaboration on the actus reus requirement and thus there remains some work to do.

Finally, *the criterion in letter c*, 'high degree of intellectual disability', was in the previous version of the rule termed 'intellectually disabled to a high degree', but it is not clear whether this terminological change was intended. Nevertheless, the criterion may, in relation to medical categories, include different types and levels of intellectual disability—a condition that is medically characterized by being innate and lifelong. A special legal issue is whether brain damage that occurs in adulthood should be included. Before the law reform in 2020, a condition caused by such brain damage was included by the criterion in letter c, provided that the symptoms were equal to that of intellectual disability.[88] The rule in section 20 then

83 Prop 154 L (n 68) 67.

84 It should also be noted here that the Ministry in its justification relies on views contained in preparatory work from 1974 'to exclude psychopaths'. See Prop 154 L (n 68) 67 with a reference to NOU 1974: 17 61.

85 Prop 154 L (n 68) 229.

86 cf The Norwegian Supreme Court (Rt 2008.549), s 34. See further Gröning and others, *Frihet, forbrytelse og straff* (n 7) 499–500.

87 cf Preparatory work of The Penal Code 'Ot. Prp. Nr. 90 (2003–2004)' 423, Prop 154 L (n 68) 229. On the English approach, see The Law Commission, 'Criminal Liability. Insanity and Automatism, A Discussion Paper', 23 July 2013 (hereafter, The Law Commission 2013) 8 and 105–10.

88 NOU 2014:10 (n 20) 131.

also allowed for a certain 'overlap' between the previous criteria 'psychotic' and 'intellectual disability to a high degree', since brain damage may also result in psychotic conditions. The preparatory work to the current rules, seems however, to have supposed that condition related to brain damage that occurs in adulthood should now be excluded from letter c, and only be relevant for letter a.[89] In my view, such a change blurs the demarcation between these different basic criteria, and may allow for unequal treatment of persons with the same type of and equally severe cognitive impairments. It also seems to imply a medicalization of the criterion in letter c, to include only conditions that can clinically be diagnosed as intellectual disability—contrary to the overall intention of the law reform. However, it remains to be seen how the Supreme Court will solve this issue.

In any case, the criterion in letter c is generally demarked by a guiding IQ limit at 60, which means that a 'high degree of intellectual disability' according to clinical characteristics also includes mild levels of disability.[90] Before the law reform, this limit was 55 and lower. Here, the criterion must, however, be understood in relation to the additional criterion that the defendant was 'unaccountable due to' his or her condition. According to this criterion, an assessment of overall functioning of the defendant is required.[91] The change to a higher IQ limit was also made in order to downplay the significance of IQ and in favour of a stronger emphasis on failure in functional capacities. Thus, in the end, the new rules will not necessarily allow for greater scope for acquittals of intellectually disabled defendants.[92]

The Criterion of 'Not Accountable Due To': An Overall Assessment

It is not sufficient for insanity that the defendant was in a condition that is included in one (or several) of the criteria in letters a to c, but it is also required that the defendant was 'unaccountable due to' this condition. What is required for accountability is not specified in the preparatory work, but here the courts are provided significant scope for discretion. Whether the defendant should be understood as accountable or not will, in the end, be assessed in a concrete evaluation of all relevant circumstances in the case.[93] The additional criterion is also, above all, meant to ensure that the courts can define a reasonable and fair demarcation of criminal incapacity,[94] and must be understood in light of the desire to delimit the power of

[89] Prop 154 L (n 68) 85, 89.
[90] Prop 154 L (n 68) 229.
[91] Prop 154 L (n 68) 89, 229.
[92] There is not yet any Supreme court judgment to clarify this issue, but to note, several district court judgments that have applied the rule as if the threshold is significantly lowered.
[93] Prop 154 L (n 68) 55, 229.
[94] Prop 154 L (n 68) 69.

the experts post the *Breivik* case. As I will return to, the preparatory work, to some extent, also gives the impression that the aim was to provide an insanity rule flexible enough to reach any desired outcome.

Among other civil law countries, Denmark and the Netherlands use insanity rules allowing large judicial discretion.[95] In contrast to the Dutch rule, *some* statutory guidance for the evaluation of whether the defendant was accountable due to his or her condition is, however, provided by the third paragraph of the rule in section 20 of the Penal Code. Here it is prescribed that the emphasis in the evaluation of whether the defendant was accountable or not shall be given to the 'person's degree of failure of perception of reality and functional capacity'.

Still, it is not fully clear from the preparatory work how incapacity should be assessed in relation to these failures and how they relate to the different criteria in letters a to c. It is explained in the Ministry's Bill that a significant failure in *one* of these capacities can be sufficient.[96] For insanity, in relation to letter a, it seems likely that a significant failure of reality perception is what is relevant, as was previously the case with the criterion 'psychotic'. When the defendant has such a serious failure, he or she will, as a general rule, be understood as insane.[97] At the same time, it is explained that it may not be sufficient with psychotic delusions if the defendant's general functioning is 'good enough'.[98] This emphasis that the failure must be of certain seriousness resembles English law on diminished responsibility under section 2(1)(b) of the Homicide Act of 1957, requiring a 'substantial' impairment.[99] It is also a common trait that the specific threshold is not clarified but left to judicial discretion.

In contrast to English law and to the insanity rules of most countries, it is clear from the preparatory work that it is not relevant whether the defendant's condition has affected his or her commission of the crime.[100] In this regard, the core characteristics of the medical model have thus survived the Norwegian law reform.

Another matter is that the character of the crime may impact on the understanding of the defendant's mental condition at the time of the act. The Ministry states, in this regard, that 'it can be hard for the public to accept that a relatively well-functioning person with the ability to plan and execute complicated crimes is not punished'.[101] It is difficult not to associate this with the 22 July case, and the view that defendants who commit such serious crimes should be held accountable,

[95] For the Danish rule, see S Kamber, 'Psykisk syge lovovertrædere i et komparativt lys' (2013) Nordisk tidsskrift for kriminalvidenskab 358–68 <https://doi.org/10.7146/ntfk.v100i3.70154> accessed 20 October 2020, and for the Dutch rule, see Ester Messina and others, 'Forensic Psychiatric Evaluations of Defendants: Italy and the Netherlands Compared' (2019) Int J Law Psychiatry 1–8 <https://doi.org/10.1016/j.ijlp.2019.101473> accessed 20 October 2020.

[96] Prop 154 L (n 68) 230.

[97] Prop 154 L (n 68) 69–70.

[98] Prop 154 L (n 68) 230.

[99] See *R v Golds* [2016] UKSC 61.

[100] Prop 154 L (n 68) 13, 54–55.

[101] Prop 154 L (n 68) 69.

regardless of whether they were severely mentally disordered or not. Hopefully, the Supreme Court's concretization of the insanity rule will be guided by the principle of equal treatment, bearing in mind also that psychotic persons may plan and commit seemingly complicated acts.

While failure in reality perception is most relevant for letter a, failures in functional capacity seem most relevant for assessment of conditions included in letter c, 'high degree of intellectual disability'. The preparatory work explains that failures in functional capacity may concern 'everyday, social and cognitive functions' and that an overall assessment must be done but does not provide any further details.[102] Hence, the court is again left with a wide room for discretion.

For letter b, 'severely impaired consciousness', the preparatory work does not include any explanation at all about how this criterion relates to failures in functional capacity and/or reality perception. From reading the preparatory work, it appears that the additional criteria have no relevance for letter b. A 'severely impaired consciousness' also affects a person so profoundly that if letter b is fulfilled, the defendant will most probably also be understood as 'unaccountable due to' his or her condition. An interesting observation, in this regard, is that this criterion was earlier legally defined and has remained unchanged over several reforms, and has, to a lesser extent than the criteria for incapacity due to mental disorder and intellectual disability, been linked to medical terms.

Thus, the additional criterion seems to fulfil different functions in relation to the different condition criteria in letters a to c. While it may delimit and adjust the relevant norm for incapacity in regard to letter a and c, it seems irrelevant for letter b. The preparatory work also provides far more explanations for letter a than in regard to letters b and c, which makes sense in light of the focus on criminal insanity and mental disorder post-22 July.

The Role of the Experts

Under the new rule, the role of the experts has been changed significantly.[103] They will now only provide a strictly clinical evaluation and should not say anything about the fulfilment of the legal criteria in section 20 second paragraph of the Penal Code. This means that the experts should not assess whether the defendant's condition fulfils one (or several) of the criteria in letters a to c, or whether the defendant was 'unaccountable due to' his or her condition.[104] They are also supposed to avoid

[102] Prop 154 L (n 68) 229.

[103] In addition to their changed role, experts are also subjected to stricter requirements concerning their qualifications and the content of their reports, cf Regulation regarding forensic psychiatric examinations and experts (FOR-2020-09-30-1921) <https://lovdata.no/dokument/LTI/forskrift/2020-09-30-1921> accessed 2 October 2020.

[104] The prosecution agency has taken the view that experts may inform the court about whether the defendant had a medical condition which, according to the preparatory work, is of such a type that it

using expressions that could be *confused* with legal criteria.[105] Their main role will be to inform the court about the defendant's *medical* condition, according to established diagnostic systems, and his or her degree of failure in perfection of reality and functional capacity.[106] On this basis, the court shall determine whether the condition is of such a character and seriousness that it implies criminal incapacity.

Through such a delimitation of the role of the experts, Norway is moving further away from many other countries that allow experts to assess the satisfaction of legal criteria. In fact, it appears that Norwegian law now emphasizes judicial discretion and the independent role of the judge even more than Anglo-American law.

It remains to be seen to what extent the new role of the experts will change how psychiatry influences the legal demarcation of criminal incapacity. After all, there will still be a need to 'translate' medical assessments to answer legal problems. It has been argued that the judges may continue to ask the experts their opinions on whether the defendant was insane or not. As the experts' evaluation will only be provided orally it will be subject to less control than before.[107]

Moreover, the elements that the courts should emphasize in their evaluations, the degree of failure of perception of reality and functional capacity, clearly reflect medical terminology. It is here noteworthy that the Ministry's Bill, while at least making some effort to explain these aspects, does not clarify the meaning of the key legal criterion, namely, that the defendant must be 'unaccountable due to' his or her condition. In this regard, an interesting aspect of the legal reform is that it seems to have a rather ambivalent approach to the significance of 'ordinary language', and how it relates to 'legal' and 'medical' terminology. While the new legal criteria for criminal insanity reflect some belief in ordinary language, the reform seems, after a closer reading still, to emphasize primarily a medical understanding of the insanity problem. To a certain extent, it seems that the reform 'legalizes' psychiatry, rather than clarifies the legal understanding of criminal incapacity. Instead of using ordinary language as a key to linking legal and medical concepts,[108] the new Norwegian position on the role of the experts also seems to uphold a sharp

may fulfil one of the basic criteria in letters a to c. See Circular from The Director of Public Prosecutions (2) (2020) 3–4.

[105] The position of the Norwegian Board of Forensic Medicine is that the experts should use the usual terminology within their disciplines. This may involve terms that are also used in law, such as 'intellectual disability', and experts should then avoid words used in the legal criteria, such as 'high degree of', to grade the seriousness of the condition, and clearly communicate that they are not assessing these. See Newsletter (no 27) (2020). Available at <http://www.sivilrett.no/nyhetsbrev.339568.no.html> accessed 19 October 2020.

[106] See attachment to Newsletter (no 27), 'Mandat for sakkyndig utredning som grunnlag for rettens vurdering av tilregnelighet og fastsetting av straff under minstestraffen eller til en mildere straffart' (2020). Available at <https://www.sivilrett.no/gruppe-for-psykiatri.423980.no.html> accessed 20 October 2020.

[107] See R Rosenqvist, 'Ytring—Et lite klargjørende lovforslag' (2018) Tidsskrift for strafferett 6 <https://www.idunn.no/tidsskrift_for_strafferett/2018/01/ytring> accessed 20 October 2020.

[108] The English position in *R v Golds* (n 99) para 38 is of comparative interest. In that case, it was held that experts should interpret the word *substantially* 'in the sense in which it is used in the courts'.

distinction between the 'medical' and the 'legal'. It is, in my view, precisely this lack of a common ordinary language notion of criminal (in)capacity that has kept the medical model tradition alive and reinforced in Norway.

Concluding Reflections

Norway is a small country on the periphery of Europe. This location might explain why Norway has developed its specific medical model approach to the regulation of criminal incapacity and insanity, and that this model has persisted for over 100 years. As in many other countries, however, legal reform in Norway has been initiated by high-profile criminal cases. The horrendous acts committed by Anders Behring Breivik on 22 July 2011, with the exception of the violence inflicted in wartime, represented the worst crime that Norway has experienced in its modern history and brought with it a strong demand for a political and legal response.

At first sight, the legal reforms post the 22 July case seem to have been profound. From being unique with its medical model it may seem that Norway has now moved closer to other countries, and maybe beyond. In fact, it may seem as if Norway has now swung from one extreme to another—from a medical model that gave priority to the experts, to a model that emphasizes the role of the judge and reclaims insanity as a legal matter.

However, this conclusion must not be drawn too hastily. The discussion in this chapter has shown that the legal reforms in Norway in many ways continue the medical model tradition, although now operationalized through different rules. Although the word 'psychotic' has been removed, insanity will still be determined by the severity of the defendant's mental condition, without any assessment of how this condition influenced the commission of the crime, and psychosis remains central. The experts will still influence the legal determination of the defendant's accountability.

Thus, while the *Breivik* case triggered changes in the legal rules and systems, the deep structural levels of the medical model seem to be more resistant to change. Similar deep structural legal cultural resistance may also explain the difficulties in reaching more radical reforms as in other countries. The attempts to change the English M'Naghten Rules is an example,[109] but generally, contemporary insanity rules are closely tied to the specific organization and development of the different national criminal justice systems.

However, the *Breivik* case also reminded us about the general problems underlying all legal doctrines that limit criminal capacity for mentally disordered offenders—about the law's conceptualization of incapacity and mental disorder

[109] For a recent attempt, see The Law Commission 2013 (n 87).

and their relation. As such, it also triggered my curiosity about unity versus cultural differences across different jurisdictions and regulation models—but it would involve going beyond the limits of this chapter to explore that problem further.

In any case, although the Norwegian medical model has been continued in its core characteristics, it has also been subject to several adjustments. Some of these provide hope for a better future. One central improvement should be emphasized: The new rule may, with its emphasis on the necessity of an overall judicial assessment, downplay the significance of diagnostic categories, in favour of a more nuanced evaluation of the seriousness of the defendant's condition. This allows for a fairer demarcation of criminal incapacity, particularly in cases with young defendants whose psychiatric diagnoses do not properly reflect the severity of the defendant's functional failures.

At the same time, the flexibility of the new rules also causes concerns. The political background for the reform has led to some compromises with requirements of legal certainty and equal treatment. In that light, it may be a good thing after all that the legislature delegated and thus postponed the concretization of the threshold for criminal incapacity to the courts. At least that left us with the hope of further development of Norwegian law in accordance with fundamental constitutional requirements.

14

The Insanity Defence in China

*Lilou Jiang**

The Qiu Xinghua Case: Thrusting Due Process into the Limelight

On 16 July 2006, Qiu Xinghua (邱兴华), a 47-year-old villager from Shaanxi province of China, killed ten people in a Taoist temple near his home, wrote 'deserved to die' on the temple wall using the victims' blood, then fried the abbot's internal organs in a wok and fed them to dogs. He was captured 35 days after the slaughter.[1]

This case aroused national attention: while the public denounced the brutality of the mass murderer, psychiatrists and legal scholars noticed Qiu's disturbing behaviours and questioned his mental state while committing the killing spree.[2] Qiu confessed that he suspected—without any proof—that the abbot had had an affair with his wife, and disclosed that he had made plans to kill his wife, his brothers-in-law, some prostitutes, and finally himself. It was reported that he was grinding his teeth with intense hatred while giving his confessions.[3]

Qiu was sentenced to death with immediate execution in the first instance on 19 October 2006. He appealed but only because he was upset that the first instance court did not confirm that his wife had been cheating on him.[4] On the advice of some psychiatrists, Qiu's wife filed a request for mental evaluation for him claiming

* The author would like to thank Professors Warren Brookbanks, Gerry Ferguson, and Ronnie Mackay for their constructive comments. The views expressed in this chapter are those of the author.

1 T Zhang, '邱兴华案二审维持死刑原判并立即执行' 'Qiu Xinghua's Death Sentence with Immediate Execution Was Upheld in the Second Instance' (*Sina News*, 28 December 2006) <http://news.sina.com.cn/c/l/2006-12-28/091811905087.shtml> accessed 20 November 2020; I Freckelton, 'Reform of Insanity Laws Needed in China: Lessons from the Qiu Xinghua Case' (2007) 14 Psychiatry Psycho & L 1, 4 (hereafter, Freckelton, 'Reform of Insanity Laws').

2 H Cai, '我不是为邱兴华一人奔走' 'I Am Not Advocating for Qiu Xinghua Solely' (*Sina News*, 30 November 2006) <http://news.sina.com.cn/c/2006-11-30/101011662464.shtml> accessed 20 November 2020 (hereafter Cai, 'I Am Not Advocating'); Y Xiao and L Zhang, '法学教授称应为邱兴华做司法精神病鉴定' 'Law Professors Call For a Forensic Psychiatric Assessment for Qiu Xinghua' (*Sina News*, 24 December 2006) <http://news.sina.com.cn/c/l/2006-12-24/030011870129.shtml> accessed 20 November 2020 (hereafter Xiao, 'Law Professors Call For').

3 H Chai and Y Shen, 'The Psychological Profile of a Mass Murderer' *Southern Weekend* (Guangzhou, 23 August 2006) <http://www.zonaeuropa.com/20060829_1.htm> accessed 20 November 2020.

4 C Chen and P Wang, '邱兴华自称身心很健康未考虑做精神鉴定' 'Qiu Xinghua Claimed Being Mentally Well and Had Not Considered Taking Psychiatric Assessment' (*Sina News*, 7 November 2006) <http://news.sina.com.cn/c/l/2006-11-17/060811539721.shtml > accessed 20 November 2020.

Lilou Jiang, *The Insanity Defence in China* In: *The Insanity Defence*. Edited by: Ronnie Mackay and Warren Brookbanks, Oxford University Press. © Lilou Jiang 2022. DOI: 10.1093/oso/9780198854944.003.0014

that his family had a history of psychiatric illness, but Qiu himself resisted.[5] On 11 December 2006, five law professors published a joint open letter calling for a psychiatric assessment for Qiu, in which they declared that they were not advocating for Qiu himself but for procedural justice.[6] In the meantime, however, a prestigious criminal psychologist and consultant to the Ministry of Public Security commented that Qiu probably did not lose control of himself while committing the crime, thus he was criminally responsible.[7] Commentators believed that this psychologist's position was adopted by the appellate court.[8]

The appellate court rejected the request for psychiatric assessment, stating that Qiu was considered to have the cognitive and volitional capacities required for full criminal responsibility in that he had a clear intention of killing, was able to set fires at the scene to cover up, successfully evaded the police, and made consistent statements about his motives and the details of the crime.[9] The appellate court upheld the first instance verdict in full. Qiu was executed on 28 December 2006,[10] three days after which, the Supreme People's Court (SPC) restored its power to review and approve all death sentences handed down by lower courts which had led to a trend of harsh sentencing in the Chinese criminal justice system.

The *Qiu Xinghua* case invoked heated debates across the country regarding (allegedly) mentally ill offenders' access to mental evaluation and their exemption from legal responsibility. The most influential state-run newspaper, *China Daily*, noted in its editorial column that Qiu's execution had 'left an essential question without a convincing answer—was he or was he not mentally ill when he committed the murders? … Justice may have been done in Qiu's case. But it would be much better had it been seen to be done.'[11] The controversies and attention provoked by Qiu's case resulted in a noticeable decrease in official rejections of offenders' requests for psychiatric assessment, which was interpreted as the 'Post Qiu Xinghua case effect' ('后邱兴华案效应').[12]

[5] Cai, 'I Am Not Advocating' (n 2); Xiao, 'Law Professors Call For' (n 2); Freckelton, 'Reform of Insanity Laws' (n 1) 1.

[6] C Xu, '五名法学专家请求司法部门为邱兴华做精神鉴定' 'Five Legal Experts Request the Judicial Authorities to Conduct a Mental Appraisal for Qiu Xinghua' (*Sohu News*, 12 December 2006) accessed 20 November 2020.

[7] Freckelton, 'Reform of Insanity Laws' (n 1) 3.

[8] ibid.

[9] Cai, 'I Am Not Advocating' (n 2); Y Wang, '司法精神病辩护中证明模式的反思与完善' 'Reflection and Improvement of Proof Mode of Insanity Defence' (2016) 24 Evid Sci 459, 463 (hereafter, Wang, 'Reflection and Improvement').

[10] 邱兴华被枪决' 'Qiu Xinghua was Executed by Shooting' (*Sina News*, 29 December 2006), <http://news.sina.com.cn/o/2006-12-29/041310886450s.shtml> accessed 20 November 2020.

[11] 'Case Raises Questions' *China Daily* (Beijing, 29 December 2006) <http://www.china.org.cn/english/GS-e/194373.htm> accessed 20 November 2020.

[12] T Zhao, '精神鉴定何时出现"珍贵范本"—重大命案中的精神病鉴定现状''When Can We Expect a "Precious Template"—The Current Status of Psychiatric Appraisal in Major Homicide Cases' *Southern Weekly* (Guangzhou, 29 April 2010) 3 (hereafter, Zhao, 'When Can We Expect'); S Chen, '论中国死刑案件中的精神病抗辩' 'The Insanity Defense in Capital Cases in China' (2015) 15 J Southwest Uni of PS & L 92, 94 (hereafter, Chen, 'The Insanity Defense').

Certain populations are eligible for leniency due to their peculiar physical and/or mental conditions under Chinese criminal law.[13] Amongst them, mentally ill offenders are the most vulnerable in that they generally do not have the knowledge, the capabilities, or even the will to assert their rights.[14] In a capital punishment retentionist jurisdiction, the insanity defence can be used as an effective tool to protect this specific population from the death penalty. The execution of Qiu, however, reveals the severity of the Chinese criminal justice system, namely that offenders with mental illness who commit homicide are subject to the death penalty in practice.

Scholarly work on the insanity defence has focused heavily on the legislation and practices in the West, whereas in China, one of the most prominent death penalty jurisdictions, it remains understudied. This chapter attempts to shed some light on the insanity defence regime in China. It will present the evolution of the criteria and procedures surrounding the insanity defence, describe the decisive role that psychiatric assessment plays in the proceedings, then reveal why the police or judicial authorities in China are less inclined to order evaluations for serious offenders claiming the insanity defence. It will further examine public perception of the insanity defence and investigate how traditional philosophical thought has shaped the historical punitive attitude towards mentally ill offenders. Finally, it will highlight that since public security concerns override the interests of this special population, this grants the courts a licence to sentence according to the judgment of the court of public opinion, which makes mental illness a matter of life or death in criminal law.

Application of the Insanity Defence

Criteria and Procedures

The first modern criminal law of China was enacted in 1934 stating that 'an act committed by a person who is insane is not punishable'.[15] However, the subsequently enacted criminal procedure law did not provide any guidance on how to determine whether an offender was, in fact, insane.[16] In practice, when questioning

[13] These populations include persons who were not yet 18 years old, or who were 75 or over when they committed their crime, women who were pregnant at the time of trial, deaf-mute or blind wrongdoers, and offenders suffering from mental illness at the time of the offence. See 中华人民共和国刑法 (2020修正) [Criminal Law of the People's Republic of China (2020 Amendment)] Arts 17–19, 49.

[14] eg they are more likely to make false confessions under psychological pressures during police interrogation; the mental issues of some offenders might not be obvious. See LL Jubilut, 'Death Penalty and Mental Illness: The Challenge of Reconciling Human Rights, Criminal Law, and Psychiatric Standards' (2007) 6 Seattle J for SOC Just 353, 353.

[15] 中华民国刑法 [Criminal Code of the Republic of China] Art 19.

[16] 中华民国刑事诉讼法 [The Code of Criminal Procedure of the Republic of China] Art 185.

the mental state of offenders, judges or prosecutors would commission a psychiatric evaluation.

The Chinese Communist Party ended the governance of the Nationalist Party in 1949 and repealed the Nationalist laws and judicial mechanism entirely—including the criminal system. Unfortunately, the Communist government was not able to provide substitute criminal laws for a smooth transition.[17] China experienced an era devoid of criminal legislation from 1949 until the end of the chaotic Cultural Revolution in 1976; the criminal justice context at that time was marked by a lack of stability, predictability, and the rule of law.[18] In a Directive issued in 1956, the SPC established a principle that offenders who had been mentally ill when committing crimes would not bear criminal responsibility. However, sentencing of mentally ill offenders was based on medical diagnosis and interviews with the offenders' colleagues and neighbours, focusing on political grounds.[19] It was not uncommon for religious and political dissidents to be labelled 'political lunatics', and for them to be imprisoned or even executed.[20]

Holding that a codified legal system was of the utmost importance in the maintenance of stability in society and the reconstruction of the country's economic situation after decades of social and political turmoil, the contemporary Chinese government launched the drafting work for major laws and regulations in 1978. Both Chinese criminal law and criminal procedure law were among the first pieces of legislation enacted in 1979.

The 1979 criminal law states that mental illness (精神(疾)病) may be used as a legal defence. In such cases, a person shall be relieved of criminal culpability for his misconduct if at the time of the offence he is unable to recognize or control his conduct as a result of mental disease.[21] This marks the recognition of the insanity defence—'not criminally responsible on account of mental disease' (NCRMD)—as a legal defence to the commission of a crime in the Chinese criminal system. The family members or guardians of offenders found NCRMD are legally obliged to keep them under surveillance and arrange for their medical treatment.[22]

The amendments in 1997 introduced for the first time the concept of psychiatric evaluation into Chinese criminal law: it specifies that mentally ill offenders are free of criminal responsibility fully or in part depending on the offenders' mental

[17] SB Davis, 'The Death Penalty and Legal Reform in the PRC' (1987) 1 J Chinese L 303, 310.

[18] ibid.

[19] The Directive of 'Reply of the Supreme People's Court on the Question of the Handling of Crimes Committed by Mentally Ill Persons' was issued by the SPC on 2 June 1956. Legal norms had collapsed almost entirely during the Cultural Revolution; the validity of the Directive was reiterated after the end of the Cultural Revolution (SPC, Document No 17 [78], 4 August 1978) until the enforcement of Chinese Criminal Law in 1979. This is cited in R Munro, *Dangerous Minds: Political Psychiatry in China Today and its Origins in the Mao Era* (Human Rights Watch 2002) 96.

[20] R Munro, 'Judicial Psychiatry in China and Its Political Abuses' (2000) 14 Colum J Asian L 1, 33 (hereafter, Munro, 'Judicial Psychiatry in China').

[21] 中华人民共和国刑法(1979) [Criminal Law of the People's Republic of China (1979)] Art 15.

[22] ibid.

condition while committing the offence, which should be ascertained through legal appraisal procedures for exemption or mitigation.[23] The wording of the standards for the insanity defence has not altered since then.

The law sets out two separate standards for raising the insanity defence in China, namely when an offender does not have control over his conduct due to mental illness; or when he does not understand that his conduct is socially harmful such that the consequence of conviction by a court is punishment. Criminal law scholars interpret the insanity defence test adopted in China as comparable to a combination of the first limb of the M'Naghten test and the irresistible impulse test used by some jurisdictions in the West.[24] However, the test in China's context does not consider whether an offender is unable to determine that his behaviour is wrong by moral standards or by a violation of law and hence has no ability to form criminal intent, which is the sufficient condition for raising the insanity defence in some western countries.[25] They argue that, by this token, focusing on an offender's awareness of the social harmfulness of his conduct as a sole criterion makes the Chinese insanity defence rule less plausible.[26]

The mental illness exemption in Chinese criminal law is interpreted as being only applicable to offenders with psychiatric disorder;[27] whereas individuals who have lost their ability to recognize or control their conduct due to their own actions (such as voluntary use of alcohol, drugs, or controlled substances) are not eligible for acquittal. There is no statutory definition of 'mental illness' in Chinese criminal law or in any other pertinent legislation.[28] A dominant theory in Chinese criminology is that mental illness falls into three categories, namely: offenders who have been professionally diagnosed with psychosis, those who suffer from moderate or severe intellectual deficiency, and those who show psychotic equivalents.[29] Some commentators have questioned the 'exhaustive' nature of the interpretation

[23] 'A mentally ill person who causes dangerous consequences at a time when he is unable to recognize or unable to control his own conduct is not to bear criminal responsibility after being established through accreditation of legal procedures.... A mentally ill person who commits a crime at a time when he has not yet completely lost his ability to recognize or control his own conduct shall bear criminal responsibility but he may be given a lesser or a mitigated punishment.' See 中华人民共和国刑法(1997修正) [Criminal Law of the People's Republic of China (1997 Amendment)] Art 18.

[24] Z Guo, '刑法中的精神病辩护美国法借鉴' 'A Comparative Study of the Insanity Defense in the US' (2016) 11 Crim System L Science 88, 94 (hereafter, Guo, 'A Comparative Study').

[25] ibid 94–95.

[26] ibid 95.

[27] It is widely acknowledged in legal circles and in society at large that the mental illness defence should apply to individuals whose state of mind, upon evaluation, is either continuously or intermittently abnormal, or individuals who display some abnormalities yet have not completely lost their ability to recognize or control their own conduct. ibid 94.

[28] The term 'mental disorder' (精神障碍) is adopted in the Chinese Mental Health Law and refers to 'disturbances or abnormalities of perception, emotion, thinking or other mental processes that lead to significant psychological distress or to significant impairments in social adaptation or in other types of functioning'. In practice, the two terms are not deemed to be interchangeable. See 中华人民共和国精神卫生法 [Mental Health Law of the People's Republic of China] Art 83.

[29] Z Hu, '精神病人的刑事责任能力(续)' 'Criminal Responsibility of Offenders with Mental Illness (Cont.)' (1998) 4 J L & Med 181 (hereafter, Hu, 'Criminal Responsibility').

of mental illness arguing that more factors that affect people's ability to identify and control their conduct would inevitably be discovered therefore analogues should be applied when determining criminal responsibility.[30] They suggested that the scope of the population with mental illness in the criminal law be expanded to include non-psychotic disorders, but the commonly accepted theory prevailed.[31] The latter is further backed by the statutory exclusion of intoxicated offenders from the insanity defence.[32] In a nutshell, mental illness is narrowly interpreted in the context of criminal prosecution, and mentally ill offenders are usually referred to as being psychotic or intellectually disabled individuals in China whereas substance induced psychosis is not considered as a basis for an insanity defence.

At the same time, the amendments of the criminal procedure law in 1996 established the legal basis for conducting psychiatric assessment by stating that 'persons with expertise shall be assigned or invited to conduct identification or evaluation' and 'medical verification of mental illness shall be conducted by a hospital designated by a provincial government'.[33] This statutory government designation was finally removed in the amendments of the criminal procedure law in 2012. All mental evaluations have been carried out by assessment agencies registered at the Ministry of Justice since 2012.[34]

A dominant legal principle with respect to the insanity defence in China is a presumption of sanity.[35] Correspondingly, a psychiatric examination shall not be initiated unless an offender displays apparent mental abnormalities before and after committing the offence or the offender has a recorded or widely known history of mental disorder.[36]

Psychiatric Assessment of Insanity

In China, only the police, prosecution, and judiciary (collectively called 'the Judicial Organs') have the authority and the duty to initiate mental evaluations in the criminal legal process. Psychiatric assessment is classified as a type of 'forensic

30 Guo, 'A Comparative Study' (n 24) 94.

31 ibid 95; Hu, 'Criminal Responsibility' (n 29) 182.

32 中华人民共和国刑法(2017修正) [Criminal Law of the People's Republic of China (2017 Amendment)] Arts 17, 18, 348, 356; '最高法：严惩吸毒诱发的严重犯罪' [Directive on Severe Punishment for Serious Crimes Induced by Drug Use], issued by the SPC on 26 June 2013.

33 中华人民共和国刑事诉讼法(1996修正) [Criminal Procedure Law of the People's Republic of China (1996 Amendment)] Arts 119–120.

34 全国人大常委会关于司法鉴定管理问题的决定 [Decision of the Standing Committee of the National People's Congress on the Administration of Judicial Authentication] issued on 28 February 2005, Art 3; 中国人民共和国刑事诉讼法(2012修正) [Criminal Procedure Law of the People's Republic of China (2012 Amendment)] Arts 144–145.

35 H Guo, '刑事诉讼中法医精神病鉴定争议的反思与理论诠释' 'Rethinking and Theoretical Interpretation of Disputes over Forensic Psychiatry Appraisal in Criminal Procedures' (2020) Chinese J Forensic Sciences 1, 4 (hereafter, Guo, 'Rethinking and Theoretical Interpretation').

36 ibid.

identification and evaluation' and an investigative measure in Chinese criminal law and follows the Chinese model of 'official-dominated' procedure.[37] A precondition for the police to order a psychiatric assessment is when the suspect is found to have committed acts of violence, endangered the public safety, but likely to be held not criminally liable; whereas the procuratorate or the court can start an evaluation if they notice mental abnormalities in a suspect/defendant.[38] This approach is different from the adversarial model dominant in the common law tradition where the court acts as a referee between the prosecution and the defence, and also from the inquisitorial model in the civil law tradition, where the court actively investigates and collects evidence and places the prosecution and defence in a comparatively subordinate position.

Initiating mental evaluation is deemed to be a legitimate exercise of statutory power of the Judicial Organs which cannot be shared or delegated because 'except as otherwise provided for by law, no other authority, organization, or individual shall exercise such powers'.[39] Additionally, the police and the procuratorates may order an assessment upon the request of a suspect if the latter is able to provide sufficient evidence to raise reasonable doubts of his mental competency and pay the examination fees in full.[40] Such evidence includes, but is not limited to, a history of mental abnormalities or a family history of mental illness; aggressive personalities, impulsive behaviours, and emotional instability in socializing; and mental abnormalities before and after committing the crime.[41] This, however, is to encourage the other party to provide pertinent information to the criminal investigation but should not be interpreted as the burden of proof being shifted onto suspects/defendants. The legal entitlement of the Judicial Organs to initiate mental examination was further emphasized in the 2016 amendments of the rules on the procedures for forensic identification and evaluation.[42] As a remedy measure, suspects/defendants and victims are allowed to request a supplementary assessment or a re-evaluation if they are not satisfied with the result of the original psychiatric

[37] Z Guo, 'Who Should Be Entitled to Initiate a Mental Examination Process? An Empirical Perspective' in M McConville and E Pils (eds), *Comparative Perspectives on Criminal Justice in China* (Edward Elgar 2013) 287.

[38] 公安机关办理刑事案件程序规定 [Procedure Regulations on the Handling of Criminal Cases by Public Security Organs] Art 342; 人民检察院刑事诉讼规则 [Criminal Procedure Rules for People's Procuratorates] Art 333.

[39] 中国人民共和国刑事诉讼法(2012修正) [Criminal Procedure Law of the People's Republic of China (2012 Amendment)] Art 3; Guo, 'Rethinking and Theoretical Interpretation' (n 35) 3.

[40] 公安机关办理刑事案件程序规定(2012修订) [Procedural Regulations on Handling Criminal Cases by Public Security Organs (2012 Amendment)] Art 244; 人民检察院刑事诉讼规则(试行) [Provisional Rules on Criminal Litigation for the People's Procuratorates] Art 367.

[41] D Sun, '对邱兴华杀人案的司法鉴定学反思' 'Reflection on Forensic Identification and Evaluation Based on the Qin Xinghua Cae' (2008) 5 Crim Rev 51, 53.

[42] 司法鉴定程序通则(2016修订) [General Rules on the Procedures for Forensic Identification and Evaluation (2016 Amendment)] Arts 2, 11.

assessment.[43] However, the official rejection of such requests is not subject to appeal.

State legislative actions in the field of forensic psychiatry began in 1984–85 in response to the advocacy of the legal and psychiatric communities for comprehensive legislation on protection for, and (compulsory) treatment of, people with mental health issues.[44] A set of provisional regulations on psychiatric appraisals was enacted between 1989 and 2007 in order to provide guidance on qualification requirements for assessors, how to set up an assessment panel, and what should be included in a psychiatric assessment report, which were further amended in 2015–16.[45]

Specifically, all psychiatric assessments are required to be entrusted to an assessment agency instead of individual psychiatrists. An assessment can be conducted by internal forensic units of the police or the procuratorates following their own ministerial guidelines.[46] External experts are encouraged to become involved to improve the impartiality and transparency of the evaluation process. An individual is deemed to have the statutory qualification to be considered as a psychiatric assessor if he or she possesses a senior professional technical title on forensic appraisal, or possesses professional qualifications related to forensic appraisal or a bachelor's degree or above in related subjects, and has pertinent work experience for more than five years, or possesses significant forensic psychiatry expertise and has more than ten years' work experience in forensic appraisal.[47]

A psychiatric assessment is generally to be conducted by two assessors, although more assessors will be designated for complicated cases.[48] The principal task of the assessors is to ascertain whether the offender was mentally ill at the time of crime; and if so, to identify the nature and severity of the offender's mental illness, explain the connection of the illness with his misconduct, and determine if the offender

[43] 中国人民共和国刑事诉讼法(2018修正) [Criminal Procedure Law of the People's Republic of China (2018 Amendment)] Arts 148, 197.

[44] V Pearson, 'Law, Rights, and Psychiatry in the People's Republic of China' (1992) 15 Int J Law Psychiatry 409, 410.

[45] Said legislation includes 精神疾病司法鉴定暂行规定 [Provisional Regulations on the Psychiatric Evaluation of Mental Illness] promulgated on 11 July 1989; 司法鉴定人登记管理办法 [Registration and Management of Judicial Authenticators] issued on 14 August 2000 and amended in 2005; 司法鉴定程序通则 [General Rules on the Procedures for Forensic Identification and Evaluation] enacted on 31 August 2001, and amended in 2007 and 2016; 全国人大常委会关于司法鉴定管理问题的决定 [Decision of the Standing Committee of the National People's Congress on the Administration of Judicial Authentication] issued on 28 February 2005 and amended in 2015.

[46] 公安部刑事技术鉴定规则 [Public Security Ministry's Regulations on Technical Authentication for Criminal Cases] which came into effect on 1 May 1980; 人民检察院鉴定规则(试行) [Provisional Rules for Forensic Evaluations of the People's Procuratorate], which came into effect on 1 January 2007.

[47] 全国人大常委会关于司法鉴定管理问题的决定 [Decision of the Standing Committee of the National People's Congress on the Administration of Judicial Authentication] Art 4.

[48] 司法鉴定程序通则(2016修订) [General Rules on the Procedures for Forensic Identification and Evaluation (2016 Amendment)] Art 18.

has full, partial, or no criminal responsibility.[49] Assessors shall jointly prepare an assessment report; any dissenting opinions should be noted in the same report.[50]

It is noteworthy that the amendments of the criminal procedure law in 2012 reclassified the conclusion of a psychiatric assessment as expert 'opinions' (意见) to replace the earlier version 'verdict' (结论),[51] and the judicial review role imposed on assessors in verifying the authenticity and legality of materials submitted for assessment was shifted to the Judicial Organs in 2016.[52] That being said, the authoritative status of psychiatric assessment has not changed substantially in practice because of the technically irrefutable nature of an assessment report. The conclusion in a psychiatric assessment report consists of two parts: a medical diagnosis of the assessed offender's mental conditions, and an evaluation of the offender's mental competency for bearing criminal responsibility. In practice, if a judge, who rarely has any medical background, is not able to challenge the medical diagnosis in the report, he has to passively accept the assessor's legal opinion on the offender's mental competency as well, because the latter is an integral part of the conclusion.[53] The probative value of psychiatric assessment and the rubber-stamping position of the courts have strengthened, as a practical matter, the widespread (mis)understanding among the Judicial Organs and the public that psychiatric evaluation has a legally binding effect on court decisions.[54]

Research shows that an average of 15,000 insanity defence cases are brought for psychiatric appraisal per year in China, accounting for 0.3% of the total criminal cases, and over 90% of these assessments were ordered by local police during investigation.[55] Of those, nearly 70% of the assessment results are positive, and over 90% of such findings are accepted by courts, indicating that most assessed offenders have received an insanity verdict.[56] Compared to the 'infrequent use and

[49] 精神疾病司法鉴定暂行规定 [Provisional Regulations on the Psychiatric Evaluation of Mental Illness] Arts 2, 9.

[50] 司法鉴定程序通则(2016修订) [General Rules on the Procedures for Forensic Identification and Evaluation (2016 Amendment)] Art 37.

[51] 中华人民共和国刑事诉讼法(1996修正) [Criminal Procedure Law of the People's Republic of China (1996 Amendment)] Arts 42, 120; 中国人民共和国刑事诉讼法(2012修正) [Criminal Procedure Law of the People's Republic of China (2012 Amendment)] Arts 48, 145.

[52] 司法鉴定程序通则(2016修订) [General Rules on the Procedures for Forensic Identification and Evaluation (2016 Amendment)] Art 12.

[53] L Jiang, 'Accessibility of Psychiatric Assessment for Capital Crime Offenders with Mental Illness in China' (2017) 5 JL Crim J 1, 6 (hereafter, Jiang, 'Accessibility of Psychiatric Assessment').

[54] ibid.

[55] Wang, 'Reflection and Improvement' (n 9) 466; Y Qi and M Kang, '司法精神医学鉴定无精神病74例案例分析及随访' 'Analysis and Follow-up Investigation of 74 Cases Found without Psychosis in Forensic Psychiatric Assessment' (2006) 22 J Forensic Med 135, 136; X Zhong and Y Shi, '司法精神医学鉴定210例的初步分析' 'A Preliminary Analysis of 210 Cases Who Received Forensic Psychiatric Appraisal' (1987) 20 Chinese J Neurology & Psychiatry 139,140; W Chen and L Cheng, '司法精神病鉴定基本问题研究' 'Forensic Examination on Mental Disorder in Criminal Process' (2012) 1 Chinese J of Law 163, 165 (hereafter, Chen and Cheng, 'Forensic Examination').

[56] Chen and Cheng, 'Forensic Examination' (n 55) 166–67; Wang, 'Reflection and Improvement' (n 9) 468; L Zhao and G Ferguson, 'Understanding China's Mental Illness Defense' (2013) 24 Journal Forens Psychiatry Psychol 634, 651.

low success rate' in North America and Europe,[57] China has taken a 'difficult entry, easy exit' (严进宽出) approach to the insanity defence.[58]

Despite the fact that suspects are not entitled to initiate a mental evaluation, studies find that most requests from offenders bearing misdemeanour charges have been approved during the investigation and prosecution process.[59] In high-profile homicide cases, however, a 'selective assessment' phenomenon is noted in that the Judicial Organs hold a tentative attitude and order psychiatric assessments selectively based on discretionary considerations.[60] In practice, the Judicial Organs tend to disregard requests for mental examination when victims are random, military, or police because such crimes generally spark outrage and fear among the public.[61] As such, serious crime offenders are more likely to receive a death sentence despite their mental conditions.[62]

A fundamental concept in understanding the actual operation of the insanity defence in China is that the main judicial yardstick in its use is the theory of harmonious society integrated into the guidelines for the Chinese judicial system at the beginning of this century.[63] The president of the SPC stressed in 2008 that all death penalty decisions should be based on the 'feelings of the people' because it is the only way to unite 'legal effects' and 'social effects'.[64] In its judicial interpretations issued in 2010, the SPC stated that the primary role of courts in sentencing is to resolve social conflicts and maintain social harmony and stability.[65] In weighing leniency and severity, the courts were required to consider 'whether the handling of a given case will win the broad support of the public, maintain social stability, and further contribute to reducing social protest and enhancing social harmony'.[66] Consequently, when handling serious criminal cases, the judicial authorities are

[57] On average less than 1% defendants raise the insanity defence, which is even more rarely successful. JA Lymburner and R Roesch, 'The Insanity Defense: Five Years of Research (1993–1997)' (1999) 22 Int J Law Psychiatry 213, 214–17; R Borum and SM Fulero, 'Empirical Research on the Insanity Defense and Attempted Reforms: Evidence Toward Informed Policy' (1999) 23 Law Hum Behav 375, 378–79.

[58] Wang, 'Reflection and Improvement' (n 9) 466–67.

[59] Chen and Cheng, 'Forensic Examination' (n 55) 166.

[60] Wang, 'Reflection and Improvement' (n 9) 463–64; Zhao, 'When Can We Expect' (n 12); Jiang, 'Accessibility of Psychiatric Assessment' (n 53) 3–6.

[61] Z Guo, 'Procedural Safeguards for Mental Examinations in China's Capital Cases' (2012) 9 Polit Science & L 35, 37.

[62] Typical cases include *Ma Zhongfu* Case (马忠富案), *Xiong Zhenlin* Case (熊振林案), *Zeng Qiangbao* Case (曾强保案), *Xiao Zengming* Case (肖增明案), *Cheng Ruilong* Case (成瑞龙案), *Zheng Minsheng* Case (郑民生案), and *Zhang Koukou* Case (张扣扣案), all of which occurred in 2008–18.

[63] 最高人民法院关于为构建社会主义和谐社会提供司法保障的若干意见 [Opinions of the Supreme People's Court about Providing Judicial Protection for the Construction of Socialist Harmonious Society] Art 18.

[64] *Xinhua News* translated by Ira Belkin. I Belkin, 'Justice in the PRC: How the Chinese Communist Party Has Struggled with Managing Public Opinion and the Administration of Criminal Justice in the Internet Age' in F Sapio and others (eds), *Justice: The China Experience* (Cambridge University Press 2017) 210.

[65] 关于贯彻宽严相济刑事政策的若干意见 [Opinions on Implementing the Criminal Policy of Combining Leniency with Severity] Art 1.

[66] ibid Art 5.

more cautious in initiating a mental evaluation because the majority of offenders who are found NCRMD will be acquitted, which may upset social harmony.

Disposition of the Legally Mentally Ill

The 1997 amendment to Chinese criminal law still placed the legal obligation onto the family members or guardians of offenders found NCRMD for supervision and arrangement of medical treatment of those offenders. Meanwhile, a supplementary provision with respect to the disposition of this population was added that, when necessary, the government shall order compulsory medical treatment for them.[67] However, no legislation or instructive guidelines had been established to define how compulsory hospitalization should be implemented until 2012. Standard procedures for involuntary medical treatment of offenders found NCRMD were codified in the amendments of criminal procedure law in 2012.[68]

Specifically, when it is determined that an offender who is likely to be found NCRMD may continue to pose a danger to public safety, the police shall submit a written request for involuntary medical treatment along with evidence and evaluation opinions to the procuratorate; the latter shall review the request and, if it agrees, shall file an application for involuntary medical treatment with the court.[69] A collegiate bench shall be convened in the court for the hearing; the prosecutor and the legal representative of the defendant are to be present. The bench is generally composed of three members—either three judges, or some combination of judge(s) and people's assessor(s).[70] If the court finds that the defendant meets the conditions for involuntary medical treatment, it shall order the defendant be detained in a psychiatric facility.[71] The police are accorded the powers—before the court renders its decision—to take temporary protective restraint measures to detain or hospitalize mentally ill offenders who have committed acts of violence.[72] The psychiatric facilities are required to regularly examine and assess the mental status of patients subject to compulsory medical treatment; they can propose a termination of the hospitalization for patients who are considered to no

[67] 中华人民共和国刑法(1997修正) [Criminal Law of the People's Republic of China (1997 Amendment)] Art 18.

[68] 中国人民共和国刑事诉讼法(2012修正) [Criminal Procedure Law of the People's Republic of China (2012 Amendment)] Arts 284–289.

[69] ibid Arts 284–285.

[70] ibid Arts 178, 286. The people's assessors in a three-member collegial panel function as judges and have the authority to decide both issues of facts and law. 中国人民共和国人民陪审员法 [People's Assessors Law of the People's Republic of China (2018)] Art 21.

[71] 中国人民共和国刑事诉讼法(2012修正) [Criminal Procedure Law of the People's Republic of China (2012 Amendment)] Art 287.

[72] ibid Art 285; 公安机关办理刑事案件程序规定 [Procedure Regulations on the Handling of Criminal Cases by Public Security Organs] Art 333.

longer pose a danger to society and discharge them upon the court's approval.[73] The procuratorate is the presiding authority to oversee the execution of the court's order and the administering of involuntary medical treatment.[74]

Notwithstanding the legal guidance on compulsory medical treatment, a significant discrepancy has been observed between the law as written and the law as applied in this respect, which is due to multiple factors. There is a total of 1,650 mental health facilities in China offering 228,000 beds with an average of 1.71 beds per 10,000 population, whereas the global average is 4.36 beds per 10,000 population.[75] Currently about 20,000 psychiatrists are practising across the country serving over 4.3 million people with severe mental disorders.[76] Scarce resources constitute a barrier to involuntary medical treatment for eligible offenders. For example, only 15.7% of eligible offenders found NCRMD were admitted for compulsory medical treatment in Hunan province in 2005–09.[77]

In addition, even offender patients who are admitted for compulsory treatment are unlikely to receive medical treatment for as long as needed. The law does not clearly indicate whether the government should underwrite—and which government agency should pay for—the hospitalization and subsequent medical treatment: offenders' families pay the bills in most cases; the majority of patients have to return home in one or two years when their families can no longer afford to pay expenses. It is noteworthy that the families or guardians of offenders found NCRMD bear the primary responsibilities to supervise and seek medical treatment for the latter; these two groups are mentioned first in the relevant provisions in Chinese criminal law whereas the role of the government is subsequent.[78]

The situation described above contributes to a pervasive belief in China that a successful insanity defence usually results in freedom. Offenders who raise the insanity defence in China are not confronting a dilemma as their counterparts do in the West: whether to go to jail or to be confined in a locked mental hospital for perhaps as much time as they would have spent in prison following a conviction.[79]

[73] 中国人民共和国刑事诉讼法(2012修正) [Criminal Procedure Law of the People's Republic of China (2012 Amendment)] Art 288; 公安机关办理刑事案件程序规定 [Procedure Regulations on the Handling of Criminal Cases by Public Security Organs] Art 345.

[74] 中国人民共和国刑事诉讼法(2012修正) [Criminal Procedure Law of the People's Republic of China (2012 Amendment)] Art 289; 公安机关办理刑事案件程序规定 [Procedure Regulations on the Handling of Criminal Cases by Public Security Organs] Art 345.

[75] 全国精神卫生工作规划 (2015–2020年) [National Mental Health Work Plan 2015–2020].

[76] ibid.

[77] Chen, 'The Insanity Defense' (n 12) 100.

[78] 中华人民共和国刑法(2017修正) [Criminal Law of the People's Republic of China (2017 Amendment)] Art 18. For further discussion, please see L Xing, 'The Rhyme of History: A Transition of Legal Culture in China Crowned by the Criminal Procedure Law 2012' (2015) 23 Asia Pac L Rev 31, 57. Word order matters when interpreting Chinese laws and policies: the families and guardians of mentally ill offenders are put ahead of the government in the related articles in Chinese criminal law. See also M Lewis, 'Leniency and Severity in China's Death Penalty Debate' (2011) 24 Colum J Asian L 303, 318.

[79] Jiang, 'Accessibility of Psychiatric Assessment' (n 53) 6.

In effect, it is not uncommon that offenders attempt to escape deserved punishment by relying on the insanity defence.[80] For example, Yang Yiyong (杨义勇), a gang chief in Hubei province, was arrested in 2000 for killing a person whom he 'disliked' (看不顺眼). Yang requested a psychiatric assessment and was assessed to be 'suffering intermittent psychosis, not to bear criminal liability' by bribing the assessors. Yang was then admitted for compulsory medical treatment but discharged in two months. Yang boasted that the psychiatric assessment report was his licence for killing. He was sentenced to death in a province-wide campaign against gang crime in 2002. By then, he had seriously injured and murdered a total of 47 people together with his gang members.[81] Additionally, one of the most notorious corruption cases in 2009 revealed that six psychiatrists at the An Kang Hospital (安康医院) in Inner Mongolia province—the only psychiatric hospital in that province qualified to conduct compulsory medical treatment—had taken bribes to provide false assessment reports over many years to help serious crime offenders evade punishment.[82]

Psychiatric assessment is the subject of much debate in China due to its decisive role in securing acquittal, regardless of the serious consequences caused by criminal behaviours. There is public concern that criminals may feign mental illness to manipulate the criminal justice system. The judicial authorities, on the other hand, have struggled with developing a balance to protect the mentally ill, to combat false claims of insanity, and to maintain public confidence in the administration of criminal justice. Although mental illness is a legitimate mitigating factor, it can turn into an aggravating factor in cases where social order and public safety are the paramount concern of the courts.

Consider, for example, the *Nanjing BMW Crash* case: Wang Jijin (王季进) crashed into another vehicle and killed two people on the spot when he was driving a BMW at 195km per hour on a road with a 60 km/h limit in Nanjing, Jiangsu province in 2015. He fled the scene but was caught soon after. The police noticed Wang's behavioural abnormalities and ordered a psychiatric assessment for him; he was diagnosed as 'suffering from acute transient psychotic disorder at the time of the crime and had limited criminal liability', which provoked a lot of questioning on whether the police were using the mental evaluation process to help the privileged offender evade a deserved punishment, as the BMW is one of the most ostentatious symbols of wealth in China. A re-assessment was conducted soon after upon the victims' request, which upheld the conclusion of the first evaluation. Nevertheless,

80 Chen, 'The Insanity Defense' (n 12) 98.

81 '湖北松滋黑团伙主犯被枪决 曾自诩有"杀人执照"' 'The Gang Chief Who Boasted Holding a Killing License Was Executed by Shooting in Songzi Hubei Province' (*Sina News*, 7 June 2002) <http://news.sina.com.cn/c/2002-06-07/1106598567.html> accessed 18 November 2020; '精神病鉴定是"犯罪执照"吗?' 'Is Psychiatric Assessment Report a License for Crimes?' *Women of China* (Beijing, 6 June 2016) <http://www.womenofchina.com/flbz/2020/1109/2531.html> accessed 24 June 2022.

82 Heyan Wang, '操纵司法鉴定: 内蒙古窝案' 'Manipulating Forensic Assessment: A Group Crime in Inner Mongolia' (2010) 2 New Century Weekly 86, 87–91.

in order to pacify the public, Wang was charged with threatening public security—a crime eligible for the death penalty—instead of the traffic offence for which he was initially arrested, generally calling for between three and seven years' imprisonment; he was eventually sentenced to 11 years' imprisonment.[83]

The general public in China is actually quite ambivalent towards lawbreakers with mental illness.[84] On one hand, they admit that mentally ill offenders should be exempted from criminal accountability fully or in part. On the other hand, they are worried that the insanity defence may be abused to shield criminals from justice.

A paradox arises whenever a serious crime involving horrific violence occurs, as demonstrated in the *Liu Aibing* case (刘爱兵案), in which Liu killed 13 of his close relatives. He was sentenced to death with immediate execution despite apparent mental abnormalities. The psychiatric assessment concluded that Liu had a paranoid personality disorder but this did not affect his full criminal responsibility. One of the psychiatrists explained in an interview that, when conducting mental assessments for high-profile cases, they would consider the special circumstances of the cases; if a heinous offender like Liu is assessed with mental illness, he would be sent to compulsory medical treatment because of his ongoing danger to society, which may ignite public indignation and impose significant financial burden to the local government.[85] This resonates with one psychiatrist's ironical critiques of the flawed psychiatric assessment system that 'when dealing with offenders who might be mentally ill but with low social standing, incarceration and even execution is the most expedient solution.'[86] In fact, the punitive attitude towards mentally ill offenders in Chinese society has deep historical roots as examined in the next section.

Stigma of Mental Illness in Chinese Society

Studies indicate that traditional Chinese people had a two-level explanation describing a person's mental illness, in which the first level was articulated in

[83] The details of the case can be found in: '南京宝马案肇事者危害公共安全判11年' 'The Offender in Nanjing BMW Crash Case Was Sentenced to 11 Years of Imprisonment for Threatening Public Security' (*Sohu News*, 2 April 2017) <https://www.sohu.com/a/131699473_260616> accessed 18 November 2020; 'Car Involved in Fatal Crash Was Going at 195 km/h' *China Daily* (Beijing, 30 June 2015) <https://www.chinadaily.com.cn/china/2015-06/30/content_21141676.htm> accessed 18 November 2020; D Tang, 'Chinese Jeers over BMW Crash Probe Highlight "Trust Crisis"' (*The Hour*, 11 September 2015) <https://www.thehour.com/nation/article/Chinese-jeers-over-BMW-crash-probe-highlight-8062103.php> accessed 18 November 2020; Guo, 'A Comparative Study' (n 24) 94.

[84] Jiang, 'Accessibility of Psychiatric Assessment' (n 53) 7.

[85] Chen, 'The Insanity Defense' (n 12) 98; L Chen, '"刘爱兵杀13人案"背后的精神病悬疑' 'Questioning the Mental Illness Evaluation behind the "Liu Aibing Killing 13 People Case"' Southern People Weekly Magazine (Guangzhou, 12 June 2010) <http://news.sohu.com/20100612/n272747582.shtml> accessed 24 June 2022.

[86] Cai, 'I Am Not Advocating' (n 2).

traditional Chinese medical theories, whereas the second level was attributing the illness to supernatural forces.[87] When someone began behaving abnormally, people in the local community would usually say that the person was sick and suggest that he or she see a doctor of traditional Chinese medicine. Traditional Chinese medicine has accumulated a wealth of knowledge concerning mental illness: as early as in the 1st century, mental illness symptoms were already described in the oldest Chinese medical text—*the Yellow Emperor's Manual of Corporeal Medicine* (黄帝内经).[88] In the following two thousand years, doctors' understanding with regard to the disease etiology and their cures was gradually added to this classic book.[89] Chinese people believed certain madness symptoms were caused by Yin-Yang imbalance (阴阳失调)—a breakdown of the internal environment of the human body and a disharmony of a person's body and soul. It was believed that such an imbalance could be relieved using Chinese herbal medicine and/or acupuncture, especially at the incipient stage.[90]

But if a patient's symptoms were not mitigated after taking traditional Chinese medicine, people would turn to the second level, seeking supernatural explanations of the origin of illness. Widely held attributions to mental illness included retribution for wrongful conduct, being possessed by evil spirits, and the soul's separation from the human body.[91] At this stage, patients and their families no longer expected much from the medical treatment; rather, they placed their hope in folk-remedies, prayers, charity, sacrifices, restitutions, and rites of exorcism.[92]

The public's attitude towards mental patients would become less empathetic and tolerant along with the deterioration of the patients' symptoms. When the patients were at the first stage, people provided them with care and sympathy. Once the patients were cured, they would be accepted by society and resume their normal life. But when the patients entered the second stage, people would think that the patients themselves were to blame for the mental illness. The prevailing belief was that the patients (or their family members) must have committed some sins in previous and present lives, or that they were possessed by some demonic spirits due to their inferior physical conditions or inappropriate desires, or that they were not able to exercise self-control because of weak personalities.[93] In this way, mental illness was stigmatized.

87 VW Ng, *Madness in Late Imperial China: From illness to Deviance* (University of Oklahoma Press 1990) 28 (hereafter, Ng, *Madness in Late Imperial China*).

88 ibid.

89 ibid 28, 33.

90 ibid 33–37.

91 ibid 51.

92 ibid.

93 T Abdullah and TL Brown, 'Mental Illness Stigma and Ethnocultural Beliefs, Values, and Norms: An Integrative Review' (2011) 31 Clinical Psychol Rev 934, 941 (hereafter, Abdullah and Brown, 'Mental Illness Stigma'). It is argued that this belief has a connection with *Samsara* in Buddhism asserting that people's behaviours in this life shall determine their reincarnation. See CS Lam and others, 'Chinese Lay Theory and Mental Illness Stigma: Implications for Research and Practices' (2010) 76 J of Rehabilitation 35, 36 (hereafter, Lam and others, 'Chinese Lay Theory').

The terms '*dian*' (癫), '*kuang*' (狂), and '*feng*' (疯) were used to describe mental illness in traditional China, and later were adopted in official standards.[94] *Dian* means 'insane without excitation or epileptic', *kuang* means 'raging, unpredictable wildness', and *feng* is 'mad or crazy'.[95] Some psychological illness, which was frequently associated with passive or non-aggressive symptoms, such as 'depression', was generally considered to be caused by weakness in the patients' spiritual strength instead of by mental illness.[96] While growing up, children were repeatedly reminded that mentally ill people were ridiculous, violent, and dangerous, and should be kept at a distance.[97] In this way, the public stigma was amplified. People with mental illness used to be described as 'a very helpless class'[98] and their families had either to hide the fact of the mental illness, or to live with shamefulness in a hostile and discriminatory environment once the truth was exposed.[99]

The historical family system in Chinese society naturally means that families are the primary care providers for mentally ill people. Living in a continental country, ancient Chinese farmers had to stick to their land for survival, and so did their descendants, because the land could not be moved.[100] Additionally, the family had to live together for economic considerations, meaning an individual lived with his grandparents, parents, uncles, and cousins.[101] With economic conditions as its basis, the ethical significance of this family system was further enhanced by Confucianism which has been the dominant philosophy in Chinese society over the past two thousand years.[102]

A primary Confucian theory is that stable social relationships can build up and maintain an orderly and harmonious society.[103] The fundamental social relations defined in Confucianism are *Wulun* (五伦, five cardinal relations), namely ruler-subjects (君臣), parents-offspring (父子), husband-wife (夫妇), siblings (兄弟),

[94] The term *dian* appeared the first time in *Shi* (《诗经》, The Book of Songs) and *kuang* in *Shangshu Weizi* (《尚书•微子》, The Book of Historical Documents). '*dian*', '*kuang*', and '*feng*' were taken as medical terms for mental illness in *Kang-Xi* Dictionary, an encyclopaedia compiled in 1716 BC pursuant to the order of Emperor Kang-Xi of the Qing dynasty. See J-K T'ien, 'Traditional Chinese Beliefs and Attitudes Toward Mental Illness' in W-S Tseng and DYH Wu (eds), *Chinese Culture and Mental Health* (Academic Press 1985) 68.

[95] ibid; Ng, 'Madness in Late Imperial China' (n 87) 37.

[96] Lam and others, 'Chinese Lay Theory' (n 93) 36.

[97] Abdullah and Brown, 'Mental Illness Stigma' (n 93) 939.

[98] RD Lamson, *Social Pathology in China: A Source Book from the Study of Problems of Livelihood, Health, and the Family* (Commercial Press 1935) 416–17.

[99] V Pearson, 'Families in China: An Undervalued Resource for Mental Health?' (1993) 15 J of Family Therapy 163, 167.

[100] F Yu-Lan and D Bodde (eds), *A Short History of Chinese Philosophy* (The Free Press 1948) 21 (hereafter, Fung and Bodde, *A Short History*).

[101] ibid.

[102] ibid 30. The Confucianist school was founded by Confucius (孔子, 551–479 BC). The body of Confucian philosophy theories was developed and expanded by his followers; Confucianism had become the main stream Chinese thought by the third century BC.

[103] Lam and others, 'Chinese Lay Theory' (n 93) 36.

and friends (朋友), three of which are family relationships while ruler-subjects is considered to be on par with parents-offspring and friends with siblings.[104]

According to Confucianism, people's humanity is verified and signified by their social relations and responsibilities;[105] a decent person is supposed to manage his social relationships appropriately based on his virtues which are rendered in his conduct in accordance with *Li* (礼)—the social and legal norms of contemporary society.[106] That is to say, a respectable person should show his humanity in his behaviours which are recognized to be appropriate and acceptable in his temporal social context. From the Confucian perspective, people with mental illness do not possess the fundamental Confucian ethics and virtues of human beings, and therefore are not able to maintain positive social relationships. Rather, they pose a threat to social order and harmony.

The low tolerance of mental illness in mainstream society certainly contributed to the harsh legal treatment of mentally ill offenders in imperial China.[107] Han Feizi (韩非子, 280–233 BC), a prestigious legal philosopher in ancient China, stressed that 'a psychotic cannot escape from punishment according to the law' (狂则不免人间法令之祸).[108] Han's strong attitude set up a cornerstone for the legal tradition in dealing with offenders with mental illness. In the Han dynasty (202 BC–220 AD), for instance, mentally ill offenders would be executed publicly for killing their parents or siblings, which was a severe violation of a Confucian ethic—filial piety.[109]

Compared to physically disabled offenders, mentally ill offenders received less leniency in criminal law since their wrongdoing was considered to be due to deviance instead of an unhealthy condition of their body or mind.[110] The mental state of offenders had not been considered in the imperial criminal law until the 17th century, and even then the added legal provisions focused mainly on isolation and punishment.[111] Since family was the core unit of the Chinese social universe, the responsibilities for mentally ill people naturally fell upon their families.[112] Taking the last imperial dynasty, Qing (清朝, 1644–1911), as an example, families were ordered to confine their mentally ill family members strictly and registered their

104 《孟子•梁惠王上》 Mencius: *LiangHuiWang Shang*.

105 M-YM Yuen, 'Human Rights in China: Examining the Human Rights Values in Chinese Confucian Ethics and Roman Catholic Social Teachings' (2013) 8 Intercultural Hum Rts L Rev 281, 292.

106 ibid 293.

107 Fung and Bodde, *A Short History* (n 100) 38; D Bodde, 'Dominant Ideas in the Formation of Chinese Culture' (1942) 62 JAOS 293; H Lu and TD Miethe, *China's Death Penalty: History, Law, and Contemporary Practices* (Routledge 2007) 29.

108 X Liu, 'Psychiatry in Traditional Chinese Medicine' (1981) 138 British J of Psychiatry 429.

109 Lam and others, 'Chinese Lay Theory' (n 93) 37.

110 T Jiang, '中国古代精神病人犯罪法探析' 'On the Law of Psychopath Crime of Ancient China' (2005) 190 The Northern Forum 151, 154.

111 Ng, 'Madness in Late Imperial China' (n 87) 67.

112 ibid 16.

names at the local government authorities.[113] Whenever a mentally ill person committed an offence, his family would be punished collectively.[114]

Although modern Chinese people no longer live in extended family relationships, the Confucian conception of the family system lives on. Thus, families are culturally obligated to supervise mentally ill people and pay for the required medical treatment. Mental health services, financial, or moral support are rarely provided by the government or society. Meanwhile, there is a lack of an understanding of the influence of mental illness on people's behaviours in contemporary China, because public mental health education is still a poorly explored area. Influenced by the stigma, most mentally ill people and their families are less respected and isolated in their communities.[115]

Conclusion

The historically punitive attitude in Chinese society towards mentally ill offenders has persisted through to the present day, as demonstrated in contemporary criminal practices: the Judicial Organs selectively omit psychiatric assessment procedures in their handling of high-profile criminal cases, and the insanity defence has not effectively guaranteed that mentally ill offenders will be treated with leniency. In a society that was immersed in a harsh legal tradition for two thousand years, promoting a more willing acceptance of the insanity defence in the mindset of people is inevitably challenging. The prioritization of social stability and the concession to popular justice in the Chinese criminal system in effect have hindered mentally ill offenders' access to a reliable insanity defence and potential exemption from the death penalty.

[113] ibid.

[114] Munro, 'Judicial Psychiatry in China' (n 20) 15.

[115] Abdullah and Brown, 'Mental Illness Stigma' (n 93) 937; G Ferguson, 'Legal Regulation of Mental Disorder: Looking East and West' in DM Johnston and G Ferguson (eds), *Asia-Pacific Legal Development* (UBC Press 1998) 279.

15

The Insanity Defence under International Criminal Law

Ian Freckelton and Magda Karagiannakis[*]

Introduction

Persons who plan, lead, and organize genocide, crimes against humanity, and war crimes are often assumed by laypersons to be insane.[1] If this were actually so, it may have been expected that the defence of insanity in international criminal law might have been invoked successfully by the leaders and middle managers of atrocities before international criminal courts and tribunals established since the Second World War. However, the opposite is true. The defence of insanity had not been explicitly recognized as a defence in the constitutive documents of the post-Second World War courts until it was included in the Rome Statute of the International Criminal Court (ICC) which came into force in 2002.[2] Even when this defence was implicitly or explicitly available, it was not often pleaded and, when pleaded, it was not successful.

The reasons for this are multifactorial and include that the leaders and middle managers of atrocity crimes are often high-functioning, intelligent, and well-organized political and military perpetrators who are unlikely to be suffering from a serious mental disorder;[3] they are more likely to be psychopaths.[4] Another reason is that the insanity defence was only implicit until the first explicit definition of insanity in the Rome Statute. This requires a very high threshold to be met

[*] Dr Karagiannakis acknowledges the assistance of a La Trobe University Social Research Platform Grant in assisting her contribution to this chapter.

[1] See I Xavier, 'The Incongruity of the Rome Statute Insanity Defence and International Crime' (2016) 14 J Int Crim Justice 793, 793.

[2] See P Chifflet and I Freckelton, 'The Mental Incapacity Defence in International Criminal Law: Ramifications from the Ongwen Judgment' [2022] Int Crim Law Rev 1–29. <https://brill.com/view/journals/icla/aop/article-10.1163-15718123-bja10138/article-10.1163-15718123-bja10138.xml>

[3] ibid 794.

[4] See M Linden and D Wetham, 'How We Discovered a Personality Linked to War Crimes' (4 February 2020) The Conversation <https://theconversation.com/how-we-discovered-a-personality-profile-linked-to-war-crimes-130622>; DA Popovic and others, 'On Behavior of Psychopaths under War Conditions' (2016) 8(8) Int J Curr Res 37489–96; SN Romanium, 'Psychopaths and Sociopaths in Wartime' in P Joseph (ed), *The SAGE Encyclopaedia of War: Social Science Perspectives* (Sage 2017); I Areh, A Sotlar, and S Zgaga, 'Some Psychological and Law Features of the Insanity Defence m War Crimes Trials in Europe' (2016) 66(1) Zbornik Pravnog Fakulteta u Zagrebu 87.

Ian Freckelton and Magda Karagiannakis, *The Insanity Defence under International Criminal Law* In: *The Insanity Defence*. Edited by: Ronnie Mackay and Warren Brookbanks, Oxford University Press. © Ian Freckelton and Magda Karagiannakis 2022. DOI: 10.1093/oso/9780198854944.003.0015

before the defence can be invoked successfully—the perpetrator's mental capacity, as discussed below,—must have been 'destroyed' at the time of committing their acts. A consequence of these factors is that defendants have been more likely to assert mental impairment as a plea in mitigation of sentence than to plead insanity. However, even in this context courts have not often been satisfied that accused persons suffered from conditions that diminished their moral culpability at the time of offending. As a result, such pleas have tended not to result in discounts in sentencing.

Because the defence of insanity was not specifically provided for by the Charter of the International Military Tribunal, which formed the basis for the Nuremberg trials, this contributed to the mixing of the concepts of incapacity for trial and criminal incapacity by virtue of insanity, both issues often being raised simultaneously. Subsequently, the statutes of the International Criminal Tribunal for the Former Yugoslavia (ICTY) and for Rwanda (ICTR)[5] also did not provide a basis for a mental illness defence,[6] thereby requiring reliance on the rules of procedure and evidence to ensure that persons who were manifestly psychotic were not coerced to trial.[7]

However, insanity (also known as 'mental impairment' and 'mental incapacity') was the subject of extensive discussion in the lead-up to the Rome Conference leading to the formation of the ICC. It resulted in the creation of a defence under Article 31 of the Rome Statute with its being framed as a 'ground excluding criminal responsibility' that has both cognitive and volitional components but is not easily invoked—a person must suffer from a 'mental disease or defect' that 'destroys' that person's capacity to appreciate the unlawfulness or nature of his or her conduct, or the person's capacity to control his or her conduct to conform to the requirements of law. The requirement of destruction of either facility imposes a very heavy burden on an accused person seeking to invoke the defence.

Another issue common across international criminal statutes is an absence of mechanisms to deal with persons should they be found not guilty by reason of their mental state.

This chapter reflects on the conceptual and practical issues arising from the impaired mental state of defendants in international criminal law proceedings, including for genocide and crimes against humanity. It notes the analysis of the diminished responsibility partial defence by the Čelebići Trial Chamber of the ICTY in the *Esad Landžo* case and considers the precedent that this potentially creates

[5] Nor did the Law on the Establishment of the Extraordinary Chambers in the Courts of Cambodia for the Prosecution of Crimes Committed during the Period of Democratic Kampuchea.

[6] See J Tobin, 'The Psychiatric Defence and International Criminal Law' (2007) 23(2) Med Confl Surviv 11.

[7] See I Freckelton and M Karagiannakis, 'Fitness to Stand Trial under International Criminal Law' in R Mackay and W Brookbanks (eds), *Fitness to Plead: International and Comparative Perspectives* (Oxford University Press 2018) 273–97.

for the use of the insanity defence. It reviews key decided cases, in particular the decision of the ICC Trial Chamber in the *Ongwen* case in 2021, and distinguishes amongst psychotic illnesses, especially those characterized by delusional ideation, personality disorders, and other mental health states that have been raised on behalf of defendants in international criminal law trials. It argues for the modernization of both the criteria for mental state defences and of the custodial and treatment procedures that apply to persons found not guilty by reason of insanity by international criminal courts.

Mental Disorder under International Criminal Law

Mental disorders can be relevant to international criminal proceedings in three ways: first, they can serve as a basis for claims of unfitness to stand trial; and second, they can be relevant to sentencing considerations and may be invoked as a basis for mitigating sentence. Third, mental disorders can form the basis of a substantive defence

First, mental disorder can serve as a basis for a claim that the accused is unfit to stand trial.[8] A psychiatric disorder leading up to and at the time of trial may give rise to a mental impairment such that the trial cannot continue because the defendant cannot meaningfully understand or participate in the proceedings. Thus a psychiatric disorder, even if it is not the basis of a substantive defence, can achieve a similar result in the sense that the accused can avoid conviction. This aspect of an accused person's mental state is highly attractive for accused persons seeking the equivalent in practice to an acquittal. Thus, although a decision on the issue of fitness to stand trial does not finally dispose of a criminal matter, it can serve to relevant intents and purposes to terminate criminal proceedings against accused persons, particularly those who suffer from age-related medical conditions such as Alzheimer's disease or dementia.[9] Such claims have also been made in relation to post-traumatic stress disorder (PTSD) and disorders which involve psychosis such as schizophrenia.[10]

[8] I Freckelton and M Karagiannakis, 'Fitness to Stand Trial under International Criminal Law' in R Mackay and W Brookbanks (eds), *Fitness to Plead: International and Comparative Perspectives* (Oxford University Press 2018) 273; I Freckelton and M Karagiannakis, 'Unfitness to Stand Trial under International Criminal Law: The Influential Decision of the International Criminal Tribunal of the Former Yugoslavia in relation to Pavle Strugar and its Ramifications' (2014) 21 Psychiat Psychol Law 445; I Freckelton and M Karagiannakis, 'Fitness to Stand Trial under International Criminal Law: Current Challenges for Law and Policy' (2014) 12(4) Int J Crim Justice 705.

[9] I Freckelton and M Karagiannakis, 'Unfitness to Stand Trial Decision-Making in the Extraordinary Chamber in the Court of Cambodia' (2014) 21 J Law Med 813.

[10] I Freckelton and M Karagiannakis 'Fitness to Stand Trial under International Criminal Law: The Ramifications of a Landmark East Timor Decision' (2014) 21 Psychiatr Psychol Law 321; I Freckelton and M Karagiannakis 'Post-traumatic Stress Disorder and Hospitalisation Syndrome as Potential Aetiologies of Unfitness to Stand Trial: The *Gbagbo* Decision' (2014) 21 Psychiatr Psychol Law 645.

Diminished Mental Capacity—A Factor in Mitigation of Sentence

Mental disorders may also be a factor in mitigation of a convicted person's sentence. As established in the *Čelebići* case, the relevant general principle of law upon which both the common law and the civil law systems have acted is that the defendant's *diminished* mental state at the time of offending is relevant to the sentence to be imposed. It is not a defence that can lead to an acquittal.[11] It is not a partial defence; it is a factor relevant to sentencing. In a subsequent ICTY judgment, diminished mental capacity was defined as an impairment to the accused man's 'capacity to appreciate the unlawfulness of or the nature of his conduct or to control his conduct so as to conform to the requirements of the law'.[12] Where an accused relies upon diminished mental responsibility at the sentencing phase of a proceeding, 'he must establish that condition on the balance of probabilities—that more probably than not such a condition existed at the relevant time'.[13]

A number of ICTY cases have considered arguments of diminished mental capacity as a factor in mitigation of sentence. These have included assertions of allegedly 'shattered' personality,[14] alcohol induced psychosis,[15] a tendency to follow orders and anxiety,[16] PTSD,[17] acute stress reaction and PTSD,[18] as well as personality disorders including borderline, narcissistic, and anti-social disorders.[19] The accused persons' sentences in these cases were not mitigated as a result. The main reason for this is that the judges were not satisfied, taking into account expert medical opinions where available, that the accused persons suffered from conditions that relevantly diminished their mental capacity at the time of offending.[20]

[11] *Prosecutor v Delalić et al (Čelebići case)*, Judgment, Case No IT-96-21-A, App Ch, 20 February 2001, para 590 (also para 839). See G-J Alexander Knoops, *An Introduction to the Law of International Criminal Tribunals: A Comparative Study* (Transnational Publishers 2003) 77.

[12] *Prosecutor v Vasiljević*, Judgment, Case No IT-98-32-T, T Ch, 29 November 2002, para 283.

[13] *Prosecutor v Delalić et al (Čelebići case)*, Judgment, Case No IT-96-21-A, App Ch, 20 February 2001, para 590.

[14] *Prosecutor v Erdemović*, Judgment, Case No IT-96-22-A, App Ch, 7 October 1997, para 12. In this case the Appeals Chamber confined its findings to the issue of duress and did not make a finding on the issue of diminished mental state for the purpose of sentencing.

[15] *Prosecutor v Vasiljević*, Judgment, Case No IT-98-32-T, T Ch, 29 November 2002, para 28. It has been held that when mental capacity is diminished due to the voluntary use of alcohol or drugs this does not constitute a factor in mitigation of sentence; *Prosecutor v Kvočka et al*, Judgment, Case No IT-98-30/1-A, App Ch, 28 February 2005, para 707. Further, according to Art 31(1)(b) of the Statute of the International Criminal Court, intoxication may constitute a substantive defence in certain circumstances, including cases of involuntary intoxication.

[16] *Prosecutor v Krnojelać*, Judgment, Case No IT-97-25, T Ch, 15 March 2002, para 521.

[17] *Prosecutor v Todorović*, Sentencing Judgment, Case No IT-95-9/1-S, T Ch, 31 July 2001, para 94. See I Areh, A Sotlar, and S Zgaga, 'Some Psychological and Law Features of the Insanity Defence in War Crimes Trials in Europe' (2016) 66 Zbornik PFZ 87.

[18] *Prosecutor v Sikirica et al*, Sentencing Judgment, T Ch, Case No IT-95-8-S, 13 November 2001, para 198.

[19] *Prosecutor v Jelisić*, Judgment, Case No IT-95-10-T, T Ch I, 14 December 1999, para 125.

[20] *Prosecutor v Vasiljević*, Judgment, Case No IT-98-32-T, T Ch, 29 November 2002, paras 285–94; *Prosecutor v Krnojelać*, Judgment, Case No IT-97-25, T Ch, 15 March 2002, para 521; *Prosecutor v*

This approach has also been adopted by the ICC. Rule 145(2)(a)(i) of the ICC Rules of Procedure and Evidence ('ICC Rules') provides that when the court is considering a sentence, it is obliged to take into account mitigating circumstances 'falling short of constituting factors grounds for exclusion of criminal responsibility, such as substantially diminished mental capacity or duress'. A plea in mitigation of sentence based on diminished mental capacity has not yet been accepted by the ICC.

In *Prosecutor v Ongwen*[21] the defence failed in its argument that the accused should be found not guilty by reason of insanity but then, at sentencing, contended that he had substantially diminished mental capacity at the time of his offending. In part, it did so on the basis that it was asserted to be probable that he experienced such incapacity because, by the time of his trial and sentencing, Ongwen was receiving treatment for symptoms of mental disease and defects. However, the Chamber rejected this inference as 'entirely unconvincing in light of reliable evidence'.[22] It rejected expert evidence that Ongwen suffered from mental diseases and defects on the basis that such diagnoses related to his condition at the time of his trial rather than at the time of committing his offence. It also rejected as 'opportunistic' the argument that because what was assessed by ICC physicians as necessary by way of procedural adjustment for the fairness of the trial process, Ongwen suffered from diminished responsibility at the time of committing a criminal offence. It concluded that:

> The evidence establishes clearly that at all relevant times for the charges, Dominic Ongwen did not suffer from a mental disease or defect. The evidence indicates that he was in full possession of his mental faculties and exercised his role as commander effectively. Persons around him at the time, who fought with him or under his command, or who were very close to him physically as women and girls abducted and assigned to his household as so-called 'wives', did not provide anything in their testimonies which would suggest otherwise. Accordingly, the Chamber finds that the mitigating circumstance of substantially diminished mental capacity does not apply.[23]

Todorović, Sentencing Judgment, Case No IT-95-9/1-S, T Ch, 31 July 2001, paras 93–95; *Prosecutor v Sikirica et al*, Sentencing Judgment, T Ch, Case No IT-95-8-S, 13 November 2001, paras 196–99; *Prosecutor v Jelisić*, Judgment, Case No IT-95-10-T, T Ch I, 14 December 1999, para 125.

[21] Sentencing, ICC-02/04-01/15, 6 May 2021.

[22] ibid para 96.

[23] *Prosecutor v Ongwen*, Sentencing, ICC-02/04-01/15, 6 May 2021, para 100.

Insanity or Lack of Mental Capacity—A Substantive Defence

Mental disorders can form the basis of a substantive defence under international criminal law.[24] Although this defence has rarely been asserted and has never been successful, it remains open to accused persons before international criminal courts, in particular before the ICC.

Nuremberg Trials

Historically, at the Nuremberg Trial, the concepts of incapacity for trial and criminal incapacity by virtue of insanity were often raised simultaneously, leading to decisions that did not clearly delineate or explain the different legal standards applied to fitness and insanity.[25]

Neither the International Military Tribunal at Nuremberg nor the International Military Tribunal for the Far East explicitly recognized any mental health defences under their charters.[26] This failure to address the mental health issues arising under international criminal law statutes continued until the adoption of the Rome Statute of the ICC. Neither mental illness nor psychiatric disorder was put forward as a substantive defence or excuse by the defendants at the Nuremberg Trial.

Fitness to stand trial, although not a defence, was raised in relation to three of the high-profile defendants: Gustav Krupp, Rudolf Hess, and Julius Streicher. In the case of Hess and Streicher, the question of insanity was incorporated into the questions which the expert medical panels were asked to address when assessing the accused men's fitness for trial.[27] Rudolph Hess was a deputy to Hitler and a Nazi government leader who claimed he was suffering from amnesia. Experts were asked to opine on whether he was sane and whether he was of sufficient intellect to comprehend the course of the trial proceedings so as to make a proper defence, to challenge a witness to whom he might wish to object, and to understand the de tails of the evidence. The four medical experts from the United States, the United Kingdom, France, and Russia found that Hess was sane and could understand proceedings to an extent but his ability to defend himself was impaired by amnesia.

[24] A Eser and K Ambos in K Ambos (ed), *Rome Statute of the International Criminal Court* (4th edn, Beck Hart Nomos 2021) Article 31; GJ Knoops, *Defenses in Contemporary International Criminal Law* (Brill 2008) 109–14; A Cassese, 'Justifications and Excuses in International Criminal Law' in A Cassese, P Gaeta, and JRWD Jones (eds), *The Rome Statute of the International Criminal Court: A Commentary*, Vol I (Oxford University Press, 2002) 951.

[25] I Freckelton and M Karagiannakis 'Fitness to Stand Trial under International Criminal Law: The Historical Context' (2014) 21 J L Med 747

[26] See PL Weiner, 'Fitness Hearings in War Crimes Cases: From Nuremberg to the Hague' (2007) 30(1) BC Int'l & Comp L Rev 185.

[27] ibid 752–53, 756.

Hess subsequently and dramatically declared himself fit to stand trial on the day of his fitness hearing.[28]

The question of whether Hess was insane was temporally connected to the time of the trial and not the time of alleged offending. As such, his mental state was relevant to the issue of fitness; insanity was not considered, as would have been the case if it had been raised as a substantive defence. The definition of insanity, albeit in the context of fitness, was not expressly set out by the Nuremberg Tribunal. Pointedly, the Tribunal judgment stated that 'there is no suggestion that Hess was not completely sane when the acts charged against him were committed'.[29] Controversially, Krabbe has interpreted this reference as an implicit recognition of the insanity defence.[30]

The mixing of the issues of fitness and insanity occurred notwithstanding that two of the four prosecutors and medical expert panels came from the common law jurisdictions of the United States and the United Kingdom. As such they could reasonably be assumed to have been aware of the M'Naghten Rules and the distinction between insanity and fitness to stand trial.[31] The consequence of this failure to distinguish between insanity and fitness is that the assertion of insanity could not have led to finding that Hess was excused from criminal responsibility on the grounds of insanity.

The Čelebići Case

The next significant case to discuss the issue of insanity as a substantive defence occurred more than half a century later at the ICTY. This was the first international criminal tribunal established after the Second World War Tribunals and was tasked with investigating and prosecuting perpetrators of international crimes committed in the former Yugoslavia during the 1990s. In doing so it was bound to apply customary international law binding on all states, as it was at the time of the offences.[32] If a rule of custom could not be found, it sought to determine the applicable general principles of law by examining the national laws and practices of leading legal systems, including civil and common law jurisdictions, to see if they took a common

[28] ibid 752–54.

[29] *Rudolf Hess* Judgment, International Military Tribunal (Nuremberg), 1 October 1946, 104.

[30] M Krabbe, *Excusable Evil: An Analysis of Complete Defenses in International Law* (Intersentia 2014).

[31] Similar issues arose in the charges brought against Shumei Okawa who, famously, dressed in pyjamas and sitting barefoot, struck the bald head of the former Prime Minister, Hideki Tojo while shouting, 'Inder! Kommen Sie!' (Come Indian) in German. The US psychiatrist, Dr Daniel Jaffe, examined him and reported that Okawa was not fit to stand trial, resulting in the presiding Judge, Sir William Webb, concluding he was mentally ill and not proceeding with the case. See E Jaffe, *A Curious Madness: An American Combat Psychiatrist, a Japanese War Crimes Suspect, and an Unsolved Mystery from World War II* (Scribner 2014).

[32] See eg *Prosecutor v Stakić*, Trial Judgment, Case No IT-97-24-T, T Ch II, 31 July 2003, para 501 (regarding genocide).

approach from which a general principle of law could be derived. If national approaches differed too much, a finding that a general principle of law was applicable would be precluded.[33]

This can be distinguished from the ICC, which is bound to apply the Rome Statute, a treaty binding on the states that have signed and ratified it. ICC judges must follow their own statute, rules, and regulations, whether or not these provisions are recognized as customary international law or as general principles of law. If the applicable law cannot be found in these sources, ICC judges may also consider customary international law, followed by general principles of law.[34] Thus, a distinction needs to be drawn between the ICTY where the applicable law, including that which relates to mental state defences, constitutes customary law or general principles, in contrast to the ICC where this need not be the case.

The statute of the ICTY, in contrast to the subsequent Rome Statute of the ICC,[35] did not make express provision for a substantive defence based on mental disorder. However, rule 67(B)(i)(b) of the ICTY Rules of Procedure and Evidence (RPE) did require the defendant to give notice to the prosecution of 'any special defence, including that of diminished or lack of mental responsibility.[36] Otherwise, it did not specify any such defences,[37] although the principle of 'nulla poena sine culpa' (no penalty without guilt) should be regarded as playing a role.

The *Čelebići* case concerned Esad Landžo, who was a prison guard at the Čelebići prison camp located in the Konjic municipality in central Bosnia and Herzegovina in 1992. Landžo was charged with murdering and seriously mistreating the detainees of the camp. He was convicted of grave breaches of the Geneva Conventions—killing, torture, and causing great suffering or serious injury to body or health. He was sentenced to 15 years' imprisonment.[38]

At trial Landžo disavowed the defence of lack of mental responsibility, namely insanity,[39] instead arguing for a defence of diminished mental responsibility based on the reference to it in rule 67. The Trial Chamber accepted that this special defence was available to the accused as a matter of law. It explained that the closest analogy to it was section 2 of the English Homicide Act 1957,[40] providing for a

[33] *Prosecutor v Erdemović*, Judgment, Joint Separate Opinion of Judge McDonald and Judge Vohrah, Case No IT-96-22-A, App Ch, 7 October 1997, paras 40ff.

[34] ICC Statute, Art 21.

[35] ICC Statute, Art 31(1)(a).

[36] ICTY Rules, r 67(A)(ii)(b). This rule was subsequently amended and the requirement can now be found in r 67(B)(i)(b).

[37] See JL Larkin, 'The Insanity Defense Founded on Ethnic Oppression: Defending the Accused in the International Criminal Tribunal for the Former Yugoslavia' (2001) 21 New York Law School Journal of International and Comparative Law 91, 94.

[38] *Prosecutor v Delalić et al*, Judgment, Case No IT-96-21-A, App Ch, 20 February 2001 (Čelebići Appeal Judgment), paras 565–71.

[39] *Prosecutor v Delalić et al*, Judgment, Case No IT-96-21-A, Trial Chamber, 16 November 1998 (Čelebići Trial Judgment), para 1156.

[40] ibid para 1164.

defence of diminished responsibility, which had been 'enacted to avoid the inevitability of a judge passing the death sentence in situations of insanity falling outside the McNaughten Rules'.[41] However, this explanation is not relevant to modern international criminal courts, including the ICTY and the ICC, because there is no mandatory sentencing and they cannot impose the death penalty.

The Trial Chamber found that an essential requirement of the defence of diminished responsibility was that the accused's abnormality of mind should substantially impair his ability to control his actions.[42] Landžo relied upon evidence given by four forensic psychiatrists who concluded that he suffered from a personality disorder and had a substantial impairment of his mental responsibility such that his capacity to exercise his own free will when given orders was diminished. One psychiatrist, who was called by the prosecution, rejected the existence of a relevant personality disorder.[43] The Chamber found the accounts that Landžo gave to the experts in his interviews with them were unreliable.[44] It also relied upon admissions made by Landžo to one of the experts that he would inflict pain and suffering on the prisoners because he was ordered to do so and because he was bored and frustrated. He admitted that he 'never experienced any difficulty in doing such things, that he actually enjoyed it and that he cannot explain why he found it to be not at all unpleasant'.[45] The Trial Chamber concluded that, despite his personality disorder, Landžo was capable of controlling his actions.[46] Thus the court accepted that he suffered from a personality disorder but held that this did not impair his ability to control his actions. However, the Trial Chamber did take into account the expert evidence of his 'personality traits' during sentencing.[47]

Subsequently, the Appeals Chamber found that the Trial Chamber was justified in discounting the opinions of the defence experts. The Trial Chamber 'rejected the views of the four psychiatrists not because it preferred the views of the one psychiatrist called by the prosecution, but because it did not accept the truth of the factual history given by Landžo upon which the four psychiatrists had based their opinions'.[48] It held that an expert opinion is relevant only if the facts upon which it is based are true.[49]

Significantly, the Appeals Chamber held that as a matter of international criminal law, diminished mental capacity did not form the basis of a special defence.

[41] ibid para 1165.

[42] ibid para 1169.

[43] Čelebići Appeal Judgment, para 592. On the issue of personality defences, see LF Sparr, 'Personality Disorders and Criminal Law: An International Perspective' (2009) 37(2) J Am Acad Psychiatry Law 168.

[44] Čelebići Trial Judgment, para 1182.

[45] ibid para 1185.

[46] ibid para 1186. See LF Sparr, 'Mental Incapacity Defenses at the War Crimes Tribunal: Questions and Controversy' (2005) 33(1) J Am Acad Psychiatry Law 59.

[47] Čelebići Trial Judgment, para 1283. This approach was approved by the Appeals Chamber at Čelebići Appeal Judgment, para 841.

[48] Čelebići Appeal Judgment, para 593.

[49] ibid para 594.

This is because the rules of the court, including rule 67, were drafted by the ICTY judges and they did not have the power to create a new defence in the absence of reference to such a defence in established customary or conventional law or in the general principles of law recognized by all nations.[50] The Appeals Chamber held that while the ICC statute and many domestic jurisdictions recognized that 'the defendant's total mental incapacity to control his actions or to understand that they are wrong constitutes a complete defence, his diminished mental responsibility does not constitute either a partial or a complete defence, but it is relevant in mitigation of sentence'.[51] In other words, a sufficient number of national jurisdictions recognize the insanity defence for it to be a general principle of law which is recognized under international criminal law but the same could not be said for diminished [mental] responsibility despite it being a statutory defence recognized by some common law jurisdictions.

In the *Čelebići* case, the appeal judges found that if an accused person asserts a *lack* of mental capacity at the time of the alleged criminal conduct, he or she is challenging the presumption of sanity by a plea of insanity. This is a defence in the true sense, in that the defendant bears the onus of establishing that, more probably than not, at the time of the offence he or she was labouring under such a defect of reason, from disease of the mind, as not to know the nature and quality of his or her act or, if he or she did know it, that the defendant did not know that what he or she was doing was wrong. If successful, such a plea is a complete defence to a charge and it leads to an acquittal,[52] as against being 'just' an issue of diminished responsibility which may be relevant at sentencing. Thus this decision at the ICTY demonstrates the incorporation of the common law M'Naghten Rules at the level of international criminal law.

During the drafting stage of the insanity defence of the Rome Statute, the first of two proposals for what would eventually become Article 31(1), the issue of diminished mental capacity was raised. The proposal stated that where a person did not lack capacity but such capacity was nevertheless diminished, their sentence should or could be reduced. The proposal raised the question as to whether this 'defence' of diminished capacity should be included in the statute.[53] It was not included in the final version of the Rome Statute of the ICC. However, this proposal did raise the distinction subsequently made by the ICTY in the Čelebići Appeal Chamber judgment which determined that diminished mental capacity, while not a complete defence, could be argued in mitigation of sentence for any crimes committed under the Rome Statute.

[50] ibid para 583.

[51] ibid paras 587–88, 590.

[52] ibid paras 581–82.

[53] Report of the Preparatory Committee on the Establishment of an International Criminal Court—Vol II (Compilation of Proposals), Fifty-first Session, Supplement No 22A (A/51/22), United Nations General Assembly, 1996 (Preparatory Committee 1996 Vol II) 97.

It has subsequently been argued that diminished mental responsibility nonetheless forms the basis of a defence in customary international law.[54] Further, it has been argued that this could have been invoked by Dominic Ongwen in his trial before the ICC.[55] Even though diminished legal responsibility was not included in the Rome Statute, the argument was advanced that it could be raised as a defence by virtue of Article 31(3) which allows unspecified defences to be asserted before the ICC if they fall under the applicable law the court is bound to apply under Article 21 of the Rome Statute. It was said that the severely traumatic effects of Ongwen's abduction and abuse as a child soldier diminished his ability to control his actions and thus reduced his responsibility for the international crimes in which he participated many years later as an adult military commander, making it potentially a partial defence. Ultimately, Ongwen did not argue diminished mental capacity as a defence at trial. Rather, he asserted two of the defences expressed in Article 31—duress and insanity (see discussion below). As a matter of law, this argument that diminished mental capacity is a defence under customary law is unconvincing as it was not based on evidence or custom or general principles of law, apart from the citation of English law as to a partial defence. By contrast, the Čelebići Appeal Judgment approach is well founded in reaching the opposite conclusion.

The Insanity Defence under the Rome Statute of the ICC

The Statute of the ICC contains express reference to mental state as a ground for excluding criminal liability. However, it is a limited defence. Article 31(1)(a) provides that a person is not criminally responsible if:

> at the time of that person's conduct . . . [t]he person suffers from a mental disease or defect that destroys that person's capacity to appreciate the unlawfulness or nature of his or her conduct, or capacity to control his or her conduct to conform to the requirements of law.[56]

The provision, therefore, has two elements. The first is that the accused person suffers from a mental disease or defect. The second is that the disease or defect 'destroys' the person's capacity to understand the unlawfulness or nature of their conduct or 'destroys' their capacity to control their conduct. As such it evokes the M'Naghten Rules and goes further to incorporate an additional and alternative volitional element to the defence.

[54] W Nortje, 'Victim or Villain: Exploring the Possible Bases of a Defence in the Ongwen Case at the ICC' (2017) 17 Int Crim Law Rev 186, 186–207.

[55] ibid.

[56] ICC Statute, Art 31(1)(a). See generally A Eser in O Triffterer (ed), *Commentary on the Rome Statute* (2nd edn, Nomos Verlag, Baden Baden 2008) Article 31.

During the drafting stage of the Rome Statute, two options were proposed for the insanity defence. The first proposal, which echoed aspects of the common law M'Naghten Rules, suggested that a person 'is not criminally responsible [is legally insane] if at the time of that person's conduct that (would otherwise) constitute a crime, the person suffers from a mental disease or mental defect that results in the person lacking substantial capacity either to appreciate the criminality [unlawfulness] of his or her conduct or to conform his or her conduct to the requirements of the law, and such mental disease or mental defect caused the conduct constituting a crime'.[57] The proposal stated that where a person did not lack capacity but such capacity was nevertheless diminished, their sentence should or could be reduced.[58]

The second proposal, which largely echoed the civil law provision of Article 122-1 of the French Penal Code, stated that a person who 'at the time of the facts, was suffering from a mental or neuropsychic disorder[59] that destroyed his judgement or his control over his actions shall not be criminally responsible'.[60] If the disorder merely altered a person's judgement or impeded their capacity to control their actions without destroying their judgement or control, that person would be criminally responsible but the circumstances would be taken into account in determining the appropriate sentence.[61]

While the proposals were expressed quite differently, they both encompassed the central concepts of the subsequent insanity defence, namely, that the accused suffered a mental disorder which caused a major impairment to his or her cognition or volition. If the impairment fell below this high threshold, insanity could not be successfully invoked but the impairment could be taken into account in sentencing.

The insanity provisions of the Rome Statute were not the subject of significant debate during the drafting period.[62] The final version of Article 31(1) is a compromise between the two main proposals. The state of mind was taken from the first proposal so that a person must be suffering a mental disease or mental defect at the time of the conduct. The level of impairment such that the person's capacity is destroyed is taken from the second proposal which is a higher threshold than that required by the first proposal.[63] The capacities that may be destroyed are broad and include the capacity to understand the unlawfulness of conduct, which is similar to the first proposal's capacity to appreciate the criminality of conduct. They also

[57] Preparatory Committee 1996, Vol II, 97.

[58] ibid.

[59] This is a French term that encompasses both neuropsychological and neuropsychiatric disorders.

[60] Preparatory Committee, 1996, Vol II, 97.

[61] ibid.

[62] For a detailed procedural history of the drafting of this provision see M Scaliotti, 'Defences before the International Criminal Court: Substantive Grounds for Excluding Criminal Responsibility, Part 2' (2002) 2 Int Crim Law Rev 1, 22–25.

[63] See J Tobin, 'The Psychiatric Defence and International Criminal Law' (2007) 23(2) Med Confl Surviv 111; P Krug, 'The Emerging Mental Incapacity Defense in International Criminal Law: Some Initial Questions of Implementation' (2017) 94(2) AJIL 317.

include the capacity to control conduct, which was referred to in both proposals. The final draft also included a new element, the capacity to understand the nature of the conduct, which is found in the M'Naghten rule. Commentators have opined that 'the requirement of a mental disease or defect encompasses impairments of both reason (cognition) and emotion (volition)'.[64] As such this element can be interpreted broadly but whatever latitude is given to it, the availability of the defence is circumscribed by the degree to which the disease or defect affected the accused's capacity at the time of the commission of the offence. A plain reading of the ICC standard requires that that capacity is destroyed and implies a total exclusion of the accused person's ability to understand or control their conduct. However, it has been argued that in order to give experts an understandable and workable definition, and a mentally ill defendant a fair chance to raise incapacity, a destroyed capacity 'may be understood as floating between the substantial and the absolute impairment of cognitive or volitional abilities'.[65] Diminished mental capacity will not be enough: an extensive and far-reaching loss of self-control or reason would be required.[66] Whichever interpretation is ultimately adopted by the court, both requirements are of a high order and thus the insanity defence will be very difficult to satisfy.

Apart from this high standard, it is unlikely that a claim of insanity is going to be asserted very often before the ICC. This is because the nature of the offences involved, such as crimes against humanity and genocide, often require the formation of policy, planning, organization, and wilful and directed action over prolonged periods of time. Further, the ICC, and other international courts before it, seek to focus their prosecutions on mid- to senior-level political and military leaders who usually plan, organize, and order the commission of complex crimes over months and years. These activities require high-order executive functioning on the part of defendants which generally is inconsistent with the total destruction of their reasoning capacity and capacity to control their actions.

These issues were touched upon in the initial discussions on the enumeration of defences at the ICC, where it was generally considered that 'only defences relevant to the type of crimes under the Statute should be included. Accordingly, it was suggested, for example, that it was not necessary to include intoxication and insanity in the Statute'.[67] This line of reasoning was also reflected in the first proposal for the

[64] Eser in Triffterer (n 56) Article 31, Margin No 23; Eser and Ambos (n 24) Article 31, Margin Nos 21–23; S Janssen, 'Mental Condition Defences in Supranational Criminal Law' (2004) 4 Int Crim Law Rev 83, 84; P Krug, 'The Emerging Mental Incapacity Defense in International Criminal Law: Some Initial Questions of Implementation' (2000) 94(2) AJIL 317, 324.

[65] Eser and Ambos (n 24) Article 31, Margin No 24.

[66] ibid Margin Nos 24–25.

[67] Report of the Preparatory Committee on the Establishment of an International Criminal Court—Vol I (Proceedings of the Preparatory Committee during March-April and August 1996), Fifty-first Session, Supplement No 22A (A/51/22), United Nations General Assembly, 1996 (Preparatory Committee 1996 Vol I) 46.

insanity provisions where it 'was observed that this defence might be more relevant for some crimes (e.g. a war crime, such as killing of a prisoner of war) than for others (e.g. crimes involving the formulation of policy, such as genocide)'.[68] The question was raised whether, if the insanity defence was included, it should only be available for some crimes.[69] Ultimately, the defence was not circumscribed in this way in the Rome Statute, but the nature of the crimes and persons prosecuted by the ICC will generally mean that the insanity defence will only be raised in a small number of cases.

The Insanity Defence Rejected in the Ongwen Case

A defence of insanity was raised on behalf of Dominic Ongwen before the Trial Chamber of the ICC. Ongwen was charged with and ultimately found guilty in 2021 of a large number of counts of war crimes and crimes against humanity—attacks against a civilian population, murder, torture, enslavement, pillaging, persecution, outrages upon personal dignity, destruction of property, conscripting children, forced marriage, sexual slavery, and rape.[70] Ongwen held a variety of senior positions in the Lord's Resistance Army (LRA) which operated against the government in Northern Uganda between the 1980s until his case was referred by Uganda in 2003.[71]

It was asserted on behalf of Ongwen that he suffered from a number of medical conditions that qualified him to be found not criminally responsible pursuant to Article 31(1)(a) of the Statute: 'severe depressive illness, post-traumatic stress disorder ("PTSD") and dissociative disorder (including depersonalisation and multiple identity disorder) as well as severe suicidal ideation and high risk of committing suicide', and from 'dissociative amnesia and symptoms of obsessive compulsive disorder'.

The Trial Chamber was at pains to distinguish between the existence of the conditions at the time of commission of the relevant conduct, in Ongwen's case many years before, and at the time of the trial—an issue relevant to an accused person's fitness to stand trial. Amongst other things, this led the Chamber to give no weight in the context of the insanity defence to an expert report that focused on Ongwen's fitness to stand trial. The decision provides a significant set of guidelines for approaches that should be avoided for the giving of expert evidence in international criminal trials, including emphasizing the need to avoid bias and to utilize rigorous

[68] Preparatory Committee 1996 Vol II, 97.

[69] ibid.

[70] *Prosecutor v Ongwen*, Judgment, Case No ICC-02/04/15, Trial Chamber, 4 February 2021 (Ongwen Trial Judgment). See further Chifflet and Freckelton (n 2).

[71] See United Nations Security Council, 'Lord's Resistance Army' (7 March 2016) https://www.un.org/securitycouncil/sanctions/2127/materials/summaries/entity/lord's-resistance-army

methodologies, as well as the importance of being critical and focused upon the questions which the court needs to determine.[72]

Helpfully, in terms of mental health jurisprudence in international criminal law, the Trial Chamber reiterated the absence of provisions in the ICC Statute concerning burden and standard of proof in relation to excluding criminal responsibility, with the onus generally being held to lie upon the prosecutor under Article 66(2) to prove the guilt of the accused. Thus the question was straightforwardly whether the Trial Chamber was able to be satisfied to the requisite degree that the guilt of the accused was proved.

Another issue traversed in the *Ongwen* judgment was the relevance of cultural considerations in determining the insanity question. The Chamber accepted the agreement amongst the experts before it that the cultural context must be taken into account in assessments of mental health but noted evidence that the core symptoms of mental illness are similar across cultures.[73] On the facts, it found that the expert reports before it had taken into account cultural considerations.[74]

Another important issue that arises in insanity contexts (as well as fitness to stand trial contexts) is where the accused person submits to examination only by defence mental health professionals. It is necessary for the expert assessors to factor this into their assessments overtly and, where possible, to have regard to collateral sources of information. The Chamber found that this was what had taken place in the *Ongwen* case as the assessors for the prosecution were explicit that a limitation of their reports was that they had not personally interviewed the accused as he had declined such an option. However, they did have regard to other relevant materials and to the reports produced by experts for the defence who had been granted access to Ongwen. This resulted in the Trial Chamber stating that it had no 'methodological concerns' with regard to the reports written by the prosecution experts.[75]

The Trial Chamber scrutinized the reports of six psychiatrists and psychologists upon which the parties relied. Professor Mezey, called by the prosecution, observed that PTSD is not 'generally associated with repeated and persistent aggression'[76] and also that exposure to trauma does not automatically result in PTSD. Ongwen was stated not to have exhibited any significant clinical distress in any symptoms associated with PTSD symptomatology.[77] Professor Mezey emphasized

[72] See generally A Appazov, *Expert Evidence and International Criminal Justice* (Springer 2016).

[73] Ongwen Trial Judgment, para 2461.

[74] ibid para 2463. Compare *Deputy General Prosecutor for Serious Crimes v Josep Nahak*, unreported, 1 March 2005, Special Panels for Serious Crimes, Dili District Court, Democratic Republic of East Timor, discussed in I Freckelton and M Karagiannakis, 'Fitness to Stand Trial under International Criminal Law: The Ramifications of a Landmark East Timor Decision' (2014) 21(3) Psychiatry, Psychology and Law 321.

[75] Ongwen Trial Judgment, para 2469.

[76] ibid para 2472.

[77] ibid para 2475.

that the evidence was that Ongwen functioned normally over a lengthy period in the LRA and that he showed no sign of significant dissociation during that time. Nor did he become socially withdrawn, lose weight, have trouble sleeping, or lack concentration. Nor could she discern any clear evidence of Ongwen experiencing a disruption of his identity; moreover, dissociative identity disorder is 'stable, static and enduring' but had not been evident in Ongwen's presentation across different contexts.

Dr Abdo, also relied upon by the prosecution, agreed with Professor Mezey and observed that a dissociative state in its severe forms would be apparent to a layperson and it was unlikely that a person would be in such a state for months or even years. She also expressed the view that dissociative flashbacks as a symptom of PTSD would be inconsistent with the ability to engage in planned premeditated action. To the extent that Ongwen had symptoms of the disorders claimed on his behalf, she concluded there was 'hardly any evidence of these leading him to commit his crimes' and found, rather, that he was 'motivated by his existential situation rather than his symptoms of mental illnesses'.[78]

The Trial Chamber was prepared to receive diagnostic evidence from a psychologist, Professor Weierstall-Pust, relied upon by the prosecution: 'The Chamber does not consider that there are any limitations to his expertise due to the fact that he is a clinical psychologist and not a psychiatrist'.[79] He accepted that Ongwen had experienced at least one traumatic event but found that the trauma-related disorder that Ongwen experienced was 'not sufficient to draw any conclusions about his capacity to appreciate the wrongfulness of his actions'.[80] To the extent that Ongwen suffered as a result of his experiences, Professor Weierstall-Pust expressed the view that it was 'highly unlikely' that his level of functioning was severely impaired and in fact concluded that the accounts of Ongwen's fearlessness and competence as a fighter were incompatible with the claimed disorder of PTSD. Similarly, the descriptions of Ongwen as a 'good administrator', 'likeable', and 'hard working' were incompatible with his suffering from a severe depressive disorder—he exhibited no signs of a significant impairment of psycho-social functioning.

Professor Ovuga and Dr Akena prepared joint reports on behalf of Ongwen. The Trial Chamber was critical of the fact that there was no clear articulation of a mental disease or defect in the body of their reports and noted that a 'structured examination of the criteria for each diagnosis is not present'. The Trial Chamber was also troubled by what it described as the two experts going 'manifestly beyond the scope of the role of experts in criminal proceedings' and espousing views on whether Ongwen was criminally liable for his actions.[81]

[78] ibid para 2482.
[79] ibid para 2487.
[80] ibid para 2490.
[81] ibid para 2524.

The Trial Chamber noted that one of the reports by Professor Ovuga and Dr Akena, as well as a report by Professor de Jong, were written to express views about whether Ongwen was fit to stand trial, so 'had a substantially different purpose than ... for determination of the issue at hand'.[82] Further, aspects of the methodology utilized by Professor Ovuga and Dr Akena led the Trial Chamber to conclude that the reliability of their evidence was adversely affected to a point where 'the Chamber cannot rely on it'.[83] It was particularly troubled by their blurring of the roles of being treating physicians with their being forensic experts and concluded that this had led to a loss of objectivity: 'In the assessment of the Chamber, there is an inherent incompatibility between the duties of a treating physician and the duties of a forensic expert. The duty of a treating doctor is primarily towards the patient, whereas an expert engaged by a court for a forensic examination is primarily in the service of the court. It is not in the role of a forensic expert to sustain a relationship of trust and confidence with the person to be examined for the court, and the expert must in fact take care to remain as objective and detached as possible.'[84] They were also concerned by the fact that, on the Chamber's analysis, Professor Ovuga and Dr Akena did not look for any sources of corroboration for Ongwen's own reports of how his colleagues interpreted his behaviour related to his experience of different personalities, in spite of the availability of such information. Finally, the Tribunal was troubled by the approach of the defence experts not to have regard to the clinical notes of the Detention Centre psychiatrist. It described this approach as 'not justifiable'.[85]

The Trial Chamber considered at length the criticism advanced by the prosecution experts that the defence mental health professionals had been too credulous and had failed to consider the possibility that Ongwen was malingering, dissimulating, or exaggerating. The Chamber rejected explanations from the defence experts for how they had excluded the potential for malingering by Ongwen and considered that their choice not to use standardized methods to detect malingering was 'questionable and undermined their analysis'.[86]

A further consideration which dissuaded the Trial Chamber from placing weight on the defence mental health witnesses' opinions was their failure to use open-ended questions, to utilize structured rating scales, rather than merely the clinical interview, and to distinguish between data and inferences and opinions. They also used an out-of-date psychiatric taxonomy, employing the Diagnostic and

[82] ibid para 2526.

[83] ibid para 2527.

[84] ibid para 2531. See too Royal College of Pathologists and Royal College of Paediatrics and Child Health (Chaired by Baroness Helena Kennedy QC), *Sudden Unexpected Death in Infancy* (2004) <https://www.sudiscotland.org.uk/wp-content/uploads/2015/06/The_Kennedy_Report_2004.pdf>; compare *Oldham Metropolitan Borough Council v GW* [2007] EWHC 136 (Fam), para 98; I Freckelton, *Expert Evidence: Law, Practice, Procedure and Advocacy* (6th edn, Thomson Reuters 2019).

[85] Ongwen Trial Judgment, para 2550.

[86] ibid para 2546.

Statistical Manual, DSM-IV, rather than DSM-5. The Tribunal also found that the symptoms recorded in the reports of Professor Ovuga and Dr Akena were at times incoherent and their diagnoses inconsistent. The Trial Chamber also noted that the two defence experts failed to take into account other sources of information about Ongwen that were readily available to them—'This is an unjustifiable and fundamental failure that in itself invalidates the conclusions put forward by Professor Ovuga and Dr Akena.'[87] The Trial Chamber also took into account the fact that the reports of Professor Ovuga and Dr Akena presented 'very general analyses and findings, and are not clearly anchored on the relevant period and the more specific factual contexts in which Dominic Ongwen acted'.[88]

It is apparent that the Trial Chamber was highly unimpressed by the quality of the expert evidence adduced on behalf of Ongwen while it largely accepted the evidence adduced by the prosecution. At the heart of the Chamber's discomfort with the expert opinions adduced on behalf of Ongwen was a perception that the expert reports from the defence witnesses were biased, went beyond what was open to them, were inadequately evaluative, utilized an out-of-date diagnostic instrument, and lacked clinical rigour. The Chamber identified multiple methodological deficits in the defence reports, including a failure to undertake a structured diagnostic process. It located a source for the partisanship in the defence reports as to the fact that there was a treating relationship which contaminated the potential for the practitioners' clinical independence. However, importantly, it did not regard expert opinion evidence from a forensic psychologist as less authoritative than such evidence from a forensic psychiatrist.[89]

Preventive Detention Arrangements for Persons Found Not Guilty by Reason of Insanity

No international preventive psychiatric detention scheme exists to deal with those found not guilty by reason of insanity before international courts, including the ICC. Similarly, there is no such scheme to care for those found not fit to be tried.[90] This issue was raised during the drafting phase of the Rome Statute, where questions were asked as to 'what should happen to a person who is found insane. Should the person be released or be detained in a mental institution? If the latter, where? Should provision for this be made in the articles concerning enforcement

[87] ibid para 2545.

[88] ibid para 2569.

[89] By contrast, this is an issue that remains live in Australian domestic law: see I Freckelton, *Expert Evidence: Law, Practice, Procedure and Advocacy* (6th edn, Thomson Reuters 2019).

[90] I Freckelton and M Karagiannakis 'Fitness to Stand Trial under International Criminal Law: Current Challenges for Law and Policy' (2014) 12(4) Int J Crim Justice 705, 724–25.

of sentences by the Court and States Parties?'[91] Unfortunately, these questions were not answered by provisions in the Rome Statute or by subsequent administrative arrangements. The absence of such provisions has drawn criticism,[92] Amnesty International for instance identifying that: 'the Statute or rules will have to establish procedures consistent with international law and standards for addressing the situation of a person acquitted on this ground who continues to suffer from that disease or defect'.[93]

These lacunae could be addressed by the insertion of provisions into the constitutive documents of international criminal courts, including the ICC, permitting the courts to issue special verdicts of 'facts proven, but not guilty by reason of mental incapacity', and authorizing a system of involuntary detention, treatment and supervision of the accused person found to lack criminal responsibility.[94]

In our view, it is important to enable international criminal courts to make findings as to the facts of the commission of criminal offences, especially if the perpetrators of such crimes are exculpated on the basis of mental incapacity. This would enable the public record to be clarified and for victims and loved ones of victims to have the vindication of a finding that serious wrongs have been committed by the accused person. In addition, with a disposition that retains the accused long term in custodial detention, albeit in mental health care, they would receive reassurance that the perpetrator of serious crimes has not been able to return to living in the community when still suffering from the mental illness that played a role in their commission of the criminal offences with which they have been charged.

The absence of a system of involuntary detention has been argued to threaten the credibility of international prosecutions. It also gives rise to the question of 'whether courts, aware of the unavailability of such a system, would give proper consideration to the mental incapacity defense despite their textual authorization (and obligation) to do so'.[95] Notably, too, the national legislation of the Netherlands, where the ICC is based, does not authorize the detention of persons acquitted by the ad hoc tribunals on the ground of mental impairment/insanity/incapacity.

The most probable result of this situation is that the Registrar of the ICC would need to find a State Party or other state which had such a scheme and reach an agreement whereby that state would take an accused person found not guilty by

[91] Report of the Preparatory Committee on the Establishment of an International Criminal Court—Vol II (Compilation of Proposals), Fifty-first Session, Supplement No 22A (A/51/22), United Nations General Assembly, 1996, 97.

[92] See, for instance, J Gilbert, 'Justice not Revenge: The International Criminal Court and the 'Grounds to Exclude Criminal Responsibility': Defences or Negation of Criminality' (2006) 10(2) Int J HR 4.

[93] Amnesty International, '16 Fundamental Principles for a Just, Fair and Effective International Criminal Court', AI-Index IOR 40/010/1998, 1 May 1998.

[94] See J Harder, 'A Future Perspective on the Disposition of the Insane and the Unfit to Stand Trial in the International Criminal Court' (2010) *8* New Zealand Yearbook of International Law 145.

[95] P Krug, 'The Emerging Mental Incapacity Defense in International Criminal Law: Some Initial Questions of Implementation' (2000) 94(2) AJIL 317.

reason of insanity. The practicalities of this scenario would be complex. What state would be willing to take, treat, and detain an insane political or military leader guilty of genocide, crimes against humanity, and/or a war criminal for an indeterminate period of time? Even if such a state was identified, what standards should be met before such a transfer was permitted? Further, in the absence of specific rules, how could the ICC supervise or enforce such detention, including appropriateness for release should a person cease to be psychiatrically unwell? All of these are matters that need consistent statutory provision to assist all international criminal tribunals and the ICC in particular.

Conclusions

Surprisingly, the role of the insanity defence remains unresolved under international criminal law. The issue has long been sensitive and it is apparent that there has been a desire on the part of those drafting international criminal law legislation to avoid perpetrators of very serious crimes from being exculpated by virtue of questionable claims of lack of criminal responsibility arising from psychotic symptomatology advanced through sympathetic mental health professionals. However, it is our contention that this leaves a conceptually unsatisfactory position with the potential for unfairness in a small number of extreme situations.

It is probable that the confusion in the Nuremberg trials between fitness/capacity to stand trial and insanity has now been dispelled and will not be repeated. However, the absence of a meaningfully available provision under the constitutive statutes of international criminal tribunals has been problematic and raises ongoing issues in relation to the integrity and fairness of the trial processes. The absence of an explicit defence under the ICTY, ICTR, and Cambodian tribunal provisions was unjustifiable, leaving mental state issues to be dealt with only by indirect and unsatisfactory means that could not properly address scenarios in which accused persons may have lacked criminal responsibility by reason of the extent of their symptomatology.

The Rome Statute, which underpins the ICC, does contain provision for an insanity defence but it is so demanding as to be almost wholly inaccessible for accused persons by virtue of its requirement for *destruction* of an accused person's capacity to appreciate the unlawfulness or nature of his or her conduct, or capacity to control his or her conduct to conform to the requirements of law. This is a much higher requirement than exists in domestic laws and is so high a threshold that it is unlikely to be satisfied.

The Trial Chamber judgment in the *Ongwen* case presented the ICC with an opportunity to enunciate the principles applicable to the mental incapacity defence. Unfortunately, that opportunity was not taken by the Trial Chamber which focused its attention on the factual issues rather than enunciating the legal parameters of the defence. The issue of Ongwen's alleged incapacity has been appealed on the basis of error in law and fact.[96] As such, the Appeals Chamber will have the opportunity for a more detailed analysis of the applicable law. However, for the present, it is apparent that trial chambers will be demanding in terms of the quality of expert evidence adduced in support of an assertion of insanity on the part of accused persons.[97]

It is our view that insanity laws as a defence should be drafted and/or interpreted broadly, implementing the M'Naghten standard that focuses upon whether there is a psychiatric condition that, at the relevant time, impaired an accused person's capacity to know the nature and quality of their conduct or that it was wrong.

Such a mental incapacity defence would allow accused persons to avail themselves of the defence only in very rare circumstances, on the basis of suitable expert evidence, but it would serve to restore conceptual legitimacy to international criminal law. There is no potential for this to open floodgates of problematic exculpations of accused persons as it will be very rare that the criteria for mental incapacity will be established in respect of persons charged with serious international criminal law offences.

In our view, provision should be made to enable a decision in such circumstances for a 'special verdict' that the person committed the offence but that they were not criminally responsible by reason of mental incapacity. Models for this exist under domestic law, in a number of jurisdictions, including in New South Wales, Australia.[98]

Should the option of a verdict of not guilty by reason of mental incapacity be introduced into international criminal law, it should be accompanied by procedures to impose a residence requirement for treatment and care of the person on a long-term basis—ideally within a neutral country's psychiatric facilities. Whether procedures should be created for the person's fitness for release on the basis of substantial amelioration in their psychiatric condition to a point where they no longer pose a risk of recidivism is a further issue for debate.

[96] *Prosecutor v Ongwen*, Defence Notification of its Intent to Appeal the Trial Judgment, Case No ICC-02/04-01/15, Trial Chamber, 21 May 2021, 12 (Grounds 27–29).

[97] Notably Judge Thompson of Special Court for Sierra Leone (SCSL) emphasized that 'the reasoning or methodology underlying the testimony must be valid and properly applicable to the facts in issue' and 'the expert must be independent': *Prosecutor v Sesay et al*, Judgment, SCSL-4-15-T, 25 February 2009, para 27.

[98] See eg I Freckelton, 'Insanity under Australian Law' in R Mackay and W Brookbanks (eds), *The Insanity Defence—International and Comparative Perspectives* (Oxford University Press 2022) chapter 8.

16
Conclusion

Ronnie Mackay and Warren Brookbanks

The idea that a person who was insane at the time he or she committed a criminal act ought not to be convicted goes back at least to the second half of the 13th century.[1] Since that time the various iterations and reformulations of a defence of exculpatory insanity have generated more debate and controversy than any other defence in the criminal law. As this book has demonstrated, it continues to be the subject of vigorous debate in many jurisdictions as legislators and policymakers struggle to formulate an appropriate rule. While in some jurisdictions the defence is rarely encountered in practice and rarely succeeds in leading to a qualified verdict of acquittal, in others, it may be more commonly raised but is equally unsuccessful for various policy and cultural reasons. While in English common law jurisdictions the insanity defence represents a fundamental tenet of criminal responsibility designed to shield those who qualify within its criteria from a criminal conviction, in other jurisdictions, like the Netherlands (discussed in Chapter 12), it does not exist as a discrete defence but exculpation is linked to an evaluation based on the use of categories of responsibility. In addition to such conceptual differences, where it is characterized as a defence the notion of insanity is deeply stigmatic and arguably breaches the requirement in Article 12 of the Convention on the Rights of Persons with Disabilities (CRPD) to equal recognition before the law. Other problems touching on questions of fairness and equal treatment relate to the disposal of insanity acquittees in terms of how to protect the public as well as to giving recognition to the rights of victims and their families.

In this book, we have confronted the fact that despite the vast literature the insanity defence has generated, most who are interested in the subject know little about how the defence operates in jurisdictions different to their own. While the M'Naghten Rules form the basis of legal insanity in many jurisdictions based on English common law, including England and Wales, Canada, New Zealand, the Australian states and territories, and many North American jurisdictions, the ways in which insanity is conceptualized in civil law jurisdictions, and in an Asian country like China, is often significantly different and unfamiliar. Nevertheless, it is our hope that the survey undertaken in this book will have filled in some gaps

[1] See eg N Walker, *Crime and Insanity in England*, Vol 1 (Edinburgh University Press 1969) chapter 1.

Ronnie Mackay and Warren Brookbanks, *Conclusion* In: *The Insanity Defence*. Edited by: Ronnie Mackay and Warren Brookbanks, Oxford University Press.
DOI: 10.1093/oso/9780198854944.003.0016

for many readers and expanded readers' appreciation of the richness and diversity of thought and practice that has surrounded the development of this most fundamental doctrine of the criminal law.

It should by now be clear, for example, that while the M'Naghten Rules are still the common law test for the insanity defence in England and Wales and continue to influence many other jurisdictions, this influence—although profound—is gradually eroding as other more modern and, arguably, more scientifically appropriate tests gain ground. In Great Britain, England and Wales is now the only jurisdiction which continues to adhere to the Rules, while Scotland, Northern Ireland, and the Channel island of Jersey have all adopted different insanity defences.

In this volume, we have succeeded in bringing together a range of domestic and international experts from a wide selection of jurisdictions to offer a broad range of perspectives on the insanity defence. This has included the international criminal law arena where insanity has become an increasingly debated issue, albeit to date, never successful. Nevertheless, as in other domestic jurisdictions, the high incidence of offenders with a mental disorder or impairment is putting increasing pressure on authorities to formulate laws and practices which best recognize the shades of criminal responsibility and are responsive to the need for therapeutic intervention while securing public safety. This is a challenge increasingly informed by developments in psychiatry and psychology, the social sciences, neuroscience, and cultural practice. It is hoped that the new and emerging insights from these specialist disciplines will ultimately help to inform the development of new insanity laws that are fit for purpose in the complex societal structures of the 21st century.

Our goal in compiling this volume has been to inform readers of the multifaceted way in which the insanity defence operates. By and large, this is an account of legal developments in the countries surveyed. Much work remains to be done in assessing the role to be played by interdisciplinary research into the causes and sources of mental dysfunction that is the 'bread and butter' of the insanity defence. However, granted the focus of this book, we hope that it will be influential in informing the current debate around the insanity defence and assisting in the development of policy and legislation in this critical area of the law. We also hope that the discussion in the respective chapters will reinvigorate the debate about the defence by demonstrating how different jurisdictions' approaches to the insanity plea have taken account of local needs and aspirations in both the formulation of an appropriate test and appropriate disposal options.

Below we review each chapter, identifying distinctive elements and common issues surrounding the insanity defence. It is our hope that the chapters will have given readers a unique comparative insight into how the defence operates in different jurisdictions and the challenges it presents for the future.

The first chapter written by the editors opens with a broad discussion of the enigmatic nature of the insanity defence and its problematical status, especially its narrowness and its potential for confusion with other statutory mental state tests. This is followed by a discussion of its theoretical basis, including the issue of causality, whether it should be a character, status, or capacity excuse together with the question of the abolition of the defence. This is followed by a description in broad terms of the origins and purpose of the law relating to the insanity defence and a discussion on how these provisions have been given effect in some of the jurisdictions surveyed. The chapter also contains a discussion on human rights aspects where it is argued that the inauguration of the United Nations' CRPD may ultimately dictate a radically different future for an exculpatory insanity defence. The chapter addresses these challenges and concludes that more work needs to be done as to how substantive criminal law might respond to disabling cognitive impairment in a CRPD-active legal environment.

In the first substantive (Chapter 2), Professor Mackay provides an overview of the insanity defence in English law. Understanding of its origins, as based upon the famous M'Naghten Rules, is now ubiquitous. Criticism of the Rules has become increasingly strident and despite a number of attempts at reform, now spanning over 100 years, the Rules themselves have remained unchanged since 1843. Criticisms have typically focused on the narrowness of the Rules, with their potential to exclude most mentally impaired offenders, and that they do not accord with modern medical thinking. The chapter traces the development of the Rules through the well-established case and statute law in order to evaluate how the insanity defence, including that of automatism, is perceived to operate, with a particular emphasis on the problematic concept of 'disease of the mind' and the difficult distinction between 'internal' and 'external' causes of automatistic behaviour. The chapter also surveys the author's empirical studies into the defence which revealed how relatively infrequently the insanity defence is successfully employed. Also discussed is how the law in the Channel island of Jersey came to reject the M'Naghten Rules in favour of a new test that incorporates volitional impairment.

The chapter concludes with the observation that although the M'Naghten Rules require urgent statutory reform, in the meantime a more expansionary approach to the Rules adopted by the appellate courts might be instrumental in feeding new life into a failing defence, in much the same way as has occurred in some other common law jurisdictions.

Chapter 3, co-authored by Professor David Ormerod and Dr Mark Dsouza, identifies the numerous failings in English law of the defence enshrined in the M'Naghten Rules which suggest that, in the authors' view, it is no longer fit for purpose. In particular, the Rules are criticized as lacking a sound psychiatric foundation, being ambiguous in terms and scope, illogical in outcomes, and stigmatizing in labelling. While the case for reform seems overwhelming, this is not a universally held view and change has not been forthcoming. However, the arbitrary distinctions created by 'disease of the mind' and the complex relationship with sane automatism and intoxication defences suggest a powerful need for reform. The

England and Wales Law Commission has already drafted proposals for a new defence based on the notion of a 'qualifying recognised medical condition' which would include a volitional (control) element in the defence. When considered in relation to a newly proposed automatism defence this would have the effect of eliminating the illogical and arbitrary distinctions based on internal and external causes, and better align the insanity defence with medical understanding. The proposals would also alter the legal burden of proof on the defendant by imposing on the defendant an 'elevated evidential burden' requiring the evidence of two experts, but reverting to the Crown to prove the accused did not suffer a complete loss of capacity by reason of a qualifying recognized medical condition.

It is to be hoped that with a more enlightened attitude to mental health issues in the criminal justice system, the Law Commission's proposed new insanity model will be favourably considered as offering a defence which deals fairly and equitably with mentally disordered offenders.

The mental disorder defence in Scots law is the subject of Chapter 4. Professor Gerry Maher explains how early Scots law on insanity depended on 'absolute alienation of reason'. In 2012 the Scottish common law defence of insanity was replaced by a statutory defence of lack of criminal responsibility by reason of mental disorder. The central element of the new defence is that, at the relevant time, an accused person was unable to appreciate the nature or wrongfulness of his conduct as a result of mental disorder. The new appreciation of conduct test is intended to have a much wider scope than the knowledge base of the M'Naghten Rules but specifically excludes any volitional incapacity or disability.

As the chapter demonstrates, reform recommendations set out in the Report of the Scottish Law Commission have been largely implemented by statute. It also considers the use made of the new defence in practice, as well as the interpretation of the law given in court decisions, and the views expressed in academic commentaries, which have been critical of various aspects of the defence. These include the exclusion of psychopathy as a qualifying condition and the imposition of a legal burden of proof on the accused to establish the defence.

In Chapter 5 Professor Paul McCutcheon traces the development of the insanity defence in Irish law, originally based primarily on the M'Naghten Rules. However, an overhaul of the law in the Criminal Law (Insanity) Act 2006 reformed the insanity defence, abandoning the traditional verdict of 'guilty but insane' to incorporate a new verdict of 'not guilty by reason of insanity'. In addition, more liberal disposal options and independent and regular review of insanity acquittees have been added to the legislation. The new defence also adds a control limb which may be open to either a broad or narrow interpretation but which nevertheless allows recognition of volitional insanity, first recognized by the Irish Supreme Court in 1974. However, the continued use of 'disease of the mind' within the definition of 'mental disorder' is curious, given the limited Irish jurisprudence on the question and the complexity of the tests developed in other jurisdictions to determine if a condition is a 'disease of the mind'; and given the concern to better align legal insanity with clinical opinion. Although the author expresses a preference for the Canadian 'holistic' test for determining insanity, it is acknowledged that further clarification of elements of the defence is desirable, in particular the scope of 'mental disorder', the nature of the knowledge element, and the scope of 'inability to refrain from acting', the control component.

A major development in Ireland has been the establishment in the 2006 Act of the Mental Health (Criminal Law) Review Board, with the power to review detention. In addition to its general review powers, the Board is also empowered to order a patient's conditional discharge. However, the absence of appropriate enforcement provisions has effectively rendered conditional discharges unconditional, creating judicial reluctance to order conditional discharges. This was remedied by a 2010 amendment which provided enforcement procedures for material breaches of a conditional discharge.

In Chapter 6 Professor Gerry Ferguson traces the growth of the insanity defence in Canada, from its origins as a model of the M'Naghten Rules to its current iteration as a substantive mental disorder defence. However, unlike the way exculpatory insanity has developed in other common law jurisdictions, the Canadian version has remained largely wedded to the M'Naghten model. Although the concept of 'disease of the mind' has been substituted with 'mental disorder', the change was largely cosmetic and the Criminal Code equates mental disorder to 'disease of the mind'—a broad definition now encompassing a wide range of mental impairments. As with the New Zealand version of the defence, the Canadian jurisprudence on insanity has been conflicted in determining whether the test in the first limb ('incapable of appreciating the nature and quality ... ') requires proof of actual incapacity as opposed to subjective knowledge, as expressed in the M'Naghten Rules.

However, as Professor Ferguson notes, senior Canadian appellate courts' current insistence that the test is one of incapability rather than simple knowledge creates the anomaly that an offender may be capable of appreciating relevant facts yet lack mens rea for failure to appreciate the nature of his act, effectively negating the social value of the insanity defence.

Professor Ferguson also argues that Canada's rejection of irresistible impulse as part of the insanity defence, in line with M'Naghten's rejection of volitional incapacity, represents a fatal flaw in the statutory defence. The argument that a morally defensible insanity defence must include consideration of both cognitive and volitional impairment is a strong one that has implications, not only for Canadian law but other jurisdictions, like England and Wales and New Zealand, that have also rejected a volitional incapacity test.

Furthermore, in relation to volitional incapacity caused by unconsciousness, Professor Ferguson notes the significant restriction of the scope of the defence of sane automatism following from the 1999 Supreme Court decision of *R v Stone*.

This has meant that only in rare cases will automatism not be caused by a 'disease of the mind', requiring evidence of strict criteria to take it out of that category. Although concerns exist around labelling epileptic, diabetic, and sleepwalking accused persons as insane, current Canadian law favours concerns for public protection over fair labelling concerns so that such labels invariably result in insane automatism verdicts.

Insanity in New Zealand, by Professor Warren Brookbanks, is the subject of Chapter 7. Since 2003, the insanity defence has been the subject of close attention, and criticism. Legislative changes to the procedures governing exculpatory insanity have rationalized its use and made it more accessible as an exculpatory defence. However, official investigation into the scope and operation of the defence by the New Zealand Law Commission in 2010 resulted in no recommendation for further change to the statutory defence, which still bears all the defects and problems associated with its conceptual predecessor, the M'Naghten Rules. As in the Canadian jurisdiction surveyed in the previous chapter, theoretical problems have focused on whether exculpatory insanity requires actual incapacity of knowing his or her act was morally wrong or whether subjective lack of knowledge will suffice. New Zealand courts are currently conflicted over this question, despite clear guidance from the Court of Appeal.

While insanity is not pleaded often in New Zealand, a number of recent homicide cases in which methamphetamine abuse has featured, have challenged the operation of the insanity laws and have highlighted the complex difficulties associated with distinguishing between acute intoxication and enduring psychosis. These cases raise the question of whether New Zealand's insanity laws are still fit for purpose, granted that they were formulated at a time when alcohol was the principal drug of choice. Although New Zealand has a methamphetamine crisis, it is doubtful whether the insanity defence offers any significant relief for those suffering from such addiction. While legislative change to the procedures applying when insanity is raised, and the disposition of persons acquitted on account of insanity has significantly changed the way in which claims of insanity are dealt with, the archaic character of the present defence and its narrow compass are significant challenges to its usefulness going forward.

The M'Naghten test still forms the basis of the insanity defence, known as 'mental impairment' in most Australian jurisdictions, although statutory formulations and disposal options vary considerably from state to state. As Professor Ian Freckelton illustrates in Chapter 8 an extensive and distinctive jurisprudence has evolved in Australia around the defence of insanity/mental impairment by reference to High Court and Court of Appeal decisions. Because insanity laws are state-based and not the preserve of the Federal jurisdiction, as in Canada, Australia formulations of the defence are subtly different across the nine jurisdictions. This means that legal controversies in relation to one jurisdiction are not necessarily common to others, giving rise to a complex diversity of approaches to various conditions, ranging from delusional illnesses to personality disorders. Varying definitions attaching to key expressions like 'mental impairment', 'mental health impairment', 'mental illness', 'cognitive impairment', 'mental incompetence', 'senility', and 'dementia', to describe the essence of insanity, illustrate the potential complexity of Australian insanity law and why it has attracted considerable judicial scrutiny. Although 'disease of the mind' is no longer an element within the various statutory formulations of the defence, it continues to be used in legal commentary to denote serious mental illness. Of interest in this regard is the inclusion in some insanity definitions of 'cognitive impairment', foetal alcohol spectrum disorder, autism spectrum disorder, and substance-induced mental disorder 'that is not temporary' as distinctive and modern elements within definitions of mental health impairment.

Of particular interest is the recent New South Wales provision requiring a special verdict of 'act proven but not criminally responsible' and the availability of an alternative procedure for determining insanity at any time of the proceedings and without a jury. This mirrors the New Zealand procedure introduced in 2003.

Criteria for the disposal of defendants when the insanity defence is made out varies across the Australian jurisdictions. It is noted that various formulations and procedures exist for decision-making concerning gradual reintegration into the community for people found not guilty by reason of their mental state. This process is made more complex with inter-jurisdictional transfers for the purposes of facilitating mental health and psychosocial rehabilitation. Furthermore, the statutory reform of this procedure has focused both upon the matters needing to be established by detainees seeking extended periods of leave from detention, or release or revocation of their supervisory status and detention. The chapter also covers the principles to be derived from the large body of case law on the subject, with a particular focus on the issue of risk prediction.

In Chapter 9 Professor Stephen Morse surveys the radical changes to insanity defence jurisprudence that followed the successful insanity defence raised by John Hinckley, Jr for the attempted assassination of President Reagan and others in 1981. That event, and the subsequent widespread negative reaction to it, singlehandedly led to a wave of legislative reform. The upshot, as Professor Morse explains, was a denigration of the control limb of the Model Penal Code eventually leading to reforms in many states aimed either at abolishing or severely limiting the scope of the defence. As a result of *Hinckley*, there has been no major change to US substantive law on the insanity defence in subsequent decades despite continued criticism of a narrow cognitive test. Through a survey of three Supreme Court cases (*Powell v Texas*, *Clark v Arizona*, and *Kahler v Kansas*), Professor Morse describes how the Court has deconstitutionalized the insanity defence, rejecting it as a matter of fundamental justice and, in the case of *Kahler v Kansas*, effectively abolishing it. While there have been few substantive changes of note to the insanity defence post-*Hinckley*, other than the elimination of a control test in a significant number of jurisdictions, Professor Morse outlines a range of procedural changes. Of particular note, in relation to the question of whether a trial judge should instruct a jury on the consequences of finding a defendant legally insane, he concludes that a defendant should be entitled to a consequences instruction on request; and that where post-acquittal commitment does occur, it should be for evaluation only and not for full commitment.

The insanity defence in France has a complex history. In Chapter 10 Dr Audrey Guinchard explains how an early practice of over-criminalization of the mentally ill has endured, despite the longstanding recognition in French criminal law that a person lacking capacity due to lack of control or a mental disorder should not be held criminally liable. It did so through a single cause of non-liability, a structure which has endured 1992 reform of the criminal code. While the term '*démence*', present in the 1810 Criminal Code, has been discarded and replaced in 1992 by the more modern concept of 'a psychological or neuro-psychological illness', Article 122-1 of the Criminal Code, continues to be the sole mechanism to exclude criminal liability for lack of capacity. This is described by the author as being as elliptic as its predecessor concerning the exact scope of the defence. Article 122-1 has also confirmed the informal practice of reduced sentencing when the defendant remains sufficiently sane to be criminally liable, but when his or her capacity has nevertheless been sufficiently altered to justify a different treatment. The chapter outlines the scope of the equivalent French insanity defence within the context of the French criminal justice system, as compared to its English law counterparts and the allied concepts of insanity, automatism, intoxication, and diminished responsibility, and suggested reforms. The chapter carefully analyses recent modifications of Article 122-1 of the Criminal Code, viewed by some commentators as introducing a conceptual shift with a greater emphasis placed on dangerousness rather than traditional concepts of criminal liability. Finally, the controversial decision in the *Halimi* case is discussed. This case has given rise to much concern and debate and could have far-reaching implications for the future of the insanity defence in France.

In outlining the scope of the insanity defence in German law in Chapter 11, Dr Regina Rauxloh observes that a conviction for a criminal offence in Germany requires the establishment of three factors: (1) the presence of the necessary subjective and objective elements of the offence (actus reus and mens rea); (2) the illegality of the action, which is assumed unless there are special circumstances such as self-defence; and (3) the culpability of the offender (*Schuld*). The term '*Schuld*', meaning guilt, culpability, or criminal responsibility, requires that the offender can be blamed for their actions at the time of the commission of the crime. The offender must have been aware that their action was wrong and must have had the ability to control their behaviour. Under German law, culpability is presumed for perpetrators from the age of 14 but can be excluded where, at the time of the commission of the offence, the offender is 'incapable of appreciating the unlawfulness of their actions or of acting in accordance with any such appreciation due to a pathological mental disorder, a profound consciousness disorder, debility or any other serious mental abnormality' (s 20 of the German Criminal Code). There are two stages to the analysis of the provision. First, whether the defendant had a mental disorder at the time of the crime, which meets the threshold of section 20 (biological-psychological level). Examples include psychoses that lead to a loss of reality perception, which could be caused by brain damage, alcohol-induced delirium, drug abuse, or psychic illnesses such as schizophrenia. Secondly, what impact did the disorder have on the defendant's capability to evaluate their acts? If, because of the mental disorder, the offender is either unable to appreciate the wrongfulness of their actions or incapable of behaving accordingly, they are not deemed culpable and consequently cannot be punished. They might, however, be admitted by a court to a closed psychiatric ward, if they pose danger to the general public. While a lack of culpability excludes criminal responsibility completely, partial responsibility, for example where the offender has only an incomplete awareness that their action is wrong, is a reason for sentence mitigation (s 21).

In 1952, the German Supreme Court declared that through 'the criminal conviction the defendant is judged for not having acted lawfully; that he sided with the wrong although he could have opted for the right'. Section 20 illustrates the underlying understanding of German criminal law that culpability is directly linked to a person's freedom of will and their ability to control their behaviour. The threshold of when a perpetrator is deemed not to be sufficiently able to either understand the wrongfulness of their conduct or act accordingly is, however, difficult to establish. The chapter examines the different problems posed by the defence of insanity, including the question of which mental disorders are included, the complications of legal and medical diagnosis, and the difficulties of evaluating the offender's cognitive ability to appreciate their actions. The chapter considers the important questions of the legal impact of a temporal mental disorder which has been induced by either negligent or intentional intoxication, the so-called *actio libera in causa*.

In Chapter 12 Professor Gerben Meynen discusses the characteristics of the insanity defence in the Dutch criminal justice system. Unlike the practice in common law jurisdictions in the Netherlands, a state with a moderately inquisitorial system, insanity evaluations can be ordered by the prosecution or by the court. Rarely is the defence raised by the defendant. Approximately four thousand insanity assessments are performed annually in a country with a total population of 17 million. Of these, a very small number (around 200 pa) are detained in a specialist observation clinic for psychopathological assessment. As a result of reforms in 2012, the former five-fold classification of degrees of responsibility was reduced to three, namely, criminally responsible, diminished responsibility, and not responsible. The insanity evaluation, in which psychiatrists have a critical role, takes place before the facts have been established in open court, meaning that insanity is not an affirmative defence. Nor is there a separate test for insanity, as in common law and other civil law jurisdictions, so that the 'sane'/'insane' binary does not exist in Dutch law.

Because of the way in which responsibility assessments are structured, forensic psychiatrists and psychologists are required to offer an opinion about the defendant's (degree of) criminal responsibility but in the absence of any statutory rule defining the legal criteria for insanity. However, neuropsychological evaluation, using the insights of neuroscience, is increasingly being used in Dutch practice to support the diagnostic process.

As with other jurisdictions, insanity acquittals in Norway are relatively rare, with around 30 successful cases a year. As Professor Linda Gröning notes in Chapter 13, current insanity law in Norway bears the heavy imprint of the massacre of 77 people by Anders Breivik on 22 July 2011. This terrible event has had a profound impact on the formulation of the insanity rule, reducing the exculpatory impact of psychosis and providing for greater judicial discretion. In particular, these changes have resulted in an apparent move away from the medical model and dependence on psychiatric experts in the assessment of insanity towards greater discretionary power of judges to determine insanity according to legal criteria. However, as Professor Gröning observes, the changes in this regard may be more apparent than real, since evaluation of key concepts in the legislation, including terms like 'severe impairment of consciousness', 'absolute unconsciousness', and 'high degree of intellectual disability', still depend on expert testimony and the application of the medical model. Furthermore, a recent proposal that the criterion of psychosis, central to the formulation of insanity in Norway, be replaced by insanity 'due to serious mental disorder' is anticipated to open up insanity determinations to wider judicial discretion, potentially downplaying the significance of diagnostic categorization. It is hoped this will signify a fairer demarcation of criminal incapacity, allowing more accurate reflection of the severity of functional failure in particular cohorts of offenders, in particular juveniles.

In Chapter 14, authored by Dr Lilou Jiang, the historical treatment of mental illness in Chinese society generally and in the criminal law, in particular, is surveyed. This includes an examination of the mental illness defence as set out in Article 18 of the Chinese Criminal Code and its similarity and differences with the insanity defence in typical western countries. While the substantive test for the mental illness defence is not very different from its western counterparts, the procedural and evidentiary rules for raising the mental illness defence in China are radically different. While state authorities are generally not sympathetically disposed to psychiatrically unwell offenders, the insanity defence has been used as an effective tool to protect mentally ill offenders from the death penalty. However, the operation of various 'official dominated' procedural and evidentiary requirements has greatly restricted the use of the defence in China. Furthermore, Chinese judges are generally less inclined to consider or to find in favour of the defence in high-profile criminal cases and the existence of the insanity defence is not an effective guarantee that mentally ill offenders will be treated leniently. The procedural and evidentiary rules and their political context are analysed in the chapter.

Chapter 15 concerns the insanity defence in international criminal law. In the chapter, Professor Ian Freckelton and Dr Magda Karagiannakis note that the defence of insanity was not specifically provided for by the Charter of the International Military Tribunal which formed the basis for the Nuremberg trials. As a result there was a mixing of the concepts of incapacity for trial and criminal incapacity by virtue of insanity, both issues often being raised simultaneously. There was extensive discussion of insanity in the lead-up to the Rome Conference, which established the International Criminal Court (ICC). It resulted in a defence under Article 31 of the Rome Statute. This contained both cognitive and volitional components but was not easily invoked. It was based on the presence of 'mental disease or defect' which 'destroys' that person's capacity to appreciate the unlawfulness or nature of his or her conduct, or the person's capacity to control his or her conduct to conform to the requirements of law. The requirement of destruction of either facility imposes a very heavy burden on an accused person seeking to invoke the defence.

Because the statutes of the International Criminal Tribunal for the Former Yugoslavia (ICTY) and for Rwanda (ICTR) did not explicitly provide for any mental health defence, defendants were forced to rely on the relevant rules of procedure and evidence to ensure that offenders who were manifestly psychotic were not coerced to trial.

The chapter also discusses the issue of the absence of preventive psychiatric detention mechanisms to deal with persons found not guilty by reason of their mental state and those found unfit to be tried. The authors suggest a solution to this problem by the insertion of provisions into the constitutive documents of international criminal courts, which would permit the courts to issue special verdicts of 'facts proven, but not guilty by reason of mental incapacity'. This, it is suggested, would authorize a system of involuntary detention, treatment, and supervision of an accused person found to lack criminal responsibility, ideally within a neutral country's psychiatric facilities. This chapter reflects on other conceptual and practical issues arising from the impaired mental state of defendants in international criminal law proceedings, including for genocide and crimes against humanity. The chapter discusses the analysis of the diminished responsibility partial defence by the Čelebići Trial Chamber of the ICTY in the *Landžo* case and considers the precedent that this potentially creates for an insanity defence. It reviews decided cases, notably the *Ongwen* case, in which the insanity defence was rejected. There is a valuable discussion of the roles of expert witnesses, and the importance of the presentation of coherent, consistent, and unbiased presentation in such cases. The chapter argues for the modernization of both the criteria for mental state defences and for the custodial and treatment procedures for persons claiming to be insane or so found by international criminal tribunals.

Final Thoughts

The approaches of the varied jurisdictions which are the subject of this volume reveal some fundamental commonalities as well as what might be described as some constant aspects.

With regard to the former, every insanity defence surveyed in this book has at its basis a mental state requirement which, in essence, requires expert medical evidence to support the fact that the accused was suffering from the mental state specified by the insanity defence in question at the time of the alleged offence. So whether it be a 'disease of the mind' within the M'Naghten Rules or a more modern medical concept such as 'mental disorder'[2] or 'pathological mental disorder'[3] or 'psychological or neuropsychological disorder'[4] or 'mental illness'[5] or 'mental impairment'[6] or 'recognised medical condition',[7] it is clear that what has also been described as a 'mental illness clause'[8] is at the root of most insanity defences. However, this approach has not gone unchallenged. These challenges have taken various forms. For example, Slobogin has argued in favour of an 'integrationist approach',[9] the basis of which is that mens rea and subjective justifications such as self-defence are better equipped to deal with the culpability of mentally disordered offenders than concepts like rationality, volition, and knowledge or appreciation. In essence, this would mean 'the elimination of the special defense of insanity and the integration of defenses for people with mental illness into the other standard defenses'.[10] In doing so it would rid the criminal law of the need for any defence based on what was described above as a 'mental state'.

One of several arguments put forward by Slobogin in support of this radical approach is that 'By integrating this latter group into the culpability framework applied to people who are not mentally ill, the Integrationist Test is not only more appealing normatively but is also less likely to stigmatize people with mental illness because it ensures that such people are no longer saddled with the double whammy associated with being called criminally insane'.[11] This issue of stigma has been at

[2] See eg Scotland in Chapter 4 and Canada in Chapter 6.
[3] See Germany in Chapter 11.
[4] See France in Chapter 10.
[5] See China in Chapter 14.
[6] As specified in five jurisdictions in Australia, see Chapter 8.
[7] As proposed by the Law Commission of England and Wales, see Chapter 3.
[8] L Malatestia, M Jurjakoa, and G Meynen, 'The Insanity Defence Without Mental Illness? Some Considerations' (2020) 71 Int J Law Psychiatry 70.
[9] Discussed more fully in Chapter 1.
[10] C Slobogin 'A Defense of the Integrationist Test as a Replacement for the Special Defense of Insanity' (2009) 42 Texas Tech Law Review 523, 528 and C Slobogin, 'Eliminating Mental Disability as a Legal Criterion in Deprivation of Liberty Cases: The Impact of the Convention on the Rights of Persons with Disabilities on the Insanity Defense, Civil Commitment, and Competency Law' (2016) 40 Law & Psychol Rev 297.
[11] C Slobogin, 'A Defense of the Integrationist Test as a Replacement for the Special Defense of Insanity' (2009) 42 Texas Tech Law Review 542.

the root of the call by the United Nations' CRPD to recognize, inter alia, that the insanity defence should be abolished, being discriminatory since it is premised on the need for a 'mental disability'. Again, therefore, this challenges the need for any mental state requirement by advocating that the insanity defence be replaced by something which is disability neutral. While this approach has attracted much discussion both for[12] and against,[13] the fundamental problem is that the CRPD is vague, to say the least, as to what precisely should replace traditional insanity defences. While it might be conceded that this should be up to individual jurisdictions which are signatories to the CRPD, one might expect some guidance as to what form this should take. The vagueness of such a fundamental challenge to the insanity defence might lead one to question its practical reality and has led Baroness Hale as the then President of the Supreme Court of the United Kingdom, in an extra-judicial article, to state 'So we are between a rock and a hard place'.[14] So while one might applaud the motivation behind this proposal, it seems unlikely that it will impact on the very existence of the insanity defence and its reliance on the need for a mental state requirement.

A second requirement common amongst the majority of the insanity defences discussed in this volume is the requirement for some link between the mental state of the accused and his alleged criminal behaviour. In short, proof of the mental state alone is generally insufficient to ground an insanity defence. Thus, most insanity defences require proof of a lack of knowledge, appreciation, and/or volition. Although this requirement has given rise to considerable debate, much of which is discussed in this book, the need for this causal link, unlike the mental state requirement, is not an essential component of every insanity defence covered in this volume. Notable exceptions are Norway, which adopts a medical model fully discussed in Chapter 13 and the Netherlands, which has 'no legal criterion specifying the conditions under which the presence of a mental illness substantiates an insanity plea'.[15] A similar type of approach was suggested in England by the Butler Report but was never implemented and has never been adopted by any common law jurisdiction. Interestingly, to support this proposal the Butler Report cited the position in France, which at that time had a formula where 'a sufficiently severe degree of mental disorder (*démence*)'[16] was of itself sufficient to ground a defence of insanity. However, as Chapter 10 makes clear, French law was altered in 1992 and now requires that the defendant 'was suffering from a psychological or neuropsychological disorder which abolished his discernment or his ability to control his

[12] See DM McNamara, 'The Insanity Defence, Indefinite Detention and the UN Convention on the Rights of Persons with Disabilities' [2018] Dublin Univ Law Journal 143.

[13] See M Wondemaghen, 'Testing Equality: Insanity, Treatment Refusal and the CRPD' (2018) 25 Psychiatry, Psychology and Law 174.

[14] Lady Hale, 'Is It Time for Yet Another Mental Health Act?' [2018] Fam Law 1282, 1285.

[15] Chapter 12 Introduction.

[16] See Chapter 10.

actions'.[17] Although this makes it clear that the 'disorder' alone is no longer enough for a defence of insanity, the fact remains that there is a divide between civil law jurisdictions, some of which like Norway rely on a medical model, or on an open criterion as in Holland, and common law countries all of which require some form of knowledge and/or volition test.

A final common requirement concerns the manner in which the legally insane are dealt with. Here there is unanimity in that all jurisdictions discussed in this book adopt a regime of detention which is often mandatory but sometimes discretionary. The important point here is the recognition that the defendant is not criminally responsible and thus cannot be punished but is instead to be dealt with therapeutically. The only exception is Sweden, which although not separately considered in this book, is a unique jurisdiction. It does not have a discrete insanity defence which means that regardless of the accused's mental state at the time of the offence he or she is held responsible and convicted.[18] However, it has been remarked that 'the defendant's mental state is relevant when it comes to sentencing, and at this level Sweden can be said to have an "insanity rule" '.[19] In this connection, Swedish law states that 'The court may not impose a sentence of imprisonment if, as a result of the serious mental disturbance, the accused lacked the capacity to realise the implications of the act or to adapt their conduct accordingly' and further provides that if 'the court finds that no sanction should be imposed, the accused is not subject to a sanction'.[20] It would seem therefore that a therapeutic disposal in such cases is also the norm in Sweden.

As far as constant aspects are concerned the one which stands out is the consistent reference to, and discussion of, the M'Naghten Rules throughout the chapters in this book. But how influential is the M'Naghten test for insanity in common law jurisdictions in the 21st century? Certainly, it is now only England and Wales which continues as part of its common law to have the M'Naghten defence of insanity as originally handed down by Lord Tindal CJ in 1843.[21] However, although the influence of the Rules may have diminished in Great Britain the same cannot be said of other common law based countries. In particular, in the United States, in the light of the *Hinckley* case, many states reverted to a M'Naghten-based test.[22] In addition, although in many common law jurisdictions such as Canada, New

[17] ibid.

[18] See P Gooding and T Bennet, 'The Abolition of the Insanity Defense in Sweden and the United Nations Convention on the Rights of Persons with Disabilities: Human Rights Brinksmanship or Evidence it Does not Work?' (2018) 21 New Crim Law Rev 141.

[19] L Gröning and others, "Constructing Criminal Insanity: The Roles of Legislators, Judges and Experts in Norway, Sweden and the Netherlands' (2020) 11(3) New Journal of European Criminal Law 390, 403.

[20] The Swedish Penal Code, ch 30, s 6.

[21] All other jurisdictions have an insanity defence which is statute-based. See eg Ireland (discussed in Chapter 5) where the M'Naghten rules are retained but with an additional limb which provides for volitional impairment.

[22] See Chapter 9 'Before and in the Wake of Hinckley'.

Zealand, and Australia, discussed in Chapters 6, 7, and 8 respectively, the Rules have been augmented with a wider test, the essence of the M'Naghten test remains. In short, the M'Naghten Rules continue to exert considerable influence despite all the criticism to which they have been subjected.[23]

Finally, we are only too well aware that the path to reforming the insanity defence is slow and complex. While the jurisdictions discussed in this book each have advantages and disadvantages we hope that the respective chapters will help to point the way to a balanced assessment of how the insanity defence might be altered and improved. If this book can assist in any small way in this process then it will have achieved its purpose.

[23] See S Yeo, 'The Insanity Defence in the Criminal Laws of the Commonwealth of Nations' [2008] Singap J Leg Stud 229, 262 who concludes, 'This comparative study of selected Commonwealth formulations of the defence of insanity shows that the basic structure of the M'Naghten formulation remains generally in good shape.'

Index

For the benefit of digital users, indexed terms that span two pages (e.g., 52–53) may, on occasion, appear on only one of those pages.

Tables are indicated by *t* following the page number